To,

Amma (Late Smt. D. A[illegible]

Nanna (Sri. D. Suryana[illegible]yana)

Anu

&

little Aparna

Creating a New Medina

State Power, Islam, and the Quest for Pakistan in Late Colonial North India

Venkat Dhulipala

CAMBRIDGE
UNIVERSITY PRESS

CAMBRIDGE
UNIVERSITY PRESS

4381/4 Ansari Road, Daryaganj, Delhi 110002, India

Cambridge University Press is part of the University of Cambridge.

It furthers the University's mission by disseminating knowledge in the pursuit of education, learning and research at the highest international levels of excellence.

www.cambridge.org
Information on this title: www.cambridge.org/9781316615379

First published 2015
First paperback edition 2016

A catalogue record for this publication is available from the British Library

Library of Congress Cataloguing in Publication data

Dhulipala, Venkat.
Creating a new Medina : state power, Islam, and the quest for Pakistan in late colonial North India / Venkat Dhulipala.
pages cm
Includes bibliographical references and index.
ISBN 978-1-107-05212-3 (hardback)
1. Pakistan–Politics and government–20th century. 2. India, North–Politics and government–20th century. 3. Uttar Pradesh (India)–Politics and government–20th century. 4. Elections–India–Uttar Pradesh–History–20th century. 5. Pakistan movement–History. 6. Nationalism–Pakistan–History–20th century. 7. Power (Social sciences)–Pakistan–History–20th century. 8. Islam and politics–Pakistan–History–20th century. 9. All-India Muslim League–History–20th century. 10. Postcolonialism–Pakistan–History–20th century. I. Title.
DS480.45.D49 2014
954.9103'5--dc23
2014018926

ISBN 978-1-107-05212-3 Hardback
ISBN 978-1-316-61537-9 Paperback

Contents

List of Photographs and Maps

Photographs

Photographs

Maps

Acknowledgements

It gives me great pleasure to thank the people whose sustained support over several years ensured that this project finally reached its fruition. I owe a great intellectual debt to David Gilmartin, who first read it in its raw form as a PhD dissertation and provided me much needed confidence at a time when I was unsure of its worth. His incisive reading, thoughtful suggestions, besides continuous support ever since have been critical as I reworked it into this book form. Few people have been as generous to me as Dilip Simeon who adopted this project as his very own after a meeting at Teen Murti in Delhi. Dilip enabled me to catch the proverbial second wind at a time when I felt exhausted by it all and kept me going over the last few years as we talked endlessly about the Partition and much else over the phone. Needless to say, he carefully read through the entire manuscript and made valuable suggestions, which have significantly enhanced its quality.

The first draft of this book was written at the Institute for Historical Studies, University of Texas at Austin, where I spent 2010–11 as a Research Fellow. I am thankful to Ben Brower and Yoav Di Capua for their friendship during my stay there and to Julie Hardwick for inviting me as a Fellow to the Institute. Philippa Levine was especially gracious and generous with her support, going out of her way to introduce me to the editors at Cambridge University Press. Imam Umer Esmail of the Nueces Mosque in Austin patiently clarified several difficult passages in the *fatawa* of Maulana Ashraf Ali Thanawi for which I am very grateful. Courtney Meador and Jose Barragan charmed me with their prompt and cheerful assistance with all the administrative paperwork during my time at the Institute.

At the University of Minnesota, Ajay Skaria, my PhD supervisor was patient, showed confidence in my abilities when I was in doubt, and gave me the greatest possible freedom to write what I wanted for which I am thankful. Professor James Tracy was a warm and compassionate mentor through graduate school. His astute comments on the project as a reader from outside the field, his care, concern and steady encouragement were crucial as I struggled to cross the finish line. Chris Isett was a critical pillar of support and my go to person right from the beginning, somebody I could always rely on for sage advice that was cheerfully delivered over the phone at all times of day and night, whenever I hit a roadblock in research, writing, and later on, teaching. Cesare Casarino kindly agreed to sit on my dissertation committee and also backed my application for the generous Harold Leonard Memorial Fellowship in Film Study for conducting archival research at the National Film Archives in Pune on Partition films – funds which proved crucial during my last year of fieldwork. I still owe him an essay in that regard. While running up the tunnel to the Social Sciences Building in the West Bank campus to avoid being late for class, I was once stopped by Allen Isaacman and encouraged to apply for a MacArthur Fellowship from the Interdisciplinary Center for the Study of Global Change (ICGC) at the University of Minnesota. The Center's munificent support in the form of a pre-dissertation Fellowship and then a Field Research grant were critical over the nearly two years I spent doing archival work in India and UK, for which I am beholden to him. I would like to thank Ann Waltner and M. J. Maynes for their encouragement and good cheer during my years in graduate school. The Department of History provided me with stellar institutional support granting me the H. R. Schoonover Fellowship during my first year of graduate study and Teaching Assistantships during the subsequent years of my coursework.

In Minneapolis, Christian Sieg was a wonderful friend, housemate and later a travel companion as we traipsed around Berlin, Prague, London, Budapest and Chicago. With Riyaz Latif, I spent many weekend evenings 'slandering God and his universe' as he put it, cooking and eating super spicy food and occasionally listening to his Urdu poetry. I must say a big thank you to Friedrike Weiss, a loyal friend whose dry humour and company to those films at Oak Street and Lagoon cinemas kept me going. I laughed a lot with Eleusio Filipe, Pantaleymon Anastasakis, Peter Mortenson, Abu Korah Ghariba, Rudolfo Gutierrez, Evan Roberts and Joel Helfrich, in the History department computer lab that was superbly run by the wise and genial Phil Voxland. It is here that I met Trond Nerland who remained supportive after returning to Norway. A big thank you is due to Don Johnson for cupcakes, good humour and help with the amazing resources of the Ames Library. Amanda Nelson cheerfully helped me with paperwork and formalities in the Department in spite of my exasperating absentmindedness. Jason Eden gave me many rides in his car between Minneapolis and Madison during which we discussed Zen Buddhism, the Bible and life in general as the Midwestern snows stretched endlessly around us.

At UW Madison where my American journey began, Velcheru Narayana

Rao (VNR) was a stimulating teacher, full of refreshing ideas, amazing insights and bubbling energy. I would like to thank Andre Wink, Michael Chamberlin and Thongchai Winichakul for getting me started on journeys into the histories of India, Islam and nationalism, which all finally came together and culminated in this project. I was the recipient of immense kindness from Rajagopal Vakulabharanam who was a pillar of support during some particularly trying circumstances at Madison. He and Rukmini Kethireddipalle provided me with a home every Friday evening during my last semester where I met them for great food, fun and laughter along with Aloke Thakore. I would also like to express my gratitude to my housemates at the Rochdale International Co-op, especially Cristina Hogetop, Tim Moye, Susan Nossal, Oscar Hernandez, Chris Ng, Priamo A. Melo Jr., Leeta Kim and Julio Pereira for their warmth and affection. My special thanks also go to Alan Ajaya for his wisdom, kindness and support during my Madison days. David Johnson, my homeopath in Madison, kept me healthy and spirited over all these years for which I am very grateful.

Several friends in India helped me generously while I researched this project. Pradhanji kept me going with his earthy humour and genuine goodwill after I rented a room at his house. Later, Siddharth Mallavarapu put me up and put up with me in his apartment inside the JNU campus. I owe an unpayable debt to Jasvir Singh, who invited me to stay with him at his residence in Lucknow after our very first meeting. I will always remember the many evenings we spent discussing UP politics, the Indian Police Service, or listening to his dhol. Ram and Darshi Advani provided me with much warmth and friendship during my Lucknow days. I spent several evenings at their bookshop browsing through new titles, meeting Lucknowis or scholars passing through town. I am grateful to Sumit Awasthi, uncle, aunty and Eesha for taking care of me after my road accident which temporarily put me out of action. I will be forever beholden to Azra Kidwai for graciously offering to translate *Islam ka Siyasi Nizam* when I was really pressed for time and could not work on the translation myself.

Archivists, librarians and friends, at various institutions were enormously kind and considerate. At the Nehru Memorial Museum and Library, Shri Dharam Singh Rautela, Sardarji and Mr Sartaj Abidi were extremely helpful. Maulana Mahmood Madani generously allowed me access to the archives of the Jamiatul Ulama-i-Hind in Delhi. In Lucknow, Shri Amitabh Pandey at the UP State Archives was cheerfully prompt in clearing all of my file requests.

At the CID Headquarters, Pradeep Mishra kept me going in the dusty record room with his dry humour while he oversaw my note taking from the Police Abstracts of Intelligence. The National Archives of Pakistan, Islamabad, supplied me with digital copies of photographs for the book for which I am very grateful. I would like to especially thank its Deputy Director, Mr Irshad Ahmad, for his prompt and cheerful help in this regard. Muhammad Naveed, out of the goodness of his heart for a stranger who he met only over the phone, personally went over there to expedite matters. Hafeez Jamali, Faiza Moatasim, Matthew Hull and Mr Muneer Jan pitched in to help with these processes in Pakistan for which I am very grateful. Prashant Keshavmurthy allowed me access to the riches of the Islamic Institute Library at McGill University and patiently put up with numerous requests to translate lines of Persian that kept cropping up in the Urdu texts I read. Gopalkrishna Gandhi kindly gave me permission to use a photograph from the Rajagopalachari collection at the Nehru Memorial Museum and Library and also identified all the people in the picture.

Several friends and colleagues gave me an opportunity to present this project at various locations and asked searching questions that allowed me to sharpen my arguments. Pralay Kanungo and Bhagwan Josh invited me to deliver talks at the History and Political Science departments at JNU where Neeladri Bhattacharya, Radhika Singha, Indivar Kamtekar, Zoya Hasan and Gopal Guru asked useful questions or commented on my presentations. Ranjeeta Dutta and Mujibur Rahman invited me to make a presentation at Jamia Millia Islamia where Mushirul Hasan and Dilip Simeon again joined a lively debate on the Partition. Pradeep Dutta invited me to present this project at the India International Centre where an enthusiastic audience asked me several interesting questions. At Teen Murti, Mahesh Rangarajan and Srinath Raghavan invited me to give a talk on this book. Dr N. Balakrishnan helped me acquire photographs from the rich collections at the NMML. B. M. Chandana Gowda and Arvind Susarla invited me to Azim Premji University and the University of Hyderabad respectively to give talks before keen audiences for which I am grateful.

I am beholden to Professor C. M. Naim who answered numerous questions about personalities and places in the UP and kindly went through my translations of Urdu poetry in the last chapter even when he often found the poetry quite awful. I learnt the rudiments of the Urdu script from Blain Auer at a time when this project was nowhere in the horizon. Professor

Muhammad Umar Memon, an inspiring, passionate, and sensitive teacher got me truly started on my journey in the world of Urdu letters at Madison. I would like to thank Sanjay Palshikar, A.V. Satish Chandra and Satish Deshpande, early exemplary teachers at Hyderabad, who encouraged me to pursue an academic career when I myself was not so sure. At UNCW, Paul Townend and Sue McCaffray were supportive Chairpersons; Mark Spaulding accompanied me on those lovely trips to NARA while Michael Seidman exhibited an active interest in this project. I would like to thank Lisa Pollard, Lynn Mollenauer, Larry Usilton, Chris Fonvielle, Yixin Chen, Bill Mc Carthy, Candice Bredbenner, Taylor Fain, Tammy Gordon, Jarrod Tanny, Monica Gisolfi, and Eva Mehl for their support in the department. At the front office Catherine Johnson, Allison Lawlor, and especially Tammie Grady were immensely helpful with paperwork and administrative issues. I would like to thank Suvadip Bhattacharjee, my editor at Cambridge University Press, for his cooperation and for making the publication process a really smooth affair.

I wrote my PhD thesis in the sublimely beautiful setting of Monterey, California where I joined my wife after completing archival research in India. Dr Glynn Wood kindly provided me with visiting scholar privileges in their library where I sat from morning to evening everyday trying to write. For their kindness and courtesy, I would like to thank Ann Thompson the Institute librarian, as well as the staff of the Monterey Public Library, where I spent countless hours going through microfilms of English and Urdu newspapers. Khalid Hayat Khan Jamaldini, a generous friend who I met at the Monterey Institute, sent me several volumes of photocopied materials from the Archives of the Freedom Movement after going back to Islamabad.

Close friends kept me going with their affection and kindness through the years without which I could not have crossed the finish line. Vasu Sreekakolapu, childhood friend, has kept me going with our daily phone call whether from his home in Nashua or from distant cities around the world when traveling. Ravi Hirekatur has been a conscience keeper over the last decade and our weekly talks on phone allowed me to keep my sanity, faith and composure during some really stressful times. Neeraja Voruvoru was of great help during my fieldtrip in Delhi and generously put me up at her Mansa residence after my Lucknow road accident. B. M. Chandana Gowda and I spent numerous hours on phone discussing Indian politics, talking shop and shoring up each other's spirits as we ploughed through graduate school. Arvind Susarla egged me past the finish line while I was struggling with the PhD thesis. My heartfelt thanks go to the monastics of the Self Realization Fellowship, especially Brahmachari Sarat for his friendship, prayers and support over the last several years.

Finally, I can never thank my family enough for literally carrying me along during the nearly eleven years that it has taken to complete this project. Anu resolutely refused to read a single page of this manuscript preferring to instead read William Dalrymple on Indian History. Yet, she took care of everything else at home even after coming back from long tiring days at work, gave me countless weekends over the past decade to work on the project, and tried to instill some of her sound common sense into me whenever I was assailed by doubts and anxiety. The book would never have happened without her. My brother Srinivas lavishly wrote out a big cheque to fund my London research trip besides regularly enquiring about the book's progress, while Nancy, Neel and Anika welcomed us at their home whenever we visited New Jersey. My mother-in-law Ramadevi Kilaru was of immense help at a time when our family got bigger and I was scrambling to finish my PhD thesis. Sudheer Kilaru, Jyothi Gudavalli, Vindhya and Safdar gave us a second home whenever we visited them at Santa Clara. My greatest though is to my father who I left alone in Hyderabad, a year after my mother's death, to come as a graduate student to the US. I can never repay my debt to him or to my late mother for their love and countless blessings. Finally, my daughter Aparna brought us great joy and happiness, and did her own bit of egging by periodically enquiring: 'How many pages left?' I am glad to be done since I can now spend more time playing with her.

List of Abbreviations

AFM	Archives of the Freedom Movement, Karachi
AICC	All India Congress Committee
C.P.	Central Provinces
CWMG	Collected Works of Mahatma Gandhi
GOI	Government of India
IAR	Indian Annual Register
JUH	Jamiatul Ulama-i-Hind
JUI	Jamiatul Ulama-i-Islam
ML	Muslim League
MUB	Muslim Unity Board
NAI	National Archives of India, New Delhi
NAP	National Agriculturalist Party
NARA	National Archives and Research Administration, College Park, Maryland
NMML	Nehru Memorial Museum and Library, New Delhi
OIOC	Oriental and India Office Collections, London
PAI	Police Abstracts of Intelligence
QA Papers	Qaid-i-Azam Papers
SHC	Shamsul Hasan Collection
SWJN	Selected Works of Jawaharlal Nehru
U.P.	United Provinces (of Agra and Oudh) in British India, later Uttar Pradesh, India
UPML	United Provinces Muslim League
UPMLPB	United Provinces Muslim League Parliamentary Board

Glossary

Achhutoddhar	uplift of untouchables taken up by the Congress under Gandhi's influence
akhlaq	ethics, moral or mannerly correctness
alim (pl. *ulama*)	a religious scholar trained in the Islamic sciences
anna	one-sixteenth of a rupee
anjuman	a voluntary public association or society
ansar	the 'helpers', companions of the Prophet in Medina
asabiyat	group/tribal loyalty
ashraf	high-caste respectable Muslim communities
barakat	blessing; good fortune; abundance
ba'yat	pledge of allegiance or public acknowledgement of the caliph or ruler
bid'a	innovation
badshah	king
bande mataram	national song sung at Congress meetings or sessions composed by Bankim Chandra Chattopadhyay praising the glories of the motherland
biradari	endogamic kinship group
chillakashi	a forty day period of seclusion for mystic communion
crore	ten million
dal-bhat	daily bread
dar al harb	lands not under Islamic rule
dar al Islam	lands under Islamic rule
darul uloom	an abode of knowledge
dastarbandi	convocation for honoring a qualifying student by tying a turban on his head

dhimmi	category of Islamic law signifying non-Muslims who were protected by the Islamic state
dhoti	dress covering the lower part of the body
din	religion; faith
din-i-illahi	faith inaugurated by the Mughal Emperor Akbar
duniya	world
diyanatdar	honest, faithful, conscientious
faqir	dervish, saint, mendicant, mystic
fatwa (pl. *fatawa*)	a legal opinion issued by the *ulama*
fiqh	the science of Islamic jurisprudence
fitna	civil war, violent factional strife, rebellion that leads to schism
ghair	opposite, other
ghat	riverbank
ghulam	slave
hadith	written traditions of the Prophet revealing what he did, said, or of his tacit approval for something said or done in his presence
haj	pilgrimage to Mecca
hazrat	Muslim notable, elite
hijrat	migration; in Islamic history the migration of the Prophet from Mecca to Medina
hukumat	government; rule
ibadat	worship; religious practice
ijtihad	lit. 'exerting oneself'; used in Islamic law to refer to the use of independent reasoning in the interpretation of a point in the *sharia*
ijma	ideally connotes the consensus of the Muslim community; it is generally used, however, to describe consensus of the *ulama*

ilham	revelation
Imam	in Shi 'ism one of the descendants and legitimate successors of the Prophet
iman	belief; faith
ishtaraqiyyat	socialism
istifta	query sent to a *mufti* seeking a *fatwa*
jahiliyat	the times of ignorance or paganism before the manifestation of Islam
jadid	new; modern
jamiat	organization
jamhooriyat	democracy
jihad	effort or struggle; often used in the context of holy war in defence of Islam
jizya	poll-tax paid by non-Muslims to an Islamic ruler
kafir	infidel; non-Muslim
kalima	Islamic creed
khaddar	homespun cotton popularized by Gandhi
khilafat	office of the Caliph
khilafat-i-rabbani	God's rule
khulafa-i- rashidin	Golden Age of Islam during the reign of the rightly guided caliphs
khutba-i-sadarat	presidential address
kisan sabha	peasant association
kripan	sword
lakh	one hundred thousand
lashkar	army
maatam	mourning rituals
madrasa	school or seminary
majlis	council or gathering
maktab	school for young children

markaz	centre; headquarters
mashaikh	shaikhs; elders, holy persons
maulana	designation of religious distinction and authority
mazdoor	labourer; worker
mazhab	religion
millat	religious community
momin	believer in Islam
mufti	juri-consult in Islam
muhajir	migrant; the companions of the Prophet who migrated with him from Mecca to Medina
mujtahid	one who is qualified to perform *ijtihad*
mulk (pl. *mamalik*)	country
munafiq	someone who pretends faith in Islam; hypocrite
murid	disciple
murshid	spiritual guide
musalman	Muslim
muttahida qaumiyat	composite nationalism
nawab	ruler
nazim	organizer; administrator
nechari	materialist, atheist; term often used by the *ulama* to refer to Sir Syed Ahmad Khan and his followers or students at Aligarh
pir	spiritual guide
purna swaraj	complete independence
pesh imam	leader of the congregational prayer
purdah	the veiling or seclusion of women
Qaid-i-Azam	Great leader
qasba	Muslim towns and rural settlements in north India

qaum	community or nation
qazi	Muslim judge
qiyas	process of analogical reasoning in *fiqh*
qurbani	sacrifice; refers to sacrifice of cow by Muslims in north India during *Eid*
raja	king; title also used by several large landlords in India
raj'at pasand	conservative; retrogressive
ravayat	narratives; reports
rozah	fasting
sangathan	organization
sarmayadari	capitalism
sarparast	patron
shura	council; consultative body
sunna	traditions; practice of the Prophet
shaikhul Islam	pre-eminent *alim* in a Muslim society
sadaqat	charity, propitiatory offerings
shahadat	martyrdom
sharia	the law of Islam
sharif	well born
swaraj	independence; self-rule
tabligh	proselytization of Islamic knowledge
tafsir	the science of Quranic exegesis
taluqdar	a large landowner
tamaddun	culture; civilization
tanzim	organization
taqlid	lit. imitation; refers to the acceptance of a religious ruling from someone who is regarded as a higher religious authority without necessarily asking for technical proof

taqsim	partition; division
taraqqi pasand	progressive
taziya	an effigy of the tomb of Imam Hussain symbolically revered and interred during *muharram*
tehzeeb	culture, etiquette
ummah	worldwide community of Muslims
vifaq	federation
waqf	a religious endowment directed towards the upkeep of institutions such as mosques, *madrasas*
watan	homeland
wataniyat	territorial nationalism
zahniyat	mentality
zakat	obligatory Islamic alms; one of the five pillars of Islam
zamindar	landholder
zat	caste

Introduction

Towards the end of a rather long day of research in the India Office Collections at the British Library in London, I stumbled upon a rather unexpected document. It swam into view in the middle of one of the many microfilms containing the private papers of *Qaid-i-Azam* Mohammad Ali Jinnah. The handwritten document, with its ink fading, was the record of a special séance with the spirit of the *Qaid-i-Azam* (*Great Leader*) held at 6 pm on 13 March 1955, nearly seven years after his death and eight years after the birth of Pakistan.[1] The séance was conducted by a spiritualist hired by a government officer, a certain Mr Ibrahim, who was present on the occasion to direct the questions. The spiritualist began the proceedings by politely offering a seat to his esteemed guest. The spirit tartly responded that it was already seated, also reminding him that they had previously met there for another such session. The spiritualist solicitously enquired about the *Qaid's* well-being since on that occasion the spirit had complained about being 'in a dark and cold place', which it did not like very much. It replied that it was much happier now for it was 'in a very good place' that was 'brilliantly lighted and had enough flowers'. As a final courtesy before the proceedings started in right earnest, the spirit was asked if it wanted to smoke a cigarette since the *Qaid-i-Azam* in life had been a heavy smoker. On the basis of an affirmative answer, a cigarette was lit and fixed on a wire stand for the spirit to smoke while it answered questions. Mr Ibrahim began, 'Sir, as a creator and father of Pakistan, won't you guide the destiny of the nation now?' The *Qaid's* spirit reacted testily, stating that it was not for it to guide Pakistan's destiny any more, even though, it ominously added, it often saw 'flashes of evil pictures about Pakistan'. A worried Mr Ibrahim enquired, 'Don't you think there is a prosperous future for Pakistan?'. The spirit responded icily, 'I don't think so. Prosperity of a country depends on the selflessness of people who control its Destiny. None at all is eager to be selfless there.' Mr Ibrahim pressed further. 'What advice would you give to the present rulers of Pakistan?' Prompt came the response — 'Selflessness, selflessness. That is the only advice I can give them now.' The spirit then made a telling remark. 'It is

1 *Qaid-i-Azam Papers*, Neg10811, File 1067, Oriental and India Office Collections (henceforth OIOC), British Library, London.

easier to acquire a country, but it is extremely difficult to retain it. That is in a nutshell the present position of Pakistan to gain which rivers of blood flowed.'

The story of how the transcript of the séance found its way into the archive would no doubt be fascinating and also raise interesting questions about procedures involved in the constitution of the archive. But what is striking about the document, as also of the spiritual testimony contained therein, is the sense of crisis it communicates about Pakistan not long after its birth. Jinnah's death a little over a year after the Partition on 11 September 1948, war with India over Kashmir, Liaquat Ali Khan's assassination in 1951, inconclusive deliberations between 'secularists', *ulama*, Islamists, and regional groups over Pakistan's Constitution, political instability in East Pakistan, musical chairs over government formation at the centre – all these finally culminated in the first declaration of martial law in 1958. Pakistan's martial law administrators justified the short shrift given to its sputtering democratic experiment in the name of preserving the nation's unity and integrity threatened by venal and 'rascally' civilian political elites.[2] Successive martial law administrators have trotted out some of the same reasons to justify the abrogation of democracy or violently quell threats to national integrity over much of Pakistan's history.

Yet, such decisive military interventions have not resolved, and indeed worsened, Pakistan's post-colonial crisis marked not just by fragility of democratic institutions, but a vexed relationship between Islam and State, secessionist and insurgency movements, internecine sectarian conflicts, not to mention violent death, assassination or forced exile of four former or serving heads of state. Security analysts, journalists as well as a burgeoning body of scholars have sought to make sense of Pakistan's troubled post-colonial condition.[3] It is a trend that has intensified over the past decade as the country's internal security environment has deteriorated significantly in the context of a complex evolving relationship between its regime and Islamic militants, leading to exaggerated fears that this nuclear armed nation might become the first failed state of the twenty-first century.

2 See K. J. Newman, 'Pakistan's Preventative Autocracy and its Causes', *Pacific Affairs* Vol. 32, No. 1 (March 1959), 18–33; Wayne Ayres Wilcox, 'The Pakistan Coup d'état of 1958', *Pacific Affairs* Vol. 38, No. 2 (Summer 1965), 142–63.

3 See among others, Anatole Lieven, *Pakistan: A Hard Country* (New York, 2011); Farzana Shaikh, *Making Sense of Pakistan* (New York, 2009); Shuja Nawaz, *Crossed Swords: Pakistan, its Army and the Wars Within* (Oxford, 2008); Stephen Cohen, *The Idea of Pakistan* (New Delhi, 2005); Husain Haqqani, *Pakistan: Between Mosque and Military* (New York, 2005); Owen Bennett Jones, *Pakistan: Eye of the Storm* (New Haven, 2002).

Much of this scholarship invariably locates the roots of Pakistan's precarious condition in the circumstances surrounding this nation-state's traumatic birth in the bloody Partition of British India in August 1947. It is broadly understood that this nation-state emerged accidentally in the context of a sharp disjuncture between inchoate aspirations of Indian Muslim masses and secret politics of their pragmatic and ambivalent political elites who may not necessarily have even wanted Pakistan. As Pakistan came into being against the backdrop of the breakdown of negotiations between the British Government, Indian National Congress and Muslim League (ML) over transfer of power, it has been assumed that it remained an exceedingly vague idea in both elite and popular consciousness. Scholars enquiring into the roots of Pakistan's post-colonial instability have, therefore, grounded their explanations in the 'insufficiency' of its nationalist imagination especially after Benedict Anderson when emphasis on nationalism's seeming artificiality or illegitimacy has been replaced by enquiry into its fecund imaginative dimension.[4] In this regard, it has been pointed out that while the ideology of Pakistani nationalism – the strident two nation theory – was spectacularly successful in rallying together the Indian Muslims, it was inadequate in as much as it lacked any programme around which the nation could coalesce subsequent to its realization. It has also been noted that while ML rallies resounded with the popular but vague slogan, '*Pakistan ka Matlab Kya, La Ilaha Il Allah*' (What is the meaning of Pakistan? There is no god but God), Pakistan was not articulated any further beyond this emotional slogan. An inchoate anti-Indianism, it is presumed, became the default mode for this new nation-state after its creation in the absence of any substantial content or futuristic vision in its national imagination that particularly solidified following the violence accompanying the Partition. It is in this vein that the political scientist Christophe Jaffrelot conceptualized Pakistan as a 'nationalism without a nation' since it does not possess a 'positive' national identity but only a 'negative' identity in opposition to India.[5] More recently, the political scientist Farzana Shaikh has extended this argument by arguing that this lack of positive content or consensus in its nationalist ideology is indeed the primary reason behind Pakistan's nearly continuous post-colonial travails.[6]

4 The phrase that Pakistan was an 'insufficiently imagined' nation-state has been coined by the writer Salman Rushdie.

5 Christophe Jaffrelot, *Pakistan: Nationalism without a Nation* (New York, 2002).

6 Farzana Shaikh, *Making Sense of Pakistan* (New York, 2009).

This book challenges these fundamental assumptions regarding the foundations of Pakistani nationalism and questions the current understanding of its post-colonial identity crisis. It charts a new direction by analysing how the idea of Pakistan was developed and debated in the public sphere and how popular enthusiasm was generated for its successful achievement in the last decade of British rule in India. In this regard, it examines the trajectory of Pakistan movement in the United Provinces of Agra and Oudh (now Uttar Pradesh, U.P., India), whose Muslims played a critical role in this nation-state's creation despite their awareness that U.P. itself would not be a part of Pakistan. U.P. presents a particularly appropriate site for exploring popular underpinnings of Pakistani nationalism for it is here that the idea of Pakistan arguably found the earliest, most sustained and overwhelming support, much before it found traction in the Muslim majority provinces of British India where it was ultimately realized. My study argues that far from being a vague idea that accidentally became a nation-state, Pakistan was popularly imagined in U.P. as a sovereign Islamic State, a New Medina, as it was called by some of its proponents. In this regard, it was not just envisaged as a refuge for the Indian Muslims, but as an Islamic utopia that would be the harbinger for renewal and rise of Islam in the modern world, act as the powerful new leader and protector of the entire Islamic world and, thus, emerge as a worthy successor to the defunct Turkish Caliphate as the foremost Islamic power in the twentieth century. This study specifically foregrounds the critical role played by a section of the Deobandi *ulama* in articulating this imagined national community with an awareness of Pakistan's global historical significance, a crucial narrative that has been written out of most accounts of the Partition. Moreover, it highlights their collaboration with the ML leadership and demonstrates how together they forged a new political vocabulary fusing ideas of Islamic nationhood and modern state to fashion the most decisive arguments for creating Pakistan.

As Pakistan became the focus of raucous debates in the public sphere, ML propagandists were not just keen to defend its economic, political and military viability, but to portray Pakistan as potentially a far more powerful state than India and indeed the largest and most powerful Islamic state in the world replacing Turkey. Over time, in public meetings, through columns of the Urdu press and widely dispersed popular literature on Pakistan, they publicized its maps, listed its natural resources and infrastructural assets, highlighted its strategic location alongside contiguous and powerful Muslim allies in the Middle East, and celebrated the boundless potential of its inspired population once it was free from both British and Hindu domination. Moreover, Pakistan was hailed as the first step towards a broader solidarity in the Islamic world culminating in its ultimate political unification under Pakistani leadership. This celebration of the nation's 'geo-body'[7] was accompanied by invocation of the 'hostage population theory', which held that 'hostage' Hindu and Sikh minorities inside Pakistan would ensure Hindu India's good behaviour towards its own Muslim minority. But while this theory was frequently invoked in U.P., what was emphasized above all was Pakistan's strength as a potential 'first class power' surpassing Turkey, thus enabling it to extend its protective umbrella not only over Muslims in Hindu India, but over the Islamic world at large in a setting dominated by western powers.

These secular conceptions of territory were intertwined with theological conceptions of utopian space by the *ulama* to theorize Pakistan as an Islamic State under God's law that would renew Islam and revive Muslims for the new era, a move that proved critical in bridging the gap between politics of the ML elite and aspirations of the Muslim masses. Generally identified in the existing historiography as opponents of Pakistan, prominent Deobandi *ulama* led by Maulana Shabbir Ahmad Usmani (founder of the *Jamiatul Ulama-i-Islam* and later acclaimed as Pakistan's *Shaikhul Islam*) declared that Pakistan would recreate the Islamic utopia first fashioned by the Prophet in Medina, inaugurating an equal brotherhood of Islam by breaking down barriers of race, class, sect, language and region among Muslims and establishing an example worthy of emulation by the global *ummah*. Usmani further prophesized that just as Medina had provided the base for Islam's victorious spread in Arabia and the wide world beyond, Pakistan would become the instrument for the *ummah's* unification and propel its triumphal rise on the global stage as a great power, besides paving the way for Islam's return as the ruling power in the subcontinent. These ideas meshed with the Pan-Islamist ambitions of the ML leadership and also helped resolve the contradiction between the ideal of Islamic nationhood whose category of belonging is the global *ummah*, and the territorial state that revives the divisive category of national belonging for Muslims. The run up to the Partition witnessed osmosis of ideas between the *ulama* and the ML leadership. Thus, while the *ulama* borrowed the ML's vocabulary of the modern state to project Pakistan as a powerful entity that would make its mark on the global stage, the ML leadership hailed Pakistan as the new laboratory where definitive solutions to all the problems of the modern world would be found

7 See Thongchai Winichakul, *Mapping Siam: A History of the Geo-Body of a Nation* (Honolulu, 1994).

within Islam, thus inaugurating a new rhetoric that would find echo in other parts of the Islamic world.[8]

These heady ideas about Pakistan as a powerful twentieth century Islamic state were bitterly but unsuccessfully attacked by opponents. Most prominent were a section of the Deobandi *ulama* aligned with the Indian National Congress led by Maulana Husain Ahmad Madani, who himself first utilized the metaphor of Medina to conceptualize a common nationhood of Hindus and Muslims in an undivided India. This *Muttahida Qaumiyat* (composite nationalism/nationality) of Hindus, Muslims and other Indian communities, he argued, had an auspicious precedent in the common nationality forged by Muslims and Jews during the Prophet's era under the Covenant of Medina.[9] Insisting that Muslims could form a common nationality with Hindus just as they had done so with the Jews at Medina under the Prophet, Madani summarily dismissed the ML's Islamic vision of Pakistan and scorned the ability and intentions of its non-observant leaders in bringing about its realization. He and his associates also contested ML's assessments regarding Pakistan's viability in terms of its economy, security, social and political stability, its place in the international community of nations, and warned of its disastrous ramifications for Indian Muslims in general and U.P. Muslims in particular. Madani was a respected *alim* who had spent over a decade of his life as a renowned teacher of Hadith in the holy city of Medina. He articulated the metaphor of Medina at a time when the ML began a protracted public campaign that Hindus and Muslims were separate nations. His views were pounced upon by *ulama* allied to the ML such as the redoubtable Maulana Ashraf Ali Thanawi, the poet Muhammad Iqbal, and the Islamist Abul Ala Mawdudi among others, who publicly savaged his interpretation of the Covenant of Medina, and affirmed the ML's claim that the Muslims constituted a separate nation in India. Later, Shabbir Ahmad Usmani, Thanawi's disciple, would fashion the vision of Pakistan as the new Medina against Madani's vision. The bitter contest over Pakistan led to a major split in the *Jamiatul Ulama-i-Hind* (JUH), the premier organization of the Indian *ulama*. Questions regarding problems and prospects of the Partition exercised the minds of not only English-speaking political elites but also a larger public

8 See Richard Mitchell, *The Society of Muslim Brothers* (New York, 1993); Brynjar Lia, *The Society of Muslim Brothers in Egypt: The Rise of an Islamic Mass Movement, 1928–1942* (Reading, 1998).

9 See Maulana Hussain Ahmad Madani, *Composite Nationalism and Islam* (*Muttahida Qaumiyat aur Islam*), translated by Mohammad Anwer Husain and Hasan Imam (New Delhi, 2005).

inhabiting the vernacular public sphere. Pakistan was thus intensely debated and vigorously contested within the Indian Muslim community as it was outside. In highlighting the extensive public debates which fed popular conceptions regarding Pakistan and the accompanying hopes, apprehensions and questions that confronted U.P. Muslims who indeed led the struggle for its creation, this book contends that Pakistan was not always 'insufficiently imagined' in the process of its creation as has been assumed thus far in Partition historiography.

Partition Historiography and the 'Insufficient' Imagination of Pakistan

Pakistan, by most accounts, seems to have happened in a fit of collective South Asian absent-mindedness, the tragic end result of the 'transfer of power' negotiations gone awry, hastily midwifed by a cynical, war weary Britain anxious to get out of the morass of an imploding empire, leaving unsuspecting millions to face its brutal consequences. The most powerful argument in this regard has been made by the historian Ayesha Jalal, who began her seminal work with the question, 'how did a Pakistan come about which fitted the interests of most Muslims so poorly?'[10] In addressing this puzzle, Jalal analysed the struggle for Pakistan through M. A. Jinnah's 'angle of vision', primarily taking into account the actions and imagined political strategy of this 'sole spokesman' of the Indian Muslims in the cause of what she claims was a vaguely defined Pakistan. In a novel and controversial thesis that has become the new orthodoxy, Jalal argued that a separate sovereign Pakistan was not Jinnah's real demand, but a bargaining counter to acquire for the Muslims, political equality with the numerically preponderant Hindus in an undivided post-colonial India. Jalal contended that the British government's Cabinet Mission Plan, which envisaged a weak Indian federal centre where Muslims and Hindus would share political power equally, came close to what Jinnah really wanted. This was rejected by the Congress leaders, who Jalal implied, were thus the real perpetrators of the Partition. A fundamental assumption underpinning Jalal's thesis was that this was a secret strategy that Jinnah pursued that remained hidden from even his closest lieutenants, let alone the general public. As regards popular conceptions of Pakistan, Jalal dismissed them tersely, noting that 'a host of conflicting shapes and forms, most of them vague, were given to what remained little more than a catch-all, an undefined slogan.'[11]

10 Ayesha Jalal, *The Sole Spokesman: Jinnah, the Muslim League and the Demand for Pakistan* (Cambridge, 1985), 4.

11 Ibid.

While Jalal's Cambridge thesis challenged existing common sense about Pakistan's creation, the spirited counter-response by her Oxford counterpart Anita Inder Singh steered the argument towards more conventional Congress party waters. Contesting Jalal's thesis, Singh contended that Pakistan, as it finally emerged in 1947, bore a close resemblance to the demand that was couched in the ML's 1940 Lahore Resolution and indeed corresponded to the logic of the resolution.[12] Arguing that Jinnah's vision of Pakistan was based on the repudiation of any idea of a united India, Singh charted in great detail the process by which a determined Jinnah outmanoeuvred a war weary British establishment and Congress led by 'tired old men', as Nehru put it, to successfully accomplish his goal of partitioning India and carving out a sovereign Pakistan. Yet, while refuting Jalal's thesis, Singh nevertheless agreed with her that as far as ordinary Muslims were concerned Pakistan was an extraordinarily vague concept and that it 'meant all things to all Muslims'.[13]

This view, ironically, has also found support from the subaltern studies scholar Gyanendra Pandey, a fierce critic of Great Man history and the concurrent tendency to reduce South Asian history to a teleological biography of the nation state. Thus, while foregrounding 'fragmentary' histories involving ordinary Hindus and Muslims possessing 'un-partitioned' selves, multiple identities, shared life-worlds, along with a topping of hard-nosed political rationality, Pandey has noted that 'the Muslims had fairly widely supported the movement for Pakistan, though, as was already becoming evident, few had clear ideas about what that goal meant'.[14] The most recent general historical account of the Partition largely echoes this theme, emphasizing the confusion and uncertainty that gripped India regarding its future at the end of World War II, with the only certainty being that Britain would quit India sooner rather than later.[15]

This line of thinking finds further support if one were to turn to regional studies of the Pakistan movement, especially those concerning Muslim majority provinces of British India such as Punjab and Bengal that were partitioned. These studies point to Pakistan's late popularity in these provinces, besides its insufficient and uncertain comprehension amongst its Muslims. In the case of Punjab, Ian Talbot's studies have moreover downplayed the role of religious ideology and popular agency, and instead explained Pakistan's

12 Anita Inder Singh, *Origins of the Partition of India, 1936–1947* (Delhi, 1987).

13 Ibid., 107.

14 Gyanendra Pandey, *Routine Violence: Nations, Fragments, Histories* (Stanford, 2006), 135.

15 Yasmin Khan, *The Great Partition: The Making of India and Pakistan* (London, 2007).

creation primarily in terms of its rural Muslim elites 'rationally' switching loyalties in the treacherous sands of Punjabi politics to a rising ML as Jinnah gained prominence at the centre, and the Unionist Party hemorrhaged almost continuously in late-colonial Punjab.[16] Neeti Nair's recent monograph on the politics of Punjabi Hindus again emphasizes uncertainty about Pakistan as well as the sheer unexpectedness of the Partition.[17] These studies on Punjab have been complemented by similar studies on Bengal. Thus, Haroon-or-Rashid's monograph on Muslim Bengal has again underlined the lack of clarity or consensus over Pakistan, arguing that its imagination by influential sections of Bengal ML was very different from that of Jinnah, for they saw it more in terms of an independent Eastern Pakistan or an undivided and sovereign greater Bengal.[18] For Rashid, the struggle for Pakistan therefore 'foreshadowed' the arrival of Bangladesh in 1971. Joya Chatterji's subsequent study has affirmed this thesis besides adding a further dimension by arguing that it was Bengal's Hindu *bhadralok* who were primarily responsible for partitioning the province by ruling out alternative approaches to Bengal's unity.[19]

Given that these partitioned provinces witnessed unprecedented human displacement ethnographies exploring personal histories of ordinary people, especially women and refugees caught up in its violence, has constituted the newest wave of Partition scholarship. Studies by Urvashi Butalia, Ritu Menon and Kamla Bhasin have brought to light rape and abduction of women by men belonging to the 'Other' community, their murder by family patriarchs to save familial and community honour, besides the grossly paternalistic attitude adopted by Governments of India and Pakistan as they got down to the task of recovering these abducted women, often against their will, in the years following the Partition.[20] Even as they attempt to recover the agency of these women in these trying circumstances, these studies ultimately point to

---

16 Ian Talbot, *Punjab and the Raj 1849-1947* (Delhi, 1988); *Provincial Politics and the Pakistan Movement* (Karachi, 1988).

17 Neeti Nair, *Changing Homelands: Hindu Politics and the Partition of India* (New Delhi, 2011).

18 Haroon-or-Rashid, *The Foreshadowing of Bangladesh: Bengal Muslim League and Muslim Politics, 1936–1947* (Dhaka, 1987).

19 Joya Chatterji, *Bengal Divided: Hindu Communalism and Partition, 1932-1947* (Cambridge, 1994).

20 Ritu Menon and Kamla Bhasin, *Borders and Boundaries: Women in India's Partition* (Delhi, 1998); Urvashi Butalia, *The Other Side of Silence: Voices from the Partition of India* (Durham, 2000).

the absurdity of the concepts of nationhood or nationality in relation to their shattered lives. In the same vein, the anthropologist Vazira Zamindar's sensitive monograph on Partition refugees has explained the Partition primarily as a long, *post-1947* phenomenon during which post-colonial states of India and Pakistan actively produced 'Indians' and 'Pakistanis' by demarcating borders, establishing passport and visa regimes, and managing forced migrations and evacuee properties of displaced Muslims and Hindus.[21] Zamindar's provocative thesis thus implies that 1947 marks the beginning of the process of partitioning the land and its people and not the end point, as assumed by almost all of the existing historiography. Recent works by Willem van Schendel and Lucy Chester have emphasized this point further by highlighting the seeming lack of comprehension among 'Indians' and 'Pakistanis' about their national status, and the confusion on the ground that followed the drawing of the Radcliffe Line. They underline the massive human tragedies that accompanied this cartographic exercise in Bengal and Punjab executed by a British lawyer who had never been to India before, how it never resolved the 'national problem' in South Asia and instead created new ones for those living in the borderlands.[22] The anthropological turn has been accompanied by an increasing interest in Partition literature and cinema, now deemed more suitable than the 'historian's History' for articulating the pain, suffering, violence and displacement caused by the Partition.[23] It marks an ethical critique of the discipline of History for largely ignoring the suffering of millions, primarily concerning itself with mapping the biography of the nation-state in South Asia, endlessly searching for causes of the Partition by identifying its heroes and villains, apportioning praise and blame – an endeavour now deemed endlessly futile if not callous and puerile. What this newest wave in Partition scholarship again emphasizes is the utter bewilderment and helplessness of the people at what was happening as their worlds collapsed around them as a result of unfathomable political decisions taken at the top in the twilight of the Raj.

The picture gets muddied further if one turns to scholarship regarding the

---

21 Vazira Zamindar, *The Long Partition and the Making of Modern South Asia: Refugees, Boundaries, Histories* (New York, 2007).

22 Willem Van Schendel, *The Bengal Borderland: Beyond State and Nation in South Asia* (London, 2004); Lucy Chester, *Borders and Conflict in South Asia: The Radcliffe Boundary Commission and the Partition of Punjab* (Manchester, 2009).

23 Pandey, *Routine Violence*, (Stanford, 2006); M. U. Memon, *An Epic Unwritten: The Penguin Book of Partition Stories from Urdu* (Delhi, 1998); Bhaskar Sarkar, *Mourning the Nation: Indian Cinema in the Wake of Partition* (Durham and London, 2009).

ideological moorings of the Pakistan movement. While the role of religious ideology and religious leaders such as the *ulama* and Sufi *pirs* in the process of popular mobilization in Punjab has long been recognized, their appeal has largely been associated only with the emotional dimension and a vague vision of Pakistan, lacking any clear territorial grounding.[24] Even Jinnah's appeals to Islam in the cause of a vaguely defined Pakistan have largely been viewed as tactical manoeuvers and not based on any firm conviction. Thus, Hamza Alavi, the Marxist theorist has argued that Muslim *salariat* leading the struggle for Pakistan's creation had secular objectives and their vision of Pakistan had nothing to do with religious ideals.[25] Again, Faisal Devji's recent intellectual history of the idea of Pakistan has disregarded the importance of religious beliefs and piety in Pakistan's imagination, while at the same time cavalierly dismissing voices other than those of Jinnah and some Muslim League elites, for whom Pakistan could become meaningful primarily as an Islamic state.[26] Moreover, while Jinnah and the 'secular' ML elite occupy a central space in the Partition drama, the *ulama's* contribution to the Pakistan movement has largely been ignored. If they make an appearance in Partition historiography they largely figure as a resolutely determined group implacably opposed to Pakistan. And here the Deobandi *ulama* and their premier organization the JUH are especially singled out as staunch defenders of composite Indian nationalism. Their plea for protecting the integrity of Muslim sacred geography in the subcontinent and their eloquent valourization of the land that would be left behind in 'Hindu' India – dotted with mosques, shrines, graves of saints and martyrs – as *more* sacred to Muslims than the land of Pakistan, has been celebrated on the Indian side as the most resounding rebuttal of the ML's two-nation theory.[27] On the other hand, their opposition to Pakistan has been cited to make the case that Muslim nationalism under the leadership of the *Qaid* was 'secular' in its nature.

If the view from the centre and partitioned provinces of Punjab and Bengal makes the Partition seem like a rather confused and murky affair, there is some consensus that the road to 1947 may well have been paved from U.P.. Some

---

24 David Gilmartin, CSSH.

25 Hamza Alavi, 'Ethnicity, Muslim Society and the Pakistan Ideology', in Anita Weiss (ed.) *Islamic Reassertion in Pakistan* (Syracuse, 1986), 21–48.

26 Faisal Devji, *Muslim Zion: Pakistan as a Political Idea* (London, 2013).

27 Ziaul Hasan Faruqi, *The Deoband School and the Demand for Pakistan* (London, 1963); Peter Hardy, *Partners in Freedom and True Muslims: The Political Thought of Some Muslim Scholars in British India 1912-1947* (Lund, 1971). Also see Barbara Metcalf, *Husain Ahmad Madani: The Jihad for Islam and India's Freedom* (Oxford, 2009).

of the earliest scholarship in the field, therefore, traced Pakistan's origins to local political feuds in this province in the decade preceding the Partition.[28] The centerpiece in this regard was the fiasco over ministry making in U.P. after the 1937 elections, the bitterness it created against the Congress in the minds of U.P.'s social and political Muslim elite and how in turn they started a mass campaign to discredit its provincial Congress government as 'Hindu Raj', by raking up controversies over *Vande Mataram*, Hindi-Urdu, and the Wardha scheme of education. While historians have furiously argued over which side – the Congress or the ML – was responsible for this debacle, it is widely believed that the years of Congress Cabinet Raj were critical in reviving Jinnah and the ML's sagging political fortunes and transforming U.P. into an ML bastion from where the Pakistan movement began its successful journey. The reasons behind overwhelming support for Pakistan among U.P. Muslims and the critical role they played in its creation soon became the focus of an intense debate between the political scientist Paul Brass and the historian Francis Robinson. Brass attributed Pakistan's popularity in U.P. to its *ashraf* Muslims' quest for political power through symbol manipulation and myth creation while claiming to defend the rights and interests of north Indian Muslims.[29] In response, Robinson pushed back against this 'instrumentalist' position by arguing that the acute sense of separate religio-political identity among the U.P. Muslims provided the fundamental rationale and impetus to the Pakistan movement in the province.[30]

Robinson further substantiated his case by charting the emergence in colonial north India of a new self-conscious community of Muslims in late-nineteenth and early-twentieth centuries, united by an acute awareness of its distinct

---

28 See the essays in C. H. Phillips and M. D. Wainwright (eds.), *The Partition of India: Policies and Perspectives, 1935-47* (London, 1970). Later works include Deepak Pandey, 'Congress-Muslim League Relations, 1937–39: The Parting of Ways', *Modern Asian Studies* Vol. 4, No. 12 (1978), 626–52; Sunil Chander, 'Congress- Raj Conflict and the Rise of the Muslim League, 1937-39', *Modern Asian Studies* Vol. 21, No. 2 (1987), 303–28; Salil Misra, *A Narrative of Communal Politics, Uttar Pradesh, 1937–39* (Delhi, 2002).

29 Paul Brass, *Language, Religion and Politics in North India* (Cambridge, 1974).

30 Francis Robinson, 'Nation Formation: The Brass Thesis and Muslim Separatism', in *Islam and Muslim History in South Asia* (New Delhi, 2000), 156–76. Robinson's initial work though had discounted the power of ideas and relied on the Namierite 'loaves and fishes of office' model to explain politics in colonial India. See Francis Robinson, *Separatism among Indian Muslims: The Politics of United Provinces Muslims, 1860-1923* (Cambridge, 1975).

religious and political identity in a predominantly Hindu society marked by its own revivalisms.[31] This Muslim community, led by the *ulama* after Mughal collapse, developed in the context of an incipient 'print capitalism' involving mass publication of the Quran and Islamic classics in Urdu translations, new methods of Muslim mass education through revamped *maktabs* and *madrasas*, and the rise of a new autonomous individual Muslim self that began to directly access the holy texts.[32] Combined with improved transport and communication links between South Asia and core lands of Islam that facilitated greater movement of scholars, pilgrims and ideas, these developments intensified trends towards more orthodox versions of Islam in India besides deepening the Indian Muslim sense of belonging to the *ummah*, the global community of Muslims. In the light of these historical processes, Robinson argued that it was hardly surprising that South Asian Muslims tended to organize politically on the basis of their religion, adding that this was the very reason why the Congress party was unable to gain confidence of the bulk of the Indian Muslims who gravitated towards the ML.[33] Subsequently, Robinson's thesis was amplified by Farzana Shaikh's monograph on the development of *ashraf* Muslim political culture in colonial north India. Retraining the focus on Muslim political elites, Shaikh contended that this culture was 'based on an unmistakable awareness of the ideal of Muslim brotherhood, a belief in the superiority of Muslim culture and recognition

31 It must be noted that Robinson drew upon and extended the influential research of C. A. Bayly that explicated the rise in eighteenth century India of distinct social identities and ideologies coalescing around Hindu and Muslim elites in north India whose mutual antagonisms intensified in the context of a fading Mughal Empire, much before the British began to consolidate themselves in India. Bayly has, therefore, argued that South Asian nationalisms were not just European derivatives but built upon local patriotisms with indigenous concepts, symbols, and sentiments. See, C. A. Bayly, *Rulers, Townsmen and Bazaars: North India in the Age of Imperial Expansion* (Cambridge, 1983); *Empire and Information: Intelligence Gathering and Social Communication in India, 1780*-1870 (Cambridge, 1996); *Origins of Nationality in South Asia* (New Delhi, 1998).

32 Francis Robinson, *Islam and Muslim History in South Asia* (New Delhi, 2000), paperback edition.

33 In making some of these arguments, Robinson again drew upon insights from path breaking works by Barbara Metcalf on Islamic revival pioneered by reformist *ulama* from Deoband, David Lelyveld on the development of *ashraf* Muslim solidarity at the Muslim University in Aligarh in late-nineteenth and early-twentieth century, and Gail Minault on the Khilafat movement in India at the end of World War I. See Barbara Metcalf, *Islamic Revival in British India: Deoband, 1860-1900* (Princeton, 1982); David Lelyveld, *Aligarh's First Generation: Muslim Solidarity in British India* (Princeton, 1978); Gail Minault, *The Khilafat Movement: Religious Symbolism and Political Mobilization in India* (New York, 1982).

of the belief that Muslims ought to live under Muslim governments.'[34] Pakistan, therefore, appeared inevitable given the incommensurability of these foundational values of *sharif* Muslim political culture with those of liberal democracy (numerically dominated by the Hindus) upon which an undivided India would presumably have been predicated.

However, if Shaikh pushed the scholarly pendulum in the direction of theologically ordained Muslim political separatism, Ayesha Jalal responded strongly by 'exploding' the scholarship on 'communalism', squarely criticizing the tendency to assume a unified Muslim approach to politics in the course of blithely charting a linear process of the rise of Muslim separatism.[35] Jalal argued that neither the Muslim self nor Muslim collective interest in South Asia was ever pre-determined by Islam since Muslims were divided over a range of issues, both religious and non-religious. Moreover, Jinnah's insistence on separate Muslim nationhood was not 'an inevitable overture to exclusive statehood', and that it was compatible with the confederal idea allowing the 'possibility of an all India entity reconstituted on the basis of multiple levels of sovereignty.'[36] Jalal, therefore, reiterated that his maximal demand for Pakistan needed to be seen as a bargaining counter. And as far the place of U.P. in the Partition story is concerned, Jalal argued that while a separate sovereign Pakistan may have been the favourite hobby horse of some Punjabis, the idea was never popular among Muslims from the 'minority provinces' such as U.P. who had a more inclusive worldview.[37]

Jalal's indignant thrust can be placed alongside another strand of Partition scholarship that has highlighted the heroic but tragically unsuccessful efforts of prominent U.P. Muslims working for a united India. The most visible corpus of writings in this regard has been produced by Mushirul Hasan, who in his many books has underscored the contribution of 'Nationalist Muslims' to the cause of an undivided and secular India.[38] Hasan has also pushed the historiographical

34 Farzana Shaikh, *Community and Consensus in Islam: Muslim Representation in Colonial India 1860–1947* (Cambridge, 1989), 230

35 Ayesha Jalal, *Self and Sovereignty: Individual and Community in South Asian Islam Since 1850* (New Delhi, 2001).

36 Ibid., 400.

37 Ibid., 394–396.

38 Among his many works, see Mushirul Hasan, *Legacy of a Divided Nation: India's Muslims since Independence* (New Delhi, 1997); *India's Partition: Process, Strategy, Mobilization* (New Delhi, 1993); *A Nationalist Conscience: M. A. Ansari, the Congress and the Raj* (New Delhi, 1987); *Nationalism and Communal Politics in India, 1916–1928* (Delhi, 1979).

tiller in a new direction by arguing that the growth of communalism and ultimately the Partition was not just due to the ML's communal politics, but also the result of Congress's failure to adequately challenge the ML with a rigorously uncompromising brand of secular politics. However, in line with the thinking of both 'elitist' and 'subaltern' historiography, Hasan ultimately locates the ML's successful achievement of Pakistan 'not so much in the realm of ideas' or popular Muslim upsurge for achieving that desired goal, as in the realm of high politics. He has therefore called for greater scholarly attention to be paid to the 'performance and subsequent resignation of Congress ministries in 1939, the fluid political climate on the eve of and during the [World] War, the Congress decision to launch the Quit India movement, and the government's readiness to modify its political strategy towards the League.'[39]

Hasan's insight regarding the impact of Hindu nationalist politics on Muslim separatism has been lent some substance by William Gould whose monograph contends that the Congress party in U.P. (including its socialist wing) was dominated by Hindu nationalists, whose ideology, public posturing and political practices created conditions that arguably provoked and sustained the Muslim drive towards Pakistan in the last decade of British rule in India.[40] This monograph needs to be seen as part of a growing literature on Hindu nationalism in India that again pushes one towards a more contextual understanding of Muslim separatist politics, in terms of a reaction to emerging Hindu revivalisms, thus pushing back against attempts to portray Muslim separatism as an essential condition or an autochthonous phenomenon.[41]

Given the difficulties in 'making narrative sense of 1947' in spite of rich scholarly efflorescence in the field, in an influential review essay on the state of Partition studies to mark the fiftieth anniversary of the event, David Gilmartin tried to reconcile its divergent viewpoints in order to come up with a more

---

39 Mushirul Hasan, *Legacy of a Divided Nation: India's Muslims since Independence* (New Delhi, 2001), 55–56.

40 William Gould, *Hindu Nationalism and the Language of Politics in Late-colonial India* (Cambridge, 2004).

41 See among others, Sumathi Ramaswamy, *The Goddess and the Nation: Mapping Mother India* (Durham, 2010); Christophe Jaffrelot, *The Sangh Parivar* (New Delhi, 2005); *The Hindu Nationalist Movement in India* (New York, 1996); Manu Goswami, *Producing India: From Colonial Economy to National Space* (Chicago, 2004); Charu Gupta, *Sexuality, Obscenity, Community: Women, Muslims and the Hindu Public in Colonial India* (New Delhi, 2001); Tanika Sarkar, *Hindu Wife, Hindu Nation: Community, Religion and Cultural Nationalism* (Bloomington, 2001); Thomas Blom Hansen, *The Saffron Wave: Democracy and Hindu Nationalism in Modern India* (Princeton, 1999).

adequate framework for explaining the Partition.[42] The key for him lay in linking 'High Politics' of Partition to 'actions and agency of Muslims in their varied contexts', thus, explaining popular influences on momentous political decisions that came to be taken at Delhi, Shimla, or London. Gilmartin, therefore, posed the question as to why Muslims with local, multiple identities coming from diverse contexts provided such overwhelming support to an 'extraordinarily vague' idea like Pakistan. In addressing this puzzle, he contended that Pakistan was understood by most Muslims primarily as a 'transcendental symbol of Muslim solidarity' rather than as a 'territorial nation state located in any specific part of India.'[43] The two nation theory, in his interpretation embodied a fundamentally '*non-territorial vision of nationality*' thus explaining its overwhelming popularity *even* among Muslims belonging to the 'minority provinces' that would remain outside Pakistan.[44]

But if Pakistan was a non-territorial symbol for the Muslims that Jinnah purported to lead, the question remains as to how, why and when it was transformed into a demand for a sovereign territorial nation-state. To explain this problem, Gilmartin fell back on the realm of elite politics arguing that as Nehruvian Congress nationalism increasingly harped upon territorially defined nationhood and citizenship, Jinnah too was forced to face up to the territorial implications of the Pakistan demand in the dying days of the Raj. It therefore seems evident that if an earlier generation of Partition scholarship was trapped between Indian nationalist historians hailing the Congress party's secular nationalism and Pakistani nationalist historians swearing by the ML's two-nation theory, between the divergent emphases of the next two waves of scholarship over the past three decades, Partition studies remains largely stuck at the incongruous and unyielding polarities of Mohammad Ali Jinnah and Saadat Hasan Manto's eponymous hero, Toba Tek Singh.

Between Jinnah and *Toba Tek Singh*: Rethinking the Struggle for Pakistan in Late-Colonial North India

The assumption that Pakistan remained an extraordinarily vague idea begs the question as to whether Muslims across India simply rallied behind

42 David Gilmartin, 'Partition, Pakistan and South Asian History: In Search of a Narrative', *Journal of Asian Studies* Vol. 57, No.4 (November 1998), 1068–95.

43 Ibid., 1071; also see David Gilmartin, *Empire and Islam: Punjab and the Making of Pakistan* (Berkeley, 1988).

44 Ibid., 1081–82.

potent symbols of their faith be it the Green Flag or cries of Islam in danger, disregarding the specificities of their local situation. That, in turn, raises a more important question– about the seeming absence of public debates, discussions, or contestation over Pakistan, a strange anomaly for a society as famously 'argumentative' as India with its vibrant public sphere.[45] One should be left in no doubt that Pakistan became the most pressing political issue confronting the subcontinent as soon as the ML lobbed its bombshell at Lahore in March 1940. It would be talked about, discussed, debated and fought over in the popular press, through books and pamphlets, in public meetings and political conferences held in cities, towns, bazaars and *qasbahs* across the length and breadth of India. The Lahore Resolution led to especially fierce controversies in U.P., for its wording denoting Muslim majority areas in the northwest and the east as Muslim homelands that were to be 'autonomous and sovereign', clearly placed U.P. (and other Muslim minority provinces) outside Pakistan's territorial domain and firmly in the realm of Hindustan. It is precisely this assumption that U.P. would remain outside Pakistan that informed public debates on the Partition in this province.

The earliest critiques of Lahore Resolution appeared in the Urdu press within weeks of its passage. The first such critique titled *Hindu India aur Muslim India par Ek Ahem Tabsira* by the JUH *alim* Maulana Saiyyid Muhammad Sajjad 'Bihari' in the weekly *Naqeeb* angrily questioned how ML could designate Pakistan as an Islamic state since both Pakistan and Hindustan would remain composite states with substantial non-Muslim and Muslim minorities respectively. More, importantly Sajjad assailed ML for its willingness to consign 'minority provinces' Muslims to a life of perpetual 'slavery' under Hindus in the name of liberating 'majority provinces' Muslims into the brave new world of Pakistan. This incendiary essay was followed by longer, more exhaustive critiques of Pakistan by JUH *ulama* such as Maulana Hifzur Rahman Seoharvi or the scholar Maulvi Tufail Ahmad Manglori that again debunked the claim that Pakistan would become an Islamic State. They also darkly warned about Pakistan's disastrous practical implications not just for the minority provinces Muslims but for Indian Muslims in general and the Islamic world at large. The JUH *ulama* carried the bulk of the burden of publicly fashioning and articulating the case against Pakistan since the Congress response remained mostly cursory given the imprisonment of much of its top leadership during the Quit India movement and their release at the end of the War in 1945.

[45] See Amartya Sen, *The Argumentative Indian: Writings on Indian History, Culture, and Identity* (New York, 2005).

However, these nationalist *ulama* as well as the most ardent supporters of Pakistan were greatly indebted to someone, who more than anybody during the 1940s shaped the debate on Pakistan imparting it with coherence, discipline and stability. This was the other constitutional lawyer from Bombay, B. R. Ambedkar. His enormously influential *Thoughts on Pakistan* was quoted by both Gandhi and Jinnah as the authoritative treatise on Pakistan when they met for their famous series of meetings in Bombay in 1944. If one were to combine Ambedkar's treatise with critiques of the *ulama*, one can see a number of interesting questions that became the staple for public debate. Would Pakistan be an Islamic state or would it be cast in the mold of a western liberal democracy? Could Pakistan maintain financial solvency, or raise revenues for the purposes of administration, defense and development? What would be the territorial boundaries between Hindustan and Pakistan? How would Pakistan defend its territorial borders against a much bigger India? How would Pakistan control its powerful Hindu and Sikh minorities which dominated education, civil service, trade, commerce and industry and were against Partition? What would be the fate of Muslim minorities left behind in Hindustan? Would there be transfers or exchanges of population between Hindustan and Pakistan for the purpose of achieving national homogeneity? How might post-colonial Pakistan count as a factor in the realm of international relations? It is precisely due to public controversies started by opponents of Pakistan through questions such as these that it did not remain 'a host of shapes and forms, most of them vague', but an idea that progressively assumed clarity, substance and popularity in late-colonial north India.

The ML leadership and its local supporters in U.P. were forced to respond in this surcharged political atmosphere. ML propaganda first built a detailed case to convince domestic supporters as well as an international audience that Pakistan would possess adequate territory and natural resources, a hardworking, enterprising, and martial population, adequate revenues from taxes and duties, besides immense potential for developing into a great power. They repeatedly harped upon how it was *already* a far more powerful and resourceful state than modern Turkey and therefore the most obvious candidate for assuming leadership of the entire *ummah*. As a top ranking ML leader Khaliquzzaman declared, 'Pakistan would bring all Muslim countries together into Islamistan – a pan-Islamic entity'.[46] This marked a significant reversal in Indian Muslim discourse on Turkey, long hailed as the central Muslim power in the world and symbol of

46 Quoted in Husain Haqqani, *Pakistan: Between Mosque and Military* (Washington DC, 2005), 18.

global Muslim solidarity for whose preservation a powerful Khilafat movement had been organized in India to warn the Raj against anti-Turkish adventurism in the aftermath of World War I. Moreover, Pakistan was characterized as the bulwark for Islam against both Hindu and western imperialisms. As Jinnah himself proclaimed during his visit to the Middle East in December 1946, if Pakistan was not created 'the whole of the Middle East and Egypt in particular would be threatened by Hindu imperialism.'[47] The contribution to the Islamic world was however conceptualized in more ambitious terms that extended beyond its mere physical defense. Pakistan was hailed as the 'laboratory of Islam' that would creatively blend Islam with Indian Muslim experience of modernity to take the lead in finding definitive solutions to the problems of the modern world and in the process inaugurating an Islamic renaissance in the twentieth century. Shaukat Hayat Khan, son of the Unionist Party leader and Punjab Premier Sir Sikandar Hayat Khan recalls Jinnah telling him that Pakistan would be the base where Muslim scientists, doctors, engineers, economists would be trained, and from where they would spread throughout the entire Middle East to 'serve their co-religionists and create an awakening among them.[48]

Within the subcontinent, ML propaganda claimed that besides liberating the 'majority provinces' Muslims it would also guarantee protection for Muslims who would be left behind in Hindu India. In this regard, it repeatedly stressed the hostage population theory that held that 'hostage' Hindu and Sikh minorities inside Pakistan would guarantee Hindu India's good behaviour towards its own Muslim minority. It also insisted that Pakistan would go to war with Hindu India to protect Muslims, besides taking matters before international bodies and world opinion if necessary. Thus, the Sind ML leader Abdullah Haroon drew a parallel with the situation of Sudetan Germans under Czechoslovakia and admiringly referred to Hitler's actions to liberate them.[49] Jinnah himself noted that 'if Britain in Gladstone's time could intervene in Armenia in the name of protection of minorities, why should it not be right for us to do so in the case of our minorities in Hindustan if they are oppressed?'[50] The seriousness with

---

47 Dispatch No. 2077, 21 December 1946, Memorandum of Conversation between Mr Jinnah, Head of the Indian Muslim League and Mr Ireland First Secretary of the American Embassy, Cairo, 845.00, *US State Department Papers.*

48 Sardar Shaukat Hayat Khan, 'The Commander I Served Under', in Jamiluddin Ahmad, *Quaid-i-Azam as Seen by His Contemporaries* (Lahore, 1966), 42.

49 *Indian Annual Register*, Vol. 1 (1940), 313; also B. R. Ambedkar, *Thoughts on Pakistan* (Bombay, 1941) to see the widespread use of this metaphor.

50 Ibid. Vol. 2, 286.

which the idea of Pakistan was articulated can be discerned from the *Qaid*'s warning to ML's supporters that 'it would be a great mistake to be carried away by Congress propaganda that the Pakistan demand was put forward as a counter for bargaining.'[51]

As regards the ML's Islamic credentials, these were first attested to by the redoubtable Maulana Ashraf Ali Thanawi who from 1937 onwards made it clear that this was the sole representative organization of the Indian Muslims as against the Congress whose membership, he insisted, was *haraam* (forbidden). Subsequently, after the 1940 Lahore Resolution, local ML functionaries repeatedly emphasized that Pakistan would be established as an Islamic state. Jinnah himself maintained an ambiguity on this question in public as evident from his speeches, while in private he could go along with such promises. A functionary of the *Jamaat-i-Islami* who met Jinnah in the days following the Lahore Resolution narrates a fascinating incident in this regard. When pressed by this functionary to clarify on the nature of Pakistan, the *Qaid* used a telling metaphor to articulate his position. He told his visitor, 'I seek to secure the land for the mosque; once that land belongs to us, then we can decide on how to build the mosque.'[52] The collaboration between ML elite and the *ulama* developed steadily over time and its extent can be gauged from the fact that soon after the 1940 Lahore session the U.P. ML leadership constituted a committee comprised of its representatives as well as the *ulama* for the purpose of crafting an Islamic constitution for Pakistan.[53] The committee under the Chairmanship of Syed Sulaiman Nadwi, another reputed *alim* belonging to the *Nadwatul Ulama* of Lucknow, came up with a report that was to be internally discussed and debated before publication but for reasons never adequately explained was not published until 1957. However, its significance can be gauged from the fact that Nadwi was invited by the Pakistan government in 1949 to head the 'body of experts' to help the Pakistan Constituent Assembly frame an Islamic Constitution for the nation, and this report became the basis for recommendations that he submitted.[54]

51 Jamiluddin Ahmad, Vol. 1, 206; *The Leader*, 4 January 1941; *Star of India*, 4 January 1941.

52 See S. V. R Nasr, *The Vanguard of the Islamic Revolution: The Jamaat-i-Islami of Pakistan* (Berkeley, 1994), 113.

53 See the 'Introduction' by Maulana Abdul Majid Daryabadi in Muhammad Ishaq Sandelvi, *Islam Ka Siyasi Nizam: Jis Mein Islam Ke Siyasi Nizam Ka Asasi Khaka Pesh Kiya Gaya Hai* (Azamgarh, 1957).

54 For an account of the work of this committee, see Leonard Binder, *Religion and Politics in Pakistan* (Los Angeles, 1961). Also see Sayyid Sulaiman Nadwi, *Fundamental Principles of the Islamic State* (Karachi, 1951).

The relationship between ML leadership and the *ulama* became especially close on the eve of 1945–46 elections that were widely seen as a referendum on Pakistan. Prominent Deobandi *ulama* led by Maulana Shabbir Ahmad Usmani, a protégé of Ashraf Ali Thanawi, came out in open support of the ML's demand for Pakistan, which proved critical for its success. Usmani's theological justifications for creating Pakistan, his crushing rebuttal of the theory of *Muttahida Qaumiyat* (composite nationality) of all Indians, and his defence of the religiously unobservant ML leadership were all greatly effective in nullifying claims of the nationalist *ulama* that Pakistan was un-Islamic or that ML leadership was neither capable nor desirous of creating an Islamic Pakistan. What needs to be noted is that the common drive of these *ulama* and ML leadership towards Pakistan was predicated on a consensus that an Islamic Pakistan under God's law would emerge only *gradually* on the basis of their mutual deliberations and negotiations. It is perhaps these continuing negotiations between Muslim modernists, *ulama*, Islamists and others or rather the lack of their resolution that explains the cohabitation, collaboration, as well as the ongoing struggles between Islamic groups and Pakistan's political establishment over the definition of Pakistan's identity, as well as its evolving domestic and foreign policy imperatives.

Pakistan's sovereignty and territorial boundaries, far from being vague became the focus of much debate and discussion and clearly brought out the stakes in this matter. Gandhi himself raised the issue in a column in *The Harijan* on 12 July 1942, wherein he distinguished the Pakistan demand from separation demanded by Andhra from Madras Presidency. As the Mahatma wrote

> There can be no comparison between Pakistan and Andhra separation. The Andhra separation is a redistribution on a linguistic basis. The Andhras do not claim to be a separate nation having nothing in common with the rest of India. Pakistan on the other hand is a demand for carving out of India a portion to be treated as a wholly independent sovereign State. Thus there seems to be nothing common between the two.[55]

Responding to Gandhi, Jinnah made clear his own position in a public statement declaring that 'he (Gandhi) has himself has put the Muslim demand in a nutshell.'[56] Full sovereignty was thus fundamental to the Pakistan demand as reiterated by numerous ML leaders in public. Jinnah also made it amply clear

[55] *Collected Works of Mahatma Gandhi* (henceforth *CWMG*), Vol. 83, 78.

[56] Ibid., 120, fn. 2.

that it excluded any loose federation or confederation with Hindu India. The 1944 talks between Jinnah and Gandhi also brought territorial conceptions held by both the parties into the public eye. The Mahatma held on adamantly to the Rajagopalachari formula (which itself was clearly derived from Ambedkar's maps of Pakistan) claiming that it gave concrete expression to the Lahore Resolution. Jinnah, on the other hand, reiterated that the ML expected nothing short of six full provinces which had Muslim majorities. Even if Jinnah publicly rejected the formula since it conceded only a 'mutilated, truncated, and moth-eaten Pakistan', the battle lines between the two sides over the question of Pakistan's territory had become clearly drawn.

Maps of Hindustan and Pakistan with their borders appeared in the burgeoning literature on Pakistan whether drawn by Ambedkar, whether as part of the Rajaji formula or those drawn by ML propagandists that reflected the ML's inflated demands. The map assumed added significance in popular culture that was produced and contested during this period. The trade journal *Film India* reported an incident in a movie theatre in Bombay in April 1946 during the screening of a film titled *Forty Crores* that reveals heightened tensions over the map in the run-up to the Partition. Written by a Congress sympathizer and famous writer-lyricist Pandit Indra, this was a film on India's indivisibility and unity of its forty crore inhabitants. It included a particular scene in which a map of India is brought out by the Hindu and Muslim protagonists who then stand around it and deliver strong dialogues on the theme of Hindu–Muslim unity, also 'threatening those who came in the way of such unity.' As the magazine noted, during the 4 pm show on 14 April 1946, some ML supporters 'fired a few crackers, stood up shouting and one of them ran up to the screen and cut the screen across with a six inch blade.'[57] The significance of the act would not have been lost on the votaries of a united India or those supporting its partition.

Structure of the book

The book consists of eight chapters besides an Introduction, an Epilogue and a Conclusion. Chapter 1 explores the divisions that developed in U.P. Muslim politics in the aftermath of the Government of India Act of 1935 that introduced a limited democracy in British Indian provinces while maintaining British control at New Delhi. Chapter 2 examines the contest between the Congress and Muslim League for the hearts, minds and votes of the U.P. Muslims

[57] *Film India*, Vol. XII, No. 5, May 1946.

following the collapse of attempts at forming coalition government in U.P. and consequently charts the process of the ML's rise as the sole representative organization of the Indian Muslims. In this regard, it explores the developing relationship between the ML leadership and an important section of the Deobandi *ulama* that was critical for the former's rising prestige in U.P. Chapter 3 examines the public debates that were inaugurated on the issue of Pakistan and particularly highlights the hitherto underappreciated but seminal role played by B. R. Ambedkar in defining the terms of this public debate. It also charts Jinnah and the ML's response to Ambedkar's challenge in the context of growing public clamour for clarifications regarding Pakistan. Chapter 4 specifically examines the thinking of the U.P. Muslim League leadership on Pakistan and looks at how the idea of Pakistan was articulated in the localities of U.P. by them as well as local ML functionaries as they built up support for this 'ideal goal' of the Indian Muslims. Chapter 5 introduces detailed public critiques of Pakistan made by 'Nationalist Muslims' including *ulama* from Deoband through pamphlets, columns of the Urdu press, and in public meetings held across the towns and localities of the province. Chapter 6 tracks the impact of public debates regarding Pakistan on the general public by analysing a series of articles sent in by readers on this issue that were published in the Urdu bi-weekly newspaper *Madina* in 1942-43. Chapter 7 analyses Maulana Shabbir Ahmad Usmani's vision of Pakistan as a new Medina and highlights his critical contribution to the success of the ML's election campaign during the 1945–46 elections. Chapter 8 analyses election campaigns of both ML and the Congress during these elections that were widely seen as a referendum on Pakistan and demonstrates how they further clarified the stakes involved in Pakistan's creation. The Epilogue looks at the aftermath of the Partition in U.P. besides throwing light on how it affected subsequent politics in India and Pakistan.

1

Nationalists, Communalists and the 1937 Provincial Elections

I was a Congressman and I was proud to be so. The moment I find the Congress represents every community, I and lakhs of Muslims will join it again, and believe me I am sincerely working for that.[1]

Maulana Shaukat Ali

I am extremely doubtful of the efficacy of the proposal and am definitely and strongly opposed to the formation of communal parties inside the legislatures... I do not think any province will follow Mr. Jinnah's new and startling program. Our most prudent policy lies in working with other communities as a team and at the same time safeguarding our interests.[2]

Sir Shafaat Ahmad Khan

The United Provinces of Agra and Oudh (U.P.) occupy a special place in narratives of India's Partition for the existing historical common sense sees 'Muslim separatism' originating from U.P. as responsible for the eventual division of British India in 1947. In this regard, scholars inclined to take a longer view have attributed the emergence of a distinct Muslim identity and separatism to the work of Sir Syed Ahmad Khan and his clique at Aligarh in the late nineteenth century if not earlier. However, those skeptical of such accounts have often identified the Nehru Report of 1928 as the decisive point of rupture between the Congress-led nationalist movement and the Muslims leading to their 'parting of ways', with fatal consequences for India's unity.[3] It has been pointed out that subsequent mass struggles initiated by the Congress, such as the Civil Disobedience campaigns of 1930–33, invoked lukewarm

1 Statement by Maulana Shaukat Ali, *The Leader*, 9 January 1936.

2 Statement by Sir Shafaat Ahmad Khan, *The Leader*, 11 May 1936.

3 The Nehru Report, an attempt by the Congress party to create a constitution for free India independently of the British, was rejected by all shades of Muslim opinion. The report was seen as not providing adequate safeguards for India's Muslim minority and justifying Hindu Raj. See, Mushirul Hasan, *Nationalism and Communal Politics in India, 1916–1928* (Delhi, 1979).

Muslim response in the U.P. (as also in other provinces) in sharp contrast to the community's vigorous participation in the Non-cooperation Movement a decade earlier. This was therefore not just a temporary estrangement, but 'a political separatism of a more abiding kind, the mutual hardening of attitudes between the two communities, and the loss of faith by each in political leaders hailing from the other.'[4]

While these failures in the 1920s and 1930s to achieve Hindu–Muslim unity seem like logical links in the chain of events leading to the Partition, this was by no means evident to contemporary observers and politicians in the U.P. in the aftermath of the Government of India (GOI) Act of 1935. With impending provincial elections under this Act in early 1937, fledgling political parties, assorted political groups and individual politicians in the U.P. got busy trying to forge local level electoral alliances or adjustments that would give them the largest number of seats in the new provincial legislatures. In doing so, they nonchalantly criss-crossed the communal divide notwithstanding tensions, conflicts and riots at the base. While ideology was an important factor in some of the cross-communal political alignments taking place, pragmatism contributed to this process in equal measure, creating strange sets of political bedfellows. U.P. political elites were not alone in this regard, for similar processes were at work in almost all provinces of British India. Even at the centre, politicians with national reach, ambitions, or pretensions belonging to both the Congress and Muslim political groups, opened negotiations with each other as they scrambled to contain the effects of the GOI Act and come up with a cohesive response to this latest move by the British government on the Indian political chessboard.[5] In this context, what an examination of U.P. Muslim politics makes very clear is that the question of who was a 'nationalist' and who was a 'communalist' was by no means a settled one at this point in time. And rather than developing as the imminent seedbed for Muslim separatism, U.P. at the advent of the 1935 GOI Act held some of the best prospects for constructing a national political front of India's major communities in the battle against the Raj.

---

4 Gyanendra Pandey, *The Ascendancy of the Congress in Uttar Pradesh: Class, Community and Nation in Northern India, 1920–1940* (London, 2004), 95–96.

5 See for example the negotiations between Rajendra Prasad and Jinnah over a comprehensive communal settlement that could be held up as a substitute for the Communal Award of 1932. For details of the negotiations see *AICC Papers File G-63/1937* with Prasad's daily notes regarding his negotiations with Jinnah and others.

The GOI Act of 1935 and Divisions in Muslim Politics

These prospects however need to be set against changes being wrought in Indian politics by the GOI Act of 1935. The Act certainly marked a further step in the process of devolution of power by the colonial state to its Indian subjects. Diarchy in the provinces made way for fully responsible governments as hitherto 'reserved subjects' handled by British officials were transferred to ministers responsible to popularly elected legislatures. But the replacement of diarchy in the provinces was also accompanied by its restoration in Delhi with the Viceroy and his officials continuing to hold all the vital powers of government and remaining responsible only to the British Parliament.[6] The intentions behind the 1935 Act, for all the devolutionary gloss put on it by the British government were clear. Rather than being an act of generosity on part of the rulers, it was an attempt to hold on to the Empire in the face of determined nationalist agitation for Indian independence led by the Congress.[7] Thus, on the one hand, it shut out constitutional advance at the centre for not only was the Congress demand for *Purna Swaraj* ignored, even the lesser term Dominion Status was avoided in the language of the Act. The opening up of provincial politics to electoral competition, on the other hand, was an obvious ploy to pin down the Congress in the provinces. As the Viceroy, Lord Linlithgow confessed, the government was banking on the 'potency of provincial autonomy to destroy the effectiveness of the Congress as an all India instrument of revolution'.[8] It was indeed its fond hope that the lure of offices would pit provincial Congressmen against one another and more importantly against a Congress High Command that was certain to oppose such limited reforms which accentuated divisions in the provinces while simultaneously blocking any advance at the centre.[9] It also

6 For commentaries on the 1935 GOI Act, see *The Indian Problem: Report on the Constitutional Problem in India* (Oxford, 1944); Shafaat Ahmad Khan, *The Indian Federation: An Exposition and Critical Review* (London, 1937); Z. A. Ahmad, *The Indian Federation, Congress Economic and Political Studies No.10,* Published by K. M Ashraf on behalf of the Political and Economic Information Department of the All India Congress Committee (Allahabad, 1938).

7 R. J. Moore, *Endgames of Empire: Studies of Britain's Indian Problem* (Delhi, 1988); Gowher Rizvi, *Linlithgow and India: A Study of British Policy and Political Impasse in India* (London, 1978); Carl Bridge, *Holding India to the Empire: The British Conservative Party and the 1935 Constitution* (New Delhi, 1986).

8 Linlithgow to Zetland MSS EUR F 125/4/12, 5 March 1937. Also quoted in Gowher Rizvi, *Linlithgow and India*, 6.

9 See chapters 2 and 3 in B. R. Tomlinson, *The Indian National Congress and the Raj, 1929–42: The Penultimate Phase* (London, 1976).

calculated that Congressmen interested in working the reforms would ward off the extremists wedded to the politics of agitation outside the legislatures, and coax the Congress organization back into a cooperative mode with the British Raj. Furthermore, the provincial scheme was heavily stacked in favour of the Raj's collaborators, especially the landlords. The lion's share provided to rural representation in the new provincial assemblies was intended to provide these landlords a chance to capture the councils and firm up their support bases in the countryside. In the end, the special powers invested in the office of the Governor were meant to ensure that no serious threats to the stability of the Raj would ever be allowed to materialize.

But if hemming in the Congress in the provinces was the primary aim of the Act, its aims with regard to Muslim politics were no less important. As Ayesha Jalal has pointed out, the Act opened up divisions between landed Muslim political groups from the Muslim majority provinces, which welcomed the new reforms and Muslim politicians hailing mostly from the Muslim minority provinces who expressed strong reservations about the Act, and whose 'nationalist' priorities seemed similar to those held by influential sections within the Congress.[10] The former were best represented by the principal beneficiary of the GOI Act, Mian Sir Fazl-i-Husain of Punjab who emerged as a central figure in Muslim politics in the interwar years.[11] The reasons for Fazl-i-Husain's contentment with the GOI Act were not difficult to discern. The Act provided the provinces with increased autonomy, but more importantly, the Communal Award, an integral part of the new Act, strengthened the Muslim position in Punjab, besides greatly improving it in Bengal. Thus far Muslims from both these provinces had paid a heavy price for securing 'weightage' for their brethren in the 'minority provinces', but assertive politicians such as Fazl-i-Husain were now more intent on consolidating power in their own provinces, rather than be distracted by such fraternal concerns. It is in this scenario that he formed his Unionist Party, a loose cross-communal combination led by Muslims, with Hindu Jat and Sikh landed elites as allies. Riding on the support of a predominantly rural electorate that was sharply limited by income and property

10 Ayesha Jalal and Anil Seal, 'Alternative to Partition: Muslim Politics between the Wars', *Modern Asian Studies*, Vol. 15, No. 3 (1981), 415–54.

11 Fazl-i-Husain quit the Congress in the early 1920s in protest against Gandhi's policy of extra-constitutional agitation outside the legislatures as part of his efforts to overthrow colonial rule. For an analysis of the politics of Sir Fazl-i-Husain see Jalal and Seal, 'Alternative to Partition: Muslim Politics between the Wars'; Azim Husain, *Sir Fazl-i-Husain: A Political Biography* (Bombay, 1946); David Page, *Prelude to Partition: The Indian Muslims and the Imperial System of Control 1920–32* (Delhi, 1982).

qualifications, this combination secured a potentially unassailable majority in the upcoming Punjab assembly.

Fazl-i-Husain signalled his aversion to the creation of an all India Muslim communal party that would centrally nominate candidates for these provincial elections. This constituted interference by 'busybodies' from the outside that he felt would disturb delicate local political alliances and power sharing agreements he had forged with Hindu and Sikh groups in Punjab. Thus, while opening his party office in Lahore on the eve of the elections, he declared that the Unionist Party was a 'non-communal party that stood for self-respect and patriotism but eschewed racial animus or malice of any kind'. Evaluating his politics, even the Congress leaning *Bombay Chronicle* was compelled to call Fazl-i-Husain 'a realist first and a communalist next'.[12] Mian Sahib's 'provincial thesis' was amplified by his friend, the Aga Khan, who after a lifetime spent in pursuing Muslim communal concerns, solemnly warned Muslims against the formation of parties on a communal basis, piously observing that political groups needed to be formed with the sole objective of raising the economic condition of the masses.[13] He further brought together like-minded landlord allies from other provinces under the umbrella of the All India Muslim Conference (AIMC).[14] New personnel were appointed to overhaul its functioning.[15] Following this lead provided by Fazl-i-Husain, Haji Seth Abdullah Haroon, a leading Muslim politician and business magnate in Sind observed that the formation of joint Hindu–Muslim parties on economic lines would not in any way undermine the solidarity of the Muslim community. On the contrary, it would promote a 'sense of tolerance and respect for each other's rights.'[16] A series of local level cross-communal political alliances also came into effect in Bengal, Bihar and Central Provinces (C.P.) as provincial Muslim groups prepared for elections. In U.P., the National Agriculturalist Party (NAP), made up of Hindu and Muslim landlords along with sections of business capital, was founded on the Unionist Party model with active encouragement from the government. With these arrangements in place, Fazl-i-Husain and his allies were willing to

12 *The Leader*, 29 April 1936.

13 *Indian Annual Register*, Vol. 1 (1936), 9.

14 For a detailed analysis of the politics of the AIMC see David Page, *Prelude to Partition: The Indian Muslims and the Imperial System of Control 1920–1932* (Delhi, 1982).

15 The Nawab of Chhatari was appointed the Chairman of the AIMC. Haji Seth Abdullah Haroon from Sind, Shafaat Ahmed Khan from the U.P., Shafi Daudi from Bihar and the poet Sir Mohammad Iqbal from Punjab were appointed permanent Vice Presidents.

16 *The Leader*, 23 June 1936.

countenance divisions in Muslim politics for the time being. It was hoped that once the old guard had refurbished its popular credentials at the elections, the upstarts hoping to centrally control Muslim politics would be cut to size paving the way for the takeover by the AIMC of the new revamped All India Muslim League (AIML) led by Jinnah. Thus, at the AIMC meeting held in February 1936, the Aga Khan observed that the question of amalgamating the AIMC and AIML had been considered by Fazl-i-Husain but it had been decided to postpone the matter and take it up after the elections to the new legislatures.[17]

The counterpoint to this conservative strand of Muslim political opinion was to be found most conspicuously in U.P. The strongest party here was the Muslim Unity Board (MUB) formed in 1933, comprised mostly of Muslim politicians with close links to the Congress party, and *ulama* belonging to the *Jamiatul Ulama-i-Hind* (JUH). Khaliquzzaman, the Secretary of the MUB, was also the main mover of the resolution that had given birth to the Congress Swaraj party at its Ranchi meeting in 1934.[18] The party, not surprisingly, was vituperated by its adversaries as a front for the Congress.[19] But in spite of such allegations, the strength of this combine became evident in 1934 elections for the Central Assembly, for it won half the seats in combination with the Congress, in the process defeating both the Muslim League and the NAP.[20] It was to this group that Jinnah, the freshly elected President of the new Muslim League, turned after his return to India in 1934 from a four year self-imposed exile in London. Jinnah had taken over a party that led a precarious existence with few members, fewer subscriptions and an unsettled policy and programme.[21] Hoping to stem this slide, he outlined a new vision

---

17 *Indian Annual Register*, Vol. 1 (1936), 303.

18 Thus, the MUB in its resolution openly welcomed the revival of the Swaraj party making it possible for 'progressive sections of all communities to co-operate and work unitedly for the country.' *Indian Annual Register*, Vol. I (1934), 320.

19 The *Hamdam* during the election campaign further described Shaukat Ali and Tak Sherwani, the leading lights of the MUB, as 'Malaviya's henchmen'. See *Notes on the Press, The United Provinces of Agra and Oudh*, 4 August 1934.

20 Of the six seats in U.P., the MUB won two seats, the Congress one, the NAP one, while the remaining two were won by Independents. See P. D. Reeves, B. D. Graham, J. M. Goodman, *Handbook of Elections in U.P. 1920–51* (Delhi,1975), xlvi–xlvii.

21 'In 1933, with a total income of ₹ 1318.11.6 its annual expenditure showed a deficit of some ₹ 564. Out of the total of 300 members on its council ninety two were under notice to pay arrears of membership. See Z. H. Zaidi, 'Aspects of the Development of Muslim League Policy 1937–1947', in C. H. Phillips and M. D. Wainwright, *The Partition of India: Policies and Perspectives, 1935–1947* (London, 1970), 246.

for the Muslim League (ML). He declared that his aim was to revive it as a vehicle for accelerating nationalist consciousness among the Muslim masses and unifying Muslim groups in different provinces on a nationalist platform. He, therefore, underlined the new party's ideological affinities with the Congress and, by extension, with the MUB fairly clear.

Jinnah clearly spelt out his points of convergence with the Congress high command, dominated at the time by its putative 'right wing'. To begin with, he expressed his willingness to negotiate an alternative Hindu–Muslim settlement that would replace the Communal Award, thus, addressing the Congress' deepest objections to the existing system of separate electorates that lay at the heart of the Award and were seen by it as the biggest obstacle to the development of a united Indian nationalism. Additionally, echoing Congress concerns, Jinnah expressed strong criticism of the GOI Act at the 1936 Bombay ML session, asking Indians to deal with it as the Germans had done with the Treaty of Versailles. At the same time, in sync with the views of the Congress right wing, Jinnah clarified that the 'provincial scheme of the constitution should be utilized for what it is worth in spite of the most objectionable features contained therein which render the real control and responsibility of the ministry and legislature over the entire field of government and administration nugatory.'[22] As he pointed out, an armed revolt against the Raj was impossible while non-cooperation at the moment appeared ineffective. In this context, constitutional agitation inside the legislatures was the only effective political strategy on the path to Indian independence.

Jinnah reminded the Congress that by itself it could never hope to achieve the goal of national independence and it therefore needed to make a fresh approach to the Muslims. Earlier attempts at Hindu–Muslim unity, he reasoned, had failed since they had been made only at the level of elites. This time around, Jinnah wanted 'to build the foundation and carry the community with him so that real and genuine unity could be achieved. It was not proper that a handful of men at the top should decide the question.'[23] With his new ML, he was hopeful that 'we may be able to hammer out a strong block to march together with the Hindus for the freedom of the country.'[24] The task could only be begun in U.P., which Jinnah declared, was 'the heart of Muslim India', whose Muslims were politically the most advanced in the country in

22 S. S. Pirzada, *Foundations of Pakistan*, Vol. 2, 261.

23 *The Leader*, 30 July 1936.

24 *The Leader*, 5 November 1936.

contrast to Punjab, a 'hopeless' and most 'official ridden province' dominated by the Unionists. With the expansion of the electorate owing to a relaxation in franchise qualifications, greater opportunities seemed available to Muslim nationalists for generating support in U.P. and sending more members into the legislatures.[25] But while Jinnah's ideological sympathies lay with the MUB, he was too much of a pragmatist to shut the door on other elements willing to join his fledgling party. The immediate goal was to infuse some life into the party in all possible ways and his ML was therefore open to whoever was willing to affirm, even for appearances sake, the party's new programme.

The Formation of the U.P. Muslim League Parliamentary Board (UPMLPB)

Jinnah and his allies however had much work to do if the ML was to get off the ground in U.P. Early press reports on the party's prospects were not very encouraging. Even the *Madina* of Bijnor, which was sympathetic to nationalist concerns, noted that the

> Muslim League has lost its importance since 1918 and now it can be said to be neither dead nor alive. Today, truly speaking, the League has no existence beyond the brain and mind of Mr. Jinnah. Muslims do not know where its office and branches are located. Nor do they know what its goals and policy are. It is evident that under such circumstances neither the League can serve its community nor is the community prepared to take any steps for keeping the League alive. Mr. Jinnah is no doubt an eminent politician but he cannot move with an active community nor can the community reach its goal by following him.[26]

---

25 For the rural voters, the qualification included either payment of ₹ 5 per annum as land revenue or ₹ 10 per annum as rent on agricultural land. For the urban voters, those paying income tax or those paying municipal income tax of ₹ 150 per annum were given the vote. In addition, those enfranchised included retired soldiers, those who had passed upper primary examinations, women who were deemed literate or whose husbands held property qualification, or pensioned wives, widows, or mothers of retired military personnel. All in all, the 1935 Act vastly expanded the electorate including a number of new voters. Whereas the electorate for the 1930 elections to the U.P. legislative council under the 1919 act consisted of about 1.6 million voters, the number of voters for the 1937 elections stood at over 5 million voters, a nearly five-fold increase. See P. D. Reeves, B. D. Graham, J. M. Goodman, *Handbook of Elections in U.P. 1920–51*, xlvi–xlvii.

26 *Notes on Newspapers: The United Provinces of Agra and Oudh*, 25 April 1936.

The party desperately needed an overhauling in terms of its organization and mindset but its provincial President, Hafiz Hidayat Husain, speaking at the UPML's annual session in 1935, expressed the view that political parties in the new provincial legislatures should not be formed on a communal basis. Husain further argued that communal matters needed to be solved on a provincial basis since attempts at an all India settlement were usually unsuccessful due to 'the impossible nature of the task'.[27] He, therefore, demanded the appointment of a provincial committee to negotiate an agreement with non-Muslim parties regarding safeguards for Muslims. This position was diametrically opposed to Jinnah's new plan that envisaged a central Muslim organization negotiating an all-India settlement to resolve the communal question.

To counteract such drift, Jinnah moved swiftly after the ML's 1936 Bombay session. He convened a meeting of nearly fifty important Muslim leaders from all over India in Delhi in late April 1936 to set up a central Muslim League Parliamentary Board (MLPB) along with provincial parliamentary boards that would select candidates to be put up in Muslim constituencies for the forthcoming elections.[28] At this meeting a nine-member U.P. MLPB was also set up to oversee the distribution of party tickets in U.P. It included Nawab Mohammad Ismail Khan, Khaliquzzaman, Shaukat Ali, Maulana Husain Ahmad Madani, the Raja of Mahmudabad, the Nawab of Chhatari, Sir Muhammad Yusuf, Nawabzada Liaquat Ali Khan and the Raja of Salempur.[29] While the first four who were either serving or ex-Congressmen, belonged to the erstwhile MUB and comprised its 'left wing', the last five were landlords who were members of the recently created NAP and embodied its 'right wing'. The Raja of Salempur however had a foot in both the camps and often mediated between them while the Raja of Mahmudabad represented the only personal ally that Jinnah had on the board.

While the MUB group had merged itself into the ML as a result of its ideological affinities with Jinnah, the landlords had joined it in order 'to take over the organization of the party and blunt its radical edge.'[30] They, therefore, retained their membership of the NAP even after joining the U.P. MLPB. The ML was thus a ramshackle coalition of disparate Muslim groups beset with conflicts right from its inception and not surprisingly tensions between

27 *Indian Annual Register*, Vol. 2 (1935), 313.

28 *The Leader*, 30 April 1936.

29 *The Leader*, 23 May 1936.

30 Haig to Linlithgow, 21 May 1936, *Haig Papers*.

the MUB and NAP groups soon burst out into the open. At the April 1936 Delhi meeting itself, Nawabzada Liaquat Ali Khan of the NAP group objected to the heavy representation given to the MUB members on the central and provincial boards, noting that they 'belonged to a school of thought not generally approved of by a majority of Musalmans.'[31] Keen to placate Liaquat, who had been instrumental in persuading him to return from exile, Jinnah persuaded the U.P. members present at Delhi to sit together and hammer out a mutually acceptable compromise. Shaukat Ali and Nawab Ismail Khan, representing the MUB group, and Chattari and Liaquat, representing the NAP group finally met and arrived at an agreement. It entailed convening a new conference in U.P. whose participants would then elect a new U.P. MLPB. The membership to this conference was to be open to all the U.P. members of the council of the AIML, besides any other person or persons about whom there was a unanimous agreement.

The agreement however did not last long. The MUB group started a war of words with the NAP group hoping to push it out of the ML with Khaliquzzaman inaugurating this battle between the 'left' and the 'right' wings of the ML. In a press statement, Khaliq stated that even though the 'progressive' MUB group had a majority in the central MLPB, the body had been 'disfigured' by the inclusion of the NAP's Nawab of Dacca and Nawab Sir Mohammad Yusuf.[32] Khaliq disparagingly noted that the NAP was a creature of the government and set up at the instance of Sir Malcolm Hailey, the former Governor of U.P. He claimed that the landlords had wanted the freedom to contest on a separate NAP ticket even after becoming members of the ML. This move however had been stymied by the MUB group and he insisted that Chhatari, Liaquat and Yusuf had been allowed into the U.P. MLPB only after giving an undertaking that they would not contest the elections on the NAP ticket. Having made clear the inadmissibility of dual membership, Khaliq cleverly suggested that for practical purposes the NAP no longer existed and happily concluded that 'its political end is doubtless good both for the nation and the country.' And tellingly, he added that the NAP 'as it stood was never a match for the Congress, but its dissolution has cleared the path of the Congress.'[33] Finally, Khaliq asked the ML's supporters to look forward to the party manifesto that would be released on 8 June as it would clarify its 'progressive' character. This election manifesto

31 *The Leader*, 8 August 1936.

32 *The Leader*, 3 June 1936.

33 *The Leader*, 3 June 1936.

was quite similar to the one released by the Congress Parliamentary Board and led K. M. Ashraf, a prominent socialist and Nehru's trusted lieutenant, to hail it as 'progressive and liberal in spirit'.[34]

The NAP members on the UPMLPB were now placed in a rather uncomfortable situation. Denying that they had ever promised to dissociate themselves from the NAP completely, Chhatari and Yusuf sent their letters of resignation to Jinnah.[35] Chhatari explained that he had resigned since teamwork had become impossible in the UPMLPB given the divergent ideologies of its members. This divergence, he claimed, revolved around the interpretation of the Communal Award and its implications for the Muslim community. Chhatari argued that since the Award carried all the necessary safeguards necessary for the Muslims 'there was no exclusive Muslim issue which called for the presentation of a united Muslim front.'[36] He further warned that the ML's decision to elect Muslim representatives on a communal basis was dangerous since the community would be reduced to a state of a permanent minority under the new parliamentary form of government. Muslim communal parties inside legislatures would also be detrimental to the community's interests since they would be a constant irritant to other communities.[37] He also asserted that the creation of communal parties would create plenty of opportunities for Governors to use their special powers, something that every political party wanted to avoid. Mixed parties on the other hand would lead to fewer occasions for the Governor to use his special powers and hence reduce them to a dead letter.[38] Chattari further questioned Jinnah's nationalist credentials noting that if the latter was indeed a nationalist he would rather form a non-communal party than sow mistrust between India's various communities through his communal politics.[39] In the same breath though, Chhatari had no problem in accusing the MLPB of being a front for the 'Hindu' Congress. Finally, alluding to the UPMLPB's radical proclivities, Chhatari claimed that the formation of mixed parties involving Hindus and Muslims was essential for preventing U.P. from becoming a centre of 'socialistic and communistic movements.'[40] His colleague, Nawab Muhammad

34 *The Leader*, 25 June 1936.

35 *The Leader*, 17 June 1936.

36 *The Pioneer*, 22 July 1936.

37 *The Leader*, 11 May 1936.

38 *The Leader*, 3 August 1936.

39 *The Pioneer*, 22 July 1936.

40 *The Leader*, 20 June 1936.

Yusuf was more candid, stating that he had decided to resign from the ML and stay on in the NAP since Muslim interests could be best protected only by a combination of Hindu landlords and Muslims.[41] Another U.P. landlord, Sir Mohammed Yamin Khan, piously noted that an election campaign by a combined party of Hindus and Muslims would create good feelings and arouse patriotism instead of communalism. He further alluded to how Hindus and Muslims in U.P. had always lived in perfect harmony, co-operating with each other both inside and outside the legislature, and advised that they should now use the existing separate electorates only for electing the best candidates, 'and carry communalism no further.' Finally, Yamin Khan declared that more than anything, it was economic interests, which were the basis of unity among social groups in India. As he noted, 'a zamindar whether he is a Musalman or a Hindu has to unite with other zamindars and socialists of different religions will unite among themselves. It is preposterous to think that a socialist returned on an ML ticket will work harmoniously with a conservative zamindar returned on the same ML ticket'.[42]

The departing leaders were sent off in a hail of criticism by the MUB group. Khaliquzzaman pointed to the glaring contradiction between Chhatari's fierce advocacy of separate electorates and his simultaneous efforts to form a mixed party of Hindu and Muslim landlords on a non-communal basis.[43] Salempur echoed Khaliq by pointing out that Chhatari had been a recent President of the AIMC, which was built on a communal programme and wondered as to what metamorphosis had occurred in the Nawab's thinking within such a short period of time. Responding to Chhatari's interpretation of the Communal Award's implications, Salempur responded that the Award was not sacrosanct as it still had influential detractors within the Hindu community. To think that the Muslims were safe because of the Award was foolhardy as it could be abrogated at any time. Recent history had after all shown that such protections or legal covenants were fragile and could be easily violated, for even a body such as the League of Nations had been unable to stop the illegal Italian invasion of Abyssinia. Muslims, therefore, needed to unite in order to protect the gains of the Award. Salempur further argued that a mixed party would severely test the loyalty of Muslims to their own community whenever issues such as representation in services, protection of religious, educational and cultural

---

41 *The Leader*, 20 June 1936.

42 *The Leader*, 9 May 1936.

43 *ThePioneer*, 28 July 1936.

interests came up. Reacting to Chhatari's jibe about the MUB group's alleged socialist orientation, Salempur asserted that the ML on the contrary was pledged to the protection of private property and was against socialism since it was an anti-Islamic doctrine. As he pontificated, the whole structure of Islam was 'built on a firm belief in God and a major portion of the Shariat law relates to inheritance, distribution and use of private property.'[44] Shaukat Ali rounded off this criticism by castigating the NAP group members as 'weaklings' who were more interested in securing the Chief Ministership and other ministerships for themselves rather than safeguarding the rights of the Muslim community.[45]

The next meeting of the central MLPB was held at Lahore in June 1936 after Chhatari and Yusuf's exit. It led to further wrangling between the MUB group and a rump of the NAP group that still remained in the MLPB and was represented by Liaquat.[46] When the draft rules regarding the formation of provincial parliamentary boards came up for discussion at this meeting, the Nawabzada pointed out that the U.P. members had already devised a method at the Delhi meeting for electing provincial parliamentary boards. The MUB group however refused to stand by the Delhi agreement after Chhatari and Yusuf's exit. The new stalemate led to a fresh round of discussions presided over by Jinnah at his room in Lahore's Hotel Nedou on 9 June as he sought to bring peace between the warring factions yet again. After protracted discussions, the two groups arrived at a new agreement. Under this agreement it was decided that the total number of members attending the conference to elect the UPMLPB in early July should not exceed one hundred. In addition to the fifty six members already invited, another forty four members were to, therefore, be invited. It was also decided that the invitees were to be carefully selected to maintain the balance between the different factions in the UPMLPB. Liaquat was allowed to invite eighteen of his nominees while Nawab Ismail Khan was allowed to nominate the remaining twenty six members. The concession to Liaquat was Jinnah's signal that the door was still open for Chhatari and other Muslim landlords to leave the NAP and come back to the UPMLPB.[47]

Liaquat did not attend the meeting that was scheduled for 9 July but postponed to 11 July, since he was informed that it was being held to primarily choose the twenty six members assigned to Nawab Ismail Khan. The 11 July

44 *The Pioneer*, 24 July 1936.

45 *The Pioneer*, 22 July 1936.

46 *The Leader*, 8 August 1936.

47 *The Leader*, 8 August 1936.

meeting however departed considerably from the agreement struck between Ismail Khan and Liaquat by deciding to convene a conference of 300–400 persons to elect the UPMLPB. These primarily included loyalists of the MUB group.[48] Salempur justified this new move on the ground that the MLPB wanted to send 'progressive Muslims' to the legislatures and keep out people who were pledged to support the NAP. He further remarked that the Nawabzada could not complain against the 'progressives' since he himself had enthusiastically supported the ascendance of the 'progressive' group at the 1936 AIML Bombay session and had been happy to become a member of the UPMLPB in spite of knowing the antecedents of the MUB group. Salempur concluded his defence by claiming that the discussions between Chhatari and Nawab Ismail Khan at Delhi were informal and tentative and hence the agreement reached between them was not binding.[49] Liaquat's strong protests at this innovation led to another meeting on 20 July which also ended in failure. Some members now left for Bombay to confer with Jinnah and a final meeting to resolve the matter was held in early August at Lucknow. Liaquat now indicated that that if a larger board as conceived by the MUB group was to be created, 'the members should be real representatives of Muslim opinion.' He therefore proposed a new set of invitees.[50] These proposals were rejected and the MUB group unilaterally decided to invite only those people who it thought were 'suitable'. This was the final straw for Liaquat who therefore resigned from the UPMLPB in protest against the tactics of a 'cabal and a clique', whose actions, he asserted, would 'prove fatal to the very ideology and interest of the League'. He claimed that instead of 'uniting the Musalmans into a politically homogeneous mass', the MLPB would 'create fissiparous tendencies and divide the community into factions and mutually repellant, warring, but suicidal sections.'[51] Nawab Jamshed Ali Khan of Baghpat, another big landlord from western U.P., also quit the

---

48 *The Leader*, 16 August 1936.

49 *The Leader*, 16 August 1936.

50 The invitees were to be members of the AIML from U.P., members of the UPML, five representatives of elected Muslim members of the municipal and district boards of the province and Muslim Chairmen of notified and town areas, members of the court of the Muslim universities from U.P., ten representatives from *Jamiatul Ulama-i- Hind*, ten representatives from *Jamiatul Ulama* Cawnpore, ten representatives of *Jamiatul Quresh*, members of the standing committee of AIMEC from U.P., members of the managing committee of the provincial educational conference, ten representatives from *Nadwatul Ulama*, and ten representatives from All India Shia Conference.

51 *The Leader*, 8 August 1936.

UPMLPB along with Liaquat.[52] The departures did not cause much anguish in the MUB group for a triumphant Khaliq welcomed Liaquat's departure noting that 'his right place is with the Nawab of Chhatari. I broadly divide the Muslim political groups into progressive and reactionary. If he is neither, what is he? Divided loyalty will serve no end.'[53]

The battle lines were now clearly drawn between the UPMLPB and the NAP thus ending Jinnah's dreams of forming a united Muslim party in U.P. for the provincial elections. The former's conference was finally held in mid-August 1936 at the Ganga Pershad Memorial Hall in Lucknow.[54] It was presided over by the Raja of Salempur and attended by four hundred delegates from different parts of U.P. Jinnah, the main speaker at the meeting used the platform to reiterate the ML's new ideology. Deploring the fact that the ML for the past thirty years had been nothing more than an academic body with no real contact with the Muslim masses he urged the delegates to make it an active mass-based organization. Jinnah insisted that the 1935 Act provided the best opportunity for the Muslim community to organize itself and it was therefore the duty of every Muslim to become a member of the League. He also clarified the party's ideological position claiming that it was wrong to view the ML as a 'communal' body. The organization of Muslims as a separate entity was natural, given the institutional reality of separate electorates. The ML was only trying to unite 80 million Muslims of India under one banner, making 'patriotic, progressive and nationalistic citizens' out of them, thus making the greatest contribution to the freedom of the country. Jinnah sardonically remarked that there were only two non-communal bodies in the country – the Unionist Party in Punjab and the NAP in U.P., but both these organizations were the most reactionary.[55] In closing, Jinnah reiterated that the ML would allow any Muslim who subscribed to its creed to join the party, irrespective of past affiliations provided that he promised to adhere to the ML's programme. He would only exclude 'job hunters and self-seekers who thought of nothing but personal aggrandizement at the expense of the community.'[56]

This was the last signal to Muslim landlords in the NAP to leave that organization even if they could not join the ML. The Raja of Jehangirabad

52 *The Leader*, 14 August 1936.

53 Ibid.

54 *The Pioneer*, 16 August 1936.

55 *Zulqarnain*, 21 August 1936.

56 *The Pioneer*, 16 August 1936.

became the first to break from the NAP ranks by deciding to stand as an independent candidate from Barabanki rural Muslim seat after a meeting with Jinnah.[57] In return, the ML decided to withdraw Mubashir Husain Kidwai as its candidate against him, shifting him instead to the Sitapur rural Muslim constituency. Salempur and Mahmudabad now proceeded to resign from the NAP which they had joined at its inception under official encouragement.[58] A meeting of the Working Committee of the UPMLPB comprising twenty five members followed at Salempur house with Salempur as President, Khaliquzzaman as the Secretary and Mahmudabad as Treasurer. Four subcommittees were appointed to deal with Election Manifesto, Finance, Propaganda and the Election Fund. Thereafter, donations were solicited for the MLPB election fund. The young idealistic Raja of Mahmudabad, who affectionately addressed Jinnah as 'uncle' given their long standing and close family ties, was by far the biggest donor contributing ₹ 10,000 to the fund.[59]

While attempts to set up a party organization and collecting funds for electioneering were steps in the right direction, all was not well even within the MUB group inside the ML since the Raja of Salempur, the Chairman of the MLPB, and Khaliquzzaman, its secretary, were involved in a tussle for leadership of the party. The U.P. Governor Harry Haig reported to the Viceroy that each of these ambitious men was working to get the other defeated in the elections.[60] He further noted that the Raja of Mahmudabad seeing the disarray in the party was 'beginning to regret his association with the Muslim League and is not very likely to take a very active part in the elections on its behalf.'[61] On the outside, the ML had to contend with the withdrawal of the Shia Political Conference from its ranks. The organization was angry that strong Shia applicants had been overlooked in favour of Sunni candidates. It also alleged that wherever the NAP had nominated Shia candidates, the ML was putting up strong Sunni candidates against them to ensure their defeat.[62] The Shias also suspected some ML leaders of attempting to stoke the *Madhe Sahaba* agitation led by the Sunnis.

---

57 *The Pioneer*, 18 August 1936; Haig to Linlithgow, 29 October 1936, *Haig Papers*.

58 *The Leader*, 16 September 1936.

59 *Zulqarnain*, 21 August 1936; *The Pioneer*, 18 August 1936.

60 Haig to Linlithgow, 2 December 1936, *Haig Papers*.

61 Ibid.

62 *The Pioneer*, 5 January 1937.

Muslim and Hindu Landlords Combine in U.P.: The National Agriculturalist Party (NAP)

The NAP began as a rather loose association of landlords, united by their class interests and fear of the Congress's radical rhetoric of land reform. But the NAP always remained a party on paper as the landlords were a disunited lot owing to mutual jealousies and conflicts and did not see much necessity in forming a cohesive political organization. They smugly believed that personal influence in their estates was what finally counted and that it would secure them the necessary votes of their tenants.[63] Not surprisingly, the party faced difficulties in raising funds, setting up district organizations and beginning a propaganda offensive against their rivals. Nevertheless, Harry Haig, the U.P. Governor, felt that if the NAP leaders were able to prevent their supporters from fighting each other, they would be able to defeat the Congress in a majority of the constituencies. As Haig explained to the Viceroy, the interests of Hindu and Muslim landlords were identical and they could greatly help each other 'through the influence the Muslim landlord has over his Hindu tenants, and vice versa.'[64]

This, however, was a fond hope, for the party also came to be divided along communal lines in addition to suffering from personality conflicts between its members. Thus, Jinnah's policy of setting up the UPMLPB caused much consternation among Muslim landlords who appeared reluctant to compete electorally against it since its 'name carried considerable influence in the U.P.'[65] The landlords' initial strategy was to 'capture the machinery of the provincial electoral board and having done so, render it nugatory.'[66] They could not however succeed in this endeavour, thanks to the vigilance of the MUB group and due to the fact that the NAP leaders lacked strength to stand up to Jinnah.[67] When the latter made it clear that MLPB members could not run on any other ticket in the elections, the landlords finally had to make a choice and resigned from the MLPB. However, even after their resignations they continued to hedge their bets. Thus, Chhatari made it clear that he continued to be a member of the council of the ML even though he was no longer a part of the UPMLPB.[68]

---

63 Haig to Linlithgow, 29 October 1936, *Haig Papers.*

64 Ibid.

65 Haig to Linlithgow, 21 May 1936, *Haig Papers.*

66 Ibid.

67 Ibid.

68 *The Pioneer,* 22 July 1936.

If the ML's attempts to wreck the NAP from the Muslim side presented one set of problems for its leaders, the same headache was presented from the Hindu side by the Hindu Mahasabha. Pandit Madan Mohan Malaviya led these efforts at pulling away Hindu landlords from the NAP but his attempts ended in failure as powerful Hindu landlords led by Raja Rampal Singh and the industrialist Sir J. P. Srivastava pushed back against these attempts and, in turn, captured the Hindu Mahasabha organization ousting Malaviya in the process.[69] The victorious NAP Hindu landlords now proceeded to display their Hindu credentials in a robust fashion in an attempt to woo the Hindu vote. Thus, J. P. Srivastava never failed to trumpet loudly that the Hindu landlords were in a majority in the NAP. This fact was further underlined by Raja Rampal Singh, the head of the Oudh branch of the NAP and also the President of the Hindu Sabha in U.P., a man described by Haig as 'a very strong Hindu.'[70]

Chhatari and his associates were therefore caught in a bind, as on the one hand they were stuck in a party dominated by Hindu landlords who did not care to hide their Hindu sympathies and on the other they had lost credibility for not throwing in their lot completely with the ML. Suspicion between the Hindus and Muslims in the NAP was further accentuated by competition between Chhatari and Srivastava for the expected Premiership of the Province. Chhatari had been a member of the U.P. government for many years and had also acted as the Governor on a couple of occasions. With his seniority and experience, he saw himself as the obvious choice for the Premiership. However, his candidature was opposed by Hindu landlords backing J. P. Srivastava on the ground that a province which was 80 per cent Hindu could not have a Muslim Premier.[71] The row over the selection of candidates made matters worse for the NAP, with the selection of candidates being determined primarily on the basis of loyalty to either Chhatari or Srivastava.[72]

The landlords sought to paper over the communal divide in a number of ways. To begin with, the NAP was openly divided into Hindu and Muslim wings, with J. P. Srivastava and Nawab Mohammad Yusuf appointed as their respective leaders.[73] The NAP also declared that its members were free to vote on communal matters according to their conscience. That the NAP was

69 Ibid.

70 Haig to Linlithgow, 29 October 1936, *Haig Papers.*

71 Ibid.

72 Haig to Linlithgow, 6 January1937, *Haig Papers.*

73 *The Leader*, 18 November 1936.

hedging its bets in all possible ways became evident when it too decided to not put up a candidate against Jehangirabad. It made a similar gesture towards Salempur who was standing on an ML ticket, hoping to lure him back into their fold after the election. This led to the ML adopting a similar strategy as it did not set up any candidates against Liaquat, who ultimately contested as an Independent from Muzaffarnagar,[74] or Chhatari in Bulandshahr, or his cousin Abdus Sami Khan who contested from Aligarh on NAP tickets.[75]

The NAP relied heavily on the government to bolster its morale as well as for help in its propaganda activities through its Rural Development Programme that was funded by the central government. The programme was based on the ICS officer F. L. Brayne's work in the Gurgaon district of Punjab.[76] Under the programme, 270 development circles were established in U.P. with each circle comprising twelve villages. A central organizer was appointed for each circle, and village committees were set up in each village, while a rural development association was set up for each district.[77] These bodies included zamindars besides local officials. The activities under this programme were coordinated by a Rural Development Officer in the district who was given a discretionary grant of ₹ 5000. The scheme sought to involve the villagers in a big way in its activities that included opening night schools and libraries in the interiors of the district, providing them regular funds for maintenance, building halls in rural centers to hold meetings, digging wells, providing rewards for owners of the best sanitary houses, training *dais* in each village, replenishing medicine chests already supplied to various villages and subsidizing shops for local products.[78] A Haig Shield competition was also instituted, to annually honour a village in each of the commissioner's divisions in U.P. for achieving the greatest annual village improvement.[79] It was hoped that this developmental work would earn the government and the NAP the gratitude of the rural population. As C. S. Venkatachar, a senior ICS officer in U.P. at the time noted

---

74 Liaquat to Jinnah, 11 November 1936, in Muhammad Reza Qasimi (ed.), *Jinnah-Liaquat Correspondence* (Karachi, 2003).

75 P. D. Reeves, B. D. Graham and J. M. Goodman, *A Handbook to Elections in Uttar Pradesh, 1920–1951* (Delhi, 1975), 292–95.

76 MSS Eur 180/85 *Memoirs of C. S. Venkatachar*, ICS, U.P., OIOC, British Library, London.

77 *The Leader*, 13 November 1936.

78 *The Leader*, 4 May 1936.

79 *The Leader*, 28 July 1936.

> The government was not concerned with the long term prospects of the project....[T]he immediate object of the project was to use it as an adjunct to the electoral campaign on behalf of the landlords. In 1936 the development plan I was operating from Lucknow became a front to promote the electoral prospects for the landlords of Agra and Oudh. . . . Divisional meetings ostensibly for the purpose of giving impetus for development work were avowedly political rallies for furthering the cause of NAPs.[80]

J. P. Srivastava was actively involved with the logistics of the scheme. In the winter of 1936, he organized two shows to further boost the election campaign of the NAP. One was an Industrial Exhibition in Lucknow, which drew large crowds. The other was a visit by Lord Linlithgow to a few villages outside Lucknow which were given wide publicity.[81] Further publicity was gained by taking credit for the remissions granted by the government to peasants for loss of crops owing to frost in January, hail in February and untimely rains in March. These remissions were to the tune of ₹ 407 lakhs in rent and ₹ 112 lakhs in revenue.[82] Later, when floods struck the province, the NAP organized relief efforts in an effort to gain political mileage for the elections. The government also facilitated the withdrawal of a number of independent candidates in order to avoid division of anti-Congress votes and facilitate straight contests between the Congress and the NAP. The government also utilized the provision that returning officers had powers to decide on the validity of nominations, with no provision for appeal against their decisions. Thus, the NAP's Chhatari and Maheshwar Dayal Seth were returned unopposed because the nomination papers of the Congress candidates opposing them were rejected. Finally, the government efforts in this regard could often be direct for a circular sent to the Court of Wards plainly ordered them to oppose Congress candidates.[83]

The Provincial Assembly Elections of 1937 in U.P. and Local Alliances

If the MLPB and the NAP flirted with each other, the advent of elections in U.P. saw a series of informal local level alliances and seat sharing adjustments, reflecting the desire of all parties to maximize their chances. Thus, the U.P. Congress also came to an informal arrangement with Malaviya's Congress

80 MSS Eur 180/85, *Memoirs of C.S. Venkatachar.*

81 Ibid.

82 *The Leader*, 9 June 1936.

83 B. R. Nanda (ed.), *Selected Works of GB Pant*, Vol. 7 (New Delhi, 1997), 101.

National Party (CNP), known for its Hindu credentials, which came to be known as the Malaviya-Rafi Kidwai pact. The Congress hoped that this agreement would help prevent some of its Hindu voters from walking into the Hindu Sabha camp. The CNP, on the other hand, hoped to consolidate its position within the Congress as a pressure group and push the party into adopting a hard line on the question of the Communal Award. According to the terms of this pact, CNP candidates were free to act according to their own party rules and discipline on matters relating to the Communal Award, while on every other matter they would abide by the Congress party discipline.[84] Similar deals were struck between the CNP and the Congress in other provinces.[85]

The U.P. ML and the U.P. Congress too came to a widely known informal arrangement with regard to their common enemy the NAP. This understanding between the two was evident as only three seats saw contests between the Congress and ML candidates.[86] The main opponent as far as both were concerned was the NAP. Nehru campaigned vigorously during these elections for the Congress. On his tour of Muslim areas, Nehru expressed regret at the lack of sufficient Congress Muslim candidates, but asked his audience to vote for ML candidates if there was no Congress candidate in the fray, as the League candidate was against the colonial government.[87] The level of cooperation between the Congress and ML can be gauged from the CID report that claimed that Rafi Ahmed Kidwai, the chairman of the U.P. Congress Parliamentary Board, had given ₹ 5000 to the ML candidate from Allahabad, Abdul Rahman, to defeat the prominent NAP candidate Nawab Sir Mohammed Yusuf.[88]

On the ML side, Shaukat Ali at Allahabad recalled the days of the Non-Cooperation movement and prophesized that Hindus and Muslims would again join in a similar movement to overthrow colonial rule. The veteran Khilafatist also predicted that both Congress and the ML would be successful

---

84 *The Pioneer*, 7 March 1937.

85 These pacts were also concluded in C.P. and Punjab but both fell through as elections approached. See *The Pioneer*, 8 January for a report on the C.P. and 13 January 1937 for a report on the Punjab.

86 *Oral History Transcript*, NMML, interviews with Ajit Prasad Jain and Sampurnanand. Also see the memoirs of Abdul Latif Bijnori, *Latif ki Kahani* (Bijnor, 1967). Latif was a Muslim member of the Congress and a candidate for the Bijnor District South East Muslim Rural seat in the 1937 elections. See also the memoirs of Muzaffar Hasan, *Meri Siyasi Sarguzasht* (Lucknow, 1983). Hasan was the President of the City Congress Committee, Allahabad, between 1936 and 1946.

87 *PAI for the week ending 30 January 1937.*

88 *PAI for the week ending 9 January 1937.*

in the elections and would soon come to an honourable compromise.[89] Again at Jhansi, while campaigning for the ML candidate Zahur Ahmad, Shaukat Ali asked the Muslims to be sympathetic to the Congress and pointed to the possibilities of a Jawaharlal-Jinnah agreement on the Hindu–Muslim question. He also reminded the voters of the services rendered by the ML candidate to the Congress during the Non-Cooperation movement.[90] The Congress got Muslim cooperation in a number of places during the elections as a result of this understanding with the ML. At Gonda, many influential Muslims and Muslim zamindars assisted the Congress candidates at polling stations.[91] At Aligarh, the students of the Muslim University campaigned enthusiastically for the Congress/Ahrar candidate Hafiz Imamuddin against Chattari's cousin Abdul Sami Khan, who was running on an NAP ticket. The Vice Chancellor of the Muslim University at Aligarh, Sir Ziauddin was heckled by his own students for supporting Sami Khan during the election campaign.[92]

The *ulama* took active part in these elections and campaigned extensively for both the ML and Congress candidates, invoking a number of issues to rally the electorate. A *Jamiat-i-Falastin* was set up to take up the cause of Palestine, with an executive of fifteen members drawn from diverse range of Muslim opinion. It included *ulama* such as Maulana Husain Ahmad Madani and Maulana Hifzur Rahman, nationalists such as Nawab Mohammed Ismail Khan and Khaliquzzaman and socialists such as K. M. Ashraf.[93] Madani, in particular, campaigned extensively for the ML in these elections. His election speeches, mirroring those of Nehru, focused on the poverty and deprivation caused in India due to colonial rule and the necessity therefore of throwing the British out of India. As Madani pointed out, several famines had occurred since the advent of British rule and the treasury was empty as a result of British exploitation of the Indian economy. Besides holding the British responsible for draining India's wealth, he accused them of fostering Hindu–Muslim enmity. In various election meetings, Madani assured his audience that the Congress was not a Hindu organization, reminding them that both Hindus and Muslims had commonly founded the Congress. He further explained that the present object of the Congress was to join the assembly so that 'they might amend and

89 *PAI for the week ending 16 January 1937.*

90 *PAI for the week ending 23 January 1937.*

91 *PAI for the week ending 13 February 1937.*

92 *The Leader*, 10 February 1937.

93 *PAI for the week ending 2 January 1937.*

protest against the new constitution for the benefit of future generations.'[94] The *ulama's* support for the ML can be gauged from the fact that when a candidate, Hakim Mian Mohammad, standing against Nawab Ismail Khan in Meerut claimed that he was a candidate of the JUH, the organization's central leadership quickly swung into action. Its top ranking leader, Maulana Ahmad Said declared that the JUH was backing ML candidates during these elections and anyone claiming to be a JUH candidate was only there to do grave harm to the Muslim community.[95]

The main opposition to the Congress and the ML came from the NAP and the Hindu Sabha. The U.P. Hindu Sabha, while taking care to avoid contests with the NAP, declared that it would not be affected by the Malaviya-Kidwai pact and would set up candidates against Congress nominees. This decision was subsequent to a motion of no-confidence that was passed against Malaviya at the working committee meeting of the Hindu Mahasabha in Delhi, which also authorized his *bête noire* Bhai Parmanand to take charge of the election campaign.[96] The Hindu Sabha candidates sought to portray the Congress as an organization, which was against Hindu interests. Thus, in Benares, Jhingan Sahu, who stood as a rebel candidate against the official Congress candidate Sampurnanand, claimed that the Congress was contesting the elections with the object of wiping out Hindu religion. He further pointed to the socialist leanings of Sampurnanand who, he claimed, had no faith in God or Hindu scriptures. Similarly, at Fyzabad the Congress leader Narendra Dev's socialist leanings were publicized to show that he was an atheist and not a Hindu. In Mathura and Vrindavan, the Varna Ashrama Swarajya Sangh launched a vigorous campaign against the Congress's candidates citing the party's support for an anti-untouchability campaign and the Temple Entry Bill, which, it was argued, would destroy the Hindu religion.

Seasoned observers of U.P. politics such as Sir Tej Bahadur Sapru and C. Y. Chintamani, the editor of the *Leader*, felt that the Congress would at most garner 80 seats.[97] It was also believed that the NAP, along with Muslims and other Independents, would be able to cobble together a working majority in the new assembly. The election results therefore came as a huge surprise for everyone, including the Congress. The party won 133 seats out of the total of

---

94 Ibid.

95 *The Pioneer*, 8 January 1937.

96 *The Pioneer*, 13 October 1936.

97 Haig to Linlithgow, 6 January 1937, *Haig Papers*.

159 general seats that it contested, putting it in a position to form a government on its own without any outside help. Its candidates defeated a number of Hindu landlords, thus decimating the Hindu wing of the NAP. Neither the NAP nor the Hindu Sabha for that matter could any longer claim to be the exclusive guardians of Hindu interests.

Jinnah's attempts at organizing Muslim nationalists in U.P. proved reasonably successful as the party bagged 29 out of the 66 Muslim seats in the U.P., making it the largest Muslim party in the U.P. legislative assembly. However, the question remained as to what role this group would end up playing in the new dispensation. The Governor, Sir Harry Haig, felt that the Muslim position was still obscure at this point in time. He, however, noted rumours that the Congress would make efforts to 'win over at least the whole of the Muslim League group, realizing that if they do this and thus split the Muslims seriously, they will render the whole opposition ineffective.'[98] He was, nevertheless, doubtful whether the Congress would 'pass over the handful of genuine Congress Muslims in favour of those who are clearly not in real sympathy with the Congress aims; and even if, to begin with, they attach a fair number of Muslims to themselves, I doubt whether this attachment will last.'[99] Haig's calculation turned out to be rather prescient.

98 Haig to Linlithgow 17 February 1937, in Lionel Carter (ed.), *United Provinces Politics 1936–1937: Formation of the Ministries and Start of Congress Government, Governors Reports and Other Key Documents* (Delhi, 2008), 81.

99 Ibid., 82.

2

Muslim Mass Contacts and the Rise of the Muslim League

I do not subscribe to the belief that Muslims can be united on the basis of a common political belief. Politics is essentially dictated by class interests and every effort to obscure class differentiation will result in the suppression of the class elements.

K. M. Ashraf [1]

When the slogan 'Workers of the World Unite' is raised, nobody has a problem. However when the slogan 'Muslims of the World Unite' is raised, everybody has a problem!

Unknown ML supporter [2]

Given the obvious affinities between Jinnah and a section of the central Congress leadership, as well as the local level understanding in U.P. between their two parties during the 1937 elections, the failure of the Congress to include the ML in a coalition ministry has generated much controversy among historians and remains one of the most hotly debated issues in Partition historiography. The *dramatis personae* involved on both sides in the Partition drama themselves had no hesitation in declaring that the pathway to Pakistan was paved from U.P. in the aftermath of this failure, even if they differed on the causes that led to it.[3] While the episode therefore clearly merits the scholarly attention it has received till now,[4] far greater attention needs to be paid to the actual process by which the ML gained strength in U.P. during the subsequent two years of Congress cabinet rule. Shut out of power and, at the same time, faced with an ambitious Congress drive outside the legislatures to enrol Muslim masses as

1 Letter from K. M. Ashraf to Habib Hassan, 15 July 1938, AICC File G-68/1937.

2 *Zulqarnain*, 28 July 1938.

3 See M. A. K. Azad, *India Wins Freedom* (Delhi, 1988); Chaudhry Khaliquzzaman, *Pathway to Pakistan* (Lahore, 1961).

4 For the latest discussion of the ministry making fiasco which closely evaluates all of the existing literature on the subject, see Salil Misra, *A Narrative of Communal Politics, Uttar Pradesh 1937–1939* (New Delhi, 2001).

its four *anna* members, ML began its own mass mobilization campaign in a desperate bid for survival. In the ensuing battle over the hearts and minds of the Muslim public the ML overcame heavy odds and came out victorious in the end. This first becomes evident from the much larger number of Muslims that were enrolled in the ML ranks clearly dwarfing its rival's more modest achievements. During this growth spurt, the ML itself was transformed from an elite moribund organization into a mass-based party that gave itself a new constitution, a more radical ideology and a revamped organizational structure. Also symptomatic of the party's rise were the pulverizing victories it scored over the Congress in almost all the by-elections that were held for Muslim seats in U.P. during this period. Along with these victories that gave it a commanding presence in the province, the influx into the ML's tent of influential Muslim groups and parties from all over British India, especially at the crucial 1937 Lucknow session, enabled it to stake its claim as the 'sole representative organization of the Indian Muslims.' Needless to say, an important consequence of these successes was Jinnah's elevation to the position of the *Qaid-i-Azam*.

A critical, but lesser known, factor in the ML's successes in the by-elections as well as its mass mobilization campaigns, was the support it received from an influential section of the, Deobandi *ulama* which was perturbed by the Congress dominance over national politics. Led by the redoubtable Maulana Ashraf Ali Thanawi, this group aligned itself with the ML and as a result increasingly came into conflict with fellow Deobandis, especially the faction led by Maulana Husain Ahmad Madani that was allied with the Congress. By 1945, the developing cracks within Deoband caused a split in JUH, the premier organization of the Indian *ulama*, with the former group providing critical support to the ML in its campaign for Pakistan. For now though, there is a need to closely attend to the process of the ML's resuscitation in U.P. and its emergence as an all India party that neither the Congress nor the British government could ignore by the time the Congress ministries resigned in late 1939.

The Congress, Emerging Left Wing, and the Muslim Mass Contact Program

Two factors determined the Congress party's mass contact strategy, as part of which the Muslims were also targeted. To begin with, even as large sections of the Congress were savouring its overwhelming success in the 1937 elections that underlined its reputation as the premier nationalist organization in the country, Nehru, their chief election campaigner, expressed strong opposition to the party entering the new assemblies or accepting offices. This stance reflected Nehru's ideological orientation as also that of the left wing that was becoming increasingly assertive within the party. Nehru feared that such a move would infect the Congress with an effete reformist mentality and lock it in a collaborative enterprise with the British Raj. With the 'right wing' pushing in the opposite direction, the Congress initially was deadlocked on these questions. But even after it tentatively decided to enter the provincial legislatures and form governments, Nehru steadfastly insisted upon keeping up the revolutionary momentum outside the legislatures gained during the election campaign and mobilizing the Indian masses with the object of preparing them for a decisive confrontation with the Raj.

Muslims were specifically targeted for 'mass contact' since the 1937 elections had made it clear that the Congress held little sway over the community. All of the nine Congress candidates who had contested Muslim seats in U.P. had been unsuccessful in the elections. The result may have subdued a lesser man but Nehru maintained a sunny optimism, claiming that the Muslims were not opposed to the Congress as throughout the election campaign he had come across Muslim voters asking him for directions on how to cast their votes.[5] The Congress, he opined, would have done better had it only put up more Muslim candidates or campaigned harder in Muslim constituencies. Undaunted by the electoral failure, Nehru declared that the elections had, in fact, awakened the Muslim masses and they were looking for 'the right leadership and direction'. He went further by grandly announcing that the time had come to cast aside the older tactic of pacts and agreements with a 'reactionary' Muslim leadership and instead reach out to the masses directly.[6] When asked to explain how he planned to make millions of Muslims rally behind the Congress party, Nehru once declared that he would do so by approaching them as 'non-Muslims, i.e., approach them with the economic issue '… My appeal will not be to the top leaders but to the masses with whom the economic reality is bound to prevail.'[7] As Nehru explained, the communal problem was essentially a conflict between upper middle class Hindus and Muslims for jobs in the services, seats in the legislature and power under the new constitution. It had no connection with the masses for not a single communal demand made any reference to

5 S. Gopal, (ed.), *Selected Works of Jawharlal Nehru*, Vol. 8 (New Delhi, 1975), 22 (henceforth SWJN).

6 *SWJN*, Vol. 8, 128.

7 *SWJN*, Vol. 7, 277.

them.[8] The masses themselves were, therefore, not in the least bothered by the communal question. Nehru therefore refused to take cognizance of the 'so-called communal problem.' As he elaborated, the fundamental problems facing Hindu and Muslim masses alike were those of poverty and starvation. They required urgent economic relief and the only way in which these problems could be overcome was by achieving political independence. And the most expeditious way for achieving this result was for all Indians to rally behind the Congress, the only genuine nationalist organization in the country as it engaged in a decisive struggle against the Raj. All other organizations either did not matter, or were impediments in the process of attaining national independence, given their narrow concerns and susceptibility to the Raj's blandishments.

Nehru set up separate department to run the Muslim Mass Contact Program (MMCP) at Anand Bhavan in Allahabad under his communist lieutenant Kunwar Mohammed Ashraf.[9] Ashraf was a Meo from Alwar, a community famous for being neither fully Muslim nor Hindu, borrowing from the traditions and practices of both these religious communities. Ashraf was an arresting choice for other reasons as well. Before earnestly taking to Communism as a young man he had been a devout Muslim in the habit of saying his prayers regularly and keeping fasts. In a later autobiographical essay, Ashraf recalled a fascinating episode from his late teens that paved the way for his disavowal of religion and his evolution into a dedicated Marxist. At the time he had enrolled under a *Murshid* and started the arduous Sufi practice of *Chilla Kashi* that involved reciting a particular prayer 26,000 times over a period of forty days amidst fasting. As he reminisced, he had already had visions of the Prophet Muhammad and Hazrat Ali during his school days, and was convinced that this arduous practice would allow him to 'perceive the Holy light of God.'[10] The

---

8 *SWJN*, Vol. 8, 7.

9 In his personal message for a volume put together in memory of Ashraf after his death, Nehru in declining health seems to have forgotten Ashraf's role in the MMCP. In his message he wrote, 'I came in contact with Dr Ashraf in the middle thirties. I invited him to join the office of the All India Congress Committee when I was President of the organization. He was a hard worker and he did his work conscientiously. He was chiefly concerned with our contacts with countries of Western Asia and his knowledge of the Persian language especially helped him in his work. Nehru perhaps forgot that the foreign department at this time was handled by Ram Manohar Lohia.' See Horst Kruger (ed.), *Kunwar Mohammad Ashraf: An Indian Scholar and Revolutionary, 1903-1962* (Bombay, 1969), 339.

10 'K. M. Ashraf on Himself', in Horst Kruger, (ed.), *Kunwar Mohammad Ashraf: An Indian Scholar and Revolutionary, 1903-1962* (Bombay, 1969), 393.

whole ritual however ended in a disaster. On the thirteenth night of the practice, Ashraf reported to his teacher a dream in which he saw himself sitting with his Hindu friend Shankar Lal drinking cheap wine at their village, which ended with the two intoxicated young men collapsing to the ground and passing out. The *Murshid* on hearing the dream was less than impressed and asked Ashraf a number of questions ranging from whether he had fallen in love just before he started the practice to whether his father's income had ever been tainted by bribery. At the end of the interrogation, young Ashraf was firmly told that spiritual development was not a part of his destiny.

This strange episode marked his gradual turn away from spirituality and a growing inclination towards more secular pursuits. But Ashraf's academic trajectory too was not destined to be smooth for after enrolling for his B.A. at the Muslim University at Aligarh he quit midway through his studies once the Non-Cooperation movement under Gandhi gained momentum. He subsequently joined the Jamia Millia Islamia following the call of the Ali brothers but once Non-Cooperation had petered out, he rejoined the Muslim University taking his B.A. in 1924, an M.A. in 1926, and an LLB in 1927. A scholarship granted by the state of Alwar to study law in England in 1927 was perhaps the turning point in the young man's life for he finally found Marxism in England. His belief in the new ideology was strengthened on a trip back to Alwar to participate in the silver jubilee celebrations of his benefactor, the Maharaja, for he was revolted by the enormous amounts of money being spent on the affair even as there was desperate poverty all around. Returning to England with money given by his father, he proceeded to complete a PhD in history on social conditions in India between 1200 and 1550 under the supervision of Sir Wolseley Haig in London.[11] Among Ashraf's fellow students, friends and communist comrades in London were Z. A. Ahmad and Sajjad Zaheer. On returning to India, the three dedicated communists joined the Congress Socialist Party before joining the AICC office under Nehru when he became the Congress President in 1936. As Sajjad Zaheer reminisced, 'Nehru was very proud of our group. He introduced us to Gandhiji and Sardar Patel saying, people say Muslims are not coming in the Congress. Here is this brilliant group of young Muslims which went to England and took degrees there and had come back and joined the Congress.'[12]

The MMCP under Ashraf took upon itself the task of lifting the Muslim

---

11 This was later published as K. M. Ashraf, *Life and Conditions of the People of Hindustan* (Delhi, 1959).

12 *Oral History Transcript*, Sajjad Zaheer, NMML (New Delhi).

masses out of the rut of communalism and encouraging them to abandon their old style leaders. This was to be done by enlightening them about their true interests and explaining how these would be fulfilled by joining the Congress, which would usher them into a new socialist utopia after leading them to a glorious victory over imperialism. At the more mundane level it involved boosting Muslim enrollment in the Congress as four *anna* members and for this purpose the cell organized membership drives and public meetings in order to reach out to the Muslim masses. Along with Nehru, Ashraf and his comrades sincerely believed that the primary reason for Muslim aloofness from the Congress was the lack of effort by the party to educate them about its own radical policies and programmes. The resulting disconnect was deemed as primarily responsible for the party's debacle in the Muslim seats in the recent elections. In order to therefore publicize Congress policies and programmes, they started a new Urdu newsweekly *Hindustan*.[13] In doing so, the protagonists of the MMCP were only following the tactics of the leaders of the erstwhile Khilafat Movement who had skillfully utilized their Urdu newspapers to educate and mobilize Muslims against the British government's alleged design to undermine the Caliphate. The articles published in the *Hindustan* thus explained the historic reasons for Muslim political backwardness, the rationale behind the new policy of Muslim 'mass contacts', the advantages that would accrue to the community and the country at large by joining the Congress party in large numbers, besides justifying the Congress decision to reject communal pacts with 'reactionary' leaders. Close attention needs to be paid to this overall message that the MMCP communicated to the Muslims and the idiom that was employed in this regard, for it is in response to this message that the ML fashioned its own more successful response that ultimately destroyed the Congress initiative.

Z. A. Ahmad made the initial case for this special Congress pitch towards the Muslims arguing that it was a long overdue and necessary step for radicalizing the Muslim community, which was politically backward and under the control of conservative leaders.[14] Muslim backwardness, he lamented, was particularly reflected in their lack of participation in any anti-imperial activities or their inability to set up any anti-imperial organizations. He contrasted the Muslim condition to the progress of the Hindus who had created the Congress, the

13 The newspaper was started as a limited liability company with a paid-up capital of ₹ 10,000 and individual shares of ₹10. The directors of the company were G. B. Pant, Rafi Ahmad Kidwai, Narendra Dev, Husain Zaheer, K. M. Ashraf and Abdul Aleem. See K. M. Ashraf to Mian Iftikharuddin, 5 May 1937, *AICC Papers File G-68/1937.*

14 Z. A. Ahmad, 'Congress Aur Muslim Awaam', *Hindustan,* 26 September 1937.

premier anti-imperialist organization in the country and also played a dominant role in its political activities. To explain this phenomenon, he relied on a Marxist theory of history that was heavily shot through with economic determinism. Ahmad explained that the critical factor that determined the political and cultural consciousness of any community was the nature of the class that economically dominated it. The Hindus had become politically advanced because they had been dominated in their recent history by the vital progressive force in the current stage of historical development – the capitalist class. This class had emerged by the end of Mughal rule holding a monopoly over trade, commerce and the professions, and fortuitously, was again the first to come into contact and collaborate with the East India Company when it arrived on the country's shores. Ahmad pointed out that while this collaboration may have been motivated by the desire for profits, it had had the crucial effect of introducing Hindu capitalists to modern education that led to the development of a new modern bourgeois consciousness among them, including a greater awareness of their own economic self-interest. The Hindu bourgeoisie were therefore the first to protest against British domination of Indian trade since it hurt their economic interests. Indeed, it is in pursuit of these interests that this class had gone on to form the Indian National Congress. To underline the class origins and character of the Congress, Ahmad pointed to the nature of economic demands made by the early 'moderate' Congress in petitions to the British government, a feature that the later 'Extremists' would call political mendicancy.

In contrast to the Hindus, Ahmad claimed that the dominant economic class among Muslims since Mughal times was the retrograde feudal class of jagirdars and zamindars that stayed away from trade and commerce and served mostly in the Mughal army and administration. This class dominated both the Muslim masses, overwhelmingly peasants who were neo-converts from Hinduism, and Muslim artisans, labour, shopkeepers, professionals and traders that lived in towns and *qasbahs*. Ahmad conceded that this urban Muslim class may have had the potential to propel the Muslim community in the same progressive direction as Hindus but rued the occlusion of this historical possibility due to its smallness in comparison to the larger rural Muslim population. This historical Muslim handicap that led to Muslim political backwardness was further compounded due to the community's delayed introduction to colonial modernity as a result of its active participation in the Revolt of 1857. The brutal British retribution had further alienated them from modern civilization as they sought to isolate themselves from the ways of the British. But the community's biggest misfortune, according to Ahmad, was its betrayal at the hands of putative modernizers like Sir Syed Ahmad Khan who thwarted political modernization of the Muslim community by keeping it away from struggles against British imperialism and its indigenous collaborators such as the zamindars. These urban Muslims thus did not have a progressive imprint on the Muslim mind. In explaining Sir Syed's reactionary attitude, Ahmad again fell back on economic determinism by attributing it to the fact that loyalist rural notables were the biggest donors backing Sir Syed, whose financial contributions had been instrumental in setting up the Mohammedan Anglo-Oriental (MAO) College. The zamindars themselves were steadfast in supporting British rule since it granted them additional privileges at the expense of the rights of their peasants.

While acknowledging the Congress party's inauspicious origins in Hindu capitalist leadership whose forebears had collaborated with the English East India Company that led to India's subjugation in the first place, Ahmad explained how the logic of history had slowly transformed it into the best vehicle for securing India its freedom from colonial rule. It was evident for all to see that the Congress-led 1921 Non-Cooperation Movement had transformed politics in India into a mass phenomenon for the first time, spreading far beyond the towns and penetrating into the countryside. Ahmad understood this development in terms of the sharpening economic contradictions between the Hindu capitalist Congress leadership and the British. This class, cautious earlier, had been emboldened by economic strength it had gained due to booming profits it had made during World War I and was now beginning to search for new and more effective techniques to put pressure on the government. It found a ready ally in a new Muslim leadership that was emerging from the middle class and was frustrated since its economic position had declined over the War. Together, they invited the masses on both sides to perform civil disobedience who, he claimed, responded readily given the severe economic distress they themselves were facing.

Yet, in the end, Non-Cooperation had failed, repressed by British batons and bullets. In order to explain this failure, Ahmad delved into the reasons as to why, even though the objective historical conditions were seemingly ripe, participation of Hindu and Muslim masses in a joint movement had not resulted in overthrowing British rule. In the first place, he blamed the leaders of this movement who, he claimed, were reformists with limited ambitions. These leaders had wanted to bring about a mere regime change without forcing any revolutionary economic or social changes that would disturb status quo in Indian society. But the more important reason for the movement's failure, according to Ahmad, lay in the state of popular consciousness. The masses participating in these struggles had ultimately failed to see their objective class interests and had instead been driven into even deeper and separate channels of false consciousness by their respective bourgeois leadership through their use of the religious idiom. Instead of mobilizing on the basis of real economic and social issues, they had been swayed by the language of Ram Raj or cries of Islam or the Khilafat in danger. Thus, when Non-Cooperation/Khilafat campaign failed in the end due to government repression, it was not surprising that mutual recriminations and horrific riots ensued between Hindus and Muslims since they had marched under the separate flags of their respective leaders.

K. M. Ashraf, the lynchpin of the MMCP, extended the analysis from this point to its contemporary context. Ashraf saw Congress victories in the 1937 provincial elections, as the first opportunity since 1921 for forging a unity between Hindu and Muslim masses so that they could jointly overthrow British rule and achieve economic and political independence under a free socialist state. The objective conditions were again ripe for a revolution since India had been thrust into the throes of a deep economic crisis as a result of the Great Depression. There was widespread hostility against the British and the ordinary man in India was experiencing the destruction of India's economy at a very personal level.[15] The global economic slump, itself a result of sharpening economic contradictions in world capitalism, would inevitably force sweeping transformations in all aspects of human existence breaking down older forms of community, politics, culture and indeed human consciousness. Given this gale force sweeping across the globe, Ashraf was confident that India would not be bypassed by the currents of history. Like Ahmad, he foresaw the coming of a free socialist state in India as inevitable in the face of this new era unfolding in human history.[16] The significance of this era for Ashraf can be discerned from his view that human beings were awakening from a barbaric (*haivaniyat*) phase and entering into the age of humanism (*insaniyat*).

While objective conditions were favourable for overthrowing British imperialism, Ashraf believed that the mistakes of 1921 had to be avoided at all costs so as to not repeat that failure. The MMCP, therefore, needed to urgently awaken Muslim masses to their real economic and political interests, radicalize them on the basis of a new programme that promised land for the landless,

15 K. M. Ashraf, 'Muslim League Ki Siyasi Ahmiyat aur Hamara Tariqeqar', *Hindustan*, 11 September 1938.

16 *Pratap* (Lahore), 15 June 1937, under the headline 'Hindustani Gharibi aur Ghulami ki Zimmedari Imperialism Par Hai. Imperialism ke Bhoot ko Marne ke liye Taaqat ko Paida Karne ki Zaroorat', *AICC Papers File 48/1937.*

security of tenure for peasant proprietors, fair wages and working conditions for workers, employment for the unemployed and freedom from hunger, poverty and starvation. Ultimately, the Muslim masses had to be awakened to an awareness of their class consciousness to enable them to embrace their true *qaum* – that of peasants and workers. This would also make them fully conscious of their class solidarity with Hindu peasants and workers. It is this combined class of Hindu and Muslim workers and peasants that the MMCP wanted to explicitly invite into the Congress fold to make it an effective agent of the revolution.

A New Definition of the Qaum

As evident, this redefinition involved a radical repudiation of existing ideas of the Muslim *qaum* as a community of believers in Islam, with its own distinctive politics or culture. Ashraf emphatically repudiated this existing notion, insisting that he did not subscribe to the belief that the Muslims constituted a natural unity with common economic and political beliefs. As he wrote to a friend, 'politics is essentially dictated by class interests and every effort to obscure class differentiation will result in the suppression of class elements.'[17] Thus, conflict between a Muslim peasant and a Muslim landlord was inevitable since their class interests were distinct and indeed antagonistic to one another. In his many essays, Ashraf continuously harped upon the fundamental contradiction between the so-called leaders of the Muslim community, compradors who propped up the system of foreign exploitation and were allied to indigenous feudal and reactionary vested interests on the one hand, and the Muslim workers and peasants opposed to these interests on the other.[18] Pointedly referring to the ML, Ashraf argued that its leaders had never played a progressive role since its formation by landlord elites in 1907, and it was evident as to which side they would join during the new round of mass struggles.[19] For him, the ML was undoubtedly an agent of British imperialism that wanted to channelize Muslim revolutionary consciousness into a civil war (*khana jangi*) with the Hindus. Its anti-kisan, anti-labour, anti-democratic credentials were evident as its government in Bengal had

17 Ashraf to Habib Hassan, 15 July 1938, *AICC Papers, File G-68/1937-38.*

18 *Searchlight*, 27 April 1937, *AICC Papers File G-18 (iii)/1937.* For a similar argument, see K. M. Ashraf, 'Congress ki Shirkat se Kya Murad Hai', *Hindustan*, 2 August 1938.

19 K. M. Ashraf, 'Muslim League ki Siyasi Ahmiyat aur Hamara Tariqeqar', *Hindustan*, 17 September 1938. See also 'Hamara Kaam', *Hindustan*, 20 February 1938.

crushed civil rights, not released political prisoners and presented no concrete economic or political programmes for alleviating the misery of peasants or working classes. In his view, the ML as a whole was only trying to weaken the Congress led anti-imperialist front even as it claimed to be patriotic and the true political representative of the Muslim community.[20] Ashraf, therefore, accused the ML leadership of perpetuating a 'false' view of politics. It had led Muslims to believe 'through poetry, false history, and through many other such influences' that they could on their own, achieve freedom for India besides building up a strong and disciplined community. He dismissed them as patently false promises, which could never come to fruition. Independence for the country and rejuvenation of the Muslim community with its millions of peasants and workers, he insisted, could only happen by joining the Congress and uniting with forces 'dictated by the logic of history'.

Ashraf was, however, confronted with the task of convincing Muslims to join the Congress in large numbers for they had largely stayed away from it ever since the collapse of the Non-Cooperation/Khilafat Movement due to fears and suspicions of the latter being a Hindu body. At the outset, he acknowledged that there was indeed some truth behind the impression that Congress was dominated by a Hindu mentality (*zahniyat*). However, this impression, he argued, was superficial since it focused solely on the presence in the party of a Hindu capitalist class whose mentality was indeed communal. It was this Hindu capitalist class, which brought discredit to the Congress as a whole and gave it the appearance of a Hindu organization.[21] Muslims needed to make a distinction between such superficial appearances and the real nature of the Congress. Here, Ashraf took pains to point out that the Congress of today was not like the early Congress, which was indeed a party of Hindu capitalists. Now, it did not include just this single class, but a number of other groups, classes and interests which had joined the party ever since it entered into the phase of mass politics in 1921. Emphasizing this diversity in the Congress he wrote to a skeptical friend that, 'those outside the Congress do not know what a keen struggle goes on amongst the elements inside the Congress.'[22]

20 Ibid.

21 K. M. Ashraf, 'Congress Mein Musalmanon ki Shirkat aur Hindu Zahniyat ka Sawaal', *Hindustan*, 12 September 1937. Ashraf here also made an appeal that the Congress delink itself from *acchutoddhar* and other similar Hindu social reform activities and remain a purely political anti-imperialist organization in order to remove the impression from Muslim minds that it was a Hindu organization.

22 Ashraf to Habib Hassan, 15 July 1938, *AICC Papers, File G-68/1937-38.*

Given this current historical conjuncture wherein the Congress was a vastly different political organization and indeed open to further transformation in a radical direction, Ashraf pointed to the historic role that lay in store for the Muslim masses. The time had come to purge the Congress of its capitalist, Hindu reactionary elements so that it could become a more suitable vehicle for bringing about a revolution in India. If only the radicalized Muslim masses joined the Congress in significant numbers, they could capture the party organization along with their Hindu counterparts already inside it and decisively overturn the domination of Hindu capitalists, reactionaries and right wingers. The Muslim working class and peasants were therefore a key factor. Their joining the Congress would have the additional salutary effect of destroying Muslim reactionaries who had arrogated to themselves, the leadership of the Muslim *qaum*. The resulting political revolution would bring an end to old style politics of pacts and agreements between self-styled leaders of religious communities geared towards dividing the spoils of office.

Ashraf, therefore, appealed to the Muslim masses to join the Congress in large numbers to be on the side of the progressives. [23] Their participation in its activities would not only alter the priorities of the Congress in the right direction but also provide the right channel for their revolutionary energies as it had during the Khilafat Movement. It would also give them better leverage in negotiating safeguards for their religious and cultural rights. In any case, he pointed out that the Congress party's Karachi declaration of fundamental rights had already guaranteed freedom of religion to the minorities and also included provisions for protecting their cultural and religious rights. This resolution was in marked contrast to the 1935 GOI Act which did not have any clause on fundamental rights for the Empire's Indian subjects. The MMCP, thus, was not simply a programme to attract the Muslim masses into the Congress but an attempt to change the very face of Indian politics by anchoring it in a new socialist, secular foundation.

Ashraf optimistically pointed to many positive signs to claim that history in India was moving in the right direction. Political consciousness among Indian Muslims was at an all-time high given their extraordinary poverty and employment. Muslim labour was showing visible signs that it was not communal in its outlook any more by declining to participate in communal rioting. Instead, it had demonstrated its class consciousness by assuming leadership of labour strikes in the city of Kanpur. Muslim peasants had shown the same level of

---

23 K. M. Ashraf, 'Congress ki Shirkat se Kya Murad Hai', *Hindustan*, 28 August 1938.

political maturity as evident from their overwhelming support to Swami Sahajanand in Bihar even though he was a Hindu. In Bengal, Muslim peasants had ignored communal Muslim parties and instead backed Fazlul Haq's Krishak Proja Party. Finally, Muslim students, too, were full of revolutionary fervour for they had taken the lead in forming the secular All India Students Federation (AISF).[24] Even the Congress, Ashraf approvingly noted, was moving in the right direction. While its critique against imperialism was earlier limited to the Drain Theory, it had now been expanded to recognize contradictions between capital and labour under the influence of the left wing.[25] What was needed now was for the Congress to start work afresh among the Muslim masses, a task it had ignored since the end of the Khilafat agitation.

Critique of Congress Left and Right Wings

In placing their own version of a Bread, Peace and Land programme before Muslim masses, the protagonists of the MMCP expressed their strident opposition to any return by the Congress to old style politics involving pacts with self-styled Hindu or Muslim leaders claiming to be at the head of their religious communities. They also opposed participation in the new constitutional reforms instituted under the 1935 GOI Act, portraying such participation as a reformist move that would betray revolutionary ideals. These two positions however put them at odds with not just the Congress 'right wing' but even with some of their own comrades on the left. Ashraf and his colleagues, therefore, went on to articulate their critique of the positions held by both these groups on these issues. In the first place, they condemned the 'right wing' for its willingness to sign communal pacts with the so-called leaders of the Muslim community arguing that such tactics would push back the Congress movement by twenty years.[26] They went on to belittle the argument that another Lucknow Pact between the ML and Congress was necessary. Ashraf pointed to the simple fact that the current circumstances were not comparable to those of 1916. At that time the Congress was like the ML, a club of upper class gentlemen who were reformist in their mindset and modest in their aims. Now, the Congress was a radicalized party whose rank and file aimed at nothing less than a revolution. To go back to an earlier day and age was therefore nothing short of

24 K. M. Ashraf, 'Musalmanon Mein Congress Ka Kaam aur Ishtarakiyyat Pasandon ka Aitraz', *Hindustan*, 10 October 1937.

25 'Muslim League aur Congress', *Hindustan*, 22 August 1937.

26 K. M. Ashraf, 'Hamaara Kaam', *Hindustan*, 20 February 1938.

a travesty. Ashraf wanted the Congress to continue with its current strategy of radicalizing the masses and organizing them on class lines by spreading the web of *kisan* and *mazdoor sabhas* under its own umbrella throughout the country. He also urged Congressmen not to lose heart due to the party's defeat at the hands of the ML in a few by-elections to Muslim seats. There was no reason why the economic programme would not succeed. It would perhaps take time given the centuries of *jahiliyat* in recent Indian Muslim history. But change was around the corner as shown by the extremely encouraging results of work over just the last year. The Congress had just within a year enrolled 100,000 new Muslim members and if the present effort was persisted with, Ashraf was confident the ML would be slowly demolished just as surely as the Congress had succeeded against the communal Hindu Mahasabha. Ashraf further warned the Congress to not be taken in by the ML's new progressive political creed that declared complete independence as its goal, dismissing it as a plain farce and fraud.

MMCP propaganda also attacked the right-wing for trying to hoodwink the masses into believing that the best way to destroy the new constitution was by making jejune threats of civil disobedience while at the same time striving to avoid a confrontation with the government at all costs. Rajagopalachari's statement in Madras during his meeting with the provincial Governor was acidly commented upon in this regard.[27] It was pointed out that his stance was identical to that of the ML leadership, which was not surprising since neither wanted a revolution, but wanted to merely tinker with the constitution while happily sharing fishes and loaves of office. Ashraf was, therefore, harshly critical of the 'reformism' of Congress governments in the provinces that were dominated by right-wingers. He dismissed them as incapable of revolutionary change for they seemed happy with marginal increases in workers' wages or reductions in peasant tax. As he noted, whenever peasants and workers resorted to any independent or direct action, Congress ministries allowed the coercive apparatus of the imperial state to crush them. He excoriated the Congress right wing for actively trying to discipline peasants and workers, for giving them lofty sermons on the virtues of non-violence. He warned that the greatest danger lay in the Congress getting transformed into the liberal party full of reform minded, rather than revolutionary minded, members.[28]

---

27 Sajjad Zaheer, 'Congress ki Wazaratein', *Hindustan*, 8 August 1937.

28 K. M. Ashraf, 'Hamaara Kaam', *Hindustan*, 20 February 1938.

More than the perfidies of the 'right wing', it is the ideological backpedalling by sections of the left that upset the protagonists of the MMCP the most.[29] Thus, when the international Marxist ideologue M. N. Roy declared that the 'Hindu dominated' Congress should accept all 'Muslim' demands, Ashraf chided him for thinking along old lines. As he insisted, there was nothing like a Hindu–Muslim problem. There were only two choices before the Congress – either to accept all 'Muslim minority' demands and continue with old style politics, or to get rid of capitalists and landlords in the Congress who were a major cause for the problem itself being framed in a 'communal' manner. Socialists, he insisted, could not afford to be confused about the right solution. Similarly, Ashraf dismissed calls by fellow socialists for winding up the MMCP on the grounds that it was giving greater fillip to communalism, as evident from the vigorous activities of the Muslim League. As he noted, their objection seemed to imply that the Muslim masses were not ready for any radical programme for they had not yet reached the required level of political maturity. For Ashraf, such an attitude reeked of a defeatist mentality and he castigated socialists for behaving like Congressmen of the yore. Just like the latter were embarrassed by what they saw as the ignorance of their countrymen, socialists seemed to be embarrassed by the very existence of communalism. Both were also fearful of being cast as opponents of Hindu or Muslim culture (*ghair tamadduni*) respectively by their detractors and hence were content to stick to elite politics staying away from mass mobilization. He exhorted socialists to shed such fears and seize the Muslim question in the manner shown by the MMCP, instead of letting Congress right wingers and Muslim communalists reinstitute old style politics of communal pacts between elites.

New Cultural and Political Vocabulary

Finally, the ideologues of the MMCP were not just economic determinists in their understanding of historical development. Instead of waiting for economic contradictions of capitalism to bring about its own destruction they wanted the Congress party to forge a new revolutionary consciousness that would reflect the concerns of the masses who would be its agents. Their protracted 'war of position' thus extended to creating a new political vocabulary which would make terms such as 'progressive' (*taraqqi pasand*), 'reactionary' (*raj'at pasand*), 'socialism' (*ishtarakiyyat*), 'capitalism' (*sarmayadari*), part of the emerging common sense and the building blocks of this new political consciousness. Ashraf and his

[29] K. M. Ashraf, 'Musalmanon Mein Congress Ka Kaam aur Ishtarakiyyat Pasandon ka Aitraz', *Hindustan*, 10 October 1937.

colleagues also attempted to construct a fresh cultural consensus about what constituted the nation and national culture in order to supplant existing sectional and 'communal' ideas with their emphasis on narrow identification with pre-existing community and its culture. Thus, in one of his essays Ashraf controversially denied that there was anything like a 'Muslim culture' that could be identified with the seventy million Muslims of India.[30] A great majority of Indian Muslims, he argued, derived their origins and culture from the Hindus. The culture of these neo-Muslims who formed 85 per cent of the country's Muslim population was thus different from what was popularly known as 'Muslim culture'. 'Muslim culture', he further explained, was a category that changed according to historical contexts. In pre-British times it was the culture of the 'Badshahs', while now, it had become the culture of feudal elites, a microscopic minority who claimed descent from the Arabs. Hence, 'Muslim culture' in both its medieval and modern contexts was elitist and had nothing to do with the culture of the Muslim masses.

Elaborating on this idea, Ashraf made a distinction between medieval 'Muslim' culture and the existing modern one. The 'Muslim' culture of the Badshahs, he noted with some approval, was marked by great internal diversity and openness, there being no rigid uniformity among Muslims at that time. Arabic, Farsi, Chinese, Tartari were all languages of Muslims. High class Muslims delighted in wearing Western, Eastern, Roman, and Indian clothes. In matters of faith, doctrine and devotion as well, there was great diversity among Muslims for Shias, Sunnis, Kharijites, had their own sets of beliefs, rituals and practices. And yet, Ashraf emphasized, this diversity had never threatened these Muslims and was indeed a symbol and source of their strength. In contrast, he witheringly noted that 'Muslim culture' of the feudal elites under colonialism represented by Sir Syed Ahmad Khan's school was so feeble that it felt threatened if someone wore a Gandhi cap or a few Hindus began to propagate Hindi. This culture therefore stressed a stifling uniformity and rigidity. As Ashraf sharply commented, 'If you don't wear a particular type of dress or don't speak high flown Urdu it becomes difficult for you to be seen as a proper Muslim. The truth is that pure and minted (*taksali*) Muslims are only those fortunate people who were raised in the atmosphere of Delhi or Lucknow or if they wear the dresses of Deoband or the Firangi Mahalis.'[31]

30 K. M. Ashraf, 'Congress ki Shirkat aur Musalmanon ki Tehzeeb ka Sawal', *Hindustan* 5 September 1937. Also see *Searchlight* 25 and 27 April 1937 for a report of Ashraf's speeches in Bihar and his clarification, *AICC Papers / File G-68 /1937.*

31 Ibid.

Ashraf traced the enfeeblement of medieval 'Muslim' culture to Muslim loss of their ruling status and subordination under colonialism. The older Muslim culture of the Badshahs was dealt a death blow in 1857. It was further compromised by Sir Syed's school that had grown up in the shadow of the colonial educational system and had no organic connection with genuine older traditions of Muslims.[32] Thus, Ashraf lamented that all that now remained in the name of 'Muslim culture' were dead traditions. Yet, even if Ashraf saw some virtues in the older Muslim culture of the Badshahs, he was quite unsentimental in asking for both these 'dead traditions' to be abandoned and be replaced by a new national culture which would serve the demands of this day and age. This new national culture would be forged in the crucible of struggle against British imperialism and its indigenous support structures and would primarily be led by the middle and working classes. In this context, Ashraf saw the Muslim middle and working classes as possessing far greater revolutionary potential than any other social group because of their greater material and cultural impoverishment under British rule.[33] As part of the revolutionary vanguard, Ashraf and his comrades saw their role in terms of generating a new intellectual culture to meet the demands of the new age. As he wrote, 'we are today engaged in constructing a new and living *tamaddun*. Our political and social struggle is a prelude to this new *tamaddun*.'[34] This new culture, however, would not be a totally new invention. A composite culture had been shared by common Hindus and Muslims in the times of the Badshahs.[35] What was needed was its reinvention in the light of current demands.

The MMCP stalwarts therefore pioneered a number of initiatives in this regard. The most important one was their effort at developing and popularizing Hindustani, which, they claimed, had historically been the language of the masses in north India and the meeting ground between Hindi and Urdu.[36]

---

32 *AICC Papers, File G-68/1937.*

33 See K. M. Ashraf, 'Firqaparvar Siyasi Anjumanon ke kaam Karne ke Tariqey aur Hamara Farz', *Hindustan* 29 August 1937.

34 K. M. Ashraf, 'Congress ki Shirkat aur Musalmanon ki Tehzeeb ka Sawal', *Hindustan* 5 September 1937.

35 'Hamari Qaumi Zabaan', *Hindustan*, 15 August 1937. The rhetoric of the MMCP stalwarts matched the new nationalist historiography being written in this period, which stressed the composite Hindu–Muslim mass culture, the Ganga-Jamuni tehzeeb that developed in north India during the medieval period. Ashraf's own work *Life and Conditions of the People of Hindustan* (Delhi, 1959) reflected this trend.

36 Sajjad Zaheer, 'Congress Ki Wazartein', *Hindustan*, 8 August 1937.

They saw their task at hand to be the further development of this language, making it linguistically capable of absorbing the latest developments in all the areas of arts and sciences. This became an ambitious nationalist project and involved creating everything from a basic primer in Hindustani to instituting a literary canon for this new language. While Dr Zakir Husain at Jamia Millia Islamia at Delhi got busy with the former, the Progressive Writers Association (PWA) arose to meet the latter demand. The manifesto of the PWA clearly stated its revolutionary aims. It was to produce literature, which drew its inspiration from the basic problems of the masses – hunger, poverty, social backwardness and political subjugation. The declared task of this literature was the arousal of critical spirit and the examination of existing institutions and customs in the light of reason.[37] The PWA also signaled its repudiation of older social identities based on religion and its espousal of new social identities grounded in rational class interests. Ashraf and his comrades coupled such efforts with strident criticism of ML's indifference towards matters pertaining to 'Muslim culture' over which the party had been raising such an enormous hue and cry. As Ashraf carpingly noted, old organizations such as *Anjuman-i-Taraqqi-i-Urdu* of Hyderabad and Muslim Educational Conference of Aligarh were 'dying out of sheer decay in spite of so much talk of Urdu and Muslim culture.' He bemoaned that 'there is an appreciable decrease in the quality and quantity of Urdu literature every day and our knowledge of Muslim classics and Islamic history is diminishing'. Muslims these days were usually content with 'third rate productions in Urdu and very few of us have either the leisure or the equipment to look into the originals.'[38] The MMCP, therefore, marked a hard hitting ideological campaign by Muslim Congress socialists to capture the imagination of the Muslim community, which had stayed aloof from the Congress at least since the time of the Civil Disobedience movements. The ML, caught in a pincer attack with the MMCP trying to capture the Muslim political base outside the legislatures and the Congress government's trying to win over its members of legislative assemblies (MLAs) was certainly not going to take it lying down.

---

37 Hafiz Malik, 'The Marxist Literary Movement in India and Pakistan', *Journal of Asian Studies*, Vol. 26, No. 4 (1967), 649–64; Shabana Mahmud, 'Angare and the Founding of the Progressive Writers Association', *Modern Asian Studies*, Vol. 30, No. 2 (May 1996), 447–67.

38 Ashraf to Habib Hassan, *AICC Papers File G-68/1937.*

The ML Response to the Congress MMCP

Nehru had set the tone for the Congress offensive by characterizing the ML as representing 'a group of Muslims, no doubt highly estimable persons, but functioning in the higher regions of the upper middle classes and having no contacts with Muslim masses and few even with the Muslim lower middle class'.[39] Jinnah himself was castigated as an elitist and a reactionary by the organizers of the U.P. Muslim Congressmen Conference that met in Allahabad in March 1937. As their statement contemptuously asked, 'Has Mr Jinnah ever identified with the sufferings of the Mussalmans? Some of us have concluded that Mr Jinnah and his compeers are made of totally alien stuff which has nothing in common with the masses.'[40] The first signs of stirring on the ML side are evident from the letter an alarmed Sir Muhammad Iqbal wrote to Jinnah pleading with him to summon an all India Muslim convention to take on Nehru's challenge.

> To this convention you must re-state as clearly and as strongly as possible, the political objective of Indian Muslims as a distinct political unit in the country. It is absolutely necessary to tell the world both inside and outside India that the economic problem is not the only problem in the country. From the Muslim point of view the cultural problem is of much greater consequence to most Indian Muslims. At any rate it is not less important than the economic problem.'[41]

Jinnah described the Congress programme as 'massacre contact' following his earlier warnings about its intentions. 'Do not be led away by the cries of *Dal-Bhat*. You must remember that nobody in the world can solve the fundamental economic, financial and social problems of a country overnight.'[42] He appealed to Muslims to instead join the ML and make it a strong representative parliament of Muslim India, a body that may speak with unchallenged authority on behalf of eighty million Muslims of India.'[43] The AIML urgently instituted a series of changes in its organizational structure, its ideology and declared goals in order to meet the Congress challenge. The charge was led by the U.P. men. A committee was set up under the Chairmanship of Nawab Ismail Khan to draw

---

39 *Towards Freedom*, Vol. 1, 25.

40 *AICC Papers, File 12/1937.*

41 *Towards Freedom*, Vol. 1, 261.

42 *Star of India*, 4 January 1937.

43 Ibid.

up a new organizational blueprint with the intent of remaking the ML as a radical political party.[44] Here the committee borrowed several leaves from the Congress book. Under the new party constitution, Town and Tehsil Leagues were designated as primary units of the ML organization. These units were to elect District Leagues which, in turn, would elect provincial Leagues. These provincial Leagues in turn, would elect the Council of the AIML besides sending nominations for the election of the party President. Another significant recommendation called for abolishing the position of permanent President in order to underline the ML's new democratic culture. The party membership fee was now fixed at two *annas*, below the Congress party fee of four *annas* as part of this new drive to shed the ML's image as a party of landlords and Nawabs. The ML's constitution was also revised to bolster its anti-imperialist credentials with its declared goal now being the 'attainment of the status of a free and independent country for India by all legitimate means with a democratic form of government'.[45] With these changes in its party structure and declared goals, the ML now appeared no less radical or anti-imperialist than the Congress. In U.P. itself, the UPML next chalked out an ambitious programme of 'mass contacts'. At the suggestion of Khaliquzzaman, it was decided that all the twenty seven ML members of the U.P. Legislative Assembly would raise ₹ 100 each from their respective constituencies while each member of the provincial working committee would contribute ₹ 30 over the next three months for carrying out propaganda among the Muslim masses.[46] Another committee was charged with the task of enrolling 25 per cent of the adult Muslim population in U.P. as ML members over the next three months.[47]

The UPML also began a propaganda offensive bitterly criticizing the MMCP as an attempt to break the solidarity of the Muslim community by utilizing the strength of the Congress organization, its financial muscle, and the backing of its provincial governments. In contrast, it pointed out that the Congress had made extensive efforts to preserve the solidarity of the Hindu community during the crisis created by the Communal Award a few years earlier. Gandhi's fast unto death in response to the Award and the subsequent Poona Pact with Ambedkar were pointedly referred to by Nawab Ismail Khan, the UPML President, in his correspondence with Nehru that was published soon after in the newspapers.

44 *The Pioneer*, 7 May 1937.

45 Ibid.

46 *AICC Papers, File 16/1937.*

47 *Towards Freedom*, Vol. 1, 492.

> It will be recollected that when separate electorates were provided for the untouchables at their own request, the Hindu leaders were most vehement in their denunciation of the Muslim attitude towards the question. They were charged with breaking up the solidarity of the Hindu community. Muslims entertain similar resentment against the Congress leaders today for launching the mass contact movement.[48]

However, it is the ideological response to the MMCP that proved to be the most potent weapon in the UPML's armoury. One of its most prominent campaigners was the young Raja of Mahmudabad. The Raja was the one of U.P.'s prominent landlords, the youngest member of the Central Working Committee of the ML, its National Treasurer, besides being its chief financier in U.P. He was the also the chief organizer of the Muslim League National Guard that was formed to defend Muslim lives and property besides countering the MMCP. In addition, he was the chief patron of the All India Muslim Students Federation (AIMSF) formed by Muslim students who had broken away from the All India Students Federation (AISF). His Kaiserbagh palace in Lucknow was the virtual headquarters of the UPML. Even though he belonged to the landed aristocracy, the Raja cultivated an austere personal style. He habitually wore *khaddar*, was known for his generosity towards his tenants, and his piety as a practicing Shia. Finally, young Mahmudabad was one of those rare individuals in the ML who had something approaching a warm and close personal relationship with Jinnah on account of old family ties.[49]

Mahmudabad decried the Congress refusal to recognize the existence of the Muslim community and work with its accredited leaders. Warning Muslims to 'counteract efforts made in interested quarters to divide the Muslim community amongst themselves', he offered Islam as a total ideology which had answers to all the problems of modern society.'[50] Mahmudabad credited Islam as the greatest emancipatory creed that the world had ever known. As he noted, if Muslims were deeply desirous of political liberty it was because their 'religion teaches them liberty, without which they cannot truly live.'[51] Islam was also

48 Ismail Khan to Nehru, 16 January 1938 in S. A. I. Tirmizi (ed.), *Paradoxes of Partition, 1937-39* (Delhi, 1998), 320.

49 See The Raja of Mahmudabad, 'Some Memories', in Phillips and Wainwright (ed.), *The Partition of India: Policies and Perspectives, 1935-1947* (London, 1970).

50 Mahmudabad's speech at the Bombay Provincial Muslim League Conference reported in *Asar-i-Jadid*, 13 January 1938 in Syed Ishtiaq Husain (ed.), *Khutbat-i-Raja Sahab Mahmudabad: Raja Sahab Mahmudabad Mohammad Amir Ahmad Khan ke Khutbat, Irshadat, Interviews aur Chand Aham Dastavezat ka Majmua* (Karachi, 1997).

51 *The Leader*, 18 October 1937.

socially liberating since it sought to break down the barriers of class, colour, and race and considered all Muslims whether belonging to the masses or the higher classes as brothers. Mahmudabad, however, specified that Muslims wanted liberty not only for the country but also for their own community and therefore outlined the ML's programme for the Muslims. Responding to the Congress MMCP's offer of a fully-fledged socialist programme to the Muslim masses, Mahmudabad offered them a vision of Islamic socialism.[52] Addressing the Bombay Provincial Muslim League conference, he credited the Prophet with inaugurating the oldest socialist creed in the world 1300 years earlier. Mahmudabad explained that the Prophet himself had been an orphan and a poor 'commission agent' and knew what poverty meant. Islam was, therefore, quintessentially the religion of the poor. Islamic socialism was not just a chimera or a slogan but would bring about a real reduction in social disparities between the rich and poor ensuring that every individual had a comfortable existence. He further claimed that the current disparities between the rich and poor was due to greed of the capitalists who had denigrated the message of Islam to such an extent that time had come to wage a *jihad* against poverty. Stalin too, he grandly remarked, was compelled to take the path of socialism that Islam had inaugurated. However, Mahmudabad posited a fundamental difference between socialism and Islam. While Islam was based on *ijma* (consensus) socialism was not based on any such popular consent of the community. But more importantly, socialism was a result of mere intellectual enquiry and had nothing to do with the heart. Islam, on the other hand, represented both the heart and the mind and hence would be enduring.[53] An ML supporter summed up the critique of Congress socialism by remarking that when the slogan, 'Workers of the world unite' is raised, nobody has a problem. However when the slogan 'Muslims of the world unite' is raised, everybody has a problem![54]

Mahmudabad was the main mover of the socio-economic resolution at the ML's 1937 Lucknow session. The resolution was progressive and sufficiently broad-based besides being directed at specific social groups. For the industrial labour it sought minimum wages, regulated work hours and hygienic housing conditions. It also favoured state assistance for cottage and small scale industries.

---

52 Mahmudabad's speech at the Bombay Provincial Muslim League Conference reported in *Asar-i-Jadid*, 13 January 1938 in Syed Ishtiaq Husain (ed.), *Khutbat-i-Raja Sahab Mahmudabad: Raja Sahab Mahmudabad Mohammad Amir Ahmad Khan ke Khutbat, Irshadat, Interviews aur Chand Aham Dastavezat ka Majmua* (Karachi, 1997).

53 See Mahmudabad's later essay 'Pakistan ki Taarif', *Sidq*, 11 May 1941.

54 *Zulqarnain*, 28 July 1938.

The resolution's stance against Hindu capitalists and traders was evident from its demand for the establishment of a state industrial development board to develop industries and for the elimination of middlemen. For the peasants it sought reduction of rural and urban debt, abolition of usury, security of tenure, fixation of fair rents and abolition of forced labour.[55] Mahmudabad also borrowed a leaf from Gandhian constructive programmes, advising Muslims to wear *garha* cloth woven by Muslim weavers,[56] enforce picketing of liquor and toddy shops[57] and join the Muslim League National Guards to participate in social work among the Muslim masses.[58]

Resisting National Symbols Fashioned by Congress

Gandhi's Wardha Scheme of Education and the Pirpur Report

In addition to taking on the MMCP, the ML gained prominence by launching a ferocious attack against the symbols of India's national life that the Congress attempted to institute through its provincial governments. Questioning the view that India constituted a single nation, the MLthrough its indignant opposition to these symbols laid the basis for its claim of a separate nationhood for Muslims. The lightning rod in this regard was the Wardha Scheme of Education, which Gandhi laid out soon after Congress ministries had assumed office in 1937. The scheme envisaged a rural education programme spanning primary, middle and high school, extending over a period of seven years, which focused on providing vocational training to villagers that would allow them to earn their livelihoods.[59] Gandhi called the scheme 'Rural National Education through Village Handicrafts'. As he elaborated, 'rural excludes the so-called higher or English education, national at present connotes truth and non-violence, and through village handicrafts means that the framers of the scheme expect the teachers to educate village children in their villages so as to draw out all their faculties through some selected village handicrafts in an atmosphere free from super-imposed restrictions and interference.'[60]

Behind the scheme lay Gandhi's own philosophy of education that saw

55 *The Leader*, 21 October 1937.

56 *PAI for the week ending 3 September 1938.*

57 *PAI for the week ending 14 May 1938.*

58 *The Leader*, 18 August 1938.

59 'Doing Not Idle Thinking', *Harijan*, 2 October 1937, in *CWMG*, Vol. 66, 191–93.

60 M. K. Gandhi, 'Foreword', in *Basic National Education: Report of the Zakir Husain Committee and the Detailed Syllabus* (Wardha, 1938).

literacy not as the end of education but 'only one of the means whereby man and woman can be educated.'[61] What Gandhi had in mind when he thought of education was not simply various forms of handicraft being taught side by side with liberal education, but the 'whole process of education to be imparted through some handicraft or industry.'[62] He specifically recommended *takli* spinning as a useful craft through which total education could be imparted to rural children. He admitted to using the same method to teach his grandson who he said 'scarcely feels he is being taught, for all the while he plays, laughs and sings.'[63] It was at present also being used throughout the country for training people to make their own cloth. Primary education could thus revolve around *takli* but the Mahatma was open to other forms of handicraft being made the mode for his total educational scheme. Gandhi was, however, careful to point out that a balance between manual and intellectual work would be maintained in this scheme since subjects such as history, geography, arithmetic, besides elementary principles of sanitation, hygiene and nutrition would also be taught as part of this primary education programme.

An integral part of the scheme was that it had to be self-supporting, which Gandhi insisted would be 'the acid test of its reality'. This was especially imperative since funds which were currently scarce due to military expenditures, would become scarcer once drink revenues would be lost due to Prohibition. But independent of funding problems, Gandhi felt that the condition of self-sustainability had its own merits. Children would become more self-confident if they paid for their own education rather than receiving it as a dole from the government, which could make them lazy and helpless. Gandhi claimed that manual training would not involve making articles fit for school museums or useless toys but marketable articles. As far as the saleability of the articles was concerned, Gandhi noted that while nobody would be compelled to buy the children's manufactures, 'the nation is expected to buy with pardonable pride and patriotic pleasure what its children make for its needs.'[64] On another occasion, Gandhi stated that the state would take over these articles and find a market for them,[65] while another time he declared that 'the state is bound to

61 Basudev Chatterji, *Towards Freedom, 1938*, Vol. 1, 755.

62 *CWMG*, Vol. 66, 264.

63 *CWMG*, Vol. 66, 264.

64 *CWMG*, Vol. 66, 241.

65 *CWMG*, Vol. 66, 118.

find employment if needed, for all the pupils thus trained.'[66] At the same time he insisted that care would also be taken so that children's manufactures would not compete with indigenous manufactures. Khadi, village paper, palm *gur*, were mentioned as some of the many items in this regard.[67] Gandhi also welcomed the suggestion that young men and women be conscripted to work as teachers in the villages for which they would be given 'maintenance on a scale keeping with the economic level of the country.'

Finally, given his well-known position regarding the importance of religion not only in private lives of individuals but also in public life, the Mahatma surprisingly declared that he wanted religious instruction to be excluded from this educational scheme. In response to questions regarding this exclusion, Gandhi declared that he was rather for teaching the children practical religion, the religion of self-help.[68] The Mahatma also expressed his firm opinion that religious instruction could best be granted to children in their own homes. What the new scheme would however emphasize was the essential unity of all religions, the idea that they taught the same great truths. Finally, as far as inculcation of ethical values was concerned, Gandhi optimistically declared that the exemplary lives of their teachers would provide children with the best instruction in ethical and truthful living and would also help in eliminating communal strife.

Gandhi's scheme had laid out general principles, which needed to be translated into policy. This task was delegated to a committee headed by Zakir Husain, the Principal of Jamia Millia Islamia, an educationist by training who had returned to India after receiving a doctorate in Germany. It included as its members, another educationist Aryanayakam, a Jaffna Tamil who had studied in England and was teaching at Tagore's Shantiniketan, his wife Asha Devi, K. Saiyidain, Director of Education in Kashmir, and finally Gandhians such as Vinoba Bhave, J. C. Kumarappa, Kishorelal Mashruwala, Shrikrishnadas Jaju, K. T. Shah, and Kakasaheb Kalelkar. After reviewing Gandhi's ideas on education and extensively discussing and debating the matter with the Mahatma himself, the committee expressed skepticism about whether the principle of self-sustainability could be achieved in practice. It, however, acknowledged that the basic scheme of education was sound in itself. After much deliberation, it finally came up with a seven year scheme for educating rural boys and girls

66 *CWMG*, Vol. 66, 265.

67 *CWMG*, Vol. 66, 241.

68 Basudev Chatterji, *Towards Freedom, 1938*, Vol. 1, 762.

with syllabi for eight subjects. They included basic craft,[69] mother tongue, mathematics, general science,[70] social studies,[71] drawing, music and Hindustani. The medium of instruction was to be the local mother tongue. The schools were expected to work for 288 days a year, 24 days a month on an average with daily instruction spread over five and half hours. Teachers were to undergo a three year training programme, which would help them develop skills in the basic craft, knowledge of local economics of village industries, principles of physical culture and hygiene and, most importantly, a thorough knowledge of Hindustani in both Hindi and Urdu scripts.[72] Teachers were to be mostly recruited locally through a careful selection procedure while the scheme as a whole would do away with the examination system and be replaced by a new sample testing method in order to check the progress of pupils and schools. The Wardha Scheme was endorsed at the Haripura Congress session which further recommended the setting up of an All India Education Board. This body came into being on 23 April 1938 and was renamed Hindustani Talimi Sangh. It was charged with the responsibility for preparing textbooks, chalking out specific plans for each province, setting up teacher training schools, testing the existing syllabus and suggesting improvements for the future.

---

69 For basic craft the committee chose spinning and weaving, carpentry, agriculture, fruit and vegetable gardening, leather work, with a provision for any other craft appropriate for local conditions. All students though taking up other craft forms were expected to learn the basics of *takli* weaving.

70 It would include study of local ecology and environment, botany, zoology, chemistry, hygiene, physical culture with an emphasis on *desi* games, astronomy, to be topped off with inspiring stories of great scientists and explorers.

71 It would include a course on history, civics, geography and current events along with a study of different religions of the world to show their underlying unity. Knowledge of history was to be dominated by that of Indian history focusing on the 'social and cultural life of the people as they moved towards greater political and cultural unity.' The treatment of the subject was to be biographical in the lower grades and social and cultural in the higher grades. It was hoped that the study of the history of India's national awakening would prepare pupils to bear their share of burdens joyfully and to stand to the strain and stress of the period of transition. Geography would include a study of local natural and human ecology, weather phenomena, maps and map making, means of transport and communication, industries and agriculture of both the locality and the nation and their inter-linkages.

72 The scheme explicitly stated that the object of the scheme was not to produce academically perfect scholars but skilled, intelligent and educated craftsmen with the right mental orientation who are desirous of serving the community and anxious to help the coming generation realize and understand the standard of values implicit in this educational scheme.

The Wardha Scheme attracted criticism from many quarters[73] but the strongest criticism came from the ML. A party committee was set up under the chairmanship of the Raja of Pirpur, a Shia landlord from U.P., to assess its implications for the education of Muslim boys and girls. Its report charged the Congress with trying to convert Muslim youth to its own ideology and attempting to wipe out the distinct identity of Indian Muslims. It pointed to the example of Communist Russia where the state through educationist and propagandist activities had converted its citizenry to the goal of communism and wiped out religion. Fascist Italy through its education system, as well as Fascist party organizations had similarly captured the minds of the youth with its spiritual creed. The report specifically charged the scheme with spreading 'Gandhian totalitarianism' to brainwash students about the virtues of non-violence. It warned that, 'if from their childhood boys and girls are made to think in terms of superiority of non-violence, it may produce the same results as the doctrine of superiority of race has done in certain totalitarian states.'[74] Moreover, it argued that non-violence did not symbolize the final truth for Muslims and was contrary to the principle of *jihad* that was obligatory for them under certain conditions. The report also criticized the reverential study of different religions as envisaged in the scheme. It took particular exception to the idea that all religions had an essential unity when it came to their fundamental precepts, and instead asserted that 'there are many essentials of Islam which are exclusively Islamic and which cannot be harmonized with the teaching of other religions.'[75]

The Pirpur report further criticized the Wardha Scheme for not taking into account the special place of religion in Muslim life since Islam was distinct from Hinduism.[76] It argued that while religious education was restricted to the Brahmans amongst the Hindus, it was an important aspect of life for all people belonging to the Abrahamic faiths. Indeed, among Muslims every respectable

---

73 Tagore criticized the scheme as did the economist VKRV Rao besides Socialists such as Minoo Masani.

74 K. K. Aziz, *Muslims Under Congress Rule 1937-1939: A Documentary Record* (Islamabad, 1978), 180.

75 Ibid., 186.

76 Dr Ziauddin Ahmad, 'Wardha Scheme se Mazhabi Taleem ka Akhraj', *Muslim University Gazette*, 1 August 1938. Ziauddin as the Vice-Chancellor of the Aligarh Muslim University also wrote to Jinnah warning that the Wardha scheme was a serious threat to Muslim education. Ziauddin Ahmad to Jinnah, 7 May 1938, in Tirmizi, *Paradoxes of the Partition, 1937-1939*, 388.

family had to have the ability to lead the *namaz* for which it needed to be cognizant in matters of the *Shariah*. It therefore charged those who wanted to substitute ethical instruction (*ikhlaqi talim*) for religious education (*mazhabi talim*) as being totally unaware of the fundamentals of Muslim religious education. It further pointed out that when a government convened conference in 1916 debated this question, it had come to the conclusion that the former was meaningless without the latter. The government was forced to conclude that the teaching of Islam was integral to the education of Muslim boys and provisions were thus made for religious instruction among Muslims through separate institutions.

The Pirpur report came down most heavily on the History syllabus arguing that Amir Khusro, Kabir, Akbar and Dara Shikoh had been held up as Muslim heroes simply because they attempted to forge a synthesis with Hinduism, while Muslim heroes with the 'Islamic outlook', who had made seminal contributions to Islamic history or Muslim society had been ignored. The syllabus was also held guilty for glorifying only Hindu heroes such as Harsha, Prithvi Raj, Shivaji, and Ranjit Singh. Indignation was also expressed at Muslim history being broken up into 'insignificant and unimportant portions.' The Report further pointed out that in the history syllabus for grades II–IV, the first three years were devoted to teaching Hindu history alongside fragmentary histories of other ancient races such as Romans, Greeks, Chinese, Persians, etc. Only after four years of studying other peoples' histories was the Muslim child introduced to Muslim history in Grade V. The syllabus was, thus, charged with undermining the real significance of Islamic history by ignoring the fact that Islam was the dominant force in world history for a thousand years, and had introduced 'a revolution in the social, cultural and political concepts of mankind.' The report also expressed unhappiness with its treatment of the Indian national movement since it dealt almost exclusively with the Congress and its leaders ignoring the contribution of Muslim leaders. Furthermore, it expressed serious reservations about the importance given to socialism as a force against the tyrannies of imperialism and capitalism all the while ignoring its character as an anti-religious movement. In this regard, it also condemned the omission of any reference to Islamic socialism in the syllabus. Finally, it deprecated the teaching of pre-history of the primitive man and his surroundings from a materialistic point of view since the evolution of man or human society had not been given a spiritual background.

The syllabus on social studies was also deemed un-Islamic. The Pirpur Report condemned it for subordinating love for religion to the love for the motherland, which it claimed, was against the tenets of Islam. It also expressed strong opposition against music and dances in the syllabus, as also the celebration of

Hindu holidays, which it deemed to be in serious conflict with the Islamic way of life. The Report came down heavily on an alleged suggestion in the syllabus that Muslims suffered from social disabilities that were similar to Harijans. It charged that such imputations were calculated to develop an inferiority complex among Muslims. The Wardha scheme was also denounced as being detrimental to the progress of Urdu language and script. Hindustani was dismissed as a non-existent language. The Report claimed that under its garb, the Wardha scheme was trying to impose Hindi on Muslims. It pointedly referred to the U.P. Education Minister, Sampurnanand's use of Sanskritized Hindi as a sign of the dangers that lay ahead. The Report asserted that the only solution to the problem was to make Urdu the national language of India and demanded that Urdu be declared the mother tongue of all Muslim boys in the country. It also demanded the setting up of different educational systems for Muslims in which they would have complete control over their own education. For this purpose, it called for the creation of a Central Muslim Education Board along with state level Muslim education boards exclusively manned and supervised by Muslims. In order to finance Muslim education the committee further recommended that Muslim representatives in legislatures seek funds from government, solicit donations from the rich, contributions from Muslim *waqfs* and the general public. Finally, the ML decided to convene a committee under the Chairmanship of Nawab Kamal Yar Jung of Hyderabad to go into the specific problems of Muslim education and make recommendations for remedial action.

The Question of Hindustani

As part of the Wardha Scheme of education, the Congress efforts to establish Hindustani as a national language, which would replace English over a matter of time, became a hugely controversial affair. Congress attempts to justify Hindustani as occupying the middle ground between Hindi and Urdu backfired as it found itself in the firing range of both Hindi and Urdu enthusiasts. The indignation was felt not just among north Indian Urdu-speaking Muslims, for Fazlul Haq the Premier of Bengal was vociferous in his calls for Urdu being made the national language. The Lion of Bengal declared that under him the province would increase the number of *madrasas* to spread Urdu, Persian, and Arabic. Though Bengali was the mother tongue of his province and would be the medium of instruction, Haq insisted that Urdu needed to be made the compulsory language for Muslim students 'so that they may come in contact with the spirit of Islam.'[77] In what now sounds like a far cry from the position

77 Basudev Chatterji, *Towards Freedom, 1938*, Vol. 1, 368.

taken by East Pakistanis in the aftermath of the Partition, Haq warned that unless Bengalis adopted Urdu for primary religious instruction, their boys and girls would be de-Muslimized through the anti-Islamic influences of the local environment. He further lamented that the reason why the Bengali Muslims were backward in pan-Islamist revival activities was that linguistically and culturally they were cut off from the rest of Muslim India due to their lack of proficiency in Urdu. Haq therefore wanted to make them full-fledged and active members of the Islamic fraternity by having them compulsorily learn the language.

Haq's views were supported by Maulana Saiyyid Sulaiman Nadvi, the rector of the *Nadwatul Ulama* of Lucknow, known for his sympathies for the ML.[78] Nadvi wanted Urdu to be made the national language claiming that it was the joint creation of Hindus and Muslims. He argued that even if it were the language of Muslims alone, it needed to be accepted by the Hindus for it could never threaten the culture and traditions of the majority community, which could always assert itself in any case due to its numerical superiority. Nadvi dismissed Hindi as a newcomer, the product of British policy at College Fort William in Calcutta. Sanskritized Hindi, he insisted, needed to be given the same classical status as Arabic and its imposition in the name of Hindustani to be avoided at all costs or else it would lead to communal strife. He also rebutted Nehru's view that Urdu was understood in the towns and Hindi in villages, claiming that the Hindi found in newspapers and magazines was little understood in towns and even lesser in the villages. Finally, Nadvi pointed out that it was misleading to say that the use of Sanskrit words in Hindustani was necessary to carry along the south Indians or Bengalis since none of these languages had anything to do with Hindi. In this regard, he also noted that Tamil Muslims spoke Urdu while the songs of Sufi mystic Gisudaraz in the Deccan were also in Urdu.

Scholars such as Maulvi Abdul Haq, a doyen of Urdu who had been involved in the establishment of Osmania University at Hyderabad as an Urdu medium university, supported Nadvi's contention. He dismissed the claim that Hindi with its stock of words from Sanskrit would be better understood by south Indians by arguing that Sanskrit did not dominate the ordinary speech of south Indians. He further noted that the south Indians themselves had been vociferous in their protests against attempts to foist Hindi in the South.[79] Delving into the history of the language problem, Abdul Haq pointed out that when Persian

78 Z. A. Ahmad (ed.), *National Language for India: A Symposium* (Allahabad, 1941).

79 Ibid.

was replaced by Urdu in 1837, not a single voice had been raised. But later Hindus under Swami Dayanand Saraswati and his Arya Samaj began this whole controversy, which was given further fillip by Pandit Madan Mohan Malaviya through his *shuddhi* and *sangathan* movements. But the greatest villain of the piece according to him was Gandhi who had provided legitimacy to Hindi by accepting the Presidentship of the *Hindi Sahitya Sammelan*. This move had led to Hindi making great progress in Madras, North Western Frontier Province (NWFP) and Punjab where earlier there was no affinity for Hindi. He also criticized Gandhi and his lieutenants such as Rajendra Prasad and Kakasaheb Kalelkar for increasing the use of Sanskrit words in their language on the grounds that people south of the Vindhyas would be able to understand them better due to the greater stock of Sanskrit words in the Dravidian languages.

Abdul Haq foresaw problems in creating a new language like Hindustani with a new canon along with a vocabulary that could accommodate modern and scientific ideas. Hindi and Urdu, he insisted, were separate languages and that was a reality that needed to be acknowledged. Writers in these languages were bound to fall back upon their parent tongues to absorb and express new ideas that were developing in the modern scientific world. Hindustani as a language at present served only basic conversational needs. But Haq also expressed his willingness to find the common ground for the creation of a national language. In order to tackle the problem he proposed the creation of a common dictionary consisting of all Persian and Arabic words that had passed into Hindi speech and literature and a list of Sanskrit words that Urdu had adopted. This dictionary could then be placed before a representative body of writers after whose approval it would be published as the basis for further development. This body would also be responsible for the incorporating new words from Hindi and Urdu necessary for the growth of Hindustani, which could then be given adequate publicity. Haq, like Nehru, boldly suggested that the script problem could be resolved by introducing the Roman alphabet so that all languages of the country could be written in the Roman script. He concluded that in case it was not possible to achieve these different tasks, Hindi and Urdu should be left to their own devices. Haq was therefore requested by the Bihar Government to participate in a project of compiling a dictionary with common words from Hindi and Urdu. In this regard, it must be noted that voices in favour of Urdu included non-Muslim Urdu enthusiasts and aesthetes such as the constitutional lawyer Sir Tej Bahadur Sapru. Sir Tej flatly declared that Hindustani was a cover for uprooting Urdu and replacing Urdu words in Hindustani with Sanskrit words. Sapru, however, opined that he was not in favour of creating a single national language and felt that the best thing would be to leave Urdu alone and allow it to occupy the same space it had over the past two hundred years. As Sapru sagely observed, Telugu, Bengali and other languages in India were as much national languages as Urdu, Hindi or Hindustani.

From the Congress side Maulana Abul Kalam Azad attempted to reassure Muslims in various ways about the Congress government's language initiative. Maulana Azad declared that the whole controversy had arisen due to indiscriminate use of the term Hindi by people from Bombay, Madras and Bengal. In a letter to Premiers of all the Congress-ruled provinces he therefore asked them to use the word Hindustani whenever the national language was mentioned. Attempting to reassure Muslims, Azad declared that the national language of India, though called Hindustani, was 'clear and simple Urdu which is generally spoken in the cities of northern India', which could be written in both Devanagari and Urdu scripts. He noted that a Hindustani reader was being prepared by the Jamia Millia Islamia and would be published by the Madras Government in both Urdu and Devanagari scripts for the primary classes. Azad also deplored the controversy being raised by Jinnah on the language question. Referring to Jinnah's address to the Memon community in Bombay wherein he accused the Congress of being a rank communal organization seeking to impose Hindi over the country, Azad derisively declared that Mr Jinnah neither knew Hindi or Urdu for his mother tongue was Gujarati, while he had spent his entire life reading and writing in English. Whatever Jinnah had said on the language question was based on hearsay or gossip in newspapers and hence irresponsible. The controversy however refused to die down and became one in the long list of Muslim grievances against Congress rule in the 'minority provinces'.

National Flag and National Song

Finally, the ML vociferously opposed the flying of the tricolour by government institutions and in public spaces and the singing of Bande Mataram during official functions, especially in government schools claiming that these were Hindu symbols that were alien to Muslim culture. The Congress response to the ML offensive was one of incredulity and rage. It took pains to point out that the author of the Wardha Scheme, Dr Zakir Husain, was a Muslim. It denounced suggestions that the scheme was a way of brainwashing Muslim students into accepting Congress ideology. On Hindustani too the Congress pointed out that the Bihar Government had constituted a committee headed by Abdul Haq to prepare a comprehensive dictionary of Hindustani words and insisted that the U.P. and Bihar governments would follow the guidelines and recommendation of this committee. On the question of the national flag it pointed out that the tricolour represented all of India's communities. It emphasized the fact that Jinnah, the Ali brothers and other Muslim leaders who had attended several Congress sessions, had never once objected to the tricolour being unfurled at these sessions.[80] Indeed, only in March 1937, Khaliquzzaman had invited G. B. Pant to unfurl the tricolour at the Lucknow municipality building of which the former was the Chairman. And as far as Bande Mataram was concerned, the party insisted that there was nothing 'Hindu' or communal about the song. Only the first two stanzas of the song were usually sung at Congress sessions which described the beauty of the motherland and her abundant bounty. It was not intended to represent a challenge to any community or group in India. The very fact that it referred to thirty crores of Indians made it clear that it included all Indians. The Congress also pointed to the historical context in which the song assumed significance. It explained that the song, though appearing in Bankim Chandra Chatterji's *Anand Math*, was written independently of and long before the novel was published, and that it was incorporated only subsequently into the book. It noted that the song was set to music by Rabindranath Tagore in 1896 and assumed particular significance after the Bengal Provincial Conference that was held in Barisal in 1906. This session was chaired by a Muslim, A. Rasul, which was broken up by a police lathi charge. Since then the song 'had inspired innumerable sacrifices across the country' and assumed 'special and national importance'. The song had not been formally adopted by the Congress as the national anthem of India, but 'past associations, with their long record of suffering for the cause as well as popular usage may have made the first two stanzas of this song a living and inseparable part of our national movement and as such they must command our affection and respect.'[81]

The Congress however expressed its willingness to accommodate the ML's newly developed sensitivities on these issues.[82] K. M. Ashraf pointed out that the slogans and culture of the Congress only reflected the presence of various communities in the Congress. Thus, during the Khilafat movement the slogan of *Allaho Akbar* was popular at Congress meetings. Ramprasad Bismil's *Sarafroshi ki Tamanna* and Muhammad Iqbal's *Saare Jahaan se Accha*, both of which were in Urdu, had also become very popular songs at Congress gatherings. As far

80 Nehru to Jinnah, 6 April 1938, in *SWJN*, Vol. 8, 238.

81 CWC Statement on *Bande Mataram* on 28 October 1937, AICC Papers File 42, in P. N. Chopra (ed.), *Towards Freedom, 1937* (New Delhi, 1985), Vol. 1, 1089.

82 Gandhi's Draft on Congress Policy on the Communal Question, 30 July 1937, quoted in Tirmizi, *Paradoxes of the Partition, 1937–39*, 223–25.

as Congress slogans were concerned, Ashraf noted that the most popular one was *Inqilab Zindabad* which was a Farsi slogan. Muslims in the Congress were free to use *Allaho Akbar* while Sikhs could likewise use *Sat Sri Akal.* Regarding *Bande Mataram,* Ashraf again explained that the song was in Bengali not Hindi. Expressing reservations about summarily discarding the song, Ashraf indicated that the right way to approach the issue was to have poets write a new national anthem, which could then be incorporated into the national movement. In this regard he noted that his friend Azhar Karzai had sent a song to Nehru that the latter had liked immensely and forwarded it to various Congress committees across the country so that it could attain popularity.[83] As far as the tricolour was concerned, Ashraf sought to play down its importance. Interestingly, he indicated its provisional nature while also happily pointing out that the Red Flag was increasingly making an appearance besides the tricolor at several Congress meetings.

But the ML remained unrepentant. The party went in for a radical image makeover. Its most visible symbol, Mr Jinnah, discarded his western suits in favour of *sherwani, pyjamas* and a *samur* cap for his public appearances by the time of the 1937 Lucknow AIML session.[84] The ML also came out with a new flag for the Muslims, unfurled for the first time at its Bombay meeting in 1938. On this occasion, Jinnah solemnly exhorted Muslims to rally under this flag 'several centuries old, given to us by our Prophet'.[85] A new national song for the Muslims, *Tarana-i-League* was adopted and sung at the Patna ML session in 1938. And it is at the Patna session that Mr Jinnah was honoured with the title of the *Qaid-i-Azam* or the Great Leader of the Muslim community, in an attempt to raise him to a position of equality with the Mahatma. The ML's offensive against the symbols of national unity promoted by the Congress and its creation of alternative symbols of Muslim nationhood, were critical steps in the process of constructing a Muslim political community. The contrasting fortunes of the Congress and the ML and the fate of their respective campaigns to mobilize Muslim support were reflected in a series of by-elections that were held for Muslim seats between 1937 and 1939.

---

83 K. M. Ashraf, 'Congress Mein Musalmanon ki Shirkat aur Hindu Zehniyat ka Sawaal', *Hindustan*, 12 September 1937.

84 See M. A. H. Ispahani, *Qaid-i-Azam Jinnah as I Knew Him* (Karachi, 1967), 37–38.

85 *The Pioneer*, 7 June 1938; *The Leader*, 9 June 1938. For a more detailed treatment of the issue of the national flag see Arundhati Virmani, *A National Flag for India: Rituals, Nationalism and Politics of Sentiment* (Ranikhet, 2008).

By-elections to Muslim Constituencies in U.P.

The first election in Bahraich in March 1937 was won unopposed by Rafi Ahmad Kidwai, as the UPML refused to put up a candidate against him. This walkover for Rafi was facilitated by Khaliquzzaman, who at the time was parleying with the Congress leadership over ministry making, much against Jinnah's wishes. Jinnah during his talks with leaders of the JUH in fact threatened to resign as the ML President if a candidate against Rafi was not put up, even if he did not follow up on it.[86] The next election, held in the shadow of the Congress' MMCP, was for the Orai-Jhansi-Hamirpur Muslim rural seat in Bundelkhand. It was occasioned by the death of the previous victor, who had been an Independent.[87] Jhansi became the scene of a bitter fight between the Congress and the ML. The Congress nominated Nisar Ahmad Khan Sherwani, the brother of the Congress veteran Tassadduq Ahmad Khan Sherwani, who had died two years earlier. Nisar was an outsider in Jhansi, hailing from a Bilona Pathan branch of the Sherwani family that had settled in Aligarh. He had been a superintendent in the post office department before resigning his post during the Non-Cooperation Movement and joining the Congress on a full time basis. This was his second entry into the electoral battlefield for he had earlier been fielded by the Congress during the recently concluded provincial elections from another constituency but had lost. Nisar Sherwani was assisted during this campaign by his brother Fida, who was the manager of a sugar factory in neighbouring Etah district.

The Congress campaign started on an awkward note, betraying internal stresses and strains within the party over the selection of its candidate for this seat. These were reflected in the emotional letter written by Fida Sherwani to Nehru two weeks before the election as he lay bedridden in Saharanpur due to kidney pain. Fida let loose his frustrations against what he saw as the U.P. Pradesh Congress Committee's cruel indifference to his brother's all important election at Jhansi.[88] Even the Congress Muslims, he bemoaned, seemed unwilling to help Nisar's campaign. The party's most potent Muslim orator Maulana Ataullah Shah Bukhari had refused to come to Jhansi on the pretext that he was too busy with his Ahrar conference. Maulana Husain Ahmad Madani, the star Congress campaigner during the previous round of elections, had declined to come claiming rather curiously that nobody knew him in Jhansi.

---

86 *The Leader*, 30 March 1937.

87 Polling for this by-election occurred on 15 July 1937.

88 Fida Sherwani to Nehru, 30 June 1937, *AICC Papers, File G-61/1937*.

More importantly, Rafi Kidwai, the Congress campaign in-charge had become scarce and was not even traceable. Fida rued that while Pant and Mohanlal Saxena had expressed their sympathy for the Sherwanis' predicament, they had not been of any real help either with money or men. He bitterly concluded that the 'heartless neglect of us by the so-called socialist party in power has made me believe that a Musalman has no place in the Congress and that a good and true Musalman like myself has no alternative but to commit suicide. None of the general elections in February was so hopelessly neglected as this one (sic).' In a dramatic flourish, Fida warned Nehru that he was 'going to ask his brother to withdraw from the contest', and if his body permitted, immediately go to Jhansi himself and perform *Satyagraha* until Nisar actually withdrew. The previous election loss had left the Sherwani family financially broke and Fida fumed at the 'callous neglect of the Congress' in this election, which was 'nothing short of an outrage from the Congress executive'. Defeat, Fida asserted, was certain. He ended this emotional letter with a threat to release it to the press if he was not given an opportunity to prove his charges against the U.P. Provincial Congress Committee.

Nehru also received panicky letters from Nisar Sherwani. The Congress nominee feared that the Raja of Mahmudabad was going to pump in astronomical sums of money, about ₹ 15,000 as the rumours went, to ensure that the ML candidate would win.[89] The ML thus seemed willing to purchase votes if necessary. His own resources were at an end since his defeat in the previous election, and the lack of money was particularly hampering the organization of workers since mobilizing and moving them around was expensive.[90] Nisar also drew Nehru's attention to the ML slogans of Islam in danger and their communal propaganda which alleged that this election was a battle between *kufr* and Islam. He, therefore, wanted visits by prominent *ulama* sympathetic to the Congress to be quickly arranged in order to boost his election prospects.

An annoyed Nehru responded to Nisar Sherwani, first expressing dismay at Fida's extraordinary missive after having 'lost his balance due to illness.' At the same time, he tried to instill courage in the Congress candidate, assuring him that the party regarded this election as the most important one given its far-reaching consequences. He promised Sherwani that the party, though financially broke, would make all the necessary arrangements to support him.[91] Since

89 Nisar Sherwani to Nehru, 2 July 1937, *AICC Papers, File G-61.*

90 Nisar Sherwani to Nehru, 4 July 1937, *AICC Papers, File G-61.*

91 Nehru to Nisar Sherwani, 5 July 1937, *AICC Papers, File G-61.*

Sherwani was keen on having the *ulama* to campaign for him, Nehru asked Azad to request Maulana Husain Ahmad Madani to go to Jhansi. But Nehru clearly did not have much confidence in the '*maulvi* type of individuals' and told Nisar that the election could be lost if he thought too much of them.[92] He cautioned his nominee, that while it was alright to have such people plugging for him, 'the correct approach should be on economic lines.'[93] Finally, giving some advice on the nitty-gritty of campaigning, Nehru discouraged Sherwani from wasting money on motor cars as bicycles were good enough,[94] and suggested that 'quiet organization and silent workers going to the villages' was what counted in the end and 'not just flashy personalities coming for a day like myself.'[95]

Nehru also took personal charge of the campaign after expressing his annoyance with Rafi Kidwai, the Congress election in-charge, for not having sent him any news about the Congress efforts at Jhansi.[96] A sum of ₹ 700 was cobbled up for election expenses, with Nehru borrowing money on his own personal surety. Nehru also wrote letters to the Congress MLAs from Jhansi district R. V. Dhulekar and Atmaram Kher and to the Congress MLAs from neighboring Banda, Diwan Shatrughan Singh and Thakur Har Prasad Singh, besides the Jalaun MLA Manni Lal Pandey exhorting them to work hard and impressing upon them the enormous importance he attached to this election. Diwan Shatrughan Singh's wife, Rani, was asked to campaign among Muslim women so that they could be persuaded to come out and vote for the Congress. Nehru also requested Abul Kalam Azad and Ghaffar Khan to accompany him to Jhansi where he himself intended to spend two full days campaigning for Sherwani. He finally deputed to Jhansi, one of his trusted lieutenants, the resourceful Congress MLA from Jaunpur, Keshav Dev Malaviya, to organize the Congress campaign while also requisitioning Muslim political workers from his hometown of Allahabad. K. M. Ashraf too was sent to Jhansi overruling suggestions that he might invite hostility due to his communist views.[97] Dismissing criticisms levelled against Ashraf, as the handiwork of Shaukat Ali and a handful of communal Urdu newspapers who were trying to discredit a popular Congress Muslim, Nehru confidently

92 Nehru to Mohanlal Saxena, 23 June 1937, *AICC Papers, File G-61.*

93 Nehru to Nisar Sherwani, 3 July 1937, *AICC Papers, File G-61.*

94 Nehru to Nisar Sherwani, 30 June 1937, *AICC Papers, File G-61.*

95 Nehru to Nisar Sherwani, 5 July 1937, *AICC Papers, File G-61.*

96 Nehru to Rafi Kidwai, 1 July 1937, *AICC Papers, File G-61.*

97 Nehru to Mohanlal Saxena, 22 June 1937, *AICC Papers, File G-61.*

asserted that Ashraf had had a very successful tour of Punjab as part of the MMCP and also knew Bundelkhand quite well. It must also have crossed Nehru's mind that Ashraf's presence could perhaps help swing the sizable Malkhan Rajput vote in the constituency. Diwan Shatrughan Singh too was pressed to work on his Muslim Rajput relatives in the *biradari* to persuade them to vote for the Congress. Paying attention to minute details, Nehru also made arrangements for loudspeakers, now an important part of electioneering, besides making plans for Congress workers to man each of the eighty polling booths in the constituency.

Perhaps feeling that his authority was being undercut, Rafi Kidwai seemed to go into a sulk. Admonishing his protégé Nehru responded, 'I feel sometimes that you are much to blame because you imagine things and seek no explanation for them. Or some little thing happens and you magnify it enormously. Others are of course often to blame also. The only possible way to get on in corporate life is to be continuously in touch with each other, and if necessary to quarrel with each other. Danger lies in holding oneself aloof or functioning separately without constant consultation.'[98] A chastened Kidwai got into the act by reaching Jhansi to help in the electioneering. Nehru also confronted his old friend Khaliquzzaman who had lent his name to a religious appeal on behalf of the ML candidate in Shaukat Ali's newspaper *Khilafat*.[99] Nehru pointed out that this was a fight between 'progressive thought and action' on the one side, and 'sheer communalism, religious bigotry, and political reaction on the other', and wanted to ascertain where Khaliq himself stood in this regard.[100] Yet, at the same time, after requests from Rafi Kidwai and Keshav Dev Malaviya,[101] more *Maulanas* on the Congress side were pressed into the campaign.[102] Thus, while the Congress employed the slogans of its mass contact programme, the rhetoric of the *ulama* was also being utilized to fortify that message. Finally, Nehru came into Jhansi in the last stages of the campaign and along with Syed Mahmud of Bihar canvassed support for Sherwani for two full days. The extent of hostility and bitterness in this

98 Nehru to Rafi Kidwai, 5 July 1937, *AICC Papers, File G-61.*

99 *SWJN*, Vol. 8, 135.

100 Ibid.

101 Telegram to Nehru, 6 July 1937 asking for Maulvis and Khansahebs to be sent to Hamirpur; K. D. Malaviya to Nehru, 8 July 1937, *AICC Papers, File G-61.*

102 These were Maulana Hifzur Rahman of Amroha, Maulana Bashir Ahmad from Delhi, Maulana Muhammad Mian and Maulana Shahid from Allahabad.

campaign can be gauged from the fact that Nehru's car was stoned by ML supporters as it traversed this vast constituency.

The ML candidate was a local barrister, Rafiuddin Ahmed, hailing from the Malkhan Rajput caste, which comprised a quarter of the Muslim electorate in the district. The caste *panchayat* had already thrown its weight behind Rafiuddin threatening various 'pains and penalties' against anyone who would vote against him.[103] This gave the ML a huge starting advantage. The ML had chosen its candidate wisely, for Rafiuddin had contested the previous election as an Independent and lost narrowly against the eventual winner. 'Islam in danger' was the ML campaign war cry during this election and it was amplified especially by Shaukat Ali, the chief ML campaigner. The veteran Khilafatist introducing himself as *Khadim-i-Kaba* (servant of the Kaba) in the many public meetings that he addressed,[104] talked of a possible civil war in India between Hindus and Muslims, and declared that he would work towards making a 'Spain of India'.[105] The ML was also helped by a quirk of fate when Rafiuddin Ahmad was wrongfully delivered a letter that Nehru had sent to Rafi Ahmad Kidwai in Jhansi. The ML candidate now proceeded to milk it for propaganda purposes, with Urdu newspapers sympathetic to the ML carrying a purported translation of the letter in which Nehru allegedly discussed details of payments to be made to the *ulama* in return for their support for the Congress candidate. Soon, these *ulama* found themselves portrayed as betrayers of their community for the sake of money, a charge that was to stick for the remainder of their lives in British India.[106]

But even as the ML excoriated the *ulama* on the Congress side as mercenaries and betrayers of Islam, it was actively soliciting support from anti-Congress *ulama*. In this regard, they turned to the Deobandi cleric Maulana Ashraf Ali Thanawi. As the scholar Muhammad Qasim Zaman in his recent biographical work on this renowned *alim* has noted, Thanawi was a 'pivotal figure in South Asian Islam'. His enormous corpus of 'juridical writings, numerous fatwas addressing questions directed to him by Muslims from all over the Indian

[103] Nehru to Gandhi, 13 July 1937, *AICC Papers, File G-61.*

[104] Handbill from the Bundelkhand by-election under the title 'Zaim-al Hind Maulana Shaukat Ali Sahab ka Paigham Banaam Musalmanan-i-Bundelkhand', *AICC Papers, File G-61.*

[105] Nehru to Gandhi, 13 July 1937, *AICC Papers, File G-61.*

[106] *AICC Papers, File G-61.*Newspaper cutting from *The Deccan Times*, Madras, 6 September 1937, under the headline 'Did the Congress bribe the Jamiat?' carrying the text of Nehru's letter to Rafi Kidwai, released by K.M. Ashraf to repudiate the false rumours being circulated by the ML.

subcontinent, came to be influential in his own day and have continued to shape discourses on Islamic law in post-colonial India and Pakistan'.[107] Thanawi was also the author of the widely influential *Bihishti Zewar*, a book seeking to guide Muslim women on what constituted proper Islamic norms, and was a part of every bride's dower in late colonial north India.[108] Thanawi's skepticism of the Congress and Gandhi was well known since the time of the Khilafat Movement.[109] His disdain for Gandhi in particular was striking as evident from his descriptions of the Mahatma as a *taghut* (idol), *shatir* (cunning), and *ayyar* (impostor) among other things. The senior cleric received a query (*istifta*) sent by voters from Jhansi asking for his opinion over whom they should vote for in this election. Thanawi consulted his protégés Zafar Ahmad Usmani and Shabbir Ali Thanawi over the *fatwa* that he should send to Jhansi.[110] Even though he preferred the ML over the Congress, Thanawi at this point in time clearly had reservations against the ML, unsure of its Islamic credentials, and whether it would indeed 'support Islam if it became powerful.' Zafar Ahmad Usmani's counsel resolved the impasse in the elder cleric's heart. If his *Pir* had misgivings against the ML, Usmani suggested that he send a wire to the voters of Bundelkhand asking them not to vote for the Congress.[111] This after all was not against his heart's desire. Thanawi expressed his happiness at this solution and a wire was accordingly sent to Jhansi with this brief advice.

The ML won the election with a comfortable majority. The party polled 2652 votes or 60 per cent of the total votes cast, an impressive accomplishment if one were to take into account the measly 180 votes its candidate had secured in the previous election held just six months earlier, ending last in the list of candidates.[112] The victory came as an elixir of life to the ML. A jubilant Jinnah,

---

107 Muhammad Qasim Zaman, *Maulana Ashraf Ali Thanawi: Islam in Modern South Asia* (Oxford, 2008), 1.

108 See Barbara Metcalf, *Perfecting Women: Maulana Ashraf Ali Thanawi's Bihishti Zewar; A Partial Translation with Commentary* (Berkeley, 1990).

109 See Chapter 2 in M. Q. Zaman, *Maulana Ashraf Ali Thanawi* (Oxford, 2008).

110 A *fatwa* is 'a non-binding advisory opinion' given by a juri-consult (*mufti*) in response to a query (*istifta*) by an individual questioner (*mustafti*). *Fatwas* have 'carried high degree of authority' in Islamic history and its closest modern 'equivalent is Anglo-American legal mechanism of case-law precedent'. See Muhammad Khalid Masud, Brinkley Messick, David S. Powers, *Islamic Legal Interpretations: Muftis and their Fatwas* (Cambridge and London, 1996), 3–4.

111 Ahmad Said, *Maulana Ashraf Ali Sahab Thanawi aur Tehrik-i-Azadi* (Rawalpindi, 1972), 125.

112 P. D. Reeves, B. D. Graham and J. M. Goodman, *A Handbook to Elections in Uttar Pradesh,*

who had not campaigned in the election, requisitioned the car and a flag used by Shaukat Ali in this election, 'like a Napoleon collecting mementoes of his war campaigns'.[113] Flush from this victory Shaukat Ali grandly declared that he would change his name if Congress candidates did not henceforth lose their deposits.[114]Along with another Deobandi *alim* Maulana Mazharuddin he visited Ashraf Ali Thanawi to thank him for his support and a *jalsa* (public meeting) was also organized at Thana Bhawan to commemorate this epic victory.[115]

But the Congress too came away from this election with a sense of hope, for as Nehru wrote, 'it had considerably enhanced the prestige and strength of the Congress'. Explaining his optimism, Nehru pointed out that of the 4700 votes cast in the constituency the Congress had secured nearly 2000 votes, a substantial number. The constituency itself included three sprawling districts – Jhansi, Orai and Hamirpur. In the first two districts, Nehru noted with happiness that Congress had won a clear majority and it was in Hamirpur alone, that Rafiuddin, as a local resident had won an overwhelming majority. He also pointed out that if one compared the performance of the two parties in the rural and urban areas, the Congress did overwhelmingly well in the former while the ML took the towns and the *qasbahs*. The Congress, Nehru added, would have pulled in even more of the rural vote but for the fact that the rainy season had made the roads and paths often impassable in these scattered areas. Elaborating on the reasons behind the ML's success, Nehru obliquely alluded to the ML's purchasing of votes, by referring to 'undesirable practices' and 'a small electorate of poor persons as an invitation for such practices'. He also regretted that the ML had no issues to discuss and had simply raised cries of Islam in danger. Many Muslims, he bluntly noted, had been made to swear on the Holy Quran that they would vote for the ML candidate, while the Malkhan Rajput *biradari* too had piled pressure on its caste members to vote for him. Thus, in just one polling station in Hamirpur, Rafiuddin got 900 such votes, which made all the difference. The Congress, on the contrary, had 'talked the language of politics and economics'. The Jhansi result only reinforced Nehru's belief that

---

1920-1951 (Delhi, 1975), 300.

113 K. M. Ashraf, 'Congress Aur Muslim League ka Doosra Election: Bijnor ke Intekhabat par Ek Nazar', *Hindustan*, 28 November 1937.

114 K. M. Ashraf, 'Firqaparvar Anjumanon ke Kaam Karne ke Tariqey aur Hamara Farz: Bundelkhand ke Zimni Intekhab ke Baz Numayan Pehloo', *Hindustan*, 29 August 1937.

115 Ahmad Said, *Maulana Ashraf Ali Sahab Thanawi aur Tehrik-i-Azadi*, 125.

the MMCP was working since 'the Congress candidate who was a stranger to the constituency did remarkably well' in spite of such enormous handicaps. Among the many good things that this election accomplished was that it brought Muslims from all over the province to Jhansi, including students from Aligarh. Congress propaganda, which began a mere ten days before the elections, was much appreciated by many of these Muslims, thus raising hopes that they would go back to their respective hometowns and raise Muslim consciousness in favour of the Congress. Nehru therefore concluded on a remarkably positive note. 'The Bundelkhand election is one of the most encouraging signs of the times. It points to the inevitable growth of the Congress among the masses, both Hindu and Muslim.'[116]

The next election held in late October for the Bijnor and Garhwal districts seat, was seen as a test of which way the wind was blowing. It was a crucial contest held against the backdrop of the Congress ministry assuming power in Lucknow and a full blooded attempt by the party to mobilize Muslims through its MMCP. The contest would decide the fate of Hafiz Muhammad Ibrahim, the ML 'renegade', who had resigned this seat that he had won unopposed on the ML ticket a few months earlier. A protégé of Maulana Husain Ahmad Madani, Ibrahim had crossed over to the Congress along with his mentor and had subsequently been inducted as a Minister in the Congress government. He was seeking a fresh mandate as a matter of principle, this time on the Congress ticket again from his old Bijnore and Garhwal districts seat. Against him, the ML had again put up a local lawyer, Khan Bahadur Abdus Samih. The mood in the Congress was distinctly upbeat as Ibrahim was a local notable and also quite popular. The ML too however was buoyed by its annual 1937 session held in Lucknow that had brought into its fold, Sir Sikandar Hayat Khan and his Unionists from the Punjab and Fazlul Haq and his Krishak Praja men from Bengal, besides assorted Muslim groups from all over India. As the U.P. Governor Harry Haig reported to Linlithgow, Jinnah had given the Muslims 'a very strong and definite communal lead which seems to have inspired great enthusiasm, and will obviously have a most important bearing on political developments in the near future'. Sir Sikandar, the Punjab Premier, told his Governor that such was the energy generated at the session combined with hostility towards the Congress, that if any Congressman had come to the

116 See Nehru's Statement to the Press on the result of the Bundelkhand Election, *SWJN*, Vol. 8, 171–72. Nehru's sentiments were echoed by K. M. Ashraf. See 'Firqaparvar Anjumanon Ke Kaam Karne ke Tariqey aur Hamara Farz: Bundelkhand ke Zimni Intekhab ke Baaz Numayan Pehloo', *Hindustan*, 29 August 1937.

conference he would definitely have been lynched.[117] This, therefore, promised to be a cracker of a contest.

Shaukat Ali again led the ML charge but was joined this time by gifted Muslim orators from other parts of India such as Maulana Zafar Ali Khan, the editor of *Zamindar* of Lahore, and Khwaja Hasan Nizami from neighbouring Delhi. Zafar Ali Khan's verses set the tone of the ML campaign.

Hafiz Ibrahim Udhar hain, Abdus Samih Idhar,
Hardwari dars udhar hai, Shari'i taleem idhar
Us Taraf Gandhi ke farman par Sar-i-Taslim Kham,
Aur Rasul Allah ki Taslim ki Tanzim Idhar
Us Taraf Nehru Paraston ke liye Bharat ka Raj,
Hift Aqleem Idhar
Vote Dene waalon Sunon Kaan Dil ke Kholkar,
Khatra Imaan ko Udhar se Hai, Nahi yeh baham Idhar

On that side stands Hafiz Ibrahim, here stands Abdus Samih
On that side is Hardwari learning, here we have Shari'i training
On that side lies submission to Gandhi, here stands the organization that submits to Allah's Prophet
On that side is Nehru's Bharat, here you have the whole world
O voters, open the ears of your hearts and listen, the threat to your Faith comes from the other side,
There are no such dangers here.

The ML declared that a vote for Congress was a vote for *kufr*. It alleged that Hafiz Muhammad Ibrahim had committed that most reprehensible of crimes, apostasy, having gone to a temple and applied Hindu marks on his forehead and was now going around closing down mosques.[118] The Agra ML leader Syed Zakir Ali, whose responsibility for creating the fake poster with Jinnah's religious appeal during the Bundelkhand by-election had by now come to light, bombastically claimed that the Congress wanted to pull the Muslims down from the heights of *Furan* and *Sinai* and force them on a circumambulatory pilgrimage of Wardha *teertha*. He further alleged that while Europe had tried to wipe out Muslim culture and civilization through its cannons, the Hindus

117 Emerson to Linlithgow, 21 October 1937, Linlithgow Papers, in *Towards Freedom*, Vol. 1, 1059.

118 K. M. Ashraf, 'Congress aur Muslim League Ka Doosra Election: Bijnor Ke Intekhabat Par Ek Nazar', *Hindustan*, 28 November 1937.

were trying to do the same in the electoral field. Nehru was accused of banning *namaz* and *azaan* and tearing down green flags with the slogan of *Allaho Akbar* since he was an atheist. Another set of leaflets described how the Muslims would be relegated to the status of untouchables under Congress Hindu Raj, luridly portraying the scenario in 'medieval colors'.[119]

Khwaja Hasan Nizami repeated the allegations made at Bundelkhand that the *ulama* and Urdu papers supporting the Congress had been bribed by the party. He exhorted the electorate to fight the Congress, which was trying to conquer the Muslims through such paid quislings.[120] Hafiz Ibrahim was described as a Mir Jafar, while K. M. Ashraf was reviled for allegedly stating that unlike the Russians, Mussolini, or Hitler, the Congress would destroy every relic of religion and kill every religious person. It was also alleged that the Congress wanted to eliminate Urdu, stop *tazias*, end cow-slaughter and force Muslims to wear *dhotis* instead of *pyjamas*. Shaukat Ali raged that the Congress was using revenue officials to pressure tenant farmers to vote for Hafiz Ibrahim. Violence also erupted as an ML volunteer stabbed a Congress worker, Maulvi Nasir, and voters were allegedly physically intimidated by ML workers at various polling stations.[121]

Yet, in this election held on 27 October 1937, the Congress candidate won hands down, trouncing the ML candidate by an impressive margin. While Hafiz Ibrahim polled 7271 (70 per cent) votes, his opponent polled 2102 (30 per cent) votes. The voting percentage in the Bijnor election also climbed from a moderate 60 per cent during the Bundelkhand by-election to an impressive 71 per cent, demonstrating the keen interest that these elections were now generating in the Muslim electorate. A delighted Nehru in his speech to the assembled delegates at the AICC Calcutta session declared that:

> our mass contact move has succeeded beyond our most optimistic calculations, so much so that today the Congress claims a far larger number of Muslims than the ML can do. A few days ago at Bijnor there had been a test of strength between the Congress and the League nominee and you

119 *AICC File G-32/1938*: 'Some Notes on the General Approach and Propaganda Methods of the AIML with Special Reference to Communal Relations'. Hasan Nizami was taken to court by the local newspaper *Madina*, which supported the Congress. Nizami had to subsequently withdraw his allegations and issue a formal apology to the newspaper.

120 Ibid.

121 Nehru to Ismail Khan, 10 November 1937, in *Jinnah-Nehru Correspondence, including Gandhi-Jinnah and Nehru-Nawab Ismail Correspondence* (Lahore, 1960).

will hear shortly that the Congress nominee has succeeded with a thumping majority.[122]

The decisive Congress victory also sent shockwaves through the ML circles. A local notable wrote to Jinnah that 'the defeat at Bijnaur has spread a very bad effect among the Muslims all over the country and particularly in the neighbouring districts. In my own village where the majority is of Muslims, are thinking of where to go (sic).'[123] Ibrahim's opponent in the Bijnor by-election, Abdus Samih, soon resigned his membership of the ML and became a four-*anna* member of the Congress.[124]

With the rubber tied at 1–1, the Congress and ML workers began fanning into Moradabad, Saharanpur and Bulandshahr for the next three by-elections, to be held on 9, 13, 18 December respectively. These elections were expected to provide a clear indication about which party enjoyed support among the Muslim electorate and in all three seats the ML won decisively delivering a serious blow to the Congress. The losses were particularly unsettling for the Congress and Nehru himself since all three by-elections were held in predominantly rural constituencies whose Muslims, especially the lower class *Momin*, were believed to be sympathetic to the Congress. Nehru again campaigned intensively in all three constituencies even as Jinnah stayed away, with the ML campaign mostly being run by its U.P. leadership. Stunned by this reversal the Congress could only come up with stock responses expressing dismay at the ML's communal propaganda and anger at its avoidance of real economic and political issues. An article in the *Hindustan* analysing the debacle of the luckless Nisar Sherwani who was again fielded by the Congress in Bulandshahr but again bit the dust to complete a hat-trick of defeats, provides a classic example.[125] It argued that even though this was a predominantly rural constituency, the poorer Muslims only had a slight majority over the zamindars, taluqdars, and the upper classes. While the ML got all the upper class votes, the paper regretted that the Congress could not achieve the same with the poorer Muslims. The reason given was that the latter were economically dependent on the former and thus

122 *Amrita Bazaar Patrika*, 30 October 1937, in *Towards Freedom*, Vol. 1, 1093.

123 See Rao Hamid Ali Khan to Jinnah, in Mukhtar Masood (ed.), *Eyewitnesses of History: A Collection of Letters Addressed to Quaid-i-Azam* (Karachi, 1968), 95–96. Also see Shafaat Ahmad Khan to Jinnah, 70–72.

124 *The Leader*, 18 November 1937.

125 Rafiq Sehbai, 'League Jiti Ya Congress: Moradabad, Saharanpur aur Bulandshahr ke Zimni Intekhabat par ek Nazar', *Hindustan*, 16 January 1938.

could not risk their livelihoods by voting against their patrons' wishes. The article bemoaned that besides facing economic pressure, the poor were also given money for their votes, and therefore went against their hearts desire and voted for the ML. Adding up the votes of the upper classes with those of the deserting poor, the ML victory was thus a foregone conclusion. The Congress, however, took heart from the fact that its candidate still won a majority of the votes among the rural poor. It also expressed optimism that before long the MMCP would raise their revolutionary consciousness, enabling them to smash their economic shackles and overthrow their oppressors on the path to independence and a socialist state.

In the same vein, the explanation for the Moradabad debacle made particular mention of two widely circulated 'communal' cartoons. In one of them the Congress candidate for Moradabad, Maulvi Basheer Ahmad, was depicted as being carried on a Hindu bier for cremation. The cartoon portrayed Gandhi, Nehru, Malaviya and Pant conducting the bier to the burning *ghat* while the funeral pyre was ignited by Hafiz Ibrahim and Rafi Kidwai, the two Congress Muslims. At the center of the cartoon the figure of Shaukat Ali exclaimed 'contrast the beginning to the end', implying that a Muslim who joined the Congress ended up being a *kafir* (infidel) in afterlife'.[126] In another cartoon, Congress leaders were depicted in humiliating positions after being beaten by Jinnah even as the Kings of Iran, Turkey and Afghanistan applauded his victory.

But it is to the Saharanpur election that one must turn to, for it allows one to examine the critical nexus developing between the ML and a section of the Deobandi *ulama* led by Maulana Ashraf Ali Thanawi. This election had an added significance since Deoband was part of the Saharanpur constituency and the contest here was in many ways a proxy battle between the Thanawi and Maulana Husain Ahmad Madani camps at the Darul Uloom. Thanawi took a more decisive stance this time, shedding the reticence he had shown during the Jhansi election. He first debunked the alleged *fatwa* issued by Madani, which claimed that voting for the ML candidate was impermissible (*najayaz*) and cause for punishment (*maujab-i-azaab*). He further decried the claims of the 'nationalist' *ulama* that voting for the Congress candidate was not only good for liberation of the country now but also for achieving personal liberation in afterlife. Categorically supporting the ML candidate Maulvi Munfait Ali, Thanawi in his own *fatwa* (given in response to a query by a voter) declared

---

[126] Some Notes on the General Approach and Propaganda Methods of the AIML with Special Reference to Communal relations', *AICC File G-32/1938*.

that the ML candidate was someone who was personally known to him as an observant Muslim and an experienced, honest lawyer.[127] The Congress candidate, Thanawi asserted, was not a well-wisher of Muslims. Any efforts by Muslims to help the Congress candidate would be harmful to the community while support for the ML candidate was both excellent and permissible for the Muslims (*jayaz aur fazal*). Big posters with Thanawi's *fatwa* written in bold letters were put up in all the constituencies to underline his support for the ML.[128]

The Congress pushed back forcefully, condemning Thanawi's *fatwa*.[129] An essay in the *Hindustan* pointed out that the Maulana, by asking voters to vote for the ML candidate on religious grounds, seemed to think of votes as *zakat* or *khairaat*, which a good Muslim should donate. A vote, on the contrary, it argued, was a very worldly thing and in order to put it to good use, an unemployed person needed to give his vote for someone who would raise the prospects of employment, a peasant for tax reduction and a worker to effect a wage enhancement. It further asserted that the Maulana's designation of the Congress as a Hindu *jamaat* was a misnomer since the Hindus were as divided as the Muslims along class lines. Reiterating the emphasis on class as the basic marker of community as opposed to religion, it pointed to the fallacy of assuming that the Muslim community as a whole had common economic, political, or social interests. It noted that conflicts between a peasant and a zamindar or between a capitalist and a worker were imminent since they were class enemies even if both happened to be Muslim. Finally, the article ridiculed Thanawi for warning Muslims against any intimate friendship (*dili dosti*) with the Hindus on the grounds that it would destroy them. As the article dryly noted, joining the Congress was not tantamount to making friendship with Pandit Nehru. Indeed, there were several Congressmen who had never even met or spoken to Nehru. But the Congress charge again was in vain. Munfait Ali, the ML candidate, easily won the election taking in nearly 60 per cent of the votes polled against the Congress candidate's 40 per cent. The Congress was now faced with a growing nexus between the ML and an

[127] Mufti Muhammad Shafi (ed.), *Ifadat-i-Ashrafiya dar Masail-i-Siyasiyya: Siyasat-i-hazira, Muslim League, Congress Vaghaira ke Mutalliq Hazrat Mujaddid al Millat, Hakim al Ummat, Hazrat Maulana Ashraf Ali Sahab Thanawi ke Irshadat ka Majmua* (Deoband, 1945), 65–66.

[128] Rafiq Sehbai, 'League Jiti Ya Congress: Moradabad, Saharanpur, aur Bulandshahr ke Zimni Intekhabat par Ek Nazar', *Hindustan*, 16 January 1938.

[129] 'Maulana Ashraf Ali Thanawi Election Mein', *Hindustan*, 19 December 1937.

influential section of the Deobandi *ulama*, which would prove crucial for the ML's growth as a mass organization.

Ashraf Ali Thanawi and the Muslim League

Thanawi had initially been skeptical about the ML as evident from the *fatwa* he had sent to the Jhansi voters in which he merely asked them to oppose the Congress, without committing himself in favour of the ML. He had even described the ML to his associates as a one eyed man as compared to the Congress' blind man, hardly a vigorous endorsement for the party. Thanawi, however, began to show greater interest in Muslim politics and the ML in the aftermath of the assumption of power by the provincial Congress ministries in 1937. The consequent split that developed within the Muslim ranks as a result of the JUH siding with the Congress, and the ML viscerally opposing it, clearly worried the senior *alim*. This split had assumed an especially pronounced form among the *ulama*, and Thanawi, therefore, took the initiative to repair this breach by attempting to mediate between the JUH and the ML. He, therefore, sent a detailed questionnaire simultaneously to both the groups in order to ascertain their views on a variety of questions facing the Muslim community in India.

The questionnaire to the JUH enquired about its relationship to the Congress, its views on Congress policies and sought to explore the possibilities of bringing peace between it and the ML.[130] Was it better for Muslims to join the Congress in an individual capacity in order to influence its policies to their own advantage from within? Or would an overarching communal pact between the ML and the Congress be more advantageous for securing Muslim communal rights? Was the Congress serious over its demand of complete independence or did it seek to rule over India under the shadow of the British sword? Would independence be good for Muslims given that it would not result in an Islamic government, but a government dominated by the Hindus due to their numerical superiority? How could one be sure that the Hindus really wanted complete independence as they were claiming? What was the JUH doing to counter Hindu atrocities on Muslims in the aftermath of the Congress ministries assuming power? Did it have any advice for Muslims over *Bande Mataram* or saluting the tricolour which were un-Islamic activities? How was the JUH support for the Congress justified since the latter had a number of prominent socialists and other godless elements

---

130 Mufti Muhammad Shafi (ed.), *Ifadat-i-Ashrafiya dar Masail-i-Siyasiyya: Siyasat-i-hazira* (Deoband, 1945), 53.

in its ranks? Did the JUH have any plans to counter the Congress land tenancy legislation that was aimed against Muslim landlords? What was the nature of the JUH's differences with the ML? Was it aware of the harm that this split was causing to the Muslim community? Could the JUH instead of opposing the ML join it and proceed to purify it from within, ridding it of atheists and ungodly elements? The JUH however refused to respond to this lengthy questionnaire from Thanawi revealing a serious split among the Deobandi *ulama*.

The ML was sent a different questionnaire.[131] It had a dozen thoughtfully formulated questions. Why was joining the Congress by Muslims on an individual basis deemed harmful by the ML? Was independence possible without allying with the Congress, and if so, what would be its nature? Would Muslim aloofness from the Congress delay independence? Could the ML stop Muslims from joining the Congress? Many Muslims had already joined the Congress especially after it assumed power. If it was able to stop a few Muslims now, what would it gain when a greater portion had already joined the Congress? Was there any truth behind the newspaper report in the *Madina* of 13 December 1937, that most functionaries of the ML were supporters and well-wishers of the English and that the ML was an 'English poison'? How did the ML react to the allegation that it was not an active organization with any ideology or programme and had not taken any practical action so far for the benefit of Muslims? Since it was fighting the Congress would it not strengthen the English and weaken the Congress thrust towards independence? What steps had the ML taken for organizing the Muslims and for their economic, religious and cultural progress, and what were its future plans in this regard? If after seeking necessary assurances the ML were to join hands with the Congress, would it be better to dissolve itself in the Congress or continue its separate existence as an organization of the Muslims? If the *ulama* wanted to become ML members, would they be given a position in the organization only through the process of an election? And if they did not like the election method would there be any other option left for them? What honour and respect would the *ulama* receive in the ML, and in case of a disagreement among these *ulama* themselves, how would a dispute between them be resolved? How would the ML end the schisms that had emerged in the community on account of its conflict with the JUH and what was the nature of the agreement it visualized to end this conflict with the JUH? Had the ML understood the importance of *tabligh* (proselytization) among the Untouchables not just for religious but

[131] Ibid., 55–65.

political purposes? If so, what practical steps had it taken in this direction and did it have any future plans in this regard?

In stark contrast to the JUH's studied silence, Nawab Ismail Khan, the UPML President, crafted detailed responses to each of these questions. He was ably assisted in this exercise by Syed Hasan Reyaz, a party Secretary in U.P. who would go on to become the editor of the *Manshoor*, the ML's flagship Urdu newspaper that was financed by Jinnah and published from Delhi. The ML was clearly eager to convey the impression that the party attached great significance to the concerns of Muslim divines, and was keen to solicit their support in its battle against the Congress. In response to the first question, Ismail Khan was emphatic that an unmitigated disaster would befall the Muslim community if Muslims all over the country were to join the Congress on an individual basis. Muslims would always remain a small minority in a Congress dominated by the numerically superior Hindus, and their opinion would never have any impact on Congress ideology. In order to substantiate his claim, he pointed out that of the twenty one members in the existing Congress Working Committee only one was a Muslim, while of the 300 AICC members only seven or eight were Muslims. Ismail Khan also debunked the argument that Muslims would be able to capture the Congress organization, make it responsive to their concerns, and indeed bend it to their will if they joined the party in sufficiently large numbers. He dismissed this line of reasoning as fallacious, arguing that on the contrary, such a move would only trigger a massive counter response from the Hindu side as they would hurry to join the Congress in ever larger numbers in order to maintain their control over the party organization. Ismail Khan brought up another serious handicap that the Muslims would face in this numbers game. While Muslim women stayed in *purdah*, Hindu women were under no such constraints and thus were always free to join the Congress. Hindus would, therefore, outnumber the Muslims by a much larger margin of 5:1 and consequently the Muslims would never be in a position to get any of their resolutions passed against any decisions made by the Hindu majority.

Ismail Khan next turned to the provincial implications of Muslims joining the Congress on an individual basis. The logic of numbers meant that Muslims would be in a majority in the provincial Congress committees in the Muslim majority provinces like Punjab, Sind, Bengal and NWFP. But these majorities, the Nawab contended, were again going to be futile since the AICC and Congress Working Committee could always shoot down the decisions made by these provincial committees. These bodies would not be able to even protest against such decisions of the Congress High Command given its rigid code of party discipline. Besides, the Congress had explicitly ruled out provincial self-determination. Ismail Khan therefore insisted that the best course for Muslims to adopt would be to organize separately under the ML. Only then would they be able to emerge as an independent second force. Even though their numbers would be inferior as compared to the Hindus, they would be powerful due to their distinct status. While Muslim voice inside the Congress was sure to be silenced by the Hindu majority, by standing apart from it, the Muslims would be able to make their voice heard throughout the world.

Ismail Khan conceded that it was true that independence could only be gained through Hindu–Muslim unity. Yet, by joining the Congress on an individual basis, there was a great danger of Muslims losing their Islamic identity and being left with only an Indian identity. On the contrary, Ismail Khan assured Thanawi, that if the community as a whole were to join the ML their separate identity would be greatly reinforced. Such a move would also give strength and stature to the ML to negotiate with the Congress as the sole representative Muslim organization. The Congress too would be left with no option but to then come forward and present itself as the representative organization of the Hindus. Once this was achieved, the two parties could have their separate independent existence but come together on specific issues. In this regard, Ismail Khan made a significant comparison which is noteworthy. The UPML leader argued that if England and France could ally together to take on Germany without forsaking their separate identities, the Hindus and Muslims could likewise do the same. Ismail Khan, therefore, wanted the Muslims to maintain their separate identity so that the Congress would be forced to come to them for a comprehensive communal settlement. Under no circumstances could or would the ML ever dissolve its separate entity.

Responding to the third question Ismail Khan warned that Muslims finding themselves perpetually dominated by the Hindus in the Congress party would lose their passion for freedom. And just like the English regime had lost the passion of its Indian soldiers and could make them fight only by throwing money at them, Indian independence would end up getting delayed if Muslims lost their ardour for freedom. On the other hand, if Hindus and Muslims organized separately, and Muslims were assured that their Islamic identity would remain secure in a free India where they too could live as an independent nation (*azad qaum*), then Hindus and Muslims could certainly fight for freedom as allies, thus hastening independence.

In response to Thanawi's query about the ML's ability to stop the reportedly large-scale Muslim influx into Congress ranks, Ismail Khan described these claims as an absolute fabrication. He expressed confidence in the ML's ability to not only stop Muslims from joining the Congress but indeed stopping the Congress' victory juggernaut in the provincial elections. As he pointed out, the ML had in the recent past contested five by-elections and won four of them. It had lost only in Bijnor, a loss that the Nawab attributed to the party's lack of proper organization at the time and the personal popularity of Hafiz Muhammad Ibrahim, the Congress candidate. Ismail Khan had no hesitation in telling Thanawi that the ML would emerge as an equally large and mighty organization as the Congress party. As he noted, the Congress too had started off as a weak party that had to contend with the formidable might of the colonial state and its Hindu allies who were a part of the state apparatus. Yet, over time, it had grown to render those very Hindus powerless and unrepresentative. Ismail Khan compared Muslims currently in the Congress to those earlier *sarkari* Hindus. They would certainly be rendered helpless once the ML organized itself vigorously on a strong communal basis.

In response to the question about the ML being full of well-wishers of the British government, Ismail Khan reminded Thanawi that the ML was no longer the old moribund party of yore but an active mass-based party with a new programme and creed whose central motif was complete independence for India. A total revolution (*mukammal inqalab*) had swept through the party at its October 1937 Lucknow session. It was now a democratic organization whose doors were open to all Muslims and no longer restricted to an exclusive few. All of its committees were now manned by elected members. Indeed, it was now more democratic than the Congress since it had a two *anna* membership compared to the Congress party's four *anna* membership. As regards the ML being an 'English poison', Ismail Khan noted that this was a term coined by Sir Akbar Hydari, the Prime Minister of Hyderabad state. The same Sir Akbar Hydari had not given permission to even the Congress to organize in Hyderabad. As for the presence of loyalists of the Raj in the party as alleged by the ML's detractors, Ismail Khan assured Thanawi that such individuals had no chance of influencing it from within, leave alone dominating its affairs. He reminded the senior *alim* that all ML members were now required to sign the party's pledge that they stood for India's complete independence. However, if in spite of their taking this pledge, some ML members still remained loyalists of the Crown in their hearts, the ML could do not do much about the matter. Ismail Khan compared this problem to the one faced by the *ulama* themselves when it came to unobservant Muslims. It was after all customary for the *ulama* to accept as Muslims, those who affirmed their adherence to the essentials of the faith and to not question what lay in their hearts. The ML stood in a similar predicament and could not vouch for what lay in the hearts of some of their members. Ismail Khan, however, assured Thanawi that in spite of the possible presence of some *munafiq* (dissemblers) in ML ranks, given the new conditions in the party, they would not be able to bend the organization to their point of view. To further ease Thanawi's burdens on this count, the Nawab also pointed out that the Congress too had such *munafiq* and yet it had never refused them admission.

Protesting at the depiction of the ML as an inactive organization with no ideology or program, Ismail Khan strongly defended the ML's record since its formation by pointing to its strong policy vis-a-vis the British government. The ML, he reminded Thanawi, had been a key ally of the Congress in the efforts to force the government to promulgate the Montague-Chelmsford Reforms in 1919. The importance of the ML as a key player in Indian politics had never been in doubt right from its inception or else the Congress would never have signed the Lucknow Pact of 1916. Ismail Khan went on to make the astounding claim that the ML was at the very forefront of the Khilafat agitation since the Khilafat Committee was a part of the ML. Perhaps, he was retrospectively claiming that glory since Jinnah had stayed out of it while the leaders of the movement such as Shaukat Ali and Muhammad Ali became active in ML politics again only after the collapse of Non-Cooperation. But whether this claim would have impressed Thanawi or not is doubtful given the Maulana's decidedly dim view of the Khilafat agitation, and particularly of its leadership as noted earlier. Nonetheless, having underlined the ML's activist record as well as its mass following, Ismail Khan also provided reasons for why the party had not participated in the latest round of anti-colonial struggles during the Civil Disobedience Movement. The simple reason for Muslims staying aloof from this latest round of mass struggles was that they were not directed against the British Government but against the Muslims themselves, reflecting Hindu anger over Muslim rejection of the Nehru Report.

Ismail Khan next outlined the steps the ML had taken since October 1937 to organize itself in order to protect the economic, religious and cultural rights of the Muslims. The party's political programme was now clear in as much as it demanded complete independence for India while at the same time seeking to protect the rights of Muslims and other minorities against the communal designs and domination of the Hindu majority. The ML was actively organizing ordinary Muslims to build strength of the community in every town, village and *qasbah* and common Muslims were being made its members. Ismail Khan also informed Thanawi that the ML was organizing a large youth body, presumably the Muslim League National Guards, popularizing Muslim artisanal products in order to ensure their economic well-being and also agitating for banning interest on loans (*sood mansukh*). This last reference was no doubt meant to burnish the party's Islamic credentials and also please the senior *alim* who was very much in favour of such a move. Ismail Khan also asked Thanawi to look at the ML's socio-economic resolution to satisfy himself that the ML had a well-thought-out and clear-cut socio-economic programme.

Finally, addressing the crucial question about the position of the *ulama* in the ML, Ismail Khan declared that if they wanted to join party committees, they did not have to necessarily go through the process of elections in the party organization since they could always be co-opted into them by the party executive. He also solemnly promised on behalf of the ML that the *ulama*'s opinion in religious matters would receive the same importance in the party as it did in the Muslim community at large. And as far as resolving disagreements that might emerge among the *ulama* themselves on various matters, Ismail Khan played it safe by noting that they could be resolved in a manner that was in accord with the Quran and the Hadith. Responding to Thanawi's concerns over the damage that the ML's rift with the JUH was causing to the Muslim community, Ismail Khan's proposed solution was that the JUH confine itself to the religious field, leaving the political, communal, cultural and other matters to the care of the ML. Finally, on the question of *tabligh* among untouchables, Ismail Khan acknowledged the obvious importance of such a programme. He, however, pointed out that the ML had not taken any steps in this direction since it had not had any cooperation from the *ulama* thus far. The party, he suggested, would only be too happy to ally with the *ulama* whenever they commenced upon this important work.

These replies were no doubt to Thanawi's liking for a subsequent *istifta* (query) by Maulvi Munfait Ali, the Saharanpur MLA belonging to the ML, gave the *Hakim al Ummat* the pretext for expressing his close relationship with the ML as also his unambiguous opposition to the Congress. This *fatwa*, which came to be known as *Tanzim-al-Muslimeen*, was eventually read out at the AIML Patna session by his protégé Zafar Ahmad Usmani.[132] Expressing happiness at the signs of Muslim awakening in India, Thanawi emphasized the urgent necessity of politically organizing the community under its own separate organization, for otherwise its identity would get erased. Such a *tanzim* however

[132] Ibid., 67–74.

had to be modeled in accordance with the commands of the *Shariah*. Thanawi acknowledged that no organization as yet existed in the country, which could perform this task. Even the ML was not organized on Shari'i principles at the moment. Yet, Thanawi concluded that between the Congress and the ML, the latter was certainly better for the Muslims to join. After all the ML was an organization of Muslims who affirmed the *Kalima* in contrast to the Congress which was full of unbelievers. It was, therefore, easier to bring it closer to the *Shariah*, since its members saw Islam as the true faith, as against the Congress whose members did not accept it at all. He, therefore, saw Muslims joining the ML as a welcome first step in their awakening. The ML leadership needed to take the next step and start reforming the organization to bring it in line with Shari'i principles. Thanawi wanted the party's ordinary members to keep their leaders on their toes in pursuance of this task, and help them in the removal of deficiencies from the organization. The ML leadership could always turn to the *ulama* for guidance, advice, as well as practical help as they attempted to improve the overall health of the party. Thanawi expressed satisfaction that the community was getting organized in Allah's name and not in the name of nationalism (*watan parasti*). He hoped that the ML would eventually become Allah's *lashkar* (army).[133] He concluded the *fatwa* by exhorting the ML to keep their *tanzim* going, and not let it merge it with the Congress.

A letter threatening to assassinate Thanawi in his Sufi lodge if he did not withdraw this *fatwa* did nothing to budge him from his stance and only served to make the senior cleric even more determined.[134] While placing this matter before the public in a statement, he further underlined his active engagement with the ML. He now claimed that he sent regular letters of advice to the party in connection with its reforming efforts and pointed to the delegation that he had sent to the recent Delhi meeting of the ML in 1939.[135] He regretted that another delegation that was to be sent to the earlier 1938 AIML Bombay

133 Ahmad Saeed, *Maulana Ashraf Ali Sahab Thanawi aur Tehrik-i-Azadi* (Rawalpindi, 1972), 137.

134 *Ifadat-i-Ashrafiya*, 84.

135 Ibid., 86. As Mufti Muhammad Shafi in his 'Introduction' to *Ifadat-i-Ashrafiya* noted, a *majlis* of the *ulama* under the title *Daawat-al-Haq* was created whose delegates at different times and places worked to propagate religious values among the leaders of the ML as well as the vast body of ordinary Muslims. Thanawi himself wrote several letters (*khutoot tablighi*) to Mr Jinnah and other leaders of the ML. He was optimistic that if the *ulama* became united and worked hard at *tabligh* the ML organization would be transformed in a very short time. Shafi claims that in response these leaders expressed their intentions of incorporating these religious commands.

meeting under the leadership of his protégé Shabbir Ahmad Usmani, had to be cancelled at the last moment owing to Usmani's mother sudden ill health. Thanawi concluded his statement with the optimism that if Muslims in general and *ulama* in particular were to put relentless pressure on the ML leaders to compel them to become more religiously oriented, the Muslim League would become a Muslim League in the truest sense of the word.

The senior *alim* conceded that the ML leaders still had some work to do before they could be seen as conscientious and observant Muslims. However, he decried any public criticism of the ML leadership for their shortcomings in this regard as he feared that it would only make them more stubborn and unyielding. He instead emphasized the virtues of patient and quiet counseling. This method was perhaps slow but its effects, he insisted, would be long-lasting. At the same time though, Thanawi dismissed criticisms of ML leaders as being non-observant Muslims as a case of the pot calling the kettle black. This was a charge which was bound to singe the nationalist *ulama* who had been most vocal in their denunciations of the ML leadership and Jinnah in particular. The ML leaders, even if they were not practicing Muslims, were still Muslims and it was always possible for them to someday become proper Muslims. The Congress leaders, on the other hand, were not even Muslims and hence beyond redemption.

To further justify his alliance with the unobservant ML leaders, Thanawi invoked the *seerat* literature on the biography of the Prophet. He pointed out that the Prophet was quoted as clearly stating that it was permissible for Muslims to fight alongside the *Khawarij* (Kharijites) in their battles against the *Moshreks*. Thanawi, however, hastened to add that the ML leaders, even though their shortcomings were obvious, were certainly not as debased as the *Khawarij*. Hence, joining them in their battles against the Congress was eminently suitable.[136] It needs to be noted that nowhere did Thanawi make an issue of Jinnah being a Shia. From these arguments Thanawi made it clear in no uncertain terms as to where his preferences lay. Indeed, he claimed support for his position from other Deobandi colleagues declaring that he had shown the *fatwa* to several of these eminent divines and had received their wholehearted endorsement.

Thanawi's protégé, Maulana Zafar Ahmad Usmani later commented on Thanawi's impact on ML affairs while recounting his memories of the 1939 AIML Patna session, which was attended by a Deobandi delegation.[137] When the delegation reached Patna the day before the ML's annual session, Shabbir

136 Ibid., 81.

137 Ahmad Saeed, *Maulana Ashraf Ali Sahab Thanawi aur tehrik-i-Azadi*, 130.

Ali Thanawi, Ashraf Ali's nephew and a member of the delegation, made it known that the ulama would not participate in the next day's sessions till they had an opportunity to meet Jinnah and ascertain his views regarding various aspects of the ML's ideology. Reacting with alacrity, Liaquat Ali Khan arranged their meeting with Jinnah that very same evening, clearly indicating the ML leadership's eagerness to please the *ulama*. At the meeting the delegation, according to Zafar Ahmad, expressed its strongly held view that the Muslims were a religious community (*mazhabi qaum*) and until and unless religion was attached to their politics, the ML would not succeed in gaining their affection. They particularly pointed to the political careers of the Ali brothers, Mohammad Ali and Shaukat Ali, which they argued, had taken off only after they 'applied some religious color' to their politics. Jinnah too was, therefore, urged to combine religion in the ML's politics. Zafar Ahmad recounts Jinnah's initial hesitation and his view that religion and politics should be kept free from each other. The *ulama*, however, swiftly responded stating such a model of politics was European and quite contrary to politics in Islam where no such separation had ever existed, and religious and political authority were usually fused in one personality. They argued that this had indeed been the state of affairs when Islam was flourishing. It was only after political authority was divorced from its religious role that problems arose in Islamic world as in the case of Turkey under Mustafa Kamal. His abolition of the Caliphate along with other reforms had devastated Turkey, completely depriving it of all of its previous power and prestige and reducing it to just another state in the world. This line of reasoning, Zafar Ahmad claimed, had a deep impact on the *Qaid's* mind for in his next day speech at the Patna session he proclaimed that Islam was not just a religion but a total way of life. The speech prompted Maulana Mazharuddin, the editor of *Al Aman*, Delhi, to plaster the front page of the following day's newspaper with the headline, 'The impact of *Hakim al Ummat* Thanawi's thoughts on Jinnah's speech'.

The delegation finally impressed upon Jinnah that while they did not wish to make any great demands of the ML leadership, they expected them to at least become regular *namazis*. To emphasize their seriousness on this count, they suggested that Jinnah should perform *namaz* along with the whole community on the following day. The *Qaid* apprehending trouble exclaimed that disputes could arise over even the seemingly trifling matter of who should be the prayer leader – whether it should be a Deobandi, a Sunni, or a Shia? This would therefore not be good tactics especially at a time when the ML was trying to present the Muslims of India as one united political community. The

Qaid's apprehensions were however laid to rest after he was assured that given his popularity the whole community would perform *namaz* behind whomever Jinnah himself stood during the prayer session. And as Zafar Ahmad recalls, that is what exactly happened. At 1 pm on the following day, the Patna ML session was adjourned for prayers. The *Qazi* of the town assumed the role of the prayer leader. Jinnah then went up and stood behind him, and in response, the whole gathering followed suit and stood behind them to pray.

Thanawi's growing alignment with the ML was also underlined by the *fatwas* he issued on the controversial issues of Urdu, *Bande Mataram* and the tricolour.[138] On the question of Urdu, Thanawi declared that the defence of Urdu was tantamount to the defence of the faith. If indeed Urdu were to die, the combined treasures of Indian Muslims would be lost since their religious books translated from Arabic and Persian, which provided religious education to ordinary Muslims, would no longer be available. Responding to an *istifta* (query) from a correspondent from Farrukhabad district on Bande Mataram, Thanawi wrote that singing this song and saluting the tricolour at the end of its recitation were impermissible under the *Shariah*. Castigating the Congress for imposing these activities on the Muslims, he acidly commented that the English were more careful over matters concerning the religious sensibilities of people since they had been the rulers over India for a while and had thus developed some farsightedness. The Congress, on the other hand, was new to the business of ruling, and intoxicated with power, acted without care or foresight.

Thanawi's Critique of the JUH Ulama and Madani's Theory of Muttahida Qaumiyat

Even as his engagement with the ML deepened, Thanawi's ties with the *ulama* supporting the Congress grew increasingly strained. He declined an invitation to participate in the JUH's 1939 Delhi session and even refused to send a message to the convention citing the delay in sending him the official invitation.[139] He, instead, publicly reasserted that if the *ulama* joined the Congress it would prove ruinous for the Muslims. It was, therefore, imperative for them to publicly announce Muslim disaffection (*bezari*) with the Congress. In a later opinion, Thanawi laid out a more elaborate explanation to back this position. Here he categorically declared that the question of Muslims joining the Congress could

---

[138] Ibid., 34–36.

[139] *Ifadat-i-Ashrafiya*, 88.

not even be a matter for discussion. Such an act was plainly impermissible since the evils associated with joining the Congress were clearly evident. Thanawi defended this reasoning in the light of the *Shariah* which clearly laid out main principles or roots (*asl*), and secondary principles or branches (*furoo*) derived from these main principles, that provided guidance on questions of permissibility and impermissibility. Thus, under the *Shariah*, a thing in itself (such as joining the Congress) could be permissible but it became impermissible on account of the associated evils that necessarily came with such a move. But in this context, Thanawi made it clear that joining the Congress was impermissible at the level of main principles itself, for it did not fulfill conditions (*quyood*) that were necessary to allow Muslims to join it. As he explained, the main condition that needed to be fulfilled before Muslims could join any organization was that the rule of Islam had to be dominant within it. A second necessary condition was that non-Muslims had to be in a position of subservience in that organization. Thanawi concluded that since these conditions were never going to be fulfilled in the case of the Congress, it was therefore impermissible for Muslims to join the organization.

Thanawi went on to demolish all other justifications for Muslims joining the Congress that had been put forth, especially by the nationalist *ulama*. Here he specifically targeted Maulana Husain Ahmad Madani's theory of *Muttahida Qaumiyat* that posited a composite nationalism of all Indians in which Hindus and Muslims could be equal participants.[140] Thanawi admonished the nationalist *ulama* for trying to buttress this theory by turning to some reports in the Hadith, having failed to find evidence to support their position in the books of *Fiqh*. This move, he argued, was new from the Shari'i point of view for three reasons. To begin with, the *ulama* needed to possess certain qualities to perform such *ijtihad*, and as he sardonically noted, these qualities (*ausaf-i-ijtihad*) were certainly not possessed by the nationalist *ulama*. Thanawi was on solid ground here for it is one of the fundamental Deobandi beliefs that there are no *mujtahids* in this day and age. Indeed, no Deobandi would dare to claim that he was performing *ijtihad*, and could at best affirm adherence to

140 The theory espoused a composite nationalism for all Indians and insisted that Muslims shared a common nationality with the Hindus, and on that basis, exhorted Muslims to join the Congress. Madani argued that there was a famous precedent for such a Hindu–Muslim compact in the form of a pact between the Prophet and the Jews in Medina that he claimed had been recorded in the Hadith. For an analysis of Madani's thought see Barbara Metcalf, *Husain Ahmad Madani: The Jihad for Islam and India's Freedom* (Oxford, 2009).

taqlid. Secondly, Thanawi pointed out that even in the Hadith, there were two kinds of narrations (*ravayat*); those which were authenticated and thus reliable, and those that were unauthenticated and hence suspect. The narrations being utilized by the nationalist *ulama*, Thanawi insisted, fell into the latter category. Furthermore, the nationalist *ulama* had not taken the pains to ascertain the reliability of these reports. And here Thanawi placed the burden of proof on the nationalist *ulama* for finding the necessary authentication for the Hadith that they were relying on in order to substantiate their argument of *Muttahida Qaumiyat*.

Next, Thanawi went on to make a case against the nationalist *ulama*'s very interpretation of even the unauthenticated Hadith that they had been invoking. Even if these reports of the Hadith could finally be authenticated, Thanawi argued that there were conditions in these Hadith that barred deductions of the sort that the nationalist *ulama* were making. In this context, he declared that he had re-read the *Seerat Ibn-i-Hisham*, the text from which narrations of the Hadith referring to the covenant between the Prophet and the Jews had been cited by the nationalist *ulama*. He acknowledged that in the covenant, the term used to describe Muslims and those who fought alongside them was 'one people' (*ummah wahida)* in order to distinguish them from other people. However, Thanawi clarified that the covenant was also very explicit about the position of the Muslims and the Jews in their mutual relationship. The primary condition that it insisted upon was that Muslims had to be the leaders of this *ummah wahida* while the Jews could only be in the position of followers. And in case of any dispute between the two, the covenant explicitly declared that Allah and his Prophet would sit in judgment to resolve the dispute. Thanawi further emphasized that the condition that the Prophet would be the judge in such cases had been explicitly agreed upon by both the parties. Given this condition in the covenant and the absence of such a condition governing a possible covenant between the Congress and the Muslims, Thanawi asserted that Muslim participation in the Congress was clearly impermissible.

Extending his analysis of this covenant between the Muslims and the Jews, Thanawi further reasoned that it was neither extraordinary nor in a class of its own; and more importantly, it could not be construed as a precedent for the sorts of compromises that the nationalist *ulama* were advocating between the Muslims and the Congress. He argued that the Medinian covenant between Muslims and Jews was very similar to ones that later took place between the Muslims and the Dhimmis. The apparent difference between the two was only due to the misleading wording of the former, which Thanawi attributed to the conditions prevailing during the time of the Prophet. As he observed, the Prophet wrote the covenant before *Jizya* was imposed and Islam was not in a position of dominance. Thus, the earlier covenant gave the Jews a portion of the spoils of war, giving the impression that this was a covenant between equals, which, Thanawi insisted, was most certainly not the case.

In a stinging riposte ridiculing the clumsy attempts by the nationalist *ulama* at substantiating the theory of *Muttahida Qaumiyat*, Thanawi quoted the didactic tale of the grocer and the parrot from the *Masnavi-i-Ma'navi* written by the Persian mystic poet Rumi.[141]

A grocer kept a parrot in his stall,
The bird was green and talked, amusing all,

Perched on a bench it watched the passers-by,
Sharing a word with those who caught its eye,

It knew how to pronounce all human words,
Spoke fluently with men as well as birds.

The parrot hopped down from the bench one day,
Spilling a flask of rose oil on its way;

And when the grocer came back to his store,
When he sat down he stained the clothes he wore.

On seeing the spilt oil a rage took hold—
He struck the parrot's head and left it bald!

The next few days the bird refused to speak,
The grocer grieved, repentant now and meek,

He tugged his beard, 'Alas!' he cried aloud
'My sun of bounty's hidden by a cloud!

Would that my hand had broken then instead
Of striking my most precious parrot's head!'

He then gave gifts to all the needy men,
Hoping to hear the parrot speak again.

---

141 The following translation is from *Rumi, The Masnavi: Book One,* translated by Jawid Mojaddedi (Oxford, 2004).

After three nights, perplexed and desperate
He sat down on the bench, disconsolate,

Then showed the parrot wondrous tricks galore
To coax it into talking back once more;

A monk then strolled by on his daily route,
In woollen garb and balder than a coot

This made the parrot talk again at last.
It shouted at the monk as he walked past:

'How did you end up such a slaphead, friend?
Did you like me a flask of oil upend?'

At this assumption everybody laughed,
It thought the monk its equal—it was daft!

The simple yet devastating point that Thanawi was making by quoting this tale was that the nationalist *ulama* were like the foolish parrot attempting to perform *ijtihad* as if they had the same qualities (*ausaf-i-ijtihad*) to take such liberty as was possessed by their illustrious medieval forebears, represented here by the monk. What is also significant is that Thanawi deliberately omitted couplets 2, 3, 10, 11 and 12, all of which present the parrot in a complimentary light or present the grocer's affection for his parrot. This was to subtly underscore his larger framing point about people who seemingly look alike but actually are quite unlike in nature.[142]

Thanawi on the Role of Ulama in Politics

Thanawi amplified his criticism of the politically active nationalist *ulama*, and specifically Maulana Husain Ahmad Madani, by specifically addressing the issue of the *ulama's* participation in politics. His observations on the matter, in the light of his interpretation of the *Shariah*, were critical since Madani and his fellow *ulama*, as the putative 'heirs of the Prophet', were making claims for leadership over the Indian Muslim community. Thanawi's exposition came in the form of reply to a query by a correspondent who wondered as to why the *ulama*, who were experts in the *Shariah*, were not assuming a leadership role in politics. As the questioner

142 I am indebted to Prashant Keshavmurthy for bringing this point to my attention besides sending me Jawid Mojaddedi's luminous translation of Rumi.

noted, expertise in *Shariah* was tantamount to expertise in politics for the latter was a part of the former. And since the *ulama* were the 'heirs of the Prophets', they were therefore expected to fulfill their bounden duty in this regard. Thanawi in his long, detailed, and masterful exposition on this subject declared that this was a mistaken view. Instead, he made a case for their mutual dependence since their separate fields of expertise could often overlap, while making it amply clear that the *ulama* should not aspire to assume political leadership.[143]

Thanawi began by noting that the sphere of politics was made up of two parts. The first pertained to Shari'i rulings, which were relevant to politics. No *alim* was unfamiliar with this part of *Shariah* for every book of *Fiqh* that the *ulama* were trained to read, had a chapter on politics. The second area of politics, however, pertained to experience gained in politics which, naturally, was subject to change over time. This part had nothing to do with the *Shariah* and, Thanawi added that it was therefore not necessary for the *ulama* to be experts in this field. If any *alim* was indeed an expert in this field, then his expertise would have been acquired by some other means and not due to his knowledge of the *Shariah*. But such an exposition could always be interpreted in such a manner as to severely circumscribe the role of the *Shariah* in non-religious aspects of life. Thanawi, therefore, hastened to add that while this part of politics was not a part of the *Shariah*, it was not *independent* of it either. He, therefore, declared that there was indeed no matter (*vaqiya*), no practice (*amal*), no proposal, plan or scheme (*tajviz*), no opinion, view or advice (*rai*), about whose permissibility the *ulama* could not be consulted.

In order to clarify this point, Thanawi came up with an illustration. The science of medicine dealt with the constitution of the body (*siyasat-i-badaniya*), its ailments and their rectification to help restore health to the body. Nobody expected the *ulama* to be experts in the field of medicine and not being so could certainly not be assumed to be a deficiency on their part. Yet, at the same time, Thanawi asserted that it was necessary for physicians to consult the *ulama* in order to ascertain whether or not any medical procedure was ethically permissible. Physicians and *ulama* were separate groups, experts in their own fields, but they needed to consult each other and hence were mutually dependent. Thanawi, therefore, contended that politicians and *ulama* could similarly be divided into two separate groups who were dependent on each other. From politicians one learnt about how to run a city or a country (*siyasat-i-madaniya*), while from the *ulama* one could gain rulings on the

---

143 *Ifadat-i-Ashrafiya*, 89–93.

permissibility of any policy, law or procedure. In order to substantiate his position, Thanawi cited a rare past precedent that was revealed in the Quran. When Samuel was the Prophet of the Jews, he was asked by his people to appoint a King who could rule over them and lead them in battle. In response, Samuel appointed Talut (Saul) to lead them in their fight against Goliath. Thanawi asserted that the indication in the Quran on this matter was very clear. The *Banu Israel* even when they had a Prophet in Samuel had asked for a King and did not ask the Prophet himself to lead them. As Thanawi asked, if the Prophet Samuel was sufficient to the task, why would his people ask him for a King? Furthermore, why would Samuel then appoint someone other than himself for this task? Additionally, if the *Banu Israel* had made a mistake in making this demand, why did the Prophet not reprimand them? Could it thus be inferred that the Prophet Samuel had made a mistake? This last question had to be dismissed straight away since Prophets were infallible, and also because Allah would never allow a Prophet to make a mistake and would indeed send a revelation to correct any such mistake.

But Thanawi still had to explain the apparent contradiction between the example of Samuel and Talut that he cited with the case of the Prophet of Islam combining the roles of secular and religious authority in his own person. Additionally there existed other prominent examples of Prophets like David and his son who also similarly combined roles of the Prophet and the King. Finally, there was also another obscure opinion that claimed that Talut had not just been a King but also a Prophet. How could Thanawi, therefore, justify the division of roles between the *ulama*, the 'heirs of the Prophet' and politicians by invoking the example of Samuel and Talut? To get around this problem, Thanawi relied on a medieval text, the *Tafsir-al Mazhari*, written by the great Indian Hanafi scholar Qazi Sanaullah Panipati to substantiate his claim that even a Prophet need not be an expert in politics. Following its cue, Thanawi ingeniously argued that while deficiency could never be admitted in the case of a Prophet (Samuel from the above example), a case could certainly be made for different degrees of perfection attained by different Prophets. To substantiate his point, he noted that while earlier prophets had been sent by God to particular races, the Prophet of Islam had been sent by God to all of mankind. Hence, while the coming of a Prophet like Muhammad to all mankind was indeed a *kamaal* (miracle), it did not signify that other Prophets were deficient, for indeed, the very thought that a Prophet was less than perfect was impermissible in Islam. Thus, while some Prophets like Muhammad also had political expertise, others did not have to have that same capacity. Besides, as Thanawi pointed out, even the Prophet of Islam who possessed the highest level of perfection often asked for advice from others. He famously sought advice from Salman the Persian when it came to the Battle of the Trench. Similarly, the Hadith *Al Bukhari* revealed that the Prophet had once asked his people to sow seeds in a manner that was different from their usual practice. When the following crop yield was lower than usual, the Prophet acknowledged that farmers knew more about these affairs than he did.

Thanawi also tackled the obscure opinion that Talut had not just been a King but was also a Prophet, which had the potential of undermining his argument over separation of roles and/or expertise between Prophets and Kings. In this regard, he argued that whether Talut was a Prophet or not, was beside the point, for what mattered was that Samuel was the Prophet *at the time* and he chose Talut to be the King of the *Banu Israel*. The implication here was that Talut may have become a Prophet later, but he certainly was not so at the time of Samuel. To conclude his point, Thanawi contended that for the *ulama* as the heirs of the Prophet, or even a Prophet himself, lacking expertise in politics was not tantamount to their suffering from any deficiency. And since the *ulama* were not experts in politics it was best for them to work in partnership with politicians without aspiring to assume a leadership role.

Thanawi argued that active participation in politics by the *ulama* was also dangerous since it would lead them into blunders, which would harm the Muslim community. In this context, he deplored the *ulama* taking on politically active roles particularly on the side of the Congress thus placing itself in an adversarial position to the Muslim community, the ML which was their representative organization, and finally the *ulama* supporting the latter. Thanawi added that if the nationalist *ulama* had instead confined themselves to their own duties, they would not have lost the respect of the community. Such was their lamentable state today that even laymen were opposing these *ulama* leading to a loss in their dignity. Thanawi also used this opportunity to express his displeasure at Congress politics making an entry into the Darul Uloom, especially under the aegis of Maulana Husain Ahmad Madani, the institution's Principal. Madani had famously declared that participation in Congress' anti-colonial politics was equivalent to participating in a *jihad*, and thus a rightful duty for all Muslims. In response to such propaganda at Deoband, Thanawi tersely reiterated his position. The Congress was dominated by Hindus, its flag was Hindu, and Muslims would forever remain subordinated in that organization. The question of becoming a part of an Islamic *jihad* by participating in the activities of the Congress therefore simply did not arise.

Concluding his overall argument regarding the role of *ulama* in politics, Thanawi asserted that the while *ulama* were not barred from participating in politics in principle, the prevailing circumstances made it necessary that they should stay out of politics and confine themselves to giving advice to political leaders in order to prevent them from doing anything that went against the commands of the *Shariah*. He argued that this was the best possible path for the *ulama* to take since their lack of knowledge of English law or constitutional politics did not give them the necessary expertise to play an active role in politics. Thanawi, however, acknowledged that politicians did not always ask the *ulama* for advice in these times. Nonetheless, he asserted that even if they were not approached by the politicians, it was the communal obligation (*farz-i-kifaya*) of the *ulama* to still go to them and offer them guidance. This also applied to the *ulama*'s interactions with experts in other aspects of life be they economists, doctors etc. Thanawi's own efforts to offer guidance to the ML in the task of reforming their organization and making it more 'Islamic' was an example of his performing his *farz-i-kifaya*. In this regard, he claimed that when negotiations between the Congress and the ML were underway, he wrote to Jinnah asking him not to give his opinion or commit himself over any religious issues. Jinnah in his reply reportedly promised the Maulana that he would take no such step before consulting the *ulama* on such matters.

Finally, Thanawi was also opposed to political activity at Deoband since it disrupted scholarly pursuits. He was especially critical about how the Arabic department had been especially affected as a result of their political activities. Thanawi's reservations regarding Madani's active participation in politics alongside Congress soon led to his resignation from his position as *Sarparast* at Deoband. As he wrote to his *murid* (pupil), Abdul Majid Daryabadi, 'I know Maulana Husain Ahmad declares that joining the Congress is a *farz*. In this context, I do not know if he likes those who keep more obscure practices.' Mufti Mohammad Shafi, the chief *mufti* at Deoband, who migrated to Pakistan after the Partition, recounted that Thanawi resigned primarily because he did not appreciate the idea of its students participating in Congress politics, which he saw as pro-Hindu. The final straw came when he learnt that a Hindu Congress leader had been given a welcome reception at the Deoband railway station by students and staff of the Darul Uloom. In response, Thanawi swiftly sent in his resignation as the *sarparast*. When it was not accepted by Madani, Thanawi had it posted on the gates of the institution.

The Congress Closure of the Muslim Mass Contact Programme

The Congress party's stock among the U.P. Muslims hit an all-time low as a series of bloody Hindu–Muslim riots ravaged the province. The U.P. Governor did not lay much store in the ML charge that the Congress government had abetted Hindu atrocities on Muslims. Yet, as the historian Mukul Kesavan has shown, Congressmen in various districts in U.P. were well-known Hindu leaders, who if not implicated in the rioting themselves openly organized legal defenses of Hindus arrested in the rioting.[144] The Congress was widely seen by Muslims by now as a Hindu organization. The ML would go on to produce another report on Hindu atrocities in the 'minority provinces'.[145]

The Congress lost another by-election for the Badayun seat in September 1938 in which the ML's Iqtidaruddin Hasan trounced the Congress candidate Muhammad Sulaiman garnering 75 per cent of all the votes polled. The MMCP by now had ground to a halt by the middle of 1938. K. M. Ashraf wrote to Nehru that Muslim Contact work, and the Economic and Political Department had been formally abolished by Kripalani. He was mainly doing routine office work, which made him feel like a parasite. He had already sent his wife and children to his ancestral village and wanted to leave the office himself as soon as Nehru returned to Allahabad.[146] The ML's mobilization drive had already dwarfed the Congress programme by the beginning of 1938 as the ML claimed to have 300,000 members on its rolls as compared to the Congress 100,000.[147] The Congress now began to explore possibilities of opening negotiations with the ML leadership. Nehru's attempts to draw Jinnah into a dialogue were rudely rebuffed. The negotiations that ultimately began between Jinnah and Subhas Bose did not get off ground as the Congress could not accept Jinnah's conditions that the ML be recognized as the sole representative organization of the Indian Muslims. The Congress now turned to explore other options. Rajendra Prasad approached the Punjab Premier Sir Sikandar Hayat Khan while K. M. Ashraf

144 See Mukul Kesavan, '1937 as a Landmark in the Course of Communal Politics in U.P.', *Occasional Paper, Second Series, No. XI*, NMML; 'Congress and the Muslims of U.P. and Bihar: 1937 to 1939', *Occasional Paper, Second Series, No. XXVII*, NMML; 'Communal Violence and its Impact on the Politics of North India', *Occasional Paper, Second Series, No. XXIII*, NMML.

145 See Qazi Mohammad Isa, *It Shall Never Happen Again* (Delhi, 1946).

146 K. M. Ashraf to Nehru, 2 September 1938 in Basudev Chatterji, *Towards Freedom: Documents on the Movement for the Independence in India*, 1938, Part 1 (Delhi, 1999), 87.

147 *Madina*, 21 January 1938.

approached the veteran Khilafatist, Maulana Shaukat Ali, but both these attempts proved infructuous. The protagonists of the MMCP were now anxious to make peace with the ML. Sajjad Zaheer, Mian Iftikharuddin and Dr Hussain Zaheer met Liaquat Ali Khan to plead for a Congress-ML settlement. They even went as far as to declare that the left wing was willing to force the Congress High Command to accept the ML as *the* representative organization of the Muslims if the ML would give them a face saver. They further assured Liaquat that the Hindus in the left wing were with them in this regard.[148]

The ML kept up the pressure on the Congress government with its Pirpur Report that levelled charges against the Congress government for highhandedness and 'atrocities' on Muslims.[149] Muslim deputations from the Muslim majority provinces now began touring the U.P. to make further enquiries regarding atrocities committed on the Muslims by the Congress government. Thus a deputation consisting of Agha Shabbir Ahmad, *Vakil* of Ludhiana, Sajjad Ahmad Khan of Hazara, Maulvi Shariful Rahman of Panipat, and Khalil-ur-Rahman, *Vakil* of Ludhiana visited Aligarh, Bulandshahr, Muzaffarnagar and Saharanpur. A different delegation consisting of Mohammad Ismail Ghaznavi, of NWFP, Professor Dildar Khan of MAO College, Amritsar, Agha Bashir Mohammad and Fateh Mohammad Khan of Baluchistan visited Bijnor and Barielly districts.[150] A large public meeting was held by the ML in Lucknow on 2 December to thank another Muslim delegation from the Muslim majority provinces for its concern for the predicament of the U.P. Muslims. 'This delegation later split into two halves and continued their tour of the province touring Allahabad, Bahraich, Ballia, Benares, Etah, Gonda, Gorakhpur, Hardoi, Jaunpur and Sultanpur.'[151]

But even as the ML appeared to be sitting pretty, the solidity of the party's support base was seriously called into question in the ensuing *Madhe Sahaba* agitation.[152] The issue had become troublesome in the autumn of 1938 but assumed ominous proportions by the summer of 1939 that led to riots between Shias and Sunnis in different parts of U.P. and especially the capital city of

---

148 Liaquat Ali Khan to Jinnah, 16 June 1939, in Muhammad Reza Qasimi (ed.), *Liaquat-Jinnah Correspondence*, (Karachi, 2003).

149 AIML, *Report of the Inquiry Committee Appointed by the Council of the All India Muslim League to Inquire into Muslim Grievances in Congress Provinces* (Delhi, 1939).

150 *PAI for the week ending 25 November 1939.*

151 *PAI for the week ending 9 December 1939.*

152 See Venkat Dhulipala, 'Rallying the Qaum: The Muslim League in the United Provinces, 1937-1939', *Modern Asian Studies*, Vol. 44, No. 3 (2010), 603–40.

Lucknow. These disturbances threatened to snowball into a wider all-India conflict as partisans from both sides poured into Lucknow from different parts of India and clashed with each other. As these tensions rose, the ML stood aside helplessly, unable to exert its authority to bring about peace between these two warring sects of Islam. The ML's lack of initiative attracted competition from other Muslim groups keen to garner the prestige that resolving this fratricidal conflict would bring them, and consequently enable their emergence as serious political players at the U.P. and all-India level. The most prominent were the Khaksars of Punjab whose spirited intervention saw them trying to forcibly compose Shia–Sunni differences.

However, the ML received a fresh lease of life as a result of a series of changes in the political circumstances in the country. To begin with the forceful repression of the Khaksars by the U.P. government, which imprisoned their eccentric leader Allama Mashriqi, along with inconsistent efforts by the Khaksars opened the door for the ML to reassert itself in U.P. Muslim politics. But what really gave a fresh lease of life to the ML in these circumstances was the resignation of Congress ministries in November 1939, protesting against India being dragged into the War without the consent of Indians themselves. The crisis came as a tremendous blessing for the ML and could not have come at a more appropriate time. The Congress high command now sought unity between different political groups in India in order to present a joint Indian response to the British Government. Keen to get the Muslims on board, the Congress again turned to Jinnah. The Khaksar issue in U.P. was a major point of discussion during the meetings between Nehru and Jinnah. Jinnah demanded and was supplied with relevant documents related to the Khaksars by Rafi Ahmad Kidwai, the Home Minister in the U.P. Government. Nehru was optimistic after his round of talks with Jinnah, which had been most cordial, but he was in for a shock for even as the talks were progressing, the *Qaid* gave his call to the Muslims of the Muslim minority provinces to celebrate a Day of Deliverance on 22 December 1939. The day was meant for Muslims throughout India to celebrate the resignation of Congress ministries and the consequent deliverance of the Muslims from their bondage. Jinnah was enthusiastically supported by his lieutenants in U.P. and other provinces on this masterstroke. Writing to Jinnah, Liaquat informed him that it also had the support of other ML leaders such as Mahmudabad and Fazlul Haq who were present at the recent Darbhanga district ML conference. Liaquat however had some advice for his leader after his consultations with the *ulama* on this move. As he wrote:

> You should ask Mussalmans to go en masse to the mosques, and after the Juma prayers, everyone should offer prayer in thanks for deliverance from this tyrannical regime and that it may never return in the same form. According to the religion, the thanksgiving prayers will have to be offered individually as it cannot be done by a gathering all together like the juma or other prayers. I have consulted some ulema on this point and this is their opinion. You should also ask the Mussalmans to observe humility and not do anything that is likely to give offence to anyone. I suggest this be done all over India and not be confined to the Provinces where Congress ministries were functioning.[153]

The Day of Deliverance met 'mixed reception in the U.P.' as was evident from the contradictory reports regarding its success.[154] On the one hand, Mahmudabad writing to Jinnah effusively reported that 'Deliverance Day was such a success that it was celebrated even in those quarters where the League is looked upon as a vile disease. Even the most anti-League elements joined it.'[155] Its real significance, he declared, was that it had laid 'the foundation of self-respecting Nationhood for the Muslims. It was indeed 'the first concrete step that shows without ambiguity that there are not one but several nations in India.'[156] And yet, not all ML notables in U.P. were happy with Jinnah's call. Hasrat Mohani disapproved of Jinnah's suggestion that Muslims seek redress for their grievances from the Governors. He, therefore, asked Muslims to stay neutral in the present struggle if they could not favour the Congress against the British Government.[157] Karim-ur-Raza Khan, the ML MLA from Shahjahanpur, bluntly declined to observe the Day of Deliverance.[158] The Bengal Muslim leader Abdur Rahman Siddiqi, criticizing Jinnah's directive, went so far as to declare that the *Qaid* was suffering from 'senile decay'.[159]

Nehru, on the other hand, wrote to Gandhi that 'Deliverance Day was a failure in U.P. Many of the meetings started off in a very small way, but then

---

153 Liaquat Ali Khan to Jinnah, 27 November 1939, in Muhammad Reza Qasimi (ed.), *Jinnah-Liaquat Correspondence* (Karachi, 2003).

154 *PAI for the week ending 16 December 1939.*

155 Mahmudabad to Jinnah, 29 November 1939, *Shamsul Hasan Collection* (hereafter SHC) Foreign Correspondence.

156 Ibid.

157 *The Leader*, 21 December 1939.

158 Ibid.

159 Chaudhry Khaliquzzaman, *Pathway to Pakistan* (Lahore, 1961), 232.

curious sightseers, chiefly Hindus joined them find out what was happening. Some meetings were also held on that day in mosques and outside condemning the Muslim League proposal.'[160] The new Governor of U.P., Sir Maurice Hallett, concurred with this judgment. As he wrote to the Viceroy, 'I do not think that Deliverance Day, of which many reasonable Muslims disapproved, was as great a success as would appear from newspaper accounts. Some collectors report little enthusiasm and in most districts, meetings were smaller than expected.'[161] Nonetheless, the resignation of the Congress ministries, placed the ML under pressure to come up with a positive vision of the future that went beyond criticism of the Congress, the British Government and the federal scheme envisaged under the GOI Act of 1935. This became especially urgent in the context of further political reforms envisaged by the British Government at the Centre as it came under renewed pressure from the Congress in the context of the war. The Lahore Resolution held precisely such a promise.

160 Nehru to Gandhi, 25 December 1939, *SWJN*, Vol. 10, 417.

161 Hallett to Linlithgow, 1 January 1940, *Hallett Papers*.

3

Two Constitutional Lawyers from Bombay and the Debate over Pakistan in the Public Sphere

Every Indian must read a book on Pakistan, if not this, then some other, if he wants to help his country steer a clear path.

B. R. Ambedkar[1]

There is a great deal of discussion and literature on this point which is available and it is for you to judge finally, when you have studied this question thoroughly, whether the Mussalmans and Hindus are not two separate nations in this sub-continent. For the moment I would refer you to two publications, although there are many more – Dr. Ambedkar's book and MRT's Nationalism in Conflict in India.

M. A. Jinnah[2]

There is a general consensus among historians of the Partition that the Lahore Resolution marks the official starting point of the ML's struggle for Pakistan. But beyond this point the consensus does not extend much further and breaks down almost immediately. On one side are those who see Pakistan's birth in 1947 as the logical culmination of a struggle, which began at Lahore in 1940. In this story, a cool, calculating and determined Jinnah, having declared Pakistan as the primary goal of the Indian Muslims, inspired his faithful millions to shed their myriad differences and unify behind this ideal on the ground, even while he skillfully and successfully outmaneuvered both the Congress and the British government at the negotiating high tables to achieve his Pakistan.[3] This stupendous achievement may have stunned and even confounded contemporary observers, but it led not just official hagiographers, but many of these later

1 B. R. Ambedkar, *Thoughts on Pakistan* (Bombay, 1941), 10.

2 Jinnah to Gandhi 17 September 1944, in *Gandhi-Jinnah Talks: Text of Correspondence and Other Relevant Matter, July-October 1944* (New Delhi, 1944), 16.

3 See for example Khalid Bin Sayeed, *Pakistan: The Formative Phase, 1857-1948* (London, 1968); Anita Inder Singh, *Origins of the Partition of India* (Delhi, 1987); Hector Bolitho, *Jinnah of Pakistan* (London, 1954); Sharif al Mujahid, *Jinnah: Studies in Interpretation* (Karachi, 1969).

historians to marvel at Jinnah's single-handed achievement in changing the map of South Asia against seemingly impossible odds. The *Qaid* too contributed to this legend by claiming that he brought Pakistan into existence with the help of nothing more than a typewriter and a personal assistant whom he paid out of his own pocket.

These certitudes existed for nearly forty years after the states of India and Pakistan emerged in the subcontinent from the detritus of the British Empire. But this conventional wisdom was challenged by Ayesha Jalal in her seminal book, which called into question the unproblematic connection and smooth progression between the Lahore Resolution and the creation of Pakistan.[4] Drawing upon newly declassified British Government documents published in twelve massive volumes that detailed the tortuous negotiations over the transfer of power in India, Jalal controversially argued that Pakistan was not a demand for a separate sovereign state but Jinnah's bargaining counter to acquire for the Muslims, political equality with the numerically preponderant Hindus in an *undivided* post-colonial India. Her book painstakingly demonstrated how in this bargaining game the *Qaid* deliberately kept Pakistan as a vague idea allowing his fired-up base to imagine it in as many ways as possible, all the while waiting to concede it once the Congress had bid the highest possible price. According to Jalal, the Cabinet Mission, which gave parity to Hindus and Muslims at the federal Centre, was what Jinnah exactly wanted, but the Plan was rejected by a crotchety Congress leadership setting in motion the chain of events leading to the Partition. Written with flair, Jalal's book crisply recounted how a proud lonely Jinnah almost overcame the Mahatma's evil genius, the tiresome sanctimoniousness and obduracy of Nehru, the sly machinations of an astute Rajaji, besides bringing the detestable colonial government to heel; all the while holding together his own flock of petty, unimaginative and often treacherous Muslim allies and underlings in the provinces, but failed tragically in the end to stop the catastrophe.

Jalal's thesis upended existing common sense regarding the real perpetrators of the Partition, shifting the burden of that 'sin', to invoke the Mahatma's evocative words, from the tired shoulders of the *Qaid* to those of the Machiavellian Congress leadership. Unpacking some of the other implications of this explosive thesis, the historian Asim Roy has written that Jalal's 'revisionism on Jinnah's role in the creation of Pakistan questions the very legitimacy of the state by

4 Ayesha Jalal, *The Sole Spokesman: Jinnah, the Muslim League and the Demand for Pakistan* (Cambridge, 1985).

the *Qaid-i-Azam* as the universally acknowledged father of Pakistan.'[5] This startling revisionism soon came to occupy the status of the new orthodoxy in the field, but the nature of its influence needs to be seen more in terms of its two enduring legacies, which continue to cast their wide shadow over the burgeoning field of Partition studies. In the first place, it cemented Jinnah's position at the very centre of the Partition drama as the 'sole spokesman' of the Indian Muslims, completely dwarfing other figures and their voices in this process. But more importantly, it inaugurated a new common sense in the field – that Pakistan remained a vague idea till its actual realization, a vagueness deliberately fostered by Jinnah, that remained unchallenged by either the colonial state or the Congress party and was largely unquestioned by millions of his followers as they rallied behind their leader, seemingly unaware of Pakistan's meaning or implications. Even Jalal's critics, especially from the subaltern studies collective, while frowning on the Great Man theory underpinning the first legacy, agreed with this latter assumption. Moving away from high tables and plush negotiating chambers to the dry and dusty blood-soaked plains of northern India, they proceeded to consecrate the everyman figure of Toba Tek Singh as the alternate pole in the field representing the unfortunate millions killed or displaced as result of elite blundering at the twilight of the Raj. Ever since, Partition studies has largely congealed around the twin poles of Jinnah and Toba Tek Singh.

These fundamental assumptions underpinning Partition historiography seem breathtaking especially in the light of raucous public debates joined by a variety of voices that lit up and suffused the subcontinent's public sphere almost immediately after the Lahore Resolution, as Pakistan became the most pressing political issue of the day. Rather than sleepwalking into the quicksands of the Partition, true to form, 'argumentative' Indians intensively and extensively discussed, debated, challenged and fought over claims concerning both an undivided India and Pakistan. These battles were fought through books, pamphlets and tracts, through the columns of the vibrant Urdu press, as also in the numerous political conferences on Pakistan that were held in the villages, *qasbahs*, towns and cities of north India, underlining C. A. Bayly's claim that Britain's Indian empire was indeed an 'empire of opinion'.[6]

5 Asim Roy, 'The High Politics of India's Partition: The Revisionist Perspective', *Modern Asian Studies*, Vol. 24, No. 2 (1990), 385–408.

6 C. A. Bayly, *Empire and Information: Intelligence Gathering and Social Communication in India, 1780-1870* (Cambridge, 1996).

A perusal of these public debates is essential if one is to make sense of whether clarity or vagueness dogged the issue of Pakistan. What such an exercise makes clear is that while initial reactions and counter-responses on Pakistan may have been characterized by lack of clarity, reflecting either anger or disbelief of its opponents or unreflective, enthusiastic support of its supporters, this amorphousness soon gave way to sober, systematic and sustained analyses of Pakistan's rationale, implications and justifications or the lack of, on both sides of this debate. It is precisely due to these debates that Pakistan did not remain 'a host of shapes and forms, most of them vague',[7] but an idea that began to assume clarity, substance and popularity in the public sphere. Nobody did more to shape the contours of this debate, to give it coherence, stability and discipline, than that other constitutional lawyer from Bombay, Dr Bhimrao Ramji Ambedkar.

A Wake-up call for the Congress and the Hindus: B. R. Ambedkar's 'Thoughts on Pakistan'

If for nearly half a century after Indian independence Ambedkar remained safely confined in the Indian nationalist pantheon as the 'father of India's constitution', a notch or two below the Mahatma, 'the father of the nation' or Nehru 'the father of modern India', he has in the recent past found resurrection as a potent symbol for social and political emancipation for India's oppressed castes, especially in the context of the rise of Dalit politics in India. Yet, in spite of an explosion in scholarly writings on Ambedkar's insurrectionary intellectual challenge to the nationalist consensus in India patched together by Gandhi before Independence and by Nehru thereafter, what is striking is the near total silence in the existing Ambedkar scholarship on his centrality in shaping public debates on Pakistan in the aftermath of the Lahore Resolution. At a time when the ML's base provided the Lahore Resolution with spontaneous and thunderous support and the Congress leadership, along with the rank and file, reacted to it in a largely visceral, knee-jerk and tersely dismissive fashion, this other constitutional lawyer from Bombay brought a semblance of sanity, order and reason to the controversy.

Ambedkar dryly reminded an indignant Congress and the Hindus that those fulminating against the Lahore Resolution and trying to shoot down Pakistan with 'similes and metaphors' needed to realize that 'nonsense is nonetheless

---

7 Ayesha Jalal, *The Sole Spokesman*, 4.

nonsense because it is in rhyme and that a metaphor is no argument'.[8] To the emotional, rapturous supporters of Pakistan (as much as to its opponents), he presented a thorough and thoughtful treatise, with its cool, clinical and, at times, playful elaboration of the Lahore Resolution. As Ambedkar sagely observed, 'I have no doubt that the only proper attitude to Pakistan is to study it in all its aspects, to understand its implications and to form an intelligent judgment about it.'[9]

In the preface to his monograph signed on 28 December 1940, Ambedkar noted that he had first submitted it as a report to the executive council of the Independent Labor Party in Bombay in August 1940. Soon after, the manuscript was sent to the press with no further corrections, a haste that is reflected in its not few errors of spelling, punctuation and grammar. Ambedkar would find time to rectify them only five years later for the next revised edition that was given a new title as well.[10] This first 400 page edition of his '*Thoughts on Pakistan* with its fourteen appendices containing various facts and figures and three accompanying maps with clearly drawn and suitably coloured maps with proposed borders and boundaries of the two states, was thus produced within an astounding four months after the Lahore Resolution – a stunning achievement by any standards. It is no exaggeration to say that this was a prescient, prodigious work of scholarship by a brilliant mind, which would go on to serve as an indispensable reference to all the parties in the conflict, besides providing a roadmap for possible constitutional solutions as the endgame of Partition was played out in the twilight of the Raj.

Ambedkar was clearly satisfied with his labours as also from the massive reception to his work, for in the preface to the second edition of his treatise he remarked that 'thoughts, ideas and arguments contained in it have been pillaged by authors, politicians and editors of newspapers to support their sides'. But even though the book's arguments and even its language had been lifted without any attribution to its author, Ambedkar declared himself to be satisfied with the results.[11] It had been of service to the public and 'supplied a real want' even if it had consumed a lot of his valuable time and given him a 'headache'.[12] It is, therefore, with justifiable pride he pointed to the fact that

8 B. R. Ambedkar, *Thoughts on Pakistan* (Bombay, 1941), 1.

9 Ibid., 2.

10 This new title was *Pakistan or the Partition of India* (Bombay, 1945).

11 Ibid., ix.

12 Ibid.

Gandhi and Jinnah during their widely publicized 1944 talks had 'cited the book as an authority on the subject, which might be consulted with advantage, bespeaks the worth of the book'.[13]

Passing references to Ambedkar's book in the existing Partition historiography have mostly described it as an eloquent defense of the idea of Pakistan.[14] Given his unconcealed hostility towards the Congress High Command and his polemics against Gandhi, one cannot be faulted for presuming that this could only be Ambedkar's logical position. A more recent and again brief, interpretation of his book has waxed eloquent on his lofty Socratic neutrality on the question of partitioning India.[15] This again might seem self-evident since by Ambedkar's own admission, his work had been appropriated by both sides in the conflict. However, such characterizations, not based on any detailed analysis of this book, serve to only mystify his thinking on this important question. Even the valuable biography of Ambedkar by his foremost biographer Dhananjay Keer, while brimming with useful insights, is rather brief and patchy in its treatment of this important book.[16]

To gain insight into Ambedkar 'thoughts' on Pakistan one needs to turn to the preface of this treatise before going to the text itself. At the very outset, Ambedkar declared that he had written this book as an impartial commentator and that his 'thoughts' were concerned primarily with exploring the 'scheme of Pakistan in all its aspects and not to advocate it'. 'The aim is to explain, not to convert', he stated succinctly.[17] What made his 'thoughts' on Pakistan worth examining, he pointed out, was their basis in careful reasoning and the absence of 'the fixity of popular prejudice' in them – something that could not be said about existing opinions on the issue. Yet, Ambedkar also rather puckishly noted that it would be 'idle pretense' to say that he had no views on Pakistan. 'Views I have. Some of them are expressed others may have to be gathered'. He had 'an open mind, though not an empty mind'.[18] His views on the subject had to be

13 Ibid., x.

14 Ayesha Jalal, *Self and sovereignty: Individual and Community in South Asian Islam since 1850* (London and New York, 2000), 300.

15 Partha Chatterjee, *The Politics of the Governed: Reflections on Popular Politics in Most of the World* (New York, 2004).

16 Dhananjay Keer, *Dr Ambedkar: Life and Mission* (Bombay, 1971), third edition see his brief chapter 'On Federation and Pakistan', 318–37.

17 *Thoughts on Pakistan*, 10.

18 Ibid., 10–11.

discerned by a careful reader of his treatise and, therefore, demanded a serious engagement with the text on the part of its readers.

The arrangement of Ambedkar's 'thoughts' on Pakistan is revealing. The initial part of the book evaluates arguments in favour of Pakistan that are primarily based on affect, considering the tremendous sentimental value that the overwhelming majority of Muslims attached to the two-nation theory. Ambedkar conceded that these arguments clearly demonstrated that the Muslims were a nation and he, therefore, unambiguously supported the ML's Pakistan demand. While this may have been music to the ears of the ML's supporters, Ambedkar subsequently presented to the Hindus a series of arguments to convince them to concede Pakistan, arguments which could only have dampened Pakistani supporters' enthusiasm for the man as well as for his message. Appealing to reason and shunning affect, this section constituting nearly three-fourths of the book and dwarfing the much smaller section that affirmed the two-nation theory, sought to demonstrate how creating Pakistan would be in the best interests of the Hindus as well as that of other minorities inhabiting Hindustan. In a nutshell, Ambedkar argued that carving out Pakistan would be a good riddance for India for otherwise a united India would be reduced into a 'sick man of Asia'. The book was, therefore, a wake-up call for the Congress and 'sentimental' Hindus. It criticized their unscientific approach to Pakistan and urged them to examine the issue carefully and see for themselves how an undivided India would be a worse alternative than Pakistan itself, especially in the face of the ML's extreme and ever increasing catalogue of demands. Ambedkar, thus, adopted the position of a hard-headed clear eyed realist hoping to persuade similar realists on the Hindu side with rational arguments. In his realist avatar, Ambedkar ironically mirrored the *Qaid* himself, who too was never tired of excoriating the Hindus for their refusal to accept the reality of Pakistan.

Evaluating the Lahore Resolution and Demand for Pakistan

Ambedkar asked Hindus to acknowledge the fact that Pakistan was not merely a flash in the pan, which would disappear over time, but 'a characteristic in the biological sense of the term which the Muslim body politic has developed in the same manner as an organism develops a characteristic'.[19] He chided them for blaming the British for the birth of this demand and urged them to understand how unrealistic it was to expect the British to forcibly crush the movement behind it. After all, the Muslims could not be denied the right to

---

19 Ambedkar, *Thoughts on Pakistan*, 3.

self-determination when the Hindus themselves were vociferously making the same demand. Ambedkar, therefore, warned that any attempt to bury the Pakistan scheme would not bury 'the ghost of Pakistan'. It would at best suppress the symptoms rather than cure the disease itself, which would only come back in a much more virulent form later. More importantly, he insisted that the Pakistan issue needed to be resolved here and now before any fresh initiatives were undertaken to devise a new Constitution for India. If Pakistan was conceded by the British after a Constitution had been framed, Ambedkar feared that it would only lead to a collapse of the entire painstakingly built structure of British India with catastrophic consequences for everyone. In order to underline his point, he offered prominent examples of such serious disruption due to attempted secession – by the southern states from the United States of America, by Natal from the Union of South Africa and by Western Australia from Australia. This was a situation that he wanted India to avoid. Ambedkar used this opportunity to further caution the Hindus against fanciful dreams of militarily winning back the seceding Muslim provinces, just as the southern states in the US had been brought back into the fold by the northern states after a bloody Civil War. Even the British, he asserted, would be powerless to save the day in the face of such disruption in India.

Having delivered this clear warning, Ambedkar began his examination of the Pakistan demand by carefully analysing the text of the Lahore Resolution. Not surprisingly, he raised pertinent questions that have subsequently been raised by later commentators. What exactly did the Pakistan demand mean? Did it entail creation of one or two sovereign Muslim states? Would Pakistan be a federal state with its eastern and western wings joined together under a single constitution? After all, the term 'constituent units' in the text indicated that a federation was contemplated, but the use of the term 'sovereign' with regard to these units made it incongruous with a federation. Would Pakistan, therefore, be formed as a confederation of two states? Notwithstanding these problems in the text of the Lahore Resolution, Ambedkar maintained that such questions 'were not very material for the moment'. What was more important, was to consider the basic demand, 'namely that these areas are to be separated from India and formed into Independent states'.[20] Boiling down its contents, he clarified that the Pakistan scheme

> in concrete terms means that Punjab, North Western Frontier, Baluchistan and Sind in the North-West and Bengal in the East, will, instead of

20 Ibid., 17.

> remaining as the Provinces of British India, shall be incorporated as independent states outside of British India. This is the sum and substance of the Resolution of the Muslim League.[21]

The whole demand was based on opposition to one central government for the whole of India. Now there would be two central governments, one for Hindustan and another for Pakistan. Thus, Ambedkar made it clear that the ML had not exactly left the question of the centre vague or nebulous, for what was being demanded was a separate sovereign centre for Pakistan. Reflecting further on the Lahore Resolution, Ambedkar argued that the scheme was not a new one since it expressed 'in its essence and general outline' the scheme put forth by Sir Muhammad Iqbal and propagated by Rehmat Ali over the past decade.[22] The ML had however expanded upon the original Pakistan scheme by envisaging another Muslim state in the East for the Muslims of Bengal and Assam. Here, he echoed a widespread perception often supported by Jinnah himself, that it was really Iqbal who had given Muslims the idea of Pakistan.[23]

Ambedkar then turned to examine the case being made out in favour of Pakistan, given the seriousness with which the ML had raised this demand. Here, he conspicuously did not go into any detailed examination of Pakistan's economic, political, or military viability. Instead, he narrowly focused on the question of whether or not Pakistan was indeed a nation. Ambedkar insisted that this was the core question that needed to be addressed and that everything else was 'beside the point'.[24] So what constituted the nation? Ambedkar's views on this subject were avowedly influenced by Renan and he, therefore, summarily dismissed race, language and a common country as the basis of nationality. Race could not be confounded with the nation for there was no pure race in the world due to intermixing that had gone on between human beings over the ages. Language too could not be the basis for nationality. As he noted, USA and Britain shared a common language and yet did not form a nation. Besides, Switzerland was a nation even though its inhabitants spoke three or four languages. As regards the arguments for 'common country' as the basis of a nation, Ambedkar again quoted Renan to argue that land could at

21 Ibid., 16–17.

22 Ibid., 17.

23 See for example *Star of India*, 7 March 1941, Jinnah's speech at Islamia Girls College, Delhi.

24 Ambedkar, *Thoughts on Pakistan*, 25.

best provide 'a substratum, the field of battle and work'. Ultimately, it was man 'who provides the soul; man is everything in the formation of that sacred thing which is called a people.'[25] Ambedkar was therefore emphatic that

> Nationality is a subjective psychological feeling. It is a feeling of a corporate sentiment of oneness which makes those who are charged with it feel that they are kith and kin. This national feeling is a double edged feeling. It is at once a feeling of fellowship for one's own kith and an anti-fellowship feeling for those who are not one's own kith. It is a feeling of 'consciousness of kind' which on the one hand binds together those who have it so strongly that it overrides all differences arising out of economic conflicts or social gradations and on the other severs them from those who are not of their kind. It is a longing to belong to one's own group and a longing not to belong to any other group. This is the essence of what is called a nationality and national feeling.'[26]

Ambedkar, therefore, asked the Hindus to come to terms with the fact that Muslims of India had developed the will to live as a nation, which meshed with the happy circumstance of nature having found them a territory that they could occupy 'and make it a state as well as a cultural home for the newborn Muslim nation'.[27] Given this situation, it was not surprising that Indian Muslims were not content to occupy the same position as the French in Canada or the English in South Africa and demanded a separate national existence. With this astonishingly brief consideration of the arguments in favour of Pakistan that had been put out by the ML and its supporters, Ambedkar concluded the case by affirming their validity and expressing his concurrence with them.

Demolishing Sentimental Hindu Objections to Pakistan

This all too narrow and limited evaluation of the Muslim case for Pakistan was followed by an exhaustive evaluation of what he saw as the many sentimental objections to its creation that were expressed by the Hindus and the Congress. Ambedkar admonished Hindu India for feigning surprise and shock at the Lahore Resolution. He began by pointing out that there was nothing new about efforts to link up the northwestern provinces into a separate administrative unit. He reminded Hindus that Punjab and NWFP had started off as a single province after the former's conquest by the British in 1849 and had been divided

25 Ibid., 28–29.

26 Ibid., 25.

27 Ibid., 33.

into separate provinces only in 1901 by Lord Curzon. He added that Sind too would have been conjoined to this unit had its conquest preceded that of the Punjab, but due to a reversal of this sequence Sind was joined to Bombay, the only base from which it could possibly have been governed at the time. To emphasize his point, Ambedkar ran the Hindus through a brief history of the several attempts made by successive British Viceroys, Governors, or Generals over the previous half a century to amalgamate the two provinces. The earliest one by Lord Dalhousie had been turned down by Court of Directors for financial reasons. It was taken up by Lord Canning after the Mutiny but was again shelved after taking into account the 'backward state of communications along the Indus'. In 1876, Lord Northbrook had again taken up the matter followed by his successor Lord Lytton, who proposed the creation of a Trans-Indus province, comprising the districts of Punjab, NWFP and Sind. Under this plan Bombay was to have been compensated for the loss of Sind with part or the whole of C.P. Ambedkar insisted that this idea would have succeeded under Lord Lansdowne but for the British conquest of Baluchistan, which ended Sind's status as the frontier, thus removing the rationale behind its amalgamation into the Punjab. Thus, if the British had not acquired Baluchistan and Lord Curzon had not thought of carving NWFP out of the Punjab, Pakistan would have been created as an integrated administrative unit a long time ago. As regards the creation of a Muslim national state in East, Ambedkar again reminded Hindu India that there was nothing new about it since Lord Curzon had once divided Bengal into Eastern Bengal and Assam with Dhaka as its capital and western Bengal with Calcutta as its capital. If Bengal's Partition in 1911 had not been abrogated due to Hindu nationalist agitation, he was certain that East Bengal would have been a functioning Muslim state for nearly thirty five years.

Ambedkar acknowledged that while the British may have wittingly or unwittingly laid the foundations of Pakistan by their alterations of the subcontinent's map – partitioning old provinces or creating new ones – he argued that they had always made them on the basis of sound logic and after publicly providing reasoned arguments to justify their actions. The Pakistan demand on the contrary, he pointed out, seemed to have popular passion as its only sanction. While he clearly implied that the ML was responsible for this lamentable state of affairs, for the moment he let it go. Instead, he used the opportunity to turn on his old *bête noire* Gandhi, pointing out that it was the Mahatma who had introduced the concept of linguistic provinces in India and accordingly reorganized provincial Congress committees along those lines. This move, he contended, was not based upon any careful consideration of the area, population and revenues of these provinces, or concomitant analyses of their viability. It was based on a dangerous populism for it was solely motivated by the Congress party's desire to win over popular support on the basis of local patriotisms. In such a context, the Pakistan demand could certainly not be deemed anomalous or outrageous. Nonetheless, Ambedkar acknowledged merit in the Hindu argument that the separation of Bihar from Orissa, Andhra from Madras or Karnataka from Maharashtra could not be compared to what was being proposed in the case of Pakistan. The latter separation was of a qualitatively different order for it involved 'partition', 'annulment of tie' and 'legal divorce' between Pakistan and Hindustan.[28]

Ambedkar went on to clinically demolish Hindu sentimental objections against Pakistan that were putatively based on geography and history. Evaluating the Hindu claim that 'the areas which the Muslims wanted to be separated from India' had always been a part of the motherland, he initially expressed sympathy for this position. He acknowledged that the Pakistan areas had been a part of India from the time of Chandragupta Maurya in the fourth century BC through the time of the Chinese Buddhist pilgrim Hieun Tsang in the seventh century AD. He also conceded that not just the Punjab but even Afghanistan could be considered a part of India during these ancient times given the pervasiveness of Hindu and Buddhist religion and culture. Yet, at the same time, he sharply reminded the Hindus that these arguments were based on conditions, which may once have existed but were certainly not in force anymore. Ambedkar argued that Muslim invasions, which began first in Sind in the ninth century and ended with those of Ahmad Shah Abdali in the eighteenth century, had wrought violent changes in the religion, society and culture of the Pakistan areas. Besides creating Hindus and Muslims as two distinct nations, perpetually at conflict with one another, these invasions had also broken up the historical unity of northern India. Not only was there no unity any more between Hindus and Muslims, there was none between Pakistan areas and the rest of India – there being 'as a matter of fact, real antipathy between the two'.[29]

28 Ibid., 23. The Mahatma concurred with this view. As he noted, 'there can be no comparison between Pakistan and Andhra separation. The Andhra separation is a redistribution on a linguistic basis. The Andhras do not claim to be a separate nation claiming nothing in common with the rest of India. Pakistan on the other hand is a demand for carving out of India a portion to be treated as a *wholly independent state.* Thus, there seems to be nothing in common between the two.' *Harijan* 12 July 1942, CWMG, Vol. 83, 78.

29 Ibid., 58.

Ambedkar quoted at length colonial historians such as Stanley Lane Poole as also their translations of medieval Muslim chroniclers such as Minhaj-us-Siraj and others, to enumerate the violent methods adopted by Muslims in the process of their conquest of India. Muslim loot of Hindu temples, slaughter of able bodied Hindu men and sale of their women and children into slavery, he argued, had created such bitterness between the communities that 'a century of political life [under the British] had not succeeded in assuaging it or making people forget about it'.[30] Hindus and Muslims therefore shared no historical antecedents as 'matters of common joy or sorrow'. Rather than constituting a unitary nation in India sharing common history and culture, historically Hindus and Muslims were 'two armed battalions warring against one another'.[31]

Ambedkar next demolished the argument that India was one nation based on the sociological claim that Hindus and Muslims in India's different regions belonged to the same racial stock. He concurred with Gandhi that a Punjabi Hindu and a Punjabi Muslim were of the same racial stock and furthermore that there was greater racial affinity between a Madrasi Brahmin and a Madrasi Muslim than between a Madrasi Brahmin and a Punjabi Brahmin. He also agreed that Hindus and Muslims in any province shared a common language and that Muslim social life in different parts of India was 'honeycombed with Hindu customs'.[32] Hindu surnames were common among Muslims; some still followed Hindu marriage ceremonies before calling the *Qazi* to solemnize it, while some others kept genealogies in Brahmanic fashion. Caste system too, he conceded, was an integral part of Muslim society, while in the religious sphere Muslim *pirs* often had Hindu *chelas* (disciples) and Hindu *yogis* likewise were known to have Muslim disciples. But in spite of these common social and cultural practices, Ambedkar argued that it would be delusional to view Hindus and Muslims as a single nation. Indeed, he dismissed such commonalities as a result of 'purely mechanical causes', attributing these oddities variously to the subjection of Hindus and Muslims to a common environment over centuries, incomplete conversion of the Hindus to Islam, either due to 'inadequate methods of persuasion', 'insufficient priestly stuff' of the Muslims, fears of a larger Hindu revolt, or the ultimately abortive efforts of Emperor Akbar at creating a common religion for India. For Ambedkar, in the ultimate analysis, the few superficial commonalities between Hindus and Muslims were ultimately the 'result of a dead past that had no present and no future'.[33]

30 Ibid., 59.

31 Ibid., 30.

32 Ibid., 26.

33 Ibid., 27.

Rounding off his critique of sentimental Hindu objections, Ambedkar dismissed Hindu attempts at denying Muslim claims to nationhood on the grounds that it was an afterthought in the minds of their leaders and that Muslims in general had all along been content to be seen as one of India's many communities. Hindu attempts to have Muslims 'debarred from calling themselves a nation', he argued, '[was] to misunderstand the mysterious working of the psychology of national feeling'.[34] After all it was certainly possible for nations to exist in 'unreflective silence for centuries' before they burst forth in the form of nationalism and demanded a separate existence. Pakistan was a very obvious case of this kind and Hindus could not, therefore, legitimately deny that claim. At best Hindus could beg Muslims not to demand a separate state and to continue to coexist with them in an undivided India even though they were a separate nationality.

Even as he knocked off these sentimental Hindu objections, Ambedkar discerned rational reasons behind their denial of Muslims claims of being a separate nation. As he noted, any patriot who asked for self-government for his people had to prove that they were a nation and not just an agglomeration of disunited peoples. The Pakistan demand, by repudiating the claim that India was a single nation, struck at the heart of Hindu India's claims to sovereignty and state power. He reminded his readers that Hindus, for long, had stubbornly dismissed Anglo-Indian barbs that India was not a nation, refusing to yield on this question to even a figure as revered as Tagore, who too disputed such Hindu claims. Hindu propagandists, therefore, churned out popular literature for generations to whip up patriotic nationalism portraying anyone who questioned this claim as 'a tool of the British bureaucracy and an enemy of the country'.[35] Just when Anglo-Indians had ceased to reply to Hindu propaganda and it had almost succeeded, Muslim League's declaration had come as a body blow to the Hindus. Hindu politicians could no longer make credible claims for self-government for India in this situation and it is for this reason they were angrily trying to neutralize the ML's claims in all possible ways.

Pakistan and the Defence of Hindustan

Ambedkar next proceeded to address the most serious and substantive Hindu concerns vis a vis Pakistan. To begin with, he tackled Hindu apprehensions that Pakistan's creation of would endanger India's defences since it would

[34] Ibid., 32.

[35] Ibid., 24.

deprive Hindustan of a 'scientific frontier'. Countering this argument, he contended that India never had any one 'scientific boundary' since various British administrators had suggested different boundaries at different points in time. These different views were particularly based on whether they subscribed to a 'Forward Policy' or 'Back to the Indus' policy, in the context of the Great Game against the Russians. The former camp believing in an aggressive policy wanted active British control over Afghanistan extending all the way up to the Oxus. On the other hand, those belonging to the latter camp favoured a more defensive approach and were content to extend Indian control only up to the Durand Line. But more importantly, Ambedkar pooh-poohed the very idea of a 'scientific frontier' comprising easily definable geographical features, which could serve as a political boundary for any nation-state. Such a safe geographical boundary was futile since modern techniques of warfare had rendered them worthless. Rather, nations lacking natural frontiers could always create 'artificial fortifications which [were] far more impregnable than natural barriers.'[36]

Since the creation of such impregnable fortifications required resources, this brought to fore another set of Hindu fears about scarcity of resources that could endanger India's defence. To alleviate these fears, Ambedkar assured them that Hindustan was endowed with adequate resources to defend its frontiers. Laying out figures compiled from the government's revenue statistics, he pointed out that the Hindustan provinces contributed greater revenues to the central exchequer than the Pakistan provinces. As regards the revenues of even the Pakistan provinces, Ambedkar made a significant statement. Hindustan's resources would be further augmented as it would gain access to half of the revenues of Punjab and Bengal since they would have to be partitioned on the basis of Hindu and Muslim majority areas. Seven years before the Partition, Ambedkar prophetically suggested that Pakistan's creation would bring the boundary of Hindustan to the Sutlej, making clear that the Partition of Punjab would be a natural corollary of Pakistan separating from Hindustan.

Ambedkar also wanted the Hindus to take heart from the fact that in addition to gaining at least half the revenues of these partitioned provinces, most of the deductions 'would fall to the lot of Pakistan'. These calculations of savings and deductions were based on his exclusion of thirteen districts of eastern Punjab and fifteen districts of western Bengal from Pakistan, taking into account the distribution of Muslim and non-Muslim populations in these provinces. As he concluded this point, 'to put it in concrete terms, while the revenues of Pakistan

---

36 Ibid., 62.

and the eastern Muslim state will be 60 crores minus 24 crores, i.e, 36 crores, the revenues of Hindustan will be 96 crores plus 24 crores, i.e, 120 crores.'[37] Hindustan would therefore be at least three times richer than Pakistan with far greater resources and hence would not be weakened in any way.

Ambedkar finally dwelt upon what he saw as the most important question Hindus needed to consider regarding India's defence – that of the armed forces. Analysing figures from the Simon Commission Report regarding recruitment of soldiers into the British Indian army from various provinces and regions of India, he brought two critical aspects to the attention of Hindus. First, that the Indian army was predominantly Muslim in its composition. Second, these Muslims again were predominantly drawn from Punjab and NWFP making them almost exclusively responsible for defending India in the event of a foreign invasion from the northwest. Ambedkar noted that 'so patent has this fact become that the *Musalmans of the Punjab and NWF are quite conscious of this proud position* which has been assigned to them by the British for reasons best known to them.'[38]Ambedkar, therefore, asked Hindus to think about some important questions when considering the issue of Pakistan. How would Muslims in the Indian army react to invasion by a Muslim neighbour like Afghanistan?[39] Would this army fight in case India decided to invade Afghanistan for the sake of its own national interests? Ambedkar's own belief that he candidly expressed, was that Muslims would rather join their Afghan Muslim brethren than defend India and would almost certainly disobey orders if India were to ever decide on invading Afghanistan. He also pooh-poohed sentimental optimism among Indian nationalists on this question and instead made his appeal to the bold realists among them. As he noted

> The realist must take note of the fact that the Musalmans look upon the Hindus as Kaffirs, who deserve more to be exterminated than protected. The realist must take note of the fact that while the Musalman accepts the European as his superior he looks upon the Hindu as his inferior. It is doubtful how far a regiment of Musalmans will accept the authority of their Hindu officers if they were placed under them. The realist must take note that of all the Musalmans the Musalman of the North-West is the most disaffected Musalman, in his relation with the Hindus. The realist must take note that the Punjabi Musalman is fully susceptible

37 Ibid., 64–65.

38 Ibid., 89.

39 Ibid., 92.

> to the propaganda in favour of Pan-Islamism. Taking note of all these considerations, there can be very little doubt that he would be a bold Hindu, who would say that in any invasion by Muslim countries, the Muslims in the Indian army would be loyal and that there is no danger of their going over to the invader.[40]

To substantiate this point on the Pan-Islamism of Indian Muslims, Ambedkar reminded Hindus of the stand historically taken by the main Muslim political organizations in India such as the ML or the erstwhile Khilafat Committee, which explicitly demanded that the government not deploy the Indian army against Muslim countries under any circumstances. While the ML may not have prevailed upon the British to accede to this demand, Ambedkar was certain that it would succeed in dictating its terms against any future Indian government once the British had withdrawn. He, therefore, warned the Hindus that they risked getting caught between the devil and the deep sea over the question of India's defences. While an undivided sovereign India would have its own army, it could never be sure of its loyalty nor be free to use it in the face of Muslim objections, especially when faced by a hostile Muslim power. As he put the whole issue in a nutshell

> If the army continues to be dominated by the Muslims of the Punjab and N. W. F., the Hindus will have to pay them but will not be able to use them and even if they were free to use them against a Muslim invader they will find it hazardous to depend upon them. If the League view prevails and India does not remain free to use her army against Muslim countries, then, even if the Muslims lose their predominance in the army, India on account of these military limitations, will have to remain on terms of sub-ordinate co-operation with Muslim countries on her border, as do the Indian States under British paramountcy.'[41]

For Ambedkar, 'the situation was pathetic as it was precarious.'[42] To drive home this argument, he also pre-empted the contention that in independent India, the Muslim proportion in the army would come down as a result of recruitment of other communities thus creating a more balanced force that would make Hindus less dependent on Muslims for India's defence. He contended that Muslims would insist on protecting their existing

---

40 Ibid.

41 Ibid., 93.

42 Ibid., 93.

representation in the army and indeed would demand constitutional safeguards to preserve their preponderance in case they ended up not insisting on Pakistan. As he witheringly noted 'the Musalmans are sure to make this demand and as against the Hindus, they always succeed. We must therefore proceed on the assumption that the composition of the Indian army will remain what it is at present.'[43]

Ambedkar therefore wanted Hindus to carefully decide whether it was in their interest to disallow Pakistan's creation so that they could have a 'safe border' of their imagination, or to welcome its separation from India so as to have a 'safe army'. Furthermore, the Hindus needed to consider whether it was better to have these Musalmans 'without and against or if they should be within and against'.[44] For Ambedkar, the answer was clear as daylight. The best option was to concede Pakistan. As he noted, 'indeed it is a consummation devoutly to be wished that the Muslims should be without. That is the only way of getting rid of the Muslim preponderance in the Indian Army.' Once Pakistan was created, Hindustan would be free to build its own army 'with nobody dictating the question of how and against whom it should be used or not used'. He therefore concluded that 'the defence of Hindustan far from being weakened by the creation of Pakistan will be infinitely improved by it.'[45]

Ambedkar pressed his point further by referring to financial losses that Hindus were already incurring in maintaining this Muslim dominated army, besides the heavier price they would have to pay for retaining Pakistan areas in the future. As he noted, while Hindu provinces were the major revenue contributors to the central exchequer (seven times more than Pakistan provinces) that enabled the army's maintenance, yet Hindus were confined to a minority in this very army. On the other hand, while Pakistan areas contributed very little to the central exchequer, they were the main recruiting ground for the army besides also being the areas where the central government spent half of its revenues. Giving actual figures, he noted that the centre spent 52 crores out of its total revenue of 121 crores in the Pakistan areas for defence purposes. From a financial point of view, it therefore made no sense for Hindus to continue with the current arrangement. While Hindus at present had no say in the current state of affairs, Ambedkar however hoped that once they had the choice they would

[43] Ibid., 91.

[44] Ibid

[45] Ibid.

rid themselves of Pakistan to put an end to this problem.[46] As he reiterated his point, 'a safe army was better than a safe border'.[47]

Critique of Martial Races Theory and British Policy

To further ease Hindu concerns, Ambedkar sought to fortify Hindu mental defences against fears of being overrun by Muslim 'martial races' from the northwest. That this was a deeply entrenched idea in both Hindu elite and popular consciousness is evident from the persistence of this bugbear since at least the time of the Khilafat Movement. A figure no less than Gandhi had declared that if the British left India, it could very soon be overrun by Gurkhas and Punjabis, a statement Jinnah claimed specifically referred to Punjabi Muslims in the army. This bugbear had moreover been undergirded by the British theory of 'martial races' inhabiting these areas and their consequent policy of recruiting soldiers predominantly from this part of the country. Ambedkar attacked the 'martial races' theory in no uncertain terms. He pointed out that pre-Mutiny armies of the Company had very little representation from the northwest and that Company's armies till the 1857 Mutiny had been dominated by Hindustani soldiers. Directing his readers' attention to the history of British conquest over India, he explained that the Punjabis came into the picture only when Hindustanis mutinied in 1857. The Punjabis had joined the British at this juncture as they were attracted by prospects of revenge, retribution and plunder, having themselves been subjugated by Hindustani soldiers during the Anglo-Sikh wars. Since the Punjabis had helped crush the Mutiny and saved the Raj in India, it was not surprising that the British responded by recruiting soldiers preponderantly from these regions into the army. Besides invoking the historical record, Ambedkar vigorously denounced the flawed martial races theory on sociological grounds arguing that 'this division between martial and non-martial races is of course a purely arbitrary and artificial distinction.' As he derisively noted, 'it is as foolish as the Hindu theory of caste, making birth instead of worth the basis of recognition… No race can be permanently without martial spirit. Martial spirit is not a matter of native instinct. It is a matter of training and anybody can be trained to it.'[48]

---

46 Ibid., 95.

47 Ibid.

48 Ibid., 71. It is fascinating to note that this martial races theory was also believed on the Muslim side and had an afterlife as evident from this episode narrated by the historian David Page who spent a year teaching at Edwardes College in Peshawar just after the 1965 India-Pakistan war. 'It was commonly boasted by my students – and Pakistanis in general – that one Pakistani soldier was worth nine Indians; that Muslims were better

Ambedkar also took this opportunity to castigate the British for throwing overboard a cardinal principle adopted after the Mutiny – of not allowing any single Indian community or group to become dominant in the army in order to ensure the Raj's safety. Speculating on this gradual shift in policy especially after World War I, he could think of only two reasons why it had been violated to give Muslim soldiers preponderance in the Indian army. He summarily dismissed the first possible reason – that Muslim soldiers perhaps fought better than other Indian soldiers in the light of the obvious implausibility of this proposition. Ambedkar then zeroed in on the second more plausible reason. He suggested that Muslims had been given a dominating position in the army so as to 'counteract the forces of Hindu agitation' ranged against the British.[49] This was an astonishing statement from a bitter critic of the Congress, affirming the Congress refrain that the government had historically perpetuated its rule by pursuing an active divide and rule policy in India.

The Communal Problem in India and its Resolution

Ambedkar next confronted the question of whether creating Pakistan would solve the communal problem in India, a topic of fierce public discussion. Here again, he sought to convince Hindus about the major gains they would realize and as always, he meticulously laid out different aspects of the problem. The communal question in India in its 'lesser extent', he explained, related to 'the number of seats to be allotted to the Hindus and Muslims in different legislatures' and 'the nature of electorates through which these seats are to be filled in.'[50] In its greater extent it involved deliberate creation of new Muslim provinces. Together, they constituted the overall communal problem. Turning to the communal problem in its lesser extent, Ambedkar noted that since the 1917 Lucknow Pact, Muslims had demanded three things – separate electorates for electing representatives to both provincial and central legislatures, weightage to Muslim minorities in Hindu majority provinces and statutory majority for Muslims in their majority provinces. All these demands had been fully conceded in the Communal Award of 1932. For Ambedkar, these features of the Award were patently discriminatory and unjust towards Hindus, especially Hindu

---

fighters than Hindus – the kind of bravado that the experience of Bangladesh was later to silence.' See 'Introduction to the paperback edition', vi, in David Page, *Prelude to Partition: The Indian Muslims and the Imperial system of Control 1920-1932* (New Delhi, 1988).

49 Ibid., 89.

50 Ibid

minorities in Muslim majority provinces. Hindu minorities from the very beginning had demanded joint electorates for Hindus and Muslims in elections to both central and provincial legislatures, representation for minorities based on population ratios wherever they might be and had raised strong objections to any community being statutorily guaranteed a majority of seats in legislatures. The Award had nevertheless ridden roughshod over rights of Hindu minorities and denied them a choice in the matter of electorates, which by contrast had been bestowed upon Muslim minorities. It had also institutionalized statutory Muslim majorities, which Ambedkar likened to divine right to rule.[51] The Award was thus 'a perversion of democratic principles' demonstrating 'callous disregard for the safety and security of Hindu minorities' for it allowed Muslim communal majorities to rule over them without requiring the former 'to submit itself to the suffrages of the minority, especially when the minority demands it'.[52]

As regards the 'greater extent' of the communal problem involving deliberate creation of Muslim provinces, Ambedkar argued that the logic behind this move was not just an 'architectural symmetry of Hindu provinces poised against Muslim provinces', but the more sinister 'hostage population' theory. It provided 'Muslim provinces an effective means to tyrannize their Hindu minorities in case the Muslim minorities in the Hindu provinces were being tyrannized by their Hindu majorities.' Ambedkar did not hesitate to denounce this line of thinking as a 'dreadful one, involving the maintenance of justice and peace by retaliation' and derisively dubbed it 'a scheme of communal peace through a system of communal hostages'.[53] But Ambedkar blamed not just the British for this situation but also the Muslims for they were only too aware of the logic of 'hostage populations' and indeed welcomed it. As evidence, he cited a speech made by none other than Maulana Abul Kalam Azad who extolled this theory during the 1927 Calcutta ML session.[54]Ambedkar ominously noted that similar

---

51 Ibid., 102.

52 Ibid., 101–02.

53 Ibid., 104.

54 Ibid., 105. In his speech Azad declared that 'the Delhi proposals gave them for the first time five provinces of which no less than three (Sind, the Frontier Province and Baluchistan) contained a real overwhelming Muslim majority. If the Muslims did not recognize this great step they were not fit to live. There would now be nine Hindu provinces against five Muslim provinces and whatever treatment Hindus accorded in the nine provinces, Muslims would accord the same treatment to Hindus in the five provinces. Was not this a great gain? Was not a new weapon gained for the assertion of Muslim rights?'

threats had recently been reiterated by the Bengal Premier Fazlul Haq in his recent speeches against Hindu minorities in his province.

But why had the communal problem degenerated to such an extent that it now rested on the basis of such a mad theory? Ambedkar contended that the problem did not exist either because Muslims were 'extravagant or insolent in their demands' or because Hindus were 'mean and grudging' in conceding them.[55] He saw the problem as inevitable whenever a minority was pitted against a majority. The best solution, he insisted, therefore lay in avoiding such a situation in India. But the question remained whether the Pakistan scheme with its idea of partitioning India was the ideal solution to the communal problem in the subcontinent. Here, Ambedkar made a crucial argument. He contended that if the Pakistan scheme were to be based on the existing boundaries of Punjab and Bengal, it would still pit a minority against a majority and the communal problem would, therefore, continue to fester. More alarmingly, the problem would further assume 'a new malignity'. As of now the power of communal majorities in the provinces to do mischief on their 'hostage minorities' was restrained by the power of the Centre. But if Pakistan became 'a Muslim state with full sovereignty, it would be free from the control of the Central government to which Hindu minorities could appeal.' In such a situation, the position of Hindus in Pakistan would be reduced to that of the Armenians under the Turks, or of the Jews in Tsarist Russia or Nazi Germany; a forbidding prospect to say the least. He, therefore, did not blame Hindus for finding such a Pakistan scheme intolerable or refusing to leave their co-religionists in the Pakistan areas 'as a helpless prey to the fanaticism of a Muslim National state.'[56] Strikingly, Ambedkar did not claim that the Muslim minority in India would face a similar predicament.

Partitioning Punjab and Bengal and Population Transfers

Ambedkar argued that this problem could however be overcome to a great extent if existing provincial boundaries of Punjab and Bengal were altered so as to create Hindustan and Pakistan as 'ethnically homogenous' states and to avoid the problem of mixed states with antagonistic majorities and minorities. He therefore asserted that existing provincial boundaries of Punjab and Bengal could and should be altered in order to practically implement the Pakistan scheme. To make his case, he invited his readers to take a look at the figures he

---

55 Ibid., 106.

56 Ibid., 106.

provided in Appendices I–III that highlighted population distribution in the Pakistan areas and also carried maps that showed how the new boundaries he proposed would create homogenous Muslim states. Ambedkar pointed out that in the Punjab, Hindu dominated districts were located in eastern parts of the province, adjacent to Hindustan. These districts were separated from and not interspersed with Muslim majority districts in the western part of the province. Similarly, he noted that Muslim majority districts of Bengal and Assam in the eastern part formed contiguous areas, separate from Hindu majority districts in the western part. As he confidently prophesized, it was 'perfectly possible to create homogenous Muslim states out of the Punjab, Bengal and Assam, by drawing their boundaries in such a way that the areas which are predominantly Hindu shall be excluded'.[57] The question of Pakistan therefore involved 'a mere question of changing the boundaries'.[58] As regards NWFP and Sind, Ambedkar explained that the Hindus were scattered in both these provinces with no majority in any contiguous piece of territory. The only possible way for creating homogenous Muslim provinces in both these cases was through a transfer of Hindu populations to Hindustan.[59] Significantly, in the case of Punjab and Bengal where homogenous states could be created merely by altering boundaries, Ambedkar envisaged the exchange of population to be of a 'very small degree'.[60] The two most contentious issues of the Partition, of redrawing the national boundaries of the two states following the Partition of Punjab and Bengal, along with the exchange of populations was thus already up for public discussion by early 1941. The map and the census, far from being fuzzy notions, were central to the understanding of the issue of Pakistan.

Ambedkar acknowledged that the idea of such population transfers had its critics, but he dismissed their views, claiming that they lacked any awareness of the many complications that the minority problem could create. Furthermore, he derided them for not taking into account the abysmal failures of European states in trying to create friendly relations between majorities and minorities even though they prepared long lists of fundamental rights for minorities or guaranteed them a number of constitutional safeguards. In spite of these measures, 'the same old policy of exterminating the minorities continued to hold the field' even in Europe. It had finally led to the realization that the

57 Ibid., 108.

58 Ibid., 107.

59 Ibid., 109.

60 Ibid.

only way to resolve the minority problem was 'for each to exchange its alien minorities within its border for its own which was without its border to bring about homogenous states.'[61] In this context, Ambedkar argued that if countries such as Turkey, Greece and Bulgaria possessing limited resources could manage the exchange of close to twenty million people, there was no reason why it could not be achieved in India. As he sunnily remarked, 'after all, the population involved is inconsiderable and it would be the height of folly to give up a sure way to communal peace because some obstacles in it require to be removed.'[62]Ambedkar's calculations regarding the numbers that were expected to move across borders were perhaps made in terms of their proportion to the overall population of India. Besides, he expected such population transfers to be conducted by the governments of Hindustan and Pakistan on a voluntary basis and in an orderly manner over an agreed period of time. What he did not perhaps expect was the complete breakdown of the law and order machinery that would occur and the large scale violence and ethnic cleansing that would totally alter the demography of whole regions.

But there still remained the question of Muslims who lived in different parts of Hindu India and would be left behind after the Partition. Ambedkar clarified that the Muslims had already made their position quite well known on this question.

> They say we are not weakened by the separation of Muslims into Pakistan and Hindustan. We are better protected by the existence of separate Islamic States on the Eastern and Western border of Hindustan than we are by their submersion in Hindustan. Who can say that they are wrong? Has it not been shown that Germany as an outside state was better able to protect the Sudeten Germans in Czechoslovakia than the Sudetens were able to do themselves?[63]

Ambedkar argued that Hindustan, therefore, did not need to bother itself with the Muslim minority question, which had to be solely left to Muslims themselves to consider. Instead, he wanted Hindus to carefully evaluate whether or not Pakistan's creation would resolve the communal question in Hindustan. Surveying the issue, Ambedkar agreed that no amount of redrawing of boundaries would make Hindustan an ethnically homogenous state since

---

[61] Ibid.

[62] Ibid., 110.

[63] Ibid., 111.

Muslims were distributed all over its domains. It would therefore continue to remain a composite state and Pakistan would thus not provide the complete solution to the communal problem. Yet, he strongly urged the Hindus to accept Pakistan since its creation would greatly reduce the magnitude of the communal problem in India. As he noted, the communal problem without Pakistan would involve 6.5 crore Muslims while after its creation it would involve only 2 crore Muslims in India. The communal problem would thus be reduced to a minor issue, rendering it much more tractable and easier to resolve in any situation. Ambedkar also held out other carrots to the Hindus. He indicated that Pakistan's creation would greatly reduce the proportion of Muslim to Hindu seats in central and provincial legislatures in Hindustan and this would fall even further once weightage was cancelled. Thus, while Pakistan would not entirely solve the communal problem for Hindustan, Ambedkar strikingly noted that Pakistan would at the very least 'free the Hindus from the turbulence of Muslims as predominant partners.'[64]

The question however remained whether Muslims of Punjab and Bengal would agree to the redrawing of their provincial boundaries to facilitate the creation of a sovereign Pakistan. Ambedkar contended that they ought not to have any objections on this count. If they did, it could be said that they did not quite 'understand the nature of their own demand.' While this was quite possible, given that the talk on Pakistan was often of a 'very loose character', Ambedkar was quick to claim that even Muslims did not contemplate creating Pakistan along the existing boundaries of the Punjab and Bengal. He noted that Sir Muhammad Iqbal had expressed his willingness to exclude the Ambala division besides a few other Hindu majority districts from Pakistan, so as to make it more ethnically homogenous. Nonetheless, if the Muslims insisted on retaining the existing borders and boundaries of these two provinces, Ambedkar pleaded with the Hindus to flatly refuse such unreasonable demands. This was imperative because the ML objective in this context could only be construed as a sinister plan to perfect the 'scheme of Hindu hostages in Muslim hands' that went beyond merely creating a Muslim national home or a national state.[65] He, therefore, urged Hindus to resist such ML moves at all costs.

Reacting to one view which held that Pakistan was Jinnah's bargaining counter to improve upon the gains that Muslims had already realized through the Communal Award, Ambedkar dismissed it as 'wishful thinking'. He

---

64 Ibid., 114 .

65 Ibid., 117 .

reminded adherents of this view that all such suggestions had been vehemently repudiated, insisting that Muslims would settle for nothing less than Pakistan.[66] Furthermore, given Hindu sentimentality on this question, Ambedkar cautioned the Congress against getting carried away by a spirit of bargaining and settling for an alternative that would be worse than Pakistan. Speculating on the heavy price the Congress would have to pay for persuading ML to give up Pakistan, Ambedkar conjectured that it would need to give 50 per cent share to Muslims in the executive, legislative and judiciary at the centre as well as the provinces. He further speculated that Muslims would also try and retain their dominance in the army, secure constitutional guarantees about maintaining existing provincial boundaries and hold inordinate veto powers over all matters pertaining to both domestic and foreign policy.[67] In no uncertain terms, Ambedkar declared that giving in to such immoderate Muslim demands or appeasing Muslims too much would lead to an alternative that would be worse than Pakistan. As he concluded his point

> What may be conceded with safety to a community may not be conceded to a nation and what may be conceded with safety to the weak to be used as a weapon of defence may not be conceded to the strong who may use it as a weapon of attack. These are important considerations and if the Hindus overlook them they will do so at their peril.[68]

Partition as the Best Answer to Muslim Communal Aggression

To press his point further, Ambedkar was quick to remind Hindus of Muslim 'communal aggression'. He particularly emphasized three features of this aggressive Muslim mentality. First, was the ever growing catalogue of Muslim political demands for there was no knowing 'where the Muslims are going to stop in their demands.' Here, he reminded Hindus of recently added 'extravagant and impossible, if not irresponsible [Muslim] demand' for a 50 per cent share in everything.[69] For Ambedkar, Muslim intentions were clear. They wanted to reduce Hindus from a majority in India to a minority in real terms while at the same time 'cutting into the political rights of the [other] minorities'. He, therefore, had no hesitation in stating that 'the Muslims are now speaking the language of Hitler and claiming a place in the sun which Hitler has been

66 Ibid., 191.

67 Ibid., 192–3.

68 Ibid., 200.

69 Ibid., 261.

claiming for Germany. For their demand for 50 per cent is nothing but a counterpart of the German claims to *Deutschland Uber Alles* and *Lebensraum* for themselves irrespective of what happens to other minorities.'[70] These were strong words and certainly would not have endeared Ambedkar to the *Qaid*.

In the same vein, Ambedkar announced that the demand for making Urdu India's national language was 'equally extravagant'. Since Urdu was not spoken all over India and indeed was not even spoken by a majority of Indian Muslims, he objected to the language of 28 million Muslims being imposed on 322 million Indians. What he found even more alarming was that these endless Muslim demands were compounded not just by an increasing British inability to resist them, but by their willingness to grant Muslims even more than what they themselves had demanded. He alluded particularly to the example of the Communal Award. As he noted, when Muslims demanded that they be granted either one of the two options in the Muslim majority provinces – statutory majorities with joint electorates or minority of seats with separate electorates – the British took statutory majority from the first demand and separate electorates from the second and gave them both.

The second feature of Muslim aggression, Ambedkar elucidated, lay in their desire to exploit Hindu weaknesses. He noted that whenever Hindus objected to anything, Muslim policy was to concede the point only if they received some additional concessions in return from Hindus. Ambedkar saw a prominent instance of this 'spirit of exploitation' in Muslim insistence on cow slaughter and stoppage of music before mosques. He pointed out that Islamic law did not recommend cow sacrifice nor did Muslims who went on Haj to Mecca or Medina usually slaughter a cow. But in India they insisted on sacrificing the cow and would not be content with sacrificing any other animal. As regards music before mosques, Ambedkar again argued that it was not an issue in any Muslim country. In particular he gave the example of Afghanistan, hardly a secularized Muslim country, which still allowed music before mosques. However, within India, Muslims insisted on music being stopped before mosques just because Hindus claimed it as a right.

The third feature that Ambedkar elaborated upon in this regard was what he termed Muslim 'gangster methods' in politics. He saw them as consciously imitating Sudetan Germans in their tactics against the Czechs. As proof, he specifically referred to the AIML Karachi Session, where Mr Jinnah and Sir Abdullah Haroon had described Muslims of India as 'the Sudetans of the

70 Ibid., 262.

Muslim world'.[71] Ambedkar therefore warned Hindus and the Congress that their policy of appeasement and concession would only exacerbate Muslim aggressiveness for they would interpret it as a sign of Hindu defeatism. The Hindus could thus find themselves in same fearful situation that the Allies found themselves in as a result of their appeasement policy towards Hitler. The only remedy to put an end to the limitless Muslim political appetite was to arrive at a settlement. And, 'if Pakistan is a settlement, then as a remedy it is worth consideration'.[72] This comparison of the ML to Nazi fascists made amply clear the threat that Ambedkar saw it as posing to India as also his firmly held view that Pakistan would be a good riddance for India.

Ambedkar adduced other reasons as well to explain why the Congress needed to concede Pakistan. Quite simply, he saw it as the only way to rid Hindustan of retrograde and anti-modern politics represented by the ML.[73] He bluntly noted that given Islam's importance in the worldview of Muslim politicians, Muslim politics took 'no note of secular categories of life, namely, the differences between the rich and the poor, capital and labor, landlord and tenant, priest and laymen, reason and superstition.' Muslim politics, he claimed, was essentially clerical and recognized only one difference – between Muslims and Hindus. If indeed, secular categories of life did end up finding a place in Muslim politics, they were 'subordinated to the one and only governing principle of the Muslim political universe, religion.'[74] To therefore avoid its ill-effects, he saw Partition as the best remedy.

In this regard, Ambedkar emphasized that only a clear settlement that created Pakistan would secure India's freedom or else it would be endangered once British rule ended. To substantiate his point, he pointed to utterances of Muslims leaders wherein they did not 'accept the obligation to maintain India's freedom'.[75] He particularly referred to a speech given in Sylhet by an ML *alim* and leading spokesman from Kanpur, Maulana Azad Subhani, in January 1939 even before the War had begun. In this speech, Subhani compared the Hindus to

---

71 Ibid., 267.

72 Ibid., 268.

73 Ambedkar's biographer Dhananjay Keer writes that 'some penetrating and caustic paragraphs describing the regressive bent of Muslim mind were deleted, it is said, at the instance of Ambedkar's close admirers.' See Dhananjay Keer, *Dr Ambedkar, Life and Mission* (Bombay, 1971), 334.

74 *Thoughts on Pakistan*, 229.

75 Ibid., 270.

Quranic *Yuj* (Gog) and *Majuj* (Magog) who were intent on swallowing up not only Muslim India but even 'Egypt, Kabul, Mecca, Medina and other Muslim principalities.[76] Subhani, had no hesitation in declaring that it was Hindus who were the real enemies of Muslims and not the British who were weak and on their way out of India. He wanted Muslims to resist Hindus in every possible way in order to protect not just Muslim India but the whole Islamic world.

Ambedkar also drew Hindu attention to the sorry fate of countries that forcibly tried to maintain their geographical unity disregarding conflicting nationalist impulses in their domains. He pointed to the example of Turkey where Arab nationalism had reduced the once massive Ottoman Empire to a fraction of its former size. He also alluded to the case of Czechoslovakia, where Slovak nationalism burst forth once it witnessed Sudetan German demands for autonomy on Czechoslovakia. He therefore delivered a blunt warning to the Hindus.

> If experience of other countries teaches that this is the inevitable consequence of pent-up nationalism, why not profit by their experience and avoid the catastrophe by agreeing to divide India into Pakistan and Hindustan? Let the Hindus take the warning that if they refuse to divide India into two before they launch on their career as a free people they will be sailing in those shoal waters in which Turkey, Czechoslovakia and many others have foundered. *If they wish to avoid ship-wreck in mid-ocean they must lighten the draught by throwing overboard all superfluous cargo.*'[77]

Ambedkar prophesized that if Hindus failed to learn from this experience and Hindustan and Pakistan remained tied together, India would become the 'sick man of Asia'.[78] He therefore wanted Hindus and Congress to take ideological pronouncements of ML leaders seriously since he did not see them

---

[76] Ibid., 271. Maulana Azad Subhani's long political innings included roles such as a veteran Khilafatist, a leader of the Kanpur mosque agitation, a socialist and finally a staunch ML supporter. For his activities during the Khilafat Movement and Kanpur mosque agitation see Francis Robinson, *Separatism Among Indian Muslims: The Politics of United Provinces Muslims, 1860-1923* (Cambridge, 1975); Gail Minault, *The Khilafat Movement: Religious Symbolism and Political Mobilization in India* (New York, 1982); and Naeem Qureshi, *Pan Islam in British Indian Politics: A Study of the Khilafat Movement, 1918-1924* (Karachi, 2008); and for his influence on Bengal ML leaders such as Maulana Bhashani, see Peter Custers, 'Maulana Bhashani and the transition to secular politics in Bengal', *Indian Economic and Social History Review*, April/June 2010, 231–59.

[77] *Thoughts on Pakistan*, 214.

[78] Ibid., 217.

merely in terms of a 'dishonest drift in their opinion', but a 'genuine ideological transformation'. As he eloquently concluded

> It appears to be the dawn of a new vision pointing to a new destiny symbolized by a new name, Pakistan. The Muslims appear to have started a new worship of a new destiny for the first time. But this is really not so. The worship is new because the sun of their new destiny which was so far hidden in the clouds has only now made its appearance in full glow. The magnetism of this new destiny cannot but draw the Muslims towards it. Its magnetism is so great that even men like Mr Jinnah have been violently shaken and have not been able to resist its force. *This destiny spreads itself out in a concrete form over the map of India. No one who just looks at the map can miss it. It lies there as though it is deliberately planned by Providence as a separate National State for Muslims.* Not only is this new destiny capable of being easily worked out and put in concrete shape, it is also catching because it opens up the possibilities of realizing the Muslim idea of linking up all the Muslim kindred in one Islamic State and thus avert the danger of Muslims in different countries adopting the nationality of the country to which they belong and thereby bring about the disintegration of the Islamic brotherhood. With the separation of Pakistan from Hindustan there is nothing to prevent Pakistan from joining Afghanistan, Iran, Iraq, Arabia, Turkey and Egypt and forming a federation of Muslim countries constituting one Islamic State extending from Constantinople down to Lahore. A Mussalman must be really very stupid if he is not attracted by the glamour of this new destiny and be completely transformed in his view of the place of Muslims in the Indian cosmos.[79] (emphasis mine)

Thoughts on Pakistan 'rocked Indian politics for a decade.'[80] Its immediate impact is evident from responses to it by important sections of the ML as well as mention of this book in Pakistan conferences held in various towns and districts across north India. Malik Barkat Ali, Jinnah's chief lieutenant in Punjab, in his presidential address at the 1941 Lyallpur Pakistan conference commended Ambedkar's book to all 'votaries of the New Destiny'.[81] Pir Tajuddin, the Punjab ML leader, publicly welcomed the book in spite of his misgivings about Ambedkar. As the Punjab ML veteran noted

> Dr Ambedkar has done a very great service to the Muslims of India in spite of his non-Muslim propensities and we should be very grateful to him. He

79 Ibid., 333

80 Dhananjay Keer, *Dr Ambedkar: Life and Mission* (Bombay, 1962), 336.

81 *Indian Annual Register*, Vol. 2 (1941), 229.

> has fully supported the idea of Pakistan as adumbrated by the AIML. I think it is an honest attempt to solve the great riddle of India at this critical juncture especially when it is from the pen of a non-Muslim.[82]

Commenting on the tenor of Ambedkar's book, *Eastern Times of Lahore* explained it in terms of the fact that the Untouchables 'look upon the Muslims with the same eye of suspicion as the caste Hindus do... they identify themselves with the Hindus and in any political arrangement would go with the Hindus rather than with the Muslims.'[83] Finally, as far as Jinnah was concerned, he voiced his views regarding *Thoughts on Pakistan* in a chat with the journalist Frank Moraes. The *Qaid* suspected that Ambedkar was keen to see Pakistan come into existence since it would allow Untouchables to take over the Muslim share in government jobs, representation in legislatures etc. in independent Hindustan since they would become its largest minority constituting 20 per cent of population.[84] Whatever Jinnah's private reflections may have been regarding Ambedkar's *Thoughts on Pakistan*, he still needed to respond to them by putting up a robust public defence of Pakistan. The response was not long in coming.

Responding to Ambedkar's Challenge: Jinnah, the Home Study Circle and the Public Defense of Pakistan

Ambedkar's exposition set the stage for a chorus of demands asking Jinnah and the ML to elaborate upon their idea of Pakistan. If Jinnah was to emerge as the 'sole spokesman' of the Indian Muslims and the ML as their 'sole authoritative and representative organization', they needed to respond to this criticism and take firm charge over the message of Pakistan besides disciplining the multiplicity of voices and messages in this process. This was vital given the plurality of Pakistan schemes floating in the public arena authored by a variety of individuals, which neither enjoyed the *Qaid's* blessings nor carried the ML's imprimatur. Jinnah, therefore, embarked upon a concerted drive to forge a propaganda machine that could give the widest possible publicity to the idea of Pakistan, especially after the unsuccessful Cripps Mission gave him and Pakistan a new prominence in Indian politics. This also became an imperative need due to the existence of a powerful Congress 'nationalist press' which was trying to effectively discredit the ML's platform within India and

82 *Star of India*, 6 May 1941.

83 Ahmad Saeed, (ed.), *Eastern Times on the Qaid-i-Azam* (Islamabad, 1983), 169.

84 Frank Moraes, *Witness to an Era* (New York, 1973), 46.

more importantly in the eyes of an outside world that seemed anxious about the state of British India in the context of the War.

Jinnah took three important steps as part of his efforts to convey the party's message to its domestic supporters besides communicating its position to the outside world. First, he started *The Dawn* from Delhi, an English newspaper that would faithfully mirror the views of the Muslim League and publicize its political, economic, social and educational activities. Writing to Mahmudabad, Jinnah optimistically observed that 'this is the first time that Muslim India is going to have a really first class English daily and I sincerely hope that it will fully satisfy the public and thus secure their wholehearted support throughout India.'[85] After some deliberation, he hired as its editor, the inimitable Pothan Joseph, a legendary figure in the world of Indian journalism. Joseph first met Jinnah as a young struggling subeditor at the *Bombay Chronicle* while the latter sat in its board of directors. The promising young journalist had served notice to the newspaper intimating his intention to move to Calcutta as the Assistant editor of *The Capital*. Jinnah tried to persuade Joseph to stay on but the latter had already booked his passage to Calcutta. As Joseph writes, 'I took my leave with Jinnah's customary remark: If you are happy, well, Joseph, I am happy, but I fancy we shall meet again.'[86] When they did meet again a couple of decades later in Delhi in 1942, Joseph readily accepted Jinnah's offer to join *The Dawn* as its editor on terms that the *Qaid* offered 'without the solemnity of a contract', for his new employer, 'though exacting, always inspired confidence.'[87] Joseph makes a particularly keen observation regarding the close attention that the *Qaid* paid to the press and his acute awareness of its potential in the arena of politics.

> He read papers carefully sifting wheat from chaff. He had no time to waste on Tom, Dick and Harry professing incredulity on ideological conflict in India when his statements were in cold print for all to know. He kept a large book of newspaper cuttings and he had a sure ear for wireless news, upon the strength of which he would casually enquire why some story had not been found in print. Once he sensed that you had the hang of the case, conversation was virtually over and the Editor was virtually free to follow his own technique of exposition.'[88]

---

85 Jinnah to Mahmudabad, 3 October 1942, *SHC UP* Vol. 4.

86 Pothan Joseph, *Looking Back* (Bangalore, 1950), 54.

87 Ibid., 55.

88 Ibid., 57.

Besides *The Dawn*, the other English language newspapers the ML counted as its own included *The Morning News* owned by the family of the Nawab of Dacca, *The Star of India* owned by his trusted lieutenants, the Ispahanis of Calcutta and *The Eastern Times* which was published from Lahore. In Urdu, the party's official organ, the *Manshoor* of Delhi, had been started in 1938, edited by Syed Hasan Reyaz, the erstwhile ML party Secretary in U.P., who had helped Nawab Ismail Khan craft the party's responses to the questionnaire sent by Maulana Ashraf Ali Thanawi. The *Wahdat* and *Al Aman* were the other Delhi-based Urdu papers that backed the ML. In the provinces too, the ML could count on the firm support of a number of devoted Urdu dailies and weeklies. In Punjab, Hameed Nizami, an ML student activist, started the *Nawa-i-Waqt* in Lahore in March 1940 purely 'for the propagation of Pakistan', for upholding the ML banner in the province and not as a commercial venture.[89] All of its initial staff members were honorary workers. Other important papers that supported the ML in the Punjab included the already established *Zamindar*, *Inqilab* and *Ehsan*, while in Bengal the major ML Urdu newspaper was the *Asr-i-Jadid* of Calcutta. In the U.P., the *Hamdam*, *Sitara* and later Khaliquzzaman's *Tanveer* and in Bombay *Al Hilal* and *Khilafat*, were firmly pro-ML papers. The *Deccan Times* of Hyderabad was the ML's English language newspaper down south, popular among Muslims in Hyderabad state and Madras province. Its editor M. A. Ravoof went on to write a biography of Jinnah that was part of the posse of publications that were sold as ML's propaganda material.[90] Besides putting together an array of newspapers the ML also started its own Orient News Agency to free itself from the stranglehold of Hindu owned news agencies in India. The extent of hostility and suspicion between the Congress and the ML over press coverage by the other side can be gauged from the fact that Maulana Azad expelled from his press conference the Orient news agency's representative on the grounds that he had been 'unfair to him in the manner of reporting his speeches.' Jinnah returned the compliment when the *Hindustan Times* correspondent, Krupanidhi, was banished from his press conferences for the paper's 'misleading reporting of a meeting of the ML Working Committee which was held in camera.'[91]

---

89 Hameed Nizami to Jinnah, 23 January 1944, in *QA Papers* Vol. 10, 132.

90 M. A. Ravoof, *Meet Mr. Jinnah* (Lahore, 1944).

91 *Eastern Times*, 24 April 1942, in Ahmad Saeed (ed.), *Eastern Times on Qaid-i-Azam* (Islamabad, 1983), 5–7.

Secondly, in addition to expanding the Muslim footprint in the world of Indian journalism, ML functionaries also began to publish Jinnah's public speeches and statements, his correspondence with Congress leaders such as Gandhi, Nehru, Bose, or Rajagopalachari, his exchange of letters with the poet Muhammad Iqbal, biographies of the *Qaid*, besides pamphlets on the Lahore Resolution and Pakistan. The Lahore firm of Shaikh Muhammad Ashraf published most of these materials. In an address to Jinnah during a public meeting at Lahore, its proprietor declared that

> nobody could be better acquainted than you with the part that the literature of a people plays in disseminating new ideas, creating new forces and awakening the masses and the important role the publisher plays in the making of a nation…We have also produced a good amount of literature on Pakistan and the reception it has got is a testimony, if at all one were needed, to the popularity and appeal that Pakistan has for the Muslims of India.[92]

The popularity of these materials can further be gauged from the number of advance orders placed for Jinnah's official biography, authored by Matlubul Hasan, his then personal secretary.[93] The rush for it was clearly the result of extensive publicity in the party's newspapers, attesting yet again to how propaganda materials were developing synergies in conjunction with party newspapers to become a crucial force multiplier for the ML. Jinnah himself assisted in this biography's publication by supplying his photographs taken by prominent photographers such as Zaidi of Lahore, Sequeira of Karachi and Udit Gopal of Bombay.[94] He also seriously considered publishing his own memoirs, which were to be put together by Pothan Joseph, but this project never materialized in the end.[95] Urdu translations of many of these materials was also undertaken to reach out to the party's base.

---

92 Sh. Muhammad Ashraf to Jinnah, 2 April 1944, *QA Papers*, Vol. 10, 248–49.

93 Matlubul Hasan Syed, *Mohammad Ali Jinnah, A Political Study* (Lahore, 1945).

94 Sh. Muhammad Ashraf to Jinnah, 31 December 1943, *QA Papers*, Vol. 10, 112.

95 Pothan Joseph to Sh. Muhammad Ashraf, 16 May 1944. *QA papers*, Vol. X, 401. Jinnah's busy schedule and his disinclination to commit his thoughts on paper in the form of essays or journalistic pieces in contrast to Nehru, perhaps explains the lack of his autobiography. The journalist Frank Moraes who, at the time, worked as the India representative for the *News Chronicle* of London notes in his memoirs that Jinnah's articles to English and American newspapers were usually ghosted by his lieutenant, Rashid Baig. This included the famous article which appeared in the *Time and Tide* of London in 1940. Baig told Moraes that Jinnah changed the draft of this article in only one place. In the phrase 'Hindu and Muslim communities', Jinnah substituted 'nations' for 'communities'. See Frank Moraes, *Witness to An Era* (New York, 1973), 59.

But the most direct response to Ambedkar's book as well as to the growing public clamour on the question of Pakistan is contained in the propaganda material that was produced under the auspices of the Home Study Circle. In this literature, a twin volume set consisting newspaper articles by a Punjabi journalist Mohammad Sharif Toosy – *Pakistan and Muslim India* & *Nationalism in Conflict in India* – are of particular importance. The *Qaid* himself wrote the foreword to these volumes to

> commend these two books to all readers who want to understand the problem of India's future constitution and its solution and I feel that anyone who reads them dispassionately and with an open mind will find by sheer facts and figures and historical arguments that partition of India is in the interests of both the major nations, Hindus and Muslims.[96]

Their importance can also be gauged from the fact that the official address for these publications was Jinnah's own residence in Bombay. Syed Shamsul Hasan and Syed Budrul Hasan from the ML's office helped with proof-reading and supervising the printing, further indicating how a small unit around Jinnah functioned closely together to create these volumes. Some of Toosy's articles from the *Eastern Times* had earlier been published by Jinnah in a collection titled *India's Problem of Her Future Constitution* in October 1940, just six months after the Lahore Resolution.[97] But in spite of Jinnah's assurance to Rajkumari Amrit Kaur that this volume 'will explain to you fully the Lahore Resolution of the AIML and the basic principle laid down therein', this was a disparate collection of essays without much cohesion or a focused message.[98] In the context of Ambedkar's treatise, Jinnah and the ML had to respond with much greater precision and depth. Serious preparations for a more systematic and robust defense of the Pakistan idea began even as Ambedkar's book was in the works. Jinnah's secretary Matlubul Hasan, presumably on his leader's directive, collected Toosy's remaining articles and placed them before him for perusal and approval in 1941. Having perused the writings, in the summer of 1942, Jinnah finally summoned Toosy and ordered him to put together the two volumes of his essays before the end of the year. Toosy, who wrote under the initials MRT, later reminisced that Jinnah himself

96 Foreword, by Mohammed Ali Jinnah in *Pakistan and Muslim India*, Home Study Circle (Bombay, 1942).

97 The Urdu version was published as, Muhammad Ali Jinnah, *Hindustan Ka A'indah Kanstityushan (dastur-i-Siyasi) kya Hona Chahiye* (Delhi, 1940).

98 Jinnah to Amrit Kaur, 23 December 1940, *QA Papers*, Vol. XVI, third series, 151.

suggested the titles for these volumes besides their organizational scheme.[99] The task was completed within the stipulated time for Jinnah to sign the book's foreword, just a day before his sixty sixth birth day on 25 December 1942, almost exactly two years after Ambedkar had signed the preface to his own book. The importance that Jinnah attached to these volumes can be discerned from the letter Matlubul Hasan wrote on his *Qaid*'s behalf to the Punjabi journalist. Lavishing praise on his writings, Matlubul Hasan assured Toosy that 'you are doing a much greater service to the community by placing before them the correct interpretation of the viewpoint of the AIML than you could in any other way.'[100]

Even if it were to be argued that this published propaganda may not have constituted Jinnah's 'real' aims, or the disclaimer that this was not the ML's 'official' policy taken seriously, it still provides readers an idea of how Pakistan was explained and justified to the ML's core constituency of supporters as well as to a wider public across British India. Arrangements were made to get this propaganda translated into Urdu further underlining the seriousness with which Jinnah and the ML approached the task of disseminating these ideas.[101] The first of these volumes was translated into Urdu by 1944 and published by the ML central office in Delhi.[102] These volumes were aimed at not just the domestic constituency but a worldwide audience. In the foreword Jinnah explicitly noted his concern about how the struggle for Pakistan was perceived around the world. He used the opportunity to, therefore, decry attempts by the Congress to 'misguide foreign opinion' that India's case 'has a parallel in China, Soviet Russia, or even the United States of America and that its problems can be successfully tackled in the light of experience gained by the peoples of these countries.'[103] The *Qaid* made it unequivocally clear at the very outset

---

99 M.S. Toosy, *My Reminiscences of Quaid-i-Azam: A Collection of Interviews and Talks with Quaid-i-Azam during November 1942 to May 1943* (Islamabad, 1976), 3.

100 Matlubul Hasan to M. S. Toosy, 8 January 1941, *QA Papers*, Vol. XVI, 191–92

101 Shamsul Hasan to Jinnah, 29 November 1943, *QA Papers*, Vol X, 58. Jinnah also accepted the offer of a 'fixed royalty of Rs. 300 to be paid out of the surplus sales proceeds of the said books.' Jinnah to Shamsul Hasan, 3 December, 1943. These volumes and their Urdu translations were further advertised by the ML during the 1944 Gandhi-Jinnah talks as also on the eve of the 1945–46 elections, especially in *The Dawn* and *Star of India*.

102 *Pakistan and Muslim India* was translated as *Pakistan aur Musalman* (Delhi, 1944). The translator Muhammad Zafar Ahmad Ansari had earlier translated Indulal Yajnik's *Gandhi as I Know Him* (Delhi, 1943) under the title *Pir-i-Sabarmati* (Delhi, 1943).

103 Ibid.

that he wanted the northwestern and eastern zones of the subcontinent where the Muslims were in a majority to be 'separated from the rest of India and constituted into *sovereign independent states*.' Jinnah repeatedly affirmed all of the ideas expressed in these volumes through his numerous public speeches and statements, which again were eagerly followed, discussed and debated in the popular media. The battle for Pakistan was thus fought as much in the public arenas as it may have been in the inner corridors of power in New Delhi, Simla, or London during the 'transfer of power' negotiations.

Pakistan and Muslim India and Nationalism in Conflict in India

Ambedkar's treatise had addressed in impressive detail how Hindustan would benefit economically, politically, militarily and socially by separating itself from Pakistan. It also left the readers in no doubt that the former would be far more powerful and prosperous than the latter, after having presented comparative sets of facts and figures regarding the financial and material resources at the disposal of both these nation-states. But even if he conspicuously ignored the question of Pakistan's viability, Ambedkar implicitly raised a serious question mark on Pakistan's ability to survive. As Congress barbs on a fragile, poor and possibly stillborn Pakistan began to animate public discussion, the ML was left with no choice but to respond forcefully to these claims. To counter this argument, the abovementioned Toosy volumes besides reaffirming the two-nation theory, produced facts, figures and statistics compiled from various official reports to emphasize the nation's sovereign 'geo-body'.[104] They portrayed Pakistan as not only a politically, economically and militarily feasible state, but potentially a far more prosperous and powerful entity than Hindu India. In this regard, this propaganda introduced a critical and significant shift in the Indo-Muslim discourse as far as its relationship to the Islamic world was concerned. If the end of World War I saw Indian Muslims agitating for the preservation of the foremost Muslim power and the pre-eminent symbol of Islam – Turkey and its Caliphate – as crucial for their own survival and well-being in the subcontinent, ML propaganda increasingly portrayed Pakistan as the worthy successor to that defunct world power in the run up to Partition.

National Territory and the Two-nation Theory

Toosy made a strong case for creating Pakistan in contiguous Muslim majority areas in the northwest and the northeast of the subcontinent by embedding

[104] The term 'geo-body' is borrowed from Thongchai Winichakul, *Mapping Siam: A History of the Geo-Body of a Nation* (Honolulu, 1994).

it in the vocabulary of international law that emerged in the aftermath of the Versailles treaty. He argued that the right to self-determination could not be denied to the Muslims in the Pakistan areas as they were a nation that occupied compact territories and this right had been granted to various nations after World War I on similar grounds. As far as justifying the partitioning of territories was concerned, he invoked the example of Syria that the French had divided into Syria and Lebanon for Muslim and Christian Arabs respectively, even though Arabs shared similar language and culture. He also ridiculed the British for ignoring their own history and continuing to insist on India's essential unity since the Protestants in Ireland, a minority of 20 per cent, had been granted their own state after refusing to accept constitutional safeguards. Toosy also repudiated various objections to denying sovereignty to the Muslims. In response to the argument that Pakistan would be a weak entity as compared to Hindu India and hence incapable of fulfilling its sovereign status, he observed that France too was much smaller and weaker than neighbouring Germany but that condition had not come in the way of her sovereign status. British insistence on Indian unity even after Burma, Nepal, Bhutan and Ceylon had been granted separate political existence was thus untenable and extremely unjust.

Having invoked the principle of self-determination, Toosy further built his case for Pakistan by asking whether the Indian Muslim would be best served by 'an assurance of full protection of his religion, culture and language on the part of the Congress, or a complete separation and independence of those parts of India where the Muslims form a majority.'[105] This second available option involved 'forming independent sovereign states in the North-West and the North-East where they [Muslims] occupy compact areas with distinct geographical limits.' Surveying the situation, he expressed a clear preference for the second scheme over the first one. The first scheme would have been appropriate had the Muslims been scattered all over British India, but since two thirds of its Muslim population was concentrated in their 'majority provinces' the second option was most compelling. He substantiated his case by pointing out that in the northwestern zone comprising Punjab, Kashmir, Sind and the Frontier province, Muslims constituted nearly 28 million out of a total population of 42 million. This two-third majority could be further be raised 'by a readjustment of the eastern frontier of the Punjab.'[106] In the northeast too, he claimed that Bengal's proportion of Muslim population

[105] MRT, *Pakistan and Muslim India* (Bombay, 1942), 1.

[106] Ibid., 2.

could be raised to 70 per cent if the frontiers were readjusted since Muslims constituted a majority of 75 per cent in the eastern Bengal districts and the Assam districts of Goalpara and Sylhet. He additionally claimed a few districts in western Bengal that were contiguous to eastern Bengal arguing that they too had Muslim majorities and would therefore become a part of the Muslim state. The new state of eastern Bengal and Assam would thus have 70 per cent majority in a population of 40 million.

Toosy, however, acknowledged that divisions existed within the ML over the question of territorial adjustment. One section wanted to preserve the present boundaries of Bengal and Punjab since it believed that this was the only way that the economic interests of these provinces and ultimately of Pakistan could be safeguarded. It, therefore, supported 'the principle of territorial nationalism based upon an appeal to the common interests of Muslims and other minorities living in two distinct parts of India'.[107] On the contrary, the other section, 'by far the most influential one', desired the separation of the Hindu majority Ambala division from the Punjab besides the Hindu majority districts of west Bengal to make the Muslim areas more compact and homogenous. This section saw this rearrangement of provincial boundaries as the only way for giving the Muslims effective majorities in the new sovereign states and also minimizing the problems of communal conflict in their domains. Strikingly, Toosy declared that the ML *more truly represented the interests of this section* and hence the Lahore Resolution had explicitly declared that 'geographically contiguous units are demarcated into regions which should be so constituted with such territorial adjustments as may be necessary.'[108] No compromise was possible between the ideas of complete separation on the one hand and subordination of Muslims under a common federation, on the other. He also dismissed as futile, all schemes of confederation under which participating units would join on the basis of equality, since the Muslims did not want any Centre which would obviously be dominated by the Hindus.[109] Moreover, a confederation did not have any stronger claims than a federation since the desire for unity was lacking on the part of Muslims. Like Ambedkar, Toosy, thus, placed geography, maps and their alteration to create new sovereignties at the very centre of the public debates on Pakistan.

107 Ibid., 55.

108 Ibid., 55.

109 The confederal idea was implicit in the schemes put forward by Sir Sikander Hayat Khan, the Punjab Premier and Dr C. R. Reddy, the Vice Chancellor of Andhra University. All such schemes contemplated a centre with control over vital subjects and hence were rejected.

Toosy justified creating a sovereign independent Pakistan by claiming that Muslims and Hindus did not represent mere majorities and minorities but distinct nations with clear social, economic and political divisions. He provided different examples of how Hindu and Muslim social and political imaginaries clashed with each other on a range of issues. Indian Muslims had 'distinct political aspirations' which motivated them to work for the political regeneration of the Muslim world in general and not just of their own narrow community. A Muslim's first concern was, therefore, the rise of Islam as a political power in the world.[110] Hindu interests on the other hand, he argued, were mostly confined to India since the Hindus had no cultural or religious links with other countries in the world. Hindus and Muslims were also socially distinct since they followed two completely different social systems – the Hindus with their hierarchical caste system as opposed to the Muslims who made no distinctions based on birth or blood. Toosy further claimed that Hindus and Muslims differed in their economic mindset as well since they took to different occupations and occupied different class positions in society. The interests of the Muslim peasant and the Muslim middle class were opposed to those of the Hindu money lender and shopkeeper. Comparing the position of the Punjabi Muslim to that of the Turk in Asia Minor before the emergence of modern Turkey, he claimed that the Turk too, like the Punjabi Muslim had either been a soldier, a debt ridden peasant, or a government servant.[111] He too was economically far behind the Jew, the Greek and the Armenian. Banking, trade, medicine, learned professions were all dominated by the non-Turkish races. A similar situation in India existed since Hindus dominated the professions, education, trade, commerce and industry. In the villages, especially in the Pakistan areas, Hindus were usually the money lenders. More importantly, with an eye to the future, Toosy insisted that Muslims could not trust the Hindus to do economic justice after they assumed political power, since they had economically enslaved them in the first place. Separation was therefore imperative for Muslims to prosper economically.

Economic Defence of Pakistan

Ambedkar had left his readers with the impression that the Pakistan areas, especially in the northwest, would struggle economically once they stopped receiving funds from New Delhi for the purposes of defending the frontier and maintaining the army stationed there. This situation was expected to get

---

110 Ibid., 3.

111 Ibid., 6.

worse once Delhi's annual subsidy to the revenue deficit provinces of NWFP and Baluchistan was curtailed. Toosy, therefore, had to bolster the economic case for Pakistan and strongly defend its economic viability. But before he embarked upon this exercise, he declared in no uncertain terms that economic principles could never be a touchstone for national sovereignty. If such criteria were established they would have disqualified several small European nations from ever gaining statehood under the Wilsonian principle of self-determination. Thus, for example, the Baltic nations would never have been granted statehood nor would the Austro-Hungarian Empire have been split up if the economic principle was made the determining criterion. Moving to his case for Pakistan, he repudiated the charge that revenue-deficit provinces such as Sind, Baluchistan and NWFP would drag Pakistan into an economic quagmire by demonstrating on the contrary, their potential to become economically self-sustaining. Sind, he asserted, would become self-sufficient once the Lloyd barrage scheme was completed and vast amounts of its agricultural land was brought under irrigation. Sind would prosper even further if customs revenue from Karachi port and income tax currently being mopped up by Delhi were to be held back locally. He further claimed that floriculture and sericulture and allied industries could be developed in Baluchistan and NWFP while oil wells in Sind and Baluchistan would be sufficient to meet the petroleum demands of all of Pakistan.[112] He was greatly optimistic about the development of agriculture and industry in Punjab and Kashmir, while expecting the Mundi Hydro-electric Works to generate ample electricity for the industrial requirements of the region besides helping Punjab and Kashmir to better exploit their mineral wealth and forest resources.[113] He saw East Pakistan too as possessing great potential for development, especially due to its textile and jute industries and expected other industries based on mineral processing to develop in these parts given its proximity to a variety of minerals in the neighbouring Chhotanagpur area.[114] Additionally, the rising population in East Pakistan was expected to provide a ready market for its industrial products.[115] Having made a case for the economic stability of Pakistan's provinces, Toosy reasoned that the central government in Pakistan states would also be financially stable with the ability to generate total revenues of over

112 Ibid., 156–7.

113 Ibid., 154.

114 Ibid., 155.

115 For a discussion on Pakistan's anticipated economic development, see Ian Talbot, 'Planning for Pakistan: The Planning Committee of the Muslim League, 1943-1946', *Modern Asian Studies* Vol. 28, No. 4 (1994), 875–89.

350 million rupees each, higher than those of Turkey and other Muslim states like Egypt, Iran and Afghanistan.'[116] Finally, if size of territory and strength of population were criteria for statehood, Pakistan was amply qualified to become a strong state. It was twice the size of France while its population was equal to that of Italy. It also possessed enough natural resources which, if properly developed, would enable it to sustain a population twice or three times its current size. He took this opportunity to also point out that in Hindu India by contrast, population had 'reached the limits of congestion.'[117] Pakistan was free from such dangers and furthermore was interested in guarding its territory from 'forced immigration' from other parts of India bursting with excess population.

The economic defence thus constituted a robust response to Ambedkar's seemingly willful disregard of Pakistan's economic prospects. More importantly, it was a point by point rebuttal of prognoses by the Indian nationalists who predicted that an economically feeble Pakistan would either be stillborn at birth or die a premature death. However, there still remained unresolved tensions in Toosy's economic defense of Pakistan. While contemplating on the sources of capital for Pakistan, he expressed hope that wealthy Hindu industrialists would invest their capital and develop industries in Pakistan. This hope was based on the assumed selfishness of the Indian *bania* and his desire to maximize his profits. Yet, at another place, he expressed strong distrust of Hindu capitalists. After all, one of the reasons adduced for the separation of Pakistan was that if it were to remain a part of India, Hindu financiers and capitalists, with active support from the Congress right wing, would take over its whole economy and reduce Muslims to an even more backward position. In this scenario, Toosy darkly warned that Pakistan would be

> at the mercy of factory owners of Bombay, Ahmedabad and Cawnpore, who will influence the Indian government to adopt a policy of protection, which will necessitate the imposition of heavy taxes upon imports and the subsidizing of their concerns. The result of this policy will be that Pakistan will be forced to buy Indian goods without being given any chance of its own industrialization while its peasantry will be starved for not finding ready markets for the sale of its raw materials.[118]

Pakistan's economic interests were thus antagonistic to those of Hindu India and it was in its best interests to rather have more wide ranging economic

---

[116] MRT, *Pakistan and Muslim India*, 148.

[117] Ibid., 24.

[118] Ibid., 23–24.

relations with Europe. Pakistan would prefer European capital to Hindu capital and Europe rather than Hindu India as its main trading partner. He, therefore, concluded that Pakistan could trade its primary goods for the industrial goods of Europe, till the time that Pakistan started its own industries.[119]

Pakistan and India's Defence

If Ambedkar had urged the Hindus to not be weighed down by concerns about India's defence and to let go of the Pakistan areas, Toosy performed a similar task of allaying fears regarding Pakistan's defence. The argument he had to contend with was that an economically fragile Pakistan might be militarily weakened and hence unable to defend itself. Thus, a charge made in the nationalist press was that the Pakistan states were not in a position to bear the financial burden of defending their borders and would therefore crumble under the military pressures of the frontier tribes or of the states beyond. Another argument made in this regard was that the two Pakistan states cut off from each other by a hostile Hindu India would not be able to withstand the latter's immense power and resources. Finally, a factor that was played up was that Hindu and Sikh minorities in the Muslim states would keep looking for opportunities to secede from the Muslim states and would, therefore, be a constant source of trouble for an already weak Pakistan. Pushing back against these arguments Toosy first noted that

> a nation that cannot maintain its independence by its own strength has no right to live and if in a future combat, after India has achieved independence, Muslim states will not be able to hold their own against Hindu India, they will not blame their new victors but will tacitly accept the consequences of the defeat.[120]

Confidently asserting that Pakistan would have ample financial resources, he predicted that they would be sufficient to enable it to emerge as not just a militarily viable state but indeed as a powerful state. To begin with, the expenditure for defending Pakistan's territorial integrity would be greatly reduced as the expensive British frontier policy involving warfare with frontier Muslim tribes would be terminated after independence. The tribes themselves were expected to lose their fervour for *jihad* against a Muslim state like

[119] Ibid., 23.

[120] Ibid., 176.

Pakistan resulting in mutual peace and friendship. Furthermore, since frontiers between Muslim states such as Afghanistan and Persia or Persia and Turkey were defended by small armies, he insisted that the same would apply to the frontier between Pakistan and Afghanistan. Toosy also anticipated significant savings by curtailing salaries and pensions of British troops and substituting arms imports from England with indigenous armaments production. But the most important factor ensuring Pakistan's security for him were its martial races, which had a strong representation in the British Indian army, making Pakistan a militarily powerful nation. It was indeed this strength, he gloated, that compelled Gandhi to remark that if the British were to leave India the Gurkhas and Punjabis would overrun the country. Concluding his defense of Pakistan from the military viewpoint, contrary to Ambedkar's view, he warned Muslims of the disadvantages they would face over recruitment into the army in the event of India remaining undivided. He prophesized that the Congress would reduce Muslim strength in the army, currently half of its force, to less than one-tenth, by recruiting soldiers from other parts of India, in the process emasculating the Muslim nation's military strength. Hence, Muslims needed to have their own state with their own army.

Toosy's conjectures regarding Pakistan's defense were however not without their equivocations. On one hand, he argued that Hindu and Muslim India would both join the British Commonwealth and sign non-aggression pacts with each other to provide a stable security order for the region. He also visualized a friendly Afghanistan as an ally against Soviet incursions with the British Navy helping to guard the seas till both the countries set up their own navies. Yet at the same time, while addressing the question of threat to the Pakistan states from a potentially hostile India, he insisted that Pakistan would have to enter into a permanent alliance with Muslim countries of West Asia in order to preserve a balance of power against Hindu India.

Pakistan and Pan-Islam

Notwithstanding Jinnah's denials that Pan-Islam was the motivating factor behind Pakistan's creation, Toosy saw it as an important element in Pakistan's defensive strategy. He claimed that a powerful alliance of all the Muslim countries of the world would materialize under Pakistan's leadership and act as a force multiplier thus making it more than Hindu India's equal. While conceding that pan-Islamism as an ideology was as yet insufficient to bring the global Muslim community under one government, he was confident that it would continue to inspire Muslims all over the world. Muslim world was already awakening to political consciousness and wanted Indian Muslims to take the lead in forging unity among the world's Muslims. In this regard, Toosy wistfully quoted Syed Ameer Ali who in his *Spirit of Islam* a few decades earlier had written

> who shall say that the Muslims of India may not, under the auspices of a great European power, be destined to restore to western and central Asia something of what their forefathers gave to Europe in the Middle Ages.[121]

Toosy further pointed to the dangers that would confront the Islamic world in the event of India remaining undivided and its foreign policy being controlled by Hindus. If Muslims in Turkistan and Azerbiajan in Soviet Russia or Muslims in the western provinces of China were at some point to demand right to self-determination due to their growing political consciousness, free India would most likely enter into pacts with China and Russia in order to suppress the Muslims in their respective territories. Furthermore, the imperial states of India, Russia and China would unite in a common policy towards their Muslim neighbours and even dismember these Muslim states to divide them among themselves with India getting Afghanistan, and Russia adding Iran, Iraq and Turkey to its sphere of influence. The triumph of Muslim nationalism in the subcontinent and the creation of Pakistan, on the other hand, would provide a beacon light of inspiration to these Muslims besides acting as a check on the aggressive designs of these existing hegemonic states. Toosy, therefore, pointed out that the creation of a new state comprising Chinese and Russian parts of Turkistan would

> strengthen the bloc of Muslims states in the west of India, as together they will command allegiance of 80 millions of Muslims including the three most virile and warlike races of Islam, the Turks, the Afghans and the Arabs. If to this bloc is added the Muslim state of Pakistan, in the Northwest of India with its Muslim population of 30 millions, it will magnify the Hindu fear into a permanent nightmare and probably this may be one of the reasons why the Hindu is opposed to the idea of Pakistan.[122]

Toosy also warned against dangers posed by Hindu imperialism to the Islamic world since history was replete with examples of nationalisms spilling over territorial boundaries. Dismissing the Congress' professed anti-colonial nationalism he pointed out that Italian nationalism too had very idealist origins

---

[121] Ibid., 81.

[122] Ibid., 46.

under Mazzini. Yet, the same Italy had brutally invaded Abyssinia and justified Italian expansion in the name of the smallness of Italy's territories and the consequent need for more land and resources for the Italian population. Toosy argued that there was no reason why Hindu nationalism too would not turn out to be imperialistic for the same reasons. Hindu expansionism was indeed imminent since India's population was increasing and it needed more land. The Muslim Northwest was still sparsely populated while the Hindu areas adjoining it, such as the U.P. were congested and without enough food to feed its present population. The U.P. with a smaller territory than Punjab already had twice its population, while Rajputana abutting Sind was a desert and could never feed its population. Punjab and Sind were therefore greatly threatened by migration from these population surplus areas of India. In any case, the Punjab already had a large population of people from U.P. who were involved in businesses such as shoe making. Hindu industrialists in Punjab were also busy recruiting Hindu labour from U.P. in order to increase the Hindu element in the work force. Toosy, therefore, warned that in a united India, the Muslim areas would be helpless to prevent the migration of Hindus from the surplus areas such as U.P. and Rajputana and swamping their territories. Hence, independence for Pakistan was imperative for its self-preservation. Also, Pakistan alone stood in the way of Hindu imperialism extending all the way to the Suez Canal and the Islamic world beyond

Toosy further explained that India already had strained relations with Burma and Ceylon due to Indian settler populations in these two countries. Indian labour in the past had also flooded British East Africa, South Africa and a number of islands of the Indian Ocean. The Malay Peninsula too had been predominantly Muslim, but the Hindu influx from South India coupled with that of the Chinese, had reduced the proportion of Muslim Malays to one-third of its total population. Moreover in Africa, Europeans and Indians had ousted the Arabs from their position of dominance in trade and commerce. Indian colonies had come up along the coast of Africa as a result and Toosy warned that these could act as the agents to an Indian colonial advance in the future. Toosy, therefore, argued that the creation of Pakistan was extremely essential in these threatening conditions involving Hindu outmigration and settler imperialism.

Regional Specificities of Pakistan

Besides general differences between Hindus and Muslims at the all India level, Toosy underlined another set of local particular factors that necessitated the separation of the Northwest Zone from Hindu India. He contended that the peoples of the northwest had more in common with each other than with the rest of India. To begin with, the Sikhs and Arya Samaj Hindus, with their views regarding the unity of God and revealed religion, had more in common with the local Muslims than with Hindus in other parts of India.[123] People of this region were also distinct from those of India in terms of their complexion, physical features, dress, social customs and ways of life, which they shared with each other in spite of religious differences.[124] Hindus, Sikhs as well as Muslims of this area were racially of the same stock, belonging to the Aryan race, used the same language – Urdu-written in the Persian script and also did not have to deal with issues like untouchability, music before mosques, or cow protection that plagued other parts of Hindu India. Toosy particularly sought to reach out to the Sikhs while subtly downgrading the place of Hindus in Pakistan. He observed that being part of a smaller Pakistan would be much more advantageous to the Sikhs as a community where they would have higher proportions allotted to them in terms of seats in legislatures, jobs in government etc. In undivided India, on the other, they would at best be a drop in the ocean. He further reminded the Sikhs that they had had lived together with Muslims for centuries in the region and that their interests too had become more and more interdependent. In Pakistan there was no danger of either of them losing their distinct identity, while in India they would be reduced to the status of helpless minorities.

This exploration into the regional sociology of Pakistan was followed by a repudiation of Indian nationalist claims about India's civilizational unity throughout history, arguments that were in line with those articulated by Ambedkar. Toosy next claimed separateness of Pakistan on the grounds regional geography, arguing that it was a natural region comprising the basin of the Indus and its tributaries, which flowed in a direction opposite to that of the Indian rivers and had a separate drainage system.[125] Pakistan was also connected internally by a separate railway system known as Northwest railway while all of its foreign trade passed through Karachi, which, Toosy declared, was more important for Pakistan than any other port in India.

The Lahore Resolution and the Minority Problem

Toosy gladly agreed with Ambedkar's contention that partitioning India would greatly diminish the minority problem in the subcontinent. He claimed that in

---

[123] Ibid., 20–21.

[124] Ibid.

[125] Ibid.

Hindu India the Muslim minority would be reduced from 90 million to less than 30 million. The Hindu proportion in population would correspondingly rise to 90 per cent while that of Muslims would be reduced from 25 per cent to 10 per cent. Pakistan too would have Muslim majority of over 70 per cent making it a viable Muslim state. He, therefore, asked a pertinent question.

> Is this not a tremendous gain for Hindu India? The stability and peace of India can only be best assured if the discontented parts are separated from it. India is too big to suffer any appreciable material loss by the separation of one fourth of its total area and population. Hindu India with a population of about 280 million after the creation of the two Pakistan States, can yet possess sufficient resources and means to play an effective part as an independent state. Thus it is apparent that the League resolution does not aggravate the minority problem; rather it removes the sting from it and reduces it to the narrowest possible limits.[126]

But Toosy was not just content with enumerating the benefits that Pakistan would bring to the 'majority provinces' Muslims. He went on to outline the benefits Pakistan would bestow upon Muslims left behind in Hindustan. In the best case scenario once Pakistan and Hindustan had gained independence from Britain, their mutual bitterness would disappear, the majorities in the new states would be satisfied, while their minorities too would strive to become model minorities. Yet, taking a realist perspective for the worst case scenario, he invoked the 'hostage population' theory.

> The Pakistan scheme introduces a balanced system of checks.... It is quite natural if Muslim minorities are oppressed in Hindu India, it will lead to repercussions in Muslim India. But the fear of provoking reprisals will exercise a detrimental effect on the majorities. The liability before world's moral opinion as well as the responsibility of the oppressing state before the neighbouring state will be quite sufficient to hold in check the danger of communal tension.[127]

Toosy, however, emphasized that Pakistan would act as a responsible state actor and not unleash indiscriminate punitive action against its non-Muslim minorities in reaction to Muslims being ill-treated in Hindustan. In the first place, Pakistan would try to exert moral pressure on Hindustan in such an eventuality. But if Hindu India was 'absolutely callous to all moral appeals for

---

[126] Ibid., 118.

[127] Ibid., 166–7.

betterment of the lot of its minorities, force may be used as a last resort.'[128] In such a situation the Indian Muslim minority could also 'use all measures possible in defense of its own interests or invoke the help of a neighboring country sympathetic to its cause and strong enough to give material assistance.'[129] In this regard, he pointed to Czechoslovakia's ill-treatment of Sudetan Germans and how that had provoked its invasion by Hitler. This contemporary example, however, threw into sharp relief the impotence of a great Muslim power such as Turkey in protecting its Muslim subjects in Palestine, let alone protecting the Indian Muslims. Toosy was forced to, therefore, acknowledge that Muslim minorities around the world had not been protected thus far according to this logic. He explained this failure in terms of the lack of strength of Muslim countries and insisted that Pakistan as the largest Muslim state in the world would never permit Muslims to be ill-treated anywhere in the world. What was implied was that Pakistan would do better than Turkey, which had let down oppressed Muslims around the world ever since it went into terminal decline. Pushing this argument further, Toosy repudiated the notion that sovereign states could not interfere in each other's internal affairs as it was against the principles of international law. Taking a realist view, he hypothesized that if the American minority in Shanghai were killed by the Japanese, America would surely go to war with Japan. The fact of two countries being sovereign states thus 'would not prevent one from interfering in the affairs of the other'.[130]

Toosy also dismissed as specious the Congress plea that Muslims should accept the idea of a united India since Muslim interests in 'minority provinces' could be maintained by constitutional safeguards while in the 'majority provinces' they could protect themselves by their numerical strength. Such pleas, he argued, only betrayed an ignorance of what was meant by full independence. He therefore noted that

> When a nation aspires for full independence, it seeks to have full power to decide all questions affecting the multifarious activities of a modern state. It does not simply want self-government as understood in a limited sense, but supreme control of all national organs of the state, including defence, foreign affairs, finance, communications, etc. Now it is a simple conclusion that if the Muslim provinces remain part of a future Indian National state they will undoubtedly enjoy a limited kind of provincial autonomy but the

128 Ibid., 181.

129 Ibid., 178–9.

130 Ibid., 184.

final voice in the army, navy and other important central subjects will be held by a Central Cabinet responsible to a central legislature which will be dominated by a Hindu majority.[131]

Toosy claimed that Muslims in Hindu India too would rather choose full independence for their co-religionists than accept the permanent enslavement of the whole Muslim community in India.[132] Besides, even if that were not always the case, Muslims of Hindu India as a sub-national group needed to 'suppress their aspiration for independence because they are not entitled to claim independence on the principle of self-determination.'[133] He, therefore, concluded that Pakistan was the only solution for India's Hindu–Muslim problem. In the northwest it would consist of Punjab, Sind, Baluchistan, Kashmir state, North West Frontier Province and all the native states that lay within that zone. As far as Punjab was concerned, the six districts of Ambala division with a Hindu majority could be merged with U.P. or joined to Delhi to create a new province. Along with the Ambala division, the princely states of Nabha, Patiala, Faridkot, Jind, Simla hills, Sirmur and Kalsia in that zone would be removed from Pakistan. The population of Punjab would be reduced by 7 million with the result that Muslim proportion would be raised in Punjab from 57 per cent to 66 per cent. The proportion of Hindu population in Punjab would be reduced from 27 per cent to 19 per cent but the percentage of Sikh population would go up from 12.9 per cent to 14.8 per cent. Overall, in the Northwestern zone proportion of Muslim population would go up from 60 per cent to 69 per cent and if independent tribal territories were added, it would go up to 71 per cent. In the entire northwestern zone Hindu population would be a mere 18 per cent. Pakistan would thus satisfy the criteria of national homogeneity that was a necessary feature of the modern state.

Toosy also held out carrots to the Sikhs, a crucial community whose cooperation the ML needed if it wanted to achieve Pakistan. He calculated that while at present they comprised 1 per cent of India's population, in the new Muslim state their proportion would be 9 per cent. They would therefore be guaranteed a permanent seat in the central cabinet. While the Sikhs currently enjoyed representation to the tune of 20 per cent in the services and the provincial legislature he assured them that Pakistan would affirm the weightage they currently enjoyed thus ensuring representation at the new centre over

---

131 Ibid., 192.

132 Ibid., 190.

133 Ibid., 191.

and above their ratio in the existing population. They would in fact have equal number of ministers as the Hindus in the cabinet. But while Toosy sought to appease the Sikhs, he firmly scotched ideas of an independent Sikh state consisting of the five districts of Gurdaspur, Amritsar, Jalandhar, Ferozepur and Ludhiana where Sikhs had a substantial presence. He pointed out that in this proposed state Sikhs would form only 45 per cent of the population, hardly a convincing majority. Furthermore, the new state would become a nerve-centre of intrigues by both Hindustan and Pakistan and never enjoy internal peace and security, thus making it completely unviable. He also held out the warning that if this scheme was somehow accepted, it would lead to further demands for similar independent states in Hindu India by sub-national groups such as the Moplahs in Malabar or the U.P. Muslims who formed 14 per cent of that province's population. This would lead to 'a piecemeal division of India, which will neither be agreed to by the Hindus nor by the British government.'[134] The Sikh demand was, therefore, untenable.

As far as Eastern Pakistan state was concerned, Toosy declared that it would consist of eastern Bengal where Muslims had majority in thirteen out of the fifteen districts barring Darjeeling and Jalpaiguri and the Sylhet and Goalpara districts of Assam. He also claimed that in Western Bengal Muslims were in a majority in three of the eleven districts – those of Jessore, Murshidabad and Nadia – while they constituted 49 per cent of Khulna district's population. Khulna, 24 Parganas and Calcutta therefore needed to be included into the East Pakistan state as they were immediately south of it. Calcutta though not having a Muslim majority, had to be given to East Pakistan as it was an essential seaport. Calculating the total area of Eastern Pakistan at 70,000 square miles with a population of 40 million in which Muslims would have a 70 per cent majority, Toosy acknowledged that Hindus would still constitute a substantial minority in East Pakistan at 30 per cent of its population. He therefore suggested that if this population remained dissatisfied with the proposed arrangements, 'a mutual exchange of population with Muslims in Bihar and excluded districts of Bengal and Assam can easily be arranged.'[135] This would involve a transfer of 5–6 millions on each side. Such figures though failed to deter ML propaganda from toying with the idea of transfer of population and it was affirmed by none other than the *Qaid*.

---

134 Ibid., 130.

135 Ibid., 137.

Affirming the Message of the Home Study Circle: Jinnah's Public Clarifications on Pakistan

The basic reasoning behind the assumption that Pakistan was a bargaining counter and not a demand for a separate state is that such a state would have been disastrous for the Muslim minority in Hindu India. As the argument goes, Jinnah as the *Qaid* of all of the Indian Muslims was hardly going to abandon the 'minority provinces' Muslims.[136] However, Jinnah's own public utterances on the matter of these Muslims seem to point to the different ideas he held regarding nations and minority groups. Never the abstract theoretician, the meticulous constitutional lawyer gave concrete examples to clarify what he meant by nations, sub-national groups or minorities. For Jinnah, Muslims in the 'majority provinces' were a nation with concomitant rights to self-determination and statehood since they constituted a numerical majority in a contiguous piece of territory. On the other hand, Sikhs, though distinct enough to be a nation, did not fulfill either of these criteria and hence were a sub-national group with no option but to seek minority safeguards in Pakistan. Jinnah specifically compared the position of Sikhs to that of U.P. Muslims. He argued that U.P. Muslims though constituting 14 per cent of the province's population could not be granted a separate state because

> Muslims in the United Provinces are not a national group; they are scattered. Therefore, in constitutional language, they are characterized as a sub-national group who cannot expect anything more than what is due from any civilized government to a minority. I hope I have made the position clear.'[137]

The *Qaid* was aware that his public utterances had created not just a slippage, but a cleavage between the purported Muslim nation and Pakistan. He, therefore, tried to bridge this crucial gap in a few ways. To begin with he lauded the great sacrifices made by the 'minority provinces' Muslims and how they selflessly demanded liberation for their 60 million majority provinces brethren from Hindu Raj.[138] They had readily supported the Lahore Resolution since they realized that they would remain a minority 'in perpetuity' and, therefore, did not want to reduce their brethren to the same fate. Indeed, Jinnah would

---

136 Ayesha Jalal, *The Sole Spokesman*, 2–5.

137 Jamiluddin Ahmad, *Speeches and Writings of Mr. Jinnah* , Vol. 1, 492. Speech at the Annual Session of the All India Muslim Students Federation at Jalandhar, 15 November 1942.

138 Ibid., 165–66, Statement on the Lahore Resolution.

call them 'the pioneers and first soldiers of Pakistan'.[139] He further pointed out that he himself belonged to a minority province and that

> as a self-respecting people, we in the Muslim minority provinces say boldly that we are prepared to undergo every suffering and sacrifice for the emancipation and liberation of our brethren in regions of Muslim majority. By standing in their way and dragging them along with us into a united India we do not in any way improve our position. Instead we reduce them also to the position of a minority. But we are determined that, whatever happens to us, we are not going to allow our brethren to be vassalised by the Hindu majority.[140]

Jinnah's speech to the Muslim Students Federation at Kanpur a few weeks later went a little further causing a furor in the Urdu press in U.P. He declared that in order to liberate 7 crore Muslims of the majority provinces, 'he was willing to perform the last ceremony of martyrdom if necessary and let 2 crore Muslims of the minority provinces be smashed.'[141] At the same time though, Jinnah tried to soften the blow for minority province Muslims by arguing that Pakistan's creation would entail a reciprocal *treaty* with Hindu India to safeguard rights and interests of minorities in both states.[142] In this regard, he pointed to the presence of large Hindu and Sikh minorities in Pakistan who too would require similar protection in Pakistan. He, therefore, asserted that 'when the time for consultation and negotiations comes, the case of Muslims of the minority provinces will certainly not go by default.'[143] Jinnah himself affirmed one of the two supporting strands of this 'hostage population' theory when he declared that if Muslim minorities in Pakistan were ill-treated, Pakistan would not 'remain a passive spectator'. As he elaborated, 'if Britain in Gladstone's time could intervene in Armenia in the name of protection of minorities, why should it not be right for us to do so in the case of our minorities in Hindustan- if they are oppressed?'[144]

---

139 Ibid., Vol. 2, 285.

140 Ibid., Vol.1, 267, Speech at Aligarh Muslim University, 10 March 1941.

141 Ibid., 271, Speech to Muslim Students Federation, Kanpur, 30 March 1941; *PAI for the week ending 4 April 1941.*

142 Ibid., 267, Speech at Aligarh Muslim University, 10 March 1941.

143 Ibid., Vol. 1, 267 Speech at the Aligarh Muslim University, 3 January 1941.

144 Ibid., Vol. 2, 286. This idea could have a long afterlife as evident from this fascinating vignette narrated by the journalist, Shekhar Gupta regarding his friend, the liberal Pakistani politician Salman Taseer who was shot dead in 2011 by his own bodyguard for speaking out against Pakistan's infamous blasphemy law. Gupta wrote, 'Sometime

At the same time, Jinnah assured adequate safeguards for Hindu minorities in Pakistan and also gave assurances about adequate representation in the government.[145] He was, however, quick to reject the argument that Hindus in Pakistan could not trust assurances that their rights would be safeguarded since Muslims themselves had refused to accept such assurances at an all India level. Such reasoning was fallacious since it assumed that the whole of India belonged to the Hindus. As Jinnah noted

> are the Muslim minorities in the Hindu majority provinces entitled to enforce their verdict that there should be no union of any kind just as the Congress puts forward the plea that the Muslim majority provinces should be forced into the union because of the Hindu minority verdict in these provinces? And it is quite obvious that the Muslim minorities in the Hindu provinces will be under the double yoke of Hindu raj both in Hindu majority provinces as well as in the centre under the proposed central government. Is the view or opinion of Muslim minority in the Hindu provinces to prevail? Is similarly the opinion of Hindu minorities in the Muslim provinces to prevail? In that case it will be the minority that will be dictating to the majority both in Hindustan and Pakistan which reduces the whole position to absurdity.[146]

Finally, if these assurances were not enough, Jinnah held out further hope for the Muslim minority in India by declaring that they could yet belong to Pakistan since they had the option of migrating to the new nation state. As he noted soon after the Lahore resolution, 'exchange of population, on the physical division of India as far as practicable would have to be considered.'[147] It was a theme that he repeated over the next few years. In a later interview, he spelled

---

in 1993, I took him out to lunch on one of his visits to Delhi and we talked the usual stuff for a couple of hours. He came back with me to my office (at *India Today*) for some more gossip and as we were climbing the narrow Connaught Place steps to the second floor, he asked me what would be the problem if a plebiscite was held and the Kashmiris opted for Pakistan. I said it would be a mortal blow to the secular nationalism we were building as, thereon, all other Muslims will be seen as suspect and may even be victimized. His jaw tightened, he made a mock gesture to roll up his sleeve and said, 'if you victimize your Muslims, you think the fourteen crore Muslims of Pakistan will sit like cowards and do nothing? (His exact expression: *Hum 14 crore Pakistani Musalman bhi chudiyan pehen ke nahin baithe rahenge*).' See Shekhar Gupta, 'This Death in Pakistan', *Indian Express*, 8 January 2011.

145 Ibid., Vol. 2, 431, Interview to the Associated Press of America, 8 November 1945.

146 Ibid., Vol. 2, 435, Rejoinder to Vallabhbhai Patel's Statement, 18 November 1945.

147 Ibid., Vol. 1, 183, Statement on the Lahore Resolution, 1940.

out three courses available to the Muslim minorities in Hindu India. 'They may accept the citizenship in the state in which they are. They can remain there as foreigners; or they can come to Pakistan. I will welcome them. There is plenty of room. But it is for them to decide.[148] Jinnah, however, recognized the limits of such a scheme, which still entailed a substantial number of these Muslims being excluded from Pakistan. He, therefore, made it a point to repeatedly laud sacrifices made by the 'minority provinces' Muslims and their selfless support for Pakistan. As he declared in his Presidential Address to the annual session of the AIML held at Karachi in 1943

> Don't forget the minority provinces. It is they who have spread the light when there was darkness in the majority provinces. It is they who were the spearheads that the Congress wanted to crush with their overwhelming majority in the Muslim minority provinces, for your sake, for your benefit and for your advantage. But never mind, it is all in the role of a minority to suffer.[149]

If the creation of Pakistan was to provide the 'authoritative sanction' for the fulfillment of Muslim minority rights in Hindu India, Pakistan needed to be a viable and powerful entity. Jinnah in the months subsequent to the Lahore Resolution squarely addressed questions regarding Pakistan's feasibility in terms of its defense capabilities as well as economic sustainability echoing the arguments adduced by ML propaganda. He first repudiated the charge that creating Pakistan would lead to a worsening security environment in the subcontinent, declaring that on the contrary it would improve the situation in the subcontinent as Hindus and Muslims would settle down in their respective national states. He also rejected the argument that if Pakistan were to become a separate sovereign state it would soon overrun all of India. He found it ridiculous that a country of 200 million could fear being overrun by their neighbour with a population of 70 million.[150] Jinnah also tried to damp down on fears of a Pan-Islamic threat to Hindu India due to an alliance of Pakistan and Muslim states of the Middle East by rejecting the idea that Pakistan would harbour such extraterritorial affinities. As he declared:

> Surely when we have constituted our national homelands and developed our territorial sovereign government it is unthinkable that we shall not guard

[148] Ibid., Vol. 2, 383–84, Interview with Daniel Edwards, BBC New Delhi, 3 April 1946.

[149] Pirzada, *Foundations of Pakistan*, Vol. 2, 407.

[150] *Speeches and Writings of Mr. Jinnah*, Vol. 1, 257; *The Leader*, 3 March 1941 reported the figures as 250 million and 90 million for Hindus and Muslims respectively.

> our frontiers just as in the Middle East exist territorial Muslim states side by side.[151]

Getting into specifics, Jinnah further pointed out that more than Hindu India it was Pakistan which would be in greater danger of being invaded since it was located at the frontiers in the northwest and the northeast.[152] Hindu concern was, therefore, not justified. Additionally, he asserted that land frontiers had ceased to be of importance in the modern world since history had shown that later invasions of India by the Portuguese, the French and even the English were not from the northwest but from the sea. Hindu obsession with land frontiers was therefore unnecessary. Additionally, Jinnah indicated that modern warfare was about acquiring supremacy in the air and that land and sea powers would become increasingly secondary.[153] He also expressed hope that once the Hindus and Muslims had resolved their differences a Monroe doctrine could be laid down for India as a whole.[154] The Hindus could guard the coastline in the south and the west while Muslims could guard land frontiers.[155]

Jinnah was also confident that though Pakistan would be divided into two wings, it would be capable of defending its territorial sovereignty. Drawing a parallel, he noted that Britain had been a strong power even though its Empire was scattered all over the globe. Pakistan, by contrast, had the added advantage of being 'more closely knitted than the British Commonwealth of Nations'. He therefore noted that

> when you travel from Britain to other parts of the British commonwealth you pass through *foreign territory* – the Suez canal for instance. It is all done by amicable arrangement. We travel from the Muslim areas of the north-east to the Muslim areas of the northwest across this so-called Hindu corridor without any difficulty today. Why should that arrangement not continue? The Hindus must not be allowed to put difficulties in the way of a state that wants to be their neighbor in a friendly way. They must not be allowed to close the doors of communication between the Muslims of the northwest India and the Muslims of the north east. This must be one of the terms of

151 *The Leader*, 26 May 1940; *Speeches and Writings of Mr. Jinnah*, Vol. 1, 190.

152 *Star of India*, 12 March, 1941.

153 *The Leader*, 14 March 1941; *Speeches and Writings of Mr. Jinnah*, Vol. 1, 266.

154 *Star of India*, 11 January 1941.

155 *The Leader*, 14 March 1941. Jinnah in an earlier interview on 2 January 1941 to Professor Radhakumud Mukherjee of Lucknow University reiterated the same point. See *Speeches and Writings of Mr. Jinnah*, Vol. 1, 241.

the *treaty*.[156]

In any case, Jinnah reminded his audience that 55 per cent of the Indian army came from the Punjab and most of these soldiers again were Muslims.[157] He, therefore, concluded that Pakistan would defend itself 'like any other sovereign state'. If it could not defend itself, nobody else would be able to defend it. In a later interview though, he expanded further, holding out other possibilities.

> Naturally no nation stands by itself. There will be other nations whose interests will be common with those of Pakistan. On being asked what nations? Jinnah smiled as he replied: I will tell you when I get the government in my charge.[158]

This remark brings us to Jinnah's other view regarding Pan-Islamism. While he tried to allay Hindu concerns regarding the threat of Pan-Islamism, he also saw Pan-Islamic unity undergirded by Pakistan as the only way to balance the power of Hindu India. As noted earlier, during his visit to Egypt in 1946, he raised the prospect of a rampaging Hindu imperialism threatening the sovereignty of the Islamic world if Pakistan was not allowed to come into existence. The journalist Ziauddin Ahmad Suleri, who was covering Jinnah's visit to Punjab in 1942 for the *Dawn* reminisced about a particularly interesting episode in this regard. At Lahore, Jinnah was given a tea party at which it was suggested that he should visit Iqbal's grave. As Suleri writes

> Half an hour later, five people quietly got out of two cars and stood by the grave of the great poet, thinker sage and philosopher of Islam. It was dusk. There was chill in the air. Jinnah stood motionless and said his *fateha*. He was in a reflective mood and everyone held his breath. ... What was Jinnah thinking?... Then one of us mustered courage and addressed to Jinnah one of Iqbal's verses; and also said something about Islam and the world. Abruptly Jinnah halted and said: My friend, Pakistan holds the key to the liberation of the entire Islamic world. I had never seen in him such visible emotion. Jinnah has his dreams.[159]

Jinnah also expressed confidence in Pakistan's ability to sustain itself

---

156 Ibid., Vol. 2, 382–83, Interview to Daniel Edwards, BBC New Delhi, 3 April, 1946; also *The Pioneer*, 5 April 1946.

157 Ibid., 432, Interview to Associated Press of America, 8 November 1945.

158 Ibid., 384, Interview with Daniel Edwards BBC New Delhi, 3 April, 1946.

159 See Z. A. Suleri, *My Leader* (Lahore, 1982) (fourth edition), 179.

economically brushing aside arguments that questioned Pakistan's viability as Congress propaganda.[160] He pointed out that bulk of the revenue in India at present was siphoned off by the Centre. After Partition, sovereign Pakistan zones would gain that revenue. But 'if worse comes to the worse, like a sensible man we will cut our coat according to our cloth', he concluded.[161] The seriousness with which Jinnah approached this question can be discerned from the fact that he set up a Planning Committee comprising technical experts to ascertain Pakistan's economic feasibility. This committee was charged with surveying mineral and natural resources of Pakistan zones and creating a plan for the development of its economic and industrial life.[162] This followed the 1943 AIML Karachi session that asked this committee to prepare

> a comprehensive scheme for a five year programme for economic and social uplift; State industrialization in the Pakistan zones; the introduction of free primary basic education; reform of the land system; stabilization of rent; security of tenure; improvement in the condition of labour and agriculture and control of money-lending.[163]

Jinnah in his opening speech to the committee made clear his own view over the controversy regarding the viability of Pakistan. 'All I can say as a layman is that in my opinion Pakistan will not be bankrupt; it will be a powerful

---

160 While the British Government and Congress remained skeptical about the economic sustainability of Pakistan a report by the Sapru Committee noted that Pakistan would be economically viable. Jinnah expressed happiness that the theory of Pakistan being a bankrupt state had at last been exploded.

161 *Speeches and Writings of Mr. Jinnah*, Vol. 1, 256.

162 Ibid., Vol. 2, 69–70; See also the essay by Ian Talbot, 'Planning for Pakistan: The Planning Committee of the All India Muslim League, 1943-46', *Modern Asian Studies*, Vol. 28, No. 4 (1994), 875–89.

163 Z. H. Zaidi (ed.), *Qaid-i-Azam Mohammad Ali Jinnah Papers: The Quest for Political Settlement in India I October 1943-31 July 1944,* second series, Vol. X, Islamabad, 1993, 644. The idea of a planning committee though was first contemplated at the AIML's Madras session in 1941 where Jinnah proclaimed the need for a five year plan for Muslim social and economic development. The resolution at the 1943 Karachi session was moved by the UPML leader from Gorakhpur, Zahirul Hasnain Lari. The resolution noted that 'as the first step towards consolidating the strength of the Muslims in Pakistan areas and preparing them for the heavy and onerous responsibilities inherent in the status of an independent sovereign state, the AIML has succeeded in establishing its governments in all the Pakistan provinces.' Ibid., 646.

state-though it may not be as rich as Hindustan.'[164] A twenty three member committee was constituted by August 1944, comprising economists, engineers, businessmen, industrialists, administrators and some ML politicians.[165]

Following Jinnah's lead, Khaliquzzaman and Mahmudabad told British officials in private that they wanted Britain to provide 'brains and capital', so that 'Pakistan being poor and under-developed would be able to develop its natural resources.[166] Jinnah too expressed these views in private, specifically referring to the examples of USA and Turkey as having been 'developed industrially and otherwise by foreign capital'. As an American diplomat noted, it constituted 'a partial explanation of his resolute refusal to elaborate publicly the details of Pakistan, as to do so would immediately expose him to the charge from nationalist quarters that he contemplated the establishment of a Muslim state dominated by British capitalists on the borders of Hindu India.'[167] Jinnah's conviction on these matters was noted by the American Ambassador in Delhi, William Phillips, who wrote about a long meeting with Jinnah that stretched to over three hours and forty minutes. As Phillips noted, Jinnah 'insisted that Pakistan is in every way practicable and the only solution to the Indian problem'.[168] The journalist Frank Moraes records a similar experience when he met Jinnah in Bombay just before his departure for the ML's Nagpur meeting in December 1942.

> I ventured to ask him whether he really thought Pakistan was practicable. That set him going. Listening to him I thought how much he sounded

164 Ibid., 702–06.

165 Ibid., Jinnah made it clear to the committee that its 'ideal should not be capitalistic, but *Islamic* and the interests of the welfare of the people should be constantly kept in mind.' The planning committee developed differences at its fourth meeting held between 30 June–2 July 1945 over the draft report with one section seeking to prepare it for India as a whole and the other section wanting the report to focus on the Pakistan areas. The impasse was resolved with the report being divided into two parts with the first part 'dealing with general principles and broad outlines of policy to be pursued from the point of view of Muslims who are spread all over the country'. The second part was to 'deal more fully and directly with the problems of the Pakistan areas', once the necessary data was collected.

166 Hallett to Wavell, 9 October 1944, *L/PJ/5/276*, U.P. Governors Reports to the Viceroy.

167 Airgram from Merrell, American Mission New Delhi, to Secretary of State, Washington DC, 30 November 1943, 845.00/2177, Box 5075, *US State Department Papers*, National Archives and Research Administration (NARA), College Park, Md.

168 Telegram from Ambassador Phillips to Secretary of State, 7 April 1943, *U.S. State Department Papers*

> like a lawyer arguing to his brief. He marshaled his arguments in sequence, sometimes challengingly, sometimes persuasively: he was really bent on convincing me about Pakistan and the thought flattered me. He must have spoken uninterruptedly for about half an hour. At the end I said as quietly as I could that I was not convinced and that Pakistan could never materialize. His hackles rose. Well, he said abruptly, I have no more time. I have got to leave for Nagpur. Good night.'[169]

On such occasions, Jinnah usually accompanied Moraes to his car but this time he walked back to his writing table. As he was leaving, the veteran journalist wished Jinnah a happy birthday. While he waited for his car he felt Jinnah's hand on his shoulder. 'That was a nice thing to say', said Jinnah, referring to the birthday greeting. As Moraes writes, 'Who could help liking him?'[170] Jinnah also exhorted his fellow Muslims to set up commercial and industrial enterprises to uplift the community. As he sharply remarked, 'have the Muslims any ghost of a chance in Hindu corporations? They only look upon you for your votes. A Hindu wants to be your brother only in the ballot box.'[171]

In any case, Jinnah vehemently defended himself against charges that that he had not 'defined Pakistan with sufficient precision', that many details regarding defence, economics, minorities etc. had been left deliberately vague. Such criticism, he shot back

> is neither just nor intelligent, particularly if it is made by an Englishman with any knowledge of his own history. When Ireland was separated from Britain, the document embodying the terms of separation was approximately ten lines. Ten lines of print to settle a dispute of incredible complexity which had poisoned British politics for centuries! All the details were left to the future-and the future is often an admirable arbitrator. Well, I have already given the world a good deal more than 10 lines to indicate the principles and practice of Pakistan, but it is beyond the power of any man to provide, in advance, a blueprint in which every detail is settled.[172]

Jinnah's refusal to provide a detailed scheme of Pakistan led some contemporary observers to see Pakistan as 'a bargaining counter' and that he would settle for far

---

[169] Frank Moraes, *Witness to an Era* (New York, 1973), 97–98.

[170] Ibid., 98.

[171] *Deccan Times*, 12 November 1944.

[172] Z. H. Zaidi (ed.), *QA Papers*, Second Series, Vol. X (Islamabad, 1993), 128–31.

less than a separate sovereign Pakistan. Later commentators too have followed on this path and argued that the Pakistan demand was kept deliberately vague since it would afford Jinnah the maximum room for manoeuvre in his bargaining game with the Congress and the British Government. However, Jinnah himself publicly declared that 'it would be a great mistake to be carried away by the Congress propaganda that the Pakistan demand was put forward as a counter for bargaining.'[173] He reiterated it several times. Addressing a special session of the Punjab Muslim Students Federation, he noted that

> the vital contest in which the Muslims were engaged was not only for material gain but also for the very soul of the Muslim nation. It was a matter of life and death for the Muslims and not a counter for bargaining.[174]

Even as late as 1945 he told a public meeting that

> Opposition to Pakistan might be due to false notions or sentiments or because it was a new idea. Some said that it was a hoax and worse still that it was a bargaining counter because Mr Jinnah was an astute politician.... It was neither a hoax nor a slogan for bargaining.[175]

He, therefore, asked his followers not to be distracted by extraneous details that would make them lose sight of their single most important goal – the formation of sovereign Pakistan. Rest of the issues could be settled after this goal had been achieved. Jinnah's unequivocal stance on Pakistan's sovereignty is brought out in his exchange with the Mahatma in 1942. Gandhi, in response to a question as to whether he regarded the Andhra bid for separation from Madras province in the same light as Pakistan, declared that

> there can be no comparison between Pakistan and Andhra separation. The Andhra separation is a re-distribution on a linguistic basis. The Andhras do not claim to be a separate nation claiming nothing in common with the rest of India. Pakistan on the other hand is a demand for carving out of India a portion to be treated as a wholly independent state. Thus, there seems to be nothing in common between the two.[176]

Jinnah in response declared that Gandhi 'has himself put the Muslim demand

173 *The Leader*, 4 January 1941; *Star of India* 4 January 1941.

174 *The Leader*, 3 March 1941.

175 Jamiluddin Ahmad , (ed.), *Speeches and Writings of Mr. Jinnah*, Vol. 2, 354.

176 *Harijan*, 12 July 1942, *CWMG*, Vol. 83, 78.

in a nutshell.'[177] The *Qaid*, therefore, had no difficulty in dismissing the plural 'states' in the Lahore Resolution as a typographical error when the convention of ML legislators was held in 1946. Even during the 1945–46 elections, he clearly stated that

> Geographically, Pakistan will embrace all of NWFP, Baluchistan, Sind and Punjab provinces in northwestern India. On the eastern side would be the other portion of Pakistan comprised of Bengal and Assam.... [The provinces would] have all the autonomy that you will find in the constitutions of USA, Canada and Australia. But certain vital powers will remain vested in the central government such as the monetary system, national defence and other federal responsibilities.[178]

For Jinnah, Pakistan was also not a 'non-territorial conception of nationality' for he repeatedly emphasized its territoriality.[179] As he noted rather tersely

> what is the use of merely saying we are a nation? [A] Nation does not live in the air. It lives on land, it must govern land and it must have a territorial state and that is what you want to get.[180]

He was also not averse to pointing out where Pakistan existed. As he once noted sardonically, the League was fighting for its creation not in Bombay but in Punjab which was the keystone of Pakistan.[181] On another occasion Jinnah asked 'why don't you give me the desert land of Sind, only the wheat growing lands of the Punjab and only the fruit growing land of NWFP? [182] To

---

177 Ibid., 120; Gandhi responded to Jinnah's statement in turn noting that 'I have read with attention Quaid-e-Azam's reply to my article in *Harijan*. Pakistan,' according to him, 'in a nutshell,' "is a demand for carving out of India a portion to be wholly treated as an independent and sovereign State. This sovereign State can conceivably go to war against the one of which it was but yesterday a part. It can also equally conceivably make treaties with other States. All this can certainly be had, but surely not by the willing consent of the rest. But it seems he does not want it by consent. For he says: "Pakistan is an article of faith with Muslim India and we depend upon nobody except ourselves for the achievement of our goal." How is one to offer one's service in these circumstances?"

178 *Speeches and Writings of Mr. Jinnah*, Vol. 2, 429–31.

179 See David Gilmartin, 'Partition, Pakistan and South Asian History: In Search of a Narrative', *Journal of Asian Studies*, Vol. 57, No. 4 (November 1998), 1068–95.

180 *Speeches and Writings of Mr. Jinnah*, Vol. 1, 247.

181 Ibid., Vol. 2, 98, Speech at a public meeting in Lahore, 2 April 1944.

182 Ibid., Vol. 2, 99–100, Speech to students at Christian Forman College Lahore, 31 March 1944.

emphasize Pakistan's separate territorial entity, Jinnah repeatedly dismissed the idea that India constituted a geographical unity. India, he insisted, was divided and partitioned by nature and Muslim India and Hindu existed on the 'physical map of India'.[183] Besides, 'geography had been altered in the case of the Suez canal, the Panama canal, Spain, Portugal, Sweden, Norway, Ulster in Eire and Sudan in Egypt' and there was no reason why the same could not be done in the case of British India.[184] There was thus no unified country that was being divided, no nation that was being denationalized for India was composed of different nationalities and the singular nation existed only in the imagination of Congress leaders who were 'recklessly indulging in such mental luxuries'.[185] It was only such critics, he derisively observed, who called Pakistan an impractical idea. Pakistan on the contrary, was indeed more practical than *Ram Raj* or *Swaraj* that Gandhi was advocating for India. Jinnah therefore had no trouble in dismissing Gandhi's warning about a civil war breaking out in India in the event of a Partition. He insisted that there would be no conflict unless the Congress and its peace loving Mahatma desired it.

Jinnah also quelled any talk of a loose federation or a confederation between Pakistan and Hindu India. As he noted, the question had been put forth by some constitutional pundits as to

> why there cannot be some sort of loose federation or confederation? People talk like that. I shall read out to you what I have written on this point, because it is important. There are people who talk of some sort of loose federation. There are people who talk of giving the widest freedom to the federating units and residuary powers resting with the units. But they forget the entire constitutional history of the various parts of the world. Federation in whatever terms it is described and in whatever terms it is put, must ultimately deprive the federating units of authority in all vital matters. The units despite themselves, would be compelled to grant more and more powers to the central authority, until in the end the strong central government will have been established by the units themselves – they will be driven to do so by absolute necessity, if the basis of federal government is accepted. Taking for instance the United States and her history, the Dominion of Canada and Australia, the Union of South Africa and Germany and of other lands where

183 Ibid., Vol. 1, 189, Message to the Bombay Presidency Muslim League Conference 26–27 May 1940.

184 Ibid., Vol. 2, 90, Speech at the concluding session of the Punjab Muslim Students Federation Conference, Lahore on 19 March 1944 in which Jinnah was responding to a speech by Lord Wavell that emphasized India's geographical unity.

185 Ibid., Vol.1, 190.

federal or confederal systems have been in existence, necessity has driven the component members and obliged them to increase and delegate their power and authority to the connecting link, namely the central government. These ideas are based entirely on a wrong footing... Therefore remove from your mind any idea of some form of such loose federation.[186]

The only solution to India's problem, he asserted, was 'to partition India so that both the communities could develop freely and fully according to their own genius.' Jinnah once described his proposal to partition India in terms of partitioning of a joint family even if he was to stay away from such metaphors later. As he remarked, even brothers found it impossible to live together beyond a point and that friendly relations were often restored between the two after partitioning.[187] He also never failed to point out that he was only demanding one-fourth of India for Muslims while Hindus could keep the remaining three-fourth and castigated the Congress for being miserly in its dealings with Muslims.

Gandhi-Jinnah Talks of September 1944 and Clarifications on Pakistan

The significance of ideas expressed by Ambedkar and Toosy can be discerned from their explicit invocation in the correspondence between Gandhi and Jinnah that paralleled their talks in September 1944 to end the communal deadlock in India. In his letter to Jinnah, dated 15 September, Gandhi expressed incredulity with the basic assumption of the two-nation theory. As he wrote

I find no parallel in history for a body of converts and their descendants claiming to be a nation apart from the parent stock. If India was one nation before the advent of Islam, it must remain one in spite of the change of faith of a very large number of her children.'[188]

Rejecting Gandhi's remarks, Jinnah in his letter dated 17 September curtly noted that

---

186 Presidential Address at the Karachi session of the ML in 1943, Pirzada, *Foundations of Pakistan*, Vol. 2, 426–27.

187 *The Leader*, 30 December 1940.

188 The Hindustan Times, *Gandhi-Jinnah Talks: Text of Correspondence and other Relevant Matter, July-October 1944, with a preface by Mr. C Rajagopalachari* (New Delhi, 1944), 12.

> there is a great deal of discussion and literature on this point which is available and it is for you to judge finally, when you have studied this question thoroughly, whether the Mussalmans and Hindus are not two separate nations in this sub-continent. For the moment I would refer you to two publications, although there are many more – Dr Ambedkar's book and MRT's Nationalism in Conflict in India.[189]

Ambedkar's book must have been readily available and the Mahatma probably read it furiously, for in his next letter dated 19 September, he wrote back that 'Dr Ambedkar's thesis, while it is ably written, has carried no conviction to me. The other book mentioned by you, I am sorry to say, I have not seen.'[190] The Toosy volume too was found and read by the Mahatma soon after, for in his subsequent letter dated 22 September, Gandhi flatly stated that 'the book recommended by you gives me no help. It contains half-truths and its conclusions are unwarranted.' He also added that while he could 'see somewhat clearly what you (Jinnah) are driving at, the more I think about the two-nation theory, the more alarming it appears to be'.[191]

A correspondence, initiated by Jinnah, followed involving clarifications and counter-clarifications, assertions and counter assertions, before talks finally collapsed on account of fundamental incongruence between the C. R. formula that Gandhi stuck to and the Lahore Resolution.[192] Jinnah meticulously

---

189 Ibid., 16.

190 Ibid., 18.

191 Ibid., 22.

192 *Jinnah-Gandhi Talks,* with a Foreword by Liaquat Ali Khan published by the Central Office of the All India Muslim League, (Delhi, 1944), 117–18. Basis for terms of settlement between the Indian National Congress and the All India Muslim League to which Gandhiji and Mr Jinnah agree and which they will endeavour respectively to get the Congress and the Muslim League to approve.

1) Subject to terms set out below as regards the Constitution for Free India, the Muslim League endorses the Indian demand for Independence and will cooperate with the Congress in the formation of a provisional interim government for the transitional period.
2) After the termination of the War, a commission shall be appointed for demarcating contiguous districts in the northwest and east of India, wherein Muslim population is in absolute majority. In the areas thus demarcated, a plebiscite of all inhabitants held on the basis of adult suffrage or other practicable franchise shall ultimately decide the issue of separation from Hindustan. If the majority decides in favour of forming a sovereign State separate from Hindustan, such decision shall be given effect to, without prejudice to the right of districts on the border to choose to join either State.

specified his objections to the formula. First, it meant 'immediate grant of independence to India as a single national unit' without conceding Pakistan, which was clearly unacceptable to the ML. Second, the proposal for provisional interim government was unacceptable. After all, it meant the establishment of a 'central Unitary or Federal government in charge of the entire civil administration with an overwhelming majority of Hindus in the legislature, which will not be less than 75%, to which the cabinet will be responsible.' Third, this national government dominated by the Congress would 'draft the treaty and agreements as regards the administration of matters of common interest… namely in matters such as foreign affairs, defence, internal communications, customs, commerce and the like', which Gandhi maintained 'must necessarily continue to be matters of common interest under an efficient and satisfactory administration of a Central authority or government.' An outraged Jinnah pointed out that this meant that 'all these vital matters which constitute the lifeblood of a State will remain vested in the National federal government proposed by him [Gandhi] to which finally full powers and responsibility for the Government of India will transferred.'[193] This amounted to nothing more than an offer of provincial autonomy to the ML and a complete negation of a sovereign independent Pakistan. As he noted, there were twenty five independent sovereign states in North and South America, which had treaties and agreements with regard to their mutual interests. Agreements and treaties were entered into even between countries that had no physical contiguity. 'Here the two nations are neighbors and have physical contiguity.'[194] Fourth, Jinnah pointed out that Gandhi wanted Pakistan areas to be demarcated district wise in which Muslims would be in an 'absolute majority' in Punjab, Bengal and Assam. This first meant that 'present boundaries of these provinces would be maimed and mutilated beyond redemption and leave us only with the husk and it is

---

3) It will be open to all parties to advocate their points of view before the plebiscite is held.
4) In the event of separation, mutual agreements shall be entered into for safeguarding defence and commerce and communications and for other essential purposes.
5) Any transfer of population shall only be on an absolutely voluntary basis.
6) These terms shall be binding only in case of transfer by Britain of full power and responsibility for the governance of India.

[193] *Jinnah-Gandhi Talks,* with a Foreword by Liaquat Ali Khan, published by the Central Office of the All India Muslim League (Delhi, 1944), 101.

[194] Ibid., 106.

opposed to the Lahore Resolution.'[195] The *Qaid*, therefore, made it amply clear that he wanted the division to happen on the basis of the existing boundaries of the six provinces of NWFP, Punjab, Sind, Baluchistan, Bengal and Assam. He could never agree to 'sheer vandalism' by a commission appointed by a central government dominated by the Congress. What was worse was that even in the 'mutilated areas', the right to self-determination would be exercised by all inhabitants of the area and not just the Muslims, in a 'promiscuous plebiscite'. The reasons why Jinnah may have been opposed to such a plebiscite were specified by the ML newspaper, *Eastern Times* of Lahore.

> A plebiscite in which all the inhabitants took part would open the gates wide for corruption. Money would flow freely; petty bodies of adventurers like the Ahrars and the Khaksars would be purchased with cash and Unionists of the types of Khizer Hayat and Leghari would be bought over otherwise and every effort would be made to disrupt the community and cheat it of its political goal.[196]

A later column added

> Also, in order that Hindu-Muslim relations be put on a stable basis, the demarcation of Pakistan areas will have to be done by agreement and not by a plebiscite. A plebiscite following a wearing a tearing campaign which Mr Rajagopalachariar's formula provides, will be anything but a true reflex of what the people really want; it will be anything but a true measure of their enlightened judgment. Nowhere in the world and least of all in India is the average adult politically enlightened to give a rational opinion as to what is really good for the country on a long or short view. The average voter casts his vote as his leader bids him to. Why not then let the leaders sit together and come to an agreement between themselves instead of raising communal passions to fever heat by virulent communal propaganda campaign? Plebiscite will not decide the issue on the basis of justice or fairness. It will at best be a trial of the propaganda skill of the two communities and the amounts of money they can scatter. Left to themselves, the Sikhs would vote for Pakistan. In Akhand Hindustan they would be nobodies. They will count after depressed classes and Christians while in Pakistan they will be the second largest minority. But exposed to a plebiscite they will likely vote against Pakistan.[197]

Finally Jinnah pointed out that Gandhi's condition of 'absolute majority' was not just unreasonable but extravagant. It meant that 'only that district will

---

[195] Ibid., 77, Jinnah to Gandhi 25 September 1944.

[196] *Eastern Times*, 12 July 1944, in Ahmad Saeed, (ed.), *Eastern Times on Quaid-i-Azam* (Islamabad, 1983), 139.

[197] Ibid., *Eastern Times*, 6 August 1944, 159.

be recognized (as falling in Pakistan) in which the Muslims have something like 75% of the population'. Jinnah stated that he had looked up the dictionary meaning of 'absolute majority' and it meant 'a majority of all members of a body (including those voting and not voting)'.[198] He, therefore, concluded that the C. R. formula was 'a veritable trap and a slough of death' that would lead to 'the burial of Pakistan'.[199] In private, Jinnah told the American Consul in Bombay that the 'negotiations broke down over the question of interim government and plebiscites.'[200] He did not make any mention of 'moth eaten' Pakistan that he had raised in public. Jinnah perhaps may well have been amenable to partitioning Punjab and Bengal if matters were decided across the table without a messy plebiscite ratcheting up tensions and Pakistan was granted full sovereignty rather than being controlled by a Hindu-dominated centre. These ultimately were accepted under the 3 June Plan in 1947.

Gandhi and Rajagopalachari's objections to the Lahore Resolution were equally clear. Gandhi declared that if it 'means utterly independent sovereignty so that there is to be nothing in common between the two, I hold it is an impossible proposition. That means war to the knife. It is not a proposition that resolves itself into a voluntary or friendly solution.'[201] He was clear that interests such as defence, foreign affairs etc. needed to be commonly safeguarded. Jinnah's rejection of a plebiscite involving participation by all inhabitants was unacceptable. As Rajagopalachari succinctly noted

> the wishes of the people of these two zones in the north-west and the east must be ascertained. The minority communities in those areas must be allowed to participate in the plebiscite inasmuch as it would be a most unpromising start for a new State claiming to be constituted for the progress of liberty, to keep large bodies of people away from the ballot box on the score of their religion or other grounds.[202]

In addition, trying to solve the problem 'by mere agreement and bargain, would be to try to treat citizenship as mere property that belongs to political organizations.'[203]

---

198 *Jinnah-Gandhi Talks, With a Foreword by Liaquat Ali Khan*, 102.

199 Ibid., 103.

200 845.00/10-744, Howard Donovan, American Consul, Bombay to Secretary of State, Washington DC, 7 October 1944, Box 5076, *US State Department Papers*.

201 *The Hindustan Times, Gandhi-Jinnah Talks*, 45.

202 Preface to *The Hindustan Times, Gandhi-Jinnah Talks*, iv–v.

203 *Hindustan Times*, 7 October 1944.

Though embittered by the failure of these talks Rajaji still saw some positives emerging from the process.[204] In conversation with an American diplomat, the cerebral Madras Congressman observed that Jinnah had been forced for the first time to precisely state the territories he was claiming for Pakistan. His claim for the inclusion of all of Punjab, Bengal and Assam despite an absolute Hindu majority in Assam and significant non-Muslim areas in Punjab and Bengal and that too without a plebiscite, was now visible to all as an extreme demand. Rajaji felt that Jinnah's failure to compromise would diminish his support among those of his followers who would have been willing to settle for far less. He therefore prophesized, rather prematurely, that the Pakistan idea had been 'killed historically' by Jinnah's 'political ineptitude' and that there would be no more Congress-League negotiations on Pakistan.[205] On the other side, Liaquat, who wrote the preface to the ML edition of the Jinnah-Gandhi correspondence, too saw some positives, though for different reasons. Above all he expressed satisfaction that 'the exchange of ideas and explanations were put in black and white' thus providing 'an education to the public'.[206] Liaquat concluded with the hope that 'Mussalmans of light and leading will find this book a valuable work of reference and will explain to their followers the meaning of the differences that came to the surface.'[207]

Ambedkar's Concluding Remarks

But the last word here needs to be given to Ambedkar. Before the Gandhi-Jinnah meeting, the constitutional lawyer had called on the British Parliament to pass an Act 'providing for a referendum among Muslims in Pakistan areas to determine whether they wanted a severance from the rest of India'.[208] Simultaneously, non-Muslims in the Pakistan could participate in a referendum to determine whether

204 The C. R. formula was, however, a move by Rajagopalachari to torpedo Pakistan. As a DIB Report noted, Rajaji maintained that 'the implied concession of the principle of Pakistan is not really as dangerous as it appears on surface: by accepting a "valueless gift" Jinnah may delude himself for a time that he has won, but he will soon find out that he has actually lost.' L/PJ/12/484 *Weekly Report of the DIB Home Department, Government of India, New Delhi, 4 April 1942* , OIOC, British Library, London.

205 845.00/9-2844, Incoming Telegram from Bombay, 28 September 1944, 845.00/9-2844, *US State Department Papers.*

206 *Jinnah-Gandhi Talks, With a Foreword by Liaquat Ali Khan*, 12.

207 Ibid., 19

208 *The Times*, London, 13 May 1943.

they preferred Pakistan or wanted to remain in Hindustan. If a majority decided to not remain in Pakistan, a Boundary Commission could be set up to delineate the *districts* in which the Muslims had a majority. When the Gandhi-Jinnah talks failed, Ambedkar re-invoked the phrases that he had used so brilliantly in his preface, to observe that Gandhi and Jinnah 'did not meet each other with empty minds, but it is equally true that neither had an open mind.' He did not lose an opportunity to highlight the personal failings of the two protagonists, which he believed had a lot to do with the talks' failure. When Gandhi adopted Gujarati to communicate with Jinnah asking for an interview, Ambedkar claimed that he immediately suspected the outcome. After all by writing in Gujarati, the Mahatma in his own inimitable way was telling the *Qaid* that he was nothing more than a mere Lohana. Similarly, Jinnah knew that the C. R. formula was very different from the Lahore Resolution; he had publicly repudiated it and yet had decided to meet Gandhi. Ambedkar attributed it to Jinnah's vanity, which had been stroked on receiving Gandhi's communication.

But besides these personality issues, Ambedkar also saw fundamental faults with the C.R. formula that doomed the talks. To begin with, it invited Jinnah to enter into a bargain under which if the ML helped Congress in achieving independence, the latter would consider the former's proposal of Pakistan. Ambedkar felt that the communal question could have been settled without making it contingent upon the attainment of independence. Secondly, he found fault with the C. R. formula's insistence on an interim government for giving effect to its provisions. The problem with this proposition was that 'by consenting to a provisional government, the Muslim League would have executed its promise to help the Congress win independence. But the Congress promise to bring about Pakistan would remain executory.'[209] Jinnah could not be expected to place himself in such a position and was therefore right in demanding that both promises remain concurrent. Another difficulty with an interim government was that after its creation as a sovereign entity, if it failed to give effect to the Hindu side of the agreement, there was no superior authority that could force it to honour commitments made to the Muslim League. The only way out for Muslims in such a situation would be an all out rebellion. The third major fault with the C. R. formula was its provision for a central authority to safeguard subjects of common interest such as defence, foreign affairs and the like. The problem with this provision was obvious since it negated a sovereign Pakistan.

[209] *Times of India*, 4 October 1944.

Ambedkar did not seem unduly bothered that the talks had failed in contrast to the general atmosphere of gloom in the country. He did regret though that some important questions still remained unanswered by Jinnah. Thus, if the Lahore Resolution contained the words 'subject to such territorial adjustments as may be necessary', Jinnah needed to publicly clarify what territorial adjustments he had in mind about which he was quite vocal in private. Again, what did the word, 'finally' which occurred in the last part of the Lahore Resolution mean? Did the ML contemplate a transition period during which Pakistan would not be a sovereign and independent state? And finally did Jinnah still want a corridor running through U.P. and Bihar that would connect eastern and western Pakistan? Ambedkar felt that unequivocal answers to these questions would have served a useful purpose of informing public opinion.

He concluded by declaring that both Gandhi and Jinnah were making a serious mistake by proceeding on the assumption that Hindus and Muslims were the only two parties in the dispute. Just as Jinnah had once reminded Nehru about the existence of a third party in India, this other constitutional lawyer from Bombay reminded the two leaders that the Scheduled Castes were a third party in the current dispute. Neither Gandhi nor the Hindu Mahasabha was entitled to speak on their behalf nor could Mr Jinnah be 'allowed to walk away with so large a population of the Scheduled Castes without their consent.' Ambedkar therefore insisted that

> the Scheduled Castes could not be allowed to be included in Pakistan without their express consent either in the western zone or in the eastern zone, that consent being given expressly and in the most positive terms such as a free referendum of their own![210]

The 1945 edition of Ambedkar's treatise provides us with another window to understand his evolving position on Pakistan. After all, he added an entire new section to make his position much more explicit in response to criticism that he had not been entirely forthcoming on the matter.[211] It must be noted that in this new edition, Ambedkar agreed with the Congress claim that India was indeed a single geographical unit. He argued that there was no reason why Hindus and Muslims could not live together in a single nation-state just as the French and English coexisted in Canada or the English and Dutch in South Africa, or the many nationalities in Switzerland. He also expressed skepticism about Hindu Raj emerging in India given the solid constitutional safeguards

---

210 *Times of India*, 4 October 1944.

211 See Part V. B. R. Ambedkar, *Pakistan or the Partition of India* (Bombay, 1945), 343–414.

enjoyed by Muslims. As an instance he pointed out that nowhere else in the world did minorities enjoy weightage as did the Muslims in India. Moreover, he squarely blamed the Muslims for the rise of Hindu communalism in India. As the learned doctor asserted, the 'Hindu Mahasabha and Hindu Raj are inescapable nemesis which the Muslims have brought upon themselves by having a Muslim League. It is action and counter action. One gives rise to the other.' More importantly, he declared that not Partition but abolition of the Muslim League and formation of a mixed parties including Hindus, Muslims and other communities was the only way to 'bury the ghost of Hindu Raj'.[212] Significantly, he added that if such parties based on 'an agreed program of social and economic regeneration' were to emerge, he prophesized that

> the many lower orders of Hindu society whose economic, political and social needs are the same as the majority of the Muslims... would be far more ready to make a common cause with the Muslims than with the high caste Hindus who have denied and deprived them of ordinary human rights for centuries.[213]

Moreover, Jinnah could lead such a party of likeminded Hindus and Muslims. Ambedkar ended his argument by stating that Pakistan was 'unnecessary' for the majority provinces Muslims since they had no fear of Hindu Raj and 'worse than useless' for the minority provinces Muslims given the obvious dangers to which Pakistan would expose them. These statements astonishingly, were much in line with the views of Congressmen and critics of Pakistan within the Muslim community.

While Ambedkar may have made clear his view that partitioning India was unnecessary, he reiterated arguments he made at the very outset when he first wrote his treatise in 1940. 'If the Musalmans are bent on having Pakistan then it must be conceded to them.'[214] He claimed that he arrived at this conclusion not because of the strength or weakness of the logic of Pakistan; indeed, the Muslim case for Pakistan suffered from significant weaknesses. He repeated the two factors that determined his outlook. First was his concern for India's defence for he believed that it could be secured only if it had an army that was non-political and was unaffected by the 'poison of Pakistan'. A political army posed the greatest danger to India's liberty and was indeed 'worse than having

[212] Ibid., 355.

[213] Ibid., 356.

[214] Ibid., 360.

no army'. After all, besides being responsible for defending the borders, the army was also the last resort for maintaining internal security in the country. If the government outlined a policy that ran into significant Muslim opposition, could it 'rely on the army to obey its orders and shoot down the Muslim rebels?' Ambedkar concluded that 'if the Muslims in the army had caught the infection of the two nation theory, India could not have a safe and secure government.'[215]

The second factor that Ambedkar considered important was that Muslim sentiment regarding Pakistan remained very high. The Hindus could at best plead with the Muslims to drop their demands and co-exist with them in an undivided India. Muslims would surely refuse if they were issued an ordinance to this effect. In this regard, Ambedkar asked Hindus to consider whether they were willing to extract Muslim obedience by employing bayonets. This was going to be futile and the Hindus needed to keep in mind that force was the 'medicine of the body politic' to be administered when it became sick and not to be 'used as daily bread.'[216] India could not carry on with Hindus and Muslims scheming against one another seeking to conquer each other. If Muslim sentiment remained high behind Pakistan he was all for a Partition so that the defence of both could be secured.

Ambedkar acknowledged that his fears regarding loyalty of Muslims in the army were perhaps exaggerated and even 'imaginary'. But he defended his own alarmist tendency on the matter. As he wrote

> I may be wrong. But I certainly can say without any fear of contradiction that, to use the words of Burke, it is better to be ruined by too confident a sense of security. I don't want to leave things to chance. To leave so important an issue as the defence of India to chance is to be guilty of the grossest crime.[217]

He again reiterated his belief in partitioning provinces of Punjab and Bengal through the method of self-determination by people and transfer of populations in order to resolve the issue of minorities. Here, rather than simply downplaying the numbers that would be involved, he now claimed that '*there will be no question of transfer of population so far as the population of these two provinces are concerned.*'[218] The reason behind this new formulation was Ambedkar's belief that men loved property more than liberty and would 'prefer to endure tyranny at the hands of their political masters than change

[215] Ibid., 361.
[216] Ibid., 363.
[217] Ibid., 364.
[218] Ibid., 378.

the habitat in which they were rooted'. He quoted Adam Smith in this regard that of all the things, 'man was the most difficult cargo to transport.'[219] In the second place, he noted that Muslims in India did not want to be transferred to Pakistan and neither did the ML want their transfer. Likewise, Hindus in NWFP, Baluchistan and Sind did not want to migrate. In this scenario, the 'transfer of population would not even be a problem.' In any case he reiterated that the scheme of transfer of population had been successful between Greece and Turkey as well as Greece and Bulgaria and there was no reason it would not be successful in India provided it was made voluntary.

While the question of whether or not Ambedkar's views on Partition and Pakistan had truly evolved between 1940 and 1945 is debatable, there was no ambiguity in his views after the event. As he bluntly noted ten years later

> I was glad that India was separated from Pakistan. I was the philosopher, so to say, of Pakistan. I advocated partition because I felt that it was only by partition that Hindus would not only be independent but free. If India and Pakistan had remained united in one State Hindus though independent would have been at the mercy of the Muslims. A merely independent India would not have been a free India from the point of view of the Hindus. It would have been a Government of one country by two nations and of these two the Muslims without question would have been the ruling race notwithstanding Hindu Mahasabha and Jana Sangh. When the partition took place I felt that God was willing to lift his curse and let India be one, great and prosperous.[220]

An analysis of the public debates on Pakistan makes it clear that one needs to look beyond secret strategies and political machinations of elites if one wishes to understand how the idea of Pakistan was understood, discussed and assumed shape in the public eye and why it began to attract either popular support or opposition. Deducing Pakistan's popularity merely to its putative potency as an affective religious symbol does injustice to the richness and intricacies of such public debates. These discussions were simultaneously accompanied by similar debates in the world of Urdu letters as evident from the searing critiques levelled against Pakistan by the Deobandi *ulama* belonging to the JUH. But before one gets to those critiques one needs to pay attention to how the idea of Pakistan was articulated in U.P. by the leadership of the UPML as well as local level leaders in the towns and *qasbahs* of the province.

---

219 Ibid., 382.

220 B. R. Ambedkar, *Thoughts on Linguistic States* (Delhi, 1955), 16.

4

Muslim League and the Idea of Pakistan in the United Provinces

Support for Pakistan is strongest in the provinces with Muslim minorities where the Congress was in power and weakest in the Punjab and Bengal where there are Moslem majorities.

New York Times, 8 September 1942

Pakistan is the birthright of the Muslims.

Chaudhary Khaliquzzaman[1]

Jinnah may have complained that the word Pakistan was nowhere mentioned in the Lahore Resolution and actually had been fathered by the Hindus and subsequently thrust upon the Muslims. Yet, even before the Lahore session had begun, there was anticipation about it in Bareily district in western U.P. as evident from a treatise published here in late February 1940, succinctly titled 'Pakistan'. Authored by one Anis al Din Ahmad Rizvi, it presented a cogent case for creating Pakistan besides outlining the expectations harboured by Muslims in western U.P. about this 'ideal goal'.[2] A map of the Indian subcontinent with Pakistan areas clearly marked out stood right behind the title page of the treatise. One does not have much information about Anis al Din himself except that he had earned a Bachelor's degree in law (LLB) as well as an M.A. (Honours) from the Muslim University at Aligarh. From his surname, Rizvi, one can infer that he was most likely a Shia, while from his Aligarh education one may further deduce that he perhaps came from a respectable family with at least a modest amount of landholding and could be counted as part of the *ashraf* elite in Muslim north India. While one may not know much more about Anis al Din, what his treatise unmistakably indicates is that Pakistan had become an object of much critical discussion in the Urdu public sphere, a world of letters based on a robust print culture involving circulation and contestation of ideas that was inhabited by a large pool of readers across northern India.

In his dedication, Anis al Din credited the idea of Pakistan to the poet

1 *Star of India*, 16 March 1942. Speech at Ahmedabad.

2 Anis al Din Ahmad Rizvi, *Pakistan* (Bareily, 1940).

Muhammad Iqbal, who at the 1930 Allahabad ML session had floated the idea of establishing a Muslim state in the northwestern Muslim majority provinces of British India. While Iqbal may have visualized this state within the confines of an all India federation and even disavowed Pakistan in a subsequent communication to the British historian Edward Thompson, Anis al Din clearly interpreted it as a separate independent state (*alahida azad hukumat*). The young man from Bareily marvelled at the power of Iqbal's idea for it had given rise to nine schemes authored by various individuals that spelt out how Pakistan could become a reality. He, however, made it clear that since the ML's sub-committee was currently scrutinizing these schemes to come up with the best possible proposal to submit to the British Government, he had no desire to add another one to the mix. Nevertheless, he justified his treatise on Pakistan claiming that he had written it to primarily argue why Partition (*taqsim*) was so necessary to establish peace in the subcontinent and also explain how any proposal that did not support the Partition was anti-Muslim and against Allah. As he insisted at the very outset, Hindustan was neither one country (*mulk*) nor its inhabitants, one single nation (*qaum*). One of the most noticeable features of the text is therefore the constant use of the term *Barr-i-Azam* (continent) to describe India. While he could at times still relapse into using the term *mulk*, the emphasis throughout the text is to foreground India as a continent or a subcontinent (*chhota sa barr-i-azam*) with a number of nationalities residing in it.

Anis Al Din's treatise is spread over six chronological chapters following the Introduction. The first two chapters set up the historical background for the steadily deteriorating relationship between the Hindus and Muslims from 1857 to the present. They go over familiar themes beginning with British fears about Muslim plots to oust them from India, consequent government policies favouring Hindus in education and jobs, Hindu contentment with their role as indigenous collaborators of the British and the rise of the Congress as a Hindu organization. The next set of themes include Congress hostility to the Partition of Bengal in 1905 since it was favourable to Muslims, ephemeral Hindu–Muslim unity that developed during Non-Cooperation/Khilafat Movement and its collapse accompanied by Hindu–Muslim riots across India. Finally, the text dwells on Congress schemes for fashioning Hindu Raj in India through the Nehru Report, Civil Disobedience Movement of 1930–32, which it claimed was an indignant Congress reaction to Muslim rejection of the Nehru Report, concluding with an account of atrocities committed against Muslims under Hindu Congress governments between 1937 and 1939. Such surveys were quite commonplace in Muslim political discourse in India by this point in time. It is however the latter four chapters of the treatise that are of interest to one for they build a case for creating Pakistan as an independent Islamic state under the rule of God (*khuda ki badshahat*). In the process, they make clear the impossibility of a composite nationalism/common nationality (*Muttahida Qaumiyat*) in India due to fundamental philosophical differences between Hindus and Muslims, emphasize the necessity for partitioning the subcontinent and suggest the method by which it could be realized.

At the outset, Anis al Din peremptorily dismissed Muslim demands for a fixed number of seats in the councils, a proportion of jobs in government services, or adequate safeguards in the constitution guaranteeing their religious, cultural, social and economic rights. He insisted that this was an extremely limited and egregiously flawed perspective on the question of Muslim liberation and warned that until Muslims saw their goal in such starkly wrong terms they would continue to suffer. For Anis al Din the only correct goal that Muslims should aspire for was the creation of Pakistan as an Islamic state (*Islami Nizam yani khilafat-i-ilahi*), for only in such a state could they truly achieve liberation. He justified this goal by arguing that it was a central tenet of Islam, a necessary and distinguishing feature of the faith that set it apart from other religions and indeed made it superior to them. Highlighting the state's centrality in Islam, he reminded his readers of the context in which Islam emerged as a beacon light for mankind. It was a time when God's message sent through the ages through different prophets had become neglected and religion was reduced to a few external rituals (*zahiri rasoom*) and forms of worship (*ibadat*). Man's life had become divided into separate spheres of religious life (*mazhabi zindagi*) and worldly life (*duniyavi zindagi*) causing a rapid decline in the human condition. Anis al Din pointed out that it is in this context that Islam came into this world as a complete religion (*takmil din*), to not just provide human beings with the right creed but to also end the distinction between religious and secular worlds (*din aur duniya*). Islam was thus a total way of life (*mukammal nizam-i-zindagi*), containing principles encompassing all aspects of religious and secular life, providing answers to all of mankind's problems from birth to death – whether they related to the state, family, social life, property and the relations between states among other things.

Given Islam's superiority over other religions and the state's centrality in achieving the perfection of its message in this world, Anis al Din distinguished the Islamic state from humanly inspired forms of government. Non-Islamic forms of government were of three types. First was the government by an individual (*shaksi hukumat*) or kingship that was based on the institution of the family in which an individual held power whose command was law. He quickly dismissed this form of government by reminding his readers of how in the past, some kings like Nimrod had the temerity to claim divinity even though they were mere fallible mortals. The second was government by democratic majority (*jamhooriyat*) and entailed powers earlier vested in the king being vested in the nation (*qaum*). Anis al Din did not repudiate this system right away for he acknowledged that it worked well in places where populations were homogenous or had arrived at an ideological consensus. But in a country where people belonged to different religions, he contended that it no longer remained a democratic system but a government by the majority. This majority could be oppressive over its minorities as was the case of the 'Hindu' Congress government in U.P. that had oppressed Muslims over the past two years. It was an example that would certainly have evoked strong emotions among his readers. Finally, the third form of human government he presented was dictatorship (*Amiriyat*), in which one individual was elected by the nation as its ruler. While considering dictatorship, Anis al Din most likely had in mind Hitler, who came to power through the electoral method but exercised supreme power in Germany. He carefully noted that the Dictator was different from a king since he was elected and had a fixed term in office and then proceeded to provide a critique of these human forms of government by contrasting them to the Islamic state.

Anis al Din declared that the Islamic state represented the Kingdom of God on earth (*khuda ki badshahat*) for the right to rule in this state belonged to no one except God. This state was not just a theoretical construct but had been practically implemented during the reign of the Prophet and rightly guided Caliphs (*Khulafa-i Rashidin*). Power in this form of government was wielded by one individual, the *Amir*, who was selected by the people. Yet, unlike in a dictatorship, this *Amir* was not above the law nor was he the source of laws. His distinguishing mark was that he was the most pious of all and kept God's commands sedulously, for such indeed had been the distinguishing mark of the first four Caliphs. Though an ardent supporter of the ML, Anis Al Din here echoed ideas articulated by Syed Abul Ala Mawdudi at the time. It is possible that Anis al Din may have heard or read Mawdudi's speech on the Islamic state that was delivered at the Muslim University in Aligarh in October 1939.[3] What therefore becomes clear is that that Pakistan was being sold in the localities of U.P. as an Islamic state.

3 See Syed Abul Ala Mawdudi, *The Islamic Conception of State* (Aligarh, 1940).

Anis al Din was in no doubt about Pakistan's historic significance since he saw it as instrumental in retrieving and restoring the Islamic state. He claimed that the Islamic state had disappeared once the Golden Age in Islam ended and was replaced by monarchical system of rule under Muslim kings. Its disappearance had been nothing short of a catastrophe since it had led to a marked deterioration in all aspects of Muslim collective existence. Anis al Din gave the example of *zakat*, pointing out that the institution had fallen into bad times since mechanisms for collection and proper expenditure of *zakat* money had been allowed to fall into disrepair. This decline had, in turn, led to deterioration in Muslim charitable institutions and degeneration in the education of ordinary Muslims who relied on such institutions. The lack of Islamic education, in turn, led to Muslim collective ways of life and habits becoming un-Islamic. In the final analysis, for Anis al Din, the decline of Muslims from their erstwhile greatness could ultimately be traced to the end of the Islamic state. He, therefore, reiterated that Indian Muslims could become totally free and reclaim their former greatness only when they had the power and choice to set up the Islamic state and live according to the teachings of the Quran. Muslims, therefore, could no longer be content simply with the rights to read *namaz*, keep *roza*, go on a Haj or give out *zakat*. These rights, he pointed out, were already available in all non-Islamic regimes as religious rights.

Anis al Din dismissed modern social and political models as remedies for the Muslim nation to regain its vitality (*hayat-i-millat*) and communal glory (*azmat-i-milli*), claiming that it did not need any other foundation (*tasis*), but *tajdid* (renewal) that would revitalize the fundamental principles of Islam. In order to substantiate his point, he made a brilliant manoeuvre by quoting the ML's *bête noire*, Maulana Abul Kalam Azad from his pan-Islamist days. He noted that Azad in this previous avatar had once declared that

> there cannot be a greater death for the followers of Islam but to believe that in a major part of their everyday life Islam is inadequate and helpless and becoming dejected they have to look into the stores of other communities. If such is the case it is better at the very outset to say farewell to Islam. What is the use of a religion which is useful merely for conducting marriage ceremonies or for reciting the *sura-i-yasin* on one's death bed? There can be no greater blot on Islam than Muslims taking lessons from others on national welfare or human liberation. The only way Muslims can revive themselves is by becoming Muslims and not by becoming Hindus or Christians. When

the lamp is burning brightly why would you need to go to the hut of an indigent *faqir* and look for his flickering lamp?[4]

If Anis al Din was all too brief about the contours of the Islamic state he wanted in Pakistan, he was more expansive while dismissing alternative models proposed by the Congress and its President Maulana Azad that were based on the principles of territorial nationalism (*wataniyat*) and composite nationality of all Indians. He summarily rejected territorial nationalism for having wreaked havoc in Europe through disastrous World Wars. More importantly, he noted that division of people according to this principle was incorrect from the Islamic point of view. God had made distinctions not on the basis of nationality, race, class or language but only on the basis of faith (*Iman*), between the *Momin* and the *Moshrek*. These were separate nations, one belonging to the party of God (*Hizbollah*) and the other to the party of Satan (*Hizb us Shaitan*). Anis al Din noted that under God's division (*khuda ki taqsim*) Abu Jahal and Abu Lahab were deemed *moshreks* even though they were Arabs while Bilal the Black African and Suleyman the Persian were considered *Momin* and thus a part of the Muslim community. Again, in the Quran, the Jews, Muslims and Christians had clearly been mentioned as separate nations (*aqvam*). Muslims, thus, did not have a nation that was based on race, geography, or territory and could be roused only by terms such as Islam and God in contrast to the Hindus and the Europeans who responded to the call of a *qaum* (nation) that inhabited a *watan* (homeland). Anis al Din sealed his argument on territorial nationalism by declaring that divisions on the basis of mountains or rivers were against God (*ghair Allah*) and Islam (*ghair Islami*) and could never override distinctions decreed by God. It is evident that Anis al Din did not see any contradiction between denouncing territorial nationalism and demanding Pakistan. For him the Muslim nation was primarily defined by its people and any territory that they occupied was incidental to that definition. Moreover, territorial divisions came in the way of the larger unity of the global Muslim community. To resolve this contradiction, Anis al Din invoked the project of Pan-Islamism in the context of a lengthy critique of the ideal of *Muttahida Qaumiyat* that envisaged a common nationality of all Indians.

At the outset, Anis al Din scathingly noted that this ideal was being proposed by a people who wrote scurrilous tracts like *Rangila Rasul* or played music before mosques. Obviously, the project had a dubious basis, but more importantly, he claimed that it made sense only from the Hindu point of view

4 Anis al Din Ahmad Rizvi, *Pakistan*, 94.

and was antagonistic to the fundamental principles of Islam. Elaborating this argument, Anis al Din pointed out that Hindus had no fixed doctrines and religion for them merely meant a set of some external rituals. Moreover, Hindu religion was ever changing, lacking any steadiness or continuity, for the Hinduism of Vedic times was different from that of the time of the Ramayana and Mahabharata and changed again in the face of the successes scored by Buddhism. Even today it lacked uniformity since Hindus were free to follow varying sets of rituals, Gods, faiths and ideas. *Muttahida Qaumiyat* too was part of such fickle Hindu thinking that he warned could change tomorrow for human thinking changed in numerous ways over time. Would Muslims in response to Hindu overtures, he rhetorically asked, break with saying their *namaz*? At the same time he pointed out that Islam in contrast to Hinduism was not an individual faith but an organized social system (*jamaati nizam*) with a set of core principles which could never be changed. Even Abul Kalam Azad, he again noted, had acknowledged that Islam was the final message sent by God to mankind providing best principles for every aspect of life. However much the world might change, one could test Islamic principles to realize that they did not need to be changed. Thus, while for Hindus, religious freedom meant freedom to perform their prayers in a temple, or taking out public processions for their Gods along with musical accompaniments, for Muslims, permission to say prayers in India (*Hindustan mein sajda ki ijazat*) was not tantamount to religious freedom. Religious freedom instead meant the power to organize collective life according to Islamic principles. Anis al Din asserted that such freedom would be impossible in an undivided India, all the more since it would be led by people like Nehru who, in his autobiography, had declared that it was his heart's desire to see the organized religions of the world fading away. If Muslims, therefore, desired to preserve their Islamic identity and wanted to raise their children according to religious beliefs, customs and traditions of their forebears, they would be foolish to expect it in an undivided India where the Wardha scheme of education would become the national system of education under the ideal of *Muttahida Qaumiyat*.

Turning to Pakistan's larger aims and significance, Anis al Din argued that since Muslims saw religion as the basis of their nation, they would desire its foreign policy to be oriented towards Pan-Islamism (*Ittehad bain al Muslimeen*). Their first priority would thus be to establish such an organic unity in the Islamic world that 'if a thorn lodged itself in the foot of a black African Muslim, the Chinese Muslim would instantly blink his eye.'[5] He pointed out that the

5 Ibid., 113.

policy of Indian Muslims in the past thirty five years had been to give as much help as they possibly could in their capacity as an enslaved nation to foreign Islamic governments whenever they faced difficulties. Thus, during the Balkan war a medical mission was sent to help the Turks while after the Great War, Indian Muslims again struggled mightily for the preservation of the Ottoman Caliphate. They had also sent a delegation to England, Egypt and Palestine to work for the liberation of Palestinian Arabs besides giving them material help. He maintained that since Indian Muslims had made great sacrifices for the sake of Pan-Islamism, they would continue to do so in the future as well.

Anis al Din added that Hindus resented this Pan-Islamism since they feared Indian Muslims were forging close collaborations with foreign Islamic governments to ultimately take over India and inaugurate an Islamic state. He did not explicitly repudiate this point, but claimed that it was for this very reason that Hindus wanted Dominion Status under the protection of the British bayonet. As a corollary he pointed out that Hindu foreign policy preferences were clearly indicative of their attempts to counter the Muslim threat. He drew attention to the Hindu Mahasabha, which had gone as far as to say that Palestine was the country of Jewish people that had forcibly been occupied by Arabs and that it was the British government's duty to return it to the Jews.[6] Even in the Congress foreign policy orientation, he saw a similar attempt to reinforce Hindu power in India by establishing close relationships with non-Muslim powers such as Burma, Siam, Anam, China, Japan and Nepal. He pointedly noted that on the Palestinian issue Nehru had contemptuously declared that the Congress could not be bothered by such small problems. And yet, when it came to the civil war in Spain or enmity between Japan and China, this Congress 'Foreign Minister' sent medical missions to Spain and China. Anis al Din, therefore, insisted that Indian Muslims needed a separate Pakistan since it would allow them to place all of its resources at the disposal of foreign Islamic governments without any hindrance if they were ever in need. Or else, as had been the case under the British, Indian Muslims would be hindered from helping the Turks or Palestinian Arabs. Any such hindrance in the future would simply nullify the Muslim idea of freedom.

Anis al Din further equated Nehru's advocacy of *Muttahida Qaumiyat* with its basis in the class conception of society, with an insidious Hindu attempt to insert Muslims into Hindu caste hierarchy. He claimed that the Hindu caste system dividing the country's inhabitants into four large and several small *jatis* had been predicated on professions right from the time of the

6 Ibid., 114.

Ramayana and Mahabharata. It was on this basis that Hindu society was able to historically absorb Shakas, Huns and other foreign invaders over the ages. The Hindus had similarly tried to absorb the Muslims when they first arrived but failed. And since their more recent *shuddhi* programme too had failed to slot Muslims into various professions in the Hindu caste hierarchy after suitably cleansing and 'purifying' them, Anis al Din concluded that Nehru through his economic programme was again trying to absorb them into the caste hierarchy by making Muslims give up their faith. Nehru's seemingly irreligious programme was thus a surreptitious attempt to smuggle Hinduism and caste hierarchy into Indian Islam through the backdoor, with the aim of eventually absorbing Muslims into Hinduism. He, therefore, warned his readers to oppose Nehru and his socialist attempts to rearrange society along class lines based on economic interests and professions, for its ultimate aim was to wipe out Islam in India.

Having made his case for creating a separate Islamic state for Indian Muslims, Anis al Din went on to define it in territorial terms. Here his conception coincided with that of the Aligarh Professors M. A. H. Qadri and Zafrul Hasan. He wanted Muslims to establish not one but three states in India. First, Pakistan in the northwest consisting of Punjab, Sind, Baluchistan, NWFP, Kashmir and more importantly, the commissionerates of Meerut and Rohilkhand besides Aligarh and Agra districts. Anis al Din made it absolutely clear too that if these areas were not included in Pakistan, it would simply not be acceptable to the U.P. Muslims. These areas were the very centres of Islamic culture and had been so for a very long time. Even today one could witness ancient Islamic ways of life being practiced here. Including them in Pakistan, he added, would bring further advantage of allowing Muslims from other U.P. districts to be absorbed into them through a transfer of population. Besides Pakistan in the northwest, Anis al Din visualized a second Muslim state in the east consisting of East Bengal and Assam. His third Islamic state was Hyderabad in the south, including Berar and those parts of Karnataka, which earlier belonged to the Nizam's state before being wrested by the British.

Anis al Din declared that it was not his intention to spend too much time going into minute details of territorial aspects of these states, since the more important matter was the overall goal of establishing these Islamic states in the subcontinent. But nonetheless he went on to justify his new scheme with the help of facts, figures and historical reasoning. He pointed out that Jammu and Kashmir was 85 per cent Muslim thus necessitating its inclusion in Pakistan. But there remained the tricky question of what to do with the Hindu Maharaja of

Kashmir. Anis al Din suggested that the Maharaja could be compensated with territories in southeastern Punjab which was a Hindu majority area, or even parts of Central Provinces (C.P.), which again had a Hindu majority. The separation of Hindu areas of Punjab from Pakistan and simultaneous inclusion of Kashmir in it would also happily raise Muslim proportion in Islamic Pakistan to 60 per cent of the overall population. In this context, he was optimistic that Muslims from eastern Punjab would slowly be absorbed into Pakistan while Hindus from western Punjab would be moved to Hindu India through a programme of population transfers. As for the Sikhs, he was confident that they would opt for Pakistan since their proportion in population would be greater in Pakistan than in Hindu India thus enabling them to claim a greater percentage of seats in legislatures, ministerships and jobs in the government.

Anis al Din noted that eastern Bengal and Assam forming a new Islamic state would have a 60 per cent Muslim majority as well. This state would be equal to France in size. But as regards Hyderabad, he was keenly aware of the fact that population figures would not back his reasoning for establishing it as the third Islamic state. He therefore invoked historical reasons in support of his claim, declaring that Hyderabad had been ruled for seven hundred years by Muslims since the time of Alauddin Khilji. More than Kashmir, Hyderabad was a legitimate sovereign state, since unlike the former, which had been purchased from the English by Maharaja Gulab Singh, the latter had been conquered by Muslims on the basis of their military strength and subsequently administered with benevolence and justice. More importantly, though its population was overwhelmingly non-Muslim, he claimed that its Muslim rulers had not been oppressive and had developed a wonderfully cordial relationship with their non-Muslim subjects. Anis al Din was understandably vague about Hyderabad's population figures but declared that through transfers of population it could be made a homeland for South Indian Muslims. Hyderabad would also be a viable state since it possessed adequate resources and access to the sea through ports in Karnataka. Anis al Din did not spend much time discussing political arrangements that Hindu India needed to have in place maintaining that it was up to the Hindus to decide. Finally, as far as princely states were concerned, he saw them joining either Hindu India or Pakistan within which they would continue to function as autonomous states. Their position would be thus similar to their position under British paramountcy since they would have full internal autonomy but would be under the jurisdiction of their respective governments on more important matters.

Anis al Din concluded his treatise by arguing that partitioning India into Hindu and Islamic states would be the best possible solution to India's current problems. Like his *Qaid*, he declared that India's unity was only apparent and not real, for its landmass had never been ruled in its entirety by more than four or five rulers in its 2500 year history. Its current unity had temporarily come into existence as a result of British rule. If Europe (excluding Russia), which had the same landmass as India, had about 25 sovereign states, he claimed that creating a few Islamic and Hindu states in India would certainly not be a tragedy. He also expressed optimism that these states would become powerful and prosperous given their abundant natural resources. Finally, on the question of relations between these states, Anis al Din did not want to leave any ambiguity. He made it clear that he wanted them to be sovereign and completely independent of each other without a supervening centre. He declared that examples of federal nation-states such as USA, Canada, or Australia were most inappropriate (*ghair munasib*) and inapplicable to the Indian context. By his insistence on sovereignty, he therefore differed from the Aligarh Professors Scheme, which had envisioned a small common central body that would act as a clearing house for matters of mutual interests or disputes between Hindu and Muslim states.

Anis al Din was mindful that the question of minorities would remain an outstanding issue and would not be resolved in spite of such a Partition. As he noted, in U.P., C.P., Madras and Bombay, Muslim population was small and defending their rights would be difficult if not impossible. He, therefore, asserted that it would be the duty of Islamic states to protect their rights by using all power at their disposal. This was a thinly veiled reference to the hostage population theory that had emerged as a principal plank in the defense of Pakistan. And here, as with many other commentators, he concluded that Hindu and Muslim states would have to act as guarantors for the security of their own people in each other's territories. But if such arrangements were not functional, he suggested a total transfer of populations, with Muslims from Hindu India being moved to any one of the three Islamic states. These notions of territorial states, populations transfers and hostage populations protecting minority populations seem to have seeped down to the grassroots in U.P. Their pervasive influence in U.P. is underlined by a contemporary account by P.W. Radice, a serving ICS officer. While visiting Muslim weavers at Tanda in Fyzabad district, Radice asked them as to what they hoped to gain from Pakistan. Their blunt reply was that 'if the Hindus annoyed them, their brethren in Pakistan would be able to take their revenge on the Hindus there.' 'A pleasant prospect', Radice exclaimed grimly.[7]

---

7 MSS/Eur/F180/80, *P.W Radice Papers*, OIOC, British Library, London.

After Lahore: the U.P. Muslim League, Initial Confusions and Reservations about Pakistan

The UPML was charged with the task of propagating Pakistan not only in U.P. but all over British India. This included other 'minority provinces' as well as the NWFP where the Congress was dominant, key Muslim majority provinces of Punjab and Bengal where Sikander Hayat Khan and Fazlul Haq were lukewarm to the idea and finally Sind where the Allah Bakhsh led ministry was hostile to Pakistan. But before the UPML leadership could embark on this road it was beset by initial confusion, reservations and lack of clarity regarding Pakistan. This first becomes evident from the speech delivered by Nawab Ismail Khan, the UPML President, at the annual UPML conference at Allahabad in December 1940. A senior member of the AIML Working Committee, Ismail Khan generally presided over its sessions during Jinnah's absence. In addition, he headed the All India Muslim League Civil Defence Committee that was set up to protect Muslim lives and property during the War's duration and the Committee of Action that was meant to energize and coordinate the work of all provincial, district and city units of the ML. In remarks aimed at addressing concerns of U.P. Hindus among whom the Lahore Resolution had caused a major furore, Ismail Khan explained that if the resolution were to be examined dispassionately, 'it would be found that all it did was to group the provinces in which Mussalmans were admittedly in a majority, in zones which would be sovereign.'[8] He assured them that these units would retain their existing character and there would no exchange of populations or migrations of people. As against these Muslim zones, there would be Hindu zones with fairly large Muslim populations but decisive Hindu majorities. Ismail Khan declared that Muslims of these minority provinces were quite reconciled to the idea of living under Hindu majorities. Getting to the heart of the matter, he acknowledged that Hindus were uneasy about the Lahore Resolution due to the inclusion of the term 'sovereign' in its text. He however, reassured them that there was nothing new in this idea, for Muslims had always demanded a 'federation of fully autonomous states' whenever the constitutional question had been debated in India as was the case during the Simon Commission proceedings or the Round Table Conferences. The Muslim demand for fully autonomous states, Ismail Khan noted, 'very nearly means the same thing as sovereignty.' He also put a positive spin on the Lahore Resolution stating that

---

8 *IAR* Vol. 2 (1940), 260.

> there is nothing in the Resolution to prevent these sovereign states from confederating with other sovereign states. If goodwill prevails and suspicions are dissipated, I have no doubt that some kind of confederation will come into being. Sovereign states in other countries have confederated before now. So there is nothing in the resolution which should cause disquiet to persons not obsessed by preconceived notions about the form of India's future constitution.[9]

Ismail Khan would however remain a skeptic at heart even if outwardly he dutifully plugged the ML's official position and vigorously supported Pakistan in public. An Office of Strategic Services (OSS) report based on interviews with leading ML figures noted that Ismail Khan was a moderate who believed that Hindus and Muslims could coexist side by side. It added that 'Ismail Khan would welcome a settlement with the Congress even at the cost of modifying the demand for Pakistan.'[10] This view is substantiated in the memoir of K. H. Khurshid, Jinnah's personal secretary between 1944 and 1947. It appears that the *Qaid* along with Liaquat, Begum Raana Liaquat and Qazi Isa once went to watch the Hollywood film *Random Harvest*, which is based on the protagonist losing his memory after being hit by a car. Turning to Begum Liaquat, Isa playfully wondered what would have happened if Jinnah as a result of an injury from the Khaksar stabbing incident lost his memory and at the subsequent Working Committee meeting said, 'What is this Pakistan? What is this Muslim League nonsense?' Speculating on the Working Committee members responses, he declared that Ismail Khan would have exclaimed 'Now the old man is talking sense'.[11] Nonetheless, Ismail Khan's position on Pakistan was determined by his attitude towards his *Qaid*. As Khurshid quotes him saying to Jinnah, 'You do not take us into confidence but we have acknowledged you as our leader and we shall follow you.'[12]

If Ismail Khan's views soon after the Lahore Resolution indicate that he envisaged a possible confederation between India and Pakistan after partition, the Raja of Mahmudabad was more preoccupied with issues pertaining to his troubled Shia community. Mahmudabad skipped the historic 1940 AIML Lahore session and his initial skepticism about Pakistan becomes evident

---

9 Ibid.

10 Office of Strategic Services, *The All India Muslim League Part 1: Organization, Leadership, Strength and Program, OIR Report No.4162.1,* 1 August 1946, 8.

11 K. H. Khurshid, *Memories of Jinnah*, edited by Khalid Hasan (Karachi, 1990), 61.

12 Ibid., 50.

from a letter written by his younger brother to Jinnah soon after, in which he sought clarifications regarding safeguards that Shias would be granted in the Muslim nation.[13] Expressing anguish at having to write such a letter, the *Maharajkumar* nonetheless wanted the question to be addressed given the poisonous relations between Shias and Sunnis in India, which he claimed were akin to those between Catholics and Protestants in early modern Europe. As the *Maharajkumar* warned, just as 'the mere difference of certain beliefs' between them had resulted in the Hundred Years War, 'similar consequences' between Shias and Sunnis would arise sooner or later in India 'if no effort was made to safeguard the fundamental rights of Shias to their satisfaction.' Lamenting that 'even today as we sit together and talk of unity among Muslim ranks, the flame of hatred is being kindled all over the place', he complained that Shia candidates found it extremely difficult to counter Sunni sectarian propaganda at the time of elections to legislative or local bodies. Even those among them who successfully entered legislatures did not feel free to express the 'true sentiments of the Shias for the fear of the electorate.'[14] In the social sphere too he alleged that Sunnis were actively trying to suppress Shia religious beliefs and deprive them of liberty to perform their religious duties. And since Shia-Sunni discord was not just restricted to some pockets in India but quite widespread, Mahmudabad demanded safeguards for Shias specifying:

1. That Shias will have a voice in the elected bodies and governmental institution (sic) and that in any matter which might affect the Shias justice and equity will be applied rather than rule of the majority.
2. That the liberty of religious observances and beliefs for the Shias shall be guaranteed against any infringement thereupon by any party.
3. That as a further safeguard, the governors of provinces and the Governor General of India shall be given special powers to exercise in favour of the Shias in case any injustice is done to them by any party.
4. That all Shia *waqfs* will be exclusively under the control of Shias.
5. If any law is passed in accordance with the Muslim Hanafi Law, the special principles of the Shia Shariat must also be taken into consideration.

He concluded that unless these principles were accepted, Shias could not

---

13 Mahmudabad to Jinnah, 29 March 1940, in Rizwan Ahmad (ed.) *Quaid-i-Azam Papers, 1940* (Karachi-Lahore, 1976), 98–102.

14 Ibid.

find a 'position of honour and security in the Muslim nation.'[15] The letter drew an irate response from a furious Jinnah. The *Qaid* stiffly noted that

> I am really sorry that your mind is still working in the direction which is not likely to benefit the Shias. I have spoken to the leaders and sponsors of the Shia conference and discussed matters with them. I have also discussed the question at great length with you. I do not think I can say anything more. I still hope that you and other prominent Shia leaders will see your way and persuade the Shias to come inside the League first and then press equity and justice (sic).[16]

Jinnah also confessed to being 'rather taken aback' at the demand for intervention by the Viceroy in case Shia interests were threatened. As he continued

> Don't you realize that the hand of the British government is disappearing rapidly? Did not the minorities have experience, during the last 2 1/2 years, of the exercise of the so-called special powers of the governors and of the Governor General and don't you realize that even according to the declaration of his Majesty's government, the termination of the British regime is implicit in it. You will forgive me if I do not see eye to eye with you. I once will appeal to you that you, at any rate, should not mix yourself up with the proposed conference. The proper policy for the Shias is to join the League wholeheartedly. The League is now able to enforce justice and fair play between Musalman and Musalman whatever be his sect or section. The one thing alone that matters is that we are all Musalmans.[17]

A petrified senior Mahmudabad immediately wired back to his 'dearest uncle' pleading

> I have been lately very ill-mentally. My brain works like a wireless in bad atmospherics. I cannot think and even if some idea comes, it is so distorted and mutilated that I cannot myself understand it. I will come to Bombay as soon as I feel a little better. God only knows what is happening to me.[18]

---

15 Ibid.

16 Ibid., Jinnah to Mahmudabad, 8 April 1940, 105–06.

17 Ibid.

18 Ibid., 107.

Jinnah's forceful response swiftly brought the Mahmudabads into line with the *Qaid's* beliefs. A week later while addressing the Shia Political Conference in Lucknow, the Raja declared that differences between Shias and Sunnis were not as pronounced as those between Muslims and other communities. He added that if eight crore Sunni Muslims could not protect Shia interests, nobody else could be relied on to safeguard their interests.[19]

The Raja of Mahmudabad and Pakistan as an Islamic state

In spite of Mahmudabad's absence from the Lahore Session and his initial reservations regarding the ML's new creed, Jinnah appointed him as Chairman of the Pakistan *wafd* (delegation) that was tasked with popularizing Pakistan among Muslims throughout British India. The appointment was indicative of Jinnah's fondness for his 'nephew' who he initially saw as his heir-apparent before finally nominating Liaquat following the Mahatma's anointment of Jawaharlal as his own successor. Jinnah threw a lavish party at his residence to welcome the Raja when he came to address the annual session of Bombay Provincial Muslim League in May 1940. As a contemporary recalled, Bombay was amazed that Jinnah of all the people had asked four hundred people to dinner, adding that even the sick and the elderly on the guest list dragged themselves to it not expecting to see another such party at Jinnah's residence in their lifetimes. The contemporary also noted that usually in Jinnah's house, 'food for each person was measured out and each person would be served with that amount. Nobody was ever asked to dine at the last moment.'[20] Again, at the AIML 1941 Madras session, it was Mahmudabad rather than Liaquat or Ismail Khan who was chosen to preside over meetings of the AIML Council and the Subjects Committee after Jinnah was taken ill.

The Raja's initial hiccups over Pakistan were soon replaced by a more focused message that he articulated during his address to the 1940 Bombay Provincial Muslim League session. Lavishing praise on the 'historic Lahore session' for passing 'such a living resolution for the first time in the history of the Muslims', he claimed that contrary to the carping of critics, 'there is no camouflage of word or meaning. It is a clear cut, sharp and steel grained resolution that has definitely

---

19 *The Leader*, 16 April 1940.

20 Sharif al Mujahid (ed.), *In Quest of Jinnah: Diary, Notes and Correspondence of Hector Bolitho* (Karachi, 2007), 15.

translated the will of the Muslims.'[21] The Indian Muslims had made it clear that their ideal was no longer 'Swaraj', 'Complete Independence' or 'Dominion Status' but 'the very right of self-determination'. They were demanding a place for themselves in the Indian sun where they could 're-establish the government of Islam'. This goal would be realized 'by bringing into being sovereign and autonomous Muslim states where by virtue of their historical position and numerical ascendancy, the Muslims judged by every canon of political and ethical doctrine are entitled to exercise supreme power.'[22] Exulting that the Muslims now had a clear ideal to 'live and die for', he clarified the nature of the new state. Pakistan was going to be 'a laboratory wherein we may experiment in peace, the greatest experiment that was ever tried – re-establish[ing] the government of Islam.'[23] The Raja asked his audience to pay close attention to his words. 'The creation of an Islamic State – mark my words gentlemen – I say Islamic, not Muslim – is our ideal'.[24] For Mahmudabad this was a crucial distinction. If the first Islamic state came into existence during the reign of the Prophet in Medina, Pakistan for him was only the second such attempt in all of Islamic history to establish the Islamic state, 1300 years after the passing of the Prophet.

Quoting Iqbal who he credited with giving birth to this vision in modern times, Mahmudabad proclaimed that Islam provided a 'certain kind of polity, a social structure regulated by a legal system and animated by a specific ethical ideal'. It did not separate church and state, or divide man's life between this-worldly and other-worldly realms. Thus, in the Islamic state, the Raja asserted that, 'the unchangeable laws of Islam will ipso facto be applied and enforced. There shall be no fresh legislation in this regard to them because Islam has already legislated for them forever and ever.' (sic).[25] Prohibition 'with no chance of it ever being withdrawn' would be introduced, usury would be abolished and *zakat* would be levied on Muslims. And since Islam dealt justly with 'every community and every section of its constituent members', he proclaimed that Sikhs, Hindus, Christians would 'benefit equally from the beneficent all-pervading activities of this democratic-theocratic State'.

---

21 Speech to the Bombay Provincial Muslim League, 24 May 1940, *Shamsul Hasan Collection* (Foreign Correspondence); also see *IAR*, Vol. 1 (1940), 319 and *The Leader*, 27 May 1940.

22 Ibid.

23 *IAR*, Vol. 2, 1940, 319; *The Leader*, 27 May 1940.

24 Speech to the Bombay Provincial Muslim League, 24 May 1940, *Shamsul Hasan Collection* (Foreign Correspondence).

25 Ibid.

Mahmudabad went on to provide philosophical justifications for creating an Islamic state. His primary justification was that it was 'a work of thousands of years, which slowly evolved through generations of experiences and tests'. After all, Islam was 'a product of history' and its truths had been tested, validated and perfected as a result of the historical process.[26] To buttress this point, he reminded his listeners that Islam was not merely 'a religion founded by an individual as the modern rationalistic historian or critic will put it', or solely a religion revealed to the Prophet Muhammad as claimed by those who believed in divine inspiration. Islam was an eternal religion that had been preached to an errant world by all the Prophets who had been sent to mankind, each emphasizing particular aspects of this eternal religion according to the demands of the period in which they appeared, or as they were ordained by God. The Prophet Muhammad's distinctiveness only lay in that he finally fulfilled God's purpose, by completing his message, thus perfecting the evolution of Islam. In this context, the Raja did not lose the opportunity to also point out that unlike the perfection of Islam Hinduism was 'limited to an individual experience.'[27] Mahmudabad's enthusiasm for Pakistan as an Islamic state is evident from the way he took it up with Jinnah. Writing to his *chacha*, the Raja emphasized that the ML needed to

> be careful in expressing our views about the proposed scheme. If these views will in any way be alien or contradictory to the contemplated system of government in Islam then there will be many to oppose them tooth and nail. But if we can manage to express our opinions in strict coordination with the Islamic conception of state then there will be an Ideal substantial and dynamic enough to take the greatest amount of sacrifice from us. When I say Islamic state I do not mean Moslem state.[28]

The insistence on the distinction had to do with Mahmudabad's belief that it was the corruptions of the Muslim state that were the primary cause behind Islam's decline in the world. Echoing the sentiment expressed by ML functionaries in the locality such as Anis al Din Ahmad Rizvi, Mahmudabad lamented that the 'revolutionary message of the Prophet' had been undermined by the kingdoms founded by Muslims in Egypt, Syria, Iraq, Spain, Algeria, Turkey, Iran and finally India. These states 'were absolutely un-Islamic' as their potentates 'had crushed all Islamic institutions', 'adopted the most reactionary

---

26 Ibid.

27 Ibid.

28 Mahmudabad to Jinnah, 28 July 1940, Rizwan Ahmad, *Qaid-i- Azam Papers 1940*, (Karachi-Lahore, 1976), 111–12.

and autocratic form of government', 'unleashed tyranny and oppression' and 'persecuted all those that stood for uncompromising Islam'. That these rulers were un-Islamic and filled with 'heathen inclinations' was most evident in the 'voluptuous and licentious architecture' that they had created. Mahmudabad, therefore, contrasted the 'elaborate decoration of their mosques' to 'the rustic simplicity of the Masjid-i-Nabi in Medina.'[29] Turning closer home to the medieval Indian Muslim states, he again bemoaned that the Ghaznavids, the Ghorids and even the Mughals, were never actually conversant with Islam's doctrines. All their talk of having left their homes to propagate Islam in the lands of the infidels was hogwash for they had exploited Islam only for the purposes of maintaining state power. Mahmudabad argued that if Islam flourished in India as evident from its thriving nine crore Muslim population, it was not due to the Muslim kings but the 'saints and *faqirs*' who had preached Islam and created an 'Empire in the hearts of the millions.'[30] For the Raja, the long Middle Ages regrettably 'marked the interpretation of Islam as a commercial commodity to be used by those in power.'[31] Imperial Muslim courts were thus no different from 'European resorts of dissipation and debauchery' since they thrived in sensuality amidst poverty and hunger of their people.

Besides declaiming against the various Muslim states in history, Mahmudabad also articulated the Islamic state's distinctiveness and authenticity vis a vis its contemporary others – the modern European state and Congress nationalism. Critiquing the European state form, Mahmudabad insisted that while Islam meant the sovereignty of God, governments of all European states, be they Britain, Russia, Italy or Germany were based on 'the idea of a Godless State'.[32] Again, while Islam meant peace, European states stood for extreme aggression as evident from the destructive World Wars they had spawned besides the destructive ideologies of Fascism, Nazism and Socialism. He, therefore, taunted Europe, 'the mother of civilizations', for giving rise to the new Genghis Khan and Hulagu Khan, a thinly veiled reference to Hitler and Mussolini. Moreover, Mahmudabad contended that even democracy that the Europeans were so proud of was predicated on an unbalanced individualism

29 Speech to the Bombay Provincial Muslim League, 24 May 1940, *Shamsul Hasan Collection* (Foreign Correspondence).

30 Mahmudabad to Jinnah, 28 July 1940, Rizwan Ahmad, *Qaid-i-Azam Papers 1940.*

31 Speech to the Bombay Provincial Muslim League, 24 May 1940, *Shamsul Hasan Collection* (Foreign Correspondence).

32 Ibid.

and aggression best exemplified by imperialist Britain. Moreover, democracy was based on a hypocrisy, for while it was 'lauded to the skies' in one context, its application was denied in other contexts. He also pointed out that it was these very democracies that had given rise to totalitarianism and dictatorship in Europe. This critique of European democracy was intended to reverberate across Muslim India for it meshed particularly well with the ML's argument that it was unsuited to the subcontinent where it allowed a permanent Hindu majority to dominate the Muslim minority.

Mahmudabad combined his critique of European style democracy with a contemptuous dismissal of Congress nationalism claiming that it was 'nourished on the crumbs thrown from the table of western theorists.'[33] He declared that the Mahatma's 'conception of India as it ought to be is in its essential Western born' for he was very much 'a product of western political philosophy and thought, his anti-European externals notwithstanding.'[34] If Hitler was a 'living commentary of Nietzsche', the Mahatma, he witheringly noted, was nothing more than an 'Indianised edition of Tolstoy, brought up to date, except his Internationalism.' And just as western ideologies of nationalism, socialism and democracy had brought War to the world, he announced that 'Gandhian philosophy of narrow nationalism based on Hindu overlordism' would not bring peace to India and only exacerbate communal tensions. Censuring the Mahatma for seeking 'a Hindu Raj of Savarkarian type' through his Quit India Resolution, he also reproved him for making such 'demands of withdrawals with slogans and resolutions of Akhand Hindustan.'[35] These political actions had been combined with subtle warnings of civil strife to provoke Muslims but Mahmudabad calmly reminded Gandhi that they were not afraid of such threats. Having repudiated Gandhi's politics, the Raja presented the Mahatma with an offer.

> Let us have, as I have said on another occasion, a laboratory wherein we can experiment on our own lines. The conflict of ideologies is proceeding with slaughter and carnage and the end is not in sight. It is about time another ideology [Islam] was given a chance to prove its worth. We believe that nationalism is a curse, capitalism is a curse and above all irreligion is a curse. Allow us to translate this political philosophy into reality; and the place where it will be worked and practiced will be Pakistan. It will perhaps be a model for the whole world to copy.[36]

33 Ibid.

34 Syed Sharifuddin Peerzada (ed.), *Unpardonable Crime of Jinnah*, (Bombay, 1942), 64.

35 Ibid.

36 Ibid.

Mahmudabad combined these rhetorical flourishes with ventures into the rather nebulous terrain of Islamic democracy that would be inaugurated in the Islamic state. From his inchoate, amorphous thoughts on this subject, it appears that it entailed the rule of a single, wise, pious, all powerful Caliph in a striking echo of Mawdudi's ideas. Mahmudabad noted that this leader would have advisors to tender him advice on all important matters affecting governance. This Islamic democracy, he noted while addressing a meeting of the Muslim Students Federation in Bangalore, was already enshrined in the *Shariah* and Muslims needed to acquaint themselves with that model.[37] It would be safe to infer that the modern Caliph that Mahmudabad envisioned shouldering the onerous responsibilities of leading the new Islamic state was none other than Jinnah. The Raja expected this model of the Caliphate to be replicated at the level of provinces, towns and localities. This model seemed dangerously close to dictatorship and Mahmudabad made no bones about it as evident from the letter he wrote to Jinnah after a visit to Muzaffarnagar where the district ML had been dissolved and a dictator had been put in place. As he wrote to his 'uncle'

> Could not the same be done in other districts? And then at the Centre? We have had enough of democratic yap yapping (sic). Only one man at the head can work and does the work, the others usually just follow. Public has never decided anything for itself. It have always followed (sic). Strong men with definite ideals lead. It is in the interests of the people to accept individual genius. Is it not surprising that even our thinking public is so apathetic that when there is war and everything is topsy-turvy, it invites and appoints dictators and in time of peace it again turns to democracy. A man who can steer the ship in a storm can do it more so in calm waters.[38]

Mahmudabad did not go much further in delineating the structure of this Islamic state. The reason, as he noted, was not because the concept of an Islamic state lacked merit or substance, but because 'Islamic literature has not yet progressed enough to furnish the technical and scientific terms' for a theory of an Islamic state for the present day and age.[39] This acknowledgement reflects the fact that the quest for an Islamic state in Pakistan marked one of the earliest attempts to theorize it in modern times. A similar quest for the

---

37 *The Leader*, 27 April 1941.

38 Mahmudabad to Jinnah, 28 July 1940, in Rizwan Ahmad (ed.), *Quaid-i-Azam Papers, 1940*.

39 Speech to the Bombay Provincial Muslim League, 24 May 1940, *Shamsul Hasan Collection* (Foreign Correspondence).

Islamic state in the 'core lands of Islam' would gain momentum only after the failure of socialism, Pan-Arabism and secular nationalisms in the Arab world.

The only worthwhile competitor that Mahmudabad saw to Islam was Socialism for which he had obvious sympathies. But he quickly proceeded to co-opt it in within Islam by claiming that Socialism was first inaugurated by the Prophet Muhammad in Arabia long before it came into existence in Russia under the Bolsheviks. Stalin himself was therefore only following in the footsteps of the Prophet. In any case, Mahmudabad conceded that Socialism just like Islam was based on a new vision of the world where there would be no discrimination based on colour, class, sect, region, or language. But Islam was still superior to Socialism for two important reasons. To begin with, Socialism was a product of the mind and had no relation with the heart and hence could never be enduring or permanent. Islam, on the other hand, represented a combination of both the heart and the mind and would therefore be an eternal order. Secondly, while Socialism was not based on a democratic principle, Islam was based on the principle of *ijma* or consensus of the community. Thus, Islam rather than Socialism would emerge as the bearer of a new superior world order most suited to the individual belonging to the new age.[40]

Mahmudabad also defended the Lahore Resolution against 'misrepresentations' by the 'perverse intellects' of 'our enemies', the Congress and the Hindu Mahasabha. He clarified that the ML did not want any wholesale migration of Muslims from the minority provinces, nor did it intend to expel non-Muslim minorities from Muslim homelands. As he pointed out

> I myself belong to a minority province and much as I would like to have been born in a Muslim sovereign state of India, I do not intend to uproot myself from my home and leave my co-religionists to their fate.[41]

The principle he cited behind this position was that he did not want the rest of India to be 'denuded of Muslims'. On the contrary, he wanted Islam to expand and not lose ground in India. As he asserted, 'the outposts of Islam will go forward, they will not be withdrawn.' Yet, Mahmudabad declared that 'natural movement of population' would not be discouraged, thus making it clear that Indian Muslims in general would always have the option of

---

40 *Sidq*, 11 May 1941.

41 Speech to the Bombay Provincial Muslim League, 24 May 1940, *Shamsul Hasan Collection* (Foreign Correspondence).

relocating to Muslim homelands.[42] Like his *Qaid*, he also publicly ridiculed the Congress on a number of occasions for insisting that India was one single nation. When Rajagopalachari made a 'sporting offer' asking the ML to form a provisional government at the centre with its own premier, Mahmudabad derisively rejected it, pointing out that such a cabinet and government would be at the mercy of a Hindu majority in the legislature. The offer had been made to 'mislead foreign countries, the British people and the press' and he reiterated that the ML had no option but to reject it since it was based on the one nation theory and a unitary government at the centre.[43] He also took a direct shot at Nehru who had been talking about a world federation and portraying Pakistan as the contradictory and retrograde trend. Mahmudabad coolly noted that such high sounding ideals barely masked the desire for world domination. He thus dismissed Congress attempts to formulate the destiny of Indian Muslims by declaring that 'a slave is after all a slave and cannot liberate another slave.'[44] Moreover, like many of his contemporaries, Mahmudabad saw the Lahore Resolution as possessing global significance for he insisted that it had been passed not just for Muslims in India but for Muslims in Turkey, Iran and Afghanistan and indeed the whole Islamic world. Thus, while addressing another public meeting at Sasaram in Bihar, home to the beautiful mausoleum of Sher Shah Suri, he claimed that the ML's new idea was timely since the world's Muslims no longer wanted to be divided on the basis of nationalities but wanted 'one and only one Islamic Sultanate for all of us.'[45] He, therefore, visualized Pakistan as marking the beginning of the process of unification of the Islamic world and a revival of the Islamic Caliphate with the Indian Muslims providing the lead in this grand project.

While praising the ML leadership for giving the goal of Pakistan to Indian Muslims, Mahmudabad insisted that this was not a 'newly created ideal or one that has leapt into prominence through the efforts of a few politicians and theorists.' The urge for an Islamic state had therefore existed in the 'subconscious mind of the least intelligent of us… long before it began to take shape and

42 Ibid.

43 *The Leader*, 29 August 1940.

44 Speech to the Bombay Provincial Muslim League, 24 May 1940, *Shamsul Hasan Collection* (Foreign Correspondence).

45 *Asr-i-Jadid*, 24 November 1940, in Syed Ishtiaq Husain (ed.), *Khutbat-i Raja Sahab Mahmudabad: Raja Sahab Mahmudabad, Muhammad Amir Ahmad Khan ke Khutbat, Irshadat, Interviews or Chand Ahem Dastavezaat ka Majmua* (Karachi, 1997).

form and was put forward first nebulously and then definitely and vigorously by our political thinkers.'[46] Islam had already 'formulated basic emotions and loyalties which gradually unify scattered individuals and groups and finally transform them into a well-defined people possessing a moral consciousness of their own.'[47] The Lahore Resolution was therefore not 'merely a paper resolution drafted by dreamers and idealists' but reflected the 'mass will of the people'. Mahmudabad used the opportunity to warn fellow Muslims that if they really wanted to save the ideal of the Islamic state in Pakistan which was above all for their own benefit, they needed to ensure that after seizing power they would not let history 'repeat itself in the form of an un-Islamic state governed by Muslim rulers of the old.'[48] This was therefore a call to the people to be ready to start a revolution in case the promise of the Islamic state was sabotaged by the leadership. At the same time though, he exhorted the propertied classes to voluntarily give up their vested interests, end class divisions within the community and meet with Muslim masses on level ground for the greater glory of Islam. Pakistan could come into existence only as a result of their united efforts. The new Islamic state was after all essential for all Indian Muslims for only it could 'protect their cultural and political thought, revive Islam and protect their identity as Muslims.'[49] They would otherwise share the fate of Muslims of Spain, Poland or Bulgaria whose identity had ultimately been submerged and erased.

Pan-Islam, Sovereignty and National Territory: Khaliquzzaman and the Pathway to Pakistan

Chaudhry Khaliquzzaman utilized Islamic imagery and metaphors not dissimilar to Mahmudabad's while describing Pakistan at public meetings. Thus, in a speech at the Pakistan session of the Punjab Muslim Students Federation conference in 1941, Khaliq noted that just as the Prophet had created the first Pakistan in the Arabian Peninsula the ML now wanted to create another Pakistan in a part of India.[50] He, therefore, wondered why the

46 Speech to the Bombay Provincial Muslim League, 24 May 1940, *Shamsul Hasan Collection* (Foreign Correspondence)

47 Ibid.

48 Ibid.

49 Ibid.

50 *Zulqarnain*, 14 March 1941.

ulama aligned to the Congress were claiming that Pakistan was against the *Shariah*. In another speech in his hometown Lucknow soon after the Lahore Resolution, he underlined this Islamist vision by exploring the relationship between territorial nationalism (*wataniyat*) and Islam. The Hindus, he noted, saw *wataniyat* as a Hindu Goddess (*Devi*) that needed to be worshipped. This practice was abhorrent to a Muslim for even though he loved his *watan*, he could never worship this *Devi* and become a slave of *wataniyat*.[51] A Muslim was first and last a Muslim and if a choice had to be made between *watan* and *mazhab* (religion), a Muslim would always choose the latter. Khaliq also pointed to the dangerous implications of being a slave to *wataniyat* in the name of composite nationalism. Raising concerns that Ambedkar had alluded to in his treatise, he asked his fellow Muslims whether they would follow the orders of any Indian Premier if he suddenly decided to attack Afghanistan in the name of national interest.

The question that Khaliq posed at this public meeting is not surprising given his longstanding Pan-Islamist convictions. As a young man, he had gone on the Red Crescent Society's medical mission to Turkey led by Dr M. A. Ansari during the Balkan Wars. He was actively involved in the subsequent Khilafat Movement in India in the early 1920s while during the 1930s Khaliq led the Indian Muslim delegations to international conventions organized to defend Palestinian Arab rights in the face of the Zionist Movement and perceived British attempts to appease world Jewry. An enthusiastic Pan-Islamist, Khaliq believed that once established, Pakistan would emerge as the leader of the Islamic world and play a pivotal role in bringing about its unification as a powerful new bloc on world stage. It is a mission he would take up with much zeal after Pakistan came into existence. He made this intention clear in a famous statement wherein he bluntly declared that

> Pakistan is not the final goal of the Muslims. We want more. Pakistan is only the jumping off ground. The time is not far distant when the Muslim countries will have to stand in line with Pakistan and then only the jumping ground will have reached its fruition.[52]

Khaliq was one of the first Muslim politicians to think of alternatives to the Federal Scheme that the British government had introduced with the 1935 GOI Act. As Lord Zetland, the Secretary of State for India wrote

---

51 *Sidq*, 21 October 1940.

52 *Star of India*, 30 May 1942.

to his Viceroy Lord Linlithgow, Khaliq along with the Bengal ML leader Abdul Rahman Siddiqui met him in London and suggested the creation of three or four federations of provinces and states in India, which would be coordinated by a small body at the centre where the British would have a significant presence.[53] Khaliq's developing thoughts on the matter can be discerned from some of the 'constructive proposals' that he presented to the U.P. Governor Sir Maurice Hallett just weeks before the Lahore Resolution.[54] In this conversation, Khaliq proposed the establishment of three independent Dominions in India. Two of these would be Muslim Dominions, one in the northwest comprising Punjab, NWFP, Sind, Kashmir and any other native state in that area and the other in the east including Bengal and Assam. Khaliq quoted population figures to show that in each of these areas, the Muslims were in a majority. He was categorical that Bengal should include not just eastern Bengal but even western Bengal. In the case of Assam he was confident that through conversion to Islam or through other means Muslims would become a majority. The Hindu Dominion would occupy the remaining parts in central India. Moving further from his previous London proposal, Khaliq made it clear that the Muslims wanted each of these Dominions to have separate and direct relations with Britain. When asked by Hallett about the position of Muslims in the Hindu dominion in central India where they would be in a small minority, Khaliq argued that

> if this system were introduced, the Hindus would be forced to face realities and that the rights of Muslims and other minorities in the central area of Hindustan will be safeguarded by the fact that they would be similar to those of the Hindu minority in the two Muslim dominions; *provinces is hardly any longer an appropriate term*. (emphasis mine)[55]

In brief, this was the 'hostage population' theory that a perceptive Hallett quickly understood. As the Governor noted, 'in other words, as I bluntly put it to him, there would be retaliation.'[56] Khaliq also addressed the question of defence and suggested that the Muslim dominions could have armies of about 25,000 and 15,000 respectively, which could be assisted by a larger army of the central zone if the need arose, suggesting the possibility of a defence arrangement

53 Zetland to Linlithgow, 28 March 1939, *Zetland Papers*, quoted in SAI Tirmizi (ed.), *Paradoxes of Partition, 1937–1939* (New Delhi, 1998), 639.

54 Hallett to Linlithgow, 16 February 1940, *Linlithgow Papers*.

55 Ibid.

56 Ibid.

between the dominions and a continuing British presence in India. He impressed upon Hallett the desirability of continuing British-Muslim friendship, emphasizing that it was the only check against the Congress totally ending the British connection and establishing Hindu Raj in India. He also assured Hallett that this scheme would stop Congress demands for independence. Not surprisingly, Khaliq also expressed his intention to visit Turkey to enlist its support for the ML's new proposal. The trip would also show to the British Labour Party in particular that the ML's claim was backed by a great Muslim power, which had been an ally of the British Empire over the last fifteen years, not to talk of other Islamic powers. Hallett, in turn viewed Khaliq's proposal as a 'nutcracker scheme', which however was a lot more practical than other schemes which talked of transfers of population.[57] Besides if in these three dominions democracy could be maintained, it would find greater appeal in Britain. Thus, even though this plan was not palatable to the British who had just come up with a federal scheme for India, it could not be disregarded. As he wrote to the Viceroy, it had the germs of a settlement and the example of Ireland was a close parallel.

In public statements soon after the Lahore session, Khaliq again strongly defended the idea of partitioning British India stating that it was bound to create a healthy atmosphere for resolving the communal problem. The presence of two independent Muslim states in the West and the East, he smugly declared, would have a 'steadying influence' on the rest of India. The Muslim minorities would consequently be much better treated in the Hindu provinces than at present, as would Hindu minorities in Muslim states.[58] Khaliq backed his claims by stating that during his tours of the eastern districts of U.P. as part of the 'Pakistan deputation' he found that the 'ordinary Muslim looks on Pakistan as his only hope.'[59] In the meanwhile, in recognition of the presence of two nations in India, he wanted the government to set up separate schools for Hindus and Muslims in U.P. referring to the case of Turkey, which had allowed Greeks and Armenians their separate schools. Hallett did not respond to this suggestion made by Khaliq at a later meeting but wryly noted in his letter to the Viceroy, 'I did not ask him whether he would like to be treated in the way the Turks treated the Armenians.'[60]

57 Hallett to Linlithgow, 17 February 1940, *Linlithgow Papers.*

58 *The Leader*, 30 March 1940.

59 Hallett to Linlithgow, 23 December 1940, *Linlithgow Papers.*

60 Ibid.

Like Jinnah, Khaliq publicly defended Pakistan's feasibility. Responding to objections against Pakistan on historical, economic and geographical grounds, he pointed to the survival of Lebanon, a small country with a population of hardly 1.5 million people. He noted that Lebanon had been a part of Syria for 1300 years, but at the end of the last war, was separated from Syria and handed over to France as a mandate. When such a small country could remain a separate independent country, Khaliq asserted that Pakistan with a population of 60 million and an area greater than that of most big European countries could surely survive.[61] As regards Pakistan's economic viability, he was confident that while Pakistan would initially be 'poor and underdeveloped', 'British brains and capital' would allow it to adequately develop its natural resources.[62]

Yet, while he was vociferous in public in advocating Pakistan, Khaliq was worried about loose wording in the text of the Lahore Resolution, which he felt could have adverse consequences for Pakistan when it came into existence. In his memoirs, he made it clear that he was not responsible for this lapse pointing out that the drafting of the Resolution had been completed while he was still in Lucknow for the wedding of his youngest daughter and that he had reached Lahore just as it was about to be passed. Khaliq also noted that he had not been present at the Sind Provincial League Conference where the precursor to the Lahore Resolution calling for the establishment of separate Hindu and Muslim federations was passed and that he was again absent from the 1941 AIML Madras session when the Lahore Resolution was reaffirmed and Pakistan made the party's official creed.[63] This was a thinly veiled critique of the *Qaid* who had been present on all three occasions but had not done anything to repair the situation.

Khaliq had an alibi to back his claims. Alone among his colleagues in the ML's High Command to muster the requisite courage to write to Jinnah, he expressed his unease about the wording of the Lahore Resolution which affirmed 'territorial readjustments' as a method for creating 'independent Pakistan states' comprising 'geographically contiguous units' with Muslim majorities.[64] The canny lawyer from Lucknow feared that this wording could be interpreted in such a way as to strip Pakistan of valuable land without giving it anything in

61 Pirzada, *Foundations of Pakistan*, Vol. 2, 463–4.

62 Hallett to Wavell, 9 October 1944, *L/P&J/5/276*, OIOC, British Library London.

63 Chaudhry Khaliquzzaman, *Pathway to Pakistan* (Lahore 1961), 234–37.

64 Khaliquzzaman to Jinnah, 7 October 1942, *Shamsul Hasan Collection*, U.P. Vol. 4. The letter is also reproduced in the appendix to his memoir, *Pathway to Pakistan*.

return, gravely endangering the viability of the new state and also adversely affecting Muslims who would be left behind in Hindu India. Khaliq's foreboding arose after a perusal of newly released 1941 census figures, which laid out the spatial distribution of India's religious communities. The census for Bengal revealed that while Muslims had an overwhelming majority in the three eastern divisions of Chittagong, Dacca and Rajshahi, Hindus were in a clear majority in western Burdwan and Presidency divisions (the latter including Calcutta). Khaliq worried that if the principle of territorial readjustment was not restricted to the level of whole provinces and was applied at the level of sub-divisions of provinces, it would not be possible to claim Burdwan and Presidency divisions as parts of eastern Pakistan. These would have to be ceded to India. The only territory that Muslims could legitimately demand in return, according to this principle, was the Muslim majority Sylhet division in Assam.

Khaliq warned that such territorial readjustments in Bengal would be greatly disadvantageous to Muslims. Muslim majority area in the easternmost corner of British India held no prospects for future development and was unsuitable for 'expansion of towns and cities' as this was low-lying land between the Brahmaputra and several tributaries of the Ganges that was subject to frequent flooding. It had no known mineral resources or industries and its overwhelmingly agricultural population, dependent on jute and paddy cultivation during the summer months, 'remained idle and without work' for the rest of the year once the monsoon began. The region also lacked railways and trade in the area was mostly waterborne 'with all its consequent disadvantages.' By contrast, Khaliq pointed out that west Bengal, which had a Hindu majority, was blessed with bountiful sources of iron and coal, a developed railway system, industries and more importantly the port of Calcutta, which two decades earlier had been the capital of the Raj before its move to New Delhi. Chittagong, a sleepy coastal backwater, was undeveloped and hence poor consolation for Pakistan. What was even more worrisome for Khaliq was that Muslim losses were not going to be confined to the East. 'Territorial readjustments' would adversely affect Muslim interests in West Pakistan as well. Muslims here stood to lose significant amount of territory in eastern Punjab since the Hindus had an 80 per cent majority in the Ambala division, while in central Punjab comprising the area between the Ambala division and Lahore, the Hindus and the Sikhs again had a clear majority. What compounded matters even further in West Pakistan was that the Muslims would have to part with land without getting any compensation in return unlike in Bengal where they would at least gain Sylhet.

Khaliq underlined the critical importance of securing full provinces of Punjab and Bengal for Pakistan and the need for ML to stand obdurately against a redrawing of provincial boundaries under the principle of 'territorial readjustments'. A full Punjab was imperative for Pakistan as it would cut off direct communication between Hindu India and Kashmir and other native Punjab states. The Hindu population in these areas would thus 'be forced to ask the Pakistan union for right of transit'. In return, 'Pakistan government could claim the same right for Hyderabad and other Muslim estates to establish contact with the Pakistan union.' On the contrary, Khaliq warned that if southern and central Punjab were to go out of Pakistan, not only would 'such an opportunity be lost, but direct communication between Punjab Hindu estates and Hindu provinces will be established without any such advantages falling to the lot of Muslim estates in the Hindu dominated zones.'[65]

In this context, Khaliq also addressed the related question of transfer of populations, an issue that had been exercising the minds of political elites and ordinary Muslims alike, as the idea of Pakistan gained momentum in public consciousness. Acknowledging that 'complete segregation of the Muslim and Hindu population, as at present located, is impossible', Khaliq, nonetheless, anticipated that 'there may come a time when it may become feasible.' If Muslims were to therefore allow such 'large territories to go out of our hands in the process of territorial re-adjustment, such an exchange of population would become impossible'. The territory left with Pakistan would 'not be sufficient to receive and maintain large populations migrating from other lands.' Khaliq, therefore, reiterated that the wording of the Lahore Resolution had dangerous implications since 'if the population of sub-division is to be taken into account, why not the population of the districts and the Tahsils, the cities, the Mohallas'. He, therefore, warned Jinnah against settling for a smaller, truncated Pakistan consisting of large Muslim majorities for that would entail 'surrendering large and valuable tracts of land', which was certainly not a 'good proposition.' Referring to Bengal and Punjab as presently constituted, he wondered what numbers would 'serve to entitle the Muslims to call themselves a majority' if 57 per cent in the Punjab and 56.3 per cent in Bengal was not considered a good majority. Majorities were valuable in the constitutional sense as also for reasons of 'physical and historical fitness' and Khaliq pleaded that the existing Muslim majorities were certainly strong enough for these purposes.

---

65 Ibid.

More to the point, Khaliq bluntly noted that 'one of the basic principles lying behind the Pakistan idea is that of keeping hostages in Muslim provinces as against the Muslims in Hindu provinces.' If millions of Hindus were allowed to go out of the Muslim orbit of influence, the security of Muslims in the Hindu provinces would 'be greatly minimized'. As he elaborated, 'the illiterate millions of Hindu population in their majority provinces will be more considerate and regardful of the Muslim minorities, if they know and feel that large numbers of Hindus live happily and peacefully in the Muslim zones of influence.' The ML, therefore, needed to remember that Pakistan, besides being a 'political remedy', was also a 'psychological cure'. 'Territorial readjustments', therefore, could seriously undermine its latter use and meaning.

In this regard, Khaliq also identified another 'serious factor' that needed to be taken into account –'contact with Pakistan zones, of the non-Pakistan zones'. If Hindu majority areas of eastern Punjab and western Bengal were cut away and excluded from Pakistan, 'long and hostile distances' would intervene against 'the cultural influences of the minority provinces on the Pakistan zones.' As U.P. was the heart of Muslim India, its cultural influences, especially the spread of Urdu was necessary for creating a common national language for Pakistan. Khaliq reminded Jinnah that 'the growing cultural contact between U.P. and Punjab had resulted in practically ousting Punjabi language and introducing Urdu in its place within the last half a century.'[66] In the eastern zones too, Urdu had made much headway 'so much so that in the Burdwan and Presidency divisions, Urdu is not only understood but freely spoken, while the area to the east of Calcutta neither understands nor speaks the language at present.' It was, therefore, imperative that cultural contact had to be maintained between Urdu speaking Bihar and areas east of Calcutta so that Urdu would become the lingua franca of eastern Pakistan as well. Hence, he reasserted the importance of preserving territorial integrity of Bengal and Punjab 'if for no other reason than to keep intact the facilities of contact between the majority and minority Muslims provinces'.[67]

---

66 K. H. Khurshid makes an interesting note in his memoirs on this issue. The Nawab of Mamdot spoke to his younger brother Zulfiqar in Urdu but in Punjabi to his uncle Nawab Akbar Khan. 'It appeared that by the time the younger brothers were born, it was either the custom to speak Urdu or there was a different national consciousness which required the younger generation to be brought up differently.' He added though that 'the family also had spent some time in Hyderabad Deccan which might explain the Urdu'. See K. H. Khurshid, *Memories of Jinnah*, 17.

67 Khaliquzzaman to Jinnah, 7 October 1942, *Shamsul Hasan Collection* U.P., Vol. 4.

Khaliq pleaded with Jinnah to give up his adamant insistence that the Congress accept the Lahore Resolution, pointing to the 'dangers' that lay in taking such a position. He saw the Cripps Mission proposals, which offered 'direct common plebiscite of Muslims and non-Muslims on the question of accession or non-accession without the intervention of the vote of assemblies' as 'comparatively more advantageous to Muslim interest *than a truncated Pakistan established by Muslim plebiscite alone.*' (emphasis mine) As he elaborated further

> if in the last analysis, we have to make a choice between a common-vote plebiscite of the provinces as at present constituted and the plebiscite of Muslims alone in the provinces of Bengal and Punjab after a territorial readjustment, the former alternative is far more attractive and profitable than the latter. With an excess in population of 75 lacs in Bengal and 35 lacs in the Punjab in favor of Muslims, there can be no room for doubt in the result of a common voting in the provinces.'[68]

Khaliq, therefore, believed that an assured Muslim majority under a common plebiscite would ward off communal subdivision of the provinces.

Yet, Khaliq was keenly aware of his *Qaid's* prickliness to any interrogation or questioning on this count for he had proclaimed the Lahore Resolution as the inviolable creed of Indian Muslims. Khaliq therefore hastened to add, rather disingenuously, that having read and re-read the Resolution he had come to the conclusion that there was nothing in it that could compel Muslims to agree to the partition of Punjab and Bengal. The Resolution, Khaliq reasoned, had clearly stated that 'contiguous units of administration, viz. provinces, should be grouped together into regions, but the units which should be grouped together should be such units where the Muslims are in a majority.' Units meant complete provinces and as Khaliq reiterated, 'in the whole paragraph, unit has been used as a synonym for a province.' 'Territorial readjustment' could, therefore, not mean or be allowed to mean, readjustment of subdivisions or parts of the unit. The ML, therefore, needed to rigidly insist upon this as the only correct interpretation of the resolution. Khaliq also took heart from the fact that if territorial readjustments were to take place, it could only happen in a spirit of mutual give and take between the two parties. If the Hindus could not give up equally valuable territories to compensate losses suffered by the Muslims, they could not reasonably ask for any readjustment. In a postscript to the letter, he happily noted press reports from that very morning in which Allah Bakhsh, the

---

[68] Ibid.

Sind Premier had declared that 'units of administration should be divided on linguistic basis and have a right to decide their own future.'[69] According to this logic, Burdwan and Presidency divisions in Bengal would remain in Bengal and hence East Pakistan since their language was Bengali, while Ambala division and central Punjab would remain in Punjab and hence West Pakistan, whether the provincial language was taken to be either Urdu or Punjabi.

In his memoir, Khaliq wrote that

> although the phrase in the Pakistan resolution *with such territorial readjustment* was contrary to my cherished views, I never proclaimed my opposition to it for the fear that once a rift in our ranks started, even a truncated Pakistan might be lost.[70]

He claimed that he shared the contents of this letter with colleagues in the UPML including Ehsanur Rahman Kidwai, Jamal Mian, Rizwanullah and Ayub Qureshi who supported his stand, but this effort was in vain for Jinnah did not favour him with a reply.[71] Indeed, he bitterly noted that he had written this letter after the NAP and Hindu Mahasabha leader Raja Maheshwar Dayal Seth had divulged to him the contents of his secret negotiations with Liaquat Ali Khan to bring about an agreement between the two parties on the question of Pakistan. Khaliq claimed that Liaquat was agreeable to the Ambala division leaving Pakistan with only the question of Jalandhar division being under negotiations. Khaliq boldly asserted that Jinnah himself was quite agreeable to such a division and that the Rajaji formula presented to Jinnah in 1942 was based on the draft created by the latter on the basis of Liaquat's negotiations with the Hindu Mahasabha.[72] In any case, Khaliq's claim may not have been taken seriously thus far with historians perhaps tending to view it as part of his efforts to clear his own reputation and blaming Jinnah for territories lost by Pakistan. But a report by a US consular official in Delhi writing to the Department of State of his interview with Liaquat Ali Khan substantiates Khaliq's claim that Liaquat was amenable to a 'truncated' Pakistan. In any case, notwithstanding questions regarding Pakistan's territoriality, Khaliq passionately advocated Pakistan to foreign diplomats. An OSS report noted Khaliq's view that 'Muslims in the minority provinces stand for Pakistan for the sake of

---

[69] Ibid.

[70] Khaliquzzaman, *Pathway to Pakistan*, 273.

[71] Ibid., 287.

[72] Ibid., 314–15.

Islam; they realize that they will themselves be exterminated eventually, but it is a personal sacrifice they make for the future of Muslims in India.'[73]

Liaquat Ali Khan, 'Territorial Readjustments' and Truncated Pakistan

The inclusion of the term 'territorial readjustments' in the Lahore Resolution, which, as Khaliq feared, weakened the ML's claims to entire provinces of Punjab and Bengal, was in good measure a result of Liaquat Ali Khan's insistence.[74] The AIML Working Committee on 21 March 1940 had appointed a committee to draft the Resolution. On 22 March at 8 pm, Liaquat placed a draft before the Subjects Committee, with an Urdu translation that was provided by Maulana Zafar Ali Khan. As the committee members wanted more time to consider it, the meeting was adjourned before it reassembled at 11 am on 23 March and hammered out the Lahore Resolution after seven hours of deliberations. During the meeting, the Punjabi Leaguer Ashiq Husain Batalvi reportedly moved an amendment for deleting crucial parts of the third paragraph, 'that geographically contiguous units are demarcated into regions which should be so constituted, with such territorial readjustments as may be necessary…' and instead suggested that the provinces of Punjab, Sind, Frontier and Baluchistan should specifically be mentioned in the resolution. At this point, Liaquat intervened to say that the 'omission of the names of the provinces was deliberate for otherwise, the territory of the proposed State would extend only up to Godhgaon' and added that the term 'territorial readjustment' was 'not intended to surrender any portion of Punjab or Bengal but to claim areas of Muslim culture like Delhi and Aligarh.'[75] The resolution was finally passed after this clarification had been provided. Liaquat's contribution to the interpretation of the Lahore Resolution also lies in the special article he contributed to the Indian Annual Register about the 1941 Madras AIML session in which he characterized Pakistan as an *independent state*, thus becoming the first ML leader of any consequence to speak of it in singular terms.[76]

Coming to Khaliquzzaman's accusation, Liaquat's evolving thinking on Pakistan especially with regard to its territory can be discerned from a report

73 *The All India Muslim League Part 1: Organization, Leadership, Strength and Program*, OIR Report No.4162.1, 1 August 1946.

74 S.S Pirzada, 'The Lahore Resolution 1940', in Pakistan Historical Society, *A History of the Freedom Movement Volume IV 1936-1947 Parts I & II* (Karachi 1970), 73–115.

75 Ibid., 97–98.

76 *IAR*, 1941, Vol. 1, 294.

of his interview with the ranking American diplomat in New Delhi, Lampton Berry, wherein he explained the ML's position as expounded in its August 1942 Bombay Resolution (which was in response to the Congress' own 'Quit India' declaration).[77] Berry enquired about the 'nature of the plebiscite contemplated in the Bombay resolution' and using Bengal as an example, ventured that the ML 'could hardly expect any party to agree to a plebiscite being held only among Muslims, which if obtaining an affirmative vote of a majority of Muslims for Pakistan would force the entire province including Hindus, out of a united India.' In stark contrast to the position that he had taken at Lahore, Liaquat responded that the plebiscite was meant to be restricted only to the eastern portion of the province in which the Muslims were in a definite majority. When Berry pointed out that 'this would deprive Muslims of the port of Calcutta', remarkably, Liaquat agreed. He, however, noted that 'if the eastern zone decided to go out of united India, it was quite possible that Hindus themselves in the western portion would desire to remain in Pakistan due to strong provincial sentiment which existed in the Indian provinces.' Liaquat further maintained that 'plebiscite in the Punjab would be held only in that zone where the Muslims are in a preponderant majority and that, that area of Punjab, roughly east of the Sutlej river would be excluded from the plebiscite.'[78] Berry informed Liaquat that Nehru had told him that he would be willing to concede Pakistan only after all attempts at resolving the Hindu–Muslim problem had failed. Besides, he would 'permit self-determination to Muslims in those zones in which they formed a definite majority' and require at least a 60 per cent affirmative vote to accept the verdict. Liaquat replied that

> such a condition would be quite satisfactory to League and that it would be quite prepared to make an effort to form a constitution for a united India by means of a constituent assembly. Whatever constitution might thus be drafted could then be submitted to a plebiscite of Muslims in zones as defined above and that if they voted for constitution of a united India that would end matter. On the other hand if they voted against constitution then that must be taken by Congress as tantamount to a plebiscite in favor of Pakistan. He suggested therefore that Congress would meet Muslim League position by recognizing principle and possibility of self-determination of Muslims to be determined by a plebiscite among them in those zones in which they

77 845.00/1574, Telegram from New Delhi to the Secretary of State, Washington DC 9 September 1942 (Interview between Berry and Liaquat Ali Khan), Box 5072, *US State Department Papers.*

78 Ibid.

> are in an absolute majority, this possibility to be invoked only after every effort had been made to draft a constitution for a united India acceptable to Muslims by means of a constituent assembly.[79]

Liaquat agreed that Rajagopalachari could act as a mediator between the Congress and the ML and that 'some headway might be made' if he were to see Jinnah and 'let Jinnah explain to him the League's position as outlined above.'[80] If the Mahatma agreed to these proposals, they could become the basis for negotiations between him and Jinnah. Liaquat must have communicated the ML's willingness to make these territorial concessions for in a public speech in Madras Rajagopalachari stated that he had '*ascertained that the Moslem claim was limited to contiguous districts wherein the population was predominantly Moslem and is not taken as coterminous with the present boundaries of Punjab and Bengal.*'(emphasis mine)[81]

The *Qaid* himself, out of abundant caution, repudiated much of what Liaquat had told Berry when the latter met him a week later. As noted earlier, Jinnah was most averse to a plebiscite of any kind, especially one conducted by an interim central government in which the Congress would have a majority and instead wanted matters to be resolved through agreement that would be guaranteed by the British Government. Again, though Jinnah may have been willing to settle for a truncated Pakistan, he would not have recklessly given away territory without bargaining for any territorial gains for the Muslim side. The *Qaid*, therefore, emphasized to Berry that Calcutta would be a part of Pakistan, which would include practically all of Bengal with the exception of three districts in the west and all of Punjab barring one Hindu district adjoining U.P. and one Sikh district adjacent to the Punjab hill states.[82] Jinnah repeated the performance with Herbert Matthews, the *New York Times* correspondent, for he *twice* showed him what he wanted on a map. It included all of Punjab and Bengal, Baluchistan, NWFP, Assam and even a corridor linking both these wings 'running across northern United Provinces'.[83] This would remain the *Qaid's* public position as also that of Liaquat till the ML eventually settled for a 'truncated Pakistan' in 1947.

79 Ibid.

80 Ibid.

81 *New York Times*, 7 February 1942.

82 Ibid.

83 Ibid.

It is possible that Liaquat could at times hold views at variance with those of Jinnah. But the *Qaid* usually had the last word given his towering presence and total dominance within the ML. A sense of Jinnah's supremacy can be gained from private interviews with some of ML working committee members.[84] As an OSS report noted

> Jinnah effectively dominates the opinions of the working committee. Fairly reliable information indicates that issues are not settled by vote. Jinnah asks for opinions and then summarizes the 'sense of the meeting' in terms of his own views; this becomes the decision of the committee by consent. As Jinnah selects only his close followers to sit on the committee, the members seldom voice any disagreement with him and on the whole are a weak lot.[85]

Yusuf Haroon noted that 'many people on the committee are not good; they are there because Mr Jinnah must choose as his cabinet men who can think as he does.'[86] Abdur Rahman Siddiqi, the Bengal Leaguer speaking of his experience as a member of the ML Working Committee in 1937 reported that

> Jinnah in the Chair read out the first resolution on the agenda. Siddiqi asked a question to open discussion, but the others immediately moved that the matter be left to the discretion of the Chair. This was repeated three times after which Siddiqi moved that the rest of the agenda be left to the discretion of the Chair. He was not reappointed to the committee next year.

G. M. Syed, the Sind Leaguer, stated that

> members who wished to oppose Jinnah's views but were afraid to do so often asked Syed to take the lead, promising to support him. But they always funked it. Anyone who expressed a difference of opinion became a marked man.[87]

Syed also reported that prior to the 1944 Gandhi-Jinnah talks

> Jinnah informed the members that he had received an invitation from Gandhi to meet for discussions and asked their opinion. When the working committee advised Jinnah to accept the invitation he stated that he had already done so. He then said he proposed to issue a statement of policy on

84 Office of Strategic Services, *The All India Muslim League Part 1: Organization, Leadership, Strength and Program,* OIR Report No.4162.1, 1 August 1946.

85 Ibid., 5–6.

86 Ibid.

87 Ibid., 6–7.

> the following day. Syed asked Jinnah if the Working Committee might have the honor of seeing the statement. Jinnah replied in the negative. After the meeting Syed tried to get some member in favor with Jinnah to ask him for the statement. Liaquat Ali refused saying 'why should I displease him?' Nazimuddin agreed to try, but Jinnah declined.[88]

It is also possible that rather than there being a variance in their views, Liaquat may have been utilized by Jinnah to float trial balloons, which could be conveniently repudiated later. Unlike Jinnah, who was laconic and tightlipped, Liaquat could be a lot more candid and forthcoming. Thus, when the Congress unleashed its Quit India campaign, an incensed Liaquat told a government official that 'the ML may not hesitate to declare that the Hindus should Quit Pakistan.' He did not follow up on the threat for as the report concluded, 'the grave dangers inherent in any attempt to popularize a slogan of this nature are obvious.'[89] In public, Liaquat like Jinnah demanded six full provinces for Pakistan as evident from the meeting he addressed in Shahjahanpur on 27–28 April 1940. Insisting that partition was necessary, the Nawabzada dismissed Congress claims that a Constituent Assembly for India would be a panacea for resolving all of its problems, adding that it reminded him of medicines advertised by quacks, which promised cure for anything from snake bites to typhoid.[90] Reiterating that the Lahore Resolution did not envisage any forced migration of U.P. Muslims to the Muslim majority provinces, he alluded to the 'hostage population' theory, claiming that it would provide for a 'balance of power' between the Hindu and Muslim states and thus give minority provinces Muslims the best possible guarantee for securing their rights and interests. As the U.P. Crime Investigation Department's (CID) report noted, this meeting unanimously passed a resolution, 'supporting the Pakistan scheme, in favour of which it was rather naively urged that the maltreatment of Muslim minorities could then be prevented by repaying in the same coin, the Hindu minority in Muslim majority provinces.' [91] A prominent feature of this meeting was the conspicuous display of Pakistan maps from the main *pandal.*

It is, therefore, clear that a section of the ML leadership was willing to

---

88 Ibid.

89 *Weekly report of the DIB Home Department, Government of India,* New Delhi, 15 August 1942, No. 33, L/PJ/12/484, File 230/35, OIOC, British Library, London.

90 *Archives of the Freedom Movement,* Vol. 352, U.P. Provincial Muslim League, Part IX, 1940, Karachi.

91 *PAI for the week ending11May 1940.*

settle for a 'truncated Pakistan' quite early on, even if in public it demanded the entire provinces of Punjab and Bengal. At the local level however, UPML functionaries were beginning to talk about partitioning Punjab and Bengal based on its population geography to ensure strong Muslim majorities in these provinces. This split regarding Pakistan's territorial expanse would be mirrored in public meetings. But before focusing on how Pakistan was articulated in the localities in U.P., one needs to turn to the UPML's move to devise a blueprint for an Islamic state in Pakistan.

A Blueprint for an Islamic state: U.P. Muslim League, *Ulama* and an Islamic Constitution for Pakistan

Soon after the Lahore Resolution, Nawab Ismail Khan convened a conference of *ulama* and prominent Muslim intellectuals to draft a blueprint for an Islamic Constitution (*Nizamnama ya Qanoon Asasi*) that would inaugurate an Islamic state in Pakistan.[92] The first meeting was held at the *Nadwatul Ulama*, Lucknow. Besides Ismail Khan and Khaliquzzaman, it was attended by Syed Sulaiman Nadwi, a prominent *alim* and a celebrated student of Shibli Numani, a close associate of Ashraf Ali Thanawi, a one-time Khilafatist and associate of Maulana Azad; Syed Abul Ala Mawdudi, who was not strictly an *alim* but at the time was closely associated with the ML; Azad Subhani, another old Khilafatist and associate of both Nadwi and Mawdudi; and finally Abdul Majid Daryabadi, the editor of the newspaper *Sidq* of Lucknow and author of a celebrated multi-volume biography of his *Pir* Ashraf Ali Thanawi. Nadwi was appointed as the Convenor of the committee that was set up to execute this task.

Nadwi was an appropriate choice as he enjoyed cordial relationships with *ulama* belonging to various schools of Islamic thought in north India. A respected *alim* and a prolific writer, he was known especially for completing a celebrated six volume biography of the Prophet titled *Seerat-un-Nabi* that was started by his teacher Shibli Numani. While Nadwi had a cordial and long-standing relationship with Nehru and other Congress nationalists, he supported the ML's push for Pakistan, especially if it were established according to Islamic laws. He had a particularly high opinion of Jinnah's capabilities and composed a verse to that effect, which gained some popularity in political circles.[93]

92 Abdul Majid Daryabadi, 'Pesh Lafz' (Foreword), in Muhammad Ishaq Sandelvi, *Islam Ka Siyasi Nizam, Jis Mein Islam ke Siyasi Nizam ka Asasi Khaka Pesh Kiya Gaya Hai* (Azamgarh, 1957); also see S. V. R. Nasr, *The Vanguard of the Islamic Revolution: The Jamaat-i-Islami of Pakistan* (Berkeley and Los Angeles 1994), 112.

93 I am indebted to Maulana Salman Nadvi, his son, for kindly sending me the verse.

Ab Mareez-i-Qaum ke Jeene ki hai kuch kuch Ummeed,
Daaktar iska agar Mister Ali Jeenah Raha

There is hope of this patient (Muslim community) surviving
If his doctor were to be Mr. (Muhammad) Ali Jinnah

At this first meeting, Nadwi delegated the task of preparing a first draft to Muhammad Ishaq Sandelvi, an *alim* from the *Nadtwatul Ulama*. Sandelvi remains an elusive figure about whom not much is known. We have no idea why he was chosen to perform this important task, but he was asked to send a copy to each committee member. The members were expected to read it carefully, prepare critical essays on it and then meet to discuss it before collectively crafting the final document. In order to facilitate the committee's functioning, the Nawab of Chhatari donated five hundred rupees. Some months later, Sandelvi produced not merely a minor tract but a hefty manuscript running over three hundred pages titled *Islam ka Siyasi Nizam* (*The Political System of Islam*). Daryabadi claims that he prepared his critical essay on this draft and sent it to Nadwi expecting other members to have done the same. However, for reasons that remain unknown, the committee was never convened again to evaluate, amend and complete this painstakingly produced document.

In 1946, a certain Azizuddin, who claimed to be a functionary of an organization called *Maarif-i-Milli* from the Central Provinces, wrote to Daryabadi pleading that he be sent the precious document. It was any way lying idle with the committee and Azizuddin expressed a desire to publish it for the benefit of the community at large. Stung by the letter and discouraged by the committee's apathetic attitude, Daryabadi sent his copy to Azizuddin by registered post after informing Nadwi. To his consternation, Daryabadi never heard back from his correspondent nor could trace him subsequently and therefore despondently concluded that the document was lost forever. But as luck would have it, the copy belonging to Nadwi himself was finally traced and was published in 1957 by the *Darul Musannifin*, Azamgarh that Nadwi himself had established in 1914 as an Islamic research institute. In the meantime, in 1947, India got partitioned and Pakistan came into existence. The Pakistani government now invited Nadwi to head the *Talimat-i-Islamia*, a special committee, which was set up to give advice to the Constituent Assembly for preparing an Islamic Constitution for Pakistan. Khwaja Shahabuddin, the Home Minister and brother of Khwaja Nazimuddin, the Bengal Leaguer who succeeded Jinnah as the Governor General, personally persuaded Nadwi to come to Pakistan, given his previous involvement in the project of drafting an Islamic Constitution.

The document prepared by Sandelvi deserves close attention for it became the primary source of recommendations made by the *Talimat-i-Islamia* to the Pakistan Constituent Assembly. Political and constitutional histories of Pakistan have thus far not taken into account this important document commissioned by the ML leadership that is indicative of their quest for some form of an Islamic state, nor have they highlighted their collaboration with the *ulama* for this purpose in the run up to the Partition. Instead, they have largely focused on the emerging conflict between the 'secular-modernist' ML leadership and the *ulama*–Mawdudi combine that came to a head in the years following Jinnah's death but not before the latter extracted important concessions such as the Objectives Resolution.[94]

Sandelvi claimed at the outset that his document had two objectives.[95] First, it wanted to demonstrate that the world's political problems could be solved by Islam and in this context he offered the Straight Path to the West. Secondly, he wanted to provide a constitutional draft to Islamic societies to help them in formulating their political systems.[96] Sandelvi made it clear that the political system of Islam was the Caliphate, which he claimed was built on purely religious foundations unlike the secular state that separated religion and politics. The sovereign, the centerpiece of this system around whom the whole Constitution revolved, was God.[97] To implement His laws so that the common man could come close to God was the duty of the Islamic state. Sandelvi noted that God provided two primary sources for law – first the Quran and secondly the Sunna. The words and actions of his Companions, *Ijma* or consensus among experts in Islamic law on any particular problem on which the Quran and Sunna were silent, and finally *Qiyas* or analogical reasoning (from the command forbidding alcohol consumption, one could derive a similar command against consuming *Bhang*), were subsidiary sources of law.

Citing various verses from the Quran, Sandelvi argued that establishing an Islamic state was obligatory for Muslims and they were expected to acquire the necessary means to achieve this end. These verses made it clear that God

94 For a recent survey, see Christophe Jaffrelot, *A History of Pakistan and its Origins* (London, 2002). The only exception is the essay by Muhammad Qasim Zaman, 'South Asian Islam and the Idea of the Caliphate', in Madawi Al-Rashid, Carool Kersten and Marat Shterin, *Demystifying the* Caliph*ate: Historical Memory and Contemporary Contexts*, (New York, 2013), 57–80.

95 I am indebted to Azra Kidwai for translating this important document for me

96 Muhammad Ishaq Sandelvi, *Islam Ka Siyasi Nizam, Jis Mein Islam ke Siyasi Nizam ka Asasi Khaka Pesh Kiya Gaya Hai* (Azamgarh, 1957), 8.

97 Ibid., 17–18.

made three promises – authority and power to rule for the faithful, propagation and spread of the faith, peace and prosperity. This was a collective package and not availing it in its entirety implied ingratitude on the part of man. In this regard, he also pointed out that the Quran itself revealed that the Israelites had to face God's wrath for lacking courage to enter the Holy land and fight for it. Sandelvi further emphasized this requirement of a pious life by quoting a verse from Iqbal.[98]

> Since the Mullah has the permission to bow in Sajda
> He is stupid to think that it is freedom for Islam.

Responsibility for establishing an Islamic state based on Islamic law would lie with the *Caliph/Amir/Imam*, who was like the Prophet's Deputy. The Caliph himself required some necessary qualifications. He had to be Muslim (since only a Muslim could implement Islamic laws), male, devout, moral, fluent in Arabic, knowledgeable in *Fiqh* with the ability to interpret and explain various parts of the *Shariah*.[99] He also needed to be physically able, intelligent, mature, perceptive and well versed in politics. The Caliph was to be elected by a body comprising religious experts (*ulama*), experts in other fields of knowledge, educated and respectable people and not by the masses. His election would happen after electors placed their hand in the hand of the Caliph thus giving their loyalty (*Bai'at*).[100] Sandelvi acknowledged it was important that the Caliph should not be appointed against the wishes of the masses. Yet, he asserted that the opinion of the masses was undependable and it was therefore not necessary to always consider their wishes. The Rightly Guided Caliphs themselves, he noted, were never elected by the masses.[101] It was also quite possible for a section of the masses to be unhappy with the Caliph but this could never be a disqualification. As an example Sandelvi pointed out that many Muslims including several Companions were not happy with the appointment of Hazrat Ali. Yet, his right

---

98 Ibid., 59.

99 Ibid., 76–77. Sandelvi here quoted the Hadith Sahih Bukhari, which declared that a Nation that appointed a woman as its head never experienced success or prosperity. As he concluded, given the wide-ranging powers and duties of the Caliph, the *Shariah* made it was obvious that a woman could not become one nor did she have the necessary intelligence to become one just as a slave too lacked these qualities and could not become a Caliph.

100 Ibid., 112–15.

101 Ibid., 161.

of Caliphate was accepted. There were three other valid ways by which a Caliph could be appointed for which there were historical precedents, but Sandelvi expressed his personal opposition to these methods. These included *Istikhlaf* wherein a Caliph appointed someone as his successor in his own lifetime (like Abu Bakr appointed Umar), appointment by *Shura* from a list chosen by the Caliph (like in the case of Uthman), or *Istila* wherein a person got appointed due to his power of persuasion (like Muawiya).

Sandelvi argued that the method of appointing Caliph in the Islamic state was far superior to the way in which heads of state were elected in western democracies. These latter leaders did not require any qualifications or training. All they needed was skill at party intrigues and the ability to attract voters who were generally emotional and had a very limited worldview.[102] The Islamic state in contrast to a democracy would remain strong as the relationship between the pious Caliph and the masses was based not just on laws but on love and trust. Unlike dictators of Europe, heads of democracies or kings, who dared not live alone in their palaces for even a minute, a Caliph lived alone in an ordinary hut even on dark nights. Sandelvi added that in the Golden Age of Islam, the Caliphs used to travel for miles on a camel with one servant and they could do this because of their loving relationship with the people.[103]

Outlining the Caliph's wide-ranging duties, Sandelvi stated that he was to be responsible for the moral health of both the individual and the society. He would, therefore be obliged to control three aspects of human life – thoughts, values and deeds – for which he would have three categories of duty – correction, supervision and training. Thus, if the direction of Muslim thought strayed from the straight path, the Caliph would have to implement measures to correct it. It was also imperative that thought and learning were supervised in order to prevent the spread of non-Islamic evils, while training entailed the Caliph promoting development of Islamic thought and knowledge so that non-Islamic thought would be eclipsed. The Caliph would thus also be responsible for *Tabligh* (proselytization) and as an example, Sandelvi pointed to the efforts made by the Prophet and his Companions in this direction.[104] The Caliph would accordingly be invested with wide-ranging powers in order to perform his duties. He would head all government departments, with the power to dismiss anyone in the whole army and the police force, expand or reduce every department. He would

102 Ibid., 105–11.

103 Ibid., 100.

104 Ibid., 126–29.

also have the power to formulate rules and norms, approve or disapprove the performance of his subordinates, issue orders to them, manage finances as well as declare war and peace. It was compulsory for all people to obey his orders and disobedience was not only a crime but also a sin.[105] Sandelvi pointed out that the Quran made it obligatory for a Muslim to obey his Caliph. He quoted a Hadith in which Muhammad reportedly said, 'Listen to your leader and obey his orders, even if your leader is a Slave of Negro origin.'[106]

The Caliph could also appoint a Vazir to 'remind him if he forgets' and help him run the administration.[107] Since the defense of the Islamic state was the Caliph's responsibility, he had to establish a War department and a military. Here, Sandelvi noted that more than military training, the strength of the Islamic army derived from its piety, honesty and devotion to God. It was, therefore, necessary to enrol in it individuals with lofty aims and chaste character.[108] In this context, Sandelvi also took up the question of whether women could be given military training since women had been active in Islamic armies of the yore. He declared that since military training had been available to veiled and modest women for centuries, the same was possible in this day and age especially since Islamic states had many more resources as compared to earlier times.[109]

While the Caliph would enjoy extensive powers, Sandelvi also outlined limits to his powers. He could be opposed if he went against the *Shariah*. Offences by a Caliph could be of three types – apostasy, immorality and cruelty.[110] For apostasy, Sandelvi quoted a Hadith in which it was stated that a Muslim who abandoned Islam should be killed. As regards immorality, the Caliph could be opposed for two types of disobedience to Islamic law.[111] In the first case, if he encouraged disobedience and secondly, if he himself became disobedient. Thus, in the former case a deviating Caliph might allow his men to indulge in drinking, gambling, or marrying a non-Muslim, or allow sale and purchase of liquor, give out its contracts, or allow publication of writings that were undesirable by Islamic moral standards. But while a Caliph who was disobedient had to be

---

105 Ibid., 172–73.

106 Ibid., 136.

107 Ibid., 247.

108 Ibid., 258.

109 Ibid., 260.

110 Ibid., 137.

111 Ibid., 141.

removed, Sandelvi noted that the condition of his removal was that it should not cause trouble or *fitna*.[112]

Limits to the Caliph's power were also imposed by the *Shariah* council (*Majlis-i-Shura*),which enjoyed its own set of powers. In the first place, the Caliph was to be elected by this council thus attesting to its importance. The council was also the place where the process for deposing the Caliph could be initiated.[113] He could not curtail this power of the council. Second, the Caliph could formulate laws that were in accordance with the *Shariah* in consultation with this council. Sandelvi pointed out that according to the Hadith, the Caliph should seek guidance from religious experts for otherwise the government would no longer be an Islamic government.[114] Third, members of this council would have the right to criticize actions and opinions of the Caliph and other functionaries of the government. Fourth, the council would have the power to appoint a commission to enquire into the accounts of the public treasury or demand an account of expenditure from the Caliph. Fifth, the council would have the right to meet without the presence of the Caliph.[115] Sixth, the Caliph would not have the right to impose a new tax or impose any new expenditure on the public treasury without consulting the council.[116] Yet, in the final analysis, the Caliph was to be all powerful since he was not obliged to accept the council's advice and could disregard it on any matter.

Ulama well versed in *Shariah* were obviously going to dominate this council but it was supposed to include a variety of other experts who could advise the Caliph on various matters. Sandelvi however made it clear that non-Muslims, Shias and Qadiyanis would be barred from its membership. On the question of how the council was to be constituted, he declared that its members could be elected by the people. While election was not the method in the Golden Age of the Prophet and his Companions, the Quran, the Hadith and Rightly Guided Caliphs all accepted the people's right to elect members of the council.[117] Moreover, he cautioned that it was not advisable to leave appointment of members to the Caliph in this present day and age. While people were to elect the council's members, Sandelvi introduced an important limitation. The

112 Ibid., 146.

113 Ibid., 208.

114 Ibid., 196–97.

115 Ibid., 211.

116 Ibid., 189.

117 Ibid., 203.

popular vote was applicable only to election of experts in non-religious fields and not to religious experts who were to be elected only by fellow *ulama*.[118] As far as voters were concerned, the right to vote again could be granted only to Muslims who were mature and of normal intellect.

Laws in the Islamic state were to be formulated through a process of consultation between the Caliph and the *Shariah* Council. The draft of proposed law could be suggested by either the Caliph or a member of the council. Any suggestion that was against the Islamic law could not be presented and formulating any law against the *Shariah* was forbidden.[119] Every member of the council had the right to consider and express opinion on the proposed legislation. This was not based on party discipline as was the case in western democracies but based on unbiased and sincere understanding of the issue. Sandelvi next tackled the important question regarding the criteria for adopting a legislative proposal – whether it would be based on majority approval as in the case of western democracies or agreement by consensus. He claimed that majority opinion, which was the norm in western democracies, was a rather stupid rule. On the contrary, legislation in the Islamic state was based on strength of argument rather than strength of numbers. The Caliph could, therefore, disregard majority opinion in the *Shariah* Council on the matter of formulating Laws. Sandelvi, however, hastened to add that that majority opinion was not always ignored in Islam. After all the Imam of a mosque was selected by a majority decision of worshippers and the Caliph's selection too was also based on majority approval in the *Shariah* Council. Yet, Sandelvi pointed out that the Prophet himself had made it clear that while majority opinion was like an important argument, it could yet be secondary to other arguments. Support of the majority had become a power in itself and democracies had lamentably started worshipping it, making it the measure of right and wrong. Life in democracies had therefore become dependent on majority opinion and Sandelvi saw this as a pernicious rule. Nature after all demonstrated that right and wrong were dependent on argument and not the system of counting raised hands of approval.[120] Thus, the Caliph would have the power to reject even the unanimous opinion of the *Shariah* Council even though it was not always advisable. As regards the judiciary, Sandelvi emphasized that the *Qazi* would be independent of the Caliph's influence in the execution of his duties. The

118 Ibid., 207.

119 Ibid., 215.

120 Ibid., 218.

Qazi would have every right to summon the Caliph, accept law suits against him and pass judgments against him.[121] The *Qazi's* freedom would however be limited to his functions for his appointment and dismissal would still be controlled by the Caliph. Thus, even though the court would be independent, the position of the Caliph would remain superior.

As evident, Sandelvi had made it clear that non-Muslims could not participate in the political process, get jobs in the military, police, or civil services. Yet, he hastened to add that they would enjoy civil and religious rights in the Islamic state. The *Dhimmis* would be free to follow their faith even though in some cases the state would be well within its rights to bar certain customs that militated against Islamic sensibilities. Here he was certain that the practice of *Sati* would not be allowed in the Islamic state.[122] The *Dhimmis* would also exempt from serving in the army for which they would have to pay *jizya* (poll-tax). If however, they joined the army of their own free will, they would be exempt from it.[123] Thus, even if Sandelvi had earlier shut the door on non-Muslims, he still kept open some cracks in the system. Non-Muslims would also be free to appoint their religious head, while their property and rights would be protected on par with that of Muslims.

Sandelvi also went into details regarding the finances of the Islamic state, the kinds of taxes it could levy on people to realize income and maintain economic balance in society.[124] They included *kharaj* (tax on cultivable land), *ashar* (another land tax), *jizya* (tax paid by non-Muslims), *zakat* (tax in the form of percentage of saved wealth in currency or material form), *khams* (a percentage of booty realized during wars) and *ashur* (tax on trade of Muslims and non-Muslims). The important question he asked in this context was whether the Islamic state would have the right to impose taxes that were not mentioned in the *Shariah*.[125] Sandelvi noted that in the Prophet's time except for the taxes mentioned above, there were no other taxes. Whenever the government felt the need for additional resources, borrowing and contributions were resorted to and levying of new taxes was avoided. This precedent was a practical lesson for Islamic state and it was further supported by the Quran and Hadith. He thus suggested that an Islamic state did not have the right to put additional

121 Ibid., 249–50.

122 Ibid., 228.

123 Ibid., 259.

124 Ibid., 232–40.

125 Ibid., 240.

material burden on its people. It meant that Islam was not in favour of adding new taxes for these would be considered tyranny and a grave sin. He added that multiplicity of taxes was the characteristic of the non-Islamic states particularly those that were capitalist. Yet, Sandelvi conceded that the Islamic state had the right to implement new taxes in return for which the government had something to offer; for instance, tax on irrigation from government constructed canals, railway fares, or income from postal services. These taxes, he clarified, had the status of loan or compensation and were not really taxes. Additional taxes were also justified in emergency situations such as war when the state might require additional resources.[126] He pointed out that in Egypt taxes were levied for this purpose or for ransoming prisoners of war. The government could also levy taxes for the fulfillment of *Shariah* requirements but again these could be levied only in emergency situations and the government should not misuse these measures.

On the question of foreign affairs, Sandelvi conceded the possibility of the existence of more than one Islamic state even though ideally Islam required all Muslims to come together under one state and government.[127] He made it clear that love and friendship between Islamic states could not be replicated in the case of a relationship with a non-Islamic state. Non-Islamic states would not be looked upon as enemies as long as they did not create obstacles in preaching, practice and propagation of Islam. But *jihad* would become necessary if these governments broke this rule. The Islamic state was also obliged to fight a *jihad* to help Muslims who may have been persecuted or treated cruelly.[128] As regards Muslims living in a non-Islamic state who were not waging *jihad* because they were not in a position to do so, it was the Caliph's duty to help them migrate to the Islamic state.[129] Finally, Sandelvi made it clear that a *jihad* could be ordered only by an Amir or Caliph ruling over an Islamic state.[130]

In this context, dwelling on the question of prisoners of War, Sandelvi observed that they could be placed under slavery (*ghulami*). He, however, hastened to add that Muslims did not make anyone a slave in the English meaning of the word.[131] The *ghulam* was more like a worker or farmer in a Socialist country. He came into existence due to economic reasons, for war

126 Ibid., 242.

127 Ibid., 269.

128 Ibid., 278.

129 Ibid., 294.

130 Ibid., 281.

131 Ibid., 285.

affected the economy of the Islamic state even if it was victorious and the slave made a contribution to the economy. Economic recovery would lead to the end of slavery with the Caliph passing an order to end it. Sandelvi pointed to the example of the Caliph Umar who passed an order liberating all captives who were enslaved by the Islamic army.[132]

Sandelvi ended his treatise with a critique of non-Islamic regimes. The Islamic state, he claimed, came into being with the advent of man with Adam as the first Caliph appointed by Allah. Gradually with the increase in the population and its dispersion, people became distant from Adam and his influence was replaced by that of Satan leading to the dominance of greed and lust based on petty desires thus creating an inhuman environment based on animal instinct instead of human instinct. Men now felt themselves in command of all resources with the power to use them according to their needs and wishes without any interference or check. They believed that no power in the world had a right to impose any rule or law on them and rules were dependent on their own individual wishes and desires. This was the beginning of non-Islamic state.[133] Initially, small non-Islamic states were based on descent and tribal solidarity. In their current form, these states were of two types – those predicated on individual will and ability and those based on general will. The first kind was called monarchy while the second type included democracies and dictatorship.

Sandelvi argued that the king who ruled on the basis of descent did not require effort or ability to become a good ruler nor did he feel the need to acquire any qualifications. A monarchy devastated morals and psychology of people, engendering a slavish mentality among them, destroyed all self-respect and made them lose sensitivity towards their rights. The greatest defect of this system was that it had no moral basis since it was based on brute power. Turning to a critique of the second type of non-Islamic governments, Sandelvi described dictatorship as an uncontrolled combination of kingship and democracy. It never came into being in normal circumstances but only in abnormal conditions when some calamity struck a people disturbing their mental balance, allowing a clever person takes advantage of the situation, instigating the people, promising them favours and winning their support.[134]

Sandelvi, however, reserved his sharpest critique for democracy. He saw it as the most deceptive political system where humanity was slaughtered with a blunt

132 Ibid., 289.

133 Ibid., 296.

134 Ibid., 302–03.

knife and the poor and weak had no place.[135] While democracy was apparently based on the rule of general will, he characterized it as one of its greatest defects. After all the will of disparate individuals was not something that was stable or lasting for it could be lured with greed, aroused and disturbed by small events and ultimately crushed by the powerful. Immorality and decadence in work and behaviour developed in democracies for they lacked a moral standard for the people. Group prejudice (*asabiyat*) was an essential ingredient of democracy and involved suppression of the minority. Furthermore, in a democracy, formulation of law was in the hands of the most affluent sections though apparently all social groups were involved in law-making. This group essentially formulated laws that were advantageous to them and their prejudices and suppressed all other groups in every possible way. Sandelvi noted that capitalist democracies especially saw workers being treated like slaves with the affluent controlling society through a vast propaganda machine. In this system, the primary goal of society was further accumulation of capital, thus leading to worship of materialism and reducing people to an inhuman level. He pointed out that in England the Director of the Bank of England was more powerful than the Prime Minister. He also noted that in France as well, the frequent changes of government were due to its differences with the Director of its Central Bank. For Sandelvi, the depravity of this system was epitomized by a fact quoted in the writer John Gunther's book 'Inside Europe' that the bullet with which the German soldier killed the French soldier was manufactured in a French factory. Sandelvi's views were largely adopted by *ulama* agitating for an Islamic state in Pakistan immediately after its creation as evident from their twenty two point declaration in 1951. The *ulama* continue to actively advocate the codification of Islamic law in Pakistan under their own jurisdiction as religious experts, to make Pakistan truly Islamic.[136]

Rearticulating Pakistan in the Locality

Badayun, 19 April 1940

If we began by looking at how Pakistan was anticipated at the local level in the U.P. before the Lahore Resolution, we also need to look at how it was explained in its towns and *qasbahs after* the AIML session had concluded. The party had

135 Ibid., 304–11.

136 See Chapter 4 in Muhammad Qasim Zaman, *The Ulama in Contemporary Islam: Custodians of Change* (Princeton, 2002).

called for Pakistan Day celebrations on 19 April 1940 in order to contest the Congress claim that it did not have support beyond the 50,000 or so who had congregated at Lahore. These celebrations were widespread and Liaquat joyously claimed that nearly 10,000 meetings had been held throughout the country to affirm the Pakistan demand. Whether or not 10,000 of these events were held on that day one cannot be sure, but of the many meetings one was certainly held after the Friday prayers in Badayun, bordering Anis al Din Ahmad Rizvi's hometown of Bareily. It was addressed by the Vice President of the District ML, Maulvi Musavvir Ali Khan, who explained the Pakistan demand to the gathering. Again, as in the case of Anis al Din Ahmad Rizvi, one does not know a whole lot about him other than the fact that he too earned LLB and M.A. degrees from Aligarh. The introductory note to the text of the speech by the Secretary of the District ML reveals that a decision to publish it was made to urgently thwart false propaganda against Pakistan that was being spewed out by its opponents.[137] Musavvir Ali Khan, therefore, submitted the text of his speech to the local ML office on 9 May 1940. Money was then cobbled together to pay for the publishing costs and it finally appeared in print on 27 July 1940. While the number of published copies of this speech remains unknown, what it clearly indicates is that Pakistan had become the locus of much more vigorous debate and discussion in U.P. soon after the Lahore Resolution.

Musavvir Ali Khan's 'well received' speech, delivered in Urdu and lasting perhaps a little over an hour is striking for the clarity of its presentation, its sophisticated deployment of facts, concepts, arguments and its placing the new Muslim demand in a well-defined historical context. Finally, its delectable turn of phrase would only have served to enhance the overall performance on that hot Friday evening with the monsoon rains still a couple of months away. Before explaining Pakistan, Musavvir Ali Khan first dismantled the Congress ideal of 'complete independence'. He derisively noted that although the Congress frequently spouted phrases like *Purna Swaraj*, whenever an opportunity to overthrow British rule arose it usually ended up concluding gentlemen's agreements with them that always fell far short of that goal. He singled out Gandhi in this regard, deriding his false posturing and 'childish tantrums'. The Mahatma, before embarking on his Dandi March, had declared that he would either come back with freedom or his body would be found floating in the sea. And yet, the drama had ended with Gandhi having a pleasant tea-party

[137] Maulvi Musavvir Ali Khan, *Musalmanan-i-Hind ka Siyasi Nasbul Ain aur Jamhuriyat-i-Hind* (Badayun, 1940).

with the Viceroy at the Viceregal Lodge in Delhi, that ultimate symbol of the empire over which the sun as yet showed no signs of setting. Musavvir Ali Khan, therefore, swiftly dismissed as puerile, Gandhi's latest threat to renew civil disobedience. The British and Gandhi, he warned, were old friends and one could not take these theatrics too seriously. As he reminded his listeners, Gandhi's chief lieutenant, Nehru, had recently declared that Britain's enemies were also the enemies of India.

The Congress' real aim, he claimed, was not independence, but Federation (*Vifaqi Hukumat*) as stipulated under the 1935 GOI Act. The ML, he reminded his listeners, was sworn to oppose Federation at all costs since it would condemn Muslims to perpetual subordination under an absolute Hindu majority at the centre. As he noted in a telling phrase, in a democracy people were counted not weighed. Federation also meant subordination of the provinces under a centre that would have the power to strike down provincial legislation besides exercising several other controls over them. Musavvir Ali Khan, therefore, posed to his audience a series of rhetorical questions. Should we accept the federal scheme with a democratic system of government and submit ourselves to the Hindu majority? Would our communal identity survive if we make such a choice? Is it even necessary to preserve this identity or should it be merged into a Hindu identity to which the Congress had given the grand name of *Muttahida Qaumiyat*? The reaction of the audience is not included in the text, but it would be safe to conclude that the answer would have been a resounding no. Like his compatriot Anis Rizvi in neighbouring Bareily, he next proceeded to attack ideas of *wataniyat* (territorial nationalism) and *Muttahida Qaumiyat* (composite nationalism/common nationality).

Echoing Rizvi, Musavvir Ali Khan argued that these ideas had their basis in Hindu religious thinking. It was repugnant for Muslims to accept these Hindu ideas, more so since Islam constituted the basis for national community and disqualified any other criteria of belonging. He asserted that Islam was an eternal and comprehensive way of life (*mustaqil nazariya-i-hayat*) and entailed cultural unity (*tamadduni wahdat*) born out of a unity of religion and politics. It broke all connections with narrow solidarities such as *wataniyat* and an individual subjecting himself to the discipline of Islam's complete way of life became part of its vast brotherhood. More importantly, he averred that Islam permitted only the government of God, based on His laws, which were already fixed (*mo'ay'yaan wa muqarrar*) and could not be made by man. Thus, if Muslims accepted a common Indian nationality based on territorial nationalism they would cease to be Muslims.

Musavvir Ali Khan warned his listeners to guard against the ideology of composite nationalism especially since it had in some cases proved effective with the youth and independent minded (*azad khayal*) people. Addressing such people as also the community at large, he asked them as to how they would respond in case India in the name of national interest militarily attacked Afghanistan or Iran or if India were forced to side with allies such as Britain, China or Japan, which then attacked the Arab lands? What would the duty of Indian Muslims be in such a situation? Would they according to the ideology of composite nationalism, side with their own government against Turkey as they had been compelled to do so during the Great War or would they revolt against it? He concluded this argument by noting that these issues could not be comprehended by Gandhi who stood outside the Islamic religious imagination. Nothing else could explain his dogged insistence that a Hindu converting to Islam could not possibly lose his nationality. By contrast, he pointed out that Jinnah, who was often accused of being a non-observant Muslim, had flatly asked the Government to desist from using Indian soldiers against Muslim powers in the War.

Musavvir Ali Khan further pointed to the numerous failed efforts throughout history at forging a common nationality of Indians. Like Ambedkar would do so later, he noted that saints like Nanak and Kabir had tried but failed in this endeavour. More importantly, he pointed out that the Emperor Akbar had created a new religion called *Din-i-Illahi* for this purpose. But not only did it again fail miserably, it ultimately hollowed out the Mughal State's foundations allowing the rise of the Sikhs on the one hand and Shivaji on the other, with the latter going on to establish the first Hindu state in India. He further claimed that Shivaji's present day successors could be found in the Hindu Mahasabha and even the Congress, which was not much different from the Mahasabha. After all in the heart of their hearts all Congressmen were supporters of its ideology as evident from Dr Moonje's claim that all Congressmen would become members of the Hindu Mahasabha if Gandhi were to remove a ban on that practice. The only difference between the two, he asserted, was that between a bitter pill and a sugarcoated bitter pill.

Echoing ideas that were common currency in the ML discourse by now, Musavvir Ali Khan stated that one could find many other examples of the failure of *Muttahida Qaumiyat*. These included the existence of separate languages and literatures of the Hindus and Muslims and the lack of commensality or inter-marriage between them. Taking the argument further, he contended that the very idea of safeguards for minorities was the best proof that it was a hollow ideology. Why would the Muslims want safeguards if the majority could be trusted? Also, even if safeguards were accepted as necessary, how could their implementation be left in Hindu hands? After all, what the Hindus had done to the Untouchables throughout history was evident for all to see. More recently when the Untouchables demanded separate representation, Gandhi had gone on a fast unto death to deprive them of their rights. Musavvir Ali Khan also pointed to international examples of Poland and Czechoslovakia to demonstrate that safeguarding national rights was the nation's own responsibility and could not be left to someone else. After all even the Allies with all their combined power had not been able to save them from Nazi aggression. In this context, Musavvir Ali Khan further enquired as to what the nationalist Muslims would do in case Muslim rights were trampled upon by Hindus in India. Would they resort to *Satyagraha*, he sarcastically demanded. Muslims, therefore, could not afford to lose their separate identity. If the Hindus hoped to rule over them in a future government, they would have to contend with a civil war. Following his *Qaid*, he concluded his critique of the idea of composite nationalism by dismissing the idea that India was one single country (*mulk*), insisting that it was a collection of a few countries (*mamalik*), which were geographically and historically distinct from one another.

Given the impossibility of Hindus and Muslims coalescing into a single nationality, Musavvir Ali Khan laid down his interpretation of the ML scheme for their separation. He noted that while the Muslims had an overwhelming majority in Sind, NWFP and Baluchistan, in Punjab and Bengal their majorities were slim or nominal. The ML, he claimed, wanted territorial boundaries of these provinces to be altered in such a way that Muslims could become an effective majority. It, therefore, wanted Ambala division in Punjab and Hindu majority areas around Calcutta to be cut away and some Muslim districts of Assam added to Bengal to make up Pakistan's territory. After these territorial readjustments, Punjab, Sind, NWFP and Baluchistan in the west could be formed into one sovereign federation with Kashmir and Kapurthala joining it under the same conditions as offered to them in the all India Federation. This Muslim federation in the west would have a solid 72 per cent Muslim majority. Eastern Bengal and Muslim districts in Assam would form a second Muslim federation. The Hindu provinces in the middle could form a third federation while a fourth federation could be made up of native states. Musavvir Ali Khan was amenable to native states joining the Hindu federation if they so wished but he wanted Hyderabad to be allowed to retain its independence while also recouping Berar and those parts of Karnataka that had been taken away by the British. He estimated that together the two Muslim federations would have a population of about 6 crore Muslims leaving 2.5–3 crore Muslims behind in the Hindu federation and native states. Unlike Anis al Din Ahmad Rizvi earlier, he did not insist on any part of U.P. being included in Pakistan, signaling a shift in the position taken by ML functionaries on the ground.

Musavvir Ali Khan next dispelled misconceptions regarding the Lahore Resolution. First, taking into account the minority provinces Muslims, he argued that Partition did not entail large scale transfers of population. He clarified though that if such population transfers were easy to manage at some places there was no harm in allowing them, but these again would have to be done gradually. In any case, like Mahmudabad he declared that large-scale migration of Muslims and their shrinking into any one single territory was against the spirit of Islam whose universal message and expanding mission required their widest possible spread around the world. Yet, the question still remained as to how partition was going to be beneficial to minority provinces Muslims. In answering this question, Musavvir Ali Khan grandly declared that even though they were not getting anything out of it the U.P. Muslims would support Partition since they did not want their brethren in the majority provinces to be enslaved under Hindu domination and instead wanted them to be liberated so that they could lead an Islamic way of life. They had earlier made a grievous mistake when under the 1916 Lucknow Pact they bartered away the rights of Punjabi and Bengali Muslims to secure weightage for themselves. This safeguard had, however, not benefitted them even under the 1935 GOI Act for their position was bad under the Congress provincial governments and it would remain the same in a Hindu federation. Musavvir Ali Khan asserted that they were not going to repeat the same mistake again. The U.P. Muslims were now prepared to accept representation according to their proportion of population along with safeguards, which would likewise be granted to the Hindus in Pakistan on a reciprocal basis. The U.P. Muslims were making a sacrifice, but this was a necessary sacrifice. Here, he used a striking metaphor to make his point. He asked his audience to imagine a man whose hand had developed a cancerous growth. There was every possibility of this cancer developing and spreading to all parts of the body and threatening its survival. The doctor had advised a surgical amputation of the hand to save the person and if he was sane he would surely let the hand be amputated to save the body. Musavvir Ali Khan claimed that the body at large was that of the Muslim nation, for the Hadith had clearly stated that all Muslims were one body. The minority province Muslims were like the cancerous hand that had to be amputated as the survival of the whole body was at stake. But even if he heroically invoked the language of sacrifice, he sought to instill courage in his listeners. As he pointed out, even though Muslims in U.P. would be left behind in the Hindu federation, it would not dare to mess with them, for the creation of Pakistan would create a 'balance of power' between the two sides. Here, he echoed the hostage population theory that had become the bedrock of the ML's defence of Pakistan. Moreover, he noted that Hindu and Muslim federations could conclude mutual treaties to provide effective safeguards to their minorities. They could develop good relations on the basis of these treaties and even become allies by establishing an international body such as a League of Nations through which they could come together in order to organize India's defence. He therefore did not rule out a coming together of the two sides but insisted that it would have to be on the basis of an international treaty between sovereign nations. A common centre was thus firmly ruled out.

Second, Musavvir Ali Khan confronted emotional objections to breaking India apart. As he sardonically remarked, the creation of separate federations would not lead to an earthquake, which would tear up the earth allowing the oceans to enter into the cracks and separate the lands. Nor would a Great Wall of China suddenly emerge between them. The subcontinent would continue to remain where it always was – at the southern tip of Asia. All provinces would remain in their current place and would not go flying in separate directions. Just as one could go from U.P. to Punjab on Frontier Mail today, one could continue to do so in the future as well. Similarly, one could take the train from Allahabad to Calcutta in the future as was being done presently. Why the Hindus were likening the division of the country to cutting a live body was indeed a mystery to Musavvir Ali Khan. As he sarcastically remarked, only the destructive mentality of our Hindu brothers was capable of performing such expansive feats of strewing the parts of the imagined body of Hindustan. The more sensible way to see the Partition was in terms of two brothers deciding to lead separate lives for the sake of peace and happiness and, therefore, dividing their house. One brother could not reasonably refuse on the grounds that he did not like the house being divided into two parts. Muslims would certainly not accept such objections or give up their subordination under English masters only to become the slaves of the Hindus in an undivided India.

Third, Musavvir Ali Khan demolished the idea that partition would weaken India as a whole. As he pointed out, physically India and Europe (excluding Russia) were of the same size. If Europe divided into so many nation-states had produced several great powers such as Germany, France and Italy, there was no reason why nation-states in the subcontinent with comparable territory and population could not produce similar Great Powers. Besides, there was no reason why they could not have cordial mutual relations or even political alliances with one another. Such an alliance was currently in place between France and England against Germany, which was mutually beneficial. Yet, the alliance did not entail a giving up of their respective identities and coming under one government. In this regard, Musavvir Ali Khan responded to the lofty rhetoric from the Congress left wing and especially Nehru, who repeatedly emphasized that Pakistan was an anachronism in an age when regional federations or indeed a world federation were the future of mankind. Clearing the air, he declared that while the talk of such federations was indeed prevalent, Germans, Italians, or the French would only agree to a federation that would allow them to keep their separate national identities. As regards a world federation, it again could only be based on an international agreement (*Bain al aqwami samjhauta*) under which different nations would keep their national identities while coming together on the basis of equality. If such a federation were proposed for the subcontinent, he reiterated that the ML would not be against such a proposal. To emphasize Pakistan's sovereignty, Musavvir Ali Khan declared that the ML would not allow it to be submerged in a Pan-Islamic federation that would then try to invade India, a favorite bugbear of some sections of Hindu political opinion in India. To further illustrate his point, he noted that the Afghans had never asked the Iranians to take over their country. Similarly, Pakistan would never allow its sovereignty to be dissolved in favour of a broad Islamic front, thus echoing his *Qaid* rather than Mahmudabad. Musavvir Ali Khan also made it clear that if Pakistan ever decided to join a larger body as a sovereign state it would join the British Commonwealth along with Hindustan rather than some other federation. The federations of Hindustan and Pakistan could have good relations with each other on this basis as also with countries such as Iran and Afghanistan. Such, however, would not be the case if the Hindus sought to force the Muslims into an All India Federation. That would certainly give rise to a fifth column in the Pakistan regions, which would only threaten India's security. There was hence no reason why 9 crore Indian Muslims with their distinct religion, culture and civilization should be denied Pakistan on the grounds that it endangered Indian unity, especially when that unity itself was imaginary in the first place.

Musavvir Ali Khan saw the partition of India not only as the only way to secure Muslim political, cultural and religious freedom but also as the only path to their economic salvation. As he explained, while their insecure and pitiable condition in the 'minority provinces' was well known, even in the majority provinces, Muslim wealth was being extracted and funneled into Hindu treasuries. This was because Hindus controlled the levers of the economy. Internal and external trade was in Hindu hands and many Muslims were indebted to Hindu moneylenders. One did not find Muslim industrialists or capitalists even though one could find plenty of Muslim artisans and workers. The only way Muslims could overcome their economic problems, he insisted, was to take full control over their own areas where they were in a majority. In this context, he summarily dismissed the Congress left wing's claim that it would establish socialism to liberate all Indians irrespective of their particular identities, claiming that these modern ideologies were inadequate to solve mankind's problems. Musavvir Ali Khan saw no difference between capitalism and socialism describing both as highly exploitative systems. He noted that the pitiable condition of the masses in Soviet Russia was a clear example of how even under socialism, one party and its functionaries ruled over the rest of the people. There was thus no difference between Stalin and the Fascists.

In this context, like Anis al Din Rizvi before him, Musavvir Ali Khan grandly declared that the only solution to mankind's problems lay in Islam. His assertion reflected popular Muslim sentiment, which saw Islam as the bountiful source of ideas that could be creatively mined to find new solutions to the problems of inequality and exploitation afflicting man in the modern world, which other ideologies had failed to resolve. These solutions would presumably be tried out in Pakistan. He, however, did not delve at any great length on this issue or provide an Islamic blueprint, hoping to satisfy his listeners with a few homilies and anodyne statements. Islam, he claimed, erased extremes and created balance in every aspect of life. It neither glorified vast familial property nor did it allow for state appropriation of individual wealth while it eschewed the virtues of poverty that Gandhi was teaching. Ultimately, Islam gave the individual the freedom to earn his living and also spend his income, while at the same time making provisions for the distribution of their excessive wealth to the poor. Thus, while it encouraged people to create wealth, it discouraged people from craving for it in their hearts, in the process teaching them that wealth was not for accumulation but for expenditure on noble causes.

However, if Muslims were to be granted a separate state of their own, the question remained as to why other nationalities such as the Untouchables or Sikhs should not be granted their own states as well. Musavvir Ali Khan responded to this objection by arguing that the differences between the Hindus and the Untouchables were not as acute as the differences between Hindus and Muslims. He underlined his point by claiming that the Untouchables themselves did not feel these differences so keenly and hence had not demanded a separate state for themselves. Besides, even if they were to raise such a demand, it could not be entertained since they did not have a majority in any part of the country in any defined piece of territory where such a state could be established. Thus, no separate state could be granted to them. As far as the Sikhs were concerned, he did not directly address their potential demand for statehood. Instead, he urged them to join Pakistan for their own benefit. Their position as a minority in a smaller Pakistan would be comparatively far better than in a much bigger Hindustan. In the former their percentage of population would be greater thus allowing them higher proportion of representation in the government and the services than they could ever hope for in Hindustan. Musavvir Ali Khan's reasoning thus demonstrated how the language of nations, sub-national groups, majorities and minorities, institutionalized by the League of Nations had become a part of the political vocabulary of ML functionaries even in the *mofussil* in India.

Musavvir Ali Khan also rejected the accusation that ML leaders behind the Pakistan scheme were British stooges implementing the strategy of divide and rule by exacerbating Hindu–Muslim hatreds so as to keep Britain as the ruling power in the subcontinent. Instead, he reversed these charges and accused the Congress of committing these crimes. To begin with, if by forming an all India federation, India could become free, he demanded to know why India could not become free instead by the creation of two or three independent federations. Here he also reiterated his charge that the Congress demand for complete independence was a sham. British power, he asserted, would not withdraw from the subcontinent, for nobody wanted such a withdrawal until India was capable of militarily defending itself on its own. Thus, Musavvir Ali Khan foresaw continuing British presence in India for the foreseeable future, helping with India's defence and also playing the referee in the disputes between the separate and independent Hindu and Muslim federations that would be created in the subcontinent.

As regards exacerbation of Hindu–Muslim hatreds that the Congress was warning about, Musavvir Ali Khan argued that ML's proposal would on the contrary, bring down communal tensions and lead to better relations between Hindustan and Pakistan. Here he also blamed the Congress for raising communal tensions as evident from Rajagopalachari's statement that likened the division of India to the cutting of a cow into two halves. He also reminded his listeners that it was the Congress, which was not averse to using divide and rule tactics, as evident from its dirty tricks during the *Madhe Sahaba* agitation to divide the Shias and Sunnis. He also accused the Congress of egging the Shias to demand safeguards while also encouraging the Momins to describe themselves as the Untouchables in the Muslim community who were downtrodden and exploited by their own brethren. He finally reminded his listeners that it was the Congress again which through its MMCP and its policy of encouraging defections from the ML in the legislative assembly, had used money power and other inducements to divide the Muslim community in order to rule over it. He, therefore, warned his listeners to beware of such insidious attempts to cause splits within their ranks and urged them to remain united.

Finally, Musavvir Ali Khan sought to instill confidence in the community that Pakistan would indeed be a viable state in spite of the tremendous odds ranged against it. As he pointed out, nobody expected Germany to rise from the ashes within just twenty years of the Treaty of Versailles and rebuild itself in such a way that it now challenged all the powers of the world simultaneously. Nobody expected Turkey, the sick man of Europe, to resurrect itself under Mustafa Kamal and regain its place as one of the front ranking powers of Europe. Indeed, nobody expected a callow 18 year old youth, Muhammad Bin Qasim, leading a handful of Muslims to bring down the most powerful kingdom in western India and lay the foundations of Islamic rule in India. Even the revolution that Islam itself gave birth to was not visualized before the appearance of the Prophet. Those who saw Pakistan as impossible in the present circumstances, therefore, needed to rouse themselves by keeping such examples in mind, more so the example of the Prophet and the rise of Islam. Musavvir Ali Khan then gave his listeners the mantra that would enable them to achieve Pakistan. Total faith in the truth of their goal (*yaqin wa imaan kaamil*), passionate urge for sacrifice (*qurbani ki tadap*), practical strength (*quvvat-i-amal*) and finally, disciplined organization of the nation (*tanzim-i-millat*). He pointed out that it is these attributes that were allowing the Allies to keep up the fight against the Nazis. Thus, even though they knew that they would have to sacrifice millions of lives and spend millions of pounds to stop Hitler in his tracks, they were not letting it break their spirit.

Musavvir Ali Khan's wide ranging oration clarified four important points before the ML's base. First, that U.P. would not be a part of Pakistan as it would be left behind in Hindu India. It is an assumption that would remain notwithstanding Jinnah's later reference to a corridor connecting East and West Pakistan running through northern U.P. Second, Pakistan was envisaged as a sovereign, independent and viable state like any other nation-state, as underlined by the frequent references to nation-states in Europe against which Pakistan was seen to compare favourably in terms of its territorial expanse and population size. Even if some common defence arrangement with Hindu India was considered along with a degree of continuing British presence, this was seen as an arrangement between sovereign entities. Third, Pakistan was visualized as an Islamic state, a utopia where the Muslim nation would thrive as a moral community besides gaining political liberation and economic justice. Finally, as regards the position of U.P. Muslims, Pakistan was presented as a shining symbol of their sacrifices, which would not remain in vain for this new nation-state would act as an effective guarantor for the protection of their rights and interests. The possibility of migration to Pakistan on a voluntary basis or through mutual and orderly transfers of populations was always on the anvil given the presence of hostage minority populations on either side.

Lucknow, 29 November 1941

Pakistan conferences in U.P. were also graced and addressed by prominent politicians from the majority provinces as is the case with the one addressed by Sir Shahnawaz Khan of Mamdot,the Punjab ML President in Lucknow in late November 1941. Mamdot's address needs to be closely examined to look at how he defined Pakistan's territoriality.[138] Unlike local party functionaries in U.P. who seemed quite willing to let go of Hindu majority areas of Punjab, Mamdot publicly pitched for the entire province to be included in Pakistan. Yet, in private, like Liaquat, Mamdot seemed willing to let go of the Ambala division since economically it would not contribute anything to Pakistan. At the same time it would serve the purpose of raising Muslim proportion in Pakistan. In public though, delineating Pakistan's territorial expanse, Mamdot stated that Pakistan was that piece of India (*barr-i-azam Hind ka woh tukda*) that consisted of Punjab, NWFP, Kashmir, Sind and Baluchistan. As far as its boundaries were concerned, Mamdot explained that the dividing line between Hindustan and Pakistan was the Yamuna. This was their national homeland (*qaumi watan*) where Muslims had been living for over 1200 years and even to this day they comprised 80 per centof its population. The culture of its Muslims, he claimed, was distinct from that of non-Muslim Hindustan, giving them a unique social, political and ethical personality.

[138] Sir Shahnawaz Khan, *Khutba-i-Sadarat Jo Janab Nawab Sir Shahnawaz Khan Sahib Vali-i-Mamdot Punjab Ne Pakistan Conference Munaqidah Lakhnau mein 29 November 1941 ko Irshad Farmaya* (Lahore, 1941).

Mamdot surprisingly did not include East Pakistan in his description even though the Lahore Resolution implied Muslim majority zones on either extremities of British India.

Keeping in mind his audience – co-religionists living on the other side of the Yamuna – Mamdot explained that they were descendants of those Muslims who had gone across and conquered that land as a victorious people or those who later converted to Islam. He hastened to add that they were as much a part of the Muslim *qaum* as their brethren in Pakistan, but following Jinnah, Mamdot took care to define their status very precisely in order to underline a crucial difference in their status. Hindustan was above all an *occupied territory* where their ancestors had continued to stay even after power slipped away from Muslim hands. Thus, their descendants – Muslims who lived in these territories today – were *minorities* in Hindustan. Like his *Qaid*, Mamdot therefore introduced a qualification in the definition of the Muslim nation besides denying that India constituted a natural unity. As he stated, the claim that Hindustan was one country (*vahid mulk*) and its inhabitants one nation, that partitioning the country was tantamount to breaking mother India (*Bharat mata*) into two parts, or even cutting a child into two, was nothing short of a blasphemy (*Akhand Hindustan ka Pakhand*).

Turning to more recent history he explained how Pakistan, which had never been a part of Hindustan, was reduced to its constituent part. Muslims had unfortunately lost power to the British in 1857 since they lacked leaders blessed with political insight and wisdom. These leaders were unable to protect even their own national homeland. On their part, the British conveniently ignored the historical truth that Hindustan and Pakistan were different and driven by their lust for territorial aggrandizement (*havas-i-mulkgiri*) they jumbled them together (*khalt malt kar diya*). This trend continued till 1932 when the Round Table Conference gave birth to the idea of an Indian Federation. Continuing their disregard for these geographical, historical, civilizational and other differences stretching back over 1200 years, the British again decided to subordinate Pakistan to the Indian Federation, claiming that the former was an administrative part (*intizami juz*) of the latter. Its real effects became visible in the form of the GOI Act of 1935, a conspiracy between the Hindus and the British, which was forced upon Muslims. Mamdot was particularly bitter about the depleted Muslim majority in the Punjab where even though Muslims were 57 per cent of the population, their majority had been reduced to 51 per cent in the provincial legislative assembly thanks to weightage provided for minority province Muslims, which were also quite useless. Theirs was not an effective majority and indeed the provincial government was in the hands of non-Muslim shareholders. This was the *barakat* of safeguards, he lamented, under which even Pakistan had been reduced to Hindustan. Mamdot had no hesitation in declaring that the Muslims in the 'minority provinces' were in a far better situation than those in the 'majority provinces' – strong statement to make in front of an audience bristling with anger against the erstwhile 'Hindu' Congress government in the U.P.

Mamdot reiterated that Hindus and Muslims were two separate realities (*judagana haqiqaten*) who could not come together under the western principle of *Muttahida Qaumiyat* and warned his co-religionists to guard against its votary, Maulana Abul Kalam Azad. In this regard, he recounted that when Emperor Akbar tried his experiment in *Muttahida Qaumiyat* by creating a new religion, one of those who rejected it was Shaikh Jamaludin, an ancestor of Azad. And yet the same Azad, Mamdot regretted, was again trying to provide a new lease of life to this troubled dream. Insisting that Partition was necessary, he outlined two possible options. First, granting Pakistan the status of a new dominion while India was still under British rule. Thus, Hindustan and Pakistan would each have a separate centre. Secondly, if and when Britain decided to grant freedom to India, they could create these two as separate independent states (*judagana azad sultanatein*). Mamdot too made it clear that Pakistan would be an Islamic state (*hukumat-i-Ilahi*) since Islam did not differentiate between religion and politics (*din aur duniya*). Finally, it was again noted that at the opening of this Pakistan conference, 'the chief feature of the ceremony was a large map of India made of coloured earth, with Pakistan zones coloured green.'[139]

Contesting Pakistan in U.P.

A notable feature of U.P.'s political landscape is the number of political conferences and public meetings organized by supporters and opponents of Pakistan taking the battle to the grassroots. The ML's Pakistan Day celebrations on 19 April 1940 had 'aroused considerable popular enthusiasm'.[140] The party tried to keep up the momentum in subsequent years and articulated a variety of themes in this process. At the Pakistan day celebrations in 1941 in Allahabad, Mufti Fakhrul Islam the President of the city ML unit 'dilated at some length

---

139 *PAI for the week ending 28 November 1941.*

140 *PAI for the week ending 27 April 1940.*

on the opportunity which Pakistan would give to the Mussalmans to take revenge on Hindu minorities under their control, for atrocities perpetrated upon them by the Hindus.'[141] The Hyderabadi, Bahadur Yar Jung, who was the State's ML President, at a meeting in Dehradun compared Muslim position in India to that of the Jews in Germany and argued that 'the only way to avoid a similar treatment was to support the Pakistan scheme.'[142] Another report noted that 'in Benares small card labels have appeared for sale showing a map of India with Pakistan areas marked and reproducing the slogans Pakistan Zindabad, Muslim League Zindabad.'[143] Besides such local conferences, the party organized its 1942 annual session at Allahabad. Jinnah was star of the occasion and his electrifying performance was noted by a report prepared by the research and analysis wing of the Office of Strategic Services (OSS).[144]

> On April 3 1942 for instance he entered Allahabad in state. The Zamindars rode with him on a specially decorated truck through streets which were gala in welcome. The procession passed under 110 arches, each named for a person important in Indian Islamic history, beginning with the first Muslim Sultan to land on India's shores and ending triumphantly with Muhammad Ali Jinnah. He addressed the Momins, the poor of the Muslim community, descending from the truck to do so and speaking of mutual loyalty between them and the League. Honorific speeches were presented to him including one which brought his name in the line of the Prophet and the Asar saints. Oratory lights, pageantry and general excitement reign at League meetings. The Pakistan Flag is flown, money is collected and Mr. Jinnah's speech – a short part in unaccustomed Urdu and a long part in English – produces a near frenzy in the audience. His sense of his own importance expresses itself in ways that lead non-followers to consider him psychopathic. He assumes a position towards his followers not unlike that of Hitler and preaches Pakistan with an intensity not unlike Hitler's advocacy of National Socialism.

For Jinnah, the setting was just perfect. It was the first time after the historic 1937 AIML Lucknow session that another such session was being held in the province and here again he could proudly inform his people of the stand he had taken during the Cripps Mission negotiations in which Pakistan was

141 *PAI for the week ending 28 March 1941*. Fakhrul Islam was prosecuted and jailed for this inflammatory speech,

142 *PAI for the week ending 1 June 1940.*

143 *PAI for the week ending 29 August 1941.*

144 *Pakistan: A Muslim Project for a Separate State in India, 5 February 1943,* Office of Strategic Services, Research and Analysis Branch, 097.3Z1 092 No.700.

implicitly conceded by the British in principle for the very first time. In any case, after Lahore, the UPML backed the *Qaid* to the hilt by investing him with full authority to negotiate on Pakistan, stymieing any local dissent in the process. Thus, at the UPML Working Committee meeting soon after Lahore, the Gorakhpur Member of Legislative Assembly (MLA) Zahirul Hasnain Lari, proposed a committee of five for the purpose of formulating 'the demands of the U.P. Muslims in regard to constitutional and other safeguards for the protection of political civil and religious and other rights and interests.' Lari pointed out that after all the future constitution would be based on three principles – the creation of independent Muslim states, protection of Hindu rights in those states and safeguards for Muslims in those provinces where they were in a minority. Lari's resolution was successfully opposed by Khaliquzzaman on the grounds that it would sidetrack the main issue, which was the partition of India on the lines suggested by the AIML.[145]

The ML's biggest opponent in U.P. was JUH that cobbled together the Azad Muslim Conference, an umbrella group of Muslims sympathetic to the Congress. The Conference had its first public convention in Delhi within a month of the Lahore Resolution that observers estimated was attended by fifty thousand people, a show of strength that certainly matched the attendance at Lahore. Allah Bakhsh, the Sind Premier and one of its leading lights, condemned the Pakistan scheme as grotesque calling it 'about the most indiscreet approach to a serious problem' that had 'torpedoed the very basis of a reasonable settlement.'[146] Examining its prospects, he declared that if six million Muslims belonging to his own province of Sind, the NWFP, (where the ML had no support) and Baluchistan, were excluded from North West Pakistan since

> they had a more realistic sense of things, the Punjab, with a population of 1.5 crores of Muslims confined between Campbellpore and perhaps Lahore would constitute a problematic little Pakistan with drastically curtailed financial resources and reduced to the position of one of the bigger Indian States.[147]

He wondered how the Punjab would be able to absorb the revenue deficit of these provinces even if they decided to join Pakistan. The Sind Premier insisted that even if northwest Pakistan enjoyed a period of sustained peace

---

145 *The Leader*, 30 April 1940.

146 See *Indian Annual Register*, Vol. 1, 1940, 323–32.

147 Ibid., 325–36.

and prosperity enabling it like Czechoslovakia to develop its industries and economic as well as defence capabilities, it would still be under pressure from enemies such as Hindu India and Russia. Questioning how Pakistan could defend itself against such enemies, Allah Bakhsh pointedly asked

> if the British were asked to hold this baby until it was strong enough to stand on its own legs, in the first place what was the quid pro quo and in the second what was this smokescreen of an independent sovereign and Islamic state for?[148]

He also expressed skepticism regarding its internal security and stability arguing that Jats and Sikhs in the Punjab would never support Pakistan even if they were granted a variety of concessions. And even if 1 crore Sikhs and Jats stayed back and eventually reconciled themselves to Pakistan, he wondered how it would be any different from any of the existing provinces and in what sense it could become an independent Islamic state.

Allah Bakhsh described northeast Pakistan as 'ten times more fantastic and hundred times more fragile'. Northwest Pakistan would probably survive and possibly link up with Afghan or Russian Muslim neighbours to further its sustenance. But Bengal and Assam 'with no superfluity of martial races to its credit' would quickly be absorbed 'by its more enterprising neighbors.'[149] This would not become an independent Islamic state but another British mandate like Palestine. Bakhsh concluded his remarks by expressing satisfaction that no responsible minister in the Punjab cabinet had supported the ML's scheme nor had it found support in Bengal. He reasoned that if the majority provinces Muslims did not want Pakistan, the minority provinces Muslims could not possibly dictate terms to them. There was thus no constitutional basis on which the ML could make its demand. The Conference's Resolution moved by Mufti Kifayatullah of the JUH provided the counterpoint to the Lahore Resolution. It declared that

> India with its geographical and political boundaries is an indivisible whole and as such it is the common homeland of all the citizens irrespective of race or religion who are joint owners of its resources. All nooks and corners of the country contain the hearths and homes of the Muslims and the cherished historic monuments of their religion and culture which are dearer to them than their lives. From a national point of view every Muslim is an Indian.[150]

[148] Ibid.

[149] Ibid.

[150] Ibid., 327.

Allah Baksh ended the conference with the suggestion that the 'ulemas (sic) should be elected to the Constituent Assembly and whatever their verdict, it should be binding on the Muslim community.'[151] The statement underlined the leading role played by the *ulama* in organizing this platform against the ML. The JUH also organized a series of local conferences in U.P. At the Jaunpur meet attended by prominent Deobandi *ulama* Husain Ahmad Madani launched a frontal attack the Pakistan scheme calling it 'utterly impracticable'. The conference, however, failed to rouse popular enthusiasm and proved to be a damp squib indicated by thin attendance at its meetings. It was reported that on the last day of the conference the most of the audience began to leave even before the meeting ended.[152] The ML vituperated these efforts against Pakistan scheme condemning the conference as 'utterly unrepresentative of Muslim opinion' describing those who took part in it as 'traitors to their religion.'[153] Khaliquzzaman at a public meeting in Allahabad criticized 'the Azad Muslims and said that Muslims who had ruled India for a thousand years had no intention of surrendering their power to anyone else.'[154]

The other groups actively involved in anti-Pakistan agitations in U.P. were the Hindu Sabha, the Arya Samaj and the RSS, besides Sikh groups from the Punjab. An anti-Pakistan day was celebrated by activists of the Hindu Sabha in late April 1940 to counter the Pakistan day celebrations of the ML in nearly half the districts of U.P. The meetings were attended at many places by workers of the Arya Samaj while Sikh participation was prominent in Kanpur.[155] The Akalis under Master Tara Singh were also active in the U.P. through their proselytization and political activities. Tara Singh declared at a U.P. Sikh conference in April 1940 at Lucknow that if the ML wanted to achieve Pakistan, it would have to 'pass through an ocean of Sikh blood'.[156] A number of conversions were reported to Sikhism from various Hindu castes. Upper caste Hindus also encouraged those belonging to the depressed classes to convert to Sikhism.[157] It was reported that the Kanpur industrialist and Hindu Sabha patron Lala Padampat Singhania subscribed ₹ 2500 in funds

---

151 Ibid., 332.

152 *PAI for the week ending 22 June 1940.*

153 *PAI for the week ending 11 May 1940.*

154 *PAI for the week ending 31 August 1940.*

155 *PAI for the week ending 2 May 1940.*

156 *IAR*, 1940, Vol. 1, 61.

157 Ibid.

for the U.P. provincial Sikh conference held in the ML stronghold of Aligarh in early June 1940.This conference presided by Tara Singh turned out to be a massive affair.[158] It was reported that a procession of nearly a hundred thousand people, which was nearly a mile long, carried Master Tara Singh to the venue from the Aligarh railway station and included twenty elephants on which the principal leaders were seated. Sikh *jathas* came from Punjab, Patiala state, Delhi and sixteen districts of U.P. Surveying the scene, a police report noted that

> Anti-Pakistan placards were carried by the procession. Local Hindus were enthusiastic in their welcome for the procession. The conference opened with a religious ceremony and an appeal for religious converts to Sikhism. The response was so overwhelming that the Presidential address and other speeches were postponed to the next day and the conversion ceremony continued throughout the evening and the next day. It was estimated that nearly 23,000 persons belonging to Rajput, Ahir, Jat, Kayastha and Depressed Classes converted to Sikhism. Nearly 30,000 Kirpans were distributed for free by the Golden temple Amritsar.[159]

Tara Singh, in his speech, warned Muslims that any efforts to divide India and form Pakistan would only cause trouble and that neither Hindus nor Sikhs could remain safe under Muslim rule. Tara Singh also ridiculed Gandhi's method of non-violence and warned that the Sikhs were not afraid to use violence. The Sikh conference also expressed its support for *Akhand Hindustan*.[160] The aggressive Sikh drive supported by the Hindu Sabha further ratcheted up communal tension in U.P. The Muslims were now wary of this new upsurge since Sikhs were legally permitted to carry *kirpans* (swords) and a number of free *kirpans* were being distributed by the Sikh mission at Aligarh. Sikhs in Shahjahanpur and Bareily agitated for permission to also carry their *kirpans* into the factories where they worked.[161]

In response, the ML began a number of schemes for Muslim self-defense. It was reported that in Benares Muslims were contemplating a scheme 'whereby large numbers of low class Muslims should be enrolled as butchers to keep large

158 *PAI for the week ending 6 June 1940.*

159 Ibid.

160 *PAI for the week ending 12 September 1940.*

161 *PAI for the week ending 24 September 1941.*

knives without license.'[162] The party exhorted Muslims to enrol in the Muslim League National Guard, which was organized for the protection of Muslim life and property. It also made invigorated efforts to court the Depressed Classes in U.P., which evoked positive responses from Depressed Class groups opposed to the Congress. Thus, Swami Kaljuganand, a prominent leader in U.P., appealed to the ML to help the Depressed Classes and demanded from the British Government that on the introduction of Pakistan, the Depressed Classes should also be allotted a portion of India as Acchutistan.[163] This was an idea that Ambedkar himself entertained for a while. The ML also received support from the Communist Party of India (CPI), which called for the acceptance of the ML demand of self-determination for Indian Muslims seeing them as a separate nationality following Stalin's thesis on nationalities and their right to self-determination.[164] Thus, a party circular issued to Secretaries of District Committees asked Communists to take part in Pakistan Day celebrations. Communists made speeches from ML platforms in favor of self-determination of Muslims.[165] The 'Nationalist Muslims' opposing Pakistan were thus caught in a crossfire between radical Hindus and the ML. At the Azad Muslim Conference at Etawah on 9–10 August 1940 the police intelligence report noted that the

> Pakistan scheme was condemned and it was suggested that Hindu opposition was aimed at goading the Muslims into forcing the scheme through at all costs to their own detriment. The only solution to the problem was the establishment of provincial autonomy with joint electorates. High proportion of audience was Hindu.[166]

As evident, as Pakistan was articulated in the towns and localities of the U.P., local ML functionaries, as well as national leaders, while grappling with the idea of Pakistan reflected and spoke on issues of territory, transfers of population and the nature of the Pakistani State. Anis al Din writing a month before the ML's Lahore Resolution was in no doubt that areas of U.P. such as the Meerut

---

162 *PAI for the week ending 2May 1941.*

163 *PAI for the week ending 29 August 1941.*

164 See Gangadhar M. Adhikari, *Pakistan and Indian National Unity* (London, 1943); also see Sriprakash, 'CPI and the Pakistan Movement', in Bipan Chandra (ed.), *The Indian Left: Critical Appraisals* (New Delhi, 1983), 215–57.

165 *PAI for the week ending 24 March 1944.*

166 *PAI for the week ending 15 August 1941.*

and Rohilkhand divisions along with the districts of Agra and Aligarh needed to be a part of Pakistan. But in Musavvir Ali Khan's address in the aftermath of the Lahore session, this insistence on including these parts of U.P. into Pakistan was no longer evident. The U.P. as a whole in his understanding was now wholly excluded from Pakistan. Furthermore, he had no hesitation in giving away Hindu majority parts of Punjab and Bengal to ensure comfortable Muslim majorities in the two Pakistan federations while at the same time ensuring a functional state in Pakistan. While Mamdot and Liaquat clearly visualized U.P. as part of Hindustan and also made strident claims for all of Punjab, in private they again were willing to partition provinces. All in all, what is clear is that Pakistan was being actively imagined, thought about and articulated in the public sphere. Above all, Pakistan was acrimoniously contested in U.P. as becomes evident from the searing critiques of the *ulama* aligned to Congress which one must now turn to consider.

K. M. Ashraf (*black topi*), Z. A. Ahmad (*white Gandhi topi*), Nehru and Khan Abdul Ghaffar Khan at Northwest Frontier Province (no date)
Photograph Courtesy: Nehru Memorial Museum and Library, New Delhi

Standing : CR's son C. R. Narasimhan, CR's ADC Captain Devendra Singh
Seated: CR's daughter Namagiri Ammal, B. R. Ambedkar, C. Rajagopalachari (CR), Mrs Ambedkar, CR's daughter-in-law C. R. Thangammal

Venue: Government House (now Rashtrapati Bhavan), New Delhi, circa 1949

Photograph Courtesy: Nehru Memorial Museum and Library, New Delhi

M. A. Jinnah addressing the 1942 AIML Allahabad session. Also seated Nawab Ismail Khan, President of the U.P. Muslim League (*holding his chin in his palm*) and Raja of Mahmudabad (*dark glasses*). Other two faces in the picture are unknown.

Photograph Courtesy: National Archives of Pakistan, Islamabad

M. A. Jinnah and Liaquat Ali Khan in a procession to the 1942 AIML Allahabad session.
Photograph Courtesy: National Archives of Pakistan, Islamabad

From Left to Right: Nawab Ismail Khan (*President U.P. Muslim League*), Syed Hussain Imam, Raja of Mahmudabad, Chaudhry Khaliquzzaman, M. A. Jinnah, Saadullah Khan (*behind Jinnah*), M. A. H. Ispahani, and Nawabzada Liaquat Ali Khan, 1942

Photograph Courtesy: National Archives of Pakistan, Islamabad

M. A. Jinnah at the Head office of the City Muslim League, Kanpur in 1941.
Photograph Courtesy: National Archives of Pakistan

From Left to Right (front row): Maulana Hifzur Rahman Seoharvi, President Rajendra Prasad and Maulana Husain Ahmad Madani.

Photograph Courtesy: Maulana Anisur Rahman Qasmi, Nazim, Imarat-i-Shariah, Patna.

Jinnah, Fatima Jinnah and Maulana Shabbir Ahmad Usmani behind them on the extreme right in the white cap.

Photograph Courtesy: National Archives of Pakistan, Islamabad

Maulana Shabbir Ahmad Usmani at Jinnah's grave, 1948.
Photograph Courtesy: National Archives of Pakistan, Islamabad

Map 1: Ambedkar's Map of Punjab, 1940

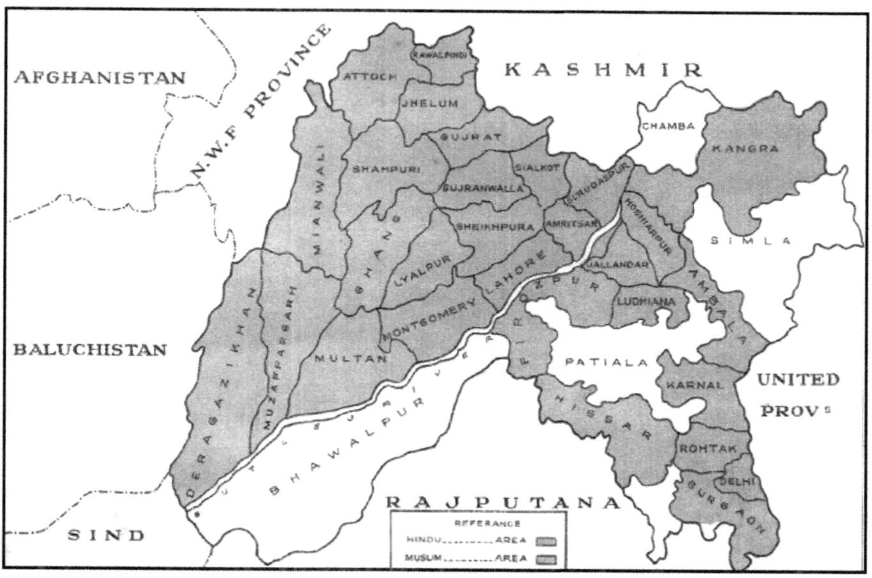

Source: B. R. Ambedkar, *Thoughts on Pakistan* (Bombay, 1940)

Note: The maps are color coded by Dr Ambedkar in the original text with the Hindustan areas in saffron and Pakistan areas in green.

Map 2: Ambedkar's Map of Bengal, 1940

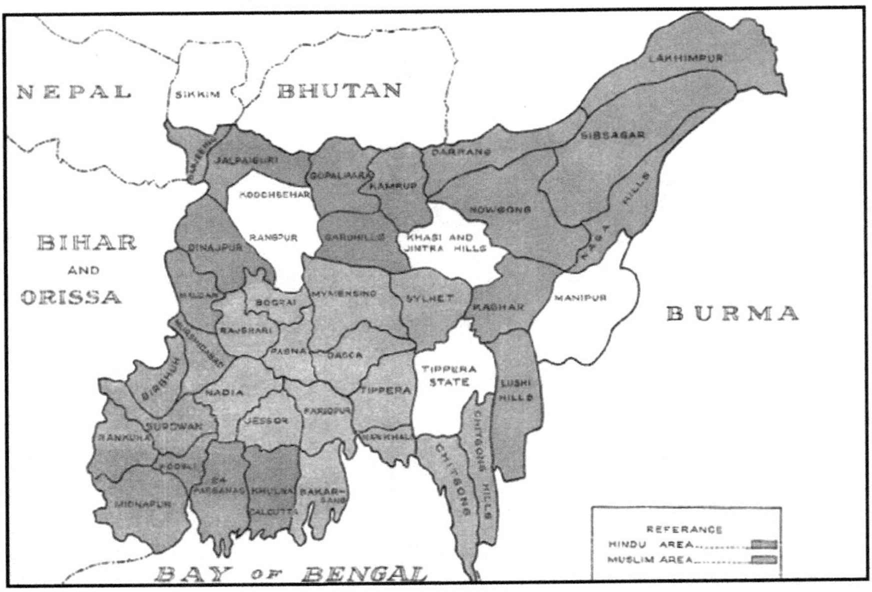

Source: B. R. Ambedkar, *Thoughts on Pakistan* (Bombay, 1940)

Note: The maps are color coded by Dr Ambedkar in the original text with the Hindustan areas in saffron and Pakistan areas in green.

Map 3: Ambedkar's Map of India, 1940

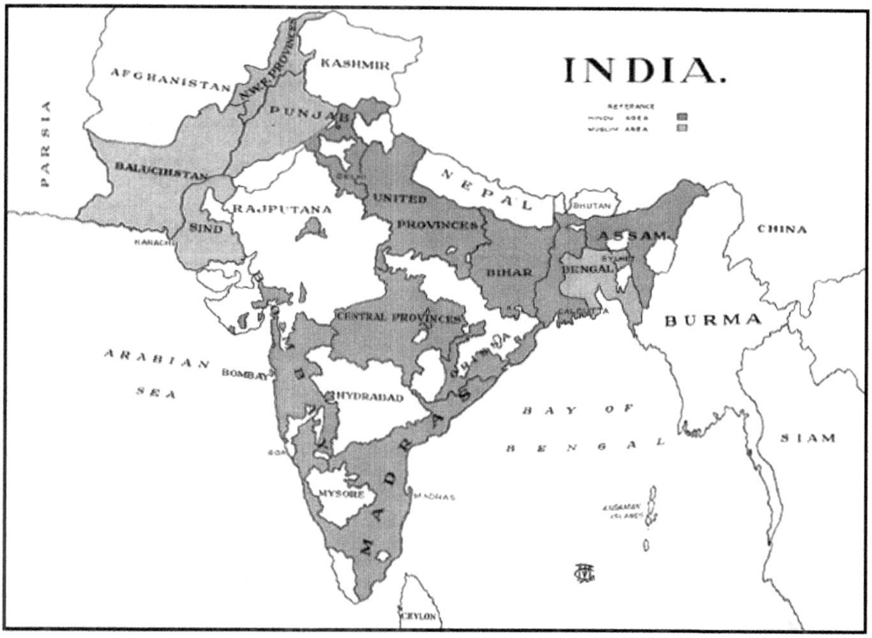

Source: B. R. Ambedkar, *Thoughts on Pakistan* (Bombay, 1940)

Note: The maps are color coded by Dr Ambedkar in the original text with the Hindustan areas in saffron and Pakistan areas in green.

Map 4: Rajagopalachari's Map, 1944

Source: Hindustan Times, 'Gandhi-Jinnah Talks: Text of Correspondence and Other Relevant Matter, July-October 1944', with a preface by Mr C. Rajagopalachari (New Delhi, 1944)

Map 5: Anis al Din Ahmad Rizvi Map, 1940

Source: Anis al Din Ahmad Rizvi, Pakistan (Bareily, 1940)

Map 6: Ambedkar's Revised Map of Bengal and Assam, 1945

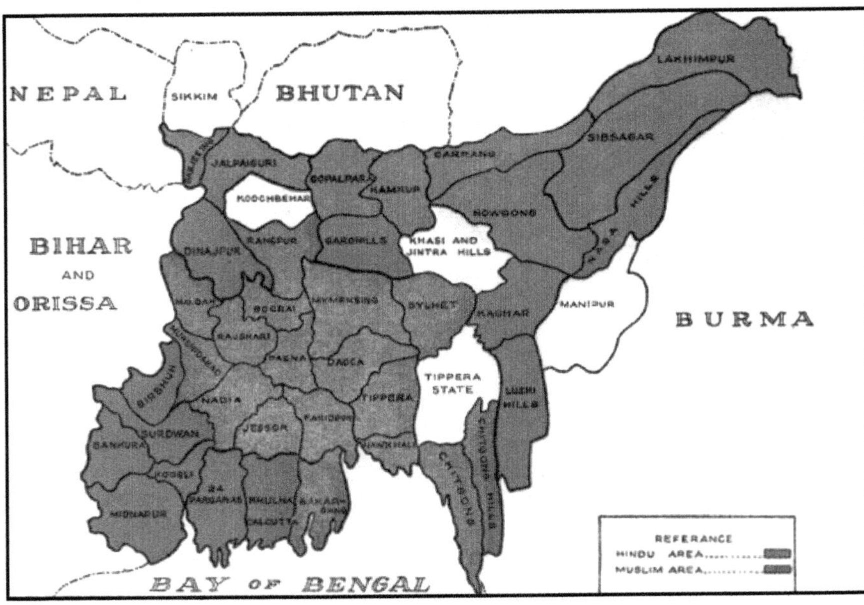

Source: B. R. Ambedkar, *Pakistan or the Partition of India* (Bombay, 1945).

Note: The maps are color coded by Dr Ambedkar in the original text with the Hindustan areas in saffron and Pakistan areas in green.

5

Ulama at the Forefront of Politics

Three Critiques of Pakistan

These days the Pakistan Movement is very popular among the masses. If it means the establishment in the Muslim majority provinces of an Islamic state based on the Prophetic traditions and the commandments of Islam, viz. 'hudud', 'qisas' and others, then it is a very noble cause and no Muslim will have objection to it. But the fact is that under the present circumstances, nobody can imagine the possibility of such a venture.

Maulana Husain Ahmad Madani[1]

During his visit to Kanpur, M.A. Jinnah addressed a meeting of Muslim Students Federation under the leadership of Mohammad Nauman Zuberi Vice President of All India Muslim Students Federation. Jinnah spoke on the usual lines and stated that he was willing to allow the 2 crores of Muslims who would fall in minority provinces under the Pakistan scheme to be smashed in order to liberate 7 crores of Muslims in the majority provinces.

U.P. Police Abstract of Intelligence for the Week ending
4 April 1941

Initial Congress reactions to the Lahore Resolution were swift and furious. C. Rajagopalachari, Gandhi's conscience keeper, insisted that India was one and indivisible and described Jinnah's call for dividing India, a product of his 'diseased mentality'. Rajaji added that even if the Muslim provinces were carved out to form a separate federation, the minority problem would remain just the same.[2] Moreover, the two-nation theory, he tersely noted, was inconsistent with the Prophet's vision of the spread of Islam.[3] Jawaharlal Nehru contemptuously dismissed the Pakistan Scheme as 'foolish', declaring that 'it would not last 24 hours'. He also derided it as 'highly anti-national,

1 Z. H. Faruqi, *The Deoband School and the Demand for Pakistan* (Bombay, 1963), 119.

2 *The Leader*, 30 March 1940.

3 *The Leader*, 6 September 1940.

pro-imperialist, which no freedom loving man would accept.'[4] A little later, an irked Nehru declared that he was pleased with the ML's new demand. This was not because he liked it, for he considered it to be 'the most insane suggestion', but because it 'very much simplified the communal problem' and the Congress could now get rid of extraneous demands regarding proportionate representation in legislatures, services, etc. He proclaimed that one thing though had become absolutely clear – Muslim Leaguers and people like him could not live together in India.[5] He, therefore, considered himself and the Muslim Leaguers to belong to separate nations.[6] Finally, the Mahatma in his reaction evocatively described the Pakistan demand as entailing the 'vivisection of India' and hence a 'sin'.[7]

While the Congress leadership launched a broadside against Pakistan, the task of opposing it on the ground was urgently taken up by their allies among the Deobandi *ulama* who controlled the JUH, the premier organization of the Indian Muslim *ulama*. Their partnership went back to the time of the Khilafat Movement at the end of World War I when Gandhi backed by the *ulama* launched the first all India mass movement against colonial rule with momentous consequences for Indian politics.[8] Beyond organizing the Azad Muslim Conference, the *ulama* took up the task of presenting Muslim public with detailed critiques of the Lahore Resolution since the battle had to be fought with ideas in the public sphere. Theirs became the most cogent oppositional voice to Pakistan especially after it became the object of far more intensive public debate following its tacit endorsement by the Cripps Mission and the top Congress leadership's imprisonment after Gandhi's Quit India call. The *ulama* and their allies dexterously performed an extremely difficult task in the changing political scenario. The Azad Muslim Conference may have

4 *Indian Annual Register*, 1940, Vol. 1, 68.

5 *The Leader*, 15 April 1940.

6 *The Leader*, 16 April 1940.

7 D. G. Tendulkar, *Mahatma: Life of Mohandas Karamchand Gandhi* (New Delhi, 1952), Vol. 6, 107.

8 For an account of their anti-colonial political mobilization see Naeem Qureshi, *Pan Islam in British India: The Politics of the Khilafat Movement 1918-1924* (Karachi, 2009); Barbara Metcalf, *Husain Ahmad Madani: Jihad for Islam and India's Freedom* (Oxford, 2009); Gail Minault, *The Khilafat Movement: Religious Symbolism and Political Mobilization in India* (New York, 1981); Z. H. Faruqi, *The Deoband School and the Demand for Pakistan* (London, 1963); Farhat Tabassum, *Deoband Ulema's Movement for the Freedom of India* (Delhi, 2006).

summarily dismissed the Lahore Resolution at its first convention, but after 1942, the *ulama* were forced to concede that the principle of self-determination had to be granted to all communities in India. After all, even Congressmen out of prison such as Rajagopalachari changed tack and wanted the party to accept Pakistan in principle in the face of its surging popularity among Muslims across India. The veteran Madras Congressman's move attracted considerable support among 'Nationalist Muslims' in the Congress. At the 1942 All India Congress Committee (AICC) Allahabad session, Rajagopalachari's resolution to this effect was supported by K. M. Ashraf, Mian Iftikharuddin, Sajjad Zaheer, Shah Omair and Abdus Sattar before being soundly defeated by the Jagat Narain Lal resolution that opposed India's partition.[9] Provincial Congress Presidents of Punjab and NWFP, besides Asaf Ali and Syed Mahmud, too openly approved of Rajaji's move.[10]

Wilfred Cantwell Smith, a perceptive contemporary observer of the developing situation was moved to write that 'by the close of 1942, then, there was no substantial organized group of Muslims opposed to the League's policy of separatism.'[11] Smith's statement, while reflecting the ML's burgeoning strength and the marginalization of its opponents, ignores the *ulama's* nuanced, stout, and sustained opposition to Pakistan even after they were forced to concede on the question of Muslim right to self-determination. A look at their critiques of Pakistan reveals the methodical way in which they constructed their arguments the eloquent ways in which they presented Pakistan's implications to the Muslim public, all the while displaying a sophisticated grasp of relevant facts, figures, and statistics. What is astonishing is how uncannily they prefigured some of the major problems that Pakistan would begin to confront once it seceded from India. A careful examination of their arguments is also imperative to realize how extensively the idea of Pakistan was debated in the Urdu public sphere in the run-up to the Partition.

'The Fraud of Islamic Pakistan': Maulana Syed Muhammad Sajjad's Early Critique of the Lahore Resolution

The earliest critique of Pakistan was published within weeks of the Lahore Resolution much before Ambedkar's seminal treatise appeared in print.

9 *Star of India*, 15 May 1942.

10 L/PJ/12/484, File 230/35, *Weekly Report of the DIB Home Department, Government of India, New Delhi, 16 May 1942, No.20*, OIOC, British Library, London.

11 W.C Smith, *The Muslim League 1942-45*, (Lahore, 1945), 4.

Authored by Maulana Syed Muhammad Sajjad, a leading member of the JUH from Bihar and the founder of the *Imarat-i-Shariah*, Patna, *Muslim India Aur Hindu India Par Ek Aham Tabsira* (A Critical Essay on Hindu India and Muslim India), was published in the 14 April 1940 edition of the weekly *Naqeeb*, the organ of the *Imarat-i-Shariah*.[12] Sajjad's origins may have been in Bihar but his itinerant life and education inextricably connected him to some of the most prominent centres of Islamic education in U.P. Born into a landowning family in Panhasa village a few kilometres down the road from the ruins of the ancient Buddhist University at Nalanda, he lost his father when he was just four years old. His biographer tells us that young Sajjad, who was raised by an older brother, was more interested in sports and games till he was almost fifteen.[13] A severe admonition from the older brother over his indifference to studies saw the rebellious teenager runaway from home to Kanpur in neighbouring U.P. The episode seems to have been transformative for the lad enrolled himself in a *madrasa* in this new city where he studied for three years before moving to Deoband. But six months into his studies at the new institution the rebel got into a fight with a Tibetan student that led to his expulsion from the Darul Uloom. Sajjad now moved to Allahabad and enrolled in *Madrasa Subhania* from where he ultimately graduated in 1905 after a colourful *dastarbandi* ceremony. Starting his first job as a teacher at *Madrasa Islamia* in his hometown Nalanda, over the next few years he shuttled between there and Allahabad before finally setting up the *Madrasa Anwarul Uloom* at Gaya.

Sajjad's political career took off from Gaya when he founded the *Anjuman Ulama-i-Bihar* in 1918 at a moment when Indian Muslims became increasingly concerned about the fate of the Khilafat. The move was motivated by the belief that the *ulama* needed to intervene in politics and provide leadership to the Indian Muslim community at this crucial moment.[14] He ultimately founded the *Imarat-i-Shariah* in 1921 that bore the particular influence of Azad's *Amir-i Hind* scheme. The scheme envisaged *ulama* in each province electing

12 It was again published by the JUH as *Pakistan ki Cheestan aur Jamiatul Ulama-i-Hindi ka Wazih Faisla* (The Riddle of Pakistan and the Verdict of the Jamiatul Ulama-i-Hind) after its 1942 Lahore session. A second edition was published in 1945 as part of the propaganda literature against Pakistan on the eve of the 1945-46 elections.

13 Syed Minatullah Rahmani, 'Muktsar Savanih-i Hayat', in Maulana Anisur Rahman Qasmi, (ed.), *Hayat-i-Sajjad: Maulana Abul Mohasin Muhammad Sajjad Rahmatullah Alaihi ki Hayat wa Khidmat wa Muntakhab Taqriren*, (Patna, n.d).

14 See Papiya Ghosh, 'Muttahidah Qaumiyat in Aqalliat Bihar: The Imarat-i-Shariah, 1921-1947', *Indian Economic and Social History Review*, Vol. 34, No. 1 (1997): 1–20.

an *Amir* who, assisted by a council of the *ulama*, would set up *shariat* courts and educational institutions in every district besides appointing district *Amirs*. All these *Amirs* were to finally elect the *Amir-i-Hind*. The overall idea was that in a free India, Muslims would exist as an autonomous, self-regulating, separate community 'maintaining a relationship with the country's government through a collective agreement' but simultaneously 'owing ultimate allegiance to the universal *Khilafat* of Islam.'[15] The *Imarat* was established in Bihar where it continues to exist but much to Sajjad's disappointment the model was not replicated anywhere else in India.

The Maulana's next significant political venture, the Muslim Independent Party (MIP) floated in September 1936, won a majority of Muslim seats in the Bihar legislative assembly in the 1937 elections. However, unlike his JUH colleagues in U.P. who split from the ML, the MIP aligned with the ML and formed the interim government in Bihar between April and July 1937, at a time when the Congress refused to assume office. Sajjad clearly saw nothing wrong in allying with the ML at this juncture since he saw the revamped party under Jinnah clearly working along the lines laid out by the Congress. He went on to condemn Congress' refusal to coalesce with any party even if they were like-minded. The MIP-ML coalition resigned after the Congress decided to assume office but Sajjad maintained his independent streak as evident from his stinging critique of what he saw as the Congress betrayal of the principles of *Muttahida Qaumiyat*. Writing after its ministries finally resigned in late 1939, he assailed the Congress for giving short shrift to Muslim representation in its decision making bodies and sharply criticized its Muslim mass contact programme for trying to wean away Muslims from their 'true leaders'.

This line was not very different from the one adopted by Jinnah before the collapse of the ill-fated attempts at forming Congress-ML coalition ministries in the provinces. However, the ML's 1940 Lahore Resolution saw the independent minded Sajjad turning against Jinnah. His moral critique of the idea of Pakistan hinged on three propositions. He first demolished the ML's claim that Pakistan would be an Islamic state where Islamic laws would regulate the lives of the faithful, instead demonstrating how and why it was impossible to establish an Islamic state in Pakistan. Second, he denounced the 'hostage population theory' with its insidious rhetoric of violence that was being bandied around by Pakistani enthusiasts, both on the grounds of religion and common sense. Finally, he launched a blistering attack on the rhetoric of sacrifice invoked by the

15 Ibid., 2.

ML leadership to attract support from the 'minority provinces' Muslims for the cause of Pakistan. As a corollary, Sajjad questioned the Islamic credentials and ethics of the ML leadership and excoriated them for utilizing false arguments and deception to popularize Pakistan merely for the sake of securing their own positions as leaders of the Muslim community.

Maulana Sajjad began his critique by pointing out that during the past two and half years the ML had been raising a hue and cry over the real or hypothetical atrocities committed by Congress governments and Hindu majorities over Muslims in the minority provinces of U.P., Bihar and C.P. However, during these years, the ML, he noted, had not once proposed a solution to the problems faced by the hapless Muslims of these provinces and had instead pursued purely 'negative tactics'. After two and half years of ritual mourning (*maatam*) for the minority provinces Muslims, the ML was finally proposing a solution for the Indian Muslims at large under the Lahore Resolution, which, therefore, needed to be examined very closely. Sajjad pointed out that even ordinary Muslims could see that Mr Jinnah's scheme contained nothing for the 'minority provinces' Muslims, and that it was concerned primarily with 'liberating' the 'majority provinces' Muslims. He found this strange since the ML had not received complaints of any kind from the latter. Indeed, if the majority provinces' Muslims had ever complained in this regard, the ML as 'the sole representative organization of the Indian Muslims' would surely not have kept quiet about it. More to the point, Sajjad asserted that the 'majority provinces' Muslims seemed quite happy with the existing 'defective' arrangement of provincial autonomy under a single unitary Centre. He, therefore, saw irony in the Lahore Resolution for it addressed non-existent complaints of the majority provinces Muslims while ignoring the very real problems their 'minority provinces' brethren for whom the original protests had been raised by the ML during the two years of rule by Congress cabinet governments.

Having dismissed the ML's rationale for liberating the 'majority provinces' Muslims, Maulana Sajjad next focused on demolishing the ML's two main justifications for creating Pakistan – (1) that Pakistan would be established as an Islamic state that would benefit the entire Islamic world; (2) that Pakistan would be a potent protector of the communal rights and interests of Muslims left behind in Hindu India. Taking on the first proposition, Sajjad argued that an Islamic state could be established in Pakistan only if two important conditions were fulfilled. In the first place, such a state could be realized if the ML promised to expatriate the substantial non-Muslim minority – almost half of the existing population – currently living in its domains. A second prerequisite in this regard was that the ML needed to explicitly declare that non-Muslims would have no role to play in the government of Pakistan. By contrast, Sajjad pointed out that Jinnah, while admitting the necessity of some population exchanges, had nonetheless ruled out large scale population transfers thus undermining the first condition. Additionally, Jinnah had publicly assured non-Muslims that they could participate in Pakistan's legislature and government, and would in fact be given a share in running it, thus demolishing the second condition as well. Sajjad declared that under these circumstances Pakistan could not be deemed an Islamic state. He therefore condemned as fraudulent, the designation of one state (Pakistan) as Islamic and the other (Hindustan) as Hindu, even though these were two composite entities. What is striking about Sajjad's critique is that it foregrounded at the very outset, the issue of transfers and exchanges of population, thus indicating the degree to which it had become a topic of public discussion, especially in the 'minority provinces' where the Muslims were confronted with the choice of either staying behind in a Hindu dominated India or migrating to the proposed new Muslim homeland.

As regards the second justification for creating Pakistan, Sajjad harshly criticized its extravagant claims about securing the lives, properties and interests of the 'minority provinces' Muslims. He particularly attacked two ideas that were being bandied around by ML functionaries on the ground in this regard. The first, which gained currency as the 'hostage population theory', held that revenge would be taken upon Hindus in Pakistan if Muslims in India were oppressed by their Hindu majority. The second idea in circulation was that Pakistan would not hesitate to declare war on Hindu India in order to protect its oppressed Muslim minority. Taking on the first idea, Sajjad strongly assailed its threat of retributive violence against religious minorities. No Muslim government, he argued, could commit atrocities on its own peace loving citizens simply because Muslims were being persecuted elsewhere. Such a policy, he insisted, was contrary to the *Shariah*, which expressly enjoined Muslim rulers to treat non-Muslims with fairness and compassion. Moreover, such a policy did not conform to conventions of international relations nor did it have any historical precedents. To substantiate his arguments, Sajjad pointed out that Muslims around the world had long been oppressed by British imperialism and yet Turkey, the foremost Muslim power of the world that Pakistan was expected to emulate, had never retaliated even once against its own Christian subjects. As regards the efficacy of the second idea, Sajjad again cited the example of Turkey, noting that it had not come to the aid of the Indian Muslims even during the 1857 Mutiny that was eventually crushed by the British. Neither

Turkey nor any other Muslim state had mustered sufficient courage to serve diplomatic notice to Britain for the atrocities it had committed against the Indian Muslims in the wake of the Mutiny, leave alone going to war for their sake. Citing a contemporary example, he elucidated that Albania had forcibly been annexed by Italy and yet all that the free and semi-free Muslim states of world had done was to sit and passively watch the show. But the most prominent example he adduced was the case of Palestine. Sajjad lamented that the Muslims of Palestine had repeatedly narrated their tale of woe to the Islamic world, specially petitioned Muslim governments to help them in their fight for freedom, and also given a call for *jihad* to overthrow imperialist domination. Yet, Sajjad bemoaned that Indian Muslims and the Islamic world generally had largely ignored Palestinian entreaties. In the light of these examples, Sajjad warned 'minority provinces' Muslims not to live under any illusion or hope that hypothetical theories regarding their protection would ever be put into practice. Such absurd ideas, he bitterly remarked, could only be entertained by the worst fool or madman (*badtareen ahmaq*). The pointer to Jinnah could not have been more obvious.

Sajjad lastly attacked the ML's residual plank on Pakistan, which called upon the U.P. Muslims to make a grand sacrifice for the sake of Pakistan. In this regard, he referred to Jinnah's startling statement about his willingness to sacrifice twenty million 'minority provinces' Muslims for the sake of liberating their sixty million brethren in the 'majority provinces'. To begin with, Sajjad charged Jinnah with deliberately reducing the number of 'minority province' Muslims from thirty to twenty million in order to downplay the magnitude of the minority problem in India. But even if Jinnah's figures were to be accepted, Sajjad pooh-poohed the extent of benefits that would accrue from such a great sacrifice by this hapless minority. Using Jinnah's logic, Sajjad argued that instead of twenty million 'minority provinces' Muslims sacrificing themselves for the sake of their sixty million 'majority provinces' brethren, it made more sense for the entire eighty million Indian Muslim population to instead accept 'slavery under the Hindus', line up behind the 'Hindu Congress', and work towards overthrowing British imperialism in India. This would be a far more meritorious act in the cause of Islam since it would have the salutary effect of destroying British imperialism and in the process liberating 250 million Muslims in the entire Islamic world. Indeed, sacrificing eighty million for the cause of 250 million was a nobler act of sacrifice than sacrificing twenty million for the cause of sixty million. Maulana Sajjad therefore demonstrated that the plank of Pan-Islam was not just a monopoly of the ML that could be used for glorifying Pakistan, but could also be appropriated and used in ingenious ways to discourage Muslim separatism and support a composite anti-colonial nationalism in India. Indeed, he pointedly sought to show how the ideals of pan-Islamism and Pakistan were incompatible at this historical juncture.

Maulana Sajjad proceeded to highlight the inconsistencies in Jinnah's position with regard to the Islamic world over the course of his long political career in order to place a big question mark on his pan-Islamic sympathies and credentials. He alleged that Jinnah had earlier advised Indian Muslims to keep aloof from the Khilafat agitation after World War I, claiming that it was a ploy by the Hindus to reduce Indian Muslims to a position of servitude after using them to overthrow British colonialism and achieving Indian independence. Sajjad recalled that the Khilafatists had opposed Jinnah on this issue at the time, fervently arguing that the Indian Muslims could never possibly be reduced to slavery under the Hindus once India gained freedom. Furthermore, they had declared that even if that were to happen, it was an acceptable price, since cooperating with the Hindus in order to overthrow British imperialism would happily lead to the liberation of 250 million Muslims of the whole Islamic world. But Jinnah, Maulana Sajjad noted, claimed that he was not convinced by this argument. Now after thirty years, Jinnah and the ML had finally accepted that India's freedom would indeed lead to the liberation of the Islamic world but were again declining to take part in the freedom struggle, this time citing non-settlement of the communal issue in India. Sajjad lamented that Jinnah was thus looking towards preserving the interests of only the sixty million majority province Muslims, and expected the minority province Muslims to forget all ideas of freedom. He, therefore, dismissed the argument that Pakistan would benefit the entire Islamic world as bogus, since it was a narrow struggle aimed at 'liberating' the majority provinces Muslims though they themselves had not sought any such favours.

In these circumstances, Sajjad submitted that the minority province Muslims surely had the right to ask Jinnah as to why, for two and half years, mourning rituals (*maatam*) had been conducted for them in public and why the lakhs of rupees that they had contributed had been wasted on meetings and processions of the ML. He further demanded to know why this mourning had abruptly stopped after the Lahore Resolution. After all Muslims were still being martyred in communal riots, there were restrictions on *Qurbani*, and life was indeed difficult for them in many ways, as was the case during the era of Congress cabinet governments. To Sajjad, it was therefore evident that the ML had abdicated its responsibilities towards the minority province Muslims and along with it the right to call itself the sole representative organization of all of the Indian Muslims.

Given the obvious problems that Pakistan would create for the 'minority provinces' Muslims, Maulana Sajjad enquired as to why the ML had still gone ahead and passed the Lahore Resolution. In order to understand this riddle (*cheestan*) of Pakistan, he analysed the history behind the idea. He reminisced that in 1922, when the Congress-Khilafat conference had been in session in Gaya, the Pakistan idea was smuggled in from overseas but fortunately Muslim leaders present at the time had dismissed it as unworthy of any attention. Then again in 1930, he recalled that Dr Mohammad Iqbal had introduced it from the platform of the ML at their annual session at Allahabad. Yet, at the Round Table Conferences, Sajjad noted that neither Jinnah nor Iqbal had cared to push it forward even though it was the best occasion to introduce it. Instead, Jinnah confined himself to harping on his Fourteen Points. While some argued that Jinnah and other like-minded Muslims had not presented the Pakistan scheme at the time since they still had faith in the Hindus, Sajjad dismissed such suggestions, claiming that trust between Hindus and Muslims was absent even at that time. This was reflected in the fact that even though only a constitutional struggle was being conducted inside the legislatures without any mass struggles outside, there were plenty of communal riots going on in the country. Furthermore, these riots were more severe than the riots that took place between 1937 and 1939. Sajjad, therefore, concluded that the Pakistan scheme was neither seen as a practical proposition nor beneficial to the Muslims and hence was not presented to the Hindus at the time by any Muslim leader.

Continuing his examination of the trajectory of the Pakistan idea, Maulana Sajjad reminded his readers that the Pakistan scheme was first accepted at the Sind Provincial Conference of the ML which was held eighteen months before the Lahore session. Between the Sind Conference and the Lahore session, there had been several meetings of the council of the ML as well of its working committee. But these meetings, the Maulana exclaimed, were again dominated by much crying and complaining about atrocities committed on the 'minority provinces' Muslims and during this entire period no outline of the Pakistan scheme was prepared. Furthermore, a constitutional committee of the ML had been in place for nearly fifteen months, but it too, till date, had not prepared any constitutional outline. Surveying this situation, Maulana Sajjad expressed disbelief that a lawyer of Jinnah's eminence did not have the capability to prepare a constitution. He, therefore, inferred that if Jinnah had not completed the task in spite of having the capability and time to prepare the constitution, it was clear that the *Qaid* still did not believe in the scheme and nor did he see it as a practical proposition.

The question, therefore, remained as to why Jinnah was still insisting on Pakistan. The answer to this riddle, Sajjad concluded, was that Jinnah and the ML were no longer left with any issues after the resignation of Congress governments in the provinces. Robbed of their only plank to rally the Muslims, they were now resorting to fraudulent concepts like Hindu India and Muslim India in order to inflame the passions of illiterate Muslims and save the ML flag. Sajjad lamented that poor, illiterate, Muslims suffering under grinding poverty that had become worse under British rule, were constantly told that the ML was going to set up Islamic Raj in a big part of India, which would protect their religion. This Islamic Raj, they were further assured, would get rid of all their material and spiritual difficulties. Sajjad bitterly remarked that this propaganda though highly misleading, would nonetheless be used by the ML to ensure its victory whenever the new elections would come up. That was the primary aim behind the ML's advocacy of Pakistan.

Ultimately, Maulana Sajjad surveyed the prospects of the three independent federations comprising Hindu provinces, Muslim provinces and Indian states, each responsible for their own respective foreign, defence and trade policies. In this context, the Maulana asserted that Jinnah had not clarified whether these proposed arrangements would secure complete freedom for these federations from British rule. Here, he referred to Jinnah's statement in which the latter had claimed that while Ceylon and Burma had been separated from Indian affairs they were still connected to India through British power. Sajjad, therefore, claimed that Jinnah wanted Britain to continue to preside over the relations between Hindu and Muslim federations and did not want it to completely exit the subcontinent as a colonial power. He therefore pessimistically concluded that the formation of three separate and independent federations would be disastrous for the so called 'Muslim India' and would only result in a triumphant Britain re-emerging as the dominant power in the subcontinent.

Maulana Sajjad's critique of Pakistan, though made primarily from an ethical standpoint, included an awareness of the sphere of practical politics and world affairs. It also reflected the shock and incredulity that the Lahore Resolution with its idea of dividing India had evoked among the *ulama*. More importantly, his analysis of the Lahore Resolution echoed the initial widespread suspicion that Jinnah and the ML were perhaps using the Pakistan demand as a bargaining counter, even if Jinnah himself had strenuously and publicly denied this charge. But subsequent critiques of Pakistan such as the one levelled by Maulvi Tufail Ahmad Manglori were accompanied by a growing realization that Pakistan was a serious demand, which now enjoyed overwhelming support among Muslims across India, including those belonging to the 'minority provinces'.

Joint Electorates and a Shining Future for Indian Muslims: Maulvi Tufail Ahmad Manglori and a Critique of Pakistan from the 'Minority Provinces'

Maulvi Tufail Ahmad Manglori was not a traditionally educated *alim* but belonged to the earliest batch of students who studied at the Muhammadan Anglo-Oriental College at Aligarh. Born in Manglaur in Saharanpur district in 1868, he completed his elementary education in a local *maktab* before joining Aligarh School in 1879 where he went on to secure an F.A. in 1889. During this decade, young Tufail Ahmad lived up to the eclectic ideals of the new institution. On the one hand, he was part of the school's cricketing eleven as its wicketkeeper, while on the other he was known for his regularity in saying prayers and an impeccable dress sense that earned him the title of 'Maulvi'.[16] In college, he was one of the founders of the Duty Society that raised funds for poor and needy students, a member of the University Union's Cabinet, and was also elected as its Secretary. A rapidly degenerative eye condition that badly impaired his vision forced him to quit Aligarh in 1890 before he could appear for his B.A. exams, thus curtailing a promising academic career. The young Aligarhian, however, quickly secured the post of a Sub-Registrar in the provincial bureaucratic apparatus in the same town. His biographer tells us that a light office workload combined with strong sense of service enabled Manglori to channelize his energies towards organizing the Aligarh's Old Boys and compiling a Directory of its alumni. As another contemporary explained, the motive behind this service was his firm belief that only 'former students of Aligarh College would complete Sir Syed's mission and raise the Muslims to a position of honor in India.'[17] As part of this mission, he opened schools for Muslim students in Muzaffarnagar and Shahjahanpur where he was posted during his service. After his retirement in 1926, Tufail Ahmad entered the provincial Legislative Council where he served till 1930.

16 Nizami Badayuni, *Yadgar-i Tufail: Maulana Tufail Ahmad Manglori Alig ki Savanih-i Hayat par Roshni ya Shama Hidayat* (Badayun, n.d).

17 See 'Extracts from the Prologue by Khan Bahadur Maulavi Muhammad Basheeruddin, an Old Boy of Aligarh, Educationist and Founder of Muslim High School Etawah', in Tufail Ahmad Manglori, *Towards a Common Destiny: A Nationalist Manifesto,* Translated by Ali Ashraf (New Delhi, 1994).

Manglori was also intimately involved with the activities of the All India Muslim Educational Conference from the very outset and was elected Joint Secretary of the organization.[18] Liaquat Ali Khan in his praise of this organization once noted that it was on the occasion of its 1906 Dacca session that the foundations of the AIML were laid with some of its most prominent sponsors being the men from Aligarh.[19] Yet, in contrast to the trend at the educational conference or at the Muslim University where Pakistan became the creed of its students and staff, Manglori became deeply critical of Pakistan, seeing it as a disaster for the Indian Muslims in general and minority provinces Muslims in particular. Not surprisingly, he was one of the founding members of the Azad Muslim Conference that met amidst much fanfare within a month of the Lahore Resolutionin April 1940 at Delhi to publicly oppose the idea of Pakistan. The organization brought together Deobandi *ulama* belonging to the Madani faction besides other prominent Congress and non-League Muslims. It is because of his close links with the Deobandi *ulama* through this organization and the fact that many of his arguments against Pakistan were in close accord with their views that Manglori's critique of Pakistan has been included alongside those of the *ulama* in this chapter.

Manglori's view of Pakistan can be gleaned from his writings that first appeared in the form of articles in Urdu newspapers, especially in the weekly *Zulqarnain* published from Badayun. These articles were later developed and sold as pamphlets and subsequently incorporated into his books, *Ruh-i-Raushan Mustaqbil* and its modified version, *Musalmanon Ka Raushan Mustaqbil.* These volumes became widely popular soon after their publication as evident from the fact that five editions of the latter were published and sold out between 1937 and 1945. Manglori began his critique of Pakistan by expressing his frustration at the ML's failure to provide clarifications regarding their Pakistan scheme since the ML had not published or sanctioned any Pakistan scheme as yet.[20] He, therefore, raised a series of pointed questions that nationalists around the country had routinely been asking about Pakistan. What was going to be the nature of government in Pakistan? Would its governments be based on the idea of God's rule (*Khilafat-i-Rabbani*)? What would be the nature of the relations

---

18 For an account of this Conference, see Abdul Rashid Khan, *The All India Muslim Educational Conference: Its Contribution to the Cultural Development of Indian Muslims 1886-1947* (Karachi, 2001).

19 Nawabzada Liaquat Ali Khan, *Muslim Educational Problems: Pakistan Literature Series No.7* (Lahore, 1945).

20 Tufail Ahmad Manglori, 'Khwab-i-Gul ki Pareshani', *Zulqarnain*, 14 April 1941.

between the units of Pakistan? How would Pakistan garner sufficient economic resources for functioning effectively? What would be the model of economic development that Pakistan would adopt? Would the ML assent to any centre with which Pakistan would have some relations? What would be the nature of its defense arrangements with Hindustan? How would the rights of minorities on either side be protected if Pakistan came into existence? Notwithstanding these outstanding issues, Manglori lamented that the ML wanted Muslims to rest assured that the *Qaid-i-Azam* was a far sighted leader who would take care of their interests. It was therefore unnecessary for them to ask such questions for they would only embroil the *Qaum* in incidental and minor disputes (*zimni aur zaili mabahas*) that were best avoided. Muslims all over the country were, therefore, expected to remain content with just raising slogans of *Pakistan Zindabad* and *Qaid-i-Azam ki Jai*. As he sarcastically noted, Pakistan after all was this strange thing that was only comprehensible to the top leaders and beyond the understanding of ordinary mortals like him.

Yet, Manglori sought to make sense of Pakistan from whatever information he could garner from ML propaganda as well as various journals and newspapers since he feared its far reaching impact on Muslims across the subcontinent. He developed his critique by zeroing in on the Pakistan scheme put forth by the Aligarh Professors, Zafarul Hasan and M. A. H. Qadri.[21] Based on his reading of this scheme, Manglori claimed that the ML wanted separate Muslim zones (*khatte*) to be created where Muslims would have their own government.[22] What was also clear was that these areas were to be hived off from other existing parts of India to form a separate Muslim federation with absolutely no connection with any central government. This new federation would thus be independent in every sense of the word (*woh har aitbar se kamil azad hon*). Contemplating this idea, a troubled Manglori drew his readers' attention to official census figures on the population numbers and percentages of Hindu and Muslim populations in the proposed Muslim zones. He pointed out that the Hindus in the northwestern Muslim zone would constitute 40 per cent of the total population and this figure would rise to 43 per cent for the northeastern zone. By contrast, he pointed out that in the Hindu majority provinces of U.P., Bihar, C.P., Madras, Bombay,

21 Zafarul Hasan and M. A. H Qadri, 'The Problem of Indian Muslims and Its Solution', in S. A. I Tirmizi (ed.), *The Paradoxes of Partition, 1937-1947*(New Delhi, 1998), 612-15.

22 *Teen Karod Musalmanon Ki Hifazat: Yani Woh Khutba jo Syed Tufail Ahmad Sahab Manglori ne Azad Muslim Conference Zila Etawah Munaqida 9, 10, August 1941 ke Iftitah ke Waqt Padha* (Badayun, 1941). This speech was published in *Zulqarnain*, 28 August 1941.

Orissa, and Rajputana, Hindus would constitute 90 per cent of the population with the Muslims coming up to a mere 10 per cent. Similarly, Muslims would constitute small minorities in Delhi (28 per cent), Malabar (27 per cent) and Hyderabad (7 per cent). Given that Muslims had slender majorities in their two majority zones, Manglori wondered how they could achieve their dream of setting up an Islamic state in these zones. Therefore, rather sarcastically, he wished the 5 crore 85 lakh Muslims of the majority provinces good luck with trying to fulfill this dream. Casting them aside for the moment, Manglori expressed greater concern about the fate of Muslims in the Hindu zone where they would become a miniscule, feeble minority. These Muslims, he claimed, were largely poor, ill-educated, with little access to either education or economic resources. What was equally important to remember, he told his readers, was that these Muslims numbering 2 crore 80 lakhs were almost half as big as the Muslim majority in the northwest and the northeast. What would happen to them in case Pakistan was established?

Manglori observed that the minority provinces Muslims were often told by ML functionaries that if they were oppressed by their Hindu majority they would always have the choice of migrating (*tark-i-watan*) to either Pakistan or Bengal and settle in either of these areas.[23] He, further, noted that the other option given to these Muslims was removal from their own villages if their numbers were small, and resettlement in places within Hindu India where they would have much larger numbers to supposedly ensure their greater safety and security. Since the problems and dangers involved in these two options seemed obvious Manglori did not bother to elaborate on them at any great length. But he did spend considerable energy in picking apart the ML's claim that the creation of Pakistan would entail a treaty with Hindustan based on reciprocal minority safeguards that would provide adequate protection for the rights and interests of the minority provinces Muslims. These proclamations were usually accompanied by open invocations of the 'hostage population' theory. Manglori dismissed this theory as absurd insisting that it would provide no security guarantees to the 'minority provinces' Muslims. Such assurances, he argued, could provide only cold comfort since the Hindus in their majority provinces could easily commit reprisals against Muslims while the same was highly unlikely in the Muslim zones against the Hindu minorities since the latter were well educated, wealthy, with a dominating presence in universities, trades and industries. He, therefore, commiserated with his listeners at the Etawah meeting bemoaning that they could not be blamed for being fearful since they

23 Tufail Ahmad Manglori, 'Pakistan Ki Nawayat', *Zulqarnain*, 28 January 1942.

were a miniscule Muslim minority in the U.P. and would find themselves in a dangerous situation under the Pakistan scheme.

An irate Manglori fumed that rather than addressing these concerns, the *Qaid* heartlessly declared that he was ready to perform the last rites of martyrdom for 2 crore minority provinces Muslims for the sake of liberating their majority provinces brethren. These Muslims, Manglori lamented, were thus condemned to live in 'Kufristan', to be crushed by the Hindu majority. An emotional Manglori now made a dramatic plea to the *Qaid*. The 'minority provinces' Muslims were ready to sacrifice themselves for his sake, but only on the condition that they be slaughtered en masse in open warfare (*alania jang*) with the enemy, for at least that way they would be able to secure eternity (*abadi zindagi*). But rather than offer them martyrdom, he bewailed that the *Qaid* was asking them to commit suicide, something that was gravely forbidden in Islam. Suicide, he bitterly concluded, was imminent, entailing the obliteration of the language, religion and culture of Muslims in these provinces, a process, which had already begun after the Lahore Resolution. To substantiate his point, Manglori referred to the case of some *ulama* who had recently gone to villages in Saharanpur to give instruction on *namaz* and *roza* to poor Muslim villagers and were staying with them. Such was the state of communal tension in U.P. that the local Hindu zamindar forced these poor Muslim peasants to cast out the *ulama* from their homes in the middle of the night. Once they were out of the village, they were set upon and assaulted by the Hindus. Islam, Manglori stated, was a proselytizing religion (*tablighi mazhab*) that could spread only through missionary activities. These would become impossible after Pakistan.

Manglori therefore asserted that it was the right of the minority provinces Muslims to ask their most powerful representative organization, the ML, to find a solution that would allow them to live in peace, just as it had devised the Pakistan scheme to putatively liberate the majority provinces Muslims. Since the ML had given a remedy that was lopsided and unsatisfactory, Manglori himself suggested a solution that he claimed would be most efficacious. The remedy was startling for it flew in the face of accepted political wisdom of over three decades in Muslim political circles in British India. It called for the restoration of joint electorates in the 'minority provinces', an ideal that the Congress had been seeking to achieve for all of India through negotiations with Muslim representatives for the past several years.[24]

24 Tufail Ahmad Manglori, 'Muslim Aqalliyat ki Hifazat ke Masley Ka Hal', *Zulqarnain*, 14 February 1942.

At the outset, Manglori defended his advocacy of joint electorates against objections most commonly raised by its opponents. He rejected the view that in joint electorates Muslim members who got elected were usually under Hindu influence, arguing that Hindu members too came under the influence of Muslims in this system. Hindus too could, therefore, be called the 'toadies' of the Muslims in such a system. At the very least, the advantage of this system was that a Hindu member who got elected with the help of Muslim votes would never be seen leading the procession that played music in front of mosques. Instead of being infected by the communal virus, the Hindu politician often saw his own advantage in passing resolutions and measures that were for public welfare and the common good of all communities. In the same vein, Manglori swiftly dismissed the second objection to joint electorates, which held that heightened communal mentality currently prevalent among the Hindus rendered them even more harmful for the Muslims. He argued that on the contrary the current communal mentality among Hindus had arisen primarily due to the absence of joint electorates. And just like Muslims often complained about Hindu communal mentality, he asked his readers to be mindful that Hindus too had similar complaints regarding the Muslims. After all it had been demonstrated that wherever Muslims enjoyed power they too harassed the Hindus, thus placing obstacles in the path of the country's political development.

Manglori backed these propositions by demonstrating how Muslim experience had been a lot better under joint electorates than under separate electorates by explaining the operation of the former in two separate contexts. First was the institutional context of the Local Boards. In this system, Manglori reminded his audience that initially Hindu voters elected Hindu members while Muslim voters elected Muslim members through separate electorates. However, when the Chairman of the Local Board had to be elected Hindu and Muslim members got together in a joint electorate to complete this process. And here the position of the Muslim members far from being helpless was often very decisive, for as he pointed out, factional fights among Hindu members saw them courting Muslim members thus giving them the decisive vote. Quite often, Muslims ended up getting elected as Chairmen in these situations. The second distinct institutional context that Manglori cited was that of the Town Areas of U.P. where the voters themselves voted in a joint electorate. He asked his readers to ponder over the fact that there were far fewer communal conflicts in these areas while at the same time they had composite political groups including both Hindu and Muslim members. The reason for this phenomenon, he argued, was very simple. In this system, a Hindu politician was compelled to approach and seek votes from not just the Hindu voters but the Muslim voters as well if he wanted to win the elections. A Hindu member who was elected in a joint electorate was therefore a lot less bigoted than a Hindu member who got elected under a separate electorate. Manglori recalled that when joint electorates were in vogue before the institutionalization of separate electorates in 1909, Hindu candidates would often be found at Muslim doorsteps and vice-versa.[25] *Mandirs*, *masjids* and *gurudwaras* were visited by all candidates and these places of worship were always safe even during communal tensions. In fact, there was no communal rioting in this era for riots generally happened between groups that had both Hindus and Muslims on each side. Even the rioting that occurred whenever *Muharram* and *Dussehra* coincided was more often the result of tensions among Twelver Shias over questions of who should lead the processions rather than Hindu–Muslim tensions.[26] Thus, the accountability of the Hindu politician to the Muslim voter and vice-versa was the greatest advantage of this system, and it ensured peace and security.

Manglori bolstered his argument in favour of a joint electorate by contrasting it to the ways in which Muslims had suffered under separate electorates over the last three decades.[27] He first pointed to the dubious origins of the system reminding his readers that it was institutionalized by the Viceroy in 1906 after a delegation of Muslim notables led by the Aga Khan successfully pleaded for its establishment after complaining that Hindu dominated joint electorates made it extremely hard for Muslims to get elected. Manglori acknowledged that the delegation may have had a point, but argued that the problem could have been rectified by reserving seats for Muslim representatives in each district as per their proportion in population. Yet, such a step was never taken and instead the British were allowed to happily implement their strategy of divide and rule. Manglori bemoaned that since then during every negotiation with the Hindus over the settlement of the communal question Muslim leaders had bargained away several rights in trying to retain separate electorates. He pointed out that the most grievous injury as a result of this policy was suffered by the majority provinces Muslims when the ML signed the 1916 Lucknow Pact with the Congress bartering away legislative majorities in Bengal and Punjab in lieu

---

25 Tufail Ahmad Manglori, 'Judagana Intekhab aur Mazhabi Balwey', *Zulqarnain*, 14 December 1941.

26 For an elaboration of this argument, see Sandria Freitag, *Collective Action and Community: Public Arenas and the Emergence of Communalism in North India* (Berkeley, 1989).

27 Tufail Ahmad Manglori, 'Musalman Awam Siyasi Daldal Mein', *Zulqarnain*, 7 December 1941.

of preserving separate electorates and weightage for Muslims in the minority provinces. Manglori pointed out that the reason for this suicidal move was not hard to understand. In anticipation of the 1919 Act, which instituted diarchy, Mr Jinnah and other minority provinces Muslims, who at the time dominated the ML, were more interested in their own political careers and therefore sought weightage for Muslims in the 'minority provinces'. They had no qualms in sacrificing legislative majorities of their 'majority provinces' brethren. For Manglori there was irony in that it was in these very Muslim majority provinces that Mr Jinnah now wanted to form his Pakistan.[28]

Continuing his historical analysis, Manglori observed that by 1927 several Muslim political leaders had come to the conclusion that separate electorates needed to be ended but they decided to do so after extracting maximum concessions from the Congress, which was desperate to bring an end to this system. Thus, as a result of further Muslim bargaining, Sind was separated from Bombay and given the status of a separate province, a council was instituted in NWFP, while in the Central Assembly the Muslims secured a good proportion of seats besides a good percentage of jobs in the civil services.[29] But rather than give up separate electorates after these gains, Muslim representatives now upped their demands even further. They now asked for legal protection for their religion, language, culture and personal laws. Manglori argued that even though these things were now protected under the law, the catch was that the Muslim voter could only go to his Muslim representative who was in a minority in the councils for their implementation. He could no longer go to the Congress members or the British Government for protection as he no longer had any relationship with them.

The second and more grievous harm caused by separate electorates in Manglori's eyes was the rise in communal tensions between the newly constructed Hindu and Muslim political communities. Manglori contended that earlier divisions that existed in society were on the basis of caste communities and class distinctions among both Hindus and Muslims. But thanks to the British, while *Qaum* was earlier used to designate *zat* (caste), *Qaum* now became the marker of religious community. If the divisions in Indian society on the basis of religion began due to competition for jobs and positions under

---

28 Tufail Ahmad Manglori, 'Pakistani Khatte Muslim Aqalliyat ke Subey Kaise Baney', *Zulqarnain*, 21 January 1942.

29 Tufail Ahmad Manglori, 'Hindu-Muslim Samjhauton ka Ghair Mutnahi Silsila', *Zulqarnain*, 21 February 1942.

British rule, separate electorates solidified these divisions even further. Hindu representatives now won elections by appealing to Hindu voters and telling them that they would protect Hindu interests vis-a-vis the Muslims and vice-versa. The Hindu politicians no longer needed to approach Muslim voters and as a result the latter's political importance declined precipitously. At the same time, Manglori pointed out that Muslim ministers too lost whatever residual influence they had on individuals belonging to the Hindu community. This initially led to alienation and was followed by mutual hatred between the two communities. In this situation if any decent Hindu minister wanted to do justice to the Muslims, the Hindu voters would be at his throat to warn him that they would punish him the next time elections were held. What was worse was that the votes of Shudras, Untouchables and Indian Christians became more valuablefor the Hindu politicians who now had to seek their votes in the elections, than the votes of the Muslim voters. Thus, all of a sudden, the Muslims were now confronted with a much bigger bloc of voters than merely the caste Hindus.

Manglori observed that the incidence of rioting also increased in this situation for soon after the introduction of separate electorates, massive riots occurred in Ayodhya and Muzaffarnagar in 1914. While earlier, Hindu and Muslim leaders risked their own lives to stop riots, now they got busy helping out their kinsmen booked in rioting cases. Poor Muslims who lived in the inner cities were the most affected by these riots. Those living in the bungalows in the civil lines were not affected and could continue with their parties, card games and tennis matches. A distraught Manglori noted that when there was a communal riot in 1929 in Badayun a police party was stationed in town for which the residents had to pay for its upkeep. However, the civil lines were exempt from this punitive tax since there had been no rioting and complete Hindu–Muslim unity existed in this locality. He also pointed out that in the council chambers too, upper crust Hindu and Muslim members could raise a lot of communal questions, make cutting speeches and hostile remarks against one another, but once in the lobbies they became thick friends. It was only poor Muslims who either rotted in their homes, hospitals, courts, or jails.

This brought Manglori to the question as to why the Muslim political leaders persisted in their efforts to preserve separate electorates if it was so detrimental to the Muslim community at large. He answered this question by arguing that even if the current system was bad for the Muslim community, it was good for the Muslim political class from the minority provinces, which dominated Muslim politics. This class demanded separate electorates since they were freed from the bother of approaching Hindu voters and thereby having to spend more money while campaigning in the elections. While Muslim elected representatives still had to approach their Hindu counterparts for election into board or council committees and getting posts, the beauty of this system was that it did not entail any additional expense for the Muslim members. And since Hindu representatives too needed the votes of Muslim representatives to be elected as Local Board Chairmen or the like, the matter was resolved to the mutual satisfaction of both these elites. From soliciting votes from one another, their relations over time progressed to being almost brotherly. Indeed, they now helped each other in every possible way, finding jobs for each other's relatives and government contracts for friends.

This system suited particularly Muslim politicians from the U.P. who tasted power and enjoyed 30 per cent of council memberships and ministerships that was far in excess of their real strength given that the Muslim population in the U.P. stood at a mere 14 per cent of the province's population. Manglori further explained that while their importance had already been buttressed due to the weightage they enjoyed after sacrificing the political interests of their brethren in the Punjab and Bengal, their disproportionate share in power arrangements was further enhanced due to the system of provincial government where Muslim ministers survived on the support of the official British contingent in the Councils. But even under this system, Manglori reminded his audience that Muslim political power was not always stable. The reforms of 1919 had meant that Muslim members in the U.P. council wielded the swing vote. Thus, if they sided with the government they could defeat Hindu proposals, while they could defeat the government's proposals on the floor of the council if they sided with the Hindu members. As a result of this shifting policy of siding with the government on some occasions and with the Hindus on other occasions in order to get proposals passed in the Councils, Muslim politicians were left with no fixed policy other than expediency. They were to also discover that when their own need arose, neither the Hindu members nor the government sided with them.

The moment of reckoning for Muslim politicians in the minority provinces such as the U.P., therefore, arrived with the GOI Act of 1935. The Hindus now had enough seats to form a majority in the assembly on their own without needing any Muslim support. Manglori recalled that while extremely friendly relations had existed between Congress and ML during the elections of 1937 and a host of other parties built on cross-communal alliances also arose in this context, after the Congress party unexpected successes in the 1937 elections, the relationship between Hindu and Muslim political elites collapsed over the distribution of ministerships and spoils of power.[30] Thus, it was only after Muslim political elites in U.P. had lost their ministerships and perks of office that Muslim policy of the previous thirty five years that revolved around 'saving' Muslims in the minority provinces from the 'oppression of the Hindu majorities' was abruptly overturned. Now, after the Lahore Resolution these very 'minority provinces' Muslims were being abandoned in the name of now liberating the majority provinces Muslims whose interests had earlier been sacrificed by these very elites. The Pakistan demand, therefore, emerged out of this context in which Muslim leaders found themselves out of power. While the ML leadership whipped up fears among Muslims that they had been reduced to an ineffectual, impotent, and permanent minority in India, Manglori argued that on the contrary it was these leaders who had become a minority under the new constitution and *not* the Muslim electorate per se.

Manglori wistfully noted that if the Muslim electorate was part of a joint electorate and had a say in the election of the Hindu representatives as well, the weight of the permanent Hindu majority would have been lessened. He,therefore, pleaded with the ML leadership to allow the system of separate electorates to be replaced by that of joint electorates. They could create Islamic government in Pakistan if they wished, but the least they could do for the minority province Muslims was to allow them to join joint electorates.[31] If Muslim representatives had enjoyed free choice and benefits under this system, he wondered why it should be denied to the Muslim voter. Indeed, Muslim voters had lost their leverage and been reduced from the position of human beings to that of insects because of the loss of opportunity to vote for Hindu candidates.[32] If even now Muslim voters were, therefore, given back this power, there would arise Hindu politicians, who if only to save their chairs, would see to it that the roads in Muslim localities were well maintained, take care of street lighting and give contracts to Muslims contractors who helped them during the elections. Manglori, however, despaired of any such development taking place, observing that it would only happen if God placed some mercy in the hearts of Muslim politicians for the Muslim general public. As he noted, there was no

30 Tufail Ahmad Manglori, 'Kaante Bo Kar Meethe Phool Ki Tawaqqo', *Zulqarnain*, 14 January 1942.

31 Manglori, *Teen Karod Musalmanon Ki Hifazat* (Badayun, 1941).

32 Manglori, 'Muslim Aqalliyat ki Hifazat ke Masley Ka Hal', *Zulqarnain*, 14 February 1942.

parallel in world history to the way in which in India the rights and interests of Muslim voters had been sacrificed by Muslim politicians. Manglori sent an essay with his views on joint electorates to Gandhi seeking its publication in the *Harijan*. But the Mahatma keeping in mind the sensitive nature of the matter in the prevailing context wrote back that 'though your argument is good I am afraid no good will come out of publishing it at the present juncture.'[33]

Finally, Manglori suggested an additional remedy to resolve the problem of protecting the culture and religion of the Muslim in the 'minority provinces', which had again been endangered due to the ML's myopic political tactics. He maintained that these could hardly be preserved by reserving jobs in government services for Muslims. Rather, they could only be preserved by giving back to the Qazis, Muftis and Maulvies, the legal powers to decide on questions of marriage, divorce and inheritance under Islamic law. These matters had been under their jurisdiction till 1860 and there was no reason why they could not decide on them again. This last remedy also reflected the view of the Deobandi *ulama*.

As evident, Manglori focused on the predicament of the minority provinces Muslims and made arguments in favour of securing their rights and interests through the device of joint electorates. He even conceded Pakistan in principle declaring that if the majority provinces Muslims wanted to create their own separate State, they were free to try their luck. But the last critique of Pakistan that we must consider next, outlined by the Deobandi *alim* Maulana Hifzur Rahman Seoharvi, made no such concessions as it proceeded to outline a comprehensive critique of Pakistan that encompassed the concerns of both the minority as well as majority provinces Muslims.

Maulana Hifzur Rahman Seoharvi's Comprehensive Moral and Pragmatic Critique of Pakistan

Maulana Hifzur Rahman Seoharvi whose comprehensive critique of Pakistan was circulated before the elections of 1945–46 was a senior cleric and *Nazim* (chief organizer) of the JUH in Delhi. His roots, however, lay in U.P. for he was born in 1901 into a *zamindar* family that hailed from Seohara village in Bijnor district.[34] His father Shamsuddin was an Assistant Engineer who first worked in Bhopal and later in Bikaner State. Shamsuddin made sure that like

---

[33] Gandhi to Tofail Ahmad, 24 May 1942, *CWMG*, Vol. 76, 144.

[34] This biographical information is drawn from Hafiz Muhammad Akbar Shah Bukhari, *Akabir-i-ulama-i-Deoband* (Lahore, 1999), 317–18; Mahbub Rizvi, *History of the Darul Uloom Deoband*, (Deoband, 1981), Vol. 2, 107–9.

him his two older sons received English education but decided that his third son Hifzur Rahman should study the religious sciences. After initial education at Seohara and Moradabad the young man enrolled at Deoband. At the *Darul Uloom*, where he specialized in the Hadith, his teachers included the celebrated scholars Anwar Shah Kashmiri and Shabbir Ahmad Usmani. He would cross swords with the latter during the elections of 1945–46. After graduating from Deoband he was sent to preach in Madras Presidency where he stayed for a year. During this stay he wrote two booklets *Malabar Mein Islam* and *Hifzur Rahman le Mazhab al Nauman*. From Madras, Hifzur Rahman went on a Haj to Mecca and also visited Medina. On his return to India he went back to Deoband but did not stay there for long as he left for Dabhail in Surat in 1927 along with Anwar Shah Kashmiri and Shabbir Ahmad Usmani following their dispute with the management at Deoband. He spent the next few years as a teacher at Dabhail as well as a preacher doing the work of *Tabligh* in the local villages. In 1930, Hifzur Rahman became active in the civil disobedience movement, but after it petered out he moved to Calcutta in 1933 on the invitation of the *Anjuman Tabligh al Islam*, at the time presided over by Maulana Abul Kalam Azad. Having taught the Quran for five years in Calcutta, Seoharvi moved to Delhi in 1938 where he was instrumental in setting up the *Nadvatul Musannefin* that published high quality Urdu books in philosophy, literature and poetry. His involvement in nationalist politics became particularly marked after the GOI Act of 1935 and he was one of the seventeen *ulama* inducted into the Muslim League Parliamentary Board by Jinnah as the party geared to fight the 1937 elections. After these elections, along with Maulana Husain Ahmad Madani, he split from the ML and moved closer to the Congress after developing differences with Jinnah. The elevation of his relative Hafiz Mohammad Ibrahim, the Bijnor MLA, as one of the two Muslim Ministers in the Congress government in U.P. drew him further into Congress politics and he campaigned for Congress candidates in the subsequent by-elections for Muslim seats.

Seoharvi's critique of Pakistan first appeared as a series of articles in one of U.P.'s most respected Urdu newspapers, the *Madina*, on the eve of the 1945–46 elections which became a referendum on Pakistan. It was also printed in booklet form and distributed as election propaganda by the Congress and the Azad Muslim Parliamentary Board, the political arm of the JUH that fought the elections in alliance with the former. While earlier critiques of Pakistan articulated the concerns of the minority provinces Muslims, Seoharvi's essay evaluated its implications for the entire Indian Muslim community. Again, while earlier critiques inveighed against Pakistan on moral grounds, Seoharvi's expanded critique combined ethical and pragmatic arguments to detail Pakistan's disastrous practical implications for the Indian Muslims.[35] At the outset, Seoharvi deplored the trivialization of the debate on Pakistan due to the ML's 'anti-Hindu sentimentalism' and 'spirit of slander'. Pakistan had not been thought through rationally, on the basis of evidence and proof. Useless questions were being asked and useless answers given. The need of the hour, he insisted, was to carefully evaluate whether Pakistan was a panacea for the Indian Muslims or a piece of fraudulent political alchemy concocted by some individuals out to make personal and party gains. Pakistan could not be supported merely because it was being opposed by the Hindus. Truth would be revealed only if this debate was conducted according to Islam's ancient ideal of rational discussion. With this opening gambit, Seoharvi cast the seemingly modern and progressive ML elites as retrograde who spread sentimental slogans and untruths about Pakistan, while at the same time claiming rationality for the *ulama*, long derided by ML leadership as purveyors of irrationality and superstition.

Seoharvi contended that it was necessary to examine ideas, which instead of leaving the minority provinces Muslims to the tender mercies of the Hindus, would give them an equal and identical freedom as the majority provinces Muslims. He wanted all Muslim political parties to get together for an exchange of opinions and achieve consensus on a common scheme, which could then be presented to both the British government and the Congress party. He pointed out that the JUH had invited the ML for such a meeting on numerous occasions but had been unsuccessful. Instead, the latter had been busy selling its own scheme as Islamic and trying to convince people about it through fraud. Given this situation, Seoharvi provided readers his own analysis of whether Jinnah's 'inspired' (*ilhami*) Pakistan scheme could actually achieve the goals it had set out for itself – of creating an Islamic State in Pakistan that would liberate majority provinces Muslims and simultaneously guarantee security for minority provinces Muslims who would be left behind in Hindu India. He, therefore, began with the question, 'What is the meaning of Pakistan?' and proceeded to lay out his own understanding of the problem. The ML, he noted, had described Muslims as an independent and separate nation (*azad aur mustaqil qaum*), which existed alongside other nations in India. It wanted the Muslim majority provinces in the northwest and northeast to be separated from the rest of India where the Hindus were in a majority. These new Islamic states would then federate and be independent from Hindustan.

[35] Maulana Hifzur Rahman Seoharvi, *Tehrik-i-Pakistan par ek Nazar* (Delhi, 1945).

Like Sajjad, Seoharvi ridiculed ML's designationof Pakistan as an Islamic state since Jinnah himself had publicly assured non-Muslim minorities that they would mandatorily be given a certain proportion of seats in Pakistan's legislature and cabinet government, and that laws in Pakistan would be passed by a European style parliament. Seoharvi pointed out that in a truly Islamic state, non-Muslims could only live as *dhimmis* and could not have any role in the functions of government. Besides, a legislature comprising such assorted members, passing laws, was unheard of in an Islamic state. Moreover, since Jinnah had also ruled out large scale exchanges of population, the prospect of Pakistan becoming an Islamic state with its enormous non-Muslim minority population was simply non-existent. To, therefore, say that Pakistan was an Islamic state, he insisted, was a grave political fraud. Seoharvi took this opportunity to address the question of population transfers, which even Jinnah conceded,were inevitable to an extent. Besides pointing to its practical impossibility, he warned that such ideas were extremely dangerous not just for 'minority provinces' Muslims who would be directly affected, but for the entire Indian Muslim community. The 'minority provinces' were after all the primary sites of Muslim culture and civilization in India, home to a greater number of mosques, shrines of saints, graves of martyrs and Muslim ancestors, than all of the Pakistan areas put together, and relinquishing this historical legacy would be nothing short of a disaster for Islam in India.

Seoharvi extended his critique with a dire prognosis regarding Pakistan's prospects as a seperate sovereign state (*Mustaqil aur Azad Hukumat*) that would be formed out of the Muslim majority provinces in the northwest and northeast 'after leaping over two provinces in the middle, U.P. and Bihar'. His understanding thus reflected the widespread perception by the time of the 1945 elections that Pakistan would be a single federal state, thus eliminating any ambiguities that may have existed earlier due to the wording of the Lahore Resolution. Like Manglori, he argued that population figures for Pakistan and Hindustan indicated that the former would be 60 per cent Muslim and 40 per cent Hindu, while the latter would be 10 per cent Muslim and 90 per cent Hindu. This meant that in Pakistan the Muslims would have a precarious majority while in Hindustan the Muslims would be a very feeble minority that would always be at the mercy of the Hindus. These being the brute facts of the situation, Seoharvi bemoaned that whenever such arguments were presented, the ML members espousing Pakistan always became very emotional. They simply declared that once Muslims secured their own independent State they would bring their non-Muslim minorities under control and also successfully exert pressure on Hindustani government to protect its own Muslim population. Expressing lofty disdain, Seoharvi claimed that the *ulama* as the guardians of rationality saw such sentimentalism as dangerous while thinking about such grave matters.

Seoharvi demolished the ML's argument that if Muslims in Hindustan were maltreated or oppressed, retaliatory measures would be taken against Hindu minorities in Pakistan arguing that it was not valid according to religion, ethics, or law. Unlike Sajjad who provided a moral critique of the hostage population theory, Seoharvi primarily pointed to its practical problems. He pointed out that when minority provinces Muslims were being 'oppressed' under Congress cabinet governments there were Muslim governments in Punjab and Bengal and yet retaliatory measures against Hindus in these provinces had never materialized. In independent Pakistan, the government again would be unable target non-Muslims in response to Muslims being persecuted in U.P. or Bihar since the former were powerful and capable of launching massive protests and creating a political deadlock that could undermine the government. Seoharvi also swiftly dismissed the other alternative of Pakistan giving an ultimatum of war to Hindustan stating that it could never happen given the evident power asymmetry between the two countries. Giving an example, he pointed out that an indignant Turkey could do nothing about Jewish immigration into Palestine or Palestinian dispossession and only wring its hands in despair since it was not strong enough to oppose European powers let alone declaring war on them. He thus questioned the purported sagacity of the ML leadership in not thinking through these issues even though it prided itself for its cold eyed political realism and knowledge of international affairs.

Seoharvi next criticized the ML leadership for spreading communal hatred in the name of Pakistan. He claimed that ML leaders, aristocratic upper class Muslims, were opportunistically resorting to these tactics for their own gain as they had done earlier. He recounted that when the ministry was being formed in U.P. after the 1937 elections, the ML and Jinnah first stood in front of Congress government with their hands outstretched like beggars, seeking positions in government. Once the Congress refused to share power, the same ML started a virulent public propaganda against its governments while at the same time continuing to privately beg Congress ministers for honorary magistrateships, Chairmanships of Village Development Schemes and other jobs in the government. As a result, he alleged that nearly 75 per cent of these positions had been cornered by *Khan Bahadurs, Khan Sahibs,*

Sirs, ML members of the Legislative Assembly and Legislative Council. In this regard, he noted that Nawab Ismail Khan and Nawab Chhatari had been appointed Chairmen of *Gram Sudhar Committees* (Village Development Committees) in Meerut and Bulandshahr respectively. Even as it continued to curse the Congress governments, Seoharvi taunted the ML leadership for not having the guts to boycott assemblies, creating a political deadlock or starting a massive agitation against Congress governments, which would have given the British an excuse to dissolve the provincial constitution or forced Congress governments to resign. All this while the poor ordinary Muslims in U.P., he lamented, had undergone great suffering while the leaders enjoyed power and pelf. He contemptuously noted that the same pusillanimous ML leadership asked the Muslim masses to celebrate a Day of Deliverance in celebration of their bravery as soon as the Congress governments resigned.

In the light of these incidents, Seoharvi concluded that Jinnah had formulated ML policy not to benefit ordinary Muslims but for personal gain and power. He reasoned that this was consistent with Jinnah and his cronies' earlier behaviour in 1916 when they sacrificed Muslim majorities in Bengal and Punjab in order to gain weightage in U.P. and Bihar and maintain their own leadership positions in the minority provinces. During the Round Table Conference these majorities could have been retrieved by Jinnah and the ML but they had not done anything about it at that point. He, therefore, found it ironical that the same Jinnah was disturbed about the fate of the Muslim majority provinces. In contrast to the ML that was full of self-seekers, Seoharvi claimed that the nationalist *ulama* had always stood up for Muslim rights in India. Thus, he took pains to point out that Mufti Kifayatullah and Maulana Azad had strongly condemned the Muslim League's decision to sacrifice legislative majorities of the Punjab and Bengal Muslims under the 1916 Lucknow Pact. Arrogant ML leaders had dismissed these protests by the *ulama* as squawks of minor Muslim clergy divorced from *realpolitik* and instead held up the ML's decision as a Divine decision (*rabbani faisla*).

Given its obvious problems, Seoharvi explained the 'irrational' Pakistan demand in terms of the British 'divide and rule' policy, arguing that it was the British who desired Pakistan even more than the Muslims. As he caustically remarked, Pakistan was not the 'political revelation' (*siyasi ilham*) that had occurred in the minds of Muhammad Iqbal or Jinnah, but a Divine Revelation (*rabbani ilham*) emanating from the Kaiser of Buckingham. Tracing its trajectory, he noted that the Pakistan idea first appeared on the political horizon when Sir Muhammad Iqbal returned from London in 1930. It reappeared when the UPML leader Khaliquzzaman stepped ashore in Bombay in 1939 after performing a Haj of Egypt and London, and was finally presented by Mr Jinnah at the ML's Lahore session in 1940. Looking at the pattern of the ML's politics, Seoharvi saw history tragically repeating itself. Thus, when Britain was trying to firm up the basis of its rule in nineteenth century India, it had patronized politics of loyalism of Sir Syed Ahmad Khan and his followers and used them to attack the anti-colonial *ulama* as retrograde and fundamental cause for Muslim backwardness. Now that the British Raj was again under threat due to the Congress led nationalist struggle that the *ulama* had joined at the very forefront, Seoharvi charged its ML 'loyalists' with using similar tactics of denouncing the *ulama* as evil in order to undermine the anti-colonial movement in India.

Seoharvi contrasted the ML elite's politics of loyalism to the long history of the *ulama's* careful stewardship of the Indian Muslim community, their patriotism and anti-colonial credentials. He recounted that when his teacher Maulana Mahmudul Hasan had visited *Hejaz* in the 1920s, he had held long discussions about strategies for liberating India with Turkish leaders such as Anwar Pasha and Jamal Pasha. These conversations, he claimed, had convinced the Maulana that Turkey or any other Muslim state could not be expected to invade India in order to free it from British imperialism. In fact, he was advised at these meetings that to get rid of the big problem (*badi musibat*) of British colonialism, the Muslims of India had to adopt the small problem (*chhoti musibat*) of allying themselves with non-Muslims in India. Only a free India, in turn would be able to liberate the Islamic world and indeed the whole colonized world suffering under imperialism.

Elaborating further on the British strategy of divide and rule, Seoharvi lambasted the two-nation theory as fraudulent and concocted by the British to divide the Indian nation in order to perpetuate their rule. In this context, he reminded fellow Muslims about the Arabs who during World War I were incited by the British to revolt against the Turks according to the ideology that they were a separate nation that had been enslaved by the Turks for centuries. However, once the Turks had been defeated and ejected out of Arab lands, the British reneged on promises made to the Arabs about their freedom, and the Arabs thus passed from the control of Turks to slavery under the British and the French. For Seoharvi the Arab example clearly showed how a powerful nation could be enslaved by inciting discord amongst its different communities so that they would demand a division of the country. He, therefore, appealed to his fellow Muslims to avoid the trap of Pakistan as it would only pave the way for the reconsolidation of British rule in the subcontinent.

Seoharvi also attacked ML propaganda regarding Pakistan's economic feasibility. He pointed out that Pakistan had few natural resources and even lesser capital to extract these resources. In this regard he repeated a common criticism that provinces such as Sind, Baluchistan and NWFP depended on federal funds for survival and whose burden would now fall on the Punjab after the partition. Similarly, he warned that the burden of Assam districts would fall on Bengal, which was again a revenue deficit province. An ML leader, he remarked, had suggested that Pakistan would reduce its civil servants' salaries to save resources for economic development. A second publicized strategy involved inviting Hindu industrialists to invest capital in Pakistan. Pouring ridicule on the unnamed ML leader's ignorance of economics, he argued that even if money was saved by reducing salaries, it would be insufficient to run Pakistan's government or to open even a single iron or coal mine. In the meantime, Hindustan would become a world power from profits produced by its many mines. As regards inviting Hindu capital, Seoharvi warned that there was no easier way for a country to become enslaved than by inviting foreign capitalists. Here he pointed out that Iranian oil fields were initially under the control of foreign oil companies but were later nationalized by Reza Shah to free Iran from their domination. Even Ibn Saud, he repeated, had cancelled similar agreements with oil companies to gain his freedom. Seoharvi, therefore, prophesized that Hindu capitalists harbouring hatred for Muslims due to the partition, would not hesitate to take over Pakistan's economic and natural resources just as Jewish capitalists had taken over Europe and become a state within the state. The only alternative for Pakistan if Hindu capital were barred would be to invite British capital, which again, he asserted, would open Pakistan to British domination. He, therefore, warned that while Pakistan would either be floundering by itself or suffering under foreign domination, India would rapidly progress like Japan to challenge Britain and America besides becoming a threat to Pakistan itself. Finally, Seoharvi laid out the disastrous impact Pakistan would have on the economic future of Muslims left behind in Hindu India. He declared that since Pakistan was being founded on the basis of religious difference and communal hatred, it was possible that after the partition Muslims in Hindu India would be deprived of capital and loans and be reduced to penury as a result of discriminatory economic laws that an indignant Hindustan would legislate.

Combining his economic critique of Pakistan with reflections on its position in international affairs, Seoharvi attacked the ML's optimism that Pakistan's main trading partner would be Europe, with the former selling primary goods to the latter in exchange for manufactured products, until the time that Pakistan became an industrialized country. He pointed out that Pakistan as a primary goods exporter would be in an extremely weak position against Britain. As a country which had taken over Chinese ports and enslaved her economically for her commercial interests, he warned that Britain would treat Pakistan in a similar manner. As he noted, weak countries were always at the mercy of strong countries, which established friendships and equal economic and political relationships only with similarly strong countries. He substantiated his claim again with the example of China. When China was being trampled over by Japan, it had no friends but now that China was rising, everybody was China's friend. Seoharvi therefore concluded his argument by posing his readers the question – whether powerful countries in the world would be friendly with India or Pakistan which would be a quarter of its size?

Elaborating on this matter, Seoharvi declared that one did not have to look for far away examples in the field of international relations, for there were plenty of examples in the domestic realm in this regard. He recounted that when the Congress started its 1930 Civil Disobedience movement and boycotted Lancashire and Manchester cloth, English companies decided to counter it. These English companies, however, soon discovered that cloth business was in the hands of the Hindus who owed allegiance to the Congress. Therefore, through a senior ML leader, Sir Abdullah Haroon, they began a huge publicity campaign in villages and towns throughout India that the English cloth trading companies were going to give cloth worth ₹ 2 crore on credits to a Muslim company so that it could establish itself in the cloth business. This Muslim company could start repaying its debt only when it could stand on its own feet. A firm was also set up in Bombay for this purpose. But the moment the civil disobedience movement was called off by the Congress, this scheme was scrapped and the Muslims were forgotten. Seoharvi warned that such would be the fate of the Muslims again if they did not think through these matters. Seoharvi's economic critique of Pakistan once again demonstrated that the *ulama* were not just men of religion but keenly aware of issues relating to modern economics and their ramifications on domestic politics and international relations.

Moving beyond secular arguments against Pakistan, Seoharvi also demonstrated how Pakistan would be detrimental to Muslim interests from the viewpoint of *tabligh* (proselytization). He warned that if Pakistan came into existence, Hindu India would pass laws prohibiting conversion to Islam or ban organizations engaged in proselytization. This would certainly lead to Malkana Rajputs and other such illiterate Muslim communities reverting to Hinduism causing a grave setback to the spread of Islam in India. Seoharvi characterized the indifference of ML elites to *tabligh* as understandable noting that just like Hindus and Christians they too did not see Islam as a special dispensation. In a clear reference to Jinnah, he vituperated such atheists (*munkir*) for whom Islam was only a social marker (*society ka mazhab)*, and whose utility was seen only in its instrumentality for securing power. Seoharvi added a novel dimension to this critique by arguing that India's partition would make Islam synonymous with the Muslim nation of Pakistan. He noted that just as a German was someone who lived in Germany, and a Frenchman was someone who lived in France, a Muslim would soon be defined as someone who lived in Pakistan. Extending the argument he noted that if a Briton was invited to become a German citizen it was only a political act without any link to a religion. But now due to the ML's two-nation theory, an invitation to a Hindu or a Sikh to accept Islam would be akin to asking him to join the nation whose centre was Pakistan. He, therefore, warned that the ML's politics would have the disastrous effect of reducing Islam from an ethical (*ikhlaqi*), cultural (*tahzibi*) and ideological (*ruhani*) programme to a mere geographical (*jugaraphiya*) programme. In this context, Seoharvi also sought to provoke majority Sunni sentiment by indicating that ML leaders were predominantly Shia. He ridiculed Jinnah, a Shia barrister for doubling as a *mufti* since *fatwas* in his name were frequently publicized in ML newspapers. Seoharvi further bemoaned that Jinnah's followers such as Sir Zafrullah Khan, a Qadiani (Ahmadiyya), and the Raja of Mahmudabad, a Shia, were held up as conscientious Muslims (*diyanatdar*) while pious, learned *ulama* such Maulana Husain Ahmad Madani and Mufti Kifayatullah were dubbed as infidels (*be'imaan*) and treated worse than *kafirs*.

Seoharvi finally criticized Pakistan from the standpoint of language. He argued that if Pakistan came into existence with Urdu as its official language, pure Hindi (*shuddh Hindi*) in Devanagri script would certainly be designated as India's official language. As a consequence Urdu would cease to be a living language of the Indian Muslims and become a 'holy' language in India like Arabic, accessible only to the *ulama*. On the contrary, if India were to remain undivided, he insisted that Urdu would spread like a tidal wave throughout the country as borne out by the experience of Bihar and Madras, where Urdu or Hindustani had made tremendous progress when it was introduced during the period of Congress-led provincial governments. As he pointed out, this had happened in spite of efforts by bigoted Hindus to strangle Urdu and promote Hindi. The creation of Pakistan would only play into their hands by weakening the cause of Urdu.

In the light of these multiple disadvantages that Pakistan would create for the Indian Muslims, Seoharvi argued that their best bet lay in a united India as envisioned in the resolutions passed by the JUH at its 1942 Lahore session. The JUH formula conceived India as a loose federation in which provinces would be fully autonomous, granting minimal powers to the federal centre while retaining residuary powers. He also emphasized that in an undivided India, freedom of religion would be protected as a fundamental right and religious matters would solely be under the jurisdiction of communities and not subject to legislative jurisdiction at either the federal or provincial levels. He concluded that this constitutional provision would adequately guarantee Muslim communal interest in India. Indeed, the Saharanpur session of the JUH held in 1945 came out with even more far reaching proposals. The JUH argued that while supporting a single federal centre for India it wanted to ensure that non-Muslim majority would not crush the Muslims' political, religious and cultural rights. It, therefore, demanded that it be constituted in such a way that Muslims would have parity at the centre.

The JUH made three specific proposals in this regard. First, that Muslims and Hindus be assigned 45 per cent each of the seats in the new Federal Assembly with other minorities occupying the remaining 10 per cent of the seats. Second, if at the centre, any bill was opposed by two-thirds of Muslim members on the grounds that it was detrimental to their political freedom or to their culture, such a bill could not be presented or passed in the legislature. Third, the Supreme Court would have equal number of Muslim and non-Muslim judges. The judges themselves would be appointed by provincial committees in which Muslims and non-Muslims would be equal in number. This Supreme Court would decide upon quarrels between the centre and provinces, interprovincial disputes and communal disputes. The Supreme Court would also adjudicate in case of a dispute between a majority and two-third Muslim majority on the question of whether a bill was injurious to the interests of the Muslims.

The JUH sought to allay fears in the minds of some doubting Muslims on questions regarding provincial autonomy and the army. It declared that provinces could have armies if agreed by all the parties. In case it was decided to have a single army under the control of a unitary Centre, the JUH promised that it would ensure that the current proportion of Muslims in the army was not only maintained but further increased. It was pointed out that Muslim position in the federal army would therefore be better than in the army of Pakistan where the 40 per cent non-Muslim minority would ask for proportional representation and it would have to be granted. Seoharvi claimed that when these proposals were discussed at a meeting between the JUH and U.P. Muslim League, a famous U.P. Muslim League leader had declared that the JUH resolution would provide better protection for Muslim rights than even the Pakistan resolution. But Jinnah's obstinacy allowed no freedom for Muslims to gather together and come to a unanimous position. Seoharvi declared that the JUH resolution was therefore the best alternative since it ensured the unity of India, addressed the fears of both minority and majority provinces Muslims and also resolved the political, geographical, economic and communal disadvantages that Muslims would have faced if India were divided. He concluded by declaring that India's unity would give a fillip to the cause of Hindu–Muslim unity, spread the spirit of friendliness and end the prospects of a civil war in India.

The critiques by Sajjad, Manglori and Seoharvi show a progression as far as the understanding and critique of the idea of Pakistan is concerned. While Sajjad's essay operates with the suspicion that Pakistan was perhaps Jinnah's bargaining counter, Manglori's articles point to a realization that Pakistan was perhaps a real demand. Manglori like Sajjad was primarily concerned with the fate of the 'minority provinces' Muslims in the event of a division of India and his essays were above all concerned with securing joint electorates for them while wishing the majority provinces Muslims good luck with their Pakistan.However, Seoharvi's critique, written from the viewpoint of the entire Indian Muslim community, clearly shows that by 1945 Pakistan was clearly understood as a demand for a separate sovereign state in the Muslim majority provinces of British. It was certainly not seen as a demand for a confederation between Hindustan and Pakistan. Any scheme, which contemplated a centre to link the Pakistan areas to Hindu India, would have been acceptable to the *ulama*. But the question remains as to why these strident critiques of Pakistan did not mention the possibility of partitioning Punjab and Bengal. Sajjad and Manglori did not publicly contemplate this scenario, nor did Seoharvi. Indeed, awareness of such a possibility would have driven home even further the grim implications of Pakistan for both the majority as well as minority province Muslims. Their reluctance in this regard can be perhaps be explained by the fact that the Deobandi *ulama* were consistently against the partitioning of these provinces. But this does not mean that the partitioning of these provinces was not being considered by a larger audience. After all, the voices of these *ulama* were part of a welter of critical voices on Pakistan that made for lively debates and controversies in the vernacular public sphere. By 1945 Madani himself in his numerous writings clearly laid out the imminent possibility of partitioning of provinces. In addition, the prospects of such partitions certainly found expression at the local level in U.P. and especially in the debates in Urdu newspapers on the question of Pakistan.

6

Urdu Press, Public Opinion and Controversies over Pakistan

Every day we eagerly wait for 'The Dawn' to see if you have issued any fresh statement or instructions. How glorious it is to be in communion with you through the Press or otherwise!

M. Suleyman Jan, *Salar*, Muslim League, Muzaffarnagar[1]

Besides the antiquity of the tradition of public debate in India as noted by Amartya Sen, India was home to a vibrant pre-colonial 'informational order' that saw the production, circulation and contestation of ideas, opinions and social knowledge. This informational order, as C. A. Bayly has demonstrated, made India a remarkably informed society in spite of its low levels of literacy.[2] Avril Powell's fascinating study of pre-Mutiny north India has delineated some of this informational order's specific, if transitory modes, especially the revived tradition of *munazara* involving public debate between *ulama* and Christian missionaries before large audiences on prearranged theological topics based on firm rules of debating.[3] Post-Mutiny India saw an exponential increase in conversations and debates among vastly increased numbers of people as civil society and public sphere emerged under the impact of colonial modernity. As Barbara and Thomas Metcalf have concisely noted, 'the railway, the telegraph, the postal service and improved steam transport together transformed the imperial system of the late nineteenth century.' If railways enabled growing numbers of Indians to travel for the purposes of visiting family or undertaking pilgrimage, telegraph 'made possible rapid transmission of information on politics, security, trade and industry', while the postal system served not only individuals but communications and fundraising of voluntary societies,

1 M. Suleyman Jan to Jinnah, 21 August 1945, *SHC*, U.P., Vol. 1.

2 C. A. Bayly, *Empire and Information: Intelligence Gathering and Social Communication in India, 1780-1870* (Cambridge, 1996).

3 Avril A. Powell, *Muslims and Missionaries in Pre-Mutiny India* (New Jersey, 1993).

organizations and publishers emerging in this period.'[4] Along with government surveys of India's land that led to production of detailed maps and the decennial census, which gave its people a sense of their numbers, these processes catalyzed the transformation of 'fuzzy' communities into 'enumerated' communities by late nineteenth century.[5] Vibrant vernacular public spheres emerged in different parts of India against the backdrop of these processes. Even if marked by regional specificities, they involved common processes integral to the rise of print capitalism and public sphere – standardization of language, a growing pool of middle class readers generated by the colonial educational system with standardized curriculum, proliferation of printed texts powered by new linguistic and cultural elites, writing of new histories, emergence of new cultures of reading and above all, the rise of the press along with a market for news.[6]

The importance of the press grew noticeably in an era marked by gradual devolution of power and slow development of institutions of representative government in India. But it is World War I that truly marked the arrival of the press on the Indian political landscape. The interwar period found the press being increasingly used by both the colonial state and the Congress as a potent weapon in their publicity battle against each other, in the process turning the daily newspaper into a 'major battlefield' between these two protagonists.[7] As Milton Israel has noted, 'at the end of World War I, both Government of India officials and Indian nationalist politicians recognized the need to reach more of the Indian people in order to support their claim to speak for all of them.'[8] The audience for this war of words and ideas was both pan-Indian and international in scope. The 'nationalist press' became the Congress party's formidable propaganda machine in its push towards India's independence and

---

4 Barbara D. Metcalf and Thomas R. Metcalf, *A Concise History of Modern India*. (Cambridge, 2006) (second edition), 96–99.

5 See Sudipta Kaviraj, *The Imaginary Institution of India* (New York, 2010).

6 See Vasudha Dalmia, *The Nationalization of Hindu Traditions, Bharatendu Harishchandra and Nineteenth Century Banaras* (New Delhi, 1997); Christopher R. King, *One Language, Two Scripts: The Hindi Movement in Nineteenth Century North India* (New Delhi, 1994); Francesca Orsini, *The Hindi Public Sphere 1920-1940: Language and Literature in the Age of Nationalism* (New York, 2002); Ulrike Stark, *An Empire of Books: The Nawal Kishore Press and the Diffusion of the Printed Word in Colonial India* (New Delhi, 2007); Francesca Orsini, *Print and Pleasure: Popular Literature and Entertaining Fictions in Colonial North India* (New Delhi, 2009).

7 Milton Israel, *Communications and Power: Propaganda and the Press in the Indian Nationalist Struggle, 1920-1947* (Cambridge, 1994).

8 Ibid., 19.

was instrumental in making Gandhi's Salt March or Nehru's Independence Day celebrations into events of national and even international importance. The prominence that Congress attached to this propaganda battle can be discerned from the fact that it started new newspapers after its governments assumed office in the provinces in 1937 to specifically highlight their achievements. This was especially the case in U.P., where it started *The National Herald* in English and the *Hindustan* in Urdu adding to the formidable array of Hindi newspapers that were owned or operated by Congressmen or those sympathetic to the nationalist programme.[9] Jawaharlal Nehru personally underwrote huge promissory notes to raise capital for these newspapers.

Jinnah himself was keenly aware of the ML's lack of resources in this regard and therefore started the Urdu weekly *Manshoor* in 1938 and the *The Dawn* the ML's English language flagship in late 1941 to counter the Congress propaganda machine that he believed was intent on maligning the idea of Pakistan, both in India and abroad. His keenness for press coverage and publicity in the battle against Congress can be gauged from this fascinating story narrated by Rafiq Zakaria about a public meeting Jinnah addressed in Bombay to celebrate the Day of Deliverance in December 1939.

> Just before the meeting Jinnah's behavior startled me beyond comprehension. He arrived at the specified time. He was always punctual. He surveyed the scene and when he could not see the press seated prominently in the front rows, he lost his temper. He turned to the organizers and shouted angrily: Where is the press? And then in the full hearing of the public since the mike was on the dais, he thundered: *Do you think I have come to address these donkeys? He wanted his remarks to be conveyed more to the world than to the assembled crowd.* The organizers ran helter-skelter and finally managed to arrange chairs and tables near the dais for the press representatives.'[10]

Milton Israel has argued that India as a nation state that emerged from the nationalist struggle was 'imagined in English print'. But this proposition does not take into account the importance of the vernacular press in disseminating

---

9 The journalist Kotamraju Rama Rao who was hired by Nehru to edit *National Herald* recalled that the paper's Board of Directors were mostly U.P. Congressmen and 'its meetings were always timed to synchronize with the meetings of the executive of the UPCC. See K. Rama Rao, *The Pen As My Sword: Memoirs of a Journalist* (Bombay, 1965), 120.

10 Rafiq Zakaria, *The Price of Partition: Recollections and Reflections* (Bombay, 1997), 39.

the meanings of the nation to vast numbers of people. Moreover, its impact was many times larger for its reach far exceeded that of the English language press. In this regard, one needs to specifically turn to the vibrant Urdu press that really came into its own by the time of the Khilafat Movement. Its leading protagonists such as the Ali brothers, Abul Kalam Azad, Zafar Ali Khan and Hasrat Mohani established their own newspapers as part of their efforts to mobilize Muslim subjects of Britain's Indian empire to rise up in defence of one of the most valued institutions of Islam – the Ottoman Caliphate.[11] Thus, Azad's *Al-Hilal*, Hasrat Mohani's *Urdu-i-Mualla*, Mohammad Ali's *Hamdard* and Zafar Ali Khan's *Zamindar* began during this period.

Another newspaper that began its innings at the same time was the *Madina* of Bijnor. Starting in 1913 as a weekly, it became a bi-weekly from 1917 onwards emerging as a prominent 'nationalist' newspaper with courageous reporting and editorials about Britain's attitude towards Turkey during the war. After the Jallianwala Bagh incident in Amritsar, the *Madina* was banned for a while from Punjab by the provincial government. Its enviable lineup of writers and poets included figures such as Akbar Ilahabadi, Muhammad Iqbal, Hasrat Mohani, Zafar Ali Khan and Jigar Muradabadi. While the other Urdu newspapers had a fitful life and slowly died after the collapse of the Khilafat Movement, the *Madina* alone survived well into the 1950s. It is no exaggeration to say that in the three decades leading up to 1947, it was easily the most prominent 'nationalist' Urdu newspaper regularly featuring writings by nationalist Muslims' and pro-Congress *ulama* whose views we have discussed thus far. *Madina* wholeheartedly supported the party's ill-fated Muslim Mass Contact Program during the period of Congress provincial governments and was one of the few newspapers that remained continuously critical of the ML's 'communal' politics.

Not surprisingly, it took the lead in facilitating a vigorous debate on the question of Pakistan in the aftermath of the Lahore Resolution. Thus, in response to the growing controversy over Pakistan in the autumn of 1942, it opened its columns to readers to send in their views on the subject – what they understood by it and whether they thought Pakistan was beneficial or harmful for Indian Muslims. The responses came from readers not just in U.P., but from places as far apart as Chatgaon in Bengal, Bombay in the west and Raichur in

[11] For an account of mass mobilization techniques used during this period including the use of political poetry, see Gail Minault, *The Khilafat Movement: Religious Symbolism and Political Mobilization in India* (New York, 1982). For a recent and more comprehensive account of the movement, see M. Naeem Qureshi, *Pan-Islam in British India: The Politics of the Khilafat Movement 1918-1924* (Karachi, 2009).

the Deccan indicating a wide readership for the *Madina* throughout India. From the flood of responses, the newspaper's editor, operating under conditions of wartime scarcity, strict quotas on newsprint and reduced number of pages in its editions, selected what he considered to be the most coherent and well written essays on Pakistan. The debate ultimately crystallized around long essays written by two figures representing the supporting and opposing views on Pakistan, which were published in a serial form over the next several months. The debate offers fascinating glimpses regarding the thinking that was going on among the educated newspaper reading public on the question of Pakistan. It clearly indicates that the vigorous and acrimonious public debate on this issue in which the ML and the nationalist *ulama* had been wrestling with each other was being eagerly followed and deliberated upon in the towns and *qasbahs* of the U.P. A perusal of this debate, therefore, provides us with a much needed counterpoint to the studies of motivations, tactics and strategies of the main players in the Partition drama that have loomed large over Partition historiography.

Maulana Syed Abu Syed Bazmi's Critique of the Muslim League's 'Pakistan'

The ball was set rolling by Maulana Syed Abu Syed Bazmi, a critic of the idea of Pakistan.[12] We do not know anything about Bazmi except that he belonged to the Urdu literati in U.P. and was obviously a supporter of the Congress led nationalist movement. Bazmi began his critique by referring to the slogan of 'Pakistan and Only Pakistan' which members of the ML had been raising with much gusto on the streets of U.P. in order to rally their supporters. Bazmi sought to enquire as to what this Pakistan was in the first place, about which the ML was raising such a hue and cry. Second and more importantly, had the Congress not already conceded its Pakistan demand? These were questions that needed to be answered in order to begin the process of dispelling the considerable confusion regarding the concept of Pakistan. Bazmi went on to lay out his understanding of Pakistan. Pakistan, Bazmi noted, simply meant that Muslims should rule wherever they were in a majority, while wherever the Hindus were in a majority they should be the rulers. Thus, Hindustan would be divided into Hindu Hindustan and Muslim Hindustan. If one were to look at the map of India, one could see that the Muslim majority existed in the provinces of Punjab, Bengal, Sind, NWFP and Baluchistan. Except Baluchistan

12 *Madina*, 25 September 1942.

the rest were all full-fledged provinces under the 1935 Act. These provinces then constituted the domain of Pakistan.

Bazmi, however, felt that the second question as to whether or not Pakistan had already been conceded by the Congress was the more important question. He argued that if Pakistan meant that the Muslim majority provinces should have the right to self-determination (*khudmukhtari*) then the Congress had clearly conceded the right of provinces to secede from the Union and given assurances that no province could be forced to join the Union. Even if they originally joined the Union, the provinces would still have the right to secede from it later. This important principle had been conceded by Maulana Abul Kalam Azad in his correspondence with Professor Syed Abdul Latif of Hyderabad and the latter seemed satisfied with the Congress concession to the Muslim demand. The Maulana, given his position as the Congress President, was an important authority while Latif was the one man who was most qualified to judge the issue of Pakistan. Latif was after all the most prominent member of the ML sub-committee that had been set up by the ML to deliberate on different constitutional 'Pakistan' schemes in 1939. His personal credentials, too, were impeccable. He had also made great personal sacrifices in order to devote himself to a full time study regarding the issue of Pakistan and for this purpose had also given up his lucrative professorship at Osmania University that paid him a handsome ₹ 1000 every month. Bazmi however regretted Latif's demonization by ML propagandists as the great seditionist (*mafsid-i-Azam)* among the Muslims after the learned professor expressed his satisfaction with Maulana Azad's clarification and was urging the ML to come to a settlement with the Congress on this basis. Bazmi saw cruel irony in such an unfair treatment meted out to a great Muslim patriot who had devoted his life to the study of Pakistan. It was especially galling at a time when the ML glorified leaders who were most unworthy and had no stature. These included people like the Raja of Mahmudabad who he alleged had property worth lakhs of rupees but had sacrificed nothing for the community, Dr Abdul Aziz of Bihar who had kicked away his position in the ML in order to take up a lucrative appointment in Hyderabad state, the Nawab of Chhatari who was more attracted to the Prime Ministership of Hyderabad state than to his membership in the ML and Sir Sikandar Hayat Khan who never lost an opportunity to snipe at Mr Jinnah besides firing on the breasts of thousands of Khaksars. Latif's only fault, Bazmi lamented, was that he had convinced Gandhi, Patel and the Congress to grant the right of self-determination to the Muslim provinces. Bazmi, therefore, declared that the Pakistan for which Muslims were agitating was already theirs for the asking.

The ML, however, Bazmi regretted, was not interested in the Congress offer and instead was looking up to the British Government for a solution. Bazmi noted that the ML had acknowledged that Pakistan had been conceded to a large extent by the Cripps Mission. The Cripps Mission in its proposals had, in principle, allowed Punjab, Sind, NWFP and Baluchistan to form a separate federation with no links to Hindu Hindustan. But Bengal had not been granted the right to join the Muslim federation since it was geographically separated from these Muslim provinces in the northwest. Bazmi pointed out that on the other hand, if one were to pay attention to the Congress resolution, it allowed every province the right to secede from the Union and hence also gave Bengal the right to join the Muslim federation. Thus, the Congress offer compared much more favourably to the Cripps proposal. Yet, Jinnah saw Pakistan only in the Cripps proposal and was fulsome in his praise for it while he had not even bothered to consider the Congress scheme as put forward by Maulana Azad. Bazmi concluded that this was because the ML leadership was simply not interested to come to a settlement with the Congress on the Hindu Muslim question and still looked up to the British for a solution. If Dr Latif was *Mafsid-i-Azam*, who, Bazmi asked pointedly, was *Changez-i-Azam* (Genghis of the Age)?

Bazmi proceeded to comment on the ML's fixation on the two-nation theory and the Lahore Resolution and how the party was damaging the interests of the Muslim community by its blind adherence to this creed. Evaluating other interpretations of Pakistan, which could flow from the Lahore Resolution, he noted that if Pakistan meant territorial readjustment of provinces as conceded by the text of the resolution, then one needed to see as to which areas would accrue to the Muslims. If Punjab were to be divided, southern Punjab stretching up to the banks of the Ravi would be lost by the Muslims since they did not have a majority in this area of the Punjab. Similarly, west Bengal along with the wonderful port of Calcutta would not accrue to the Muslims since it did not have a Muslim majority either. Bazmi opined that such territorial readjustments would be disastrous for Muslims because they would lose the fertile areas of the Punjab and be left with only the lesser hilly and desert areas. As far as Bengal was concerned, he pointed out that in addition to Calcutta, the areas of Ranigunj and Asansol with their iron and steel, the basis of any country's economic development, would also escape from Pakistan's hands. Bazmi warned that this would lead to a precipitous decline in the revenues of the Pakistan provinces and as a result it would no longer be able to bear the costs of its own functioning. In addition, Sind, NWFP and Baluchistan survived on 3 crores that were given as grants from the central budget in order to pay for the expenditure of administration. These central grants would stop with the partition and Punjab and Bengal would have to take on these burdens. But since these two provinces would be losing their fertile parts to Hindu Hindustan, contrary to helping the other poor provinces, they themselves would need help and assistance.

Reflecting the concerns earlier expressed by Khaliquzaman in his letter to Jinnah, Bazmi pointed out that Pakistan would receive no territories to compensate for the losses it was going to suffer. If one were to look at Hindustan in order to see which places the Muslims could claim, there were none as no other places had a Muslim majority. He conceded that there were a few pockets, like some cities in Rohilkhand such as Saharanpur and Deoband where Muslims were in a majority. But even if they were to be given the status of free cities like Danzig or some free cities in the Soviet Union, Bazmi warned that they would still not be able to become self-sufficient, unlike cities such as Bombay or Calcutta. Not having enough resources to set up their High Courts or Universities, these cities would instead depend on Hindustan and consequently come under its influence. Bazmi derisorily noted that there was indeed no reason why Hindustan would even want to bear their expenses. The Muslim provinces of Pakistan, on the other hand, would be too poor to help them. Furthermore, the sheer distance between the Pakistan provinces and these cities would prevent any such assistance. Thus, the territorial readjustment of provinces in order to form Pakistan would be a disaster for the Muslims.

Bazmi proceeded to intensify his economic critique of Pakistan. He demanded to know where the money would come from, to pay for the development of the poor Pakistan provinces. He contemptuously dismissed claims by its proponents that Muslims in Pakistan would live frugally and the money thus saved would be used to fund Pakistan's expenses. Indeed, if Pakistan could only live frugally, he wondered how it could possibly invest for the purposes of economic development. He was, therefore, in no doubt that Hindu India would surge ahead given its natural resources as also the fact that the Hindus were far ahead of the Muslims in education, trade, their stock of capital – the bases of economic development. As Bazmi rationalized, development in the current circumstances, depended not on physical strength (*jasmani quvvat ya pehelwani*) but on brain power and science. Indeed, he also wondered how a poor undeveloped Pakistan would be able to defend itself against an industrialized Hindustan when the wars today were wars of science, coal, steel, rubber, machines, mills and factories and victory or defeat depended on them. He, therefore, reiterated that in this machine age, man's physical strength no longer mattered for if it were simply a matter of hand to hand combat the strong men of Punjab and Baluchistan would easily win over Hindu India. Driving home the economic argument, Bazmi pointedly asked how the Muslim provinces, which were so poor as to be unable to meet their own expenses, would have any money left to pay for the setting up their federal centre (*markazi vifaq*). And if the Muslim centre could not be set up, Bazmi wondered how its provinces would be able to develop the country's defence capabilities, build diplomatic ties and goodwill with other countries. Pakistan, he therefore concluded, would end up taking loans from other countries in order to survive and this, in turn, would only enslave it economically and politically.

Bazmi went on to critically evaluate another dangerous implication of Pakistan that had become an object of public discussion. This related to the transfer of populations and he forcefully proceeded to point out its deadly consequences for everyone involved in the process. He was especially severe on Latif, who he had praised earlier, for proposing the most large scale scheme for the transfer of populations in his own Pakistan scheme.[13] Bazmi explained that in the event of the principle of transfer of populations being accepted, Muslim majorities would become possible in the newly designated Muslim zones only if 30 million Muslims came in from the outside. Correspondingly, an identical number of Hindus would have to pack up and migrate to Hindu Hindustan to make space for the incoming Muslims. Bazmi reasoned that in the thousands of years of human history, there had never been such an enormous migration of people anywhere in the world. The biggest case of human migration that had ever occurred was during World War I, involving Turkey and Greece and led to a million Greeks leaving Turkey. The world considered the migration of these million a miracle (*mojizah*). Who, Bazmi asked, had the courage to perform the miracle of migration (*naql-i-watan*) of 50-60 million people? How could God's children leave their long lived homes and go to new lands? Could Hindustan bear the expenditure for this massive event? Who would take the responsibility for the purchase and sale of lands of those who were migrating out of these areas? Would the government itself buy them and then pay the money to the sellers? For those moving into these areas, would the government compensate them for their movable and immovable properties? Would the hapless citizens be taxed for all these enormous expenditures that the government would have to bear? Given the fact that the Pakistan provinces were already poor, how

13 *Madina*, 28 September 1942

would they be able to bear the responsibility of taking care of the incoming population and giving them suitable employment?

The biggest problem with the idea in Bazmi's eyes was that it was based on the naïve assumption that the Hindus were an inert *qaum* like rocks and wood, which could be sorted, slotted and distributed at will. Such an assumption was untenable. Bazmi also explained the impact that schemes for transferring populations would have upon U.P.'s Muslims. In the first place, he noted that areas of U.P. that had been designated as Muslim cultural zones by Latif, were considered by the Hindus as their cultural homes (*tahzibi ghar*) as well. Wherever the Ganga and the Jamna flowed, these areas were holy lands for the Hindus, no less than the Hijaz was holy for the Muslims. The significance of the waters of these rivers was no less to the Hindus than the water of the *Zam Zam* was for the Muslims. The religious gatherings of the Hindus happened in these areas several times a year where they had several religious landmarks. If the Muslims on the basis of inhabiting these areas for a thousand years considered them to be their cultural homes, Hindus had been around in these parts for over a few thousand years and hence had more valid claims over these lands.

Bazmi further argued that even if the Muslims were given the unlikely right of transforming parts of the Muslim minority provinces into Muslim majority areas through a resettlement of Hindus, the Hindus too would have to be given the same right in Muslim majority areas. If this principle was accepted, Pakistan's present territorial domain (*maujooda hudood*) would become extremely deficient with disastrous effects on its economic condition. Thus, Hindu majority areas in Punjab, Sind and Bengal would have the right to have their own independent governments (*Khud Mukhtar Hukumatein*). In this context, Bazmi noted that some propagandists of Pakistan were including Hyderabad, Bhopal and other such native states ruled by Muslim rulers in the domain of Pakistan even though these had Hindu majority populations. If the same principle were to be followed consistently, he argued states such as Cooch Behar, Nabha, Kapurthala and most importantly Kashmir would have the right to join Hindu zones. This again would not be beneficial to the Muslims.

Bazmi angrily demanded answers to these questions, none of which seemed forthcoming. He further warned that if the millions of displaced people as a result of transfer of population were not gainfully employed there would be a serious deterioration in the social situation as these people would take to robbery in order to make a living. He concluded this argument by reminding his readers of a recent catastrophe when not too long ago, during the Khilafat Movement, Indian Muslims in their fervour had migrated to Afghanistan. These *mohajirs* (migrants), he sadly recalled, had undergone untold hardships and finally been cruelly driven out of the borders of Afghanistan. Thus, any and all schemes, which talked about transfer of populations were impracticable and would cause grave harm to the Muslims.

Bazmi, therefore, expressed his support for the Congress position on India's political future, which gave the right of self-determination (*khudmukhtari*) to provinces as they currently existed, without any territorial readjustments. He indicated that the JUH in its 1942 Lahore session had passed a resolution, which reiterated this Congress position. Since the British Government in the Cripps proposals too had accepted this principle of self-determination of provinces, Bazmi sought to ascertain as to what the continuing controversy over Pakistan was all about. What was the Pakistan whose non-realization was making the ML so cantankerous that in choosing epithets against the Congress, they had outdone even the *bhatyaras* (cooks)? Bazmi deduced that Muslim League hostility could perhaps be explained by the fact that even though the Congress had practically accepted Pakistan, its leaders were making a lot of hostile noises against Pakistan. Nehru had time and again stated firmly that the division of India would not be countenanced under any circumstances. C. Rajagopalachari who had openly accepted the Pakistan principle and had advocated a settlement with Jinnah had been forced to resign from the Congress. The party as a whole, therefore, seemed unduly prickly over the question of Pakistan. Bazmi, therefore, enquired as to why after having practically conceded Pakistan, the Congress was being so ambivalent on the matter and not clarifying its position.

Bazmi explained this curious paradox by examining the ideology and history of the Congress. The Congress, he elaborated, was committed to India's national unity and did not see Hindus and Muslims as two distinct nations but as two parts of one unified nation. If the Congress were to agree to the ML conditions and openly acknowledge that Hindus and Muslims were two separate nations, it would have to reconstruct its fifty two year old history on a totally different basis. It would have to remove Muslim members from its rolls and become a Hindu organization. This was impossible for the Congress to contemplate and herein lay its dilemma. The only explanation for the Congress doublespeak, therefore, was that while the Congress was not averse to Pakistan as a necessary evil, it did not wish to say it with its own tongue that the Muslims were free to form their Pakistan. Such an acceptance would imply that it accepted the two-nation theory, the fact that Hindus and Muslims were two separate nations and that the Congress was established only for the benefit of the Hindus. This was repugnant to the Congress. Furthermore, Bazmi insisted that the Congress wanted to make one last attempt to unite the Hindus and Muslims into one nation and if the effort failed, it would accept the *fait accompli*. Bazmi here utilized the metaphor of the body to describe the Congress position. The Congress recognized the Hindu–Muslim problem as an excrescence on the body politic of India but it wanted to exhaust all attempts to cure it before calling in the surgeon to cut it away from the body. Thus, given these dilemmas, the Congress could at best only *tacitly* concede the principle of Pakistan. That is why even while opposing Pakistan it did nothing to stop Muslim provinces from moving towards that goal. Hence, it had granted the Muslim provinces the right to decide their own future and had not closed the door for the formation of Pakistan.

At this point having evaluated the prospects of Pakistan, Bazmi paused to consider whether Pakistan as demanded by the Muslim League was going to be beneficial to the Muslims, especially those of the minority provinces such as U.P. and Bihar. Bazmi proclaimed that there was a popular consensus that if Pakistan was formed it would benefit the Muslims living in the 'northern' provinces while it would be catastrophic for those living in the southern provinces. He noted that when this matter was brought up before the *Qaid-i-Azam*, the ML supremo had remarked in a speech at Kanpur that for the liberation of 7 crore (majority province) Muslims he would allow the two crore Muslims of the minority provinces to get crushed. Like Maulana Sajjad, Bazmi objected to the *Qaid's* misrepresentation of the population figures of the minority provinces. But even if the *Qaid's* figures were granted and it was agreed that there were only two crores Muslims in the minority provinces, Bazmi pointed out that their population was equal to the combined populations of Iran and Afghanistan. Continuing the analogy, he noted that the population of Iraq, Hejaz, Oman – that of all of Arabia combined – came up to 2 crores. Thus, Bazmi indicated that when Jinnah talked lightly about letting the 2 crore 'minority provinces' Muslims get crushed, it amounted to finishing off the joint populations of Iran and Afghanistan or that of all of Arabia. Bazmi further noted that the irony of this statement was that it had been made in the context of the hullabaloo about Congress oppression of Muslims living in the minority provinces such as U.P., Bihar and Madras. In his eyes, the demand for Pakistan was also absurd since the Muslims of majority provinces such as Punjab, Sind, Bengal, NWFP and Baluchistan had never expressed any problems with Hindu mentality, Hinduism, or Hindu nationalism that the ML was never tired of highlighting. To substantiate his argument Bazmi pointed out that at the Patna ML session in 1938, the CPML President Rauf Shah had listed the atrocities committed upon the Muslims of his province and at the same time complained that Muslim majority provinces had not helped them. Besides, he had regretted that the ML was weak in those provinces. In response to Rauf Shah's complaint, Bazmi revealed that Fazlul Huq, the Bengal Premier, had acknowledged that the ML was not as strong in Bengal as it was in U.P. or Bihar, the reason for this being that Muslims in these provinces did not know what Hindu atrocities (*Hindu mazalim*) meant.

Bazmi observed that it was the Krishak Proja Party that was the strongest in Bengal while in Punjab it was the Unionist party that was strong and in both these provinces the ML was weak. The ML was strongest in the Muslim minority provinces where Muslims constituted only 10–15 per cent of the population and it was here that the cry for Pakistan was the loudest. This was where the Muslims felt threatened about their language, culture and religion and this was where the largest number of Hindu Muslim riots took place. However, it is in connection with these Muslims that the *Qaid-i-Azam* had stated that they must sacrifice themselves for the sake of Pakistan. And this was for the Muslims of the Pakistan provinces where even today the Muslims did not fear the Hindus or feel any threats to their language or culture. Such was the absurdity of Pakistan.

Bazmi went on to detail the problems of the Muslims of the minority provinces and the ways in which the formation of Pakistan would exacerbate these problems.[14] The Hindi-Urdu problem, Bazmi indicated, was one of the main points of contention between the Hindus and Muslims. In Punjab, Sind, Baluchistan and NWFP, the official language was now Urdu. However, in U.P. and Bihar, where the local language of the people was Urdu, the official language was pure Hindi (*shuddh hindi*). With the formation of Pakistan, this problem would not disappear. On the contrary, due to the Partition, U.P. Muslims would not be able to raise their voice in support of Urdu and the Hindus would be able to freely and forcefully spread Sampurnanandi Hindi. People, sympathetic to Urdu language or Muslim culture in Hindustan, such as the likes of Sir Tej Bahadur Sapru would be silenced and those Hindus who had till now opposed Urdu in a muted voice would do so more openly and vigorously like a Savarkar or a Moonje.

Bazmi stated that there was a similar problem that 'minority provinces' Muslims faced over the issues of dress and clothing. The fight between *dhoti* and *pyjama*, *sherwani* and coat, Turkish *topi* and felt cap, was absent in Punjab, Bengal, Sind, NWFP or Baluchistan. Even today the dress of Hindus and

---

14 *Madina*, 1 October 1942.

Muslims in all these provinces was similar. It was in U.P. that this fight was on, a fight which Muslims would surely lose in the event of a partition. The fight for government jobs, again, was in the minority provinces such as U.P. In this regard, Bazmi also pointed out that the U.P. Muslims lived mostly in cities and had a greater percentage of jobs in the government as compared to their percentage in province's population. If Pakistan as demanded by the ML was formed, they would lose this extra representation in government jobs. Indeed, their proportion in government jobs would certainly be cut down to 10–12 per cent and the rest of the jobs would be cornered by the Hindus. Bazmi acknowledged that the Pakistan Government could perhaps do the same in retaliation against the Hindus in government jobs, but he wondered how would such a policy benefit the Muslims of U.P. or Bihar.

Like Seoharvi, Bazmi warned that creating Pakistan would also bring about a setback in the work of *Tabligh*. Hinduism, Bazmi explained, was not a religion. A Hindu was a Hindustani who was not a Christian, Muslim or a Parsi. There were thousands of sects in Hindusim and they did not eat or drink with each other. Their priests, temples and marriages rituals were all very different. They did not have a common Holy Book or Shariat. And then they had the Untouchables among them. However, all these divisions among the Hindus would disappear in case Pakistan was formed and they would all gang up against the Muslims. This would also result in the work of *Tabligh* coming to a complete standstill.

Pakistan was abhorrent to Bazmi for one more reason. The proponents of Pakistan, he claimed, were supporting Muslim rulers of Indian states and calling their dominions Pakistan. The ML was thus implicitly supporting the feudal rulers of these states and condoning their continuing loot of the common people. Bazmi declared that this was not surprising given the social background of the ML leaders themselves. All of them were Sirs, Khan Bahadurs, or Nawabs. He, therefore, averred that it eminently suited them to raise the issue of Pakistan in order to obscure all questions of economic and social justice.

In the light of this analysis, Bazmi laid out what he claimed was the best solution for the Indian Muslims. The only way out, he asserted, was to stop the agitation for Pakistan as was being pursued by the ML and to work on a twin pronged strategy. First, the ML needed to affirm the idea of *Muttahida Qaumiyat*. This would greatly help the Muslims of the minority provinces who the *Qaid-i-Azam* wanted to discard as a useless limb. Instead of saying that they wanted to form a separate nation, Bazmi asked Muslims to instead turn to the Hindus and tell them that it was their Mahasabhaite and Sampurnanandi mentality, which was striking at the very root of *Muttahida Qaumiyat*. Secondly, Bazmi declared if the ML so badly wanted Pakistan, the proper way was to take up the Congress offer which gave each province the right to secede from the federation. Muslim majority provinces could then if they wished secede and form a federation of their own. This new federation would, for all practical purposes, be Pakistan.

Muslims, therefore, needed to grab the Hindus by the neck and force them to give effect to the principle of *Muttahida Qaumiyat*. This would strengthen the hands of people like Nehru and reduce the influence of people like Purshottamdas Tandon and Sampurnanand. In the name of this principle, the Muslims could also demand that in U.P. and Bihar, Urdu be declared the sole official language since it was shared by both Hindus and Muslims. They could point out that it was this language that had given rise to literary figures such as Ratan Nath Sarshar, Daya Shankar Nasim and others. Bazmi, therefore, advised Muslims that there was profit in following the policy of *Muttahida Qaumiyat* for the minority province Muslims without causing the majority provinces Muslims to incur any losses. If the Hindus still refused to change, it was they who would have to carry the bier of *Muttahida Qaumiyat* on their shoulders and it could then be legitimately stated that the Hindus had forced the Muslims to form a separate nation.

Bazmi also warned that if on the contrary, Muslims enraged Hindu sentiments and fought with them on the basis of the two-nation theory or persuaded Hindu areas in Pakistan areas to secede in the name of creating a homogenous Muslim state, they would only bring grave harm upon themselves. Muslim interest dictated that if the demand for separation were made, it had to be made only on the basis of the principles of geography and economy. In such a situation, minority provinces Muslims could still make arrangements for their own security and well-being. Thus, they could try and evolve into majorities in pockets of their provinces and then make a demand for their cultural autonomy on the model of autonomous republics (*Khud Mukhtar Jumhuriyatein*) in the Soviet Union or free cities such as Danzig. He, however, asserted that these republics would continue to be linked to the Hindu provinces in which they were situated and not with the Pakistani provinces. But the problem, Bazmi wearily stated was that these days the Muslims carried the badge of separatism on their foreheads and were thus incurring losses due to such a strategy.

If Pakistan was so harmful to the Muslims, Bazmi posed the question as to why the ML was making this demand so vociferously. After some deliberation, he concluded that the continuing advocacy of Pakistan based on the two-nation theory, in spite of its obvious disadvantages, could only be explained in terms of the selfishness of the ML leaders. They did not care for the Muslims or the *millat* but only for their own selfish interests and *izzat* (prestige). Above all they only cared about being accepted as the leaders of the Muslim community. Bazmi, therefore, denounced Jinnah as a vain and selfish man and claimed that all he wanted was to be anointed the Shah of Pakistan. He saw this as the primary reason as to why the ML and its leader were being so truculent in their dealings with the Congress and perpetrating the fraud of Pakistan on poor Muslims by raising the spectre of Hindu Raj. Finally, even if Pakistan was created, Bazmi did not see any happy prospects resulting from it for Indian Muslims in general and those of the minority provinces in particular.[15] He dismissed the 'hostage population theory' being offered as an anodyne for the minority province Muslims with its idea that if Muslims in Hindustan were ill-treated, then retaliatory measures could be taken against the Hindus in Pakistan. Bazmi maintained that if Britannia with its great might could not force *khaddar* off Indian bodies and drape them with Lancashire cloth it was naïve to imagine that the Muslims through the threat of Pakistan could force the Hindus to behave properly with them in Hindustan. A pessimistic Bazmi, however, also acknowledged that there was no trust between Hindus and Muslims in India at present. None could be expected to develop immediately either. Bazmi, therefore, speculated on the reasons behind Hindu–Muslim bitterness. He concluded that history as taught by the British was a major reason, which had sowed seeds of discord that would not go away quickly. He also zeroed in on the economic issue as a major source of problems between Hindus and Muslims. Muslims, in general, felt that they were being deprived of jobs in the services, not being employed in their mills by the Hindu industrialists and were being denied loans. Bazmi attempted to correct such an impression arguing that such an attitude was not due to Hindu narrow-mindedness but poverty. Jobs were so few, most people tended to employ their own kith and kin. He further philosophized that poverty was not restricted to Muslims, but was also widespread among the Hindus. This problem, Bazmi claimed, would only be remedied once India achieved complete independence and proceeded on the path of economic development. With this classic Nehruvian manoeuvre, Bazmi rounded off his critique of Pakistan.

Two Brief Attacks and a Supporting Response to Bazmi's Critique of Ml's Pakistan

Bazmi's critique of the ML's 'Pakistan' drew three brief responses from readers that were published by the editor of the *Madina*. Two of these attacked his

[15] *Madina*, 5 October 1942.

essay while the third supported his critique of Pakistan. Hakim Mohammad Anwar, writing from Bombay began by exclaiming that Pakistan was a dream whose interpretation nobody knew and yet every individual with his own mind translated according to his own needs.[16] Even Muslim Leaguers, the biggest supporters of Pakistan did not definitively know as to what was meant by Pakistan. This, however, did not stop Anwar from coming up with his own interpretation of Pakistan. Anwar saw Pakistan as an independent sovereign state alongside Hindustan and proclaimed that creating Pakistan was important for three reasons. First, Pakistan would help in *Tabligh* of Islam just like the United States of America helped in the spread of Christianity. Second, Anwar believed that the formation of Pakistan would lead to the liberation of Islamic countries throughout the world. Finally, he expected the creation of Pakistan to pave the way for the spread of Islamic government throughout the world.

Anwar then went on to lay out his understanding of Pakistan. Islamic India, he claimed, would be divided into two parts – northern and eastern. The Northern part would be divided into three provinces – Sind and Baluchistan, NWFP and Kashmir and Punjab. The Ambala division of Punjab would be detached from Pakistan while Mewat would be joined with it. These northern provinces together would be called Pakistan. In the east, East Bengal and South Assam would be combined to form Islamistan. Anwar described Pakistan as gift of nature forming a distinct geographical unit for it was bounded in the north and the west by the Himalayas, in the east by the desert of Rajasthan, while the river Yamuna provided its border with Hindustan. Following Toosy, Anwar finally saw Pakistan as a distinct unit since it was connected by Northwestern railway, while Islamistan was connected by the Assam and Bengal railway – both of which were important assets.

As Pakistan had become the butt of ridicule at the hands of its opponents, especially due to questions regarding its economic viability, Anwar proceeded to repudiate Bazmi's spirited economic critique of Pakistan. He rejected Bazmi's suggestion that fertile areas of Ambala division cut off from Pakistan would leave the country with only hilly and desert areas, which would not be self-sustaining. The Ambala division, Anwar contended, was not very fertile and Pakistan would not be badly affected by its separation. Again, Bazmi's warning regarding the separation of the seaport of Calcutta from the eastern wing did not cause any alarm for Anwar. He asserted that Chittagong could be developed into a first class port and along with Karachi these two ports would be much better than

16 *Madina*, 1 November 1942.

Bombay and Calcutta in Hindustan. Again, Anwar did not see the separation of coal and iron rich areas from eastern Pakistan as a major problem. Just as British India and Japan imported rubber from Dutch East Indies, he surmised that Pakistan too could buy coal and iron from Hindustan.

Anwar also reminded his readers that Pakistan too was endowed with plenty of natural resources. Punjab was blessed with wonderful water and air and excellent irrigation systems. These produced three crops a year, besides plenty of fruits. On the contrary, he pointed out that vast stretches of Hindustan, especially areas such as C.P. and Bombay were at the mercy of the monsoons and produced only one crop a year at best. Again, these crops were of lesser grains such as *jowar*, *bajra* and peanuts. He further noted that Pakistan areas besides being the most fertile were also among the most sparsely populated. While the population of Pakistan was nearly four and a half crore out of which nearly three and a half crore would be Muslim, the population of Islamistan in the east would be three crores out of which two crores would be Muslim. Thus, Pakistan would be both self-sufficient and have large Muslim majorities.

Anwar acknowledged that a central grant was the main source of income for provinces such as Sind, NWFP and Baluchistan. However, these grants, he argued, were given to them by the central government only to keep them in servitude. These provinces did not need to sustain the current levels of expenditure in the future since the most of the central grant was currently being spent on expenses concerning World War II. These expenses, he maintained, would come down by half once the War was over. Moreover, threats on the northwest frontier would end after the War with the likely defeat of Russia and this would further bring down the defence expenditure. And once Pakistan came into existence the frontier tribes could be won over due to the common religion they all shared. Anwar also suggested that the cost of guarding the frontiers could be shared by both Hindustan and Pakistan. At the same time, he averred that if Hindustan was unwilling to share the expenses of guarding the frontiers, Pakistan would be quite capable of guarding them on its own. The very word *jihad*, Anwar predicted, would do the work of an entire army. Furthermore, he asserted that all Pakistani citizens would be granted military training. He saw the Khaksars as a good example in this regard and wanted Pakistan to extend their example to the country at large.

Anwar also expressed optimism that if military and defence expenditures could be brought down, the government of Pakistan could also conceive several cost cutting measures, which would then afford it more revenues. Here Anwar mentioned what was a favourite among supporters of Pakistan – reducing the salaries paid to civil servants. But most importantly, Anwar rejected the principle of economic viability as a criterion for granting freedom to a people. Freedom, he asserted, was the birthright of any people. If the economic principle were applied as a touchstone for granting freedom, a number of countries in the world would never be free. And yet, Anwar pointed out that a number of free countries in the world straddled hilly and desert areas. He noted that even though the people inhabiting them were poor, they lived with dignity and pride, which came from their being free people. Thus, states such as Afghanistan and those in Arabia existed in the civilized world and were respected because they were free. Closer home, he indicated that states such as Jodhpur and Jaipur which, though located in the desert, were self-sufficient. Finally, he gave positive examples of native states such as Mysore and Hyderabad, which were very well-developed as compared to many parts of British India. Compared to all of these countries and states, Anwar saw Pakistan situated in a much more advantageous situation. Rounding off the economic argument, he noted that the income of Pakistan and Islamistan was more than the income of Turkey which, he declared, was the most civilized country in the world.

Having defended Pakistan as not just an ideal but also as a practical proposition, Anwar laid out a simple method for gaining Pakistan. Muslims needed to join the Muslim League en masse and make Jinnah their Dictator in the same manner as Gandhi had been made the Dictator of the Congress. This was essential as Jinnah at present was still not in complete control of the ML, which had a lot of leaders who were still toadies of the Raj. Anwar believed that such a move on part of the Muslim masses would make the attainment of Pakistan very simple. However, he differed from the ML's official policy in one crucial regard. While the ML sought simultaneous freedom for both Pakistan and Hindustan, for Anwar the overthrow of imperialism and India's independence was the first goal after which Pakistan could be attained under the leadership of the ML.

Anwar's views were supported in large measure by Mohammad Abid Sharif of Raichur in faraway Deccan who, in his brief response, expanded on aspects of Bazmi's essay, which had not been addressed by Anwar. Sharif focused on the ideal of *Muttahida Qaumiyat,* (composite nationalism) which had been emphasized by Bazmi. Sharif argued that the ideal of *Muttahida Qaumiyat* had once been creed of leaders like Jinnah, Shaukat Ali, M. A. Ansari and Ajmal Khan who had played a major role in the revival and restoration of the Congress party. But it was the treachery of the Hindus that had destroyed that ideal. In any case, Sharif declared that the concept had now assumed threatening proportions for in the name of this ideal Congress governments was encouraging co-education in schools and this had caused Muslims girls to come out and start singing and dancing on stages. He, therefore, appealed to the sense of brotherhood of U.P. and Bihar Muslims towards their brethren in the majority provinces. He enquired whether the two crore brothers in U.P. and Bihar would be happy if along with their daughters, the daughters of seven crore Muslims would also dance and sing on stage. Would they, he asked, go by the essence of the popular Urdu couplet

Ke Hum to Doobey hain sanam,
Tum ko bhi le doobenge.
(We are sinking, but we are going to take you down with us, my dear.)

Sharif therefore strongly repudiated the idea of any common centre in Delhi given the fact that Muslims and Hindus would have 25 per cent and 75 per cent of the votes respectively, effectively ensuring Hindu domination. Instead, in a separate Muslim federation the Muslims of the majority provinces would be the masters of their own fate. As regards the minority provinces Muslims, Sharif noted that their fortunes could not change for they would always be under Hindu domination. However, he assured them that all was not lost. The U.P. and Bihar Muslims needed to be aware that cooperation between majorities on both sides would happen by a process of give and take and this would ameliorate the problems of the minorities on both sides. If such cooperation did not work, Sharif warned that retaliatory measures (*Jawabi Karrawaiyan*) would certainly work. The Muslims of U.P. and Bihar needed to understand these intricacies clearly so that it would lessen their dread and horror.

The lone response supporting Bazmi's stance, came from Adil Mirza, a student from Aligarh, a holder of B.A. and B.Com degrees. In his response, Mirza noted that the ML leaders wanted their followers to not concern themselves with the political kite-flying that was going on, but to keep their focus on the slogan of Pakistan.[17] And when these Pakistani brothers sang praises of Pakistan, they said two things. First, that Pakistan would have an Islamic government. Second, that a composite government at the centre would never provide adequate security to the Muslims. Mirza acknowledged that there were no Muslims who would not support an Islamic government or rank any other government above an Islamic government. However, as Mirza tellingly

[17] *Madina*, 13 November 1942.

noted, the question was not about whether an Islamic government was good or bad, but whether it was possible or not. That was the crux of the Pakistan issue and unfortunately no Muslim Leaguer had provided a satisfactory answer to that question.

Mirza was scathing about the responses sent in by Anwar and Sharif. These people, he exclaimed, had no idea about the Indian economy or Indian politics, or the state of world affairs. He ridiculed Anwar's fond hope that the word *jihad* would do the work of a modern army. He also dismissed suggestions that Chittagong could be developed as an alternative port to rival Calcutta. Perhaps, he noted with biting sarcasm, the gentleman did not know that ports did not come free of charge but cost several crores of rupees. But it was the suggestion regarding how Pakistan would deal with the separation of coal and iron rich areas of west Bengal, which Mirza said, brought him to the brink of tearing his clothes like a crazed *Majnun*. They say, he exclaimed, that they will buy iron and coal from other countries. It was like when a Queen said – 'Let them eat cake if they did not have bread! Pakistan of our ML brothers, Mirza concluded, was like Shaikh Chilli's *Jannat* (paradise),which is so beloved because it is a place of great relief. But nobody knew how one could get to it or what to do for it.' However, it was not long before a more serious and sustained response to Bazmi's long essay would appear in the *Madina*. Five weeks later, the newspaper began publishing a long essay in a serial form from a supporter of Pakistan, Maulana Abul Nazar Rizvi Amrohvi.

Maulana Abul Nazar Rizvi Amrohvi's Defence of Pakistan

Bazmi's critique of Pakistan as also of the ML's political tactics adopted in pursuit of this goal was countered by Maulana Abul Nazar Rizvi Amrohvi, who mounted a strong defense of Pakistan.[18] Again, we do not know anything about Amrohvi and can only surmise that he was a Shia from Amroha and like Bazmi a part of the Urdu literati in U.P. Amrohvi first complimented Bazmi for his long essay on Pakistan, which he had penned immediately after being released from a *riyasati* (native state) jail. The essay therefore was also an indicator of the political ferment in the native states. Amrohvi, however, contended that while people respected Bazmi for his political services, his sacrifices, his mental acuity, critical faculties and his vigorous pen, his essay was unfortunately marred by sentiment and emotion and was short on proof and evidence.

18 *Madina*, 17 November 1942.

Amrohvi sympathized with Bazmi's strong sentiment for achieving India's freedom in the shortest possible time. He also agreed with Bazmi that the unity (*ittehad*), the humility and spirit of sacrifice (*aisar-o-qurbani*) and practical politics (*amali siyasat*), necessary to achieve Pakistan were at present missing in Muslim India. In addition, the masses lacked political training and they could be made to simultaneously support both Hindustan and Pakistan. The masses were also not interested in wasting their time in resolving problems, which were not connected with their own selfish issues and establishing Pakistan was hence not an easy task. But whatever be the hurdles, Amrohvi insisted that no one could negate the truth of Pakistan. Before proceeding to unleash his arguments, Amrohvi cautioned Muslims not to be influenced by Hindu and Sikh threats of civil war (*khana jangi*) or political chaos when they thought about Pakistan. Muslims could not afford to be misled by the propaganda of the majority community that was keen to preserve its political dominance and hence portrayed attempts to achieve Pakistan as akin to running after a shadow.

Amrohvi began by repudiating the argument often made by nationalist *ulama* that Pakistan was the product of the official British mind or was simply a passing ephemeral sentiment among excitable sections of Muslim political opinion. He, therefore, proceeded to provide a brief intellectual history of the idea of Pakistan. Amrohvi recounted that ever since the end of Islamic rule, when the flag of Islam came down in India, continuous attempts had been made by Indian Muslims to reclaim their power. But when assistance from foreign forces or the cry of jihad in a *dar al harb* did not work, they took to a new modern path. He described how they had started to cooperate with other communities and started a constitutional struggle to gain independence for the country, based on the idea of mutual reconciliation with the Hindus. But as they moved forward in this path, Amrohvi indicated that Muslims became increasingly aware that according to the principles of western democracy, they would be reduced to a minority both at the centre and in the federated provinces. Muslims, however, saw that they had relative strength (*izaafi taaqat*) in a few provinces and on that basis they, therefore, started to beg for the protection of their rights all over the country. And for a long time, as Amrohvi poignantly noted, the world never saw those outstretched begging hands falling down due to tiredness. But even such Muslim mendicancy, he regretted, did not change the Hindu mentality.

In this context, Amrohvi bitterly came down on Nehru. It was Nehru, who at this juncture claimed that there were only two forces in the country – the Congress and the British government. Referring to the *Qaid*, Amrohvi declared that it is then that one voice arose, which was the voice of the Muslim heart, that there was a third force, which was that of the Muslim nation. It is Jinnah who accelerated the development of a political idea, which first grew out of the mind of Dr Mohammad Iqbal, (and not Dr Abdul Latif), who first presented it at the ML session in Allahabad in 1930. Thus, like many others before him, Amrohvi saw Iqbal as the father of Pakistan. Amrohvi, however, acknowledged that Iqbal's idea soon died down on the Muslim political scene and few Muslims took any interest in Pakistan despite it being a unique idea. He attributed this lack of interest to the fact that Iqbal did not envisage the government of Muslims over *all of Hindustan*, which, Amrohvi argued, was the still the main Muslim concern. Besides, Muslims in general did not expect that they would have to protect themselves from the democratic majority. However, a few Muslims took a little interest in the idea and adopted it as their ideal goal (*nasbul ain*).

Tracing the trajectory of this idea further, Amrohvi noted that the first time the idea was proposed to him was by a friend of his, a certain Dr Burhan Ahmad Faruqi PhD. Dr Abdul Latif's 'cultural' (*tamadduni*) Pakistan came to the fore a long time after that and it was followed by a very different idea of 'political' (*siyasi*) Pakistan that was being currently advocated by the ML. Amrohvi clarified that Latif's 'cultural' Pakistan was never affirmed by the Muslim League, Mr Jinnah (or even Bazmi *sahib* himself), since it envisaged Pakistan's cultural evolution to happen under a central government, which would be non-Islamic. He, therefore, wanted to correct the false impression once and for all, that Dr Latif was the original proponent of Pakistan. To differentiate between the ML and Latif's ideas of Pakistan, Amrohvi further noted that Latif himself was upset with Jinnah for not endorsing his policy. Amrohvi acknowledged that Dr Latif may have given up his job in Hyderabad with the sincere wish to study and make his idea of Pakistan successful, but this did not mean that no research had been done by others on the idea of 'political' Pakistan. There were the intellectuals and students from the Muslim University in Aligarh who had expended considerable amount of time and energy in putting together a Pakistan scheme. There were other individuals who came up with their own schemes of Pakistan such as Maulana Obeidullah Sindhi and Maulana Hasrat Mohani and all these schemes had been built on the basis of the two-nation theory. But more importantly, Amrohvi declared that 'Political' Pakistan could be discerned from the speeches and statements of Mr Jinnah. 'Political' Pakistan meant an alternative Muslim centre with a Muslim government (*Musalmanon ka markazi nizam-i-hayat*). Amrohvi, however, visualized this Muslim centre in the context of dominion status and thus envisaged a continued British connection. To think of anything more than a dominion status at present, Amrohvi remarked, was nothing more than the dream of an idiot. However, unlike Latif's cultural Pakistan, political Pakistan had none of the impractical features against which any serious objections could be raised.

In this context, Amrohvi acknowledged that Jinnah had not provided details of the ML's Pakistan scheme. The reason for this omission, Amrohvi explained, was that neither the Congress nor the British government had accepted the basic principle of Pakistan. Besides, even if they did accept it to a degree, they had interpreted it very narrowly. And since Jinnah was convinced that publishing details of the scheme was simply buying trouble, he studiously avoided the task. Amrohvi, however, hastened to note that owing to this lack of elaboration on Jinnah's part, one should however not infer that Pakistan was just an ambiguous idea beyond which there was nothing in the mind of Mr Jinnah or the Muslim League. The basic ideas of Pakistan along with the necessary maps of its constituent units (*jazwiyat ka naqsha*) had already been made public by the ML. However, Amrohvi indicated that some work still needed to be done with regard to the current division of the provinces, which would be altered. Thus, those districts of Bengal, which were taken away and given to Assam in 1912 needed to be returned to Bengal. Amrohvi insisted that while this work should have been done before the two-nation theory became popular, no scheme could be declared impracticable simply for this one reason. His terse explication regarding Pakistan, however, was followed by a further elaboration on his idea of Pakistan, which emerged in his detailed point by point repudiation of the arguments made by Syed Abu Syed Bazmi.

Amrohvi argued that the biggest reason why Pakistan was so attractive to the Muslims was because they harboured a number of misgivings about living in *Akhand Hindustan* (undivided India), where they were apprehensive about the protection of their religion, language, culture and shariat by a central government dominated by non-Muslims. They, therefore, had a number of questions in their mind regarding *Akhand Hindustan*. Would the provinces have their own armies? Could they use external and internal resources to develop their armies? Was the army that was stationed at the Afghan border to be under the control of the NWFP government or the central government? Who would realize the customs duties at the ports of Karachi and Calcutta? Would the navy, responsible for protecting the coastline be under the control of the central government or under the governments of Sind and Bengal? What steps would be taken to improve the economic situation of Muslims in the minority provinces? To what extent would Muslims be allowed to take part in the politics of the Islamic world?

Would Indian government be allowed to have alliances with China, Japan or western powers if they were hostile to Muslim countries? How would Muslim weakness in trade and commerce be rectified? What would be the percentage of jobs that Muslims would be given in the army? Would recruitment be based upon fighting abilities or upon percentage in population? What steps would be taken to implement the shariat? Till the Congress produced a scheme, which answered these questions satisfactorily, Pakistan, Amrohvi felt, would continue to be alive as the ideal for Muslims in India.

Amrohvi dismissed Bazmi as naïve in thinking that one letter from Maulana Abul Kalam Azad had opened the royal pathway (*shahrah*) to Pakistan. It was possible that the Maulana may have conceded it, but then successive resolutions of the Congress had roundly rejected Pakistan. Besides, Amrohvi pointed out that what the Maulana had granted was nothing more than the right of provinces to secede from the centre. If one were to analyse his offer, two things became evident. Firstly, even though a province had been granted the right to secede, it had not been granted the right to establish a new centre. Again, it was not clear whether other provinces would be allowed by the Hindus to join the seceding province and together set up a new centre. The Hindus, Amrohvi asserted, would never allow the formation of an independent centre. Since Britain would reduce its commitments in India in the future and withdraw to a large extent, those provinces, which wanted to secede from the existing Indian centre would be frightened by the Hindus into submission. This had been the case with what were now the semi-autonomous republics of the Soviet Union. Amrohvi pointed to a similar example from American history. Thus, the right to secession though being offered would be useless in the face of the vital powers that the current Indian centre monopolized at the moment. The Maulana's concession, therefore Amrohvi concluded, did not grant even a hazy Pakistan. A war, therefore, would inevitably have to be waged if the Muslims wanted to establish a new Muslim centre.

Secondly, besides the impossibility of seceding from the centre, Amrohvi noted that Maulana Azad had granted the right of secession only to an electoral majority in the provinces. In such a referendum it was not just the Muslims but also the Hindus, Sikhs and Untouchables who would have the right to vote and decide on the question of Pakistan. He pointed out that a simple majority among Muslims would, therefore, not suffice to bring about secession and it was only a trap for the Muslims. Indeed, Amrohvi warned that if one were to take into account the demographic profile of the Punjab and Bengal, one could only infer that this principle was being introduced in order to make Pakistan an impossible prospect. Hindus and Sikhs constituted 45 per cent of the Punjab and were very well organized. The Muslims on the other hand were neither strong nor united. In addition, they had in their midst fifth columnists, who went by the name of 'nationalist Muslims', who would certainly work relentlessly against Pakistan. As a result of these divisions in Muslim ranks and potential mischief by fifth columnists, Punjab and Bengal would actually never be able to secede. If these two major provinces refused to secede, Amrohvi maintained that Sind, NWFP and Baluchistan would never dream of seceding. As a result, poor Muslims would be duped and be forced to come to the conclusion that the Congress had generously granted them all the rights that they had demanded, but that luck was not on their side. Amrohvi contended that if the Congress was really serious about granting the right to secession, it should have granted it to the Muslims and not to the provinces. The right to secession needed to be on a communal and not on a provincial basis. Otherwise, there was no point in the Congress' magnanimous gesture and courtesy. The reality was that the Congress would never grant Muslims the right to self-determination since that would bring out the overwhelming support for the two-nation theory into the open and the Congress' delicate nationalism could never tolerate such an eventuality.

Amrohvi, therefore, concluded that the division of India on the basis of the two-nation theory was the only way to bring Pakistan into existence.[19] Amrohvi agreed with Bazmi's critique of Professor Abdul Latif's scheme of transfer of populations. He pointed out that neither the ML in any of its resolutions nor Mr Jinnah in any of his speeches had called for a wholesale transfer of populations. Even after the formation of Pakistan every individual would have the right to stay wherever he was living. However, Amrohvi also declared that each individual would have the right to gather his wealth and make Pakistan his destination (*mustaqar*). He, therefore, warned that threats about wholesale transfer of populations were a part of the war of nerves (*aisabi jang*) that was being waged by the enemies of Pakistan. Thus, after partition, Hindus could live under a Muslim rule and Muslims similarly could live under Hindu rule where a 'paradise' of protected rights, as described by the nationalist Muslims, would be offered to them. What, however, should never happen in a vast country like India, Amrohvi averred, was one community becoming dominant over everyone else. Pakistan would resolve this problem besides also removing the bitterness between Hindus and Muslims, which could be exploited by others and become a danger to India's independence.

---

19 *Madina*, 21 November 1942.

Amrohvi next responded to Bazmi's spirited economic critique of Pakistan. He acknowledged that Bazmi was right in pointing out that Sind, NWFP and Baluchistan depended upon a 2 crore central grant since they were poor. However, he happily noted that the exploration of mineral wealth and opening of factories was going on at a decent pace in these provinces. He, therefore, refused to believe that Pakistan did not have mineral wealth. On the contrary, he was sure that it would abound in silver and gold. Baluchistan, he noted, had deposits of chromium and sulphur. Nature, Amrohvi thankfully observed, had prevented the British from exploiting the mineral wealth of Pakistan because it was the property of Pakistan. Amrohvi, therefore, pleaded for time and opportunity for the Muslim government to realize the enormous potential in Pakistan.

Amrohvi also sought to tackle questions regarding the sources of capital for Pakistan that would be necessary to exploit its economic resources. The answer, he cryptically explained, could be found by looking at the history of England. England was once the Baluchistan of Europe but today the sun never set on the British Empire. Without any further explanation, he concluded that there was no reason why Pakistan could not have a bright future as well. At this juncture, he went through the familiar set of few practical measures that had been recited earlier. First, Amrohvi argued that savings could be increased by reducing expenditures in the government and bureaucracy. Here he gave the devil its due by giving credit to the Congress governments in the provinces for having shown the way for saving several crores of rupees through austerity measures. Second, he suggested that national loans could be raised by the Pakistani government, which could then set up factories with that capital. Third, he conjectured that Pakistan's Hindu capitalists could also be invited to invest in this regard. Here Amrohvi drew upon the cliché of the Hindu capitalist, who was only interested in his profits and protection for his capital and nothing else. He further expanded on this theme by noting that the Hindu capitalist would never become a threat to Pakistan and instead could be easily brought under control since the germs of obedience to government were deeply embedded in the Hindu nature.

Amrohvi rationalized that even assuming that the Pakistan provinces did not have enough money to pay for the establishment of a new centre (*markaz*), a loan could always be taken from the Hindu centre. It would after all be in the interest of Hindustan to grant a loan to Pakistan not just for the purpose of improving mutual goodwill but also for its own security. Drawing again from an oft repeated proposition, Amrohvi noted that the Hindu was presently an enemy of Pakistan, but that would cease once Pakistan became a reality. After that, Hindustan and Pakistan would aspire for close cooperation because it was necessary for both of them. Therefore, to persuade Muslims to accept a semi-autonomous status in India was not right. Free unity, which would obtain from the formation of Hindustan and Pakistan, could never be compared to the forcible unity under servitude in the ambit of a united India.

Amrohvi next repudiated Bazmi's argument that since the Hindustan government had the requisite wealth from which it could produce machine power, this machine-power could be used to subjugate Pakistan and Muslims therefore needed to accept a secondary position in a united India and live in peace under a Hindu government. But how important was machine-power in deciding the fate of wars, Amrohvi asked his readers. Did a crippled China surrender its arms during the recent seven years war? The truth, he insisted, was that the defence of a country rested not so much on its armour or weaponry but on its passion for freedom (*jazba-i-Hurriyat pasandi)*. Besides, *jihad* came as a natural duty to the Muslims, who would therefore not be so easy to conquer. Further, if one were to apply the same logic to Hindustan, Amrohvi wondered why was it that Hindustan desired independence from Great Britain even as it beheld Britain's machine might. Hindustan by this logic needed to be as fearful of British Army, Navy and Air force. Besides, even if Hindustan were to import machinery from Britain to produce armaments, it would take centuries for it to produce armaments like the latter. However, in spite of all these arguments, Amrohvi noted that the Congress had still passed a resolution for total independence. This only proved that no nation could tolerate living under the domination of another nation. Even machine-power could not extinguish the passion for freedom. Muslims, likewise, could not be expected to extinguish their desire for their own freedom.

Amrohvi also tried to turn the tables on Bazmi by leveling the same critiques against Hindustan as had been aimed by the latter at Pakistan. He pointed out that Pakistan was being opposed by some sections on the grounds that British influence in the subcontinent would be revived with the formation of Pakistan. Amrohvi argued that such a fear could also be associated with a united India, which for all its unity would still be forced to live under the influence of Britain or some other power. In this regard he pointed out that the Balkan powers for all their armed might had not managed to remain independent. To, therefore, expect Hindu India to remain completely independent was a grave folly. As Amrohvi had mentioned at the very outset, dominion status was the best that India could expect from Britain. Since Hindu India was going to be under the control of some external power or another for at least another half a century, where, Amrohvi enquired, was the danger from *Pakistaniyat*? As he concluded this argument, he reiterated that while there was enmity between Hindu and Muslim India today, which would perhaps continue till tomorrow, there was no reason why India as a whole could not unite against a foreign power in the future.

Just as Bazmi had raised questions about Pakistan's centre, Amrohvi also expressed doubts as to whether the Hindu centre would be able to fulfill the needs of its provinces, in view of its own parlous situation. If, as was being argued, the Hindu centre would make progress by taking loans from America and Britain, Amrohvi argued that the Muslim centre could do the same. He also made it clear that America and European powers would find it profitable to trade with Pakistan and establish political relations with it since Pakistan had a healthy population of 150 million if one were to also include the population of Muslim native states as well. This was more than the population of America and almost equal to that of the Soviet Union. The seaports of Calcutta and Karachi would bring in a lot of wealth for the Pakistani federal centre. Besides, the land trade routes beginning from NWFP and extending through Afghanistan, Iran, Iraq, Palestine, Turkey, Balkans and going through Germany and Russia would definitely bring in many economic benefits for Pakistan.

In a related criticism regarding the Indian Union, Amrohvi noted that different and mutually antagonistic provinces were currently being brought under the aegis of the Hindu centre. This was being done under the expectation that it would foster a unified consciousness among the Indian people. If the Indian centre was expected to achieve this goal, Amrohvi wondered as to what could possibly stop the Islamic centre from similarly fostering Islamic sentiments as a unifying factor among the Pakistan provinces. The use of Islamic sentiments, he vaguely noted, would provide moral if not material support to Muslims in the minority provinces. This was especially the case since the Islamic centre would be subject to legal responsibilities and obligations and might not be able to help or assist the Muslims of the minority provinces. But then again, Amrohvi added with a rhetorical flourish, the Muslim minority did not live due to the favour of any centre and could struggle themselves for their own rights. Besides, it was not easy to suppress 4.5 crore Muslims especially since these were an awakened people. This was perhaps an indication that perhaps the minority provinces Muslims could not expect to look up to Pakistan for much assistance.

Amrohvi next dismissed Bazmi's political, economic and ethical objections to the inclusion of native states in the domain of Pakistan. On the contrary, he welcomed the inclusion of Kashmir and Hyderabad into Pakistan. Kashmir, he noted, was close to the border of Russia and was on trade routes which would be extremely helpful in sourcing precious mineral resources from Russia. Hyderabad by joining Pakistan would bring in two first class ports in the form of Kakinada and Vishakhapatnam. Since Hyderabad also had substantial mineral deposits, it would bring enormous economic benefits to Pakistan. In this regard, Amrohvi also repudiated all objections to labelling such states Islamic and elaborated upon the criteria for calling any state Islamic. For Amrohvi, Turkey, Iran, Afghanistan and Iraq were all Islamic states. This was in spite of knowing that a country like Turkey had abolished Islamic law and had laid its foundation in Roman law. A country, according to him, could be called Islamic if it fulfilled any of the three criteria – the ruler called himself a Muslim, the majority of the population was Muslim, or it accepted rule by Muslim government. This was an astonishing claim on Amrohvi's part and not easily defensible given the specific understanding of an Islamic state in the mind of someone like the Raja of Mahmudabad and others in the ML. Yet, he did not bother to provide any further reasons in order to support his use of the term. What it makes clear is that Amrohvi was a modernist who unlike many of the supporters of Pakistan, did not envisage it as an Islamic state.

Continuing with the discussion of native states, Amrohvi conceded Bazmi's point that native states were despotic and what was going on inside them could not be tolerated by any serious Pakistani. However, he declared that he was convinced that during the evolutionary stage of British India's independence, the native states (*riyasati Hindustan*) too would evolve politically. These states could also, therefore, be gradually reformed. In this regard, Amrohvi rebutted Bazmi's criticism of the ML leadership for to its toleration of the system of monarchical government in native states. He accused Bazmi of deliberately not looking at the Congress to see how undemocratic a party it truly was besides noting Gandhi's soft spot for factory owners, rajas and maharajas. If Gandhi was perfectly content with the continuation of native states, Amrohvi wondered what was wrong if Jinnah adopted a similar position. He, therefore, roundly criticized the double standards and doublespeak of the nationalist Muslims.

For Amrohvi, deviousness and doublespeak were expected of Gandhi and the Congress. This was in contrast to the honest Jinnah whom he saluted for his unimpeachable integrity. One could think of Pakistan as the worst possible idea or even believe that it would never happen, but no one could accuse Jinnah, a man of parliamentary spirit, of going against his own soul. However, Amrohvi hinted that matters would perhaps not always be carried in the same parliamentary spirit in case Muslim sentiments were sought to be crushed. And whether Mr Jinnah was alive or in his grave, he declared that the movement for Pakistan would not be affected.

Amrohvi went on to dismiss Bazmi's explanation that Congress was against Pakistan since the party had for the past fifty two years established itself on the philosophy of *Muttahida Qaumiyat* (composite nationalism).[20] The idea of *Muttahida Qaumiyat*, he asserted, was not going to help India gain independence. In fact the Congress had been using the idea to establish Hindu supremacy in India. He insisted that the 'idol' of *Muttahida Qaumiyat* needed to be smashed and replaced by the principle of *Bainul Aqwamiyat* (internationalism) in India. The fact that India was home to several nations and was not one nation needed to be clearly understood by the Congress. There was no reason for the Congress to fear that if *Muttahida Qaumiyat* was replaced by *Bainul Aqwamiyat*, it would be reduced to the Hindu Mahasabha. The Congress did not need to remove any member of any community from its rolls. All it needed to do, Amrohvi remarked tongue in cheek, was to change its name from National Congress to International Congress and that would resolve its problems.

Continuing his train of thought, Amrohvi felt that as human consciousness evolved, both *Qaumiyat* (nationalism) and *Bainul Aqwamiyat* (internationalism) with its potentialities of international government would make progress in the world concurrently. However, this did not mean that all nations should immediately subordinate their governments to one government. *Bainul Aqwamiyat* had arisen in the West but it had not been able to sweep over even such small countries such as Belgium, Finland and Romania or been successful in persuading them to cede their sovereignty to a larger entity. If even such small nations hesitated to cede their sovereignty to a larger entity, Amrohvi saw no reason why the Indian Muslims could be expected to cede their sovereignty to a larger entity. *Bainul Aqwamiyat* was good insofar as it raised hopes for the betterment of mankind, but it could not be a reason for postponing the programme of national self-government. Amrohvi, therefore, concluded this argument with an ambiguous welcome of *Bainul Aqwamiyat*. If it spread, it would help both the Muslim state and the Muslim minority in India. If it did not spread, at least the national position (*qaumi position*) of the Muslims would be preserved due to establishment of the Muslim state. On the other hand supporting a united India would be a great mistake and Muslim nationalists would only regret it in the future.

---

20 *Madina*, 25 November 1942

Amrohvi finally attempted to address Bazmi's criticism regarding Pakistan's deleterious effects on the minority provinces Muslims. Here, Amrohvi alternated between two strategies. On the one hand he pointed out that their fate under a Hindu majority would certainly not improve if a Hindu central government ruled all over India. Additionally, it would not get any worse if Pakistan came into existence. On the other hand he assured the minority province Muslims that with the formation of Pakistan their interests would be fully protected due to the reciprocal arrangements that would be made for the protection of the minorities in both the states. Thus, Amrohvi acknowledged that with the formation of Pakistan, the Muslims in U.P., Bihar, C.P. and Madras would definitely come under the subjection of the Hindus. As he flatly stated, neither you nor anyone else can change their fate (*Muqaddar ko na aap badal sakte hain na koi aur*). Amrohvi further acknowledged that given the regional sentiments of the Punjabis and the Bengalis, or legal restrictions, they would perhaps not always come to the aid of U.P. Muslims. However, it was also clear that the U.P. Hindus would never be indulgent towards the U.P. Muslims and hence they could simply not trust Hindu assurances that their interests in a united India would be preserved. Amrohvi, therefore, appealed to the spirit of sacrifice of the U.P. Muslims. The U.P. Muslims, he reminded them, had made great sacrifices for even such faraway causes like the Khilafat Movement. The U.P. Muslims had also shown their love for Afghanistan, Iran, Iraq and Turkey and prayed for their independence. These sentiments towards their brethren existed in spite of their not bringing any profit to the U.P. Muslims. The U.P. Muslims could, therefore, certainly make sacrifices for their brethren in the Pakistan provinces. Finally, Amrohvi had comforting words for the U.P. Muslims. One thing, he stated emphatically, was definite – that the servitude of minority province Muslims would be in the context of a similar servitude of crores of Hindus in Pakistan – again a thinly veiled reference to the hostage population theory that he had not uttered earlier.

Amrohvi, therefore, dismissed Bazmi's sense of outrage about Mr Jinnah's speech wherein he had stated that he would rather let two crore Muslims in the minority provinces be smashed in order to liberate the seven crore Muslims in the majority provinces from Hindu rule. Bazmi had also noted that these two crores were more than all the people of the Arab world put together. Amrohvi, however, argued that having a greater number, viz. all the nine crore Indian Muslims, in a secondary position to the Hindus in a united India was surely the worst possible proposition since it would lead to the inferiority of the whole Muslim nation. If nationalist Muslims on the one hand demanded total independence (*mukammal azadi*) for semi-autonomous governments (*neem azad hukumatein*) such as Iraq and Egypt, Amrohvi demanded to know as to how on the other hand could they demand a semi-autonomous position for the Indian Muslims.

Amrohvi also dismissed Bazmi's astonishment at the ML's indifference towards Muslim minority provinces in which Muslim culture, language etc. were under threat and its solicitousness towards the Muslim majority provinces where Muslims were already protected. Amrohvi acknowledged that in the minority provinces, Muslim processions and *azaan* (call to prayers) were still being stopped, the Hindus were propagating Hindi at the expense of Urdu and Muslims faced numerous other problems. Amrohvi, however, asked whether all this would stop if Muslims were to agree to a central government dominated by the Hindus. Since this was not going to be the case, there was no point in Bazmi's criticism. Besides, these 3–4 crores Muslims in the minority provinces would not be crushed as such by the Hindu majority. They would be granted cultural, economic, educational and religious rights which would make for a 'paradise' (*jannat*) of protected rights that had been promised by the nationalist Muslims. And since these rights would be part of the fundamental laws of the two centres, the minority province Muslims who had played such a crucial role in the freedom of their Muslim brethren had no reason to be afraid of either being abandoned, forgotten or crushed under Hindu majority rule.

Amrohvi then went on to repudiate Bazmi's arguments regarding Hindus turning their backs on Urdu in case Pakistan came into existence.[21] He argued that there would be no change in Hindu attitude towards Urdu with the formation of Pakistan. Gandhi had publicly expressed his desire for *Nagari* script and Hindi to be enforced and had also worked to make *Hindi Sahitya Sammelan* stronger. Rather than Hindu voices getting softer in their espousal of Hindi due to a greater emphasis on the ideology of *Muttahida Qaumiyat*, the Hindu domination over the centre would only lead to more strident support for Hindi. In this regard, Amrohvi asserted that one needed to look more at how languages developed and spread. He therefore explained that any language spread mostly as a result of social contact. The best prospects for the spread of Urdu therefore lay in the cessation of fighting for political power between Hindus and Muslims. This would result in the development of their social contacts, thus bringing them closer. This coming together of Hindus and Muslims would, in turn, help

21 *Madina*, 28 November 1942.

in the spread of Urdu. More importantly, Urdu would receive official status in Pakistan. Thus, even if Urdu were in a secondary status in Hindustan it would be compensated by its status in Pakistan. Amrohvi further insisted that it was naïve to think that Hindus would adopt the dress and customs of the Muslims in *Akhand Hindustan*. He flatly declared that their hatred of Muslims was too deep for such a thing to happen.

Amrohvi also attacked as fallacious, the argument that the work of *Tabligh* would be affected due to the formation of Pakistan. Islam, Amrohvi argued, could not be deterred by such impediments. Islam had found a place even amongst the enemies of the Arabs. It had impressed Europeans in Europe as well as the untouchables in India. Amrohvi expressed optimism that as prophesized by Shah Waliullah, Islam would definitely become the dominant religion of India. He further noted that the thinking and educated people who were converting to Islam in India today were not doing so under the influence of a *Maulvi* or a *Sufi* but due to their own study of Islam and their realization that the emancipation of mankind rested on Islam. Thus, the only way to further the work of *Tabligh* was through ethical conduct (*ikhlaqi kardar*), spiritual behaviour (*roohani amal*) and adherence to religious rules (*mazhab ki pabandi*). If there was a body of people adhering to these values then even in spite of the formation of Pakistan, the work of *Tabligh* would continue in Hindustan.

Continuing with his argument about religion and religiosity, Amrohvi addressed himself to the criticism made by Bazmi of ML leaders particularly Jinnah as being westernized and not being religious.[22] This accusation, he noted, had been made by the nationalist *ulama* but they had conveniently ignored the fact that many of the nationalist Muslims too were westernized. Moreover, the problem with these *ulama* was that their piety *(khuda parasti)* was tinted with political colour and they had not been impartial. For Amrohvi this was an indication of a deep malady in Muslim India. The Hindu nation, he pointed out, had learnt to respect both its reactionary and its progressive leaders. The same lesson needed to be learnt by the Muslims. Amrohvi further dismissed the importance of the nationalist *ulama* claiming that more than experts of the Quran and the Hadith, people most urgently needed by the Muslim nation were those who were intimately aware of constitutional complexities. That is why they had decided to follow those who denied God, he noted, making a pointed reference to Jinnah.

---

22 *Madina*, 1 December 1942.

In this regard, Amrohvi also addressed Bazmi's contempt for the plutocrat leaders of the Pakistan movement. Amrohvi agreed that if the reins of government were left in the hands of self-seeking leaders (*gharaz parast*), then one could not hope for a democratic revolution as in France or Russia for many years. The blame for the existing state of affairs however lay with the Nationalists (*qaum parast*) since they refused to be wise and refused to walk on the royal path of consensus. If only the nationalists had given up the policy of being such 'know-alls' they would not have laughingly dismissed delicate Muslim sentiment and the initiative would have remained in their hands. Even now they had the opportunity of admitting their weaknesses so that in their own politically inert world, a revolution may occur. In this context, Amrohvi also pointed out that the Congress too was under the influence of the wealthy. He pointed to someone like Sampurnanand as a prominent example.[23] Besides, Amrohvi justified wealth as a necessary component of politics. He wondered how any party could attain domination without commanding gold and silver. Meetings and processions of parties were facilitated by money. One needed to therefore realize that politics was based on money power. As he pointed out, America, which now dominated the world, was the hunting ground of the rich. So why, Amrohvi questioned, were such complaints being made against Pakistan? Indeed the play of wealth would continue till Muslims stopped copying western democracy and tried to change its very bases.

Amrohvi, therefore, enquired whether there was any Hindu province in which a poor labourer had been made a Premier. Poor people could not even dream of ever becoming a part of the Congress high Command. Again the Congress ministries of Allah Bakhsh in Sind or Dr Khan Sahib in NWFP were hardly those of poor Muslims. Amrohvi also dismissed the alleged sacrifices of the Nehru family for the country and deprecated their show of giving up their wealth for the national cause. In contrast to the shenanigans of Congress leaders, he noted that Jinnah was famous for his personal integrity and incorruptibility and, therefore, was indeed a great man. However, he acknowledged that the ML too had its share of sinners at provincial, district and *qasbah* levels. And here Amrohvi made a startling revelation. It was this problem that had prevented him from coming close to the League in spite of being a fervent Pakistani. However, he asked Bazmi to do some soul searching to find out why such leaders had come to dominate the ML. It was not because of machinations of the British government. Rather, it was due to the failure of the nationalist Muslims who

23 *Madina*, 28 November 1942.

had played with the sentiments of the Muslims, lost their ideological balance and tilted so far in the direction of *Muttahida Qaumiyat* that the scales needed to be balanced again.

Amrohvi, therefore, ridiculed Bazmi's recommendations that Muslims accept provincial Pakistan (*subjaati Pakistan*) in addition to free cities, recognition of Urdu language and script as official in return for accepting central control of the Hindus. The Hindus would be more than happy to accept some of these childish demands (*taflana zid*). Who, Amrohvi asked, would refuse to give such minor concessions in return for central control? Moreover, what the nationalist Muslims were demanding today as a substitute for Pakistan, had already been conceded to the Muslims and was already in Mr Jinnah's pocket. No power could stop provincial autonomy and independence (*subjaati azadi*). Residual powers (*mabqi ikhtiyar*) too had been conceded. If the Muslims had any faith in the centre, the demand for residual powers would never have been made.

Amrohvi finally dismissed Bazmi's arguments that solving the economic problem and then throwing a few safeguards to the Muslims after independence, would resolve the Hindu–Muslim problem.[24] On the contrary, he insisted that with independence the Hindus would be in complete control and they would use it to distribute economic benefits to their own brethren and the Muslims would, in the end, gain nothing. In such a situation, he asserted that Muslims would never be able to attain equality with the Hindus. If the Hindus had a sincere desire to solve the economic problems of the Muslims they would have shown generosity and selflessness since they had snatched power from the Muslims. The Muslims would no longer be beggars with their hands outstretched before the Hindus. Amrohvi proudly noted that Mr Jinnah did not extend his palms like a beggar and instead made his demands like a self-respecting person. Now the Muslims were not begging but making schemes for snatching political power (*badshahiyat)*. Success or failure was in the hands of God. Today the Muslim demand was not for Hindu selflessness but for power and partition. There was a constant constitutional struggle going on in pursuit of the goal but in case extra-constitutional effort was necessary, then the Muslims would be ready.

Besides, economic problems of big nations were complex and not solved through simple methods like currying favour with the Hindus, or partial or total independence as suggested by Bazmi. There were thorns galore on the path

---

24 *Madina*, 5 December 1942.

of economic development and centuries of modern civilization had not been able to solve this problem. For this, what was needed was a compact ideology, political power, democratic consensus in the Muslim nation and a dedicated body of pure and educated young men in order to implement this ideology. And in order to find these necessary ingredients, it was imperative to utilize the lamp of Pakistan. Thus, it was necessary for Muslims to have political and military power to begin to solve the economic problem. Strengthening the foundations of the economic system required the political system of *Khilafat-i- Rashidin*, which, Amrohvi concluded, would be established in Pakistan.

The impact of debates in the public sphere on the thinking of Muslims at the grassroots may be gauged by two letters sent to Jinnah from the U.P. in 1944 which have been reproduced here in full. The first is from the secretary of the Lucknow District Muslim League while the second is from a young student and a troubled supporter of the ML from Amroha, the town from where Amrohvi hailed. They point to bewilderment about Pakistan besides a sense of apprehension among the U.P. Muslims about their fate in a post-colonial political order in south Asia.

My Dear Qaid e Azam,

So far no one has been able to give a definite conception of Pakistan. I have thought out something about it. So I would like to tell you what it is.

Pakistan

Hindus will be enjoying all civic rights but they will have no political rights in Pakistan. They will be regarded as aliens. Muslims will be in the same position outside their zones. There is no use for Muslims to have 30% or so seats in the minority provinces because all their opposition will be a cry in wilderness as it has been during the Congress regime. Hindus will appoint puppet Muslim Ministers (like Rafi Ahmed Kidwai, or like Ibrahim, or like Dr. Mahmud of Behar)who will play in their hands. They will not be able to overthrow the Hindu government if the latter proves to be tyrant to them. On the contrary, Hindus will always be a constant source of trouble to them in the Punjab and Bengal if there they are given political rights, because there the Muslims have a very narrow majority. Muslim governments will always be weak governments. So Hindus should have no political rights in Pakistan if they choose to live there.

Gradually all Muslims living out of the two zones will migrate to their national land and the government will provide every facility to immigrants.

Hindus may do likewise. The migration will be voluntary and not compulsory for anybody. One of its two zones will consist of NWFP, Kashmir, Jammu, the Punjab, Sind and Baluchistan. The other region will comprise Bengal and Assam put together. Muslims should not accept less land than this otherwise when in the future the migration of Muslims will begin from non-Pakistan areas to Pakistani areas, there will be very little land available for Muslims to live in.

Ashique Raza Siddiqui[25]

My Dearest Quaid e Azam,

Received your kind letter of 20th May 1944 which encouraged me to write this letter to you. After my dearest wishes I first stand in need of the introduction of this letter. My father is a Congressman and he is a warm worker of the Congress. He would like to see me a Congressman, therefore he awfully objects the League in its views. He, before me, praises the Congress as the only national political party to live in India. I, though have not gone to the Congress, yet I fear that one day will come when I, out of my conscience will be obliged to see myself a Congressman. I don't even know what is Pakistan and the object in view of the League. Father, Mr Akhtar Hasan, objects so awfully that I fear answering them or I am in fact, not in a mood to reply the objections correctly. I ask you to answer them as I shall be able to make him a League admirer. The objections are

1. What is the aim of Pakistan helping Mohammedans

2. Pakistan helps Muslims to fight against Hindus as it is. Two centres will be established, one under Muslims, one under Hindus. The rulers to extend their territory will surely fight.

3. It is heard that the subhas (sic) which can produce Muslim majority shall be included in Pakistan, viz Punjab, Bengal, Assam, Sindh, NWFP. Therefore UP as it produces only 14% Muslims will be excluded of Pakistan which means we will enjoy Hindu rule. As here are 86% Hindus, they can under their Raja easily crush 14% Muslims. The answer ever given to this question is that we will adopt 'The policy of reaction'. But, my dear Qaid, it is improbable. As you see it is harder to crush 45% Hindus in Punjab than the crushing of 14% of Muslims in UP. It is hardest to crush Hindus in Bengal. Draw a line from Calcutta to Murshidabad. Now if you will go down the line, you still find Hindus awfully rich, learned and wise. But going up the line you will find Muslims quite foolish, uncivilized and

25 *Quaid-i-Azam Papers*, IOR Neg 10814, Reel 55, File 1102 Ashique Raza Siddiqui, Secretary Lucknow Muslim League to Jinnah, 25 July 1944.

ragged. Here it is, I think impossible to crush the Hindus, as you see the example of whole India which depends on an island equal to 1/100 of its own area – it is why? – only because England are wise, rich, politically civilized and educated. Therefore here it is the danger of losing the province forever. The objection arising here is under what rules we can save us from crushing?

Hoping to get this answer very soon but quite explained and yes – here is another question for you – will you give me a share of your valuable time so often to write you letters to create the feelings of Muslim League in Amroha – I conclude.

Sincerely yours

Athar Hasan[26]

[26] *Quaid-i-Azam Papers*, IOR Neg 10814 Reel 55 File 1102, Letter from a Muslim from Amroha to Jinnah, 25 May 1944.

7

Fusing Islam and State Power

Shabbir Ahmad Usmani and Pakistan as the New Medina

To the world trapped in whirlpools of materialism and wandering aimlessly in the darkness of atheism, Pakistan wants to become the lighthouse showing a beacon of light.

Maulana Shabbir Ahmad Usmani[1]

One of the truisms in Partition historiography is that the *ulama* were totally committed to the idea of an undivided India and hence were the Congress party's natural allies. In this regard, Deobandi *ulama* have been singled out for espousing a composite nationalism of all Indians ranged against British Raj. What has however remained unexplored is the significant role played by a critical section of the Deobandi *ulama* in drumming up popular support for Pakistan. This section broke away from the JUH on the eve of the 1945 elections and started their own organization the *Jamiatul Ulama-i-Islam* (JUI) in order to support the ML's election campaign.[2] This new group vigorously countered the JUH's critiques of Pakistan and claimed that a sovereign Pakistan would not just be viable but emerge as the largest and most powerful Islamic state in the world. These *ulama* defended ML's track record as the true representative organization of Indian Muslims, lionized Jinnah's personal integrity and political sagacity and also adumbrated the benefits that Pakistan would confer on even minority provinces Muslims such as those in U.P. But most importantly, besides denouncing the JUH slogan of *Muttahida Qaumiyat*, they provided ML a much needed set of theological justifications for creating the Islamic state of Pakistan. The most notable feature of this collaboration was the growing symbiosis and a marked osmosis of ideas between the ML and the *ulama*. As the election campaign unfolded, the ML leadership increasingly deployed Islamic imagery

1 Shabbir Ahmad Usmani, *Roshni ka Minar* (Multan, 1950), 6. Speech in the Pakistan Constituent Assembly on the occasion of the passage of the Objectives Resolution.

2 It came to be known as the *Jadid* (new) *Jamiat ul Ulama* as opposed to the *Qadeem* (old) *Jamiat ul Ulama*.

to describe Pakistan while the *ulama* liberally borrowed the former's vocabulary of modern politics to make their case for a separate Pakistan. A new political vocabulary intertwining both religious and secular arguments thus emerged that was commonly used by both the *ulama* and the ML elite to rouse popular enthusiasm for Pakistan.

Founding the *Jamiatul Ulama-i-Islam*

The *ulama* from U.P. did not wait for the ML to send them a formal invitation and instead took the lead in offering their services as soon as the Viceroy announced the dates for the elections. A grateful ML organized twenty four of these Maulanas into five groups and drafted them for campaigning through September and October, nearly two months before the polling dates. It demarcated specific parts of U.P. to these groups for doing propaganda work.[3] The party took adequate care to make sure that the *ulama* selected for the task were agreeable to all the factions in the party. The only suggestion that the ML gave to these committed deputations of *ulama* was to focus upon the idea of Pakistan as the birthright of the Indian Muslims and desist from touching upon any local issues. As their campaign gained momentum, they gathered support from their counterparts from Badayun and Bareily.[4] These U.P.-based *ulama* also moved decisively to set up a countrywide organization of their own to support the ML at the polls. The new organization sought to maintain its own independence and keep a distance from the factional strife within the ML. A conference was convened at Calcutta in late October in this regard,

3 The first group consisting of Maulana Hasrat Mohani (leader), Maulana Abdul Barakat, Mulla Abdus Samad Moqtadiri, and Maulana Ghulam Mustafa was responsible for campaigning in Basti, Gorakhpur, Azamgarh, Ghazipur, Ballia, Jaunpur, Benares and Mirzapur in eastern U.P. The second group with Maulana Jamal Mian (leader), Maulana Abdul Wahid Usmani, Maulana Shahibul Hasnain and Maulana Mohammad Hashim toured Bijnor, Bareily, Moradabad, Shahjahanpur, Pilibhit, Sitapur, Lakhimpur and Badayun in northwestern U.P. The third group with Maulana Abdul Hamid (leader), Maulana Sibghatullah, Maulana Azad Samdhani and Maulana Ibn-i-Hasan toured Gonda, Bahraich, Barabanki, Faizabad, Sultanpur, Unnao, Rae Bareily and Hardoi. The fourth group with Maulana Karam Ali (leader), Maulana Abdul Majid, Moulvi Mehdi Hasan Khan and Qazi Mohammad Ilyas toured Allahabad, Fatehpur, Kanpur, Etawah, Farrukhabad, Mainpuri, Etah, Aligarh and Bulandshahr. The fifth and final group with Maulvi Maudud Ahmad (leader), Maulvi Sharihuddin and Maulvi Mohammad Nasim toured Jhansi, Jalaun, Hamirpur and Banda. See *The Pioneer*, 21 September 1945.

4 See the statement of Jamal Mian that most of the *ulama* of Deoband, Farangi Mahal, Badayun and Bareily, were with the ML. *The Pioneer*, 6 July 1945.

which was blessed by Shabbir Ahmad Usmani, a senior and reputed *alim* from Deoband. His followers from U.P. came to occupy important positions in the new organization.[5] The conference was attended by nearly 5000 *ulama* from across the country. At the outset, the meeting declared that the *ulama* were against 'the evils of Gandhism, Communism, and Godless politics of Kemalism called Laicism or secularization of the state and economy and divorce of life from the Universal moral laws of the Shariat'.[6] It assured Jinnah of its 'love and sympathy' for him and exhorted the *mashaikh* and *ulama* to support the ML in its battle for Pakistan in the forthcoming elections. The ML responded in kind with Nawab Ismail Khan sending a message to the conference in his capacity as the Chairman of the Committee of Action, assuring the *ulama* that the ML recognized 'the leadership of the ulama in matters of religion and Shariat.'[7]

The political section of the JUI in its resolutions made it clear that since Pakistan would be an Islamic state, the *ulama* needed to have a greater role in passing legislation, administering law, besides regulating Muslim religious and cultural life. It demanded restoration of the institution of *Shaikhul Islam* 'to act as the ecclesiastic head of the Muslim *Millat*', and the office of the Grand Mufti working under the direction of the *Shaikhul Islam* for guiding and regulating Islamic *Qazi* courts all over India like the ones that had been in existence in India before their abolition by the British in 1864. These *Qazi* courts were to be invested with 'full authority to adjudicate cases of every recognized Muslim sect according to its own school of *Fiqh* or law' and enforce the decisions of these courts. The JUI also demanded the establishment of an Islamic *Baitul Mal* 'with statutory authority to administer *Zakat, Sadaqat,* Muslim charities and escheats, and Muslim communal properties belonging to the Muslim community as a whole, and to manage the public finances of the Millat.' The other statutory offices it wanted included the *Nizamat-i-Auqaf Islamia* (Directorate of Islamic Endowments) to protect and manage Islamic Waqfs, a *Nizamat Maarif Islamia* (Directorate of Muslim Education) to protect and promote Islamic culture

5 The U.P. was well represented in the working committee of the Jamiatul Ulama-i-Islam. Besides Shabbir Ahmad Usmani the President, it included, Jamal Mian of Farangi Mahal, Prof. Syed Zafrul Hasan of Aligarh, Maulana Sibghatullah of Farangi Mahal, Maulana Mohammad Tahir Sahib of Nanauta, Mohammad Zahid Qasmi of Deoband, Maulana Shah Abu Lais of Ghazipur, and Maulana Zafar Ahmad Usmani from Thana Bhawan. *Star of India*, 31 October 1945.

6 *Dawn*, 18 October 1945.

7 Ibid.

and Muslim education and finally a *Diwan us Shariat* to guide legislatures and Muslim communal life in matters concerning the *Shariah* and Islamic culture. The JUI made it clear that no Bill or measure legislative or executive, which concerned the *Shariah*, should be 'moved, passed or enforced unless it was discussed and approved by the *Diwan*.'[8]

The social and cultural section of the conference passed a number of resolutions championing the cause of Islam as a total ideology and condemned all modern 'isms' for having enslaved the human mind including 'capitalism, socialism and racial fascism.' It further welcomed the recommendations of AIML Planning Committee, lauding it for adhering to the principles of Islam and steering clear of both capitalism and communism. It also urged Muslims to purge the *Qaum* of evils that had crept in due to intermingling with 'anti-Islamic' communities. Warning Muslims against caste and class divisions and racial *biradari* organizations that had insidiously entered into Muslim society from '*Manushastric Varnashrama Dharma*', it alleged that they were being encouraged by the enemies of Islam to break the solidarity of the Muslim community. The conference, in an economic resolution, also resolved to save Muslim labouring classes from the clutches of Hindu capitalists and moneylenders.[9]

The JUI finally adopted an organizational charter (*Nizamnama*) to organize its branches in every town, district, province and state, which would be affiliated to the central office at Calcutta. The charter made it clear that the JUI did not wish to supplant the ML as the sole representative organization of the Indian Muslims but saw its role more in terms of guiding it in matters pertaining to religion and the *Shariah* and 'to work for the regeneration of the Muslim nation on Islamic lines.' Clearly aware of factional strife in the ML, the charter declared that 'the root of all evil in a democracy was self-seeking.' It, therefore, asked all its members to avoid power politics. Members were further enjoined to desist from canvassing for positions in the organization and told that seeking positions was contrary to the Prophet's injunctions. The organization's constitution, therefore, laid down a rule that anyone guilty of canvassing for office would automatically be disqualified from election to any office in the JUI.[10]

The JUI further decided to give battle to the JUH at its own citadel of the *Darul Uloom* at Deoband that was under the control of Maulana Husain

---

8 *Star of India*, 2 November 1945; also *Dawn*, 25 November 1945.

9 *Star of India*, 5 November 1945.

10 *Star of India*, 21 November 1945.

Ahmad Madani and his allies.[11] It, therefore, formed a committee of *ulama* and donors of the *Darul Uloom* to go to Deoband and argue against the policies of the current management.[12] The deputation consisted of men like Haji Mohammad Husain MLC of Bengal, who after the Nizam of Hyderabad was the biggest financial donor of the school.[13] This deputation met with the *Majlis-i-Shura* of the *Darul Uloom* to argue against the 'anti-*millat* activities' of the teachers and students of the school.[14] It demanded that the institution either stay aloof from politics or at least not side with the 'Hindu Congress'. To substantiate its claims, it pointed to previous instances of disciplinary action against teachers when they had hurt the sentiments of even a section of the Muslim community, as the institution was the common property of all Muslims. It contended that the activities of the *Darul Uloom's* students as Congress workers constituted a breach of trust and amounted to misappropriation of funds since Muslims all over the country donated money to the school to enable students to obtain religious education. Such political activities were thus inconsistent with those aims. The *shura* after hearing these arguments initially ruled that it would take cognizance of the matter and give it its full consideration. But subsequently, it ruled that staff and students of the *Darul Uloom* had the fullest freedom to take active part in politics, thus revealing the dominance of the Madani party in the institution.

Shabbir Ahmad Usmani and the Idea of Pakistan

The *alim* who provided the JUI with its ideological moorings and campaigned vigorously for the ML through the length and breadth of India during the election campaign was Maulana Shabbir Ahmad Usmani. He was born in 1887 in Bijnor, one of eleven children to Maulana Fazlur Rahman Usmani, a product of Delhi College who worked as a Deputy Inspector of Schools in the provincial Education Department. Saiyyid Mahboob Rizvi in his two volume history of Deoband tells us that Fazlur Rahman was a close associate of Maulana Nanautavi and among the founding members of the *Darul Uloom*, remaining a

---

11 *Star of India*, 5 November 1945.

12 *Star of India*, 26 December 1945.

13 Other members of the committee were Maulana Musleh-ud-din, President of JUI Mymensinh, Maulana Mohammad Yusuf and Maulana Zafar Ahmad Ansari.

14 *Dawn*, 3 January 1945.

member of its *Majlis-i-Shura* till his death in 1907.[15] Among Shabbir Ahmad's brothers, Habibur Rahman became a Vice Chancellor of the *Darul Uloom*[16] while Azizur Rahman became the Grand Mufti, serving as the head of the *fatwa* department at Deoband from its inception in1892 for nearly three decades.[17]

As regards Shabbir Ahmad himself, his earliest biographers tell us that this future ideologue of Pakistan was extremely serious and studious as a child, averse to playfulness or roaming around in the jungles with his friends.[18] Sent to Deoband as a youth to study the Islamic sciences, his teachers included stalwarts such as *Shaikhul Hind* Maulana Mahmudul Hasan, Maulana Obeidullah Sindhi and Maulana Barkatullah Bhopali. Highly regarded by his teachers for his intellect and subtle insights into philosophical problems, his piety too was evident by this time, for the same biographers tell us that after his studies during the day he would stay up all night praying. It induced his worried mother to successfully petition Mahmudul Hasan to intercede with her son so that his health would not be adversely affected. After finishing his studies at Deoband in 1907, Usmani was appointed head teacher of the Fatehpuri madrasa in Delhi. He, however, returned to Deoband in 1910 where he became famous for his lectures on the *hadith* Sahih Muslim. He also wrote a highly regarded commentary on it in Arabic from the Hanafite point of view titled *Fath al Mulhim*, which was published in three volumes by the government of the Nizam of Hyderabad and won praise in the pages of the Egyptian journal *Al Manar*. Young Usmani was politically active as well, collecting funds for the Turkish government during the Balkan War in 1914. He also became a prominent member of the JUH and worked actively for it during the Mahatma led Khilafat Movement. While he preached Hindu–Muslim unity at this time, a biographer notes that he did not go overboard like the Ali brothers asking Muslims to eschew cow slaughter.[19]

When his teacher Maulana Mahmudul Hasan died in 1921, Usmani

15 Sayyid Mahboob Rizvi, *History of the Dar al Uloom Deoband*, translated into English by Prof. Murtaz Husain and F. Qureshi, (Deoband, 1981), Vol. 2, 68–71

16 Ibid.

17 Muhammad Qasim Zaman, *Modern Islamic Thought in a Radical Age* (Cambridge, 2012), 179.

18 Faiz Ambalvi and Shafiq Siddiqi, *Hayat-i-Shaikhul Islam Shabbir Ahmad Usmani* (Lahore, 1949).

19 Mohammad Anvarul Hasan Sherkoti (ed.), *Khutbat-i-Usmani: Shaikhul Islam Maulana Shabbir Ahmad Usmani ke Milli, Siyasi aur Nazariya-i-Pakistan se Mutalliq Alamanah Khutbat, Maktubat, aur Mukalimat ka Majmua* (Lahore, 1972).

completed his translation of the Quran which became very famous under the title *Tafsir-i-Usmani*. Later, Usmani's supporters would pointedly note that the family of Mahmudul Hasan had chosen him instead of Maulana Husain Ahmad Madani for completing this project, thus indicating which of his two students the *Shaikhul Hind* deemed more worthy. Usmani quit Deoband for the first time in 1928 along with his celebrated friend and fellow disciple of Mahmudul Hasan, Maulana Anwar Shah Kashmiri following differences with the management at Deoband. Appointed as the chief teacher of Hadith at Dabhail after Anwar Shah's death in 1932, he returned to Deoband in 1935 on the request of Maulana Ashraf Ali Thanawi and was appointed Vice Chancellor by the *majlis-i-shura* of the *Darul Uloom*. In 1940 soon after the Lahore Resolution, he tried to bring together Jinnah and the Deobandi *ulama* controlling the JUH who were opposed to him and his Pakistan demand but their meetings did not result in any breakthrough. Usmani himself developed misgivings over the aggressive support given by Maulana Husain Ahmad Madani and his followers to the Congress and again left Deoband along with a number of his students for Dabhail in 1943. He resigned from the JUH in 1945 and started the rival JUI, which came out in open support of the ML and its Pakistan demand.

The formal break came with the formation of the JUI at a conference in Calcutta in October 1945. Usmani did not attend this conference due to ill health but his *khutba-i-sadarat* was read by Maulana Matin, one of his *murids* at Deoband.[20] The speech was translated by turns into both Bengali and Gujarati. Usmani later went on to campaign for the ML all over India during the 1945–46 elections. In his public speeches, Usmani vigorously and consistently supported the idea of Pakistan and designated the ML as the only organization that could take Muslims to their ideal goal. Usmani's importance to the ML can be gauged from the fact that he was asked to preside over the ML session held in Meerut in December 1945, the first such session after its resounding triumph in the first round of elections. From now on, Usmani was invited to all crucial meetings of the Council of the AIML as well as those of the working committee.

Usmani elaborated his vision of Pakistan in a series of speeches in support of the ML that he eloquently delivered at various election meetings. They provide important insights into the thinking of a group of *ulama* aligned

20 *Khutba-i-Sadarat*, Calcutta Session, 26–28, October 1945, Mohammad Ali Park, Calcutta, in Sherkoti (ed.), *Khutbat-i-Usmani*, 73.

to the ML whose role was greatly influential during the 1945–46 elections. Contrary to the existing historiography, which has set up an overall opposition between conservative *ulama* on the one hand and the modernist, westernized politicians of the ML on the other, a perusal of Usmani's speeches reveals that there was little difference between the thinking of these two groups regarding Pakistan. Both of them broadly articulated Pakistan as a sovereign state to be established according to the principles of the Quran and the *Shariah*, which at the same time would also be a modern state. Neither saw the Islamic state as materializing immediately after the establishment of Pakistan, seeing it instead as an evolutionary process happening over time. More importantly, they borrowed concepts from each other and forged a common vocabulary in their descriptions of Pakistan. Thus, while Jinnah and other ML leaders freely talked about the establishment of an Islamic state in Pakistan, Usmani too provided not just religious or theological rationale for creating Pakistan, but justified it in non-religious, secular terms providing economic, political, social and military arguments in a manner reminiscent of Jinnah and his lieutenants in the ML. An analysis of Usmani's rhetoric thus provides a fascinating overview of the messages communicated to the Muslim voters of U.P. during this referendum on Pakistan.

Pakistan as the New Medina

Usmani glorified Pakistan as the first Islamic state in history that would attempt to reconstruct the Islamic utopia created by the Prophet in Medina. He constantly used Pakistan and Medina interchangeably to solidify their identification in the public mind. Usmani explained Pakistan's global historical significance by invoking powerful metaphors from early Islamic history. He pointed out that instead of establishing Pakistan in his native Mecca, the Prophet had migrated to Medina to establish the first Pakistan. The Prophet's decision, he asserted, was based on his conviction that Pakistan could only be established in an area where Muslims could practice their religion with complete freedom, for it was only in such a land that the Muslim community could develop to its fullest potentiality. Given the unrelenting hostility to his teaching among influential sections of Meccan society, this would not have been possible in Mecca, thus compelling the *Hijra*. Usmani consequently argued that an Islamic state resembling Medina could never be established in an undivided post-British India even with extensive devolution of powers to the provinces, since the Hindus would always control power at the federal centre due to their numerical majority. Pakistan, therefore, needed to be a separate, sovereign Islamic state where Muslims could live under the *Shariah* and free from non-Islamic control.

Usmani outlined Pakistan's significance to Islam by declaring that it would be the first step in the process of self-purification of Muslims in the modern age, purging them of their earlier narrow identities based on race, class, sect, language and region and creating an equal brotherhood of Islam, as had happened thirteen hundred years earlier at Medina. He pointed to the many resemblances between the unity that had developed between various Arab tribes comprising the first followers of the Prophet and the dramatic solidarity that had become evident among Indian Muslims in the struggle for Pakistan. He, therefore, declared that just as Medina was created due to the hard work and close cooperation between the *muhajirin* (migrants from Mecca) and the *ansar* (helpers in Medina), Pakistan would similarly come into existence due to the close cooperation between Muslims from 'minority provinces' such as U.P. and the inhabitants of the Pakistan areas. Thanking the former for their great sacrifices for the cause of Pakistan even while they were aware that their current homelands would remain outside this new Medina, he assured them that their sacrifices would not go in vain. Invoking a glorious chapter from Islamic history, he declared that just as Medina had provided a base for the eventual victory of Islam in Arabia, Pakistan would pave the way for the triumphal return of Islam as the ruling power over the entire subcontinent. The whole of Hindustan would thus be turned into Pakistan just as the Prophet himself had turned all of Arabia into Pakistan.[21] Indeed, Arabia itself, Usmani declared, became the Pakistan of the entire world after the annexation of Mecca by the Muslims. Consecration of Pakistan's territory as a modern powerful Medina, taking care of both material and spiritual concerns of Muslims, effectively crushed competing narratives that sought to make a case for an undivided India by claiming superior sacredness for Muslim lands in the 'minority provinces'.

Usmani deepened Pakistan's significance by declaring that its creation had always been destined. He pointed to Pakistan's hidden indication (*Pakistan ka ghaibi ishaara*) in the way the Muslim population was distributed in the subcontinent. Arguing that this was a sign of Allah's unfathomable wisdom, he pointed out that instead of being a uniform minority all over the country,

---

21 *Hamara Pakistan, Khutba-i-Sadarat Punjab Jamiatul Ulama Conference*, Lahore, 25–27 January, 1946, (Hyderabad, 1946), 28.

the Muslims were in a majority in some provinces that were also pivotal from a geographical point of view.[22] He referred to other significant signs indicating Allah's secret design regarding Pakistan, in his speech at Lahore, the capital of the Punjab and the putative heart of Pakistan.[23] It was from Lahore, Usmani declared, that Shaikh Ahmad Sirhindi had launched his *jihad* against the Emperor Akbar's *Muttahida Qaumiyat* and *Din-i-Illahi* and again at Lahore that the Pakistan Resolution was passed in 1940. Connecting the earlier *jihad* of Shaikh Ahmad Sirhindi to the new one started by the ML, Usmani declared that

> It is possible that in his (Sirhindi's) revelations there may be a pointer in this direction that when in the future, Muttahida Qaumiyat in another form arises, when Din-i-Illahi in the form of Gandhism comes to the fore, it will be Lahore from where the voice for breaking these new idols would issue forth, spread and flourish.

Quranic Origins of the Two-nation Theory and the Unity of Indian Muslims

Like his *Pir* Maulana Ashraf Ali Thanawi and many other ML stalwarts before him, Usmani put the ML's two-nation theory beyond the pale of critique by arguing that it was not the invention of any man and that its origins lay in the Quran. While acknowledging that the world was currently classified on the basis of *watan* (homeland), *nasl* (race), *zabaan* (language), or *tamaddun* (culture), he reminded his listeners that the final prophecy brought by the Prophet had deemed that the only valid classification for ordering humankind was that between the *Momin* (Believer) and the *Kafir* (Infidel). Usmani underlined the special importance and uniqueness of the Prophet's final prophecy by pointing out that even before his arrival, the division between *Iman* (faith) and *Kufr* (unbelief) had always been present. In the pre-Islamic era, God sent Prophets before Muhammad to particular communities and their apostleship, therefore, could not wipe out the distinctions between different communities. The uniqueness of the Prophet of Islam lay in that his Prophecy was not limited to or by any *mulk* (country), *khandan* (family), *zabaan* (language), or *makaan* (house) but was universal and hence able to wipe out all myriad small identities that people in their ignorance and narrow mindedness had made the touchstone

---

22 Sherkoti, *Khutbat-i-Usmani*, 76.

23 *Hamara Pakistan*, 9.

of their distinctiveness. Usmani here introduced a local metaphor in order to make his message clearer. He pointed out that in India there were big and small rivers such as the Ganga, Yamuna and Narmada that had their own distinct identities. However, beyond a point these identities merged themselves into the larger identity of the ocean. In the same way, distinctions based on community, class and race may have existed earlier, but falling into the ocean of Islam, they joined in the formation of such a nation where all their previous distinctions and differentiations ended. Usmani reminded his fellow Muslims that the description of the 'great Islamic nationality' was present in the Hadith *Sahih Muslim* on which he had written a highly regarded commentary. As he noted

> It has been stated in this Hadith, that when the Prophet asked his flock what *qaum* are you, they did not reply that they were Hejazi, Yemeni, Najdi or Qureshi. All said in unison that they were Muslim. The arrival of Islam therefore meant the all the idols of *watani* and *nasli asabiyat* broke down and all that remained was their Islamic identity.

The Indian Muslims too constituted a distinct nation and to deny this fact about the ten crore sons of Islam in India was thus a grave lie.[24] The Muslims of India, he claimed, had always carried the 'revelation' of their separate nationality (*judagana qaumiyat*) in their hearts and never gave it a second thought until the Congress introduced its theory of *Muttahida Qaumiyat* with much fanfare.[25]

Usmani proceeded to demolish the theory of *Muttahida Qaumiyat* propagated by Maulana Husain Ahmad Madani, which stressed the composite nationality of all Indians be they Hindus or Muslims. Calling it false and anti-Islamic, he noted that even their common teacher Maulana Mahmudul Hasan had talked of Hindus and Muslims as two separate nations just nine days before his death.[26] But the strength of his critique lay in countering Madani's interpretation of the pact between Jews and Muslims, the presumed bedrock of *Muttahida Qaumiyat*. Following the lead earlier given by Thanawi, Usmani clarified that under the original treaty between the Prophet and the Jews, the term *qaum wahida*, as suggested by Madani, had never been used to designate Muslims and Jews as one single community. Even when the term *ummah wahida* was used, the Prophet had always given a cautionary warning that this application was only an extension, a broad interpretation that was valid only under certain

24 *Khutba-i-Sadarat*, Calcutta, 1945, in Sherkoti (ed.), *Khutbat-i-Usmani*.

25 *Hamara Pakistan*, 9.

26 Ibid., 10.

conditions. But most importantly the Prophet had explicitly declared that in case of a dispute between Jews and Muslims, the resolution of the dispute could happen only through the final judgment delivered by Allah and His Messenger. Usmani, therefore, pointedly asked the nationalist *ulama* whether the votaries of *Muttahida Qaumiyat* in the Congress would be willing to accept the condition that the Quran be the final word in disputes between Muslims and the Hindus.

Usmani declared that the theory of *Muttahida Qaumiyat* was also suspect because it was a favourite catchphrase of the Congress and used extensively by the Hindu press. Who could, Usmani asked, believe the tender solicitousness of Hindus for the welfare of Muslims?[27] Here he quoted the poet Akbar Illahabadi to drive home his point about the subordinate role played by the JUH in the service of the mighty Congress party and this ideal.

Unhi ke matlab ki keh raha hoon, Zabaan meri hai baat unki.
Unhi ki mehfil saja raha hoon, Chiraagh mera hai, raat unki
Sune jo isko usey taraddud, Jo isko dekhe usey tahayyur
Hamari neki aur unki barkat, amal hamaara najaat unki.

(I speak about things that matter to them, the tongue is mine, but the words are theirs.
I set up their party, the lamp is mine, but the night is theirs.
He who listens to this may be perturbed, he who beholds this may be surprised
Ours is the goodness and theirs is the grace, ours is the effort and theirs is the freedom.)

Usmani warned fellow Muslims that the Hindus were financing nationalist Muslims to the tune of lakhs of rupees and Muslim organizations such as the JUH were putting enormous amount of work for them in return. However, it was the Congress and the Hindus who would in the end realize the fruits of their hard labour. There were only two paths open for the Muslims – that of Islam or that of *kufr*. The JUI represented the path of Islam while the Congress and its allies were the forces of *kufr*. There was no third way.[28] Usmani thus concluded that the theory of *Muttahida Qaumiyat* was a ploy to enthrone the Hindus as the dominant force in India due to their numerical majority in the

27 Sherkoti, *Khutbat-i-Usmani*, 173; *Khutba-i-Sadarat*, AIML Meerut session, December, 1945.

28 Usmani did refer to the path suggested by the JUH as similar to the 'neutralist' third path of the Mutazila, but then asserted that it was a non-existent path since the Mutazila thankfully no longer existed and Allah was certainly not going to bring them back to life.

country, for under this theory, all ten crore Muslims of India would be forced to perpetually live on the tender mercies of the Hindus.[29] No Muslim could, therefore, support such a pernicious ideology.

Pakistan as an Islamic State

Having fashioned theological justifications for the Muslim nation, Usmani argued that this nation required its own centre (*mustaqil markaz*).[30] Such a centre, he maintained, needed to be established in an area where Muslims were in a majority and could live under their own God given laws (*khudaai qanoon*) in total freedom, backed by the requisite material resources. In this context, Usmani underlined the distinct identity of the Islamic state. It was the establishment of Islamic laws that distinguished an Islamic state from other states (or even a Muslim state) and gave the former its defining character. Thus, *Dar al Islam* or the Islamic state was one where the government was under Muslim control and its laws were Islamic. The *Dar al Harb*, on the other hand, fulfilled neither of these conditions. But more importantly, he declared that the defining characteristic of the *Dar al Harb* was not the lack of Muslim control over government, but the lack of Islamic laws governing the land. Usmani, however, did not go into any great detail about the kind of Islamic laws that he envisaged for Pakistan. In fact he warned that an Islamic state implementing Islamic laws could not materialize overnight. It could only emerge through a process of gradual evolution. As Usmani noted

> Just like the night withdraws slowly and the light of the day spreads, just like an old chronic patient takes a step towards health and does not at once become healthy, in the same way, Pakistan is a step in the direction of our national health (*qaumi sehat*), towards our high noon (*nisfun nihar*); but a gradual step (*tadriji kadam*).[31]

In order to defend this approach, he pointed out that even the Pakistan that the Prophet inaugurated in Medina had reached its crest (*hadd-i-kamal*) only in a gradual way. The Prophet, he argued, could have crushed his enemies in an instant and established Pakistan immediately, but then the demand of *Hukumat-i-Illahiya* (God's Government) was such that the *ummah* had to

---

29 *Khutba-i-Sadarat*, AIML Meerut Session, 171.

30 Sherkoti, *Khutbat-i-Usmani*, 76; *Khutba-i-Sadarat*, Calcutta.

31 *Hamara Pakistan*, 26.

arrive at it gradually receiving guidance from the Prophet at every step.[32] He, therefore, cautioned that nobody should labour under the impression that in the Pakistan areas a pure Quranic government could be established immediately. However, Usmani promised that Pakistan would certainly be the first step in the eventual establishment of such an Islamic state.

Usmani's theory of the gradual development of the Islamic state in Pakistan dovetailed neatly with the declared aims of Jinnah and the ML leadership. The significance of Usmani's gradualist approach lay in the fact that it left enough room for deliberation and negotiation in the process of establishing of an Islamic state in the future. While Usmani expected the *ulama* to have an influential voice in this process, it still kept the field open for various Muslim groups in Pakistan to discuss the shape of the constitution that would eventually govern them. This approach was in stark contrast to the far more conservative views on Islamic state held by the JUH *ulama* who claimed that there was no necessity to formulate any fresh laws in such a state since the Quran already contained all necessary laws for humankind, and no human being could in any case modify God-given laws. Usmani, therefore, was no fundamentalist demanding a literal reading of the Quran and strict implementation of Quranic law as it existed, but a pragmatist who understood the complexity involved in the process of bringing an Islamic state into existence.

Besides advocating a gradualist approach, Usmani took an astonishingly modern view of the Islamic state by cautioning Pakistani enthusiasts that the practical expression of Islamic law in such a state could, at best, only partially recover the principles of justice and freedom that existed in Islam, further extending the common ground between the *ulama* and the ML elite. He, however, expressed his firm belief that it would still be a matchless law (*bemisaal qanoon*) which would be an example to the whole world. Indeed, Pakistan would provide practical expression to the excellence of the Quranic State for it would be based on justice (*insaf*), tolerance (*ravadari*), compassion (*rehmat*) and peace (*aman*).[33] Unlike the Congress governments whose atrocities on Muslims were known and had been reported in the *Manshoor* and the *Dawn*,[34] Pakistan would be just and equitable towards all its citizens. Indeed, before long, Hindustan itself would dearly wish to have a system of government like Pakistan.[35]

32 Ibid., 14.

33 Ibid., 24

34 Ibid., 22

35 Ibid., 28

Defence of ML Leadership and Participation in the ML

Usmani stoutly defended the ML leadership and particularly Jinnah, while at the same time debunking JUH propaganda that portrayed the ML leadership as atheist, westernized and comprised mostly of self-serving Rajas, Nawabs and title holders. At the outset, he acknowledged that the ML and its leaders had weaknesses and shortcomings that were objectionable in the eyes of the *ulama*. He went so far as to call Jinnah a *fasiq* (sinner) and noted that the *ulama* were aware of the *fasq-o-fujoor* (sinfulness and debauchery) of the ML leaders. He also conceded that the reputation of the ML leaders was preventing a number of religious minded Muslims (*deendar*) from joining the ML. In this context, Usmani confessed that he himself had joined the ML after prolonged deliberation prayer and a close reading of the Quran, the *Sunna* and Hanafi law. Usmani singled out the clarification provided by the Hanafi jurist Ibn-i-Hasan Shaybani in his book *Al Siyar al Kabir* for providing him with the mental breakthrough and removing any doubts about joining the ML.[36] It pertained to Shaybani's view of the *Khawarij* (Kharijites) and their relationship to the Muslims. Usmani noted that in the Hadiths *Sahih Bukhari* and *Sahih Muslim*, the Prophet himself is supposed to have declared that the *Khawarij* were in the black books of Allah since they had been Muslims in the beginning but then had turned into *Kafirs*. The Prophet had, therefore, advised his followers to kill the *Khawarij* for their apostasy, wherever they encountered them. For Usmani, Shaybani's brilliance lay in the fact that he came up with an alternative view regarding the *Khawarij* and the way Muslims should deal with them. This medieval jurist decreed that in case the *Khawarij* were fighting *Moshreks* or the *Kafirs*, it was the duty of the Muslims to support the *Khawarij* in these battles.[37] This was because the *Khawarij*, though despicable, still upheld the *Kalimah* as against the *Moshreks* and the *Kafirs* who were fundamentally opposed to the *Kalimah*. The ML too had its share of *Khawarij*, noted Usmani, but since the party was fighting the *Moshreks*, it was vital to support this organization.[38]

36 Sherkoti, op. cit., 175; *Khutba-i-Sadarat, Meerut.*

37 Ibid.

38 The *Siyar* has been characterized as the Islamic Law of Nations, which arose in response to the question of how to deal with non-Islamic states and non-Muslim communities within Islamic territories. The *Siyar* is not a separate body of law but considered an extension of the *Shariah*. Shaybani who died in 804A.D was a disciple of Abu Hanifa the founder of the Hanafi School of law. This magnum opus is reported to have so impressed the Caliph Harun al Rashid that he ordered his two sons Al Amin and Al Mamun to study it under Shaybani's guidance. Shaybani has, therefore, been hailed as

If Usmani acknowledged the shortcomings of the ML leadership and criticized them, he also gave the devil his due. Thus, he asserted that whatever might be his faults, it was undeniable that Jinnah was personally incorruptible, unbending and could not be bought over by money and would in any case be always better for the Muslims than Gandhi or Nehru. Harshly criticizing the labelling of Jinnah as *Kafir-i-Azam* by his opponents in the JUH, Usmani declared that Jinnah's opponents were not in a position to criticize him given their own immodesty, since the JUH and nationalist Muslim stalwarts had assumed grandiose titles such as *Imam-i-Azam* and *Mufti-i-Azam* without really deserving them.[39] He also reminded fellow Muslims that the ML may have started as an undesirable organization in the past but it had, over time, evolved and transformed itself.[40] In this regard, he noted that the Congress party too had started in a manner similar to the ML, but then it too had transformed itself over time. In making these arguments, Usmani again echoed Ashraf Ali Thanawi who publicly took on the nationalist *ulama* during the years of Congress cabinet governments.

While contemplating the existing state of affairs in the ML, Usmani blamed the *ulama* for its current condition. The problems in the ML, he argued, were as much due to the aloofness and withdrawal of reformers (*muslehin*) and their hostility (*nibard azmai*) towards the ML leaders as to the ignorance and carelessness (*bekhabri aur laparwahi*) of the ML leadership. If indeed capable *ulama* joined the ML and corrected these mistakes, many of the objectionable things for which the party was now being criticized would have been minimized or even eliminated. Usmani however comforted his followers by declaring that the number of such dubious leaders (*batil parast*) in the ML was very minute (*ashr-i-ashir*).[41] Time had, therefore, come for the *ulama* to join the ML in large numbers in order to help cleanse the party of its sinners, rather than join the

---

the Muslim Hugo Grotius by the German scholar Joseph Hammer von Purgstall. An edition of the *Siyar* was published in three volumes in 1916 by the Government of the Nizam of Hyderabad, and almost certainly must have been the text which Usmani would have read. See Majid Khadduri, *The Islamic Law of Nations: Shaybani's Siyar* (Baltimore, 1966).

39 Among the titles given to Usmani by his murids and admirers was Sheikhul Islam. This was also the title by which Madani was known, suggesting a personal rivalry between the two men. Usmani also had among his titles *Janasheen Sheikhul Hind* and *Janasheen Qasmi* or the beloved of both Maulana Mahmoodul Hasan and Maulana Mohammad Qasim Nanautavi respectively.

40 Sherkoti, op. cit., 77 *Khutba-i-Sadarat*, Calcutta.

41 Sherkoti, *Khutbat-i-Usmani*, 175; *Khutba-i-Sadarat* Meerut Conference.

enemy Congress. This was also a moment for all practicing Muslims to join the ML so that they could influence the character of the party and bring it more in line with the beliefs of practicing Muslims. Together, the people and the *ulama* had to be vigilant and compel the ML leaders to acquit themselves sincerely in the positions of trust that they occupied in the premier organization of the Indian Muslims. In this regard, he also observed that ever since larger number of Muslims had been joining the ML, its leaders had indeed been conducting themselves with a greater sense of responsibility.

Usmani, however, emphasized the continuing need for the Muslim masses to bring to the notice of their leaders in as many ways as was possible that they were only supporting the ML for the sake of protecting their religion and their true nationality (*asal qaumiyat*). The masses, therefore, needed to make it clear to the leadership that their support to the ML was not absolute and was available only under certain *Shari'i* conditions.[42] The ML leadership needed to be told in no uncertain terms that in all religious matters it would have to follow the commands of the *ulama* as the final authority. Usmani then issued an ominous notice to the ML leadership. He warned that if the party did not heed this advice the masses would not rest until they had cleared the ML of all corrupt elements (*fasid anasir*).[43] He, therefore, advised the leaders of the ML to honour the promises that they had made so repeatedly during the election campaign regarding the nature of Pakistan. He reminded them of Jinnah's Eid message to Bombay Muslims in which the *Qaid* had openly declared that the programme of the Muslims was present in the Quran and hence the ML was not going to present any new programme before the Muslim nation. He also referred to similar speeches that Jinnah had made at Karachi, Sialkot, Aligarh, Delhi and Lahore during the election campaign. The seriousness with which Usmani intended to hold down the ML leaders to their promises can be discerned from his account of a meeting he had with Jinnah.[44] With the ML having won the elections so decisively, he claimed that Jinnah had told him that his work was now over and it was up to the Muslims to elect whosoever they wanted as their leader and establish the form of government that they most desired. This position was of course was in conformity with some of Jinnah's own public pronouncements. Usmani responded by stating that the *Qaid's* task was not yet complete and would be completed only after Islamic laws had been

---

42 Ibid., 77, *Khutba-i-Sadarat*, Calcutta.

43 Ibid., 78.

44 Sherkoti, *Khutbat-i-Usmani*, 233, Speech at Peshawar, 29 June 1947.

established in Pakistan. He also reminded Jinnah about the election promises that he and fellow ML leaders such as Liaquat Ali Khan had made in this regard and urged him to fulfill them. Usmani ended his story by noting that Jinnah promised to promulgate Islamic laws within two months of Pakistan coming into existence.

Taking into account all these circumstances, Usmani concluded that it was imperative for Muslims to unite under the ML's banner for only then would they be able to attain the goal of Pakistan. He darkly warned that if they missed this opportunity, they would be doomed for a long time to come. This was after all the first time in the history of the subcontinent that Muslims had gathered in such large numbers under one flag – no ordinary thing and indeed a sign of divine favour. They needed to take advantage of this special moment and get over their individual differences. In this context, he also warned that there was no greater crime than creating splits in the Muslim community (*tafriq al muslimeen*) at such a time as this when the fate of the entire community was at stake.

Individual Virtue and Pakistan

Usmani's exhortation about upholding moral probity as taught by Islam was not limited to just the leaders of the ML. He also gave the same advice to the masses involved in the struggle for Pakistan. Arguing that history was witness to the fact that whenever Muslims had perished it was by their own hand and not because any outsider was ever able to vanquish them, he declared that if Muslims wanted to preserve their freedom it was imperative that they become pure and virtuous.[45] It is only when they became pure (*pak*), and their lives were based on the commands of the *Shariah*, that they would be able to establish a strong Pakistan. Usmani lamented that Muslims at present lived in an un-Islamic slavery in which they were free to do whatever they pleased without any sense of moral accountability. If Muslims continued to stay as they were, the independence gained with the formation of Pakistan would indeed be no independence.[46] The ML had made them *ek* (one), it was now the turn of Muslims to become *nek* (virtuous). Without virtue, Muslim unity, Usmani warned, could not last.

Usmani consequently saw Pakistan as a land that would give birth to the

[45] Ibid.

[46] Ibid., 178; *Khutba-i-Sadarat*, Meerut Conference.

revival and the rejuvenation of Islam in the subcontinent and the world at large and saw the process of struggle for Pakistan as the beginning in the struggle for self-purification of Muslims. As part of the programme of raising such pure Muslims, Usmani recommended six months of military training to all young boys once they were no longer minors. He expressed satisfaction that Nawab Ismail Khan had agreed to his proposal. As he declared, in Pakistan there would be slavery only to God. *Raqs-o-surood* (dancing and music), *sharaab-o-kabab* (wine and feasts) and the other gay accompaniments of the world would be absent. Pakistan demanded a commitment so intense that Muslims had to be ready to sacrifice their very lives for its cause.[47] He himself, he told his audience, had been praying for the last thirty years for martyrdom (*shahadat*) in the cause of Islam and Pakistan.

The Role of the *Ulama*

Given the persistent suspicion regarding the ML leadership and the insistent demand in a section of Muslim opinion that the *ulama* should assume the leadership of the Muslim masses in their current struggle, Usmani attempted to clarify the role of the *ulama* in a future Pakistan. He began by asking fellow Muslims to not be upset by reference to Jinnah as *Qaid-i-Azam* since it seemed to place him on a higher pedestal than the religious elders. He declared that the term simply meant the tallest among them in the field of politics. However, there still remained the question as to whether an *alim* could lead the Muslims better than Jinnah. Usmani answered this question with the help of a metaphor. He explained that when the famous wrestler Zabisco came to India, Gandhi was not sent to fight him. Nor were Jinnah or Maulana Husain Ahmad Madani sent to wrestle with him. Usmani himself had not been sent to challenge Zabisco. All of them had been rightly ignored and instead the Indian wrestler Gama was sent to confront Zabisco. Usmani argued that this was logical since Gama was an expert in the field of wrestling. In the same way, he pointed out that Jinnah was the best expert when it came to the question of representing Muslims during complex constitutional negotiations. Muslims, therefore, needed to be eternally grateful to Allah for giving them such a capable, honest and peerless *vakil* as Jinnah.

Usmani, however, firmly circumscribed Jinnah's role to the task of tackling the British and the Congress on constitutional negotiations. The role of the *ulama*, he

47 *Sidq*, 5 June 1946, Speech at a public meeting in Lucknow.

explained, would begin once this phase of Muslim constitutional struggle against the government and Congress was completed. Here Usmani employed another telling metaphor in order to delineate the division of labour between Jinnah and the *ulama*.[48] He noted that when Muslims from India went on Haj, they usually boarded ships skippered by an English captain. This ship carrying *hajis* on reaching the vicinity of the port of Jeddah, usually stopped well short of the port given its many treacherous shoals and underwater rocks that the English captain of the ship was not competent to negotiate. At this point, an Arab mariner known as the pilot came from the shore to the ship to take charge from the English captain and safely guide the ship to the port so that the pilgrims could disembark and step on the holy land. Mr Jinnah, Usmani concluded, was the English captain who could take the Muslims only up to a certain point. After that point, an expert in the *Shariah* was required and it is here that the *ulama* would fulfill their duties like the Arab pilot. Usmani, however, warned that the work of the Muslims could be completed only through the cooperation of these two personnel and would be unsuccessful if such cooperation was lacking. He, therefore, called for the closest possible cooperation between these two groups as they led Muslims in pursuit of their ideal goal of Pakistan.

Defending Political Tactics of the ML

Rubbishing allegations that complete independence was not the aim of the ML and that the party wanted British overlordship to continue over the subcontinent, Usmani argued that the charge was absurd since even beasts craved for freedom. Thus, even a parrot imprisoned in a cage would fly away as soon as its cage was opened. But the same parrot, he continued, would stay inside its cage even if it were open if it saw a cat keeping vigil outside it. Usmani indicated that this was the situation in which the Muslims found themselves in India. Muslims were desirous of freedom and complete independence was indeed their goal, but the presence of the Congress 'cat' prevented the Muslim 'parrot' from flying out of its cage. This was the reason they could not cooperate with the Congress in mass struggles against the Raj since their ultimate goal was that of a united India. Such cooperation would be tantamount to Muslims sacrificing themselves and their ideal of Pakistan and allowing the Hindus to become dominant in India.

Usmani contended that cooperation with the Congress was against both Islam and rationality given the existing political context in India. He rubbished

48 *Sidq*, 5 June 1946.

the nationalist Muslims' plea to Muslims to join the Congress party so that they could transform its ideology from the inside. Given its Hindu dominance, it was absurd to expect the Congress to change its mentality due to Muslim entry into its ranks. On the contrary, Usmani asserted that the ML, which the nationalist Muslims dismissed as a party of landlords and title holders and hence impossible to change, was certainly more amenable to change. If Muslims could not bring about changes in an avowedly Muslim party of *kalima* reciting Muslims, it was futile to expect them to change a non-Muslim party. What therefore mattered most for Usmani was the fact that the ML was a party of Muslims. However many mistakes it leaders may have made and whatever maybe their nature, they could always be forgiven since they were Muslims. In this regard, he pointed out Turkey had not committed any fewer crimes than other countries. Yet, whenever the question of Turkey came up, Muslims tilted towards Turkey as against non-Muslim powers because it was a Muslim country.[49]

Usmani also repudiated calls for cooperation with the Congress and defended non-cooperation with it on the basis of Islamic principles. Usmani noted that every jurist right from Imam Mohammad to Imam Tahtawi to Allama Ibn Abedin had conceded that Muslims could take help or give help to the *kafirs* (infidels) in opposition to another *qaum*. At the same time though, they had always specified that such mutual cooperation was valid only under the condition that the Muslims were in a dominant position in that alliance. Any cooperation with the Congress was therefore impossible given the fact that Muslims were not in a dominant position vis a vis the Congress. In this context, Usmani concluded that the only solution to the problem of Indian Muslims was Pakistan. He, therefore, urged all Muslims to demand Pakistan unanimously, for then their demand would surely be successful.[50]

Minority Provinces Muslims

A major issue that the JUH had raised with regard to Pakistan was the disastrous consequences it would have for Muslims belonging to Hindu majority provinces such as U.P.. As a U.P. Muslim himself, Usmani sought to reassure his fellow compatriots against these fears. Here, just like the ML leaders, he alternated on the one hand between appealing to their sense of sacrifice and invoking the hostage population theory. Pointing to Pakistan's special significance for the minority province Muslims, he noted that just like the first Pakistan was created

49 Sherkoti, *Khutbat-i-Usmani*, 86, *Khutba-i-Sadarat*, Calcutta.

50 Ibid., 79.

in Medina and away from Mecca by the Prophet this second Pakistan too was being established away from their homeland in U.P..[51] The role of the minority province Muslims was therefore very similar to that of the original *muhajirin* who had accompanied the Prophet to Medina in order to help establish Pakistan. These original *muhajirin* were *ghair* Pakistanis (non-Pakistanis) who had leveled the ground in Medina and laid the foundations for the settlement of the Muslim community in that holy land. In the same way, Usmani noted with pride, the work of modern day *ghair* Pakistanis who had left their homesteads in order to cooperate with local Pakistanis who he likened to the *ansar* (helpers) of Medina, to create Pakistan. They were doing this even though they clearly knew that they would not be leaving their homeland in Hindustan for good (*tark-i-watan*), or like the Pakistani Muslims, gain anything directly from the establishment of Pakistan.[52] Usmani explained that the *ghair* Pakistanis were making tremendous sacrifices and praying for the establishment of Pakistan since they did not want to be a hindrance in the path of freedom and prosperity of two-third of their nation. Coming to the question of the status of Muslims in the Hindu majority provinces in free India, Usmani reiterated the hostage population theory:

> Just like we are worried about our minority in Hindustan, don't you think the Hindus are worried about their 3 crore Hindu minority in Pakistan?[53]

He, therefore, assured the U.P. Muslims that reciprocal arrangements for protecting minorities would become the prerequisite for subsequent cooperation between the two governments on matters relating to defense and security. Just as Pakistan would provide generous privileges and concessions to Hindus, Usmani expected Hindustan to provide similar privileges and concessions to its Muslim minority. The partition being demanded was after all a just and honourable partition (*moatadil aur mukhlisana taqseem*). Pakistan's Muslim and non-Muslim population, he promised, would be equal partners in the joys and sorrows of the country.

> The Muslim majority will be able to demonstrate *inshallah*, that power and strength does not lead to arrogance but to a spirit of service towards humanity (*khidmat-i-khalq ka jazba*). They (the ML) are not the Indian National

51 *Hamara Pakistan*, 15.

52 Ibid., 27.

53 Ibid., 44.

> Congress that ignores the minorities' aspirations and crushes their rights. They will protect the rights of their brothers in the country (*biradaran-i-watan*) because that is what their religion teaches them. Their past history is a testimonial to this specialty of their nation.[54]

While emphasizing the fact that Pakistan would not oppress its non-Muslim minorities, Usmani did not rule out active measures by Pakistan to protect its nationals in India. In order to underline this point, Usmani narrated to his audience a legend in Islamic history from the time of the Abbasid Caliph Mu'tasim. Usmani recounted that during this time when a Christian government was reigning in *Rum* (Constantinople), a Christian soldier slapped an old Muslim woman. The poor old woman in her terror began to scream for help from the Caliph Mu'tasim. The Christian soldier, therefore, slapped the old woman again and asked her whether the Caliph riding on a white horse would come to take revenge upon him for assaulting her. This little episode, Usmani recounted, gradually reached Baghdad and finally the ear of the Caliph himself. On hearing the story, the indignant Caliph resolved that he would not step into his palace without answering the old woman's cry for help. He, therefore, ordered that all white horses in the region be purchased at any price available and after raising a powerful army, attacked *Rum* and won a great victory. The wretched soldier who had assaulted the old woman was captured and presented to the old lady by the Caliph who declared that Mu'tasim had come to her aid. An *azad hukumat* (independent state) in Pakistan, Usmani noted, would confer similar advantages. Nobody would dare to molest Muslims in Hindustan once Pakistan came into existence. It was thus imperative for Muslims to have their own sovereign Islamic state. Such stories first popularized during the struggle for the creation of Pakistan would later be incorporated by Islamists battling secular regimes in the Arab world who portrayed the Islamic state as the best defender of Muslim interests in the world dominated by western powers.[55]

Usmani also insisted that Muslims in Hindustan would possess as much right over Pakistan as its own inhabitants for it was as much their national homeland as it was of its natives. Pakistan's separation from Hindustan would thus not entail snapping ties with Hindustani Muslims since geographical

---

54 Ibid., 45.

55 See Khaled al- Berry, *Life is More Beautiful than Paradise: A Jihadist's own story* (Cairo and New York, 2009), 181. Mu'tasim would be another Islamic hero to whom Jinnah was obviously being likened here given the ML propaganda that Pakistan would go to war with Hindu India to protect Muslims living there.

boundaries (*hadbandi*) were no barriers to their mutual relationships (*bahami taluqaat*). Just as Muslims in the northern and southern Africa were bound in a strong relationship with the Islamic *millat* and were two parts of the same body, there could be no break in the relations between the Hindustani and Pakistan Muslims. Usmani also explored the option of *hijrat* to Pakistan for Muslims of Hindustan to underline the point that Pakistan was also their national homeland to which they were always welcome. Reacting to objections that such a migration was not feasible, Usmani pointed out that when the Prophet along with his Companions made his *hijrat* (hegira) from Mecca to Madina, he had left behind his shrines (*mabid*) and dependents (*mustazafeen*) and that this matter had been clearly discussed in the Quran.[56] Usmani's veiled comparison of Jinnah to the Prophet here is indeed startling for he seemed to be pointing out that like the Prophet, the *Qaid* too was leaving his own home to establish a Pakistan in another Medina. In any case, Usmani clarified that *hijrat* became imperative in case Muslims were prohibited from following the tenets of their religion. Hence, *hijrat* was something that became necessary only under certain clearly defined conditions. In this regard, Usmani observed that Muslims in Hindustan did not have to fear any such conditions at present. As he noted

> Here the question is not of *hijrat* right away, nor is the state of these few crore Muslims that of utter helplessness (*bedast-o-pa*). Especially when their neighbor is a powerful Pakistan and it is fully alive to its responsibilities of helping and protecting them. And Pakistan will be on friendly terms with other Islamic countries. *God knows why people are so scared of the Hindu qaum to such an extent that if somebody talked of escaping from its slavery, everyone begins to think that we are finished.*[57]

Usmani continued to emphasize to the minority provinces Muslims the importance of Pakistan for protecting their rights and interests even as they felt shaken by the massacre of Muslims in Bihar in 1946. He dismissed any talk of Islam being exterminated in India after Partition as was feared in some quarters. He reminded his minority province brethren that Muslims around the world had faced greater crises earlier. The Tartars had tried to exterminate Muslims in medieval times but had failed. Islam was, therefore, incapable of being wiped out from India.

---

56 Ibid., 46.

57 Ibid., 48.

Non-religious Justification of Pakistan

Usmani did not just provide religious justification for the formation of Pakistan. Just like the *ulama* of the JUH who in their wide ranging critique of Pakistan used both religious and non-religious arguments, he extensively utilized rational secular arguments in his espousal of Pakistan. His clearest enunciation of these arguments were made in his speech at Lahore during which he sought to calm doubts and misgivings regarding the Lahore Resolution as expressed to him by a correspondent from Bihar.[58] These questions echoed concerns raised earlier by the *ulama* of the JUH. They pertained to the fate of Muslims of the minority provinces, Pakistan's economic and military feasibility, apprehension that dividing the country would allow the British to entrench themselves in India, and finally, skepticism about the possibility of an Islamic state in Pakistan given the powerful presence of non-Muslims in its domains. Usmani explicitly utilized the propaganda literature of the ML published by the ML in its Urdu paper *Manshoor* to address these questions.

Usmani first demolished all the arguments made by the Congress in favour of a united India. In this regard, he repudiated the Congress proposal for the formation of an all India Union to which the British would devolve powers, from which the provinces would subsequently have freedom to secede. He dismissed this Congress offer of self-determination to the provinces as a ploy meant to destroy the very idea of Pakistan, arguing that once the provinces agreed to an all-India Union, the federal government would crush any attempts at secession by provinces. If the Muslim provinces persisted with their stubborn attitude, the federal government could always send in the army to settle matters, which would still be under the control of the federal government.[59].

Usmani next clarified matters with regard to the proportion of Muslims and non-Muslims in Pakistan since JUH propagandists frequently harped on the precarious Muslim majorities in Punjab and Bengal. He contended that this wrong interpretation was based on the assumption that there would be as many Pakistans as the number of Muslim provinces. Flatly asserting that the Muslim provinces would not become separate Pakistans but constitute one single Pakistan, he argued that the Partition would make population proportions in a united Pakistan much more favourable to the Muslims. Marshalling statistics and census data, he pointed out that in the combined Pakistani provinces,

---

58 Ibid., 35–40.

59 Ibid., 31.

Muslim population would number 7 crore 20 lakhs while non-Muslim population would number between 2.5–3 crore. Even if one were generous and assumed that Muslims were 7 crore in number and the non-Muslims 3 crore, the proportion of Muslims to non-Muslims in Pakistan would be 7:3. In addition, if one were to include the Christians (as a people of the book) and Sikhs (as unitarians) along with Untouchables and Adivasis on the Muslim side of the register, then the proportion of Muslims to Hindus would be even higher.[60] Usmani argued that this was surely much more advantageous to the Muslims than the JUH formula in a free India that reduced the Muslims to a minority with 45 per cent representation at the federal Centre.[61] He also poked holes into the JUH formula as enunciated by Seoharvi, arguing that even this 45 per cent representation was precarious as there would always be Muslims who were selfish and would desert the Muslim camp, dazzled by Hindu wealth and inducements.[62] He, therefore, scorned the JUH *ulama* for advocating the idea of a united India on the basis of spurious and fallacious arguments. As he noted,

> Is'nt it strange that when we have 70 per cent majority, we are in a loss but if we have 45 per cent (representation) the keys of success and prosperity are supposedly in our hands?[63]

Usmani also defended Pakistan against searing critiques regarding its viability by the JUH *ulama*. He referred to the report of Sir Homi Modi and Dr John Mathai who were members of the Sapru Committee, which had declared that Pakistan would be an economically viable state.[64] He also pointed to Jinnah's interview to the correspondent of Associated Press of America in which the *Qaid* dismissed fears about the economic viability of

---

60 The idea of including Sikhs, Christians, Untouchables and Adivasis on the side of Muslims was popularized by the JUH when defending the idea of a united India. The JUH pushed this idea in order to argue that the Muslims would not be such a powerless minority in a free and united India. Usmani pointed to the irony of the JUH including these non-Hindu groups on the side of Muslims whenever it argued for a united India but then doing the exact opposite when it considered the idea of Pakistan. In the latter case, the JUH ranged these non-Hindu groups against the Muslims thus reducing the proportion of Muslims to non-Muslims in Pakistan.

61 Under the JUH formula, the Muslims and Hindus would have 45 per cent representation in central government while the other minorities would corner the remaining 10 per cent representation. Thus, Muslims would only have 45 per cent as against 55 per cent representation enjoyed by the non-Muslims thus reducing Muslims to a minority.

62 *Hamara Pakistan*, 43.

63 Ibid.

64 Ibid., 49.

Pakistan. Usmani went on to build Pakistan as not just a viable state but an economic powerhouse that would soon outshine India. He quoted Muslim and British experts to claim that Pakistan deposited more revenue into the central treasury than the money that it got from the central government. Thus, Pakistan would have enough financial resources to make it a viable state. Dwelling on the question of natural resources, he noted that Sind and Baluchistan had petroleum deposits while Eastern Bengal would make up for the scarcity of coal. Since a major portion of the Himalayan range of mountains was expected to fall in the area of Pakistan, Usmani was confident that they would contain deposits of precious metals and minerals. He also noted that the Makran coast of Baluchistan was famous for its fishes, Kashmir for its medicinal plants and Pashmina wool and Punjab for its cattle, which produced plentiful milk and *ghee*. Moreover, Punjab had extremely fertile soil, which produced enormous amounts of wheat. If its wheat production was organized on a scientific basis, Usmani predicted that Punjab could become the biggest producer of wheat in the world. He also claimed that Pakistan as the land of five rivers could generate enormous hydroelectric power. Even the Ganga and Yamuna, he pointed out, passed through Pakistan before they flowed into India. If the waters of these rivers could be scientifically diverted into the Sutlej and the Beas, all of Pakistan could be irrigated with water. In this regard, Usmani made a very interesting observation. He pointed out that the task of shifting rivers had been mastered by America while building the Panama Canal since the water of an entire river had been diverted for a year or two by American engineers. Pakistan, he claimed, could learn that technology from the United States. The reference to this obscure fact by this Deobandi *alim* makes it clear that the *ulama* were not just men of religion and were clearly aware of developments in the world of international politics, economy and science.

Usmani also made a case for Pakistan's defence capabilities by observing that it had a healthy population that naturally took to soldiering. This was evident from the fact that 60 per cent of the army was recruited from the Pakistan areas. Pakistan would, therefore, have no problem defending its borders. Besides, Pakistan could have a close and mutually beneficial defence treaty with India so that they could together protect the subcontinent from external invasions. However, mirroring the equivocation by the ML leaders regarding Pakistan's relations with India, in a public meeting, Usmani narrated a story about his meeting with a friend who was a Congress sympathizer in Abbotabad. The friend had asked him as to how Pakistan would respond to a Russian invasion since it was such a poor country. Usmani responded that if the Russians entered Pakistan, he would tell them that theirs was a poor country. He would then point to the railway lines going towards India and tell the Russians all the riches (*rupiyon ki tijoriyan*) lay in that direction.[65]

Usmani also argued that Pakistan's location would make it an extremely important power. Pointing to the advantages of Pakistan's strategic location, he noted that two of the subcontinent's frontiers would be in the hands of Pakistan. Hence, neighbouring countries such as China, Tibet and Afghanistan would have to conclude friendly treaties with Pakistan. He was confident that Pakistan would have a favourable balance of trade with all these neighbouring countries. For example, in exchange for grain it could import fruits from Afghanistan, while from Russia it could import machinery. Karachi, Usmani claimed, was the best seaport in the subcontinent from which wheat and cotton could be exported to many countries. Bombay by contrast, he derisively noted, would only import goods into Hindustan causing losses to the country. He was confident that the port of Calcutta, which he expected to be included in Pakistan, would be another significant source of Pakistan's trading power from which jute and rice could be exported to Australia, Malaya and Singapore. From Sumatra, and Java, which were Muslim lands, goods could be imported and then again exported to Hindustan. Again, fish could be profitably exported to the Indian interior from eastern Bengal. Pakistan, Usmani asserted, would be in a far better situation than India from the viewpoint of agriculture, mineral wealth and the economy in general. Usmani put these things in a nutshell.

> The Hindu thinks that with Bharatvarsh, the trade of Malaya, China, Japan, Burma, and Australia passes through the port of Calcutta. Once this comes under Pakistan's control, all this trade will go Pakistan. The trade of Arabia, Iran, and Iraq passes through Karachi. The oil of Iran and Mosul is close to Karachi. The oil of Burma is close to Calcutta. The oil companies of Iran, Iraq and Burma can come into the hands of Pakistanis. What will then happen to the Hindu![66]

Usmani's election appeal on the eve of the elections therefore exhorted the Muslim voters to vote for the ML as it stood for the formation of Pakistan. While casting their votes, he advised Muslims to disregard kinship (*qarabat*),

---

65 Sherkoti, *Khutbat-i-Usmani*, 233, Speech at Peshawar.

66 Ibid.

friendship (*dosti*), teacher student relationship (*talmuz pir muridi*), greed and party feeling in order to fulfill their great responsibility towards the Muslim nation. The fight, he reminded Muslims, was not between personalities but between principles. He also warned them that if they deliberately ignored the fundamental principle of Pakistan and got carried away by wrong principles and arguments, they would be responsible for damaging their nation.[67] In fact, they would be humiliating the Muslim *qaum* before the *kafirs*.[68] The ML, Usmani reminded Muslim voters, was an organization of *Kalimah* reciting Muslims. The ML's principle of Pakistan was preferable and pure (*marajjah aur beghubaar*) from both a rational and *shari'i* point of view. If the ML lost this election, it would lead to the burial of this true principle (*saccha usool*) and Muslim freedom in India would be snuffed out forever.

Meeting with the JUH Ulama

Usmani's public support for the ML and Pakistan on the eve of the 1945–46 elections caused quite a sensation leading his erstwhile colleagues at Deoband and the JUH, who strongly opposed Pakistan, to approach Usmani in an effort to persuade him to retract his position. Maulana Madani, Maulana Ahmad Said along with Mufti Kifayatullah met Usmani at his house in Deoband on 7 December 1945 after Hifzurrahman Seoharvi made the initial contact with his former teacher. A long three and half hour discussion followed as the *ulama* bid to resolve their differences.[69] Seoharvi also brought along his close friend, Usmani's nephew Atiqur Rahman Usmani from Delhi where he headed the *Nadwatul Musannifin*, to help build bridges at the meeting. After the initial pleasantries, Seoharvi broached the subject of Pakistan, which had caused a divide among the *ulama*. Reiterating his misgivings about Pakistan, he made a powerful presentation to explain the many ways in which it would cause grave harm to the Muslims in India. Seoharvi also raised the issue of the dubious origins of the JUI, claiming that it had been formed with the financial support of the government at Calcutta. He indicated that its purpose was to smash the JUH, undermine the unity of the *ulama* and ultimately torpedo the struggle for independence. He alleged that Maulana Azad Subhani, one of the organizers of the JUI conference at Calcutta had stayed at the house of Hakim Dilbar Husain,

67 Ibid., 170, Khutba-i-Sadarat Meerut Conference.

68 Ibid., 173.

69 Ibid., 93–108

a government man, where he met a functionary of the government's Political Department and received money for this purpose. He disparaged Subhani as a fickle character who at one time had been Gandhi's shadow but subsequently had turned against him and was now hobnobbing with the government.

Usmani responded that he was not interested in either verifying or contradicting the story about Azad Subhani. He himself had been informed of the same story by an anonymous letter he had received from Delhi, which also carried a threat warning him to stay away from the JUI. This seemed reminiscent of the threat sent to Maulana Ashraf Ali Thanawi in 1938 when he came out in public support of the ML and both episodes may well have been the work of government agencies. In any case, whether Subhani was in the JUI or whether the organization itself existed or died, Usmani claimed that it made no difference to his own view that Pakistan was good for the Muslims. They needed to have their own centre and a single political platform and it was the duty of the *ulama* to give it their support. Moreover even if the story of the JUI being set up by government money was true, Usmani pointed out that even the Congress was set up by the government and for a long time sang the tune of loyalty towards it. Organizations might have beginnings, which were less than ideal, but could always transform and stabilize later. Usmani also expressed his skepticism about stories and allegation that were not based on any solid proof. He reminded them that allegations had been made against their respected elder Maulana Ashraf Ali Thanawi that he received a regular six hundred rupee allowance from the government. But the Maulana himself never knew that the government was giving him money; and even if the money was sent to him he could not be held accountable since he did not know about it. Usmani grimly noted he himself had been the target of a vilification campaign by certain parties and individuals at Deoband for a rumour was recently spread claiming that Usmani had been instrumental in getting Madani arrested by the government. At this, Atiqur Rahman lowered his eyes since his uncle had indeed been targeted and the nationalist *ulama* at Deoband had done nothing to dispel such rumors. Usmani also pointed out that Madani, Seoharvi and the nationalist *ulama* themselves had been accused of taking money from the Hindus. They all, therefore, needed to move away from such toxic allegations and insinuations.

Usmani then addressed the more substantial issues, which they had gathered to discuss and asked his interlocutors three questions. He first asked Seoharvi whether the JUH's formula that had been advertised as a substitute for Pakistan, was backed by the Congress. Seoharvi replied in the negative but added that it was not their policy to fight the battle for freedom conditionally and have the Hindus agree to all their conditions before joining the struggle. Next, Usmani enquired about the assumptions on which the discussion was to proceed – whether the British government had left Hindustan, was still leaving, or whether it was still around and was not about to leave right away and that whatever Muslims wanted to take they needed to take it from the British government. Seoharvi replied that the latter was indeed the case. Usmani then enquired whether his interlocutors wanted a revolution based on a military overthrow of British rule or constitutional change. Seoharvi again replied that the latter was indeed what they all were striving for. Usmani reasoned that the only question that needed to be addressed was about the best way forward for the Muslims – whether it was the path of composite nationalism and undivided India as decided by the JUH or that of a separate Pakistan as espoused by the ML.

Seoharvi in his impassioned speech had pointed out that in the Muslim majority provinces the Hindus were a powerful and significant minority who would not allow the Muslims to achieve any of their goals. In Bengal the Muslims had a bare majority of 53 per cent while in Assam they were in a minority. In the Punjab where the Muslims had a 57 per cent majority, the warlike Sikhs on the one hand and the belligerent Jats on the other would not let the Muslims live in peace. And since Jinnah had made it clear that Pakistan would be a European style democracy, Seoharvi contended that the Muslim majorities in Pakistan would practically be under the thumb of the Hindus. Usmani quickly intervened to ask whether there would be six Pakistans based in each of the Muslim majority provinces, or one Pakistan combining all of them. Seoharvi replied that there would only be one Pakistan. Usmani countered that discussion of statistics of individual provinces was therefore useless and one needed to instead look at the proportion of Muslims and non-Muslims in Pakistan as a whole. At this Seoharvi responded that Pakistan would have six crore Muslims and three crore non-Muslims. Usmani disputed these figures claiming that the Muslims would be about seven and a quarter crores while the non-Muslims would add up to about three crores. The proportion between Muslims and Hindus in Pakistan would be 70:30. Even taking Seoharvi's statistics to be true, Usmani noted that the proportion between Muslims and non-Muslims would be 60:40. This was still better than the 40:40:20 formula outlined by Seoharvi for Muslims, Hindus and other minorities in an undivided India.

At this point the JUH side argued that Christians would join on the side of the Muslims in India thus increasing Muslim leverage. Usmani retorted that this was rather strange reasoning since whenever the Pakistan formula was put forward, the Christians were always counted in the non-Muslim bloc while if the JUH formula was put forward, the same Christians were counted on the side of the Muslims as a people of the Book. Muslims and non-Muslims, Usmani averred, should strictly be counted separately to which the JUH *ulama* were forced to agree. He next enquired as to why the Hindus were so bitterly opposed to Pakistan if as the JUH *ulama* argued it was beneficial to the Hindus and harmful to the Muslims. It seemed rather unbelievable that Hindus did not want Pakistan to come into existence since it was ruinous to the Muslims. Seoharvi had no plausible answer to this question and kept evading the issue. Cutting him short, Usmani insisted that the only reason why the Hindus did not want Pakistan was because they wanted to establish their suzerainty over all of the ten crore Muslims in India under British aegis and not let even a single Muslim escape from their stranglehold. Muslims would thus be pulverized under the double slavery of the British and the Hindus.

The JUH *ulama* again did not have any convincing rebuttal to this argument and shifted the discussion to the dreadful fate that would befall Muslims who would be left behind in Hindustan in the event of Pakistan coming into existence. Usmani saw no reason for any apprehensions on this front for he visualized the question of minority rights being settled between Hindustan and Pakistan on the basis of treaties (*moahadat*). Here again, he invoked the hostage population theory to claim that majorities would desist from oppressing the minority on their side to ensure good treatment for their own brethren on the other side.There would be no such guarantees for the ten crore Muslims in an *Akhand Hindustan*. At this point Seoharvi and Ahmad Said again changed the topic of discussion and expressed their fears that *Necharies* from Aligarh would become the leaders of Pakistan and once in power would wipe out the *ulama* and destroy Islam in the new country. Ahmad Said also raised the issue of the Aligarh students' extremely insulting behaviour towards Madani. He further pointed out that the ML was full of Rajas, Nawabs, titleholders and British toadies like Firoz Khan Noon who till the other day served in the government and was now a prominent ML leader. Usmani refused to get into an argument over Noon but instead argued that Jinnah was incorruptible and could never be enticed or purchased by anyone. As regards the Aligarh *Necharies*, Usmani acknowledged that it could indeed be a problem and in turn asked his interlocutors if they had any solution to this problem. There was silence for a while as they all looked at each other but the JUH *ulama* cleverly tossed the ball back into Usmani's court asking for his ideas on the matter.

Usmani's own solution was to invite the JUH *ulama* to join the ML so that together they could capture the party organization. They could tour around the country together for a couple of months and enroll three or four lakh two *anna* paying members into the party. Surely they had the influence among the people to meet that target. Usmani claimed that more and more people would be attracted to join the League seeing their presence in the organization. With such a heavy presence of like-minded supporters in the party they could easily bring about an internal reformation in the ML. An uncomfortable Ahmad Said, who had heard this argument before but remained unconvinced, responded that the Rajas, Nawabs and Khan Bahadurs of the League would surely secede and form another ML if the *ulama* did succeed in their gameplan. Usmani calmly replied that this would not constitute a problem since the masses would still be with them. He reminded Ahmad Said that in the past a breakaway ML had been formed by Sir Muhammad Shafi but it had faded and died with him. Such would be the fate of any breakaway section that seceded from the ML after the *ulama* had captured it.

Ahmad Said had no response to this argument and Usmani now turned to the other issue that was broached by the JUH *ulama*. He made it clear that he had publicly condemned the misdemeanors of the Aligarh students towards Maulana Madani. Usmani, however, pointed out that these students were neither their own wards nor had they been raised in a religious environment. Against this, he regretted that his interlocutors' students of Arabic at the *Darul Uloom*, who were raised at the very centre of religious learning, had outdone their Aligarh contemporaries in mean and vulgar behaviour. Filthy epithets had been shouted against him, obscene posters in which he had been compared to Abu Jahal had been put up inside the *Darul Uloom*. These students had also issued threats to kill him and scattered such demeaning letters and essays at his doorstep that had the women of the family seen them it would have greatly ashamed him. Usmani expressed his deep pain at the fact that these rampaging students had been trained by teachers at the *Darul Uloom* who had once been his own students. Admonishing his interlocutors, he pointed out that none of them had uttered a word of censure against these base and vulgar actions (*kameeni harkat*). Usmani continued that the nationalist Muslim newspaper the *Hurriyat* of Delhi had published obscene essays against him but none of the JUH *ulama* had said a word against him. At this Ahmad Said responded saying that Aziz Hasan Baqqali, the editor of the *Hurriyat*, generally wrote nonsense. Usmani shot back that he was at the moment, however writing complimentary things about the JUH *ulama* and the latter had not condemned Baqqali for his slanderous attacks against Usmani. On the other, Usmani pointed out that when a letter was recently sent to him asking whether the JUH *ulama* had joined the Hindus for personal gains and moved away from the ideology of their teachers, he had responded stating that the JUH *ulama* did not hold their existing views with a view to making personal fortunes. He had also written that they sincerely believed that they were following in the footsteps of their illustrious teachers even if in his own personal opinion, the JUH *ulama* were mistaken.

At this point, Maulana Husain Ahmad Madani who had sat quietly thus far finally broke his silence. He took out an essay and read out its contents for the next several minutes, which detailed the opinions of a British writer who had recommended that Indian be partitioned. Madani's point was that Pakistan was an English idea and the ML was taking its orders from the British Government. Ahmad Said chimed in and asked Usmani to comment on whether the British would benefit by dividing India or keeping it united. Usmani responded that Britain divided or patched countries together on the basis of its own personal interest. Thus Britain had broken up the Ottoman Caliphate and created Iraq, Syria, Lebanon, Yemen etc. but now was putting together the Arab League as a front against Russia. The JUH *ulama* reluctantly agreed with this proposition. Usmani continued that it was, therefore, not correct to say that British policy had always been to divide countries for it also tried to unite them at other times. One, therefore, needed to think about what was profitable for the Muslims irrespective of British concerns. Usmani further noted that the essay that Madani had read was an individual opinion expressed by an Englishman fourteen years earlier. In the meantime, Lord Linlithgow and Lord Wavell had publicly expressed themselves in favour of a united India and also advised against a surgical operation in the subcontinent in order to divide it. Ahmad Said retorted that these were diabolical English manoeuvres for they said one thing and did another. Usmani shot back that the same thing could be said about the English writer whom Madani had quoted.

Madani now widened the discussion asking Usmani how he thought India would be defended in the face of a Russian invasion after Pakistan had been created. He feared that the entire burden would fall on the frontier Muslims who would not be able to withstand a Russian attack on their own. In his rejoinder, Usmani first noted that the British were still in India and that it was unlikely that they would leave without any plan for defending India to counter a Russian invasion. But in any case, Hindustan and Pakistan could always come together to defend against a Russian invasion since it was in their common interests. He pointed out that only recently the English and the Russians had come together under a treaty and fought together against the Germans and the Japanese during the War. It was, therefore, very possible for India and Pakistan to enter into a treaty regarding defence arrangements for the subcontinent at large. Ahmad Said dismissed Usmani's idea saying that nobody cared for such treaties these days. Stung to the quick, Usmani shot back that the Maulana was happy to give away everything to the Hindus without a treaty. A treaty was anyday an improvement than having no treaty.

Atiqur Rahman who had stayed silent all this while finally asked his uncle as to why he was taking an interest in the elections when he had always stayed away from politics. Usmani replied that this election was different from all previous elections since the assemblies that would be elected were going to decide India's future. He had, therefore, decided to support the ML since it had demanded self-determination for the Muslims. He also denied that he had always been aloof from politics. Save the past few years, he too had made his modest contributions to the politics in the country. The reference was perhaps to his activities involving the collection of funds for Turkey during the Balkan War besides his active participation in the Khilafat Movement. Usmani also wondered why his friends in the JUH were getting concerned if his entry into politics and appeals on behalf of the ML brought another ten or twenty votes for Liaquat Ali Khan in the recent election. After all he had the status of an inconsequential Untouchable as compared to them. At this, Ahmad Said responded that this was not true for his statements had caused a commotion throughout India. Said further complained that such was the force of Usmani's statements that it left no space for those holding the opposite views. Usmani responded that none of them ever softened his stance while arguing over theological matters. At this everyone laughed.

Hifzur Rahman Seoharvi was one of Usmani's students who had followed him when the latter along with Anwar Shah Kashmiri had resigned from Deoband and left for Dabhail following their differences with the management of the *Darul Uloom*. He appealed to his former teacher not to break the JUH's unity and also desist from becoming the JUI President. Usmani quietly responded stating that while he had not yet made up his mind on the matter, he could not give them any assurances. It was not long afterwards that Usmani became the President of the JUI. Maulana Ahmad Said then asked Usmani if he was indeed leaving for Hyderabad, perhaps hoping that the Nizam's invitation to the senior cleric would take him away from the battlefield of the election campaign. Usmani responded that he had asked the Nizam for a few months of leave since his health was not very good to which the Nizam had kindly assented. The departing *ulama* finally pleaded with Usmani to remain silent and issue no further political statements since he had already said what he wanted to say on the question of Pakistan. Usmani calmly replied that he would continue to express his views on what he thought was right and hence could not remain silent. On this note, the meeting ended.

As we shall discuss in the next chapter, the JUH *ulama* stepped up to push back against Usmani's espousal of Pakistan during the 1945–46 elections that became a referendum on Pakistan. Theirs was however a losing cause. For the moment though we may conclude by contrasting Usmani's views regarding the role of the *ulama* with those of his *Pir* Ashraf Ali Thanawi. The senior cleric before his death had told one of his students that

> It seems that the Leaguers will be successful and whatever (Muslim) State will be established will be governed by those whom we call fasiq awr fajir (big sinners). If through your efforts these (Muslim leaguers) become religious and honest and if they are the ones who govern the State then it is all right. We are not interested in governing a State. Our sole aim is that whatever (Muslim) State is established that should be in the hands of religious and honest persons so that Allah's din (Islam) reigns supreme.[70]

But Usmani had a far more activist view about the role of the *ulama* in Pakistan as evident from his metaphor of the English sea captain and the Arab pilot. It is a view which would place him closer to Khomeini whose concept of the *Vilayat-i-Faqih* too held that the *ulama* should 'discharge the full range of the Imam's functions including the political headship of the community.'[71] Future research might gainfully try to analyse the influence that the Deobandi *ulama* espousing Pakistan had on Khomeini's vision of the Islamic State.

---

70 Rizwan Malik, 'Muslim Nationalism in India: Ashraf Ali Thanawi, Shabbir Ahmad Usmani and the Pakistan Movement', in *Pakistan Journal of History and Culture*, Vol. XVIII/2 (1997), 76.

71 Roxanne L. Euben and Muhammad Qasim Zaman (ed.), *Princeton Readings in Islamist Thought: Texts and Contexts from al-Banna to Bin Laden* (Princeton, 2009), 12, footnote no. 9. For a selection of Khomeini's writings, see Ruhollah Khomeini, *Islam and Revolution: Writings and Declarations of Imam Khomeini translated by Hamid Algar* (Berkeley, 1980). For views on Khomeini as a pragmatist, see Ervand Abrahamian, *A History of Modern Iran* (Cambridge, 2008); also his *Khomeinism: Essays on the Islamic Republic* (Berkeley, 1993).

8

The Referendum on Pakistan

They (Congress) say they do not understand Pakistan. If you do not understand it, then what is it that you are opposing? On the contrary, I find that even a child of 12 or 13 understands it. When I see Muslim boys shouting for Pakistan, I very often enquire from them as to what Pakistan is and believe me, I am not exaggerating, they give me perfect answers. Even Muslim children understand it but here is this great leader (Nehru) who says he does not understand Pakistan. Pakistan means partition. Pakistan means division. It means you must take Hindu provinces of yours and leave out Muslim provinces where we want to establish our own government. All these pretensions, all these excuses are simply to confound, confound, confound. Why don't you say plainly instead of going round and round? We want to take Pakistan as soon as we can and Inshallah, we shall have Pakistan.[1]

M. A. Jinnah

They fully know what Pakistan is. And let me define it once again. Pakistan means the establishment of free independent, democratic and sovereign states in those areas and zones in which the Muslims are in a majority. They ask what are the boundaries of Pakistan? I once again declare it from this platform that the boundaries of Pakistan will be the present provincial boundaries of the Punjab, NWFP, Baluchistan, and Sind in the northwest, and Bengal and Assam in the northeast. They again ask what will be the constitution of Pakistan. Pakistan will be a democratic state and its constitution will be framed by the people of those areas through a constituent assembly elected by them. Everything is as clear as daylight! I want to say it with the fullest sense of responsibility that those who think we are pitching our demand too high in order to bargain are gravely mistaken. This is not the maximum demand but the minimum demand of Muslim India.[2]

Liaquat Ali Khan

On 21 August 1945, the Viceroy Lord Wavell announced that elections to the central and provincial assemblies would be held later that year in order to elect representatives to the Constituent Assembly that would be tasked with framing a new constitution for British India. The ML responded to this announcement by declaring that these elections would be a referendum on Pakistan. The party

1 *Dawn*, 20 October 1945. Speech at Quetta.

2 *The Pioneer*, 25 September 1945. Speech at Aligarh Muslim University.

now needed an unqualified triumph in this referendum in order to demonstrate its sway over not only the Muslim voters in the Muslim majority provinces where it envisaged the creation of Pakistan but even in the Muslim minority provinces, which would not be a part of this nation-state.

Winning elections in the U.P. was, however, going to be a challenge for the party for two reasons. In the first place, it faced a determined Congress, which, confident of sweeping the general constituencies, was concentrating all of its energies on winning Muslim seats. The party exuded optimism that it would achieve much better results this time than it did in the 1937 provincial elections when it put up candidates in only nine of the sixty four Muslim constituencies in U.P. and saw all of them crash to defeat. An improved performance this time was imperative in order to bolster its own claims of being an organization that represented all Indians irrespective of their religion, region, caste, or class and dent if not demolish the ML's claim of being the sole representative organization of the Muslims.

The second and bigger challenge for the MLas it geared up for the election was rampant factionalism that festered within its ranks, threatening to mar the prospects of its candidates at the polls. The existing situation, thus, did not seem very different from the state of the party just before the 1937 election when a fledgling ML had mostly co-opted independent Muslim candidates with the requisite wherewithal to contest the elections on their own. The consequent lack of cohesion in the party's ranks became evident soon after when it faced disruption and disintegration over the question of ministry formation. However, the irretrievable breakdown of negotiations with the Congress on this issue reunited the ML besides providing a major impetus for its expansion in the villages, *qasbahs* and cities of U.P. Party membership increased sharply during the years of Congress rule, but the campaign for Pakistan brought in much larger numbers into the party fold. ML membership in the U.P. stood at 304,586 in 1944. It had sixty nine branches in the province and this number was expected to further rise to seventy seven by the time of the elections.[3] This large increase in party membership, however, resulted in schisms between the old guard and newer elements that had entered into the party. As elections drew near and a badly splintered ML struggled to pull together, contributions by two crucial groups that were independent of the party became critical to its success. The first of these groups were the Deobandi *ulama* who, as demonstrated in the previous chapter, provided a robust theological defence for Pakistan besides crisscrossing

[3] *The Pioneer*, 17 September 1945.

various constituencies in British India to address ML meetings and rally the faithful. The second group included students from the Muslim University at Aligarh who acted as the party's foot soldiers during the ML's election campaign. Jinnah, Liaquat and the top ML leadership had made regular visits to Aligarh right from the time of the 1937 provincial assembly elections. These visits would become much more regular after the Lahore Resolution. The *Qaid* after all saw Aligarh as the 'arsenal of Muslim India' and its students responded warmly to him as he called upon their services for the national cause. Together, these groups made up for the lack of cohesiveness in the ML and played a decisive role in ensuring its decisive victory in these elections. The election campaigns by ML and Congress did not just mark a continuation of debates over Pakistan that had raged in U.P. from the time of the Lahore Resolution, but brought out the stakes in this contest much more clearly.

Parties and Politics in the U.P. Muslim League

The UPML had to first set its own house in order before it could start the process of gearing up for the elections. Factional struggles intensified within the party during the run up to the 1944 Municipal Board elections over the creation of a Parliamentary Board and the distribution of party tickets to candidates. Even though ML candidates did particularly well winning 82 per cent of the nearly 900 Muslim seats, and wrested control over forty four municipalities in the process, the severity of the factional conflicts effectively split the party in the U.P.[4] The main division that emerged was between the old guard comprising Nawab Ismail Khan, Khaliquzzaman and their associates and a new group headed by S. M. Rizwanullah, the UPML General Secretary who had the backing of Muslim industrialists from the city of Kanpur. Rizwanullah also had a patron in Sir Francis Mudie, the U.P. Chief Secretary who helped his brother Irfanullah, an architect, secure government contracts and a job in its Improvement Trust.[5] The ostensible reason for the old guard's opposition to Rizwanullah was that he had not submitted proper accounts in connection with funds collected for the 1942 AIML Allahabad session. Problems spilled into the open when the newspaper *Haque* secured details of Rizwanullah's bank account

4 *The Leader*, 23 December 1944.

5 The following account is largely based on Mahmudabad to Jinnah, 11 August 1944, Z. H. Zaidi, (ed.), *QA Papers*, Vol. 11, 36–39; Ibid., 531–32, Hasan Ali Khan and Others to Jinnah (Telegram), F.701/96, 6 July 1944; Ibid., 540–43, Nawab Ismail Khan to Jinnah, 7 July 1944; Ibid., 561–62; Jamal Mian to Jinnah, 12 July 1944.

that revealed a large amount of unexplained money and proceeded to publish a series of articles charging him with misappropriation and embezzlement of funds. As the scandal over its financial affairs broke in public, the working committee of the UPML initiated an enquiry. It appointed Mahmudabad, the Treasurer, to conduct a probe into the matter and directed Rizwanullah to submit all the necessary accounts for scrutiny. The latter was also asked to file a lawsuit against the *Haque* suing for damages. Rizwanullah, however, did not help matters by adopting dilatory tactics against the enquiry. In the face of his non-cooperation, Mahmudabad summarily concluded that Rizwanullah could not account for a sum of ₹ 20,000 in his bank account.

In March 1944, at a meeting of the UPML working committee, Rizwanullah finally yielded, submitting 'some sort of a ledger' consisting of a loose assortment of papers. But a perusal of the contents revealed that the papers had been forged. An exasperated working committee turned the screws further by officially censuring Rizwanullah, but still gave him another chance to clarify his position. When Rizwanullah refused to respond, the working committee in May 1944 finally decided that although he had failed to prove that the amount of ₹ 20,000 was his own, the matter had to be buried in the larger interests of the party. In return, it asked Rizwanullah to give a written commitment that he would never stand for any office in the ML besides returning an amount of ₹ 1,148, which he himself acknowledged he had embezzled. Mahmudabad, who had been the enquiry officer, vehemently opposed this compromise and went on to record his dissenting vote against it. Writing to Jinnah, he bitterly complained that Rizwanullah had been let off since he was seen as a potential ally by the factions aligned to Ismail Khan and Khaliquzzaman who were wooing him to gain an upper hand in their own tussle for securing control over the UPML.

The old guard had made a fatal mistake in letting Rizwanullah off the hook. When the question of contesting the Municipal elections and forming a Parliamentary Board to distribute tickets to party candidates for these elections came up, both Ismail Khan and Khaliquzzaman found themselves upstaged by Rizwanullah. The latter having assiduously cultivated support in the Council of the UPML was clearly in a position to capture the Board and hand party tickets to his own supporters for the Municipal elections. Seeing the writing on the wall, at the meeting of the Council of the UPML in July 1944, Khaliquzzaman opposed the idea of the ML setting up its own candidates for the elections, arguing that the selection of candidates would exacerbate factionalism in the party. The Rizwanullah group, which had arrived in strength for the meeting, was clearly in no mood to buy this idea. When the matter was put to vote in the Council, the new group not surprisingly, outvoted the old guard. The party was now officially committed to putting up party candidates in the municipal elections. In response, a humiliated old guard withdrew from the process of electing the Parliamentary Board that was to distribute party tickets for these elections. The new group, having been given a walkover, proceeded to capture the Board and elected Rizwanullah as its Convenor.

Rizwanullah's election, however, was in contravention of the promise he had earlier given to the working committee to stay away from all offices in the UPML. The turn of events so upset Nawab Ismail Khan that he dramatically declared that he was proceeding on leave from his position as the UPML President. Citing 'personal reasons' behind this decision a miffed Ismail Khan further claimed that Jinnah himself had approved of it, clearly hinting that the old guard had the blessings of the *Qaid*. But this move did not lead to any softening in the position of opposing group for it did not, as expected, beseech Nawab Ismail Khan to withdraw his resignation. A bewildered Nawab now had no option but to invite nominations to fill the position of the Acting President of the UPML during his absence. At this point, his strong contingent of supporters proposed Rizwanullah's name and not surprisingly, he again won the contest with an overwhelming majority. A triumphant Rizwanullah now invited nominations for someone to replace him as the Convenor of the Parliamentary Board secure in the belief that one of his own lieutenants would capture the position. This was an ambitious attempt at a total power grab by the new group. At this point Aizaz Rasul, a member of the old guard, in a last moment display of wits requested for an adjournment of the meeting until the next day so that matters could be deliberated much more carefully. The request was granted by Rizwanullah. The counter move came the next morning when Khaliquzzaman, Begum Aizaz Rasul, Jamal Mian, Karimurraza Khan and Zahur Ahmad representing the old guard resigned from the Working Committee of the UPML. The new group remained unfazed and made the most of this opportunity. Going for the kill, Rizwanullah's supporters welcomed these resignations and induced their leader to accept them.

This bold move further flummoxed the old guard, which now became desperate to recoup its position in the organization. In panic, it beseeched Ismail Khan to return and get back to the helm of affairs to prevent the party from being completely captured by the upstart usurper. The next day, on 5 July

1944, Ismail Khan promptly informed Rizwanullah that he was reversing his earlier decision and no longer wished to relinquish office. A piqued Rizwanullah shot back that Ismail Khan's proposed return to his erstwhile position was unconstitutional and refused to vacate his position as the Acting President to which he had been elected only the previous day. Matters were not helped by the fact that the Council of the UPML had not passed any resolution specifying Ismail Khan's period of absence or the date at which he could resume his office. Ismail Khan conveniently interpreted this to mean that the decision on this matter had been left to his own personal discretion. He, therefore, summoned a fresh meeting of the Council of the UPML in the second week of August. In response, a defiant Rizwanullah called an extraordinary meeting of the same Council on 23 July 1944 at Muzaffarnagar. The contending groups now set up separate offices in Lucknow with the old guard operating out of the Mahmudabad house and the new group from the Bhopal House. The ML had effectively split into two parties in the U.P.

Claiming to be the true ML both parties turned to Jinnah to intervene in the dispute. An anguished Ismail Khan wrote to the *Qaid* seeking advice and guidance reminding Jinnah that he had decided to return to his position not for his own sake but to secure the best interests of the party. Rizwanullah called upon Jinnah in person to argue his case but the *Qaid* deftly refused to take sides on the matter or step into the messy factional strife in the UPML. Writing to Ismail Khan, he pointed out that there were mechanisms in the party organization to resolve disputes and referred specifically to the Council of the UPML and the Committee of Action.[6] While Rizwanullah had strong support in the former, Ismail Khan headed the latter body. The lack of any direction from Jinnah did not help matters.

The conflict between the two sides continued during the municipal elections with the Parliamentary Board, dominated by the Rizwanullah group, liberally giving party tickets to its own supporters and the old guard supporting 'rebel' candidates in the elections.[7] Referring to the factionalism in the UPML, the secret Fortnightly Report of the U.P. Government to the Home Secretary at Delhi noted that

> the ML in UP seems at present to be in a rather sorry state as nominations made by the League authorities for municipal elections have led to a large

6 Jinnah to Ismail Khan, 19 July 1944, Telegram F, *QA Papers*, Vol. 10, 578.

7 Mahmud Hashmi to Jinnah, 1 November 1944, QA Papers, Vol. 11, 276.

number of resignations from the League in several districts. Party factions within the League are rapidly disintegrating it.[8]

Once the elections had concluded, the old guard that still dominated the Working Committee made the next move by setting up a parallel body known as the Central Parliamentary Committee refusing to recognize the Parliamentary Board under Rizwanullah. It also filed a suit in a local civil court seeking to have the Parliamentary Board declared an illegal entity. The old guard and its parliamentary committee now invited leaders of ML parties in the municipalities to a meeting in a bid to display the extent of its political support. This meeting, which was declared illegal by Rizwanullah, was attended by leaders of only four out of the forty four municipalities controlled by the ML and attested to the fact that Rizwanullah and his supporters had a powerful hold in the party and were no bunch of pushovers.[9]

The contending parties finally met for a showdown in Kanpur at the next meeting of the Council of the UPML in early February 1945. Opening the proceedings, Ismail Khan 'shocked the meeting' when he claimed that he had been offered several thousand rupees by the opposing group to join its ranks.[10] The Rizwanullah group struck back with its secretary Mustansirullah alleging that Ismail Khan's lieutenant, Aizaz Rasul, had 'hampered the work of the Parliamentary Board' during the elections; a euphemism for setting up rebel candidates. He also accused Aizaz Rasul of having a hand in the injunction suit that had been filed in court against the Board. Mustansirullah further alleged that group loyalties were determining the distribution of receipt books for the enrollment of party members as also the appointment of election officers for party elections that were due in a few months. These accusations and counter accusations only added more bitterness to the proceedings. Supporters of the old guard shouted demands for Mustansirullah's resignation and these were met with loud calls for the working committee's resignation. In retaliation, an incensed working committee passed a resolution declaring that the charges levelled by Mustansirullah were baseless. The latter in response refused to leave the meeting until he wrote out a note of dissent against the Working Committee resolution. With matters approaching boiling point, both the groups decided to step back and not push matters towards a complete breakdown. The meeting

8 Fortnightly Report for the Second Half of October 1944, *L/P&J/5/273*, OIOC, British Library, London.

9 *The Pioneer*, 23 December 1944.

10 *The Pioneer*, 12 February 1945.

ended with both the groups agreeing to postpone the forthcoming meeting of the Council of the UPML as also all decisions regarding disciplinary action against those who had worked against official ML candidates in the municipal elections.

The announcement of elections to the Central Assembly and provincial assemblies, however, brought about a temporary ceasefire between the two factions. The party high command in its bid to quell the infighting within the party organization now unveiled a new constitution for the provincial ML units that also outlined the relationship of these units to the central organization.[11] A number of restrictions were now placed upon the strength of the provincial Councils. Under the previous constitution, there was one Council member for every 1000 two *anna* paying primary members of the ML. This rule had allowed those with money to enroll bogus members allowing them to swell the number of their supporters in the Council. It was, therefore, not unusual in many districts for the number of primary ML members to exceed the entire Muslim population of the district. Now under the new constitution, a Provincial Council could only have three times its quota of members who would be sent to the Central Council. Since the U.P.'s quota in the Central Council was set at seventy members, its membership in the Provincial Council was therefore restricted to 210 members. These 210 seats were further distributed according to the Muslim population in each district, which were required to enrol a minimum number of primary members in order to secure representation in the Provincial Council. In addition, the Presidents and Secretaries of the District and City MLs were to be ex-officio members while a provision was also made for a few members to be co-opted. The party high command also laid down the rules for membership of the provincial parliamentary board. This body would now consist of the provincial ML President, the ML legislature party leader, two representatives of the legislature party and three representatives of the provincial council of the ML.

The ceasefire between the different factions, however, broke down again in an acrimonious meeting of the Council of the UPML at Lucknow in mid-September 1945 that was called to elect the office bearers of the UPML besides a new Parliamentary Board under the new party constitution.[12] The old guard came better prepared for this meeting making sure that all of its supporters were attending. The proceedings began smoothly enough as Ismail Khan and

---

11 *The Pioneer*, 1 August 1945.

12 *The Pioneer*, 17 September 1945.

Mahmudabad were unanimously elected as the President and Treasurer of the UPML respectively. At this point, Rizwanullah asked for an adjournment pointing out that no consensus had been reached over other appointments in the party. An exasperated Ismail Khan now declared that his own election and that of Mahmudabad should also be adjourned until the next sitting since it seemed clear that factionalism was still alive in the party and they had not succeeded in sinking their differences. Ismail Khan warned the gathering that the ML was facing a powerful and well organized opponent in the Congress party. The party could, therefore, ill afford internal conflicts and needed to work as a united team if it wanted to defeat the Congress in the elections.

The council met again in the afternoon at which Ismail Khan announced his resignation yet again. What followed was 'a scramble for the microphone' with several names being proposed and seconded for the post of the UPML President. Khaliquzzaman's name was proposed but he withdrew from the contest. Z. H. Lari, Rizwanullah, Nawab Mohammad Yusuf and Maulana Hasrat Mohani were all proposed and seconded as candidates. At this point, a member got hold of the microphone and pointed to the unseemly nature of the afternoon's proceedings. He appealed to Ismail Khan to reconsider his decision and announced that until the Nawab withdrew his resignation, the Council would not elect anybody as the President. This proposal was immediately seconded by Nawab Jamshed Ali Khan of Baghpat. At this point Z. H. Lari again proposed Ismail Khan's name at which all the other candidates withdrew their names and Ismail Khan ended up getting elected a second time during the day as the provincial party president. A contest for the post of the General Secretary could, however, not be avoided in spite of all efforts at arriving at a consensus. In this contest, Aizaz Rasul defeated Rizwanullah by 257–178 votes. This was a victory for the old guard and the meeting was adjourned for the next day to elect members for a new Parliamentary Board.

The trial of strength during the previous day had a 'sobering effect' on the next day's meeting convened to elect the remaining five representatives on the Parliamentary Board.[13] The two parties instead of putting matters to vote fought each other with lengthy arguments. Finally, after several hours of arguments twenty four names were proposed. Feverish efforts again got underway to arrive at a consensus on the matter with each side trying to get as many of its nominees appointed as possible. Khaliquzzaman was first off the tracks and proposed a list of five names, which purported to accommodate all

---

[13] *The Pioneer*, 18 September 1945.

the sections in the party. It included the Raja of Mahmudabad, Rizwanullah, Nawab Mohammad Yusuf, Z. H. Lari and Aziz Ahmad Khan. A chastened Rizwanullah whose group had not done too well in the previous day's contest consented to most of the names but wanted Maulana Hasrat Mohani to be included in the place of Aziz Ahmad Khan. The canny Khaliquzzaman responded that he had not included Hasrat in the Board since the Maulana was not interested in parliamentary activities. Ultimately, a compromise was arrived at between the two parties and both Aziz Ahmad Khan and Hasrat Mohani were nominated. The Raja of Mahmudabad, disgusted at the continuing bargaining game, adamantly refused to serve on the Board even though he was the Treasurer of the UPML.[14] Respecting his wishes, the committee instead appointed his younger brother, the Maharaj kumar as his replacement. The Parliamentary Board finally had nine members that included Ismail Khan, Khaliquzzaman, Z. H. Lari, Rizwanullah, Begum Aizaz Rasul, Nawab Mohammad Yusuf, Hasrat Mohani, Aziz Ahmad Khan and the Maharaj kumar of Mahmudabad. The meeting also elected S.A. Ashraf and Husain Mian as the two Secretaries to the UPML.[15] The next day the old guard scored another victory when the working committee succeeded in pushing through a resolution recommending that no disciplinary action be taken against those who had worked against official ML candidates during the elections in view of their unqualified apology.[16] An uncomfortable truce, thus, prevailed in the party as it set out to give battle to the Congress and its allies in the forthcoming polls. However, more than the party itself, it was groups independent of it that made a decisive impact on the elections. These included the faculty and students from the Muslim university at Aligarh and the *ulama* from Deoband. It is to the contributions of Aligarh that we may now turn.

The Committee of Writers and the Pakistan Literature Series

Even as the UPML was caught in the throes of crisis due to its intense factional conflicts, the Committee of Action headed by Nawab Ismail Khan appointed a Committee of Writers headed by Jamiluddin Ahmad, Lecturer of English at the Muslim University, to produce a series of pamphlets that could become

---

14 *Dawn*, 20 September 1945.

15 *The Pioneer*, 18 September 1945.

16 *The Pioneer*, 19 September 1945.

part of the popular literature on Pakistan.[17] The other members included Qazi Saiduddin Ahmad, a Geographer from the Muslim University at Aligarh, Syed Hasan Riaz, the editor of the ML's flagship Urdu newspaper the *Manshoor*, and Ahmad Shafi from Lahore. Jamiluddin Ahmad was an appropriate and deserving choice for this position given his assiduous labours in producing popular literature on behalf of the ML, the most notable being his compilation of the bestselling two volume set of speeches and writings of Mr Jinnah. One of Jinnah's earliest and most devoted followers at Aligarh, Ahmad kept a regular correspondence with his *Qaid*, contributed a number of publications for the League's propaganda,[18] and helped organize student workers for the ML's election campaign in 1945–46. He also wrote extensively about the Indian Muslim struggle for freedom after he moved to Pakistan where he taught in the English Department at the University of Karachi.[19]

Ahmad grandly declared that for 'too long has the cause of Muslim India suffered due to the absence of effective presentation of their case' and the 'mendacious propaganda carried on by the Congress and other anti-Muslim bodies with powerful backing of Hindu financial magnates.' He hoped that

> the series of pamphlets we are starting will serve to some extent, to dispel misconceptions and help all fair-minded people to make a dispassionate study of the peculiar conditions of India and appreciate the position and viewpoint of the Muslim nation in India.[20]

While it is not clear how popular these pamphlets became on the basis of sold copies (and there is no evidence that these were translated into Urdu despite the presence of Syed Hasan Riaz in the committee), they are an indicator of the growing common sense about Pakistan at Aligarh and Muslim north India at large. It is also reasonable to say that these pamphlets addressed a larger international audience as evident from Ahmad's assertion that 'the demand

---

17 *Deccan Times*, 21 May 1944.

18 See Jamiluddin Ahmad, *Is India One Nation* (Aligarh, 1939); *Muslim India and its Goal* (Aligarh, 1940); *The Indian Constitutional Tangle* (Lahore, 1941); *Through Pakistan to Freedom* (Lahore, 1944); *Some Aspects of Pakistan* (Lahore, 1946).

19 See Jamiluddin Ahmad, *Glimpses of Quaid-i-Azam* (Karachi, 1960); *Early Phase of Muslim Political Movement* (Karachi, 1963); *Middle Phase of Muslim Political Movement* (Karachi, 1964); *Final Phase of Muslim Political Movement* (Karachi, 1967); *Historic Documents of the Muslim Freedom Movement* (Lahore, 1970); *Quaid-i-Azam as Seen by His Contemporaries* (Lahore, 1976); *Creation of Pakistan* (Lahore, 1976).

20 Preface to Muhammad Abdul Sattar Kheiri, *National States and National Minorities: Pakistan Literature Series, No.1* (Lahore, 1945).

for Pakistan' was 'justified by all canons of international law and all principles of most advanced political thought.'[21]

National States and National Minorities

The first pamphlet on 'National States and National Minorities' was appropriately written by Muhammad Abdus Sattar Kheiri, a Professor at the Muslim University.[22]A colorful, if minor, figure in the annals of Indian nationalism, Kheiri along with his older brother spent a long period of time in diverse locations in the Middle East and Europe working on anti-colonial or Pan-Islamist causes before returning back to India and becoming an ardent advocate of Pakistan.[23] Kheiri argued that Muslims could not expect a fair deal in an undivided India as a minority and reiterated the ML's argument that the Indian Muslims were indeed a nation. His rejection of a minority position in India for Muslims in was based on two reasons. First, he pointed out that the concept of the minority initially arose in modern international law for protecting religious freedoms of persecuted Jews in Europe. Only later was this protection extended to linguistic, and then 'national minorities' and this again happened due to demands by a section of Jews who laid stress not on their religion or their language but on their 'national' characteristics. Kheiri pointed out that this protection of Jews was not based on a special European sense of toleration, but on a peculiarly western conception of religion in which religion was merely the private affair of the individual. 'This had led to the disappearance of religion as a great motive power and reduced it to mere ceremonies and forms.'[24] This gross reduction of religion was something that Kheiri, like his *Qaid* and much of the ML leadership, was unwilling to countenance in the context of Islam.

The second reason behind his rejection of the minority status for the Indian Muslims was the visibly pitiable condition of national minorities ever since nation-states of Europe had signed treaties guaranteeing minorities rights in their territories after the Great War. These treaties, that were supposed to

---

21 Ibid.

22 Muhammad Abdul Sattar Kheiri, *National States and National Minorities*: *Pakistan Literature Series, No.1* (Lahore, 1945).

23 For a detailed account of the Kheiri brothers political activities, see Majid Hayat Siddiqi, 'Bluff, Doubt, and Fear: The Kheiri Brothers and the Colonial State, 1904–1945', *Indian Economic and Social History Review*, Vol. 24, No. 3 (1987), 230–63.

24 Kheiri, *National States and National Minorities*, 5.

grant them cultural autonomy, protection of their languages, separate courts and schools as well as a proportionate share in administrative positions and legislatures, had not been honoured in the least. Kheiri, like Ambedkar before him, quoted from the work of C. A. Macartney, the Secretary of the Minorities Committee of the League of Nations to show that these minority treaties were woefully inadequate. The minorities had in practice been 'oppressed and persecuted and all the goodwill and resources of the Great Powers and the League of Nations who had undertaken to look after these minorities proved to be of no avail.'[25] Indeed, from the inauguration of the League up till 1931 the Committee had received 525 petitions from minorities regarding their suffering and oppressions, not taking into account the worst affected minorities who were afraid to even put up such petitions. He noted that senior posts in administration were filled almost completely by the majority while the minorities were given a few junior positions. Promotion to higher ranks was almost impossible for them. In education again, minorities were denied their own schools and very few among them made it to institutions of higher education. More insidiously, in some states administrative boundaries had been redrawn as well to reduce the proportion of minorities in territories where they had significant presence.

Minorities had also suffered economically since governments gave a majority of contracts to firms belonging to the majority community. Minority landlords had been expropriated due to new legislations with inadequate or no compensation by these governments while discriminatory taxation policies were also adopted to harm them. Kheiri gave concrete examples to substantiate his point. Thus, in southern Dobrudja, which had a large Bulgarian population, the Romanian Government had turned all state schools into Romanian schools leaving the Bulgarian minority with no instruction in their mother tongue. A petition signed by 140,000 fathers of Bulgarian school children asking for Bulgarian schools to be opened was confiscated, its signatories arrested and forced to declare that they were satisfied with the Romanian schools. The League's intervention in these cases had been feeble and ineffective. Kheiri pointed out that even in cases like the expulsion of German settlers by the Polish government from the Corridor, in which the League Council had intervened, Poland had still carried out its plan of evicting two thousand of the three thousand settlers.

In contrast to the modern nation-state, Kheiri argued that the record of Islamic states throughout history was far superior given their well known and

[25] Ibid., 11.

generous treatment of minorities. The Prophet himself had guaranteed the Jewish minority in Medina 'almost the same rights as enjoyed by Muslims themselves' in spite of the fact that the Jews 'started and continued a series of acts of treason and treachery during the whole period of his life in Medina.'[26] In the same vein, the Prophet's Companion Abu Bakr had granted a charter of freedom to Christians. Minorities generally paid a 'nominal tax' for the protection and freedom they enjoyed under Muslim rule and this was often 'wholly returned when the Muslims felt themselves unable to protect non-Muslims under their rule'.[27] Coming to the Ottomans, Kheiri pointed out that Mehmed II, the conqueror of Constantinople, had invited the Greeks to return to the city by promising them freedom of worship and supervising the election of a new patriarch. He also lavished praise on the Ottoman Millet System under which the Millet-Bashy was granted full spiritual and temporal powers over his community and invested by the Sultan with his own body of janissaries, prison and torture chamber. Kheiri pointed out that the system had been admired and preferred by medieval Jews as well. In this regard, he quoted the letter written in 1454 by Isaac Zafrati, a German Jew, to the congregations of Syria, Rhineland, Moravia and Hungary inviting them to Turkey, wherein he wrote that it was better to live under the Muslims rather than the Christians for here 'every man may dwell at peace under his own vine and his own fig tree'.[28]

The Turks, Kheiri continued, had also allowed non-Muslims to establish themselves in commerce, banking, industry and the arts. Thus, the Dragomans of the Port and Fleet were almost always Greeks. By contrast, he noted that the Greeks had no hesitation in destroying the literature, historical records and national monuments of even their fellow Christians, the Bulgarians. Given the obvious superiority of the Islamic state on the question of minority rights, Kheiri quoted from the records of the twenty second session of the Mandates Commission to point out that even the Assyrians of Iraq whose minority rights had been guaranteed by the League of Nations in 1932 had demanded that they be allowed to live once again under the Millet System. He had no hesitation in therefore claiming that Ottoman laws for the protection of minorities 'have not yet been improved upon by modern Europe in any of its States.'[29] Turning

[26] Ibid., 6.

[27] Ibid.

[28] Ibid., 9.

[29] Ibid., 7.

to India, Kheiri flatly declared that 'had the Muslims in India not given wide freedom and protected the Hindus in India during their 800 years of rule, today there would have been no minority problem here.'[30]

Kheiri concluded that it was not in the interests of any national state to protect its minority by granting them cultural autonomy and avenues for development. That would be tantamount to 'conscious suicide'. After all given a chance to freely develop their own culture and community, the minorities would surely utilize it to carve out their own independent states. National states, therefore, had to assimilate national minorities for the sake of their own survival by wiping out the distinct identity of their minorities. Kheiri warned the British government against trying to prepare Indian Muslims for getting assimilated into Hindu India. He reiterated Jinnah's message by listing all the characteristics that made the Muslims in India a distinct nation. He also used the occasion to express astonishment at the recently expressed view of Sir Sarvepalli Radhakrishnan, the Vice Chancellor of the Benares Hindu University, that the communal problem could be resolved with the help of music. Kheiri remarked that 'the learned gentleman is ignorant of the most well-known fact that music is forbidden to orthodox Muslims'.[31] The Muslims wanted their Pakistan. All efforts at peace had failed and 'nothing but a major operation can help now.'[32] Kheiri claimed that he had arrived at this conclusion in 1916 and had suggested the same to Camille Huysman, the Secretary of Socialist International. The latter had also mentioned it in his book that was published in French in the following year from Stockholm.Kheiri ended his pamphlet with a verse from the Quran: 'They intend to put out light of God with their breaths, and God will not agree except to perfect His light, though it be disagreeable to the unbelievers (IX-3).'[33]

Pakistan's Distinct Physical and Human Geography

If Kheiri built up a case for creating Pakistan on the basis of his reading of world history and modern international relations, Kazi Saiduddin Ahmad, utilized insights from his discipline of Geography for the same purpose in the three pamphlets he wrote for this series. Ahmad was a fresh PhD from the University of London having submitted a doctoral thesis in 1939 on the 'Agricultural Geography of the Punjab'. An 'old boy' of Aligarh, having secured

30 Ibid.

31 Ibid., 20.

32 Ibid., 22.

33 Ibid.

a masters degree from there, he was appointed as a Reader of Geography at the Muslim University on his return from England. He soon moved to the Punjab University at Lahore in late 1944 to set up its geography department and went on to serve there until his retirement in 1966. Ahmad refuted the idea that India was geographically a single entity as had been stated in a speech by the Viceroy Lord Linlithgow. The term 'geographical unity', he asserted, was at best a relative expression since 'within the wider geographical unity for the whole of India, we have well marked diversity, and in each of these diverse units much better geographical unity.'[34] To substantiate his argument, he invoked various examples from world geography. Ahmad pointed out that while Scandinavia seemed like a well-marked physical unit with people belonging to the same Nordic stock who were Christian, yet it contained two separate political units in Sweden and Norway. Explaining this divergence in terms of differences in the local geographical environment, he noted that Sweden was oriented towards the Baltic Sea while Norway faced the Atlantic Ocean. This led the Norwegians to acquire maritime traits while the Swedes acquired continental traits. The difference in their life based on differences in natural environment had thus made them drift apart and form independent states.

Another example that he cited was that of the Iberian Peninsula, which too seemed like a well-marked physical unit with populations that belonged to the same racial stock, spoke similar romance languages, shared the same Roman Catholic religion, but again contained two independent countries in Portugal and Spain. Ahmad attributed their existence as separate sovereign states to Portugal's location in a lowland area, its separation from Spain by rough mountain country, its physiographical aloofness from Spain on the coastal margin of the Iberian plateau, besides the impact of English influences on Portuguese culture, which was absent in case of Spain. Again, in Europe, Holland was independent from Germany even though both were situated on the German Plain, were connected by the Rhine, possessed Christian populations and spoke Germanic languages. Holland had developed as a maritime power while Germany had emerged as a continental power, again as a result of environmental differences.

Ahmad's pamphlets contained another distinct argument – that there was no necessary and direct correlation between physical geography and political sovereignty. To build his case he pointed out that in North America the division

34 Kazi Saiduddin Ahmad, *Is India Geographically One?: Pakistan Literature Series No.6* (Lahore, 1945), 9.

between Canada and United States was artificial as was the case of the division of Ireland and Ulster. The Balkan Peninsula again, he indicated, was a single physical unit but had a number of states given their ethnographic differences. Closer home, Indo-China too had greater geographical unity than India but was divided into several states. Ahmad thus concluded that 'factors other than physical and geographical considerations' had determined the formation of states in different parts of the world. Geographically homogenous areas had been carved into various states and the principal factor here had been 'the will of the people inhabiting a particular region, and in the cases of subordinate states, the might of the ruling power.'[35]

In the light of these living examples, Ahmad asserted that the communal pattern in India, therefore, needed to be given political recognition, for a hundred million people 'inhabiting large contiguous areas with independent outlets to the sea' could not be forced to remain as a minority within an undivided India. He, however, added that 'the object should be to divide India not into political units which should either be in complete isolation from one another or in subordination to each other or to a common center, but into states which should function in harmony or neighborly co-operation.'[36] But the question remained as to how this division was to be achieved. Ahmad elaborated his own plan in another pamphlet that had been published earlier in the Muslim University Gazette on 1 December 1943, wherein he divided the subcontinent into Pakistan, Hindustan, Dravidastan, Bengalistan and Rajasthan. There would thus be two Hindu and two Muslim 'communo-regional' states based on Hindu and Muslim majorities respectively, in addition to Rajasthan. For Ahmad, majority implied 'not the absolute majority of a community but its being the largest single group'.[37] Pakistan would comprise Punjab west of the Sutlej, the NWFP, Baluchistan and Delhi province that would cover the whole of the Ghaggar Plain between the Yamuna and the Sutlej. Ahmad suggested that eastern Punjab be added to Delhi to create a large province where the combined population of Hindus, Muslims and Sikhs would have 'the right to self-determination and self-administration'.[38] This natural region was inhabited

---

[35] Ibid., 19.

[36] Kazi Saiduddin Ahmad, *The Communal Pattern in India: Pakistan Literature Series No.2* (Lahore, 1945), 9.

[37] Kazi Saiduddin Ahmad, *Politico-Regional Division of India: Pakistan Literature Series No. 4* (Lahore, 1945), 5.

[38] Ibid., 10.

by Turko-Iranian and Indo-Aryan races on either side of the Indus, which were different from those inhabiting other parts of India.

Ahmad saw the second state, Hindustan, inhabited by the Aryo-Dravidian race, as covering the upper Gangetic basin and including the provinces of U.P., Bihar, Orissa and C.P. He recommended the Burdwan division of Bengal to be attached to Bihar as a sub-province and further envisioned the Hooghly as the natural western boundary between Hindustan and Bengalistan, with Calcutta reverting to the latter and Howrah to Burdwan in Hindustan. This transfer, Ahmad happily noted, would also increase the percentage of Muslim population in Bengal from 54.7 per cent to 63 per cent. Bengalistan would thus comprise the provinces of Bengal (sans Burdwan division) and Assam. Ahmad justified the inclusion of Calcutta, which had a Hindu majority, into this third sovereign state on the grounds that this majority was primarily a result of the floating population of Hindus who were temporarily drawn from outside into Calcutta on account of its being a seat of government. He claimed that geographically too, Calcutta belonged to the central delta region and not to Burdwan and hence could not be transferred along with Burdwan to Hindustan. Ahmad's fourth republic was Dravidastan based in the Deccan peninsula and inhabited by the Dravidian race. It would consist of Bombay province, a new combined province of Andhra and Kanara, Madras province and Andaman and Nicobar Islands. Bombay province itself was to be reconstituted into three sub-provinces – Maharashtra, Gujarat and Berar. The fifth republic, Rajasthan, would comprise the native states of Rajputana, west Central India, Gwalior and Kathiawar. Ahmad indicated that Ajmer province lying in the center of this entity could serve as the seat for a central coordinating organization for these states. In the final analysis, he wanted each Republic to have autonomous provinces whose boundaries could be redrawn taking into account linguistic, economic, and regional considerations.

Ahmad made a distinction between his scheme and that of Reginald Coupland, the Oxford don, who had written a three volume report on the constitutional problem in India. He clarified that while Coupland had proposed a confederation of these states, his own idea was

> to have four sovereign states in British India with a statutory provision for an India Council for purposes of co-ordination with several committees consisting of representatives of sovereign states to discuss subjects of all India concern and to take any common action which may be agreed upon.[39]

[39] Ibid., 2.

The India Council was to be maintained out of contributions by the sovereign states based on a fixed percentage of revenues. The scheme would function 'within the framework of the British empire on the basis of the Statute of Westminster with the Viceroy acting as the link between the various Republics and Britain on the one hand and the Republics and the Native states on the other.'[40]

Ahmad was somewhat ambiguous about the powers and responsibilities of this India Council. While on the one hand he wanted India's defence to be vested in the Indian Defence Committee at the same time he was clear that the Republics were free to maintain separate armies whose strength during peace time could be regulated by agreement. Native states would also have to share in India's defence and even Ceylon was considered part of India for this purpose. Again, while Ahmad wanted the Republics to have freedom in foreign relations, he also noted that they could 'have separate representation or a common one through the foreign relations committee.'[41] Finally, the native states in his scheme were free to continue their relations with the Paramount Power or join the Republic in which they lay or to which they were contiguous.

Islam and Muslims in the Indian Environment

Ishtiaq Husain Qureshi, renowned Professor of History from Delhi University, contributed two provocative pamphlets to the series, the first of which provided the historical background for the development of Islamic culture in India, while the second speculated on the future development of the Islamic polity in Pakistan. Qureshi was very much a U.P. man, born in Patyali near Allahabad into a family, which had fallen on hard times ever since the 1857 Mutiny in which one of his granduncles had been hanged by the British.[42] Straitened family circumstances did not allow him to go to MAO at Aligarh and he passed his intermediate exams as an external candidate. Active during the Non-Cooperation/Khilafat Movement in the U.P. countryside, he joined the staff of the Urdu newspaper *Al Aman* in Delhi once the movement had died down. While in Delhi, Qureshi acquired a B.A. and a double M.A. in History and Persian from St. Stephens College. Later he went on to Cambridge where he wrote a PhD thesis on the administration of the Delhi Sultanate. On his return to India, Qureshi was appointed a reader in History at Delhi University before being promoted to a full professorship.

---

40 Ibid.

41 Ibid., 3.

42 See Rauf Parekh, 'The Grand Old Man of Historiography', *Dawn*, 20 January 2009.

During his Cambridge days, Qureshi had been acquainted with the group of students, who supported Chaudhri Rehmat Ali's idea of Pakistan. While it is not clear whether he was part of this group, by the time of the 1945–46 elections he was a definitely a firm supporter of Pakistan. Dwelling on the question of Indian Muslim identity, Qureshi asserted that 'the uniformity of all Muslim peoples is far more striking than their diversity. This is true to a remarkable extent of the Indian Muslims as well.'[43] If the Indian environment had played a part in influencing the Indian Muslim, it was mostly to make him more conscious of the need to preserve his identity and prevent its annihilation by the rising tide of Hinduism. Even if Qureshi acknowledged the existence of a distinct Indian Islam, he firmly believed that 'the assimilation of Hindu characteristics by Indian Islam was confined to mere superficialities of life. In deeper matters the Indian Muslim was no different from other Muslims.'[44]

Qureshi attributed the existence of Indian Islam to the very catholicity of Islam. Going back to the time of the earliest Muslim conquests of India, he pointed out that Muslim conquerors of India were proud of their Islam but not of their race since there is no sense of racial superiority in Islam. They had married Hindu women who became Muslim, but were liberal enough to not eliminate all traces of their culture as long as these did not conflict with Islam. It is this catholicity that produced the right atmosphere for cultural contacts with the Hindus. Muslim kings employed scholars to translate Hindu works into Persian. Muslim poets such as Malik Muhammad Jayasi, Abdur Rahim Khan-i-Khanan and Kabir wrote some of the greatest Hindu poetry while Amir Khusrau cultivated a taste for Hindu culture and music. Qureshi also claimed that it was due to Islam's impact that the Bhakti Movement arose in India.

While Muslims in India had, therefore, not been averse to borrowing elements of Hindu culture they nonetheless took care to see to it that none of them conflicted with Islam. The only exception, Qureshi pointed out, was in the case of Urdu, a unique product of the Indo-Islamic encounter that became the language of Indian Muslims. Urdu was based on Prakrit grammar but had an 'essentially Islamic vocabulary' consisting of Arabic, Persian and Turkish words. Qureshi claimed that the Muslim had gone more than half way in meeting the Hindu by creating and adopting this language for he 'had sacrificed the much easier, simple, more regular and logical forms of Persian verbs and

---

43 I. H. Qureshi, *The Development of Islamic Culture in India: Pakistan Literature Series No. 9* (Lahore, 1946), 1.

44 Ibid., 6.

propositions to win the understanding of the Hindu.' In this process, 'he had remained a Muslim, but ceased to be an Arab, Turk, Persian and an Afghan. He had become an Indian Muslim.'[45]

In addition, Qureshi reminded his readers that Muslim kings in their generosity also patronized other Indian languages as evident from Bengali translations of Sanskrit Hindu scriptures being dedicated to Muslim potentates. Muslim rule thus liberated Hindu masses from the 'tyranny of Sanskrit classicism and encouraged popular languages hitherto considered vulgar… Awakened into new life the Hindus became eager to assimilate new ideas and under the patronage of the Mughals, Muslim mannerisms, idioms, ideas, and etiquette became fashionable.'[46] In response, the Indian Muslims too discarded Islamic taboos about music and rejoiced in the charms of classical Hindu music, let Hindu subtleties creep into Muslim poetry, adopted Hindu dress, while Muslim architecture adopted some Hindu motifs. Even the Muslim palate changed as chilly and tamarind entered into their cuisine. A modus vivendi, therefore, developed between Hindus and Muslims, especially among the cultured sections, under which Muslims and Hindus kept their own religious beliefs, Muslims tolerated Hindu notions of the 'unclean' Muslim and Hindu aversion to inter-dining, thus inaugurating a tradition of toleration with few parallels in world history.

Qureshi contended that while the Sikh, Maratha and Rajput rebellions against the Mughal Empire shook the foundations of this structure of goodwill between the two sides, the end came only in the nineteenth century when the spell of Muslim domination was well and truly broken in India. The Hindu 'naturally changed his orientation' in the context of British rule and what followed was revivalism that idealized ancient Hindu culture before the advent of Muslims in India. The most obvious manifestation of this process was the movement for the adoption of Hindi that was purged of Muslim origin words as an official language, the adoption of Devanagri and the eschewal of the Arabic script. In response to this revival, Qureshi noted that Muslims now used Urdu with a larger percentage of Persian and Arabic words, sought to purge Hindu social customs and restore Islam's pristine purity in their lives. While the Hindu saw the pre-Muslim past as his civilization's era of glory, the Muslim exulted in the conquests of his ancestors in India, which the Hindu saw as national humiliation. The result was that 'the bridges which the Muslim had taken seven hundred years to build were burnt and in their place was left the dark,

45 Ibid., 9.

46 Ibid., 8.

deep gulf.'[47] Qureshi had no doubts that these social and cultural developments had a direct impact on the political cleavage in India for it left the Muslim in India feeling isolated. It was thus Hindu revivalism that made the Muslims a separate nation in India. But even as he placed the greater portion of the blame on the Hindus for this breakdown, Qureshi saw the process as inevitable. As he concluded, the Hindus could not have permanently reconciled themselves to 'the superiority of a culture whose foundations rested upon ideas alien to their philosophy and therefore their revolt was logical and inevitable. The reaction of the Muslims was equally rational.'[48]

Islam and Pakistan

Qureshi's other pamphlet was a bold inquiry into the problems and prospects regarding the development of an Islamic polity in Pakistan. At the very outset he declared that

> if we face facts we are a mass of heterogeneous men and women held together by our common allegiance to Islam. Weaken this allegiance and we are lost: like the seared leaves of autumn we are blown in all directions, ultimately finding our way to the manure pit to enrich the growth of other peoples, other systems, other ideals.[49]

This formulation would later be echoed in independent Pakistan by various votaries of the 'ideological state'. In any case, he defended his position.

> We cannot afford to be carried away by slogans which have no validity in our society. We cannot divorce our individual or social life from religion because it is a meaningless phrase meant to hoodwink the unwary. Life cannot be divided into watertight compartments; it is based on certain loyalties; these loyalties will dominate our entire attitude towards other men and ourselves; religion is after all a crystallization of this attitude in a clear-headed intelligible, definable manner. Those who say that politics has nothing to do with religion talk in a terminology which does not concern us – to them politics is merely the machinery of government and the laws which govern its working; to them religion is merely a Church or an ecclesiastical organization. Our politics includes a motive power behind the government,

---

47 Ibid., 11–12.

48 Ibid., 16.

49 Ishtiaq Husain Qureshi, *The Future Development of Islamic Polity: Pakistan Literature Series*, No. 8 (Lahore, 1946).

> the idealism to safeguard which a State is necessary: our religion is not the organized Church but the idealism that governs our entire life. How can we separate the two? For us a State that does not help us in our endeavors to attain our ideals is useless, meaningless; for us the State is an instrument of tyranny if it becomes an ideal in itself. My country is 'not' my God: it is only a geographical unit into which I have been born. It should be my endeavor to maintain and spread my idealism in this unit and through this unit in the world. For Islam cannot afford to be static: it is a revolutionary force: either it changes the world or it decays. A most elementary knowledge of Muslim history will bear me out in this statement.[50]

If Pakistan was going to be based on the ideals found in the Quran and the life of the Prophet, the only way that these ideals could become a governing force in society was by recognizing Muslim law as the ultimate sovereign. As Qureshi made it very clear

> on one thing we can have no difference of opinion and this has been recognized by our jurists all this time, that in a Muslim State the sovereignty can be vested only in the law and the law can only be the law of Islam. The principles enunciated by the Quran and the Prophet should form the Supreme and basic law of a Muslim State... It should be like the constitutional law of a modern state differing only in one respect, that the basic law of a Muslim state should be unchangeable, above human interference. There will have to be an impartial tribunal like the Supreme Court of the United States of America to determine if a measure in any way contravenes the dictates of Islam.[51]

Qureshi pointed out that rulers and Caliphs in the history of Islam had been legally subservient to the *Shariah*. History had also shown that their sovereignty had often been undermined when they went against its commands. But could these states ruled by Islamic rulers in history become the model for Pakistan? Qureshi rejected this idea outright for he visualized Pakistan as a modern Islamic state and not a carbon copy of its medieval forebear. Indeed, like Mahmudabad earlier, he questioned whether the medieval Islamic state was ever truly Islamic and indicated that Islam had declined as a force in the world because the medieval state betrayed its essential principles. This betrayal was most strikingly embodied in the reduction of the Islamic state to dynastic

---

50 Ibid., 7.

51 Ibid., 15.

rule by families backed by medieval jurists. Reflecting on the historical decline in Islam's political system, Qureshi pointed out that after the Prophet's death his Companions inaugurated the method of nominating the Caliph by a small high-minded, virtuous coterie to which the masses were expected to give obedience. This principle had been adopted with the laudable objective of preventing the Caliphate from becoming a family heritage and was perhaps appropriate for the time as the Islamic community was in its infancy and was beset by civil war. More importantly, the Companions themselves had been very flexible in their use of their methods and never intended to 'lay down forms and antecedents for all time to come.'[52] In this regard they were one with the Prophet who 'beyond inculcating certain fundamental teachings that Muslims were to adopt towards social and political life, did not suggest any constitution or method of election or for that matter even the form of government.' This was to provide his people a free hand to fashion their own institutions. But under dynastic rule that followed, the Caliphate became the possession of families even as the selection of the leader through a small coterie continued. Qureshi lamented that the jurists of Islam had thus 'thrown away the kernel and kept the form.'[53] This was, however, not surprising since the jurists who upheld this system were not divinely inspired, but human beings who were creatures of their environment and above all prisoners to their instincts as lawyers and hence inherently conservative. While conservatism based on respect for precedents and authority was suitable for a static, unchanging society, Qureshi contended that it

> was hardly consistent with a revolutionary and dynamic force like Islam. This was like chaining Prometheus; like mummifying a living being to save it from the cuts and bruises of the great Armageddon of life. The result was exactly the opposite to what had been the mission of Islam; instead of carrying away the straw and rubbish of privilege, vested interests, and inequalities on a surging wave of revolution, it became in its own way the bulwark of reactionary conservatism.[54]

These were strong words and Qureshi followed it up by declaring that if Muslims wanted to 'escape further consequences of this decay' they needed to start thinking of remedies. But questions remained as to who would come up with the necessary solutions for making the Islamic state a practical reality and

---

52 Ibid., 9.

53 Ibid.

54 Ibid., 10.

what those particular solutions would look like. Qureshi was of the firm opinion that 'our universities, our academic societies, and organizations, our teachers and students have to think out these problems.' As he insisted

> we cannot leave these matters to the Ulema... because however learned they might be in principles of jurisprudence, they have neither the training nor the vision to be of any use. *We may know our shortcomings but we are the only people to do it.*[55]

At the same time, Qureshi wanted modern intellectuals to be aware of their own limitations. As he asked

> are we free of blemishes ourselves? Are we not open to the great accusation that we do not know either the Quran or the Traditions of the Prophet? And of course who are we to criticize the jurists without studying them?[56]

He, therefore, wanted modern academicians to equip themselves with the necessary knowledge of the Quran, the Hadith, the writings and discussions of medieval jurists as well as Islamic history. This was easier said than done and as Qureshi himself acknowledged, mastery over each of these subjects could take up an entire lifetime of study. The key for him, therefore, lay in cooperation between specialists working in these various disciplines. He was optimistic that Aligarh could 'produce with the help of different departments some scheme which may form the basis of discussions.'[57]

As regards the features of the modern Islamic system of government, Qureshi expressed confidence that it was going to be far superior to democracy and totalitarianism, to capitalism and socialism, even if it shared commonalities with these contemporary systems. Islam was democratic in as much as it was against tyranny. He, therefore, maintained that ordinary Muslims would have 'a full and free share in the government of a Muslim State so that no vested interests may deprive them of their freedom and put any shackles on them'. The old method of a small coterie appointing the Muslim ruler who would be owed allegiance by masses was unacceptable, however reliable the coterie might be. He insisted that 'the masses must have the right of at least electing this college of electors.'[58] At the same time Qureshi was quick to express

---

[55] Ibid., 11.

[56] Ibid., 13–14.

[57] Ibid., 14.

[58] Ibid., 19.

skepticism about liberal democracy stating that there were 'evils in the western system of elections.' In this regard, he was only echoing a sentiment that had been forcefully articulated by Jinnah and the ML leadership for over a decade. Qureshi was, however, positive that with the Grace of God, an Islamic substitute free of such evils would eventually be found.

But liberal democracy posed a more fundamental problem for Qureshi since it maximized the individual's liberty defining limits on his actions as narrowly as possible. Stressing Islam's differences with the West on this matter, he contended that while Islam gave the individual the fullest freedom to ascend to his highest stature it could not allow him to 'indulge in meaningless and destructive pleasure or wield an unhealthy influence upon society.'[59] As Qureshi made it clear

> Islam cannot leave certain spheres of life strictly to the individual, any action which is likely to prejudice the healthy growth of Muslim society will have to be severely prohibited. We do not believe in unrestricted freedom to bring about a lowering of human standards, of spiritual values of allegiance to our common idealism. Anything which brings in germs of decay and degeneration in our physical, moral or spiritual life will have to be ruthlessly curbed and steps will have to be taken that loose talk and loose thinking are not allowed to exist. This does not mean censorship but an enlightened and sympathetic censorship with an appeal to the highest tribunal in the land.[60]

Qureshi went on to dismiss liberal democracy as a Jewish conspiracy and in this regard approvingly noted that

> Hitler was not wrong when he identified the democracies with international Jewry, because high finance and big business which are the backbone of social organization in the democracies are very much in the hands of the Jews; and because finance is the real master of bourgeoisie democracy, the Jews are very much in control.[61]

Underlining this point, Qureshi declared that there was a deep antipathy between Islam and capitalism since Islam and high finance could not go hand in hand. It was, therefore, not surprising that the rise of capitalism coincided with the decline of Islam.

---

[59] Ibid., 18.

[60] Ibid., 21.

[61] Ibid., 17.

As regards totalitarianism, Qureshi contended that Islam had some features in common with it and asked Muslims 'not to be afraid of this fact.' After all the Quran, he claimed, clearly stated that God had 'bought the lives, possessions and even the families of true believers'. There was not one aspect of human life which did not come under the control and guidance of Islam. This was the 'totalitarian outlook'.[62] The fundamental difference between Islam and a totalitarian state was that while the latter demanded allegiance of the individual to make itself stronger, Islam made that demand for the establishment of a balanced society and 'good life'. While totalitarianism considered the individual an automaton, Islam saw the human beings as responsible persons cooperating to achieve their fullest stature. 'The ideal of Totalitarianism was material, that of Islam spiritual.'[63]

Qureshi bemoaned the subjugation of Muslim peoples around the world by western industrialized powers and attributed it to their failure to industrialize. He, therefore, exhorted Muslims to take advantage of the new scientific methods, increase their productivity, raise standards of living and become capable of defending themselves against the aggressors and imperialists. For this purpose Qureshi did not want Pakistan to become capitalist but instead made a case for intensive economic planning and state capitalism. He saw antecedents for state capitalism on a limited scale in Islamic history. As he wistfully noted, 'will it not be better to go back to those antecedents and adopt a modern and more developed form of State Capitalism to develop our resources?'[64] He, however, hastened to add that this economic system was not tantamount to socialism for there could be 'no compromise between Islam and materialistic dialectics'. At the same time, though, he believed that there were two things that Islam had in common with Russia. First, Islam too believed in social justice and Muslims, therefore, needed to be open to learning from the Russian experiment. Second, like the jurists in Islam, Qureshi expressed his belief in the 'doctrine of human labour being the real producer of wealth.'[65]

In order to achieve the task of rapid industrial development, Qureshi wanted the entire population of the Islamic state to 'be regimented for the purpose of reconstruction which [would] have to be carefully planned.' He wanted this to continue till the Muslims became pioneers in all branches of human knowledge

---

62 Ibid., 20.

63 Ibid., 21.

64 Ibid., 22.

65 Ibid., 23.

and activity and fulfill their destiny of being 'the model nation in the world.'[66] Qureshi was passionate about the task at hand. As he waxed eloquent

> let us try to find a meaning in the Quran which leaves the progress of the world far behind. With the guidance we have in the Holy Book, we should form, as the Quran wants us to form, the spearhead of all progress. Let us be the leaders of the caravan of life, not stragglers left behind to mourn our fate.[67]

Finally, Qureshi contended that since Islam was a revolutionary force, which transcended all barriers of race and country, it 'cannot and must not be divided into independent states.' He pointed out that soon after the Prophet's death Abu Bakr established the principle of the indivisible Muslim world, the Khilafat, when he did not allow the Arab tribes to secede from central authority. These tribes had only refused to pay a tax and not relinquished Islam but even this action was seen as tantamount to seceding from the Muslim commonwealth. Qureshi himself wanted a revival of the Khilafat, a Muslim federation or a 'super-state'. He did not envisage this super-state as 'an idle body with little or no power', but a powerful entity that was 'able to make decisions and enforce them.'[68] Qureshi acknowledged that 'this ideal is not easy to achieve' for there remained 'antagonisms to conquer, prejudices to remove, fears to allay.' He was also clear that it could not be realized in the immediate future, but nonetheless wanted it to be the main goal for the Muslims. Qureshi concluded his meditations with a dramatic flourish.

> And the achievement of that goal depends on the success we achieve in this land of India in establishing and maintaining a polity in accordance with our ideals. That depends on our will to live, which depends on our willingness to die.[69]

Muslim Education and Pakistan

Liaquat Ali Khan's speech on Muslim educational problems to the All India Muslim Educational Conference held at Agra in 1945 was published as a

---

66 Ibid., 23.

67 Ibid., 13.

68 Ibid., 24.

69 Ibid., 24–25.

pamphlet in the series since the question of Muslim education was 'as much a political as a social and cultural problem.'[70] Liaquat used the opportunity to remind his audience that the Muslims were 'bound sooner or later to realize our national destiny, Pakistan.'[71] He, therefore, wanted Muslims to 'be ready with properly equipped and efficient personnel to make proper use of the power and opportunity in the wake of Pakistan and undertake and execute vast schemes for the social, economic, industrial, and educational development of our people.'[72] That required Muslim students to enrol in much higher numbers in engineering, medicine, commerce, science and industry so that the nation could have a healthy pool of doctors, engineers, scientists, men of commerce and industry. He complimented Aligarh for taking a lead in this regard and starting a college of engineering and technology and also beginning a drive for establishing a medical college. As far as the Humanities were concerned, he laid special emphasis on 'religious education and the study of Arabic, Islamic history, Islamic Philosophy, and Islamics in general' since they constituted the foundations of Muslim national life and culture.[73]

Liaquat also used this opportunity to lambast Gandhi's Wardha Scheme of Education as well as the subsequent Sargent Scheme whose recommendations were being considered at the time by the government since both 'cut at the root of the fundamentals of our faith and national ideology.' Echoing the Pirpur Report, this Oxford graduate and secular face of the Muslim League argued that the Gandhian idea of all religions being equally true propagated by the Wardha Scheme militated against the idea of Islam being the final truth and the Prophet as the final teacher. He also claimed that *ahimsa* was against the Islamic belief of fighting against evil in the cause of righteousness and meant to root out martial spirit from Muslim youth. Underlining the two-nation theory, he rejected the Sargent Report on the grounds that its recommendation for setting up a central educational authority for India as a whole was similar to the demand for a central government for India. The Report was also unacceptable since it had not recognized the Muslims as a separate nation or their claims of setting up independent sovereign states in Muslim majority areas.

---

70 Liaquat Ali Khan, *Muslim Educational Problems:Pakistan Literature Series No.7* (Lahore, 1945), 16–17.

71 Ibid., 31.

72 Ibid.

73 Ibid., 38.

Islamic Fiscal Fabric for Pakistan

The final set of pamphlets focused on Pakistan's economic, fiscal, industrial and power resources and reiterated the ML's message about Pakistan's economic viability and its future policies in the face of incessant Congress propaganda that dismissed Pakistan as an impending economic disaster. Writing about the nation's 'fiscal fabric', Ahmad Shafi, a member of the Committee of Writers, reflected on how a modern economy could be fostered in Pakistan while at the same time keeping its functions and programmes in consonance with the principles laid down in the Quran. For Shafi, this was imperative if Pakistan was to live up to the promise of an ideal Islamic society providing economic equality and avoid the heavy price being paid by the West for tremendous economic inequalities in society. He acknowledged that the complexities of the modern economy had not been anticipated in the early days of Islam when Islamic law was formulated. Thus, 'something more than the collection of Zakat and the determination of the usury or no-usury dispute would be required to tackle the situation.'[74]

Shafi, therefore, addressed the questions of interest (how it could be eliminated) and profit motive (how it could be softened), the primary sources of inequality in modern capitalist society. He pointed out that even Christian thinkers had been critical of these twin pillars of capitalism and quoted at length from G. D. H. Cole's 'Socialism in Evolution' to contend that the 'wisdom of the Quran was being verified by the experience of erring blundering Europe.'[75] Shafi wanted to make sure that interest did not make a back door entry in some other form. He, therefore, dismissed the suggestion that interest distributed by banks to finance commerce and industry was valid. He pointed out that unlike the modern bank or investor the Muslim trader of Islam's early days invested his own money at his own risk and shared both profits and losses. The modern investor, on the other hand, was only interested in his fixed rate of interest on the money invested irrespective of the fate of the business. The modern alternative to this system, socialism, involving state takeover of business, finance and industry was also not acceptable to Shafi on the more pragmatic grounds that it was progressing 'through trial and error' and had not reached a stage where it could be 'copied wholesale'. Shafi also noted that a socialist state would be marked by a concentration of political and economic power and possibly ruled by an oligarchy. Here he quoted Bertrand Russell to warn that imitating Russia blindly would be extremely dangerous.[76]

74 Ahmad Shafi, *The Fiscal Fabric: Pakistan Literature Series No. 5* (Lahore, 1945), 4.

75 Ibid., 6.

76 Ibid., 8.

Shafi, like Qureshi earlier, therefore supported a mixed economy in which state enterprise would be accompanied by private enterprise. The state would raise finances through 'profit and loss' loans in order to set up heavy industry and run public utilities and also enable devout Muslims to participate in this process as investors. The profit for these enterprises could be calculated at 'a slightly lower than normal rate and guaranteed by the government, the loss being underwritten at par by the state through its own bank.'[77] The investor would not lose unless the state bank crashed. Moreover, loss would be spread over the entire community, which would be protected by the law of averages. He claimed that theologians with whom he had discussed these matters had no objections to it. While a modern economist had expressed his doubts, Shafi wanted to give this idea a trial. He was hopeful that in 'a well-balanced economy many angularities will be rubbed off in the course of working.'[78]

Shafi also envisaged a Central Bank to handle Pakistan's finances, deal with the outside world and reflect its credit in the international money market while acting as a Reserve Bank within the country. The ordinary citizen, petty industrialist or small trader would no doubt have to rely on the services of banks of joint stock variety but the state would 'control not only the terms of their capital issue but also the composition of their directorate to save them from being monopolized by any particular section'.[79] Shafi concluded with brief speculations on sources of revenue for Pakistan. He envisaged land revenue as continuing as a major source since Pakistan would continue to be an agricultural country for a long time. He saw tariffs assuming importance with the coming of industries while he expected ports to yield adequate customs duties on both imports, and in some cases, exports. He also insisted that Pakistan would enforce total and would, therefore, forego excise duty on alcohol and narcotics. He was, however, optimistic that income tax would make good any decrease from other sources and also hopeful that a vast unexplored field of taxation could be identified and tapped to raise national revenues.

Reiterating Pakistan's Economic Prospects

If Shafi speculated on Pakistan's future economic policy, Anwar Iqbal Qureshi reiterated the ML's message that Pakistan had enough natural resources, infrastructural assets and a healthy and enterprising population to emerge as

---

77 Ibid

78 Ibid., 10.

79 Ibid., 12.

a prosperous economic entity. Qureshi was from Jalandhar in eastern Punjab. who after an initial career as a student and teacher at Punjab University, went abroad to acquire an M.Sc. in Economics from the University of London and a PhD from Dublin for which he wrote his doctoral thesis on the structure and working of the Farm Credit Administration for which he visited the US in the summer of 1935.[80] Recruited by Osmania University into its Economics department on his return to India, he taught there and wrote on issues of economic development in Hyderabad before migrating to Pakistan.[81] Qureshi's later research extended to Islamic economics wherein he strongly argued against the charging of interest on loans of any type, thus taking a position similar to the one articulated by Mawdudi.[82] Some of his last work, written in the aftermath of the secession of East Pakistan, almost twenty five later, was on the grim prospects of the new Bangladesh.[83]

Young Qureshi, however, confined himself to commenting on the prospects of West Pakistan about whose economy, he claimed, he felt better qualified to speak. Arguing that it was for the Muslim nation to decide its own economic ideals, he pointed out that just like Gandhi who laid emphasis on simple living and high thinking, Jinnah in an interview to the *New York Times* on 21 September 1942 had remarked that 'if we are willing to live sensibly but poorly so long as we have freedom, why should the Hindus object? ...The economy will take care of itself.'[84] The question, therefore, remained whether Pakistan, even if poor, would at least be an economically feasible entity. Before beginning his economic defence of Pakistan, he noted that an unbiased team of economists – Dr John Mathai and Sir Homi Modi – in their memo to the Sapru Committee had declared that Pakistan would indeed be a feasible proposition if judged by its ability to maintain existing standards of living and meet budgetary requirements on a pre-war basis, but excluding provisions for defence.

---

80 Anwar Iqbal Qureshi, *Agricultural Credit: Being a Study of Recent Developments in Agricultural Credit Administration in the United States of America* (London, 1936).

81 Anwar Iqbal Qureshi, *The Economic Development of Hyderabad* (Bombay, 1947).

82 Anwar Iqbal Qureshi, *Islam and the Theory of Interest* (Lahore, 1946); *Fiscal System of Islam* (Lahore, 1978); *Economic and Social System of Islam* (Lahore 1979); for an assessment of various positions on the issue of interest (*riba*) see Izzuddin Pal, 'Pakistan and the Question of Riba', *Middle Eastern Studies*, Vol. 30, No. 1 (January 1994), 64–78.

83 Anwar Iqbal Qureshi, *Bangladesh: Its Dark Past and Dim Future* (Lahore, 1973); *Mr Mujib's Six Points: An Economic Appraisal* (Lahore, 1970).

84 Anwar Iqbal Qureshi, *The Economic Basis of Pakistan*: *Pakistan Literature Series, No. 12* (Lahore, 1947).

Contrary to the criteria of a province's total budget or per capita income being used by economists to judge Pakistan's economic prospects, Qureshi argued that the real economic strength of a nation depended upon 'the size strength and quality of its population, the fertility of its soil, and the availability of other mineral resources, including mineral wealth'.[85] The resources of a country could also be developed very quickly if its population had the will and determination. In this regard, he claimed that West Pakistan possessed the strongest and healthiest population in all of India, for a stalwart Pathan or Punjabi could do twice as much work as a South Indian. Punjabis were also fine artisans and craftsmen besides being soldiers and agriculturalists as evident from the number of excellent small scale and medium scale industries that had come up in the province to service the war effort. As regards its natural resources, Qureshi pointed out that it had perennial rivers, an extensive network of canals,tremendous amount of potential hydroelectric power, fertile land that met all the food requirements of its people and produced a substantial surplus as well. It also produced commercial crops such as cotton and oilseeds. Average density in this area was lesser than for India as a whole thus making the pressure of population on land much lighter. Given that food constituted the main item in the standard of living in India, Qureshi exulted that it was higher in this region than in all of India. Thus, West Pakistan enjoyed a standard of living, which was already much higher than that of any other region in India.

Qureshi dismissed the idea that Pakistan would remain an agricultural state since it had no mineral resources such as coal and iron. He pointed out that some of the most prosperous states in the world like Switzerland had made industrial progress without these mineral resources. Furthermore, a country like Denmark that relied primarily on agriculture had an enviable standard of living. Indeed, no state needed to be self-sufficient in all mineral resources for it to develop economically. Besides, iron and steel could be imported given that price of minerals in India was higher than those being sold in international market. Qureshi also suggested the ways in which existing resources could be utilized innovatively to develop Pakistan. For example, he noted that extensive road building in rural areas could be accomplished within five or six months by requisitioning village labour, which was anyway unemployed for about 200 days every year. This would make sure that they were not idle and also ensure that they paid taxes in kind through such labour since they did not pay anything in cash in any case. The government could also introduce compulsory community

85 Ibid., 13.

service for the maintenance of roads for two years in addition to military service.

Qureshi also reiterated the advantages that Pakistan would enjoy in terms of very low defence expenditure since it would not need a large army to defend its western frontiers. Comparing Pakistan's situation with that of India, he noted that even a united India after independence would hardly be in a position to defend itself against a major enemy since it had practically no navy or air force and would take many years to create defence industries to supply itself with the necessary armaments. Besides no country including UK or USA relied only on their own strength to fight wars. In any case, Qureshi believed that the development of atomic energy made existing weapons useless in any case. In this regard, he heartily endorsed Gandhian proposal to make absolutely no preparations for war. In conclusion, Qureshi was confident that 'economically Pakistan had a very bright future, and considering its strong, well trained manpower and rich land, it will have a fairly high standard of living.'[86] Pamphlets on the industrial and power resources of Pakistan completed the economic defence of Pakistan reiterating arguments that had earlier been made in the twin Toosy volumes brought out by the Home Study Circle.[87] Jamiluddin Ahmad himself contributed a pamphlet in which he briefly surveyed the history of negotiations over the past decade to resolve the communal problem in India. Ahmad made it clear that Muslim India was opposed to any scheme, which had as its basis any idea of a central government – federal, confederal or union – since it wanted complete independence for the Pakistan areas. Finally, the last pamphlet written by an anonymous 'Student of International history' marshalled and reiterated all the arguments made by Jinnah and the ML leadership thus far regarding why the Indian Muslims were a separate nation.[88]

The Muslim University Organizes for the Elections

A few months before the elections, Liaquat Ali Khan, speaking at his *alma mater,* made an impassioned appeal to students to come out of their schools and colleges and work for the nation's freedom even if it entailed sacrificing a year of education. Referring to the closure of the university during the

---

86 Ibid., 19.

87 Ali Ahmed Faziel, *Power Resources of Pakistan: Pakistan Literature Series No. 10* (Lahore, 1946); Muhammad Yunus, *Industrial Pakistan: Pakistan Literature Series No. 11* (Lahore, 1947).

88 A Student of International History, *Are the Indian Muslims a Nation?: Pakistan Literature Series No. 13* (Lahore, 1947).

Khilafat Movement, Liaquat pointed out that 'if this university can render such magnificent services to fight for the freedom of another country, what services can they not render to fight for the freedom of their own nation and their own country?'[89] Mahmudabad made a similar appeal stating that every Muslim's fate in India would be decided in these elections. Dismissing fears about students losing precious time in the academic calendar, Mahmudabad noted that

> after all a few months loss of time is nothing when compared with the educative training that the Muslim youth will have in practical politics when he will be called upon to deal with the complicated administrative and legislative machineries of the state (sic).[90]

However, the disunity that characterized the UPML was also in evidence at Aligarh. It was, therefore, not surprising that the response of the Aligarh Muslim University (AMU) students to the call for serving the Muslim nation, though immediate and enthusiastic, was along factional lines with two groups emerging in this process. The first group was the Muslim University Muslim Students Federation (MUMSF) aligned to A. B. A. Haleem who had until recently been the Pro-Vice Chancellor of the University and was still a senior faculty member. This group began to collect funds to send student workers to different parts of the province to canvass for ML candidates.[91] The second group, the Muslim University Muslim League (MUML) aligned to the Vice Chancellor Dr Ziauddin was led by a youthful Manzar-i-Alam, an inhabitant of Gwalior who was a part time faculty member at the university and also practiced as a lawyer in the local courts. It is his group that seized the initiative and helped ML candidates win in the first round of elections to the Central Assembly. Manzar-i-Alam grandly declared that 'Aligarh being the arsenal of Muslim India, must also supply the ammunition in the battle for the freedom of the Great Muslim Nation.'[92] The MUML, therefore, embarked upon a programme of training student workers for the elections and laid down clear criteria for selecting students for this purpose.[93] An MUML circular specified that those desirous of becoming workers for the election needed to be at least seventeen years of age, physically and mentally alert, good speakers or good

89 *Star of India*, 24 September 1945.

90 *Star of India*, 10 October 1945.

91 *Dawn*, 29 August 1945.

92 *Dawn*, 18 October 1945.

93 Ibid.

conversationalists, besides having some contacts in the areas where they desired to work. The MUML also sought help from the AMU teaching staff in order to devise courses for the training of these student workers. These courses covered

> 1) Lectures on the ML in the light of Islam and Islamic history, brief history of the ML and its achievements; genesis and analysis of Pakistan; comparative study of the policies and programs of the Congress and the ML since 1935. 2) Study of the Objections of the Opponents against the ML and preparation of answers. 3) Study of special conditions and features of particular areas. 4) Training in publicity work. 5) Training in public speaking. Each worker would speak for at least five minutes. 6) Group reading and discussions. 7) Technique of fighting elections 8) Visits to *mohallas* of towns and neighboring villages for purposes of actual training in public speaking and canvassing.'[94]

The Aligarh students confined themselves to U.P. during this first round of elections to the Central Assembly since they had organized mostly out of their own initiative with little guidance or material support from the party high command. Manzar-i-Alam took leave from his position as a part time lecturer at the University and suspended his practice at the Aligarh bar in order to devote himself wholly to the task of organizing students for the ML's election campaign. He also paid for the expenses of the training camps out of his own pocket noting that he could not sit idle when 'Muslim India was struggling for its existence.' It drew praise from the top leadership of the ML as Liaquat publicly thanked him and the MUML for their tremendous contribution during the election campaign.[95] After all four hundred student workers from Aligarh worked for Liaquat in his Meerut constituency especially since the Congress had pulled out all stops to defeat him. Such was the enthusiasm with which the Aligarh students were welcomed in Meerut that at various places local *Pesh Imams* insisted on Aligarh boys leading the prayers at the mosques declaring that they were the real leaders of the *millat* and hence deserved to lead the prayers as well.[96] Jamiluddin Ahmad, an old lieutenant of Jinnah and Dr Ziauddin, who taught at the English department at Aligarh, noted their sterling contribution in the ML campaign.

---

94 *Dawn*, 18 October 1945.

95 *Star of India*, 8 December 1945.

96 K. R. Khan to Manzar-i-Alam, 28 November 1945, *QA Papers*, Vol. 12, 720.

> The energy, devotion, and perseverance with which student workers deputed by the MU ML are working, is eliciting all round admiration. The Aligarh students who were supposed by some people to be ease loving are astonishing friends and foes alike by their endurance hard work and self-sacrifice. In Meerut division where the Congress has concentrated all its forces, over 500 students are working day and night. They have spread out to all the remote villages of various districts. On an average they cover 30 miles every day, walking most of the time. Besides addressing meetings they contact individual workers and by their missionary spirit and convincing arguments they have been able to win over a large number of voters.[97]

It is only after the total success of the ML in the central assembly elections that Jinnah realized the utility of drafting Aligarh students into the ML's election campaign for the next round of elections to the provincial assemblies. However, his lack of familiarity with university politics was evident from his rather haphazard initial attempts at tapping into the reservoir of student energy at Aligarh. Jinnah first sent a note to A. B. A. Haleem asking him to form a Committee of three and inform him about the work done by Aligarh students in the recent elections.[98] He suggested that the committee should include Jamiluddin Ahmad, Haleem himself and Ishrat Ali Khan, Vice President of the Students Union. With the latter having left Aligarh and the former two at loggerheads, this committee was always going to be a non-starter.[99] Jinnah soon received a letter from Jamiluddin Ahmad informing him that he had been approached by Haleem on the matter but hinted that the latter was not suitable for inclusion in the committee.[100] Instead, he sent Jinnah a list of people he thought were suitable, which excluded Haleem.[101] Haleem too had other ideas about the committee, which he made clear in his response to Jinnah.[102] Jinnah

97 *Dawn*, 28 November 1945.

98 Jinnah to A. B. A. Haleem, 23 November 1945, *QA Papers*, Vol. 12, 711.

99 Ibid., 419–20, Jamiluddin Ahmad to Jinnah, 26 January 1945. Ahmad had earlier written to Jinnah that 'several Communists posing as Muslim Leaguers have crept into the local branch of the AIMSF and have found a patron in Professor Haleem... Haleem has been associated with a group responsible for disrupting provincial ML affairs'.

100 Ibid., 730, Jamiluddin Ahmad to Jinnah, 4 December 1945, 712–14; Jamiluddin Ahmad to Jinnah, 1 December, 1945.

101 Ibid. His choices for the committee were Nawab Ismail Khan, Liaqat Ali Khan, Qazi Mohammad Isa besides Manzar-i-Alam.

102 Ibid., 731–32, A. B. A. Haleem to Jinnah, 4 December 1945. He asked Jinnah to include Afzal Husain Qadri in the committee.

kept the matter up in the air by writing separately to Jamiluddin Ahmad, Haleem and Manzar-i-Alam asking each of them to form a committee to organize student workers for the elections.[103] The result was the formation of separate committees by Jamiluddin Ahmad and A. B. A. Haleem.[104] However, heeding Jinnah's directive to sink all differences, a broader committee was ultimately formed to coordinate the efforts of the two groups for the provincial assembly elections.[105]

Jinnah now provided sufficient funds for the programme of training student workers and dispatching them to different parts of the country to work for ML candidates. A greatly encouraged Manzar-i-Alam pleaded with Jinnah for additional help, requesting the *Qaid* to ask the university authorities to postpone exams for two months, reduce the minimum required attendance for students to enable students to miss classes while campaigning and also grant leave facilities to the teaching staff proceeding on election work.[106] The committee dispatched students to different provinces during their Moharram and Christmas break in December to canvass for the ML, a full two months before the provincial assembly elections in February and March. Aligarh staff too participated by taking charge over the separate branch offices set up for organizing student work in different provinces.[107]

In the first round of elections for the Central Assembly, 225 students worked in the Punjab, the 'keystone of Pakistan', 25 students campaigned in the NWFP, 7 students worked in Bengal, while 75 students canvassed for ML candidates in the U.P. In early 1946 as all parties geared for the provincial assembly elections, an additional 250 students campaigned for ML candidates in Punjab, Sind

---

103 Ibid.; Jinnah to A .B. A. Haleem, 5 December 1945, 734; Jinnah to Jamiluddin Ahmad 5 December 1945, 732–33; Jinnah to Manzar-i-Alam, 10 December 1945, 736.

104 Jamiluddin Ahmad wrote to Jinnah that he formed a committee with himself as Convenor, Obaidur Rahman Khan Sherwani as the Treasurer, Prof. M. B. Mirza and Manzar-i-Alam.

105 Ibid., 747–48, A.B.A. Haleem to Jinnah, 12 January 1946. This committee included Jamiluddin Ahmad, Manzar-i-Alam, Obaidur Rahman Khan Sherwani, M. B. Mirza from the earlier committee and Haleem, Dr Aziz Ahmad, Afzal Husain Qadri, M. M. Haq Choudhary, General Secretary of the AIMSF and Ghayural Islam, President MUMSF and Vice President, Muslim University (MU) Union, from the second committee.

106 Ibid., 746–7; Manzar-i-Alam to Jinnah, 24 December 1945.

107 Ibid., 739–40; Manzar-i-Alam to Jinnah, 17 December 1945.

and Assam.[108] The services rendered by these youthful student workers proved critical to the ML campaign not just in U.P., but also in all the provinces of British India where it contested the elections. Reminiscing about the role played by Aligarh students in rallying support for the ML and Pakistan, a writer wrote

> One of the author's earliest memories is of the arrival in our ancestral village in northern India of three young men carrying the Muslim League flag – the Islamic crescent and star on a deep green background. The three were students from Aligarh University. They planted the flag in the village square and a crowd of little boys gathered around them... Within an hour our quiet village had been turned into Pakistan village.... Every piece of green material our mother could find was made into Muslim League flags...A few months later they [parents] all walked in their bare feet and some carried their aged and sick parents on their backs to the polling booth four miles away to vote for the Muslim League and Pakistan. This was repeated all over India. Seldom in History have so few inspired so many with so little effort.[109]

As Mushirul Hasan too has noted, 'the intervention of Aligarh boys tilted the balance in several constituencies' in favour of the ML.[110]

Urdu Poetry and Popular Mobilization

ML newspapers such as the *Dawn* and *Star of India* carried brief reports of Aligarh students working hard for ML candidates in various provinces, especially in the rural areas. But the question remains as to how these college students communicated to a rural audience as they rallied support for the ML and Pakistan. During the Khilafat Movement when political activity spilled out from council houses and bar associations on to the streets, bazaars, mosques and fairs, emotional stump speeches and more importantly, recitations of poetry became the means for swaying popular emotions.[111] The referendum for Pakistan too saw poems, ditties and songs being composed that were recited or sung before large audiences besides being published and sold in inexpensive

---

108 Mushirul Hasan, 'Local Roots of the Pakistan Movement', in Kaushik Roy (ed.), *Partition of India: Why 1947?* (New Delhi, 2012), 126.

109 Kalim Siddiqui, *Conflict, Crisis and War in Pakistan*, London, 1972, quoted in Mushirul Hasan, 'Local Roots of the Pakistan Movement', in Kaushik Roy (ed.), *Partition of India: Why 1947?* (New Delhi, 2012), 116.

110 Ibid.

111 Gail Minault, 'Urdu Poetry during the Khilafat Movement', *Modern Asian Studies*, Vol. 8, No. 4, (1974), 459–71.

editions.[112] We do not have access to any poetry specifically written or recited by these Aligarh students; not surprising since much of such popular literature perished after the Partition as fearful Muslims burnt everything that could be deemed seditious by the Indian or U.P. government. Yet, some samples of this genre have survived like the rare slim volume that was released on Jinnah's birthday on 25 December 1945 from Bombay.[113] Its author and compiler, Ramzi Illahabadi, was at the time a resident of Hamidia hostel located at Bhendi Bazar in Bombay. Illahabadi appears to be his *nom de plume* and his real name or whether he had any Aligarh connections is not known. The volume was produced for the Muslim League National Guards (MLNG), in which Aligarh students too had enlisted in large numbers. In the brief dedications page Illahabadi thanks the *Salar* of the Bombay MLNG, Hashim Ali Inamdar, for his generous help in bringing out the publication. The ninety six page volume contained thirty nine poems and was priced at four *annas* making it accessible to a popular audience. We do not know if the poems in this collection attained any degree of popularity in Bombay or if they even made it to U.P., or whether they were set to music and sung by students and others in those heady days. But their importance lies in that they offer us tantalizing glimpses of the youthful enthusiasm for Pakistan that swept Muslim students across India.

Ramzi is no Akbar Illahabadi as these poems do not possess much subtlety or the many layers that characterized poetry produced during the Khilafat Movement. They lack delicate ambivalences or ambiguities and there is no attempt here to evade the colonial censor as a fading Raj stood on its last legs. The few representative poems presented here are plain, direct, and catchy and ring in a tone that is both triumphant and exhortatory. The first poem in the volume celebrates Jinnah's seventieth birthday.

Aaj khuda se Karein Dua'ein	Let's pray to God today
Sehat Qaid-i-Azam Payein	To grant good health to our Qaid
Rab ke Aage sar ko Jhukayein	Let's bow before our Lord
Qaid ki yun umar badhayein	So He may extend our Leader's life
Zindabad ke Narein lagayein	Let's shout –Long live Our Qaid
Saal girah ka jashn manayein	Let us celebrate his birthday

112 See C. M. Naim, 'A Sentimental Essay in Three Scenes', *Outlook Magazine*, 11 January 2007.

113 Ramzi Illahabadi, *Muslim League National Guards ke Taraane* (Bombay, 1945).

Sadkein Hotel aur Sarai,	Roads, hotels and Inns
ghar bhi aur dukaan sajayein	Homes and shops we should decorate
Bhookon ko kuch khaana khilayein	Feed the hungry
Nangon ko Hum Kapdey pehnayein	Clothe the naked
Duniya mein ek dhoom machayein	Let us bestir the world today
Saal girah ka jashan manayein	By celebrating our Qaid's birthday
Ai wahdat ke diwaanon	Oh believers in One God
Shamma-i-Millat ke parwanon	Moths to the Millat's Flame
Mere buzurgon aur jawanon	My elders and juniors
Chhotey bacche aur Nadaanon	Children and toddlers
Aao khelein hansein hansayein	Come let's laugh and play
Saal girah ka jashn manayein	As we celebrate our Qaid's birthday
Is Qaid ki saal girah hai	It is the birthday of our Leader
Baat mein jiski bang-i-dara hai	Whose words are like a clarion call
Jis ne hamein bedar kiya hai	They have truly awakened us
Aur yeh hum ko dars diya hai	And given us the timely wisdom
Apna ghar hum aap banayein	To create our own Home
Saal girah ka jashn manayein	Come, celebrate His birthday
Nahin hai jis ke dil mein keenah	His heart knows no malice
Jaam-i-muhabbat hai uska pina	For he drinks from love's chalice
Tum ne bachaya apna safina	He has saved the ship of the Nation
Lakhon baras hai jina jina	That it may live for many years hence
Tum ko dekar aaj dua'ein	Saying our prayers of gratitude for you
Saal girah ka jashn manayein	We celebrate your birthday
Aap mudabbir bahut badey hain	You are a great Statesman
Haq ki khaatir aap ladey hain	You have fought for the sake of Truth
Hum ko dijiye hukum khadey hain	We stand ready for your command
Lenge Pakistan adey hain	We shall not yield on Pakistan
Azadi se jiyein jalayein	Live and let live in freedom
Saal girah ka jashhn manayein	And celebrate His birthday

Ab to na Shikwe aur giley hain	No conflicts remain among us
Shia Sunni Galey miley hain	Shia and Sunni have embraced each other
Sotey karwat leke hiley hain	The sleeping have bestirred and awakened
Is Qaid ke Qurbaan jayein	Hail the Leader for this miracle
Saal girah ka jashan manayein	And celebrate His Birthday
Aanch na aaye us pe Khuda ya	May no harm befall upon him O Lord
Jis ne humein sotey se jagaya	For he has roused us from slumber
Bhoola sabaq phir yaad dilaya	Reminded us of a long forgotten lesson
Phir manzil ka raasta bataya	Redirected us to the right destination
Aise Qaid ke gun Gaayein	Let's sing the glories of this Qaid
Saal girah ka jashn manayein	And celebrate His birthday
Ramzi ab buland dast dua ho	Let us raise our hands to pray
Aur dua maqbool khuda ho	And may God grant our prayer
Qaid ki sab door bala ho	That our Qaid's problems disappear
Khizr ki Umar unko Ataa ho	May Khizr's immortality be granted to him
Qaid Pakistan Dilayein	May he deliver Pakistan
Saal girah ka jashn manayein	Come, let's celebrate the Qaid's birthday

The poem exhorts the *qaum* to come together to celebrate their supreme leader's birthday and pray for his health and long life. None of Jinnah's lieutenants finds nary a mention here as the poem consecrates a direct relationship between the great helmsman and his grateful nation. It lauds the Qaid's many sterling qualities, thanks him for ending internecine sectarian conflicts within the community and awakening it to its national self-consciousness by giving it the perfect ideal of Pakistan. It also solemnly assures him that the nation would follow his every command to bring about its realization.

The next poem 'We Shall Triumph' (*Hum Lekey Rahengey*) is a litany against Hindu Congress Raj in U.P. between 1937 and 1939 and specifically recounts the tribulations suffered by the U.P. Muslims to explain why Pakistan had become necessary.

Hum hain Musalman hum na darengey	We are Muslims and fear we shall not
Jo hai haqeeqat aaj kahengey	Whatever the truth we shall speak
Ab na kadam peeche hatengey	Never shall these feet withdraw
Aage badhengey Aage badhengey	But march ahead and march ahead
Aakhir kab tak zulm sahengey	Pray, till when can we bear their villainy
Pakistan hum leke rahengey	We will achieve Pakistan

Yaad hai jor-i-la mutnahi	Do you remember their highhandedness
dhai saal ki sikka shahi	Two and a half years of tyranny
Tadpey jun be-aab ke mahi	When we suffered like fish out of water
Denge sab akhbaar gavahi	All newspapers bear that evidence
Aakhir kab tak zulm sahengey	Pray till when can we bear their villainy
Pakistan hum leke rahengey	We will achieve Pakistan
Jab ki hukumat haath mein aayi	Since they assumed power
Gaddi mein thi aql samaayi	This was the logic that got into their heads
Aisi hui kuch haatha payi	And what followed were such outrages
Cheekh uthi phir saari khudai	That all of humanity was screaming
Aakhir kab tak zulm sahenge	Pray, till when can we bear their villainy
Pakistan hum lekey rahengey	We will achieve Pakistan
Kya sunega apni kahani	Can your ears bear our horror stories
Kaisi huin barbad jawaani	When our youth were decimated
Khun-i-Muslim ki arzaani	The blood of Muslims became worthless
Dekh chukey ai zor ke bani	We have seen it all oh Tyrant
Aakhir kab tak zulm sahengey	Pray, till when can we bear their villainy
Pakistan hum lekey rahengey	We will achieve Pakistan
Suniye Suniye bipta hamaari	Hear hear our tale of woe
Dil pe padi hai zarb-i-kari	The wounds that our hearts have suffered
Woh jo ahimsa ke hain pujari	Those devotees of ahimsa
Hum pey chalayein zulm ki aari	Have let loose the saws of oppression on us
Aakhir kab tak zulm sahengey	Pray, till when can we bear their villainy
Pakistan hum lekey rahengey	We will achieve Pakistan
Dekho Pioneer taintees sitambar	See the Pioneer of September 1933
Unki hukumat har das din par	Their government issued a curfew order
Nafuz kar ke curfew order	Every ten days
Kahti thi tayyar ho lashkar	And called in the army
Aakhir kab tak zulm sahengey	Pray, till when can we bear their villainy
Pakistan hum lekey rahengey	We will achieve Pakistan
Waqt ibadat rakhna pada tha	Our prayers were disturbed
Pesh masjid baaja baja tha	When they beat their drums at prayer times
Kisko yeh swaraj mila tha	Who was granted this Swaraj
Bolo kiska khoon baha tha	Tell us whose blood was shed
Aakhir kab tak zulm sahengey	Pray, till when can we bear their villainy
Pakistan hum lekey rahengey	We will achieve Pakistan

Shariat-i-Haqqani roki	They stopped the practices of our faith
Kar ke anakani roki	In their rising arrogance
Leke bhari jawaani roki	Cutting down our young in abundance
Eid ke din qurbani roki	Stopping Qurbani on Eid
Aakhir kab tak zulm sahengey	Pray, till when can we bear their villainy
Pakistan hum lekey rahengey	We will achieve Pakistan
Baney Madarsey Vidya Mandir	Madrasas became Vidya Mandirs
Khusk kiya Urdu ka Samandar	While the ocean of Urdu was desiccated
Wardha ki Iskim ke Andar	Under the aegis of the Wardha scheme
Hindi Bhasha banegi sundar	It is Hindi that will emerge supreme
Aakhir kab tak zulm sahengey	Pray, till when can we bear their villainy
Pakistan hum leke rahengey	We will achieve Pakistan
Band kiye akhbar-i-Millat	They stopped our national newspapers
Lekey unse Bhari zamanat	Slapping heavy penalties on them
Aisi hukumat hai ek laanat	Such a regime is a curse
Cheekh rahe thhey Haq aur Wahdat	So were screaming Haq and Wahdat
Aakhir kab tak zulm sahengey	Pray, till when can we bear their villainy
Pakistan hum lekey rahengey	We will achieve Pakistan
Yeh tha zamana ministry ka	This was the era of the Congress ministry
Ya kissa bedadgari ka	Or rather a tale of their oppression
Tanda Ballia aur Dadri ka	For the events of Tanda, Ballia and Dadri
Kya jawaab hai is Khan Khan ka	It still has no answers
Kab tak aisey zulm sahengey	Pray, till when can we bear their villainy
Pakistan hum lekey rahengey	We will achieve Pakistan
Jaanib Kaaba haath utha kar	Facing the Kaaba raise your hand
Ramzi rab se aaj dua kar	Ramzi makes a prayer to the Almighty
Aisi hukumat hum ko ata kar	Kindly grant us such a government
Adl ka jiske zikr ho ghar ghar	Whose virtues every home shall sing
Aakhir kab tak zulm sahengey	Pray, till when can we bear their villainy
Pakistan hum lekey rahengey	We will achieve Pakistan

Each paragraph in the poem ends with the refrain that Muslims will no longer bear the atrocities of Congress Hindu Raj and shall strive to achieve Pakistan. It describes Gandhi's Wardha scheme of education as a ploy to turn madrasas into *Vidya Mandirs* and recounts the government's attempts at eliminating Urdu and patronizing Hindi. It reminds Muslims of how the votaries of *ahimsa* imposed frequent curfews in Muslim areas and confiscated Muslim newspapers such as *Haq* and *Wahdat*. It talks about how emboldened Hindu mobs disturbed prayers by playing music in front of mosques, stopped *qurbani* on *Eid* and killed scores of Muslims in the riots at Tanda, Ballia and Dadri.

A third poem 'Let us Make Pakistan' (*Pakistan Banayein*) again recounts the experiences of the minority provinces Muslims under Hindu Raj but goes a step further in specifying Pakistan's geographical domains besides rebutting Congress arguments against Pakistan.

Roothe huon ko aaj manayein	Let us assuage the aggrieved amongst us
Apnon ko hum galey lagayein	Clasp our own to our breasts
Bhooley soye ko yaad dilayein	Remind the sleeping and forgetful
Bhatkey huey ko raah batayein	Show the path to the prodigals
Ligi ko vote dilayein	Get out the vote for the League
Yani Pakistan banayein	And Create Pakistan
Aksariyat ki shafqat dekhi	We have seen the tender mercies of the majority
Unki humney hukumat dekhi	Seen the ways they ruled
Aqalliyat ki durgat dekhi	Witnessed the minority's miseries
Kaisi kaisi bidaat dekhi	And beheld many heresies
Yeh jo humko aisa satayein	When they so oppress us
Kyun na Pakistan banayein	Why not make our own Pakistan
Kaan ko apne kavva samjhe	He who has fearful fantasies
Kishmish ko jo mahwa samjhe	And looks at a raisin but sees a grub
Sirf tarazoo pavva samjhe	Who understand only weights and scales
Pakistan ko havva samjhe	And regards Pakistan as an ogre
Aise ko hum kya samjhayein	How can he understand anything?
Aao Pakistan banayein	Come let us create Pakistan
Dadaji ke pootey parotey	Grandpa's darlings and his menials
Ek hi ghar mein kaise sotey	Could never live in the same house
Jhagdey hotey dandey hotey	Fights and scuffles would ensue
Aakhir mein batwaare hotey	Leading to divisions and partitions
Hum bhi apna hissa payein	We too want out share of the division
Jis mein Pakistan banayein	Where we can create Pakistan

Punjab aur Bangal chhodo	Quit our Punjab and Bengal
Assam uska himala chhodo	And the Himalayas of Assam
Sarhad Sind ko lala chhodo	Lalas leave Sind and the Frontier
Hoga nahin diwala chhodo	Fear not we won't be bankrupt
Aap na apna rang jamayein	You will not dictate to us
Yeh hum Pakistan banayein	We will make our Pakistan

Baat na saaz-o-baaz ki hogi	No intrigues or conspiracies will thrive here
Aur na hirs –o-aaz ki hogi	Nor shall greed or corruption flourish
Yaan na hukumat qaaz ki hogi	Its government will not be of cowardly ducks
Shaheen o Shahbaz ki hogi	But of hawks and falcons
Aakhir Ramzi kyun ghabrayein	Why Ramzi should we fear
Aao Pakistan banayein	Let us make our Pakistan

By mocking Hindu paranoia about Pakistan it refers by implication to the bugbear of an Islamic invasion of India from the northwest that even Gandhi acknowledged when he claimed that the Punjabis and Gorkhas would overrun the country once the British had left India. It ridicules the Hindu economic objections to Pakistan equating it with a *bania* obsession with scales and weights. Such a people, it implies cannot feel or understand the passion for Pakistan. It asks the Congress and the Hindus to quit and let go of the Muslim majority provinces, which will be the parts of Pakistan and reveals the high hopes and expectations of this new state which would be full of idealism and free of corruption.

The last poem that we may consider – 'Flag of Islam' (*Parcham Islam*) – glorifies the national flag and is interesting inasmuch as a close variant of it exists on the other side of the divide, in India, as well. This variant *Jhanda Ooncha Rahe Hamara* penned by the U.P. Congressman Shyam Lal Gupt Parshad has been immortalized in the annals of Hindi film music ever since it was first picturised in the 1948 film *Azadi ki Rah Par*.

Hara hara yeh pyaara pyaara	This beloved Green Flag of ours
Parcham ooncha rahe hamara	May it always fly high
Isko nabi ji ne hai sanvaara	The Prophet himself has embellished it
Aur Ali ne tana man waara	While Ali laid down his life for it
Chand hai khanjar dhal hai taara	Its Crescent is our Sword, its Star our Shield
Azmat-i-rafta ka hai yeh ishaara	It signifies our approaching greatness
Hara hara yeh pyaara pyara	This beloved Green Flag of ours
Parcham ooncha rahe hamaara	May it always fly high

Is Parcham pe aanch na aaye	May its dignity never be tarnished
Chaahe jaan hamari jaaye	Even if it means loss of our lives
Pakistan mein yeh lehraaye	In Pakistan shall it grandly fly
Khushi khushi har Muslim gaaye	Where every Muslim will proudly sing
Hara hara yeh pyaara pyaara	This beloved Green Flag of ours
Parcham ooncha rahe hamaara	May it always fly high
Muslim apney haq pe adega	The Muslim shall stay put on his rights
Millat ka har fard ladega	Every individual of this nation will fight
Jhelega jo waqt padega	Bearing any vicissitudes time may throw at us
Par yeh Pakistan mein gadega	To ensure the Flag is unfurled in Pakistan
Hara hara yeh pyaara pyaara	This beloved Green Flag of ours
Parcham ooncha rahey hamaara	May it always fly high
Soye huey bhai ko jagaao	Awaken the sleeping brother
League ke ab member ban jaayo	And become the League's member
Ramzi yeh parcham lehrao	Ramzi get this Flag flying
Phir sab koi mil kar gaao	And then let all of us sing
Hara hara yeh pyaara pyaara	This beloved Green Flag of ours
Parcham ooncha rahey hamaara	May it always fly high

While Ramzi's poetry may not have set U.P. on fire, this last independent composition (or rather its refrain) with which we may end this section, certainly found much resonance in the province. It was written by a member of the U.P. Muslim Students Federation, Saiyyid Yavar Husain – *nom de plume*, Kaif Banarsi, after his hometown Banaras – soon after the failure of the 1944 Gandhi-Jinnah talks.[114]

Chashm-i-Raushan Pakistan	Our bright hope is Pakistan
Dil ki Dhadkan Pakistan	Our heartbeat is Pakistan
Sahra Sahra is ki dhoom	The world resounds with its name
Gulshan gulshan Pakistan	Our lush garden is Pakistan
Apni hasti ka Hasil	It is the basis of our very being
Apna maman Pakistan	Our sanctuary is Pakistan
Leke rahenge Pakistan	We will seize Pakistan
Bat ke rahega Hindustan	By dividing Hindustan
Manzil ko sar karna hai	The goal has to be accomplished
Mushkil se kya darna hai	And every obstacle demolished

[114] Kaif Banarsi, *Dil ki Dhadkan Pakistan* (Karachi, 1990).

Azaadi ke sholay ko	Fan the flame of freedom
Dil mein raushan karna hai	So it burns bright in every bosom
Pakistan ki Ulfat mein	In this mad love for Pakistan
Apna Jeena marna hai	We will live or give up life
Leke rahenge Pakistan	We will seize Pakistan
Bat ke rahega Hindustan	By splitting Hindustan
Kis ne Shab khoon mara hai?	Who dared to ambush us
Sheron ko lalkara hai	And challenged Lions ferocious
Baccha baccha momin ka	Every child of this Nation
Shola hai angara hai	Is a blazing flame, a scorching fire
Qaum ki Khatir mar jayein	For the Nation we will Die
Bus yeh qaumi naara hai	That is our rallying cry
Leke rahenge Pakistan	We will seize Pakistan
Bat ke rahega Hindustan	By dividing Hindustan
Hind ke saare subon mein	In every province of Hind
Islami lashkar tayyar	Army of Islam be ready
Kasrat hai dushman ki fauj	The enemy's force is bigger
Wahdat hai apni talwar	But Unity is our Saber
Naam khuda ka letey hain	Chant our Lord's name
Ho jayega beda paar	And Victory will be ours
Leke rahenge Pakistan	We will seize Pakistan
Bat ke rahega Hindustan	By dividing Hindustan

The young poet claimed that he was greatly upset by the Mahatma's arrogant comment in his correspondence with Jinnah during their 1944 talks that he did not know of any 'parallel in history for a body of converts and their descendants claiming to be a nation apart from the parent stock.'[115] The anger seems to have found a creative outlet for it burst forth in this inspired poem titled *Shola-i-Azadi* (Flame of Freedom) wherein, as evident, the poet sought to demolish and ridicule Gandhi's assertion by emphasizing the distinctness of Muslims as a separate nation and their determination to establish their own state in Pakistan. A variation of the refrain in the poem as narrated by C. M. Naim in his memoir went further: '*Hans ke Liya hai Pakistan, Lad ke Lenge Hindustan*' (We took Pakistan with no effort, We will seize Hindustan by force).[116]

115 *The Hindustan Times, Gandhi-Jinnah Talks: Text of Correspondence and other Relevant Matter,* July-October 1944, with a preface by Mr C. Rajagopalachari (New Delhi, 1944), 12.

116 'Two Days' in C. M. Naim, *Ambiguities of Heritage* (Karachi, 1999).

The ML Campaign

The UPML President Nawab Ismail Khan declared that ML would consider the results of the elections as the decisive verdict of the people on Pakistan.[117] Grateful for the support that his badly splintered party was receiving for its election campaign from the outside, Ismail Khan first thanked the *ulama* 'who came out of their scholarly retirement to battle against heavy odds for the solidarity of our nation which had been seriously menaced by the conspiracy of robed – sanctimony and financed – politics.'[118] Secondly, he thanked students for carrying the message of the League to the remotest villages of the province. The UPML decided that Pakistan was going to be the single point in the ML's election manifesto with all other issues placed on the backburner in order to avoid any points of contention within the party. A meeting convened to discuss the items that should be included in its election manifesto came to a swift conclusion on this matter. At this ML meeting, Z. H. Lari, the MLA from Gorakhpur and a prominent left-winger had proposed a radical resolution that called for nationalization of banks, insurance and basic industries such as textiles, jute, sugar, iron and coal in the ML's election manifesto. His proposal also extended promises of land reform and the replacement of the zamindari system with peasant proprietorship, contemplated administrative reforms including the separation of judiciary and executive as well as a commission of enquiry to investigate into charges of bribery and corruption in the government services. It further included social items like introduction of free and compulsory primary education, enforcement of prohibition, abolition of interest except through cooperative societies and abolition of court fees. Finally, the religious section of the proposal demanded Muslim right to call *Azan* and say prayers in congregations.[119] The resolution was supported by other left wingers but opposed by the landlords who pointed out that they expected 80 per cent of the ML candidates to be *zamindars* and the ML could not, therefore, expect them to sign their own death warrants. Abdul Hai Abbasi, another right winger, opposed the resolution on the grounds that the twin issues of Pakistan and ML as the sole representative organization of the Indian Muslims were enough for the election manifesto. These, he noted, had been declared by Jinnah himself as the main election issues to be raised by the ML.[120] Abbasi further declared that

117 *Dawn*, 3 August 1945.

118 *Star of India*, 3 November 1945.

119 *The Pioneer*, 19 September 1945.

120 The MLPB and the Committee of Action met in Delhi and decided that the ML would fight the elections on the issues of Pakistan and the ML as the sole representative organization of the Muslims. See *The Pioneer*, 4 September 1945.

it would be unwise for the League to outline its parliamentary programme in an election manifesto since issues such as abolition of the *zamindari* system and renunciation of titles would only cause divisions within the ML. With the party keen to avoid anything, which could lead to a recrudescence of factional conflicts, this objection was upheld and the UPMLPB confined itself to these two issues in its election campaign.[121]

Z. H. Lari was nonetheless elected as the Secretary of the UPMLPB at its first meeting. The Board also decided to set up its main office in Meerut, the home district of the UPML President Nawab Ismail Khan rather than in Lucknow. The UPMLPB drew up an ambitious plan of mustering 50,000 workers for the elections. A pyramidal party structure was set up for the entire province with Lari at the top of the pyramid. The whole province was divided under divisional party bosses who were responsible for the conduct the election campaign in their respective divisions.[122] Under them were sixty six party candidates, who were to undertake intensive election propaganda. Each of these candidates was promised one personal secretary and an advisory committee of twenty one to assist him in his work.[123] Furthermore, a booth leader was appointed for each of the 1,372 election polling stations in the province with each of these booth leaders again having twenty one men under him to help him in the task of booth management. Apart from this core

121 The ML, nonetheless, was in no mood to cede any ground to the Congress on the question of representing the working classes. It described the Congress claim of representing the peasants and working classes as fraudulent since it was bankrolled by the likes of Birla, Dalmia and Singhania. It alleged that these Hindu capitalists after making their money in the black market and sucking the blood of the labouring classes were funding the Congress campaign to enable it to buy Muslim votes. It also reminded Muslim workers of the Congress record of broken promises, pointing out that one of the first Acts passed by the Bombay Government in 1938 placed restrictions on labour and disallowed them from going on strike. It argued that Hindu capitalists were in cahoots with British capitalists and wanted British imperialism to continue. They both wanted 'Akhand Hindustan' so that they could capture the whole country's market along with its cheap labour. If Muslims created Pakistan, these Hindu and British capitalists would no longer have access to cheap Muslim labour, the largest labouring class in the subcontinent. Pakistan would also thus be a blow against imperialism. See Ayub Ahmad Kirmani, *Congress aur Mazdoor, Shobah Nashr-o-Ishaat, All India Muslim League* (Delhi, 1945).

122 *The Pioneer*, 22 October 1945. They included Maulvi Mohammad Farooq for Gorakhpur, Mufti Fakhrul Islam for Allahabad, Maulvi Maudood Ahmad for Banaras, Syed Zakir Ali for Agra, Karimur Raza Khan for Kumaon, Nawab Aizaz Rasul for Lucknow, S. M. Ashraf for Meerut and Sharifuddin for Jhansi.

123 *The Pioneer*, 5 December 1945.

taskforce an auxiliary body of 15,000 men comprised the corps of volunteers and MLNG was planned under Suleiman Jan, Salar of the provincial MLNG. Maudood Ahmad, the Publicity Secretary of the UPML, stated that 'every small village and town in the province would have placards, charts, maps, posters explaining the League program so that vital issues of present day politics may be placed before each and every Muslim during the forthcoming elections.'[124] A women's committee was also formed to undertake tours across U.P. to reach out to Muslim women.[125] A secret service was allegedly started by the ML Parliamentary Board in all the districts in order to keep a tab on election organization. Ten election publicity vans were placed under each of the divisional bosses equipped with microphones and loudspeakers to do propaganda work. It was also proposed to start a network of miniature broadcasting stations all over the province. Training camps were also to be set up in Allahabad, Meerut and Lucknow in order to train election workers. The MLPB further decided to observe an election fortnight between 17 December and 1 January throughout the province during which election meetings were to be held, processions taken out and ML literature distributed. It was also decided to approach every Muslim to contribute at least one rupee to the League fund and buy an ML badge for one *anna*.[126]

In his first directive to the ML workers, Lari exhorted them to enrol Muslim voters in the electoral rolls, a greater number of whom were now eligible to vote, given the relaxation in the franchise rules. He also appealed to the ML workers to start collecting funds for the party to fight the elections. The UPML set a target of ₹ 300,000 for the election fund.[127] It then went about collecting funds in an innovative manner that strove at the same time to make it more popular among the Muslims masses. Thus, while addressing a public meeting in Lucknow, Jamal Mian noted that the Muslim community in India was poor and unlike the Hindus who had in their ranks a number of capitalists and industrialists such as the Birlas, Dalmias and Tatas. The ML, thus, depended upon the subscriptions of ordinary Muslims and valued 'a poor man's gift, however small, more than that of a millionaire.'[128] He then sent his cap around in the crowd and soon a total of ₹ 123 was collected mostly in *annas*. The cap

---

124 Ibid.

125 *The Pioneer*, 21 September 1945

126 *The Pioneer*, 5 December 1945

127 *The Pioneer*, 1 August, 1945. See the statement of Nawab Ismail Khan.

128 *The Pioneer*, 21 September 1945.

was then put up for a running auction with different people in the crowd bidding for it. The cap was thus repeatedly bought and the amount noted against the name of the donor, which was announced publicly. An astounding ₹ 16,302 was ultimately collected at the meeting. The UPML also printed money order forms with the address of Jinnah printed on them so that the public could send money for the election fund directly to Jinnah himself.[129] Jinnah's appeal to the Muslims to give him 'silver bullets' so that he could 'finish the job' evoked a massive response from Muslims not just across India but from different parts of the world.[130] The UPML further printed receipts worth ₹ 150,000 of ₹ 1 each so that they could be subscribed even by poor Muslims.[131] By attracting such small donations from ordinary Muslims, the ML also utilized the opportunity to negate the Congress propaganda that it was a party of rich landlords, Nawabs, Khan Bahadurs and Knights of the Raj.

Critique of Congress and JUH Nationalists

The ML launched its election campaign with a massive public meeting at Lucknow.[132] Addressing the gathering Nawab Ismail Khan noted that the nationalist Muslims who had earlier ridiculed the idea of Pakistan now were talking in terms of the right to self-determination.[133] He labelled JUH and others opposing the ML as confidence tricksters and asked the Muslim public not to be beguiled by them. Khaliquzzaman in his speech mirrored the variety of themes that came to characterize the ML's election campaign throughout U.P. He noted that Pakistan had been forced on the Muslims by the Congress as a result of the atrocities that had been committed upon them during its government in 1937–39. The Muslims were, therefore, left with only two choices. They could either find freedom through Pakistan or 'sink forever into slavery.' Every vote that was cast, he declared, had to be a vote for the ML and the *Qaid-i-Azam*. Khaliq emphasized the validity of the two-nation theory given the growing Hindu bigotry in anticipation of the impending British withdrawal. Khaliq also observed that Hindus now were ashamed of being seen in an *achkan*. He also reviled the All India Radio (AIR) as a Hindu agency and

---

129 *The Pioneer*, 1 September, 1945.

130 *Dawn*, 5 September, 1945.

131 *The Pioneer*, 18 September 1945.

132 *The Pioneer*, 21 September 1945.

133 *Dawn*, 25 September 1945.

urged Muslims to boycott it, accusing it of imposing Hindi even though the language it was supposedly using was Urdu.

The Congress idea of an Indian Federation was a special target for criticism for the ML leaders keen to stress the demand for a sovereign independent Pakistan. Z. H. Lari speaking at Allahabad decried the Congress determination to set up a single centre to rule all over India. Pakistan, he noted, was opposed to the very idea of a centre. He also repudiated the Congress argument that the idea of dividing India was absurd given the trend towards a World Federation. A federation, Lari pointed out, was a 'union of sovereign powers and not the submission of a fettered people.'[134] The Congress idea of a federation, he charged, was only a mask for Hindu imperialism. While inaugurating the Allahabad University Muslim Hostel Union the next day, Lari ridiculed the Congress suggestion that India should have an American style federal system dismissing the American system as 'medieval in character'. Any decent state he argued, provided its constituent units the right to secede, a principle he noted, the Congress was not willing to concede. He opined that this was, therefore, the best time for the Muslim provinces to secede.[135]

The ML leaders also repudiated Nehru's warning about dividing Bengal and Punjab. Characterizing such talk as 'sheer nonsense', Jamal Mian while addressing students at Lucknow's Ganga Prashad Memorial Hall, in turn, raised the prospect of partitioning every province of India if the Congress talked in such terms. He declared that

> if Pandit Nehru is prepared to concede Pakistan in terms of a town village or city and the partition of UP and CP, then we are prepared to accept a divided Bengal and Punjab...Pakistan is our ultimate goal. Even if we suffer discomfiture for the present, we shall stick to our demand.[136]

The ML leaders repeatedly denied that the formation of Pakistan would jeopardize the position of the U.P. Muslims. Nawab Mohammad Yusuf asserted that the Pakistan demand also envisaged the establishment of coalition ministries in both Hindustan and Pakistan. Such a move, he noted, would end aggressive nationalism of both Hindus and Muslims and provide the best safeguard for the security of minorities on both sides.[137] Speaking at a rally of Muslim peasants in Sitapur, Jamal Mian pointed out that

---

134 *Dawn*, 30 September 1945.

135 *Dawn*, 1 October, 1945.

136 *Dawn*, 6 October 1945.

137 *Dawn*, 14 December 1945.

> The Lahore resolution explicitly envisages the conclusion of a treaty between Hindustan and Pakistan by which the rights of Muslims where they are in a minority will be properly safeguarded. It will not be a mere verbal understanding but will be incorporated in the statutes. Presuming Hindustan does not abide by this agreement, a free Pakistan will exert diplomatic pressure.[138]

Jamal Mian further pointed out that there was no guarantee that in a united India the rights of Muslims would not be trampled upon. Besides, he pointed out that the U.P. Muslims had shown their sympathies for Muslims around the world and they could surely vote for their liberation of their six crore brethren in the Muslim majority provinces. Jamal Mian also ridiculed Nehru's views on the atom bomb noting that if it became a criterion for sovereignty, 'then most states in the world would lose their freedom.' Muslims of India were not perturbed by the atomic bomb and would 'rather perish than surrender their right to carve out a separate Muslim state for themselves.'[139] Liaquat too dismissed Nehru's take on the atomic bomb arguing that it was no reason why Muslims should not demand Pakistan. Pakistan too could join a federation of independent countries but not an Indian federation. Dr Ziauddin Ahmad, the Vice Chancellor of the Muslim University at Aligarh, chimed in as well to proudly declare that Dr Rafi Mohammad Chaudhuri, the Chairman of the Physics department at the University, had done his doctoral research work in atomic physics at the Cavendish Laboratory, 'where the greatest basic research which led to the discovery of the atomic bomb was carried out.'[140]

The ML leaders dismissed threats of large-scale violence in the event of India's partition. In addition, they did not rule out the use of violence if their demand for Pakistan was denied. Thus, Liaquat told an election meeting that the Hindus hold out the threat that blood will flow in India if Muslims persist in their demand for Pakistan. I want to remind them that Muslims are past masters at shedding their blood. In fact, Muslims have nothing except to give their lives, which they carry in the palm of their hands.[141] Mahmudabad underlined this theme when he declared at a public meeting in Kanpur that 'we may die in the battle of Pakistan without seeing even a glimpse of it but so long as a single Muslim is alive we cannot accept Hindu Raj.[142]

---

138 *Dawn*, 23 October 1945.

139 *Dawn*, 31 August 1945.

140 *Deccan Times*, 2 September 1945.

141 *The Pioneer*, 28 October 1945.

142 *Dawn*, 9 November 1945.

Mahmudabad added that Pakistan was not just an election slogan. He warned Muslims that unless they created Pakistan their position would become similar to that of Jews in Europe who despite their vast wealth did not have a homeland anywhere in this world. Ismail Khan at Shahjahanpur stated that Muslims would be forced to resort to 'a policy of blood and iron' if their popular demand for Pakistan was denied.[143] Khaliquzzaman went further by seeking an aggressive approach to the idea of Pakistan from his audience. As he noted at a public meeting at Fyzabad, 'if the Musalmans of India pursue the policy of tooth for tooth, eye for an eye, nail for a nail, no power on earth can dominate them.'[144] Dwelling on the question of the Muslims in the 'minority provinces' such as the U.P., Khaliq insisted that

> After Pakistan is established, the Hindu majority provinces will think a hundred times before they resort to any tyrannical act. They know the Indian Muslim who can shed his blood for his Muslim brethren of Turkey can also do something to save his Indian Muslim brethren of the minority provinces.[145]

But more to the point, Khaliq asked Muslims to win the fourth and fifth battles of Panipat corresponding to the central and provincial assembly elections, by casting their votes in favour of the ML.[146] The *ulama* supporting the Congress came in for special criticism by the ML leadership. Speaking at a massive rally in Meerut, Khaliquzzaman accused the JUH *ulama* of plotting to deprive the Muslims of their power.[147] Khaliq quoted from the Quran in which the Prophet had advised the Muslims not to part with the sword and the horse, which were the sources of self-defence for the Muslims. The *ulama*, by opting for *Akhand Hindustan* were depriving Muslims of precisely those defenses. Khaliq declared that the JUH *ulama* could not be considered the religious leaders of the Muslim community since they had neither protected Islam nor Muslims in India. To discredit the JUH *ulama* even further, Khaliq asked the crowd whether the JUH had ever asked them for funds. Pointing out that they had never asked Muslims for funds, he explained that this was because they were bankrolled by the enemy Congress. The ML, on the other hand, he pointed out was fighting the elections with money given by ordinary Muslims. The ML also tried to

---

143 *Dawn*, 8 December, 1945.

144 *Dawn*, 25 November 1945.

145 *Dawn*, 25 November 1945.

146 *Deccan Times*, 2 December 1945.

147 *Dawn*, 8 October 1945.

cash in on the wave of sympathy for the Muslim heroes of the Indian National Army (INA) who were on trial for treason by forming a committee of lawyers for defending them in court.[148]

The ML also sought to rebut the various allegations in the pamphlets written by Maulana Husain Ahmad Madani. Speaking at a massive public meeting at Aminuddaula Park in Lucknow, Khaliq pointed out that the Bengal ministry could not be blamed for the famine since the Food Ministry at the federal centre was under the control of the Hindu Mahasabha leader, Sir J. P. Srivastava. The Woodhead Commission set up to enquire into the matter too had not been able to pin any responsibility on the ministry. Besides, even if these charges were true, Khaliq insisted that it was hardly fair to punish the whole party for the actions of a few individuals.[149] He also avowed that Pakistan was not un-Islamic as alleged by the JUH *ulama* but valid according to the tenets of the Quran for he too had read that Holy Book. The ML also ridiculed specific items in the Congress election manifesto. Thus, Khaliq criticized the Congress manifesto on agriculture noting that it did not even mention zamindari abolition and instead talked about modernization of agriculture and industry and social control of wealth. 'The modernization program in agriculture', he alleged, 'would not be anything more than Grow More Food campaign of the Advisors regime while the social control of wealth would only go so far as rehabilitating Congress workers coming out of jail!'[150] Khaliq also dwelt upon the sorry state of Congress Muslim leaders who found it impossible to enthuse Muslim voters, pointing out that Maulana Azad was so unpopular that on his visit to Lahore he could not find a single Muslim to give him shelter and was forced to live in a European hotel. Khaliq expressed apprehensions that the Congress would use Hindu landlords to put pressure on their Muslim tenants to vote for the Congress and warned Muslims against such moves. At the same meeting, Sir Raza Ali pointed out that if the Congress was a good organization then Muslims like Punjab's Mian Iftikharuddin would not have resigned and come over to the ML. Ismail Khan at this meeting thanked God for granting him life so that he could fight the battle for Pakistan.

148 *The Pioneer*, 10 November 1945. The committee included Shaikh Karamat Ali, Mian Abdul Aziz, Shaikh Mohammad Amin, Chaudhry Nazir Ahmad Khan, Nawab Qadiruddin Ahmad, Ahmad Ashraf and Qazi Mohammad Isa.

149 *The Pioneer*, 12 November 1945.

150 Ibid.

Shia and Communist Support for Pakistan

The ML also drew some support from the Shias in the run up to the polls.[151] The Anjuman Tanzimul Momineen now declared its support for the ML in the elections.[152] Sir Sultan Ahmad also circulated an appeal among Shias to vote for the ML noting that Shias needed to sink their differences with the ML in these crucial times.[153] The Shia Political Conference also began to hedge its bets by opening itself up for negotiations with the ML. As Syed Ali Zaheer declared

> I do not consider Pakistan to be either anti-national or unattainable and thus I do not consider this to be any obstacle in the way of the Shia community joining the ML. The chief difficulty is whether the ML is willing to accommodate them or not.[154]

While the Shia Political Conference ultimately came out on the side of the Congress, the conference itself split and a significant chunk walked away from the party and into the arms of the ML. One of the leading members of this breakaway group, Nawazish Ali Khan, was given the ML ticket to contest from the Fyzabad-Sitapur-Bahraich cities constituency. A new feature of Moharram *alams* and *tazias* that year was the prominence of the Pakistan map in front of every group of processions and the mounting of ML flags on elephants. The usual Moharram slogan of *Ya Ali* was replaced by the ML war cry '*le ke rahenge Pakistan*'. As a writer noted, 'this has created a very good impression and has been educative to the Muslim masses. The Hindus were perturbed for they consider that this is most conducive to permeate the Pakistan Ideal into the minds of Muslim masses.'[155] Mahmudabad summed up the enthusiasm in the Shia community when he noted at an election meeting in Bombay that the united Muslim community was now being led by a Shia Imam to whom even the Sunnis were paying obeisance.[156] Yet, even if Mahmudabad remained publicly committed to the goal of Pakistan, privately he began to develop misgivings about its creation as an Islamic state. As he wrote to Jinnah on the eve of the elections

---

151 *The Pioneer*, 2 November 1945.

152 *Dawn*, 16 October 1945.

153 *Dawn*, 1 December 1945.

154 *Dawn*, 19 October 1945.

155 S. N. A. Jafri, (President Eastern India Railway Muslim Employees Association) to Jinnah, 16 December 1945, *Shamsul Hasan Collection*, U.P., Vol. 1.

156 *Madina*, 1 December 1945.

> Your recent statement on the form of government in Pakistan has emboldened me to pen these few lines for your perusal. I am glad, Sir, that you have dispelled, to a great extent, all doubts that were being entertained on this score. I welcome, Sir, your statement (though you only expressed your personal opinion) that the government of Pakistan will be on democratic lines with state control over the key industries. Let us hope that the constitution of Pakistan will be modeled on the latest up to date experiences of the practical working of democracy rather than vague and indefinite slogans such a Hakumat-i-Ilahiyya etc.[157]

The disillusionment may be explained due to the discomfort that he began to develop with the JUI. Complaining to Jinnah, he noted that this organization was 'purely a theo-political one and its doors are closed against all others who do not happen to be Sunnis.'[158] He explained that he had tried to get Shia *ulama* elected to it but its existing members were not allowing anyone from outside their own coterie into the organization, thus revealing its 'sectarian color'.

The UPML also found support from the Communist Party of India (CPI), which openly expressed support for Pakistan. Thus, E. M. S. Namboodiripad stated that 'the CPI would wholeheartedly support ML candidates in the forthcoming elections and put up communist candidates in general constituencies against the Congress'. He hinted that this would be the general policy of the party in all provinces.[159] Raghubar Dayal Chaturvedi, the Agra CPI leader, declared that the party was supporting the ML since its Pakistan demand was reasonable.[160] Z. A. Ahmad in a speech in Lahore declared that there was nothing wrong with the Pakistan demand and noted that the Sikhs should not be against it, as they would get their due share in the new state.[161] These developments are not surprising given the prominent role played by Communists like Daniyal Latifi in formulating the manifesto of the Punjab Muslim League ahead of the elections.[162] A young Hamza Alavi who would later emerge as a Marxist ideologue and explain the creation of Pakistan in terms of the work of a secular Muslim *salariat* leading the movement, tirelessly

---

157 Mahmudabad to Jinnah, 3 December 1945, Z. H. Zaidi (ed.), *QA papers,* Vol. 12, 1 August, 1945- 31 March 1946, 1945, 375–76.

158 Mahmudabad to Jinnah, 5 July 1946, SHC, U.P., Vol. 4.

159 *The Pioneer*, 4 October 1945.

160 *The Pioneer*, 13 October 1945.

161 *The Pioneer*, 5 February 1945.

162 See Appendix II, 'Manifesto of the Punjab Provincial Muslim League 1944', in S. S. Pirzada, *Foundations of Pakistan*, Vol. 2, 554–71.

collected facts, figures and statistics regarding Pakistan areas to help with the work of the Planning Committee set up by Jinnah of which his uncle Hatim Alavi was a member.[163] Poetry eulogizing Pakistan was composed by progressive Urdu poets such as Majrooh Sultanpuri and Asrarul Haq Majaz. Majaz's passionate *Pakistan ka Milli Taraana* vividly captures the millennial hopes of young Muslim Communists that the Islamic state of Pakistan would turn Red.[164]

Azaadi ki dhun mein kis ne hamein aaj lalkara	Who dares challenge the song of our freedom today
Khyber ke gardoon par chamka ek hilal ek taara	in the vast skies of Khyber a crescent and a star have arisen
Sabz hilali parcham lekar nikla lashkar hamara	holding Green Flag aloft our army moves forward
Parbat ke seene se phoota kaisa sarkash dhaara	like a wild turbulent stream gushing from the heart of a mountain
Sarmaaye ka sookha jangal is mein surkh sharaara	in the withered jungle of dead capitalism flares the Red spark of Revolution
Pakistan hamara Pakistan hamara Pakistan hamara	in battle readiness we thrice cry, Pakistan is Ours, ours, ours
Sau injeelon par hai bhaari ek quran hamaara	A hundred Gospels taken together stand no match for the Quran
Rok saka hai koi dushman kab toofan hamaara	no mortal enemy has ever been able to stop our storm
Har turk apna har hur apna har afghan hamaara	we count as kindred every Turk, Hur, and Afghan
Har shakhs ek insaan yahaan hai har insaan hamaara	every human here we deem a fellow and our brother
Hum sab Pakistan ke ghazi	we are all *ghazis* in service of Pakistan
Pakistan hamara Pakistan hamara Pakistan hamara	And proclaim, Pakistan is ours ours ours

The CPI's capture of the All India Kisan Sabha and attempts to use its organization and cadres to campaign in support of Pakistan led to the resignation

[163] Hatim Alavi to Jinnah, 23 July 1945, *QA Papers,* Vol. 10, 747.

[164] Sehba Lakhnavi, *Majaz ek Ahang: Zindagi, Shakhsiyat, Fann* (Karachi, 1967), 57–58.

of Swami Sahajanand, the founder of the Sabha. Sahajanand complained that the communists were deliberately using the organs of the Kisan Sabha to propagate the Pakistan policy of the party in contravention of the decision of the Sabha three years earlier to remain neutral on the question.[165] The ML, however, remained highly suspicious of the aims of the communists. Liaquat cautioned Muslims against the danger of communism to Islam. As he stated during a public meeting, Muslims were greatly mistaken if they thought that communism would secure Pakistan for them. By following such a path, the Muslims might 'secure Pakistan of the conception of communism, but they would not be able to secure the Pakistan of Islamic conception.'[166] Jinnah summed up the ML's message to the Muslim voters when he told a meeting in Allahabad that they were not to vote for personalities. They were to vote for a ML candidate even if the candidate was a lamp-post because 'he stood for Pakistan and the Muslim nation's freedom.'[167]

The Jamiatul Ulama-i-Hind (JUH) Campaign against Pakistan

The failure of the meeting with Usmani, as described in the previous chapter, left the JUH with no option but to intensify its campaign against Pakistan. It now formed a separate party, the Azad Muslim Parliamentary Board, to fight the elections and ward off the criticism that it was merely a handmaiden of the Congress. Its chief campaigner was Maulana Husain Ahmad Madani, the principal of the *Darul Uloom*, Deoband and one of the foremost Islamic scholars in the country. Madani, as his name suggests, had an intimate connection with Medina as he had been a renowned teacher of Hadith in that holy city for nearly fifteen years. But as Barbara Metcalf in her excellent new biography of this towering *alim* tells us, he was a proud native of eastern U.P., born in Bangarmau in Unnao in 1879 where his father Habibullah was the headmaster of the local primary school. The family subsequently moved to Tanda in Faizabad district, a place Madani proudly noted had been continuously inhabited by his family ever since his ancestors moved there in the early sixteenth century, even before the Mughals came into India.[168] Madani's father may have had to pursue secular education to

165 *The Pioneer*, 4 March 1945.

166 *The Pioneer*, 13 May 1945.

167 *Star of India*, 15 February 1945.

168 Barbara Metcalf, *Husain Ahmad Madani: The Jihad for Islam and India's Freedom* (Oxford, 2009).

make family ends meet after the family's landholdings had been lost due to usurpation by a local chief after the 1857 Mutiny, but he was a deeply spiritual man who wanted his sons to have a religious education. Husain Ahmad as also his five brothers were, therefore, sent to Deoband after initial education in government schools. A student of the legendary Maulana Mahmudul Hasan at Deoband and a spiritual disciple of Maulana Rashid Ahmad Gangohi, the institution's founder, he was forced to quit his studies while in his final year in 1898 as his father decided to emigrate to Medina along with the entire family. He would spend the next sixteen years abroad barring two trips to India. During the Great War, Madani was detained in a prison in Malta along with Mahmudul Hasan (1916–20) on the charges of sedition, of trying to 'involve the Ottomans against the British in India'.[169] Recognized as Mahmudul Hasan's successor after his death following their return to India, Madani became a staunch Khilafatist, a founding member of the JUH besides joining the Congress. Madani also joined the revamped 'nationalist' ML under Jinnah in 1937 and was appointed a member of the Muslim League Parliamentary Board for the 1937 elections during which he campaigned hard for the party's candidates. He, however, resigned from the ML soon after, having fallen out with Jinnah, threw his lot entirely with the Congress and had his protégé Hafiz Muhammad Ibrahim appointed as a Minister in the Congress cabinet government in the U.P.

Undergirding Nehru's belief in a unified Indian nationalism ranged against British imperialism, Madani had propounded the theory of *Muttahida Qaumiyat* or composite nationalism and located its antecedents in the pact between the Jews and Muslims at Medina under the Prophet. His views were subject to devastating critique and ridicule at first by Iqbal, Mawdudi and Thanawi and later by the breakaway *ulama* led by Usmani who came up with his own idea of Pakistan as a new Medina. But Madani remained steadfast in his advocacy of a composite undivided India and emerged as the most prominent *alim* opposed to the ML and its Pakistan demand. Reacting to the accusation that he had 'joined the Hindus', he wrote to a correspondent in Rawalpindi

> You write that I have joined the Hindus and you are stunned by that. Why do you get affected by such propaganda? Muslims have been together with the Hindus since they moved to Hindustan. And I have been with them since I was born. I was born and raised here. If two people live together

[169] Ibid., 11.

> in the same country, same city, they will share lot of things with each other. Till the time there are Muslims in India, they will be together with the Hindus. In the bazaars, in homes, in railways, trams, in buses, lorries, in stations, colleges, post offices, jails, police stations, courts, councils, assemblies, hotels, etc. You tell me where and when we don't meet them or are not together with them? You are a zamindar. Are not your tenants Hindus? You are a trader; don't you buy and sell from Hindus? You are a lawyer don't you have Hindu clients? You are in a district or municipal board; won't you be dealing with Hindus? Who is not with the Hindus? All ten crore Muslims of India are guilty then of being with the Hindus.[170]

Madani believed that the 'fundamental institution of contemporary political life was the territorial nation-state' and India was indeed such a State.[171] The main problem facing India was British imperialism, which could only be overthrown through a joint Hindu–Muslim struggle. This would have the effect of also freeing other parts of Islamic world from British yoke, since it was control over India that allowed them to hold on to their worldwide Empire. Madani opposed Pakistan since he saw it as a British ploy to divide and weaken the nationalist movement and extend British control over the subcontinent. He pointed to their dismemberment of the Ottoman Empire and reducing its component parts to colonial appendages. Madani, therefore, attacked ML and Pakistan in a number of different ways. To begin with, he accused Jinnah of deliberately not coming up with a concrete plan about Pakistan. Quoting a newsreport from the *Haqiqat* of Lucknow, he pointed out that when Jinnah was asked at a press conference in Karachi about what Pakistan meant, the *Qaid* asked for more time to provide clarifications on the matter. On being pressed further, Jinnah directed the inquisitive newsman to existing writings and his own statements on Pakistan. When a Muslim editor reportedly pointed out that he had read all the existing literature and concluded that Pakistan was suicidal for the Indian Muslims, Jinnah got upset and refused to take further questions.[172] For Madani this meant that Mr Jinnah till date had not fully thought through or worked out the implications of Pakistan.

By contrast, Madani claimed that he himself had thought deeply on the

---

170 Maulana Husain Ahmad Madani, *Muslim League Kya Hai*, (Delhi, 1945). This pamphlet was translated into English by a certain Professor Bright and published by Dewan Ram Prakash as *An Open Letter to the Muslim League* (Lahore, 1946).

171 Metcalf, *Husain Ahmad Madani*, 2.

172 Husain Ahmad Madani, *Pakistan Kya Hai*, Vol. 2 (Delhi, 1945), 4.

matter and proceeded to lay out Pakistan's devastating consequences for the Indian Muslims. While earlier JUH commentators such as Sajjad and Seoharvi had highlighted its dangers for the 'minority provinces' Muslims, Madani added that even those belonging to the majority provinces would find themselves in the lurch. If Seoharvi had desisted from mentioning the prospect of dividing the Punjab and Bengal, Madani made it clear that according to the principles of the Lahore Resolution itself, existing provincial boundaries would have to be altered. It would entail Muslims in eastern Punjab and western Bengal being excluded from Pakistan.[173] After all numerical majority was the deemed principle for partition and non-Muslim districts in the Muslim majority areas could not be forced to join Pakistan. Assam too would not be a part of Pakistan as Muslims were a small minority in the Brahmaputra Valley. Madani noted that Iqbal too had talked of severing the Ambala division from Punjab to make it more religiously homogenous. By echoing the official Congress stance on the issue of territorial division Madani further clarified it for his fellow Muslims and also squarely called into question Jinnah and Liaquat's claims that Pakistan would include six provinces in their entirety.

Madani also ridiculed the idea that Pakistan would be an Islamic state based on principles of the *Shariah*. He rejected a public statement to that effect by Nawab Ismail Khan, published in the 25 November 1945 issue of the *Manshoor* as also another such claim made earlier by the Punjabi ML Mian Bashir Ahmad in the 1 January 1943 edition of the *Madina*, by calling attention to Jinnah's own public speeches and interviews on this matter.[174] He noted that the *Asr-i-Jadid* of Calcutta had quoted Jinnah as saying that Pakistan's constitution would be created by a Constituent Assembly elected by its people. Madani also referred to the *Shahbaz* of Lahore that carried an Urdu translation of Jinnah's interview to the *News Chronicle* of London, in which he likened Pakistan to a European style democracy. Liaquat too, he claimed, had stated the same in a speech at Aligarh as reported by the *Asr-i Jadid*. Madani cited editorials in the *Dawn* that debunked ideas of *Hukumat-i Illahiya* or *Khulafa-i Rashidin* and quoted Jinnah declaring unequivocally that Pakistan would neither be a theocratic state (*dini wa mazhabi hukumat*) or have anything to do with Pan-Islamism. Jinnah had also made it clear that Pakistan's basic industries would be state controlled thus making it more akin to a socialist state. Madani's extensive and careful citation of various newspaper reports in his pamphlets against Pakistan attests

---

[173] Ibid., 3.

[174] Ibid., 9.

to the importance of the popular press not only in terms of being a critical site for debating Pakistan but also as a vehicle for dissemination of information and ideas to a wide audience.

Madani was, however, selective in quoting Jinnah since he largely ignored his many public statements wherein the *Qaid* asserted that Pakistan's government would be established according to the principles of the *Shariah*. Even if Madani quoted one such speech where Jinnah asked the minority provinces Muslims to sacrifice themselves for the purpose of establishing such a state, he dismissed Jinnah's commitment to establishing an Islamic state in Pakistan as a charade (*dhong*). After all Jinnah was not a practicing Muslim and Islamic practices had no meaning for him. The JUH *ulama* would go on to call Jinnah *Kafir-i-Azam* (great infidel) and Churchill's showboy. Madani also pointed out that Jinnah did not particularly care for even the worldly needs of fellow Muslims. Jinnah had after all sacrificed Muslim legislative majorities in Punjab and Bengal in the 1916 Pact. Closer home, Madani noted that the staff of Jinnah's newspaper the *Dawn*, included only three Muslims while it had six Hindus, two Christians, a Jew and even a Qadiani such as Z. A. Suleri.

The League's anti-Islamic character, its close association with the imperialist government, its dangerous ploy of Pakistan and the devastating consequences it would have for Indian Muslims were themes that Madani reiterated in a number of pamphlets on the eve of the elections as he tried to wean Muslim voters away from the ML.[175] These were pithily summarized in a widely circulated appeal to the Muslim voter that listed all the anti-Muslim activities of the ML over the past three decades.[176]

1. The ML had betrayed Islam by undermining a comprehensive Shariat Bill in the Central Assembly by adding conditions that rendered it useless and dead.
2. The ML toed the government line by passing the Divorce (Khula) Bill, which made it unnecessary for Muslim judges to adjudicate divorce in Muslim families. When the JUH *ulama* sought to redress this issue by introducing a Qazi Bill, the ML, at the government's behest, opposed

175 See Madani's pamphlets published 1945–6 such as *Civil Marriage aur League, Shariat Bill aur League, Mr Jinnah Ki Aath Muslim Kush Siyasi Ghalatiyan, Mr Jinnah ka pur asrar Moammah aur us ka Hal, Pakistan Kya hai, Muslim League Kya Hai, Hamara Hindustan aur uske Fazail,* that were circulated during the election campaign.

176 *Sheikhul Islam Maulana Husain Ahmad Madani Madzila Alaihe ka Maktub-i-Girami Markazi aur Subaai Councilon ke Muslim Votaron ki Khidmat Mein* (Delhi, 1945).

and killed this bill since it did not want the *ulama* to be invested with any authority.

3. The ML had cooperated with the government to enable the passage of the Army Bill even though 500 *ulama* signed a *fatwa* opposing it.
4. The ML had not objected to the transfer of the Shahidgunj court case from Punjab to Calcutta thus sinking the Muslim cause forever in the Bay of Bengal.
5. The ML supported amendments to the Civil Marriage Act allowing marriages between Muslims and non-Muslims even though it knew that such marriages were against the Quran.
6. The ML forced the Sarda Bill upon Muslims with government help even though the *ulama* protested against such an imposition.
7. The ML signed the Lucknow Pact of 1916 reducing the Muslims to legislative minorities in the provinces of Punjab and Bengal.
8. During the 1930 Round Table Conference, the ML got together with Europeans, Indian Christians and Anglo-Indians and again reduced Bengal and Punjab Muslims to a minority in their own province, making their demand for establishing Pakistan in these very areas rather ironic.
9. The ML repeated this despicable tactic again after the Communal Award of 1932.
10. The ML supported the government in imposing stiff conditions for obtaining drivers licenses making life more difficult for poor drivers.
11. The ML did not condemn the government for shooting dead 47 Muslims who were part of a public procession mourning the hanging of Abdul Qayyum by the Sind government.
12. The ML government in Bengal was responsible for the death of 35 lakh people during the Bengal famine, a majority of who were Muslims.
13. The government of Sir Nazimuddin was extremely corrupt and government contracts were mostly handed over to friends and relatives of the high and mighty including many Hindus.
14. The central government dropped 700 bombs from the air upon the NWFP as part of its offensive against the rebellion killing a number of Muslims. When the Congress member from Madras, Mr Satyamurthy introduced a motion to condemn these wanton acts of the government, the ML did not support him and instead kept silent.

15. While the ML raised a hue and cry over atrocities perpetrated upon Muslims in the minority provinces by the Congress governments, when Rajendra Prasad offered an enquiry to be headed by the Chief Justice of the Federal Court, the ML flatly declined and instead demanded a royal commission to probe the charges.
16. The ML did not raise even a murmur of protest when the government itself declined to set up a Royal Commission for this purpose.
17. The ML did nothing for the cause of the Palestinians or the Muslims of Zanzibar.

The *ulama* of the JUH fanned out into the countryside and campaigned extensively throughout U.P. in favour of the Congress-Nationalist Muslim alliance and their programme of a united India. Hifzur Rahman Seoharvi, speaking at Gonda, described Pakistan as a British invention and argued that the British objective was to retain Calcutta and Karachi after Hindustan had slipped out of its hands.[177] Seoharvi maintained that Pakistan would be politically dependent on the British and economically bankrupt. Jinnah, he claimed, had left the Congress not because it became a Hindu organization, but because it had become anti-British. Afraid of jail, lathis and bullets that had become the lot of the Congress leaders and workers, Jinnah had thus decamped from the party. A vote for the ML was, therefore, described as a vote for British subjugation. Seoharvi tried to persuade Muslim voters that the Quran and Hadith permitted pacts with non-Muslims. The *ulama* were assisted by the Khaksars and Ahrars besides the Khudai Khidmatgars from the NWFP in this campaign. The latter campaigned extensively for Rafi Ahmad Kidwai in Bahraich, one of the three constituencies from which he contested but lost in these elections.[178]

The difficulties encountered by Congress Muslim candidates and their allies among the JUH *ulama* in this election campaign are captured in a pamphlet written by Maulana Muhammad Manzoor Numani, a Deobandi scholar who edited the journal *Al Furqan* from Bareily. Numani was founding member of the *Jamaat-i-Islami* and a close associate of Mawdudi who had resigned from that organization after irreconcilable differences emerged between them.[179]

---

177 *National Herald*, 24 February 1946.

178 Ibid.

179 For a discussion of Numani's association with Mawdudi and Jamaat-i-Islami see Seyyed Vali Reza Nasr, *The Vanguard of the Islamic Revolution: The Jamaat-i-Islami of Pakistan* (Berkeley and Los Angeles, 1994), 22–26.

Numani was not associated with either the JUH or the ML at this point in time and the former, therefore, used this pamphlet by an 'impartial' observer to flay the ML. He provides an eyewitness account of an election meeting that was addressed by Maulana Husain Ahmad Madani in Bareily on 20 November 1945.[180] Observing the meeting from a distance instead of sitting at the enclosure that had been created for the purpose, he wrote about the way in which it was disrupted by a crowd of ML supporters.

> What I saw subsequently is something that cannot be described by the pen. Crazy and animal like behavior, vile epithets, and vulgarity were on full display. One wanted to cry at the ethical and religious decline of Muslims. Along with the goondas there were hundreds of those who seemed respectable by their looks and dress, wearing Sherwanis; school and college educated folks, no doubt *sharif* born. They looked as if they had lost their senses and acted in such a disgraceful and debased manner that they looked like professional goondas. Some were flailing their shoes, some raising hockey sticks, some thrashing canisters, some pounding sign boards of shops, sometimes all of them were clapping together or making animal like sounds and raising a ruckus. There were a few piles of stones close to the meeting for laying a road. In the beginning an odd stone or two were thrown at the meeting. Then the gas lights were smashed so that the meeting was enveloped in darkness. And then a few groups standing on those piles of stones began to rain stones on the meeting mercilessly. I saw this macabre *tamasha* with my own eyes.[181]

Numani darkly warned that if Maulana Husain Ahmad with his magnificent record of sacrifices for the community and country was attacked in such a shameless manner, the same could happen to anyone in the future. He also gave an example of the ML's fraudulent electioneering tactics by recounting a meeting addressed by a student delegation from the Muslim University at Aligarh which came to Bareily. Numani recounted that one of the students in a speech boldly proceeded to make a statement about Maulana Ashraf Ali Thanawi. He claimed that Thanawi once had a dream in which he saw the Prophet, his Companions and other elders seated together in a *durbar*. The most striking feature of the *durbar* was that Mr Jinnah too was present, sitting

---

180 Muhammad Manzoor Numani, *Ilekshani Jihad aur Uske Hathyar: Az Moazzam Mohtaram Hazrat Maulana Muhammad Manzoor Sahab Numani Madzila Mudabbir Al-Furqan Bareily Jisko Hasb-i- Farmaish Haji Muhammad Yunus Sahab Dehlavi, Muhammad Haidar al Din Qasmi Ne Dilli Printing Press Dehli me Tab Kara Kar Daftar-i- Markaziya, Jamiatul Ulama-i-Hind (Gali Qasim Jan) Dehli Se Shaya Kiya*, n.d.

181 Ibid.

right next to the Prophet who was treating him with great love and kindness. Astounded at this sight, Thanawi in his dream reportedly enquired from the Prophet: 'Huzoor, this individual was most non-practicing (*bad amal*), never said his *namaz* or kept his *roza*, so why is he in such an exalted situation today?' The Prophet is reported to have told Thanawi in the dream that while Jinnah was undoubtedly non-practicing, yet when the ship of the *ummah* was sinking it was he who had been instrumental in saving it. It was this act, which has brought him to this exalted status.

Numani bemoaned that this false story of Thanawi's dream had been published in a number of newspapers and expressed anger at the satanic lies being spread during the election campaign dragging even the Prophet into this quagmire. What was worse was that they were being peddled by students from the Muslim University who were mostly communist and were against God and religion. The elections had been a revealing process since it showed the degenerative impact that a 150 years of British rule had on the collective life of the Muslim community. As he noted, the existing trend was to besmirch the opposing candidates with low and baseless allegations, roll their honour into mud, set *goondas* upon them, exult at the mischief and vulgar antics against them, not to talk of the ceaseless babbling that went on in the Press. What was more distressing for him was that this had become common not only among the common masses of Muslims but had become mother's milk (*shir-i-madar*) for even the *sharif* Muslims. He deplored these activities conducted by the ML in the name of Islam and the best interest of the Muslim community, and expressed horror at their being dignified by the label of *Jihad*. As Numani wrote eloquently

> God, is this Jihad? (*Hai Hai, yeh jihad hai?*) This is not Jihad in the path of God (*fi sabil Allah*) but in the path of idolatry (*fi sabil al taghut*). I wish you people could see that the strings of your heart are in the hands of Satan. Oh Mujahids of this election, if you truly have any connection with the Islam brought to us by the Prophet, for God's sake for a few moments step back from the hell of your ire and fury and think with a cool heart. You will realize that whatever you are doing in this heated passion is Kafir like behavior which would sadden the Prophet. You have uttered lies and spread falsehood during these elections. Don't you know that Allah in his exalted book has cursed liars. Only those who do not have faith in God's commands speak untruths.It is a crime which is close to *kufr*, *shirk*. In Sahih Bukhari and Sahih Muslim Hazrat Abu Bakr says that one day the Prophet said to him, Shall I tell you the greatest sin of all? It is lying.[182]

[182] Ibid.

Numani claimed that his fears were shared by a large number of people and quoted from a letter that a friend from Aligarh, who was an old boy of the institution and an ardent ML supporter, had written to him.

> Ever since I saw the baseness of the Muslim University's students my soul quivers at the very mention of education. Seeing their antics I have reached the conclusion that the speciality of the modern educational system is that it makes man into an animal and an animal into a ravenous brute. The illiterate and uneducated are far better than these specimens. A scoundrel of Rampur is more *sharif* than these boys in that he at least does not call himself a *sharif*. I struggle to find words to describe the behavior of these enlightened folks. When I see them I curse modern education. The abuses they throw around: Maulvi, you son of a pig, bastard. If they see a dog, they laughingly say, Look there goes the Maulvi. And ever since they have stepped out during the election time, the earth trembles under them.[183]

The Congress Campaign in U.P.

The Congress under Nehru also made a determined push against Pakistan. Nehru was convinced that if the Congress educated the Muslim voters during the election campaign, the ML would stand exposed as an organization of upper class Muslims that was using Pakistan as an election slogan in order to protect their own interests. He, therefore, declared that the Congress was resuming its MMCP.[184] Nehru launched a multifaceted critique of Pakistan on his tours throughout India. As an internationalist surveying the world affairs of the day, Nehru described the formation of a separate small country like Pakistan as anachronistic. In his view, in the emerging international scenario small countries of the world had no future and would have to perforce federate into three or four big confederations. Failure to do so would reduce them to the status of satellites of the great powers.[185] Nehru saw large federations as imperative especially in the decolonizing world. In this regard, he further noted that the atom bomb had finished the idea of small states.[186] Even an undivided India, he was convinced, needed to federate with neighbouring countries in order to save itself from utter

---

183 Ibid.

184 *The Pioneer*, 24 September 1945.

185 For Nehru, there were only two great powers at present – America and Russia while India and China were the rising powers that would be added to this list in the near future. Britain, according to Nehru, was no longer a world power.

186 *The Pioneer*, 25 August 1945.

annihilation. He, therefore, called for a federation of India, Iran, Iraq, Afghanistan, Burma and Siam.[187] Nehru also justified the existence of larger units as opposed to smaller countries from the viewpoint of development. The vivisection of India would thus only weaken India and arrest her development.

Nehru also dismissed the idea of Pakistan as impractical from the viewpoint of India's internal security, given the fact that there would always be 'a foreign element in both Pakistan and Hindustan.' He scoffed at the ML for demanding the right to self-determination for the Muslims of Punjab and Bengal while denying the same right to the non-Muslims in those provinces. He, therefore, declared that there would be no Pakistan without dividing Punjab and Bengal, reiterating this point in the many speeches that he made throughout the election campaign.[188] Pointing out that a large number of non-Muslims and Muslims including ML members were opposed to partitioning these provinces, he declared that it was up to the ML to decide whether it wanted such a division or if it would coerce a large number of unwilling people to remain in Pakistan in order to make it a feasible proposition. While the former was difficult, the latter, Nehru declared, was absurd.[189]

Nehru also vituperated the idea of Pakistan for the damaging consequences it would have for the U.P. Muslims. Speaking at a Congress rally in Lucknow, Nehru pointed out that U.P. would not be a part of Pakistan and therefore asked the Muslims to consider, 'What kind of *stan* do you want? Would the Nawabs of U.P. migrate to Pakistan leaving behind their zamindari and taluqdari?'[190]

A few days later in a speech in his home town of Allahabad Nehru again reiterated this message. Referring specifically to the landlords, he again asked 'Will they go and live in Pakistan? If so what will happen to their landed property and other interests in the province? They could certainly not lift these things and take them to Pakistan.'[191]

The tone of these speeches unleashed an indignant response from the ML newspaper *Dawn*. Referring to Nehru's Lucknow speech, the editorial entitled *Lucknow Hysterics*, noted that

---

187 Nehru also made an approach to Ceylon to be a part of this arrangement. See *The Pioneer*, 14 November 1945.

188 *The Pioneer*, 27 August 1945.

189 *The Pioneer*, 27 September 1945.

190 *Dawn*, 7 October 1945.

191 *The Pioneer*, 18 October 1945.

> These are significant words for two reasons. First, the taunting challenge is to the Muslims of UP as a whole and not to mere Muslim Leaguers indicating that the local Congress leaders are fully aware that the Muslims of the province are as a body with the League in their support of Pakistan. Secondly, the Muslim zamindars and talukdars are threatened that if Pakistan is established in India, Muslim property will be seized and expropriated by the Hindus in provinces ruled by them. Pandit Nehru is gravely mistaken if he believes by such threats he will succeed in cowing down the spirit of the Musalman whose lot is cast in the Hindu majority areas. The Pandit only reveals the extent of desperation to which he has been driven by the complete failure of the wiles and intrigues of the Congress to keep Muslims forever in its toils. Whether living in a majority or a minority area Muslims everywhere are resolutely bent on a course from which the voice of neither siren nor satan will divert them. The rise of Muslims to legitimate power in their majority zones will in itself be the surest guarantee of security for those of their compatriots who may be living in other areas and that alone can save the Muslim minorities from ruthless oppression to which unchallenged Hindu supremacy all over India would inevitably subject them.[192]

Nehru's trusted lieutenant Rafi Ahmad Kidwai, who was also the Convenor of the U.P. Congress Parliamentary Board and a candidate in three Muslim constituencies, made similar speeches in his election tour of the U.P. In one speech, Kidwai stated point blank to his audience that

> we Muslims living in these provinces will become aliens if Pakistan is established. Are the Muslims of UP ready to share the burden of administration or remain aloof and be treated like Kabulis, Chinese, and Japanese, with no rights? Even the Muslims in Punjab and Bengal would achieve no advantages by Pakistan. The time had come to tell Jinnah frankly that Muslims did not want a Pakistan in which either they would have to become aliens in their own country or leave it altogether.[193]

At Rae Bareily, Kidwai laid out a radical programme that the Congress intended to implement once it had assumed power involving abolition of *zamindari*, employment opportunities for people, and full wages to workers. While these measures would benefit Muslim workers and peasants, Kidwai pointed out that the ML was an organization of landlords and feudals whose class interests

192 *Dawn*, 8 October 1945.

193 *The Pioneer*, 14 October 1945.

overrode all other concerns. In this regard, he stated that the local ML candidate the Raja of Mahmudabad was being assisted by Raja Maheshwar Dayal Seth, another landlord, who was also a leading light of the Hindu Sabha in the U.P.[194] In a speech at Sandila, Kidwai again pointed out that the local ML candidate and a notable landlord of the district Nawab Aizaz Rasul had not found Islam to be in danger in 1936 when he contested the elections on a NAP ticket. Kidwai explained that since the NAP was finished, the Nawab had shifted to the ML in order to protect his own interests.[195] Nehru hoped that the Congress campaign would weaken the ML in the Muslim minority provinces where it was the strongest while undermining its position in the Muslim majority provinces where it was already weak. He calculated that in the Punjab, while the ML was strong in urban areas, it would fare poorly in the rural constituencies that constituted the bulk of the Muslim seats in the legislative assembly. The extent of Nehru's miscalculation can be gauged from his expectation that the ML would at best win only 25 per cent of the seats in the Punjab and would be forced have to join a coalition in order to form a government.[196]

The Election Results

The first round of elections to the Central Assembly saw the ML score a complete victory sweeping all six Muslim seats in U.P. The Congress, however, did not seem disheartened by this performance since the election was based on a highly restricted franchise. In the next round, it set up half of the candidates to oppose the ML candidates leaving the other half to the pro-Congress nationalist Muslims. Kidwai expressed confidence that the Congress would win 50 per cent of the seats in the provincial assembly elections that were based on a wider franchise. These hopes too were belied even though the ML performance was less impressive in the second round. As the OSS, the forerunner to the CIA, in its report on the election results noted

> the ML fared relatively poorly in the United Provinces, the historical heart of Muslim culture in India, winning only 65% of the popular Muslim vote. 14% of the Muslim vote went to Congress candidates and another 14% went to pro-Congress Nationalist Muslims.

---

194 *National Herald*, 25 February 1946.

195 *National Herald*, 27 February 1946.

196 *The Pioneer*, 27 September 1945.

It attributed the League's weak showing 'to the strength of religious orthodoxy which diverted votes to nationalist Muslim candidates, conflicts between Sunnis and Shias which swung votes to the Shia Political Conference and recent internal dissensions in the provincial League organization.'[197] A letter from Abdus Sattar Butla, a supporter of the ML, to the editor of *Dawn* summed up the U.P. situation – 'The Muslims of U.P. have proved that though their province is not in Pakistan yet they are solidly behind the Muslim League which rightly claim to represent the Muslims of India (sic).'[198]

[197] *The All India Muslim League Part 1: Organization, Leadership, Strength and Program*, OIR Report No. 4162.1, 1 August 1946, 21.

[198] *The Dawn*, 14 December 1945.

Epilogue

The Aftermath of the Partition

This is very tragic – but very thrilling.[1]

M. A. Jinnah

Leave aside conspiring against Partition, if at this time Pakistan were to ask for a reunion, we shall definitely refuse it and resist any such move.[2]

Jawaharlal Nehru

In a column in the *Dawn*, ten days after the 3 June declaration, Qamaruddin Khan, a Lecturer of Aligarh Muslim University, contemplated upon the future of Muslims who would be left behind in Hindustan.[3] He noted that 'it was nakedly clear that the fifty million Muslims who have been forced to remain in Hindu India will have to fight another battle for freedom.' But Khan asked his readers to take heart from the fact that 'when this second battle is staged, anyone can easily guess that the geographical and strategic situation of Pakistan on the eastern and western frontiers of Hindustan will be of immense advantage to us.' The Aligarhian elaborated that while the U.P. Muslims were not about to invite and help Pakistan invade Hindustan,'the presence of Pakistan in our vicinity will exert a great moral pressure on the Hindus and persuade them to give us a fair deal.' Also, as a member of the United Nations Organization (UNO), Pakistan could always put any 'fundamental issue concerning the Muslims of Hindustan before the bar of world opinion' and also count on 'the sympathy and support of the Muslim peoples of the world can be mobilized for our cause.'

Apart from this 'negative consolation' Qamaruddin Khan added some positives. First, he noted that 'we must frankly admit that the Muslims of

1 Letter from Sir Francis Mudie to Hector Bolitho, 30 August 1953, quoted in Sharif al Mujahid (ed.), *In Quest of Jinnah: Diary, Notes, and Correspondence of Hector Bolitho* (Karachi, 2007), 143.

2 *The Leader*, 20 January 1948.

3 *Dawn*, 13 June 1947.

Hindu majority provinces never expected to be included in the Pakistan state as envisaged by the ML.' Second, they were still a substantial nation of fifty million whose population was greater than the population of any country in Europe except Russia. They could continue to 'live here as a great and formidable nation' as their 'national resources', 'educational advancement' and 'cultural supremacy' could 'very well be organized to give us an honorable status in Hindustan.' Third, the severance of Pakistan did not, in any way, affect their position for while in 'the greater India of yesterday' Muslims were a minority of about 25 per cent, now in Hindustan they would be a minority of about 15 per cent. There was no difference 'for all practical purposes' between these two figures, for their voice, which was ineffective earlier, would continue to be ineffective in the new system. Fourth, he also reminded his readers that despite the inability of the majority provinces Muslims to come to their rescue, 'we did remarkably even without them' and there was 'no reason why we should not pluck courage and rejoice in the good luck of our own resources, solidarity and strength, to maintain our integrity, dignity and honour.'

Khan then bluntly noted that Muslim participation in the political sphere was going to be quite useless and he therefore outlined what he called a 'constructive programme' for them in Hindustan. This involved giving up 'the political fight with the Hindus', eschewing claims to representation in the government, assemblies or services, giving up claims to special minority status and 'living like Parsis and Christians in Hindustan.' They now needed to 'concentrate on nation-building work in the economic and cultural spheres', educate all their people as quickly as possible, build up industries and 'become a nation of artisans and industrial and skillful workers'. An institution like the Muslim University at Aligarh had to now revert to purely academic work, become a centre of excellence and continue to draw Muslims from the world over, thus providing Hindustani Muslims with a link to the outside world. Muslims in Hindustan also needed to keep 'as intimate relations with Pakistan as possible and count on it for the maintenance of our central institutions of all kinds.' Khan further suggested that they needed to get back to their original mission of converting people to Islam once 'these abnormal times gave way to quieter times' – especially the Untouchables who, according to the 1941 census, numbered 50 million, whose conversion to Islam would enable them to double their numbers, greatly adding to their strength. He was optimistic that this mission would succeed since he expected Hindustan to witness a rapid revival of Vedic culture and the caste system, driving the Untouchables into the Muslim fold. In the short term though, Qamaruddin Khan advised Muslims to congregate in concentrated pockets in Hindustan in order to escape butchery at Hindu hands. He specifically encouraged the U.P. Muslims to congregate in western U.P. as it would enable them to secede from Hindustan, while counseling Muslims of North Bihar to congregate in Purnea district to enable their amalgamation into East Pakistan. Khan concluded his essay by exhorting his compatriots to not be overcome with despair but to work towards an even greater destiny than what they had achieved so far, ending with Iqbal's rousing couplet

> Come and let us ordain the destiny of this nation,
> Let us play the game of life like men.[4]

Early Responses to the Partition in U.P.

These were brave last words before the catastrophe of the Partition unfolded. Apprising the Viceroy of local reactions to the 3 June Plan, the U.P. Governor Sir Francis Wylie noted that after

> taking a thoroughly belligerent line over the Congress Panchayati Raj bill, much talk of fights to death for Pakistan, much marching and countermarching by the [ML] National Guards...our Leaguers in the Legislature have begun to coo like doves...seemingly the whole attitude now is that in the U.P. we must now forget the past and become all brothers together.[5]

Wylie explained that this was understandable since local ML leaders were mostly right wing people belonging to the privileged classes who had been 'pretending to show their teeth' under Jinnah's orders, putting it out that the U.P. Muslims were in favour of nothing less than Pakistan and the last thing they wanted was 'real trouble'. He added that 'whether they will be able to persuade our urban and usually very low class Muslim populations to take the same line remains to be seen.'[6] The U.P. Chief Secretary's Fortnightly Report tersely noted that 'the jubilation of the Muslims for getting Pakistan later got moderated by the realization amongst the more sober elements particularly the Nationalist Muslims of its logical implications for the Muslims outside Pakistan.'[7]

---

4 Ibid.

5 Wylie to Mountbatten, 9 June 1947, *Governor's Fortnightly Report, U.P.-83.*

6 Ibid.

7 *Fortnightly Report for the First Half of June 1947,* Chief Secretary U.P. to Home Secretary GOI, 25 June 1947.

Communal tensions were already high after the large scale killings in Calcutta, Noakhali, Bihar and Garhmuktesar and the 3 June declaration only fuelled a new rash of rioting in U.P. with the Muslims bearing a heavy brunt. Riot figures for June alone showed that of the 149 people killed 145 were Muslims, while of the 138 injured 119 were Muslims.[8] Matters only got worse in July with serious rioting in Aligarh, Bulandshahr, Badayun, Kanpur, Pilibhit, Mathura and neighbouring Gurgaon. 'Volunteer Organizations' in the U.P. boasted of ever larger numbers and seemed more organized than before. The Rashtriya Swayamsevak Sangh (RSS) was the biggest organization in this regard with 36,649 volunteers in the province as compared to the ML National Guards with 24,134 members and the Congress Seva Dal with 29,203 members.[9] Communities seemed to be organizing themselves for the worst as government reports noted the greater circulation of small axes, choppers, spades and swords. At Lucknow, the police arrested two residents from Rampur with a large assortment of its famed knives.[10] There was a 'phenomenal number' of conversions of Hindus to Sikhism in many towns for the purpose of getting the benefit of exemption under Arms Act which enabled a Sikh to carry a *kripan*.[11] The next two months witnessed rioting across many districts in the province. When rioting started in Delhi in September, railway services connecting U.P. to West Pakistan were disrupted and 'all north bound trains stopped at Mathura with goods trains being parked on the sidings of small stations up and down the district.' These became an open invitation for looting by mobs with the first case being a train 'of about 60 wagons containing mostly property of refugees which was on its way to Pakistan.'[12] Appearance of Hindu and Sikh refugees in Haridwar, Dehradun and Mussoorie from West Punjab and subsequently their entry into Lucknow only heightened communal tensions.[13] Seizures of Muslim properties as Evacuee Property could happen on the mere suspicion of its inhabitants leaving or desiring to leave for Pakistan as depicted in M. S. Sathyu's brilliant film *Garam Hawa*.

8 Wylie to Mountbatten, 2 August 1947, *Governor's Fortnightly Report, U.P.-88.*

9 Wylie to Mountbatten, 9 June 1947, *Governor's Fortnightly Report, U.P.-83.*

10 *Fortnightly Report for the Second Half of July 1947*, Chief Secretary U.P. to Home Secretary, GOI.

11 Wylie to Mountbatten, 22 December 1946, *Governor's Fortnightly Report, U.P.-69.*

12 *Memoirs of Channing Pearce of Communal Disturbances in Muttra in 1947*, OIOC, British Library, London.

13 Wylie to Mountbatten, 9 June 1947, *Governor's Fortnightly Report, U.P.-83.*

While the government passed the U.P. Communal Disturbances Prevention Ordinance, 'a savage enactment' in the words of the Governor, to prevent large-scale massacres, it was under some strain as a result of British and Muslim officers deciding to leave for Britain or Pakistan.[14] G. B. Pant, the Premier, 'was particularly angry with Muslim officers asking to go to Pakistan.'[15] The provincial administration was going to be almost completely in Hindu hands as a result, with U.P. also set to further receive a batch of twenty two Hindu ICS officers from the Punjab. Furthermore, while the proportion of Muslims in the lower ranks of the police was roughly 50 per cent, the government was under tremendous pressure to reduce Muslim representation in the services especially after the Sind government decided to reduce Hindu representation in the provincial services. Communal tension now was 'invading the ranks of the government itself'[16] even though it was noted that Pant himself 'keeps a fairly even communal balance in the day to day working of the administration so that the likelihood of the Governor having to interfere to protect minority interests is remote'.[17] Pant came under additional pressure from his own party and the Hindu Mahasabha when the U.P. Advocate General Mohammad Waseem appeared as counsel for Pakistan before the Boundary Commission. The Premier ultimately bowed to popular outrage and retaliated against the Sind measure by abolishing weightage for Muslims in the provincial administration.[18] Expressions of protest, lament, and pleas by UPML to the Sind government to desist from such an unwise policy, followed.[19] Syed Aizaz Rasul, the party general

---

14 Wylie to Mountbatten, 2 August 1947, *Governor's Fortnightly Report, U.P.-88.* There were 54 Indian and 19 European Indian Civil Service (ICS) officers in the U.P. Of these, 48 Indian officers including 2 Muslim officers decided to stay, with the remaining 6 Muslim officers opting to leave for Pakistan. 10 European officers decided to leave for Britain at once while 8 agreed to stay for some months and 1 opted for transfer to Pakistan. Out of the 54 Indian Police Officers – 31 Indian and 23 British – five British and one Indian (Anglo-Indian) officer opted to leave immediately, 15 volunteered to serve for a few months while 4 offered to serve indefinitely. Of the remaining 30 Indian Police Officers, 24 (Hindus) decided to stay on while the remaining 6 (Muslims) opted for Pakistan.

15 Ibid.

16 Wylie to Mountbatten, 18 May 1947, *Governor's Fortnightly Report, U.P.-81.*

17 Wylie to Mountbatten, 26 April 1947, *Governor's Fortnightly Report, U.P.-77.*

18 *The Leader*, 23 May 1947. The U.P. government decided that henceforth Muslim representation in the services should not exceed 15 per cent.

19 *The Pioneer*, 26 May 1947. Khaliq argued that the Sind assembly resolution in this regard was a non-official one and he would fight the move for reduction of Muslim

secretary, bitterly remarked that his Sind counterparts 'were all an egocentric crowd, they do not care what happens to us in the Muslim minority provinces.'[20] A UPML delegation met Jinnah and claimed that the *Qaid* disapproved of the Sind government's decision since it would be detrimental to the interests of the minority provinces Muslims who had sacrificed themselves for creating Pakistan.[21] But it was of no avail as both the Sind and U.P. government decisions were not reversed.

Police morale in this context hit a new low as evident in the big decline in the number of preventive detentions. As the Governor noted, a 'police station officer is afraid to run in bad hats under these sections and when he does so, finds his efforts to get convictions stultified by the interference of local Congressmen.'[22] Desertions by Muslim police officers and flight of skilled personnel to Pakistan was widespread in the weeks and months after the Partition. Many others began to leave. As C. M. Naim has noted in his little gem of a memoir

> it was happening in all the *sharif* families that we knew of, or identified with in what we locally called our *javaar*, our own special 'region'. The sons and sons-in-law were moving away; the relatively younger in age were moving away; the men, more than the women were moving away.[23]

The ML had prepared a list of critical personnel necessary for the new nation-state who could be approached to serve the Muslim homeland.[24]The Pakistan Government now spent a phenomenal fifty five lakh rupees transporting 7,000 such personnel along with their families from Hindustan.[25] Some incentives had, over the previous year, been offered to U.P. Muslims with Premier G. H. Hidayatullah reportedly offering them free agricultural land if they were willing to settle in his province.[26] Many though, simply fled from the violence or from

representation in services. Besides, he pointed out that Hindus in Sind were hardly a minority being 43 per cent of the population while they enjoyed a 50 per cent share in government.

20 *The Leader*, 26 May 1947.

21 *The Pioneer*, 15 June 1947

22 Wylie to Mountbatten, 2 August 1947, *Governor's Fortnightly Report, U.P.-88*.

23 See his essay, 'Two Days' in C. M. Naim, *The Ambiguities of Heritage* (Karachi, 2003).

24 *Dawn*, 28 June 1947. Liaquat set up a committee under I. H. Qureshi, Professor of History at Delhi University to make a list of scientists, technicians, specialists and other men of distinction, who would like to serve in Pakistan and could be approached in this regard.

25 *The Pioneer*, 21 September 1947.

26 *Dawn*, 5 December 1946.

fear of violence that swept through north India with Bihar and Garhmuktesar serving as savage warning signs.

Hindu Mahasabha and the Congress in U.P.

In this context, the Hindu Mahasabha gave a call for 'Direct Action' in the province on 1 August if its nine point charter of demands was not met.[27] It included disparate items such as prohibition of cow slaughter and the dismissal of the efficient and effective Rafi Ahmad Kidwai, the Home Minister who had done much to keep U.P. mostly free of large-scale communal rioting.[28] His own brother, Shafi Ahmad Kidwai, would be killed during these riots. The government initially appointed Sampurnanand to conduct negotiations with Mahant Digvijaynath of Gorakhpur to persuade him to call off the agitation but when the talks failed, it arrested Digvijaynath, Kunwar Guru Narain and Suresh Prakash Singh of Tikra along with other Mahasabha leaders and also issued an ordinance enabling it to attach properties of agitators and place it under receivership. The official report claimed that the movement fizzled out soon after.[29] But the Mahasabha's resilience was evident from the fact that Suresh Prakash Singh sensationally defeated the Congress candidate Mohanlal Gautam by one vote in the by-election for the Sitapur rural assembly seat. Gautam was later accommodated into the Constituent Assembly as a replacement for Vijayalaxmi Pandit who was sent as the Ambassador to Moscow, but it was alleged that he had lost due to massive internal sabotage.[30]

The U.P. Congress itself displayed open Hindu communalist sentiment. Purushottam Das Tandon, the new Speaker of the U.P. Legislative Assembly, openly repudiated Gandhian non-violence exhorting his countrymen to resort to arms in order to 'fight communal aggrandizement, gangsterdom, and manslaughter which [had] been let loose by the Muslim League.' At Talbhet in Jhansi district, he urged the establishment of rifle clubs, training of an armed force of at least 5000 young men in each district, liberal distribution of arms among people by the government, setting up *akharas* for physical training of young Hindu men and the creation of a Hindu Raksha Dal. Later, addressing

---

27 *Fortnightly Report for the Second Half of July 1947,* Chief Secretary U.P. to Home Secretary, GOI.

28 Wylie to Mountbatten, 2 August 1947, *Governor's Fortnightly Report, U.P.-88.*

29 *Fortnightly Report for the Second Half of July 1947,* Chief Secretary U.P. to Home Secretary, GOI. Also see *The Pioneer*, 1 August 1947.

30 *The Pioneer*, 13 and 17 September 1947.

Harijans in Bareily at the residence of Dharam Prakash, a Constituent Assembly member, he called for caste distinctions to be eliminated in Hindu society and asked Harijans to behave like *kshatriyas*, by learning to wield the lathi and sword so that they could protect their hearths and homes.[31] His statements caused such a commotion that even the stridently 'nationalist' *Pioneer*, in its editorial felt compelled to ask the government to either substantiate Tandon's claims and take stringent measures to curb ML gangsterism, or initiate criminal proceedings against him for spreading such false and dangerous rumours calculated to disturb peace and tranquility in the province.[32]

New Partition Schemes

The UPML began to think of ways and means to secure the safety of Muslims in Hindustan after the acceptance of the 3 June Plan. Nawab Ismail Khan appointed a committee to report on the prospects of forming a 'Muslim homeland' in U.P. by carving out Rohilkhand and Meerut divisions and adjoining tracts since its combined population of the Depressed Classes and Muslims was projected to exceed that of caste Hindu population.[33] Shaukat Ali Khan, an ML MLA, claimed that the nationalist Muslims had assured the ML of their cooperation in this scheme for the creation of an 'autonomous unit' in northwest U.P.[34] A number of schemes of this kind began to be floated by this point in time. The Lucknow District ML called for the creation of a 'sovereign independent state consisting of Rohilkhand and Lucknow district'.[35] S. M. Rizwanullah demanded the creation of five separate, sovereign, independent Muslim states in the Hindustan area if Punjab and Bengal were to be partitioned.[36] ML socialists called for the formation of a middle Pakistan

---

31 *The Pioneer*, 15 May 1947.

32 Ibid.

33 *Fortnightly Report for the First Half of June 1947*, Chief Secretary U.P. to Home Secretary, GOI,25 June 1947.

34 *Dawn*, 26 April 1947.

35 *Star of India*, 5 May 1947.

36 *Dawn*, 7 May 1947. Two of these were to be carved out of U.P. One would comprise the districts of Saharanpur, Moradabad and Bijnor and *tehsils* of Muzaffarnagar, Jansath, Meerut, and Mauna in western U.P. The other would include the district of Lucknow, Sitapur and Biswan *tehsils* of Sitapur district, Sandila and Hardoi *tehsils* of Hardoi district, Lakhimpur *tehsil* of Kheri district, Tanda *tehsil* of Fyzabad district, Nawabganj *tehsil* of Barabanki district. The other two Muslim states would be in the province of Bihar. The first would include Purnea district, which was contiguous to Bengal. The other would include the districts of Ranchi, Singhbhum, Palamau and Santhalpargana. The fifth

that would connect West and East Pakistan.[37] This followed Jinnah's support for the idea of a corridor between the two wings in a press interview.[38] But the Congress emphatically rejected this demand for a 1000 mile corridor.[39] In this melee, Prince Yusuf Mirza, the grandson of Wajid Ali Shah the last King of Awadh, also threw his hat into the ring declaring that he would approach the UN to regain his kingdom, which he pledged he would rule on a non-communal and democratic basis.[40] He found support from the Maharaj Kumar of Mahmudabad, who claimed that Awadh belonged to the 'royal family, Taluqdars, Zamindars and tenants.' The British government, he added, had never conquered Awadh but merely annexed it temporarily and taken over its management, just as the Court of Wards took charge of small *taluqdaris* on grounds of mismanagement.[41]

These proposals generated similar proposals from other parts of India. Mohammad Ismail, the Madras ML President demanded a Moplahstan on the grounds that Moplahs were 'racially different from Hindus, being mostly the descendants of the Arabs', and that 'their religion, culture, civilizational aspirations and outlook on life was different from those of the other inhabitants of the west coast of Madras.'[42] He claimed that the Moplahs formed a majority in Moplahstan in which they were 9 lakhs out of a population of 15 lakhs. This state would be 3000 square miles in area, larger than states such as Cochin and considerably larger than the European state of Albania.But this claim was going to cut into territories demanded for Dravidastan by E. V. Ramaswami Naicker whose Dravidian Federation expressed support only for the independence of Hyderabad and Travancore states in southern India.[43] Naicker now appealed to Muslims to join the Dravida fight against both British and Aryan domination arguing that Muslims in south India too were Dravidians. In response, Mohammad Ismail expressed sympathy for Naicker's demands and indicated that there was a rethink in the Madras ML on this

---

Muslim state would be based in the district of Malabar barring Kottayam and Palghat.

37 *Fortnightly Report for the First Half of June 1947*, Chief Secretary U.P. to Home Secretary, GOI, 25 June 1947.

38 *Dawn*, 23 May 1947. Interview with Doon Campbell of Reuters.

39 See the statement by Rajendra Prasad, *The Leader*, 24 May 1947.

40 *The Pioneer*, 14 August 1947.

41 *National Herald*, 8 July 1947.

42 *Dawn*, 18 June 1947.

43 *The Pioneer*, 4 July 1947.

matter.[44] The C.P. and Berar League though decided to oppose the Nizam on the Berar issue and stated that the Muslims of C.P. would be loyal citizens of the Indian Union and participate in Independence Day celebrations.[45] Meos also claimed a separate homeland in Mewat in southeastern Punjab, claiming they did not want to suffer Hindu domination and that their case was superior to that of the Sikhs since they occupied a compact zone.[46] A meeting of some Delhi Muslims passed a resolution demanding the inclusion of Delhi in Pakistan.[47] It argued that Delhi was originally a part of the Punjab and was separated from the province only to undermine Muslim strength. It further contended that Muslims also held a unique position in Delhi province in terms of their political importance, ownership of property and numerical strength inasmuch as they comprised 4.5 lakhs out of Delhi's total population of 10 lakhs. Together with *acchuts* who constituted 1 lakh of Delhi's population and 50,000 other minorities, the Muslims would be a majority in Delhi over the 4 lakh Hindus residing there. The resolution also argued that Delhi had been the seat of Muslim power, the capital of Muslim kings for seven centuries, the seat of Islamic culture and civilization and home to tombs of 22 saints, which could not be handed over to non-Muslim rule. Sindhi Hindus joined this chorus demanding a partition of Sind, suggesting that Hyderabad, Tharpakad and parts of Karachi be amalgamated to Jodhpur State with the other part of Sind amalgamating with Baluchistan.[48]

Scaling Back and its Challenges

As the date for British withdrawal from India drew closer, strains emerged within the UPML over future party policy in the province. Tensions had been brewing ever since the Gaon Hukumat Bill was introduced in the provincial legislature by the Pant government and the UPML had strongly opposed it on the grounds that a key provision involved the introduction of joint electorates for Hindus and Muslims. Ehtesham Mahmud Ali, a League MLA, broke from the official party line by welcoming joint electorates and was promptly

---

44 Ibid. Other reports however claimed that Mohammad Ismail had finally come out with statement pledging loyalty to the Indian Union claiming that he was an Indian first and a Muslim next. See *The Leader*, 1 July 1947.

45 *The Pioneer*, 10 August 1947.

46 *Dawn*, 17 May 1947.

47 *Dawn*, 7 May 1947.

48 *The Leader*, 17 May 1947.

expelled.[49] Khaliquzzaman reiterated that only separate electorates would save the interests of Muslims in the U.P.[50]A meeting of fifty leading lights of the party, held on 5 July to resolve these tensions, saw one section making a strong plea for a reorientation in the UPML's policy, arguing that if the Muslims wanted to live honourably in U.P. they needed to be responsive to the progressive programmes launched by the majority community. The other section opposed this 'surrender' arguing that this question could be settled only after Hindustan and Pakistan came into existence. It further argued that forcing the issue at this juncture would only lead to defeatism among Muslims and hence it was inadvisable to constitute a committee to negotiate Muslim safeguards at the present juncture.[51] The next day elections to the council of the UPML saw divisions publicly re-emerge in the ML ranks and rival factions soon began intriguing against each other.[52]

By late July though, Khaliquzzaman joined the Indian Constituent Assembly and asked everyone to work for the country's future and forget the bitterness of the recent months.[53] While the UPML policy had not yet crystallized in early August, the dominant section of the ML after a meeting on 2–3 August decided to cooperate with the government and celebrate 15 August as a day of rejoicing given that the party high command had also issued instructions to that effect.[54] Ismail Khan declared that 'political parties' would now replace 'communal parties' in the country.[55] Z. H. Lari the ML left winger and MLA from Gorakhpur, echoing Ismail Khan, declared that the ML should cease to exist as a political party and devote itself to social and economic uplift of Indian Muslims. He also opined that separate electorates were positively harmful to the minorities and untenable specially after Jinnah's speech on 11 August. On the issue of Vande Mataram, he observed that an unnecessary fuss had been created about the song. He had read and re-read the first two stanzas of the national song and found nothing objectionable or repugnant in it to Islamic principles.

49 *Dawn*, 11 March 1947.

50 *Dawn*, 29 March 1947.

51 *The Pioneer*, 6 July 1947.

52 *Fortnightly Report for the First Half of July 1947*, Chief Secretary U.P. to Home Secretary, GOI 29 July 1947.

53 *The Pioneer*, 23 July 1947.

54 *Fortnightly Report for the Second Half of July 1947*, Chief Secretary U.P. to Home Secretary, GOI.

55 *The Pioneer*, 6 August 1947.

He also agreed to join the zamindari abolition committee and acknowledged that the ML would have to change its decision on the matter.[56]

Lari cleared the air further by claiming that even while supporting the right of self-determination, ML members in U.P. had always thought of India as their motherland and cherishing their citizenship of the Indian Union, had never aspired for citizenship of Pakistan.[57] He, therefore, assured the U.P. Assembly that League Muslims did not look to Pakistan for protection of their rights in the Indian Union. AIML was dead and the organization of which Mr Jinnah was President had no hold over the ML in India. Referring to Kashmir's invasion by Pakistan, attitudes towards which had become a litmus test for Indian Muslim loyalty, Lari declared that he had no sympathies for feudal lords and that the Maharaja and the Nizam had to go. Finally, while expressing support for a secular democratic state in India, he made clear his disagreement with the Congress on three issues. First, instead of Hindi, he wanted Hindustani with both Devanagari and Urdu scripts to be made the state language as was the case of Switzerland where there was more than one state language. Second, he claimed that while the ML was against separate electorates, it also did not want joint electorates and wanted a third system to be put in place. Third, contrary to Congress government's assertions, Lari claimed that its officials were not impartial, hinting at bias when it came to dealing with particular communities. But the climate in U.P. in those extraordinary times was hostile to such nuanced positions. Responding to Lari's speech, the Editorial in the *Leader* bluntly stated

> We recall a speech given by Mr. Ismail in Allahabad before the elections. 'Let us have a Hindu homeland and a Muslim homeland. The Hindus will be entitled to shape their homeland according to their culture. He proceeded to give a sarcastic illustration. If the Hindus want that the national dress of India shall be Mahatma Gandhi's *langoti*, they will have the right to prescribe *langoti* as the national dress of India. But let the Muslims have the right to shape their homeland according to their culture.' Our advice to Messrs Ishaq Khan and Z. H. Lari is simple: you made your bed; you had better learn to lie on it without creating trouble.[58]

Pant himself rebuffed Lari and publicly defended Hindi as state language in

---

56 *The Pioneer*, 31 August 1947.

57 *The Leader*, 4 November 1947.

58 *The Leader*, 6 November 1947.

the U.P. Assembly. Quoting Grierson, he averred that Hindi was spoken and written by a vast majority of people in Avadh, Gorakhpur, Benares, Allahabad, Agra and Kumaun divisions, and was more widely spoken than Urdu in Rohilkhand and Meerut divisions. He noted that 44 out of 47 million people of U.P. spoke a dialect of Hindi according to the figures available in 1919, that 9116 out of every 10,000 people spoke Hindi while only 853 spoke Urdu. Pant further explained that the total circulation of periodicals in U.P. was 133,685 out of which only 17,120 was for Urdu publications. Finally, while Devanagri script could be learnt by a man of average intelligence in 15–20 days, Pant claimed that this was not the case with Urdu.[59] Even if Pant pledged to protect Muslim minorities in the province, the Congress leadership in U.P. publicly demanded 'absolute loyalty' from its Muslims even in the event of a conflict with Pakistan. Pant on a tour of western U.P. noted that 'we will not tolerate a single fifth columnist in India and those who grudged loyalty to the state should better leave for Pakistan.'[60] U.P. Muslims were also asked to 'cross the borders and ask their co-religionists to stay their hand'.[61] A UPML peace delegation led by Rizwanullah consequently left for Pakistan and 'appealed in the name of Islam to make Pakistan a safe place for minorities', referring to Jinnah's 11 August speech to make its case.[62]

New Setbacks and the ML in Disarray

As Muslim refugees from East Punjab streamed into Pakistan following the Partition massacres, Jinnah initially reiterated his oft repeated belief in exchanges of population, something he had first articulated soon after the Lahore Resolution and would repeat following Bihar and Garhmuktesar. As he noted, 'if the ultimate solution to the minority problem is to be mass exchange of population let it be taken up on a governmental plane and not be left to be sorted out by blood-thirsty elements.'[63] But as Pakistan faced a flood of refugees, Ghazanfar Ali Khan, the Pakistan Rehabilitation Minister, made it clear that it did not want any exchange of population.[64] Liaquat's statement that the government of Pakistan was absolutely opposed to migration of Muslims from

---

59 *The Leader*, 5 November 1947.

60 *The Pioneer*, 21 September 1947.

61 *The Pioneer*, 20 September 1947.

62 *The Pioneer*, 19 October 1947.

63 *The Pioneer*, 12 October 1947.

64 *The Pioneer*, 28 September 1947.

Delhi, west U.P. and areas outside east Punjab came as a major psychological blow to the U.P. Muslims.[65] Khaliquzzaman's exit to Pakistan after having joined the Constituent Assembly as the leader of the opposition and pledging his loyalty to the Indian Union, was the last straw on the camel's back. Two chartered planes carried the family and its possessions to Pakistan.[66] In his telegram to H. S. Suhrawardy wherein he declined to attend a peace conference called by the latter, Khaliq now stated that he had

> resigned from the U.P. assembly and the Constituent assembly of India to make room for younger blood to shape and implement policies in the new setup. Besides, I cannot reconcile myself to learning Hindi which has been made the official language in spite of Gandhiji and Jawaharlal's efforts to the contrary at this stage.[67]

Unlike the party supporters at the base, Khaliq and the UPML elite could make these choices quite conveniently. Begum Raana Liaquat represented the attitude of this class, telling Ambassador Grady that she had 'strong doubt that the Muslim minorities in Hindustan would receive proper treatment.' She added that 'regardless of the financial sacrifice' that the Liaquats were making 'she herself would prefer to beg in Pakistan than to live in Hindustan in comfort.'[68] Incensed Congress members in the U.P. Assembly asked ML MLA's to resign, forfeit their citizenship and move to Pakistan.[69] Charan Singh declared that the

> inexorable logic of Partition of Mother India on a religious basis can admit only of two peaceful solutions of the problem, namely an exchange of population or an unqualified denunciation of the two nation theory by the Muslim Leaguers and the launching of an active enthusiastic campaign by them for the unification of the two dominions. There is no other middle path. Not all the efforts of our Nehrus and Pants can bring peace to this unfortunate land otherwise.[70]

---

65 *The Pioneer*, 15 October 1947.

66 *The Pioneer*, 24 October 1947.

67 *The Pioneer*, 6 November 1947.

68 845.00/77-1447 Incoming Airgram from Ambassador Grady to Secretary of State, 14 July 1947, *US State Department Papers*.

69 See the statement by R.V. Dhulekar, the Congress MLA from Jhansi in *The Leader*, 4 November 1947.

70 Lionel Carter, *Partition Observed: British Official Reports from South Asia 16 October–31 December 1947*, Vol. 2 (New Delhi, 2011), 520.

The U.P. Congress President, on the other hand, added that the Congress could not be fooled by the professions of loyalty to India so freely and frequently made by Muslim Leaguers nowadays. Their sole aim seems to be to enter the Congress by backdoor methods and get a share in the administration. 'I want to tell the Leaguers your infiltration tactics and sabotaging would not succeed. We know you have always betrayed the country, you stabbed us in the back and so we will give you your proper place.'[71]

The ML also faced Ambedkar's wrath since the Pakistani government was barring scheduled castes from migrating to India as it cited the maintenance of essential services in Pakistan as the reason.[72] He condemned Pakistan and Hyderabad for violence against scheduled castes and attempts to forcibly convert them to Islam. Significantly, Ambedkar added that 'the union of Hyderabad with India must be insisted upon because the geographical unity of India is indestructible and no state can be allowed to violate it.'[73]

Jinnah did not help matters by sending a telegram to the U.P. government seeking details of incidents involving violence against Muslims. Pant angrily denounced it as outside interference.[74] It led to a renewed chorus for the ML's burial in India even by Leaguers. The Maharaj Kumar of Mahmudabad now resigned from the ML and demanded its termination. He bitterly remarked that League leaders had left for Pakistan leaving Muslim masses to their fate.[75]Supporting this view, Karimurraza Khan, the ML MLA from Shahjahanpur added that 'Muslim Leaguers should be given freedom to join any political party they like based on economic grounds.'[76] Even as the party was rocked by these developments, nationalist Muslims met at the residence of Hafiz Muhammad Ibrahim and expressed their faith in the leadership of Maulana Abul Kalam Azad. Accusing the ML of 'infusing the spirit of separatism, rowdyism, and popularizing the two nation theory' and holding it responsible for the existing plight of Muslims in India, the meeting asked the

71 Ibid.

72 Sriprakasa, the first Indian High Commissioner to Pakistan, notes that when he asked Liaquat why these people were being barred from going to India for a month to see their families, he responded, 'who would clean the streets and latrines of Karachi if they did not come back?' See Sriprakasa, *Pakistan: Birth and Early Days* (Meerut, 1965), 76.

73 *The Leader*, 29 November 1947.

74 *The Leader*, 5 November 1947.

75 *The Leader*, 22 October 1947.

76 *The Pioneer*, 9 December 1947.

party to adopt the ideas of nationalist Muslims.[77] As the nationalist Muslims made preparations for their conference that was to be held in Lucknow in late December. The AIML met for one final time in Karachi towards the middle of December. It led to some fireworks. Jamal Mian launched a frontal attack on Pakistan Government and objected to the use of the term Muslim state in the official resolution of the Council of the ML. The young man reportedly burst out

> For God's sake do not call yourself a Muslim state and thereby blemish the fair name of Islam. You have exploited Islam enough. I beg you to call a halt now. The ways of your government and the behavior of your Governors and Ministers are not those of Muslim states. If you persist in calling yourself a Muslim state, we would expect the same standard of behavior from you as those of our pious Caliphs. You know, you cannot lead the life of those pious men when bribery and corruption reigns supreme under your aegis.' He also launched a frontal attack on Jinnah. "We put you on the highest pedestal. We acknowledged no other leadership. We put complete faith in you to guide our destiny. When you unceremoniously bid us farewell, leaving us in the lurch, our ship became rudderless and destruction stares us in the face. We are not afraid of our annihilation provided we are assured that Pakistan which you have built by sacrificing us will be worth living for those who are there. Unfortunately, what we see now gives us no such hope.'[78]

It was reported that he was lustily cheered when he attacked the Ministry and the behaviour of its members. Jinnah had earlier swatted away such arguments by deploring the 'insidious propaganda' that 'minority provinces' Muslims had 'been let down by the ML, and that Pakistan is indifferent to what may happen to them.' He bluntly stated that

> they were fully alive to the consequences they would have to face remaining in Hindustan as minorities but not at the cost of their self-respect and honor. Nobody visualized that a powerful section in India was bent upon ruthless extermination of Muslims and had prepared a well-organized plan to achieve that end. This gangsterism, I hope, will be put down by the Indian government.[79]

The next day, Jamal Mian dropped his amendment for the deletion of

[77] *The Leader*, 3 November 1947.

[78] *The Pioneer*, 10 December 1947.

[79] *The Pioneer*, 24 October 1947.

the term 'Muslim state'.[80] The Karachi meeting also decided to split the organization into Pakistan Muslim League and the Indian Union Muslim League (IUML) each of which was free to frame its own policies and follow its own political future. But rather than choosing a leader from U.P. as the IUML President, the Karachi meeting appointed Mr Mohammad Ismail the Madras ML leader for the position.

The new party leader decided that UPML members should stay away from the Lucknow conference, a move which was immediately resisted by a section of the UPML leadership including Z. H. Lari and Begum Aizaz Rasul. The latter bluntly stated that 'Muslims in the U.P. who are 14% of the population certainly do not like to be guided by Madras where Muslims are only 4% of the population'.'The real problem of the Indian Muslims', she added,'is in the U.P. and the lead should therefore come from the U.P. Muslims.'[81] But another section of the UPML, led by Rizwanullah, affirmed the new President's position claiming that the conference agenda as outlined by Azad was unacceptable.[82] Rizwanullah particularly objected to Azad's diktat that all Muslim political organizations should be dissolved and all decisions taken at the conference must be binding on all those participating in it. He shot back that the ML alone could take any decisions regarding the future of Muslims in India.

At the Lucknow Conference, Azad declared that the ML should be wound up and all Muslims should join the Congress.[83] He further made it clear that a non-communal committee would be formed to address the immediate problems of the Indian Muslims. Taking a strongly secular stand, Azad also asked the JUH to withdraw from the political field and primarily concern itself with the religious and cultural life of the Indian Muslims, leaving it to the nationalist Muslims to take over the mantle of leadership of the Indian Muslims. The JUH *ulama* had paid a heavy price in the run up to the Partition. The family of Maulana Syed Muhammad Sajjad was butchered during the Bihar riots in 1946. The torching of their property also meant that the fire consumed the few photographs that existed of the Maulana.[84] In these trying circumstances,

80 *The Leader*, 16 December 1947.

81 *The Pioneer*, 27 December 1947.

82 *The Pioneer*, 28 December 1947.

83 *The Leader*, 28 December 1947.

84 Email communication to the author from Maulana Anisur Rahman Qasmi, General Secretary, Imarat-i-Shariah, Patna.

Maulana Madani and Maulana Hifzur Rahman Seoharvi busied themselves in the task of working for the rehabilitation, safety and security of Muslims in Delhi, U.P. and all across India. Seoharvi came to be known as *Mujahid-i-Millat* for his services to the community in those trying times.

The Nationalist Muslims however helped Z. H. Lari get elected to the Constituent Assembly in January 1948 where he claimed he would sit as an Independent member. The Muslim League in U.P. soon folded up as most of its lights over the next few months and years migrated to Karachi, including finally, Lari himself. Of those who remained, some like Nawab Ismail Khan retired from politics while others like Begum Aizaz Rasul or the Raja of Pirpur joined the Congress thus leaving the IUML with influence only in parts of Madras province. The Congress now had a clear field to appropriate the Muslim vote. At a by-election for the Lucknow seat, Hafiz Muhammad Ibrahim asked Muslims to vote for the Congress candidate if they wanted to strengthen it to fight for democracy in India against those intent on establishing Hindu Raj.[85] On its part, the ML withdrew its candidate claiming that it was doing so to save Gandhiji's life as he was on a fast.[86]

Patriotism in Question and Muslim Pledges of Loyalty

C. M. Naim, in two exquisite pieces, has evocatively described those days when history was made sensitively dwelling on the fears, dilemmas and trials faced by common Muslims in U.P.[87] We would no better than begin at Naim *sahib*'s Barabanki. A letter to the Editor of the *Pioneer* by Dildar Husain, member of the Municipal Board, Barabanki, reflects the fragility of their situation and the ways in which they made attempts to belong in the new India. As Husain wrote

> I now fully realize my blunder in supporting the demand for Pakistan. May God and Indian nationals forgive me. I also pledge and declare most solemnly my determination never to falter in any service to the cause of our state—the Indian Union. I also appeal to the better sense of my co-religionists and implore them to fully rally round the Congress and to strengthen the hands

85 *The Leader*, 18 January 1948.

86 *The Leader*, 25 January 1948.

87 See 'Two Days' in C. M. Naim, *Ambiguities of Heritage* (Karachi, 1999); 'A Sentimental Essay in Three Scenes – 1906 All India Muslim League Formed; 1945–46, elections that settled the political fate of South Asia; 3 June 1947: Jinnah's speech broadcast on radio…', in *Outlook Magazine*, 11 January 2007.

> of those two most human of men, Mahatma Gandhi and Pandit Jawaharlal Nehru who are devoted today to the tending of wounds inflicted by our preaching of the two nation theory to the masses. I would also earnestly request my brother Musalmans not to sacrifice cows on the coming Id festival as atonement for past blunders and as a gesture of their love towards the other nationals of the Indian Union.[88]

Muslims were by now largely seen as fifth columnists and their loyalty to the Indian Union was demanded through public obeisance to the symbols of the new nation. The *Leader* reported that three assistant masters of government Jubilee high school in Gorakhpur Abdur Rahman, Abdur Rahim and Shabbir Hasan had been pulled up by the authorities for their failure to salute the national flag on 15 August. Explanations were demanded for their behaviour, and when given deemed inadequate. The report noted that they were going to be given another opportunity to clear their names by saluting the flag in front of staff and students.[89] Two hundred railway men from Eastern Indian Railways who had opted for Pakistan and now wanted to revoke their choice, publicly swore that 'India was their home and they would dedicate themselves to the services of their country without the slightest tinge of communalism.'[90] It is doubtful if their prayer was heeded by the government. Muslims in different parts of the province passed resolutions condemning violence against Hindu and Sikh minorities in Pakistan and reminding its leaders how it was affecting the Muslim minority in India. A public meeting in Benares urged Pakistan to create a *Gulistan* for its Hindu and Sikh minorities.[91] Deploring the existing suspicion against the Muslims, Nawab Jamshed Ali Khan of Baghpat, a leading ML leader and landlord, declared that a plebiscite held among the U.P. Muslims would make it clear that they had no desire to go to Pakistan.[92]At the 'arsenal of Muslim India', Nawab Ismail Khan now in his new avatar as the university's Vice Chancellor, pledged its 'loyalty to the Indian State, its constitution and all the implications and consequences which the allegiance of states involves.'[93] While making it clear that 'this loyalty will be the loyalty of self-respecting and free citizens and not of abject slaves', Ismail Khan laid out the tasks that

---

88 *The Pioneer*, 14 October 1947.

89 *The Leader*, 29 October 1947.

90 *The Pioneer*, 10 September 1947.

91 *The Pioneer*, 8 September 1947.

92 *The Pioneer*, 15 October, 1947.

93 *The Leader*, 28 October 1947.

the university and its denizens now had to fulfil in the new India, which was intensely suspicious of them.

> We shall therefore have to create an atmosphere of goodwill and fellowship so that their doubts and suspicions as to our aims and objects may be dispelled. It is my firm conviction that politics should be altogether divorced from this university and it should now revert to its primary role as a seat of learning pure and simple with no political leanings or affiliations. Not many of the students who will pass out from here can hope to secure employment under the government. The abolition of weightage may not be an unmixed evil but may on the contrary be a blessing in disguise if it thereby makes our students more self-reliant and enterprising and ready to explore other fields and direct their hopes and aspirations from stagnant careers in government services to channels more productive of material good. We must now learn to stand on our own fate (sic).[94]

His comments were echoed by Muhammad Habib, Professor of History at the Muslim University. Habib stated that the U.P. Muslims were 'thoroughly repentant of the League vote of 1945 and stand aghast at its consequences.' He added that the unity of Indian Islam was 'broken forever and within a generation or less the Musalmans of India and Pakistan will be as distinct as the Persians and the Turks.' He claimed that the process of separation had already begun and was proceeding 'at a rapid pace.' He also vehemently rejected Master Tara Singh's demand that Muslim peasantry from western U.P. needed to be transferred to west Punjab to make up for the losses of Sikh lands. Habib insisted that 'no power on earth can make us Punjabis or Pakistanis.' Echoing K. M. Ashraf from the days of the MMCP, he added that 'heir to the great Muslim culture of the Middle Ages, we simply refuse to be moved into that cultureless land where an alleged devotion to Islam begins and ends with the hatred of Hinduism.'[95] Other voices in the community counselled a withdrawal from politics, a return to Islamic learning and self-improvement. That is what Muslims, it was claimed, had done following the Treaty of Hudaibiya, the destruction of Mughal Empire and defeat at Balakot in 1857.[96]

Jinnah and Pakistan's Dual Imperatives

In contrast to their position in U.P., the *Mohajirs* went on to wield

---

94 Ibid.

95 *The Leader*, 10 October 1947.

96 Vahid Ahmad, *Musalman Kya Karein* (Lucknow, 1948), 81–91.

considerable influence in Pakistan in its early days, shaping the idea of Pakistan in ways that would have a lasting impact on its identity. We may begin this side of the story with the *Qaid-i-Azam*, who though not a *mohajir* from U.P., was certainly a migrant from Bombay. A few days before the Viceroy's momentous June 3 declaration, confidently remarked to an American diplomat taking leave of him: 'I tell you we are going to have Pakistan – there is no question about it. Delhi will soon be of no importance whatsoever.'[97] But as independence approached, the *Qaid*, mindful of the incredibly tense communal situation following the horrific massacres of Muslims in Bihar and Garhmuktesar and the apprehensions felt by Muslims in Hindustan made a soothing remark. He grandly declared that

> I am going to Pakistan as a citizen of Hindustan. I am going because people of Pakistan have given me the opportunity to serve them. But this does not mean I cease to be a citizen of Hindustan. Just as Lord Mountbatten who is a foreign citizen has accepted the Governor Generalship of Hindustan in response to the wishes of its people, similarly I have accepted the Governor-Generalship of Pakistan. But I shall always be ready to serve the Muslims in Hindustan.[98]

The same sentiment, more than his touted secularism, would motivate Jinnah's 11 August speech a few days later. But this statement itself was in sharp contrast to earlier remarks wherein Jinnah flatly noted that 'I do not regard myself as an Indian.'[99] Before leaving for Karachi, the *Qaid* sold his Aurangzeb Road residence to his old friend Seth Ramkrishna Dalmia who promptly converted it into the headquarters of the Cow Protection League and asked 10 August to be celebrated as Cow Day in the country.[100] Jinnah had tried to sell his Malabar Hill residence in Bombay in 1944 to the Nizam of Hyderabad but the deal never materialized and the property was ultimately sealed by the Government of India. On the other hand, Liaquat's property was leased to the Government of India by Begum Raana Liaquat for two years and hence was not requisitioned.[101]

In any case, Jinnah's bold optimism about a 'moth eaten, truncated Pakistan'

---

97 Telegram from American Consulate New Delhi to Secretary of State, 29 May 1947, 845.00/5-2947, *US State Department Papers*.

98 *Star of India*, 1 August 1947.

99 *The Pioneer*, 1 April 1946.

100 *The Pioneer*, 9 August 1947.

101 *The Pioneer*, 12 August 1947.

that he had rejected a few years earlier, echoed the sustained confidence and public enthusiasm that both ML elites and cadres displayed in the run-up to the Partition. Jinnah was not alone in his optimism as evident from the rather upbeat assessment of Pakistan by Henry Grady, the American Ambassador to India.[102] Fiercely protective of Pakistan's sovereignty Jinnah made it clear that Pakistan would never agree to a constitutional union with India.[103] The American journalist and photographer Margaret Bourke-White, who met Jinnah at his Viceregal residence soon after, described his demeanour in terms of 'a fever of ecstasy'. As she wrote, his 'deep sunken eyes were points of excitement' and 'his whole manner indicated that an almost overwhelming exaltation was racing through his veins.'[104] Jinnah reminded her that Pakistan was 'not just

[102] Enclosure to Dispatch No.40 11 July 1947 from Henry Grady American Ambassador on the subject of 'The Economic Viability of Pakistan', M-1448, Roll 4, *US State Department Papers*.Grady noted that even West Pakistan with an area larger than France and a somewhat smaller population, would 'rank with the world's medium powers.' Agriculturally, it was already self-sufficient giving 'its people adequate nutrition on a sufficiently varied diet' and leaving it with a large margin for export; and 'this is true of nowhere else in India.' The separation of southern Punjab, would not affect Pakistan since this area was a desert tract, with little irrigation, greater pressure of population on land and producing inferior grains like *bajra*. Pakistani Punjab would have more fertile land, greater irrigation facilities and much lower pressure of population on land thus making it 'definitely the richer for not having to carry South Punjab'. As regards its industrial prospects, Grady felt that 'separation from Hindustan and a tariff barrier' would kickstart its industrialization. And on the question of its defence, he remarked that it would 'be better protected than anyone else from Cairo to Peking, particularly if Great Britain were to recruit a certain number of Punjabi soldiers for her overseas posts.' Grady also saw Pakistan possessing adequate financial resources, enough to pay for the conduct of its foreign affairs and defence and also have a steady favourable balance of payments that 'would enable the new state either to embark on further large development programmes or considerably to improve its standard of life by further imports of consumer goods.' He was equally upbeat about the prospects of East Pakistan since its land was 1.5 times as productive as that of West Bengal and it had 'enough rice, meat, eggs to make it slightly more than self-sufficient in food, some hides, some tea, and nearly all the jute in India, which means nearly all the jute in the world'. While West Bengal with 'most of the tea, hydroelectricity, and coal would still be a serious loss' the real issue Grady noted, was 'whether it would be ruinous for East Bengal to lose Calcutta. For Grady, the answer was a surprisingly emphatic No. As he concluded, 'it is hoped that a certain amount of faith may be placed in the final conclusion that both Northwest Pakistan and East Bengal will benefit from a very favorable balance of trade, and that East Bengal will be more prosperous in every way by being freed of the incubus of Calcutta.'

[103] *The Pioneer*, 24 October 1947.

[104] Margaret Bourke-White, *Halfway to Freedom: A Report on the New India in the Words and Photographs of Margaret Bourke-White* (New York, 1949), 91.

the largest *Islamic* nation but the fifth largest nation in the world.'[105] This dual emphasis on Pakistan as the leader of the Islamic world and a major modern state in the world of nations, a new Medina as it were standing on the vista of breathtaking possibilities, reflected a widespread sense of excitement about the prospects of this new nation-state. But balancing these twin imperatives in a creative roadmap that would enable Pakistan to realize its potentialities posed a formidable challenge to the new nation-state.

Jinnah himself struggled to find the right balance or give content to this new project as he shepherded Pakistan's early destiny. When Bourke-White pressed Jinnah to reveal his plans for Pakistan's constitution, the constitutional lawyer most suited to 'correlate the true Islamic principles with the new nation's laws' stuck to generalities, remarking

> Of course it will be a democratic constitution; Islam is a democratic religion... Democracy is not just a new thing we are learning. It is in our blood. We have always had our system of *zakat* – our obligation to the poor... Our Islamic ideas have been based on democracy and social justice since the thirteenth century.[106]

This reference to 'Islamic democracy' echoed the idealism of people like Mahmudabad, or the young Anis al Din Ahmad Rizvi from Bareily, who had used similar justifications for Pakistan in the pamphlet he wrote in February 1940. Jinnah's famous 11 August 1947 speech, praise for which would land L. K. Advani in hot water sixty years later, was perhaps an attempt at restoring some balance, but it only created much confusion and consternation in Pakistan. The statement though was immediately welcomed in U.P. *The Pioneer* in its editorial called it a transition 'from Philip drunk to Philip sober, from Jinnah the partisan to Jinnah the statesman'.[107] Jinnah however soon reverted to his artful ambiguity on the matter. As Farzana Shaikh has noted:

---

105 Ibid.

106 Ibid., 92; Jinnah reiterated these points in his radio broadcast to the American people in February 1948 in which he declared, 'I do not know what the ultimate shape of this constitution is going to be, but I am sure that it will be of a democratic type embodying the essential principles of Islam. Today they are as applicable in actual life as they were 1300 years ago. Islam and its idealism have taught equality of man, justice and fair-play to everybody.' See Jamiluddin Ahmad, 'Pakistan as the Quaid Visualized' in Ziauddin Ahmad, (ed.), *Mohammad Ali Jinnah: Founder of Pakistan* (Karachi, 1976), 98.

107 *The Pioneer*, 13 August 1947.

in a speech to the Sind Bar Association in Karachi on 25 January 1948, he even seemed ready to abandon his earlier stance which had called for religion to be kept out of politics, denouncing as mischief, attempts to ignore Shariat Law as the basis of Pakistan's constitution.[108]

His ambivalence on the matter can further be gauged from his refusal to throw the ML's doors open to all of Pakistan's religious communities stating that 'time had not yet come for a national organization of that kind'.[109] Jinnah's own colleagues, especially from U.P., were far from ambivalent on the matter. As Sriprakasa, the U.P. Congressman who was sent to Pakistan as India's first High Commissioner noted, he was taken to public meetings large and small by 'friends he had known in India who would ask the audience, Do you want to be ruled by the Indian Penal Code or the Quran? And they would reply, the Quran.'[110]

Along with Islamic democracy Jinnah called for the inauguration of an Islamic model of economic development arguing that Pakistan needed to work out its destiny in its'own way and present to the world an economic system based on the true Islamic concept of equality of manhood and social justice.'[111] This model of Islamic development or social justice was at times presented in terms of Islamic socialism but the state in Pakistan was far from approximating this ideal in part due to Jinnah's own conservative instincts and in part due to the class composition of ruling elites.The *Charge' D Affaires* in the American Embassy in Karachi noted with astonishment, that salaries of provincial governors in Pakistan ranked 'far above the salaries provided for almost all the Governors in the United States.' He found this ironical 'in view of the great

[108] Farzana Shaikh, *Making Sense of Pakistan* (New York, 2009), 83.

[109] *The Pioneer*, 20 December 1947. As he stated 'the time has not yet come for a national organization of that kind. Public opinion in Pakistan is not yet ready for it. We must not be dazzled by democratic slogans that have no foundation in reality.'

[110] Sriprakasa, *Pakistan: Birth and Early Days* (Meerut, 1965), 50.

[111] Jinnah continued that 'the adoption of Western economic theory and practice will not help us in achieving our goal of creating a happy and contented people.The economic system of the West has created almost insoluble problems for humanity and to many of us it appears that only a miracle can save it from the disaster that is now facing the world. It has failed to do justice between man and man and to eradicate friction from the international field. On the contrary it was largely responsible for the two world wars in the last half century.The Western world, in spite of its advantages of mechanization and industrial efficiency is today in a worse mess than ever before in history.' See Jamiluddin Ahmad, 'Pakistan as the Quaid Visualized' in Ziauddin Ahmad (ed.), *Mohammad Ali Jinnah: Founder of Pakistan* (Karachi, 1976), 99

lack of capital in Pakistan, the poverty of the overwhelming majority of the people, and the fact that the new government will probably apply to the US for financial assistance in the near future'. It was 'more startling' since one of the main criticisms directed against British rule in India was the exorbitant salaries paid to governors and other officials at the expense of the masses. [112]

Pakistan and Early Foreign Policy Orientations

Pakistan's foreign policy is often explained in terms of its obsession with India, but it should not blind us to the operation of the above-mentioned dual imperatives. In the first place, the regime actively pursued a pan-Islamist policy as promised during the freedom struggle.[113] Even before the Partition Jinnah set the ball rolling by proposing a World Muslim Conference as a preliminary step to bringing about the creation of an Islamic bloc involving Muslim countries of the Middle East and Far East. The proposal was immediately welcomed by Iraq, Syria and Lebanon.[114] Consequently, on his tour of the Middle East to build relationships with the Islamic world in late 1946, Jinnah expounded on the great dangers an undivided post-British India would pose to the Islamic world. He warned that if Pakistan was not established, 'there will be a menace of Hindu imperialist Raj spreading its tentacles right across the Middle East.'[115] This Hindu Empire, Jinnah claimed 'would be as great a menace for the future if not greater as the British imperialistic power has been in the past. If it were achieved, it would 'mean the end of Islam in India and even other Muslim countries.'[116] There were press reports in the Middle East that Jinnah

---

112 Airgram from Charles D. Lewis, Charge D' Affaires, American Embassy Karachi to the Secretary of State, Washington DC, 4 September 1947, 845F.01/9-447, *US State Department Papers*

113 As the veteran Pakistani foreign policy commentator Samuel Martin Burke has noted, the creation of Pakistan 'was thus not viewed by the founding fathers of Pakistan as the culmination of their efforts but merely as a necessary milestone on the journey towards the ultimate goal of universal Muslim solidarity.' Burke quoted Liaquat who declared that 'Pakistan came into being as a result of the urge to secure a territory where Islamic ideology could be practiced and demonstrated to the world, and since a cardinal feature of this ideology [was] to make Muslim brotherhood a reality, it was a part of her mission to do everything in her power to promote fellowship and co-operation between Muslim countries.' See S. M. Burke, *Pakistan's Foreign Policy: An Historical Analysis* (London, 1973), 65.

114 *Dawn*, 27 November 1946.

115 *Dawn*, 18 December 1946.

116 *Dawn*, 21 December 1946.

'was discussing in Egypt projects for setting up a worldwide Islamic League and that Saint John Philby adviser to King Abd al-Aziz Ibn Saud of Saudi Arabia, was in India on the King's behalf paving the way for the establishment of a Pan-Islamic League'.[117] While this talk was politely rebuffed in Egypt, the AIML was heartened by the proposal of Trans-Jordan's King Abdullah, calling for the creation of a Turco-Arab bloc comprising Turkey, Iran, North Africa, Afghanistan, Pakistan and various the Arab states.[118] Jinnah also actively took up the Palestinian issue to bolster Pakistan's Pan-Islamic credentials. On the eve of the 1945–46 elections, he enquired why Palestine should be 'the dumping ground for such a large number of Jews'[119] while in a subsequent meeting with Lord Ismay, Jinnah frankly noted that he would not be averse to Pakistanis fighting for the liberation of Palestine in their individual capacities alongside their Arab brethren. This attitude was in consonance with the AIML's umpteen resolutions in support of the Palestinian cause over the previous decade when Pakistan Day celebrations were often combined with Palestine Day commemorations. In Pakistan at large, there were calls for 'sending a liberation army to Palestine to free the Holy Land from the Jews', and establishing a 'united front of Muslim countries in the military as well as spiritual sense.'[120] During the Kashmir crisis as well, Jinnah asked Pakistanis to cultivate the spirit of the *Mujahids*.[121] Looking East, Jinnah also extended his support to Indonesia and its Sultan Shariar in the face of attack by the Dutch forces on behalf of both 'Pakistan and Muslim India'.[122] It drew a stinging response from the U.P. leader Chaudhry Charan Singh who angrily noted that

> the Muslim left here in the Union will be a national of India and Mr. Jinnah being the head of a foreign state has absolutely no business to give assurances on their behalf or to represent them to the outside world.'[123]

Norman D. Palmer, a respected commentator on Pakistani foreign policy, has noted that 'disillusionment with Muslim states forced Pakistan in 1953–55 to

[117] Jacob M. Landau, *The Politics of Pan-Islam: Ideology and Organization* (Oxford, 1994), 268–69. Saint John's son Kim Philby would later attain notoriety as a spy.

[118] *Dawn*, 13 January 1947.

[119] *The Pioneer*, 10 November 1945.

[120] Bourke-White, *Halfway to Freedom*, 93–94.

[121] *The Leader*, 1 November 1947.

[122] *The Pioneer*, 27 July 1947.

[123] *The Pioneer*, 1 August 1947.

turn to the West for support.'[124] But attempts to establish close relations with the United States to help Pakistan against India took place simultaneously with the policy of Pan-Islamism. Jinnah told Margaret Bourke-White that 'America needs Pakistan more than Pakistan needs America.'[125] Pointing to Pakistan's strategic geographical position, he claimed that 'Pakistan is the pivot of the world, as we are placed [on] the frontier on which the future position of the world revolves.'[126] The man who once aspired to be a stage actor dramatically leaned towards the famed reporter and dropping his voice to a confidential note confided, 'Russia is not far away.'[127] Given that the United States was pouring money into Greece and Turkey as the Cold War with the Soviet Union got underway, Jinnah expected that US would 'be much more interested in pouring money and arms into Pakistan.'[128] Government officials in Pakistan echoed their *Qaid's* thesis and eagerly waited for indications of Russia's interest in Pakistan, hoping that it would galvanize the US to build Pakistan's armed forces.[129] On his maiden visit to the US, Liaquat would again present Pakistan as a firm anti-communist ally and portray its Muslim soldiers as providing the best fighters against the godless communists. While anxious to gain American military aid, Liaquat was an eager visitor to the US for other reasons as well. Indeed, if Begun Raana is to be believed, Liaquat initially asked Jinnah to send him to Washington DC as the Pakistani Ambassador, but the *Qaid* turned it down deciding to keep him in Pakistan.[130]

---

124 Norman D. Palmer, 'Pakistan: The Long Search for Foreign Policy', in Ziring, Braibanti, Wriggins (ed.), *Pakistan: The Long View* (Durham, 1977), 426.

125 Ibid., 92.

126 Ibid., 92.

127 Ibid., 93.

128 Ibid.

129 Bourke-White was unsparing in her criticism of these attitudes in Pakistan. As she wrote, 'In Jinnah's mind this brave new nation had no other claim to America's friendship than this – that across the wild tumble of roadless mountain ranges lay the land of the Bolsheviks. I wondered whether the *Quaid-i-Azam* considered his new state only as an armored buffer between opposing powers.' Trying to understand 'whether the purpose was to bolster the world against Bolshevism or Pakistan's own uncertain position as a new political entity', she harshly concluded that 'it was more nearly related to the even more significant bankruptcy of ideas in the new Muslim state – a nation drawing its spurious warmth from the embers of an antique religious fanaticism fanned into a new blaze.' Ibid.

130 845.00/7-1447, 14 July 1947 Incoming Telegram from Ambassador Grady to Secretary of State, Washington DC, *US State Department Papers*.

The U.P. Wallahs in Pakistan

Given these twin imperatives, the direction in which Jinnah would have taken Pakistan has been a source of much speculation with some claiming him on behalf of a secular Pakistan and others seeing him as the father of its 'ideological State'. But what is undeniable is the close association he developed with the *ulama*, for when he died a little over a year after Pakistan was born, Maulana Shabbir Ahmad Usmani, in his funeral oration, described Jinnah as the greatest Muslim after the Mughal Emperor Aurangzeb.[131] More strikingly Usmani compared Jinnah's death to the passing of the Prophet. Consoling the stricken nation, Usmani reminded it that when the Prophet had died, his Companion Abu Bakr had asked Muslims to take heart, for the message Muhammad had brought from God still lived and it was now their duty to carry forward his message. Similarly, Usmani asked Pakistanis to remember the *Qaid's* ceaseless message of Unity, Faith and Discipline and work to fulfil his dream

> to create a solid bloc of all Muslim states from Karachi to Ankara, from Pakistan to Morocco. He [Jinnah] wanted to see the Muslims of the world united under the banner of Islam as an effective check against the aggressive designs of their enemies. This is the hour of trial for Muslims. Those who face it with courage and determination will reign supreme.'[132]

On this occasion, India's canniest politician and its serving Governor General C. Rajagopalachari sent his official condolences not to Liaquat Ali Khan, but to Usmani, who by this time was acclaimed as Pakistan's *Shaikhul Islam*.[133] Usmani too did not live long after his *Qaid's* death but in that short time was responsible for some important political initiatives that would shape Pakistan's post-colonial destiny, his signature achievement being the Objectives Resolution, which would become the lever for those who sought to uphold the 'ideological State' as opposed to a secular state in Pakistan. Usmani also gave a push to Pakistan's Pan-Islamic ambitions by convening a World Muslim Conference (*Motamar Alam-i-Islami*) under the auspices of a new organization that he founded – the Islamic World Brotherhood

---

131 *The Dawn*, 13 September 1948. Usmani migrated to Pakistan along with other Deobandi *ulama* associated with the JUI who supported Pakistan. These included Mufti Muhammad Shafi, Zafar Ahmad Ansari, Zafar Ahmad Thanawi, Azad Subhani and Shabbir Ali Thanawi, among others.

132 Jamiluddin Ahmad, *Quaid-i-Azam as Seen by His Contemporaries* (Lahore, 1966), 238–39.

133 Ibid., 246.

(*Akhuwwat-i-Islamiya*).[134] His associates in this endeavour were other U.P. men like Khaliquzzaman and A. B. A. Haleem, the latter, now the Vice Chancellor of the new Sind University after his migration from Aligarh. The Ladies Section of the conference had as its patron, none other than Jinnah's sister, Miss Fatima Jinnah. As a report on the conference noted

> most of the speakers at the conference expressed the hope that with the unification of Islam, Muslim countries would be able to repel the incursions of outside powers. Certain of the speakers declared that Islam could act as a 'third force' between capitalism and communism.[135]

What was also noteworthy was that Pakistani speakers at the conference did not fail to claim full credit for their country for having convened the meeting in an attempt to highlight Pakistani leadership in Islamic affairs.[136]

Chaudhry Khaliquzzaman had led the procession of UPML leaders leaving for Pakistan after having first joined the Constituent Assembly of India and pledged his loyalty to the Indian Union. Khaliq's move was motivated by the possibilities of a political career in Pakistan, and before his exit, was already being tipped off as Pakistan's ambassador to the Middle East due to his avowed interest in promoting Pan-Islamic unity.[137] Appointed the President of the

---

[134] See Airgram from Charles Lewis, Charge D' Affaires, American Embassy, Karachi to the Secretary of State Washington DC, 25 February 1949, 845F.404/2-2549, *US State Department Papers.*

[135] Ibid.; The formal aims of the conference included the 'removal of racial, national and other discriminatory tendencies among Muslims, the promotion of Islamic fraternity, the encouragement of greater educational and cultural exchange between Muslim countries, the popularization of Arabic as the international language of Islam, the development of Urdu as the popular language of Pakistan and neighboring countries, and the general reeducation of masses in the tenets of Islam.'

[136] Ibid.; A brochure at the conference titled 'Muslims of the World Unite' stated that 'it was but natural that such an effort is made by Muslims of a country who do not subscribe to the theory that a nation is based on geography or race, but whose country's very foundation is laid on a theory of religious nationality.' The government, though closely associated with the conference, had to officially declare that it had nothing to do with it after the French Embassy asked for a clarification since it was exercised about the news that the legendary guerilla leader Abdel Karim el Khattabi of Rif, at the time resident in Cairo, would preside over the conference. The conference was deemed something of a damp squib for some of the above reasons besides organizational issues and did not find much coverage in the English language press, though press coverage by Urdu press would certainly have been different.

[137] *Dawn*, 26 June 1947.

Pakistan Muslim League a year later, Khaliq affirmed the *Motamar Alam -i-Islami* promoted by Usmani, as the first step in the creation of a permanent world organization, which would have branches not only in Muslim countries of the world but also in countries with Muslim minorities. It could soon be extended to become an organization similar to the Organization of American States. Expressing the long term aims of the Conference, he noted that in the context of the failure of the Arab League and Arab racial sentiment, he expected the 'natural reaction' of Muslims in Arab countries to work for the creation of a 'central authority for Muslim States which can protect them against further political and economic inroads of other powerful States.'[138] He conceived this supervening authority in terms of the 'Quranic State', which he believed could be brought about through 'political associations, social contacts, economic co-operation, and linguistic changes.'[139] This state would embrace any and all Muslim countries that wished to join and would be structured as 'a loose federation of autonomous states bound together alike by adherence to the principles of Islam and mutuality of interests.'[140]

Khaliq drew a sharp distinction between this Islamic state and a Muslim state. He claimed that as of now Pakistan was only a Muslim state in view of the majority of its population being Muslim, and indeed could never be an Islamic state by itself. It could certainly fulfill its promise and destiny by bringing together all the believers of Islam into one political unit and it is only then that an Islamic state would be achieved. Khaliq, therefore, argued that designating existing Muslim states as Islamic states was not only a misnomer but dangerous since it would divide 'Muslim polity for all time to come and making further progress in the direction of unification of the Muslim states into any form of association, federal or otherwise, an impossibility.'[141] He, however, saw encouraging signs in Pakistan itself that would kickstart this process. Thus, he pointedly emphasized to a US embassy officer the Objectives Resolution passed by the Constituent Assembly, given the great importance it placed on the provision that 'Muslims may be enabled to live Muslim life and

---

138 Airgram from Charles Lewis, Charge D' Affaires, American Embassy, Karachi to the Secretary of State Washington DC, 25 February 1949, 845F.404/2-2549, *US State Department Papers.*

139 Ibid.

140 Airgram from Charles Lewis, Charge D' Affaires, American Embassy Karachi to Secretary of State, Washington DC, 845F.404/3-849, *US State Department Papers.*

141 Ibid.

follow Muslim laws as enunciated in the Quran and the Sunna.'[142] Begum Raana Liaquat laid similar emphasis on the proper Muslim life in Pakistan even before she left Delhi. She told the US Ambassador Henry Grady that alcoholic beverages would not be served in any public place in Pakistan and that similar restrictions would apply to the use of pork and pork products.[143] Foreigners though would not be subject to these restrictions. In any case, Khaliq had to contend with the fact that without at least the tacit approval of the US, the organization would be a non-starter and, therefore, looked for its approval. He, therefore, proposed in the initial phase a semi-official conference of representatives of Pakistan, Iran, Turkey and Egypt, following which it could be extended to other countries of the Middle East.[144] These initial attempts, however, failed and saw Pakistan turn towards cementing its ties with the US in order to hold India at bay.

If Khaliquzzaman had a political career in Pakistan, his final appointment being the Governor of East Pakistan, the Raja of Mahmudabad proceeded on a very different trajectory. The Partition and its accompanying violence had sickened the young Raja and as Pakistan and India celebrated independence he along with his family crossed the border at Zahedan into Iran. They traveled from there to Mashhad , then Tehran and finally on to Karbala where the holiest shrines of the Shia are located. They still had Indian passports. The Raja stayed on in Iraq for ten years.[145] In the meantime he sent his son and wife back to Lucknow where the young man would get educated in an Anglo-Indian school. In 1957, the Raja went to Pakistan and changed his Indian passport for a Pakistani one. He had thought of going into politics but then Pakistan was a different country. He was a *Mohajir*, a refugee in Pakistan, a Shia in a predominantly Sunni country. The Raja left Pakistan again and traveled to London where he finally settled down. Here he served as the Director of

---

142 Airgram from Charles Lewis, Charge' D Affaires, American Embassy Karachi to Secretary of State, 7 March 1949, 845.011/3-749, *US State Department Papers.*

143 Incoming Airgram from Ambassador Grady to Secretary of State, 14 July 1947, 845.00/77-1447, *US State Department Papers.*

144 Ibid.; Khaliq was aware that limiting the attendance to this conference would upset Saudi Arabia and Afghanistan but was prepared to take the risk if the US provided its approval. As far as Israel was concerned, Khaliq was a realist agreeing that it was there to stay. He wanted the world Muslim body to be free of any aggressive intent against Israel but to 'come into defensive operation the moment Israel attempted to exceed the territorial boundaries allotted to it by the UN.'

145 V.S Naipaul, *India: A Million Mutinies Now* (New York, 1991), 371–80.

the Islamic Cultural Centre in Regents Park and was also instrumental in successfully pushing through the plans for the construction of the London Central Mosque near Hanover Gate.[146] In an interview to a Pakistani newspaper, the Raja declared that he had not settled in Pakistan as he felt he was not needed there. He had also transcended nationalism. As he told his interviewer, 'I am less interested in nations and more interested in people. And one can serve people in any country.'[147]

His son told the writer V. S. Naipaul years later that his wandering around the world was like a penance. He needed to go through the same process of homelessness that other people had gone through when they left India and went to Pakistan. In 1965 when the second Indo-Pak war broke out, the Raja's property was sealed and all the income from it was confiscated by the Government of India through the Custodian of Enemy Property. The India-Pak war over Bangladesh in 1971 and the birth of Bangladesh was the final straw for the Raja for it struck at the heart of the two-nation theory. It was a blow from which he never recovered. He died two years later at the age of fifty eight and was buried in Mashhad first in a cemetery next to the great shrine. The final reburial was intended to be at Karbala but it was never to happen. When in 1976 the Shah of Iran ordered the cemetery to be converted into a park, the Raja was reburied within the inner shrine thanks to the intervention of Zulfikar Ali Bhutto, then Prime Minister of Pakistan.

Muslim socialists such as Sajjad Zaheer and K. M. Ashraf were ordered by the party to go to Pakistan to foster the Communist Party in the new country. Travelling to Pakistan on ship, Ashraf poignantly described the scene as refugees approached the Promised Land.

> I can never forget the scene we witnessed when on reaching the coast of Pakistan the Islamic green flag with a crescent and star first appeared before our eyes. The whole atmosphere immediately and spontaneously reverberated with the recitation of the *Ayas* from the Holy Quran and people shouted the *Takbir*. All the immigrant passangers had tears in their eyes as if the caravan of those performing hijrat from Mecca had reached Medina on the invitation of the Ansars and now wealth would be equally distributed among the people according to their needs....In that situation if I would have said to anyone that, like Indian self-serving leaders, the

[146] J. D. Latham, 'The Raja of Mahmudabad (1914–1973)', *Bulletin (British Society for Middle Eastern Studies)* Vol. 1, No. 1 (1974), 41–43.

[147] Interview with Iqbal Ahmad Siddiqui on 12 April 1955, in Syed Ishtiaq Husain, ed., *Khutbat-i-Raja Sahib Mahmudabad* (Karachi, 1997).

Pakistani leaders are also involved in the struggle for wealth, my life in this sea of honest believers would have been in danger; I had no option but to keep quiet and observe.

The Fate of the Mohajirs

These ordinary U.P. Muslims, the *Mohajirs*, who were forced to migrate to Pakistan underwent much suffering. While they struggled to rebuild their lives in a new land they came to be a major political force and exerted a great influence on Pakistan's outlook towards India in its early years. As an American diplomat stationed in Karachi noted about the politics of the community

> It is clear nevertheless that the *mohajireen* remain a considerable political force though not as great a one as once seemed likely. In any major political speech, campaign or election, the interests of the *mohajireen* must be referred to most solicitously especially by politicians out of power, like Mr. H.S. Suhrawardy.... Finally with respect to international relations the refugees may be expected to continue to stand for a tough policy with the Indian Union.....Over a period of more than a year and a half there has been a noticeable decline in the emotional content of the refugees remarks on the Indian Union. There remains nevertheless something perhaps more serious – a fixed pattern of thinking according to which India and Pakistan are always in an inverse relationship. What is good for Pakistan will probably be bad for India; and what is bad for India is almost certainly good for Pakistan. If a third country shows a spurt of interest in the one country it is ipso facto becoming hostile to the other. If there is serious criticism of Pakistan in either neighboring or distant countries it must be due to Indian machinations and propaganda. If India woos one big power, Pakistan must woo the other to save face if nothing else, and also in sheer desperation for equal aid and prestige. To some extent these ideas seem to have permeated into all of the population of Pakistan and are certainly not the exclusive property of the refugees. The Urdu newspapers of West Pakistan, in particular, give the impression that these reactions are universal, but it must be remembered that virtually all of the important Urdu papers of West Pakistan are refugee staffed and in some cases refugee owned as well. There is no doubt that refugees have no more powerful ally than the press of West Pakistan.... Those rare qualities of forgiveness and repentance seem to be as far removed from refugee thinking as is possible, however, and it will be many years, probably a generation, before psychological traces of the refugee influx into Pakistan have been effaced.[148]

[148] 'Status of Refugee Problem in West Pakistan' by Franklin W. Wolf, Counselor of Embassy for Economic Affairs, Karachi, 9 November 1949, 845F.48/11-949, *US State Department Papers.*

It was a prescient statement. While these patterns got inscribed into official thinking on both sides and continue to be devil Indo-Pak relations, the *Muhajireen* over time did leave them behind. Nearly fifty years after that fascinating séance with the *Qaid*, Altaf Husain, the exiled leader of the *Muttahida Qaumi Movement* (MQM) made headlines after an impassioned speech at a high profile conference in New Delhi.[149] Referring to the internal political situation in Pakistan, he excoriated the Pakistani state in front of a distinguished audience for the atrocities it was perpetrating upon his people, the *Mohajirs*. In a dramatic moment, an emotional Husain declared that the Partition of India 'was the greatest, greatest blunder in the history of mankind' and that the division of the subcontinent was not just a division of the land but 'the division of the blood.' Publicly repudiating the two-nation theory, Husain made a sensational request to the Government of India, its opposition parties – to the entire Indian establishment. He asked them to forgive the *Mohajirs* and pleaded for giving them refuge (*panah*) in case the Pakistani establishment ever persecuted them again.[150] This was not the first time that the mercurial *Mohajir* leader had made such remarks, but the delivery of such a speech on Indian soil led to considerable furore in Pakistan. The former cricketer Imran Khan, who heads a rising *Tehrik-i-Insaf* party, was incensed enough to go to court to press charges of treason against Altaf Husain. The wheel, it seems, had turned full circle.

---

149 The occasion was the Leadership Initiative organized by the *Hindustan Times* newspaper in New Delhi on 5–6 November 2004.

150 *The Hindu*, 7 November 2004; a video clip of Altaf Husain's histrionic filled speech at the HT summit can also be found on youtube.

Conclusion

The idea of Pakistan may have had its share of ambiguities, but its dismissal as a vague emotive symbol hardly illuminates the reasons as to why it received such overwhelmingly popular support among Indian Muslims, especially those in the 'minority provinces' of British India such as U.P. While the aspect of symbolism cannot be denied, Pakistan was a symbol with substance, which needs to be unpacked if one wishes to understand its concrete realization. As evident from the above analysis, the Lahore Resolution set in motion rich debates in which views regarding Pakistan were articulated, evaluated, challenged and wrestled over in the public sphere. Pakistan assumed substance and popularity in U.P. and across India *precisely* as a result of such debates in which political elites and the general public came together.

Popular articulations of Pakistan blended both secular and religious arguments. Thus, Muslim League propaganda valorized Pakistan's 'geo-body' waxing eloquent on its natural resources, infrastructural assets, strategic location and a human population with unbounded potential once freed from both Hindu and British domination. Bigger than most European nation states in terms of both territory and population and as the world's largest Islamic state, Pakistan was expected to assume leadership of the Islamic world (thus replacing Turkey) and protect the global *ummah* in a twentieth century dominated by non-Muslim powers. Some with deeper Pan-Islamic convictions dreamed that it would not just significantly enhance the Islamic world's unity but indeed catalyse its reunification into a single political unit. In the subcontinent itself, Pakistan was expected to not just survive, but to emerge as a far more powerful state than Hindu India that would liberate the 'majority provinces' Muslims while at the same time extending a protective umbrella over the Muslim minority who would be left behind in Hindu India.

While the nation's geo-body was to provide Pakistan with material strength, Islam demonstrably constituted its soul and spirit. Historians riveted by the political performance of the elegantly suited Mohammad Ali Jinnah and consequently prone to seeing Pakistani nationalism as a species of secular nationalism have not paid adequate attention to the religious impulse animating the struggle for its creation. As the book has demonstrated, local ML functionaries, (U.P.) ML leadership, Muslim modernists at Aligarh, the ulama and even Jinnah at times articulated their vision of Pakistan in terms of an Islamic state. The renowned historian of Islam and comparative religion, Wilfred Cantwell Smith, who lived and taught at Lahore between 1940 and 1946, and was thus a close contemporary observer, was among the first scholars to acknowledge that Pakistani nationalism was above all a struggle for the creation of an Islamic state in the modern world and indeed a significant milestone in Islamic history.[1] Smith faulted himself for not having paid adequate attention to this impulse earlier but was quick to note that 'one of the advantages, however, of studying contemporary rather than past history, is that one may fairly quickly learn where one is wrong.' As he wrote, 'the economic, sociological, psychological, and other factors conditioning this separatist movement were there, operative and important; only they did not add up to explain the full cataclysm of what happened in 1947, nor the vibrant stamina and creativity of Pakistan in the constructive years since.'[2]

Smith argued that Pakistan was 'already an Islamic State not because its form is ideal, but because, or in so far as, it's dynamic is idealist'. Just like 'one becomes a Buddhist not by living up to the teachings of the Buddha or the principles of Buddhism but by undertaking to do so; one might say that man is a Buddhist who tries to be a Buddhist.'[3] He also drew parallels with the Communist state which, though as yet unachieved in the ideal form, was something which Communists around the world aspired to reach. As evident from this formulation, he simultaneously added that Pakistan was also trying to *become* an Islamic state, approximating its transcendental ideal, which however vague or contested, was an ideal nonetheless. Pakistanis had 'an enthusiasm and commitment to the actual as well as to the transcendent.'[4] As regards the transcendental ideal, Pakistanis broadly saw it in terms of the ideal Islamic community that would be enabled and brought into existence under the Islamic state. That this project constituted

1 W. C. Smith, *Pakistan as an Islamic State* (Lahore, 1951).

2 Ibid., 34–35; This analysis, therefore, marks a revision of the ideas expressed in his earlier book, *Modern Islam in India: A Social Analysis*, first published in Lahore in 1943 and later in London in 1946.

3 Ibid., 32–33.

4 Ibid.; Mawdudi, Smith claimed, had fallen foul of public opinion in Pakistan since he did not take into account the first sense in which Pakistan was already an Islamic state, instead denying it in the absence of the realization of its ideal transcendental form of his imagination.

a huge challenge and could not be achieved overnight was conceded by most Pakistanis including the *ulama* who pointed out to Smith that the Prophet himself in the first several years of his life at Mecca confined himself to moral teaching and that the ideal Islamic state and community at Medina was built only slowly.

Not least of the problems that Pakistanis faced in this regard was the vast variation in the conception of the Islamic state even though they overwhelmingly wanted its establishment. Even if there was widespread agreement that it was a state whose laws would be based on the *Shariah*, it raised the vexing problem as to what the *Shariah* meant, for it could mean different things to different people besides raising questions about how it could be implemented. It could thus either mean the accumulated legal tradition of Islamic legal scholars (*fuqaha*), or a complete rejection of this corpus and a recourse to the fundamental texts of Islam especially the Quran, or recourse to law codes worked out in the Golden Age of Islam that could be suitably modified to fulfil the needs of the modern era, or creating a unitary Pan-Islamic state covering the entire *ummah*. Pakistan was witness to a growing contest between groups espousing these various ideas making it clear that there was no consensus as to what it entailed.[5] Smith, however, cautioned that even in the absence of clarity or consensus, one could not cavalierly dismiss the ideal of the Islamic state. In the final analysis, the Islamic state was an 'impossible state' as it could never be realized since ideals were never realized in the real world.[6] Yet, for Smith, it was critical that Pakistanis pursued this ideal since it was 'their way of saying that it shall be good.'[7] More importantly, he presciently noted that Pakistan would not survive in the absence of its foundational ideal, a sentiment echoed by thoughtful Pakistanis whom he interviewed even in those early days.

Islam became the language of politics in Pakistan precisely as a result of the trajectory of the Pakistan movement in the last decade of the Raj.[8] Even if it has been argued that language is inherently pluralist inasmuch as its existing

5 For an elaboration of contemporary debates on Islamization of Pakistan especially among the *ulama*, see Muhammad Qasim Zaman, *The Ulama in Contemporary Islam: Custodians of Change* (Princeton, 2002).

6 For a recent argument about the impossibility of the Islamic state in the modern world in a different and far more sophisticated form, see Wael Hallaq, *The Impossible State: Islam, Politics, and Modernity's Moral Predicament* (New York, 2012.)

7 W. C. Smith, *Pakistan as an Islamic State*, 98.

8 See, Dale Eickelman and James Piscatori, *Muslim Politics* (Princeton, 2004) on how Islam becomes a language of politics in Muslim societies.

vocabulary can be used by various groups to advance vastly different and competing agendas thus allowing a contestation of ideas, Islam still set the limit on public debate in Pakistan. Political groups were compelled to define themselves in Islamic terms. Groups not seen as adequately Islamic found themselves marginalized as became evident in Pakistan's early days when the Ahmedis came under attack. Even Muslim Modernists who were among the founders of this nation-state espousing secularism as state ideology could be delegitimized given that the term secularism itself is translated as atheism (*la-diniyat*) under the existing vocabulary.[9] W. C. Smith noted that the reins of the state in Pakistan were in the hands of those who wanted to build it into a 'prosperous, modern industrialized semi social welfare state.' While they could persuade the electorate that they were competent to implement their programme, the question remained whether they could 'persuade it that what they are trying to do in Pakistan is actually good. And as we have seen this consists in part in showing that it is Islamic. A major crisis, both within the country and within the development of Islam as a religion would occur if any sizable group, or any sizable portion of educated leaders, should come to feel that the modernist program were good but not Islamic.'[10] Smith quoted one modernist telling him 'There is the nightmare of Pakistan's going back to a rigid, backward, narrow country. I share that nightmare. For us intellectuals the problem is that Pakistan shall not go back, that it shall not become an extension of Afghanistan.'[11]

The pervasive popularity of the Islamic state in Pakistan from its very inception ties in with one of the central arguments of this book that its vision was integral to Pakistan's popularity in the run up to the Partition. The multiple voices that articulated this vision and also framed popular debates on Pakistan, need to be highlighted as a corrective to studies of Pakistani nationalism that have long been dominated by the politics of its 'secular elite' or a 'sole spokesman'. In this regard, the book traces a more long-standing relationship between the Muslim League leadership and men of religion, the *ulama*, in contrast to the existing wisdom that the latter were implacable foes of Muslim League and Pakistan. The book tries to show how they utilized a common political vocabulary that intertwined

9 See Humeira Iqtidar, *Secularizing Islamists? Jama'at-e-Islami and Jama'atud-dawa in urban Pakistan* (Chicago, 2011). Her thesis that Islamists could become agents of rationalization and secularization due to their emphasis on the modern rational individual's direct relationship with Islam's fundamental texts and his/her critical meditation on the role of religion in public life, while intriguing, seems unconvincing.

10 W. C. Smith, *Pakistan as an Islamic State*, 105–06.

11 Ibid., 99.

concepts of modern politics and Islamic political theology in order to make the most compelling arguments in favour of Pakistan. Indeed, their collaboration during the struggle for Pakistan needs to be examined much more seriously if we are to make sense of post-colonial Pakistan's complex identity. The importance of Islam or the role of religious groups in nationalist movements in the Islamic world as well as their continuing relevance after the creation of post-colonial nation states has, over the past decade, been highlighted in revisionist studies of contemporaneous Indonesian and Egyptian nationalisms.[12] These studies, too, have called into question previous models that similarly highlighted the centrality of westernized elites and the secular anti-colonial nationalisms that they led while marginalizing the role of religious actors and their values.

The study of how Pakistan was imagined and contested in a Muslim minority province like U.P. is important given the leading role the U.P. Muslims, and indeed those belonging to the 'minority provinces', played in the struggle for its creation. However, a further task awaiting historians of the Partition is to analyse the valence possessed by issues raised in these debates – of sovereignty, territoriality, economy, international relations, Islamic foundations of Pakistan – in the 'majority provinces' where Pakistan actually came into being. Furthermore, while not denying that the imagination of Pakistan became associated with rich sets of meanings at multiple sites, this book argues that its dispersal into several local imaginations of community without the central focus of the state has been overemphasized. The book therefore makes a case for 'bringing the state back in' if we are to understand the overwhelming popularity that Pakistan attained in the last decade of the Raj.[13]

In this context, it also needs to be remembered that the public sphere, in part comprised Urdu newspapers and a reading public, encompassed the whole of India and was not just confined to U.P. Its breadth, depth and reach has been demonstrated by historians who have analysed popular mobilization during the Khilafat Movement to show how its leaders such as Mohammad Ali or Abul Kalam Azad used their pointed pens through the medium of newspapers to

---

12 See Michael Laffan, *Islamic Nationhood and Colonial Indonesia: The Ummah below the Winds* (London, 2002); Israel Gershoni and James Jankowski, *Redefining the Egyptian Nation 1930-1945* (Cambridge, 1995).

13 For a recent argument about the centrality of the state in modern Muslim political imagination in the late nineteenth and early twentieth centuries,see 'Introduction' in Francis Robinson (ed.),*The New Cambridge History of Islam Vol. 5: The Islamic World in the Age of Western Dominance* (Cambridge, 2010). Also see the burgeoning literature on Islamism that has analysed the centrality of state for some of these groups for realizing the ideal Islamic community.

successfully whip up popular Muslim sentiment against the British government. Analysis of the Urdu press during the Pakistan movement makes clear that Urdu newspapers from different parts of India carefully scrutinized each other's reportage, shared and commented on stories and articles appearing in each other's issues, thus keeping up lively conversations on what became the most pressing political issue of the day for Muslims in India. Individual papers too were not just confined to the provinces of their origins. Thus, a newspaper like *Madina* from Bijnor in U.P., which opened up its columns for a debate on Pakistan to its readers received responses from places as far apart as Bombay in the west, Chatgaon in the east and Raichur in the south. If indeed we are to take seriously C. A. Bayly's idea of the presence of an informational order in India making it a remarkably informed and argumentative society in spite of its low levels of literacy, we could infer that debates over Pakistan reached a wider public than just the newspaper reading literati.

In closing, tropes of insufficient national imagination, secular nationalism and accidental state formation have long dominated explanations regarding not just Pakistan's origins, but also its post-colonial trajectory. Thus, Pakistan has been primarily seen in terms of a bargaining counter never intended to be achieved, whose accidental achievement set the tone for the trajectory of the post-colonial state. It has further been understood that this was a secular nationalism led by secular political elites whose appeals to Islam in the cause of Pakistan were tactical at best and never out of conviction. The state's birth in the trauma of the Partition, the early deaths of Jinnah and Liaquat Ali Khan, the weakness of the ML's organization in the provinces where Pakistan came into existence, the fractiousness and venality of its second-rung politicians, the insecurities that it experienced *vis-a-vis* its hostile neighbour India – all these factors have been added up to explain its structural weaknesses and the consequent rise of the 'ideological' state in Pakistan, often led by the army. This has further been described in terms of a tragic betrayal of Jinnah's vision. While not denying the importance of some of these factors in explaining Pakistan's post-colonial trajectory, my argument is that the origins of the 'ideological' state in Pakistan lie not just in its post-independent insecurities, but at the very core of its nationalist ideology that developed in the run up to 1947. Studies of Pakistan that emphasize its 'insufficient imagination' therefore overstate the case. Pakistan was not insufficiently imagined, but plentifully and with ambition. It is this fact, coupled with the failures (and successes) of the state in fulfilling the expectation of a new Medina, which accounts for the crises that confront Pakistan today.

Select Bibliography

Private Papers

Nehru Memorial Museum and Library, New Delhi

B. R. Ambedkar Papers
Harry Haig Papers
K. M. Ashraf Papers
Hallett Papers
Nawab of Chhatari Papers
C. Rajagopalachari Papers

Oriental and India Office Collection, British Library, London

Fazl-i-Husain Papers MSS/EUR/E. 352
Hailey Papers, MSS. EUR/E. 220/F. 220
Linlithgow Papers MSS/EUR/F.125
P. W. Radice Papers MSS/EUR/F.180/80
Quaid-i-Azam Mohammad Ali Jinnah Papers, MSS IOR Pos 10760–10826

Institute for Third World Studies, Jamia Millia Islamia, New Delhi

Shamsul Hasan Collection

Ames Library, University of Minnesota

Hector Bolitho Papers

Records of Political Organizations

Nehru Memorial Museum and Library, New Delhi

All India Congress Committee (AICC) Papers

National Archives of Pakistan, Islamabad

Archives of the Freedom Movement

Government Records

Oriental and India Office Collection, London

Public and Judicial Department Proceedings (L/PJ)

United Provinces Native Newspaper Reports (UPNNR)

National Archives of India, New Delhi

Government of India, Home Department Files: Judicial, Public, Political, Revenue and Sanitary Proceedings

Uttar Pradesh State Archives, Lucknow

Proceedings and Files of the Government of the United Provinces: Education, General Administration, Political, Public and Public Information Department Files

Central Record Room, CID Headquarters, Lucknow

Police Abstracts of Intelligence, 1937–1946

National Archives and Research Administration (NARA), College Park, Maryland

RG 59 Records of Department of State, Central Files India, 1940–1949

Newspapers and Periodicals

English

Dawn

Deccan Times

National Herald

Star of India

The Leader

The Pioneer

Urdu

Aligarh Institute Gazette

Al-Jamiat

Hindustan

Madina

Qaumi Awaz

Sidq

Zulqarnain

Oral History Transcripts

Nehru Memorial Museum and Library

Interview with Ajit Prasad Jain

Interview with Hajrah Begum

Interview with Sajjad Zaheer

Interview with Syed Ali Zaheer

Interview with Sampurnanand

Interview with Sir Sita Ram

Urdu Sources

Abbasi, Qazi Jalil, *Kya Din They* (Nai Dilli, 1985).

Ahmad, Chaudhry Habib, *Tehrik-i-Pakistan Aur Nationalist Ulama* (Lahore, 1966).

Ahmad, Waheed, *Musalman Kya Karein* (Lucknow, 1948).

Ambalvi, Faiz and Shafiq Siddiqi, *Hayat-i-Shaikhul Islam Shabbir Ahmad Usmani* (Lahore, 1949).

Badayuni, Nizami, *Yadgar-i Tufail: Maulana Tufail Ahmad Manglori Alig Ki Savanih-i hayat Par Roshni Ya Shama Hidayat* (Badayun, n.d).

Banarsi, Kaif, *Dil Ki Dhadkan Pakistan* (Karachi, 1990).

Bijnori, Abdul Latif, *Latif Ki Kahani* (Bijnor, 1967).

Bukhari, Hafiz Muhammad Akbar Shah, *Akabir-i-ulama-i-Deoband* (Lahore, 1999).

Daryabadi, Abdul Majid, *Tamaddun-i-Islam Ka Payam Bisvin Sadi Ki Duniya Ke Naam* (Aligarh, 1938).

Ghazi, Hamidul Ansari, *Mukhtsar Tarikh Jamiatul Ulama-i-Hind, Shubah-i-nashr-wa Ishaat, Subah-i-muttahidah Ka Trekt 4: Khutbah 9,10,11 Aprel 1945* (Moradabad, 1945).

Hāmid, Afirah, *Tahrīk-i Pākistān Men Muslim Sahāfat Kā Kirdār, 1930 ta 1947* (Lahore, 1989).

Husain, Muzaffar, *Meri Siyasi Sarguzasht* (Lucknow, 1983).

Husain, Syed Asghar, *Matalibah-i-Avadh: Avadh Restoreshan Mishan* (Lakhnau, 1947).

Husain, Syed Ishtiaq (ed.), *Khutbat-i-Raja Sahab Mahmudabad: Raja Sahab Mahmudabad Mohammad Amir Ahmad Khan Ke Khutbat, Irshadat, Interviews Aur Chand Aham Dastavezat Ka Majmua* (Karachi, 1997).

Ibrahim, Hafiz Muhammad, *Ruidad Muslim Kanfarans Lakhnau Munaqidah Disambar 1947, Zer-i-Sadarat Hazrat Maulana Abul Kalam Azad* (Lakhnau, 1948).

Ilahabadi, Ramzi, *Muslim National Guards Ke Taraane* (Mumbai, 1946).

Jamiatul Ulama-i-Hind, *Islami Parcham va Nizam-i-Razakaran* (Dehli, 1946).

____, *Shirkat Kangres Ka Jawaz Aur Izala –i-shukuk* (Dehli, 1945).

Jinnah, Muhammad Ali, *Hindustan Ka Aindah Kanstityushan Ka Hona Chahiye* (Dehli, 1940).

Kalkattiyah, Ghulam Rasul, *Kaljug Ki Bahar Urf Desh Ki Pukaar* (Kalkattah, n.d).

Kazmi, Hasnain, *Tehrik-i-Pakistan Ki Taasurati Tarikh* (Karachi, 1988).

____, *Manzil Pakistan* (Karachi, 1985).

Khaliquzzaman, Chaudhry, *Shahrah-i-Pakistan* (Karachi, 1967).

Khan, Muhammad Sadat Ali, *Muslim Yunivarsiti Ke Maujudah Haalat Rahmatullah Kameti Ke Bad* (Badayun, 1942).

Khan, Muhammad Shuaib, *Islami Hind Par Ek Nazar: Hindustan Ke Musalman Duniya-i-Siyasat Mein is Waqt Kis Maqam Par Hain Aur Kya Kar Rahe Hain* (Aligarh, 1937).

Khan, Munshi Abdurrahman, *Tamir-i-Pakistan Aur Ulama-i-Rabbani* (Lahore, 1975).

Khan, Musavvir Ali, *Musalmanan-i-Hind Ka Siyasi Nasbul Ain Aur Jamhooriyat-i-Hind* (Badayun, 1940).

Kirmani, Ayub, *Kangres Aur Mazdoor* (Dehli, 1945).

Lakhnavi, Sehba, *Majāz Ek āhang: Zindagī, Shakhsiyat, Fann* (Karachi, 1967).

Madani, Husain Ahmad, *Muslim League Kya Hai: Muslim League Aur Kangres Ki Mukhtsar Haqiqat, Unke Fawaid Aur Nuksanat* (Dehli, 1945).

____, *Pakistan Kya Hai: Tehrik-i-Pakistan Ka Pas-i-Manzar*, 2 volumes (Dehli, 1946).

____, *Mr. Jinnah Ka Par Asrar Muammah Aur Us Ka Hal* (Dehli, 1944).

____, *Shariat Bill Aur League* (Dehli, 1945).

____, *Civil Marriage Aur League* (Dehli, 1945).

____, *Muslim League Ki Aath Muslim Kush Siyasi Ghalatiyan* (Dehli, 1945).

____, *Muttahida Qaumiyat Aur Islam* (Dehli, 1939).

____, *Hamara Hindustan Aur Uske Fazail* (Dehli, 1946).

____, *Maktub-i-girami Markazi and Subayi Councilon Ke Muslim Votaron Ki Khidmat Mein* (Dehli, 1945).

Manglori, Tufail Ahmad, *Ruh-i-Roshan Mustaqbil* (Badayun, 1946).

____, *Musalmanon Ka Roshan Mustaqbil* (Dehli, 1945).

____, *Teen Karod Musalmanon Ki Hifazat* (Badayun, 1941).

____, *Hukumat-i-Khudikhtiyari Aur Hindu Muslim Masle Ka Hal* (Badayun, 1940).

Miyan, Muhammad, *Jamiatul Ulama-i-Hind Kya Hai* (Dehli, 1947).

____, *Ulama-i-Hind Ka Shaandar Maazi*, 3 Volumes (Dehli, 1957).

Nadvi, Abul Hasan Ali, *Yeh Ikhlaqi Giravat Kyon?* (Lakhnau, 1949).

____, *Hindustan Samaj Ki Jald Khabar Li Jaye* (Lakhnau, 1949).

Nadvi, Hasan Musanna, *Pakistan Mukhalifeen Ki Nazar Mein* (Haidarabad, 1946).

Nadvi, Masud Alam, *Hindustan Ki Pehli Islami Tehrik* (Rawalpindi, 1960).

____, *Ishtirakiyat Aur Islam* (Karachi, 1949).

Nadvi, Syed Sulaiman, *Yad-i-raftgan* (Karachi, 1955).

Numani, Muhammad Manzoor, *Ilekshani Jihad Aur Uske Hathyar* (Dehli, 1945).

____, *Musalman Qaum Ki Haalat Aur Hamilan-i-din Ka Farizah* (Lakhnau, 1947).

Qadri, Abu Mushtaq, *Muslim League Ki Taid Mein Hazrat Allamah Usmani Ke Dalail Aur Tahriri Sarqe* (Dehli, 1946).

Qadri, Muhammad Afzal Husain, *Musalmanon Ki Taalim* (Aligarh, 1940).

Qadiri, Mahmud Shah Khan, *Swaraj Ya Hindu Raj Ki Haqiqat* (Agra, 1938).

Qasimi, Anisur Rahman (ed.), *Hayat-i-sajjad: Maulana Abul Mohasin Muhammad Sajjad Rahmatullah Alaihi Ki Hayat Wa Khidmat Wa Muntakhab Taqriren* (Patna, n.d).

Qasimi, Muhammad Fazlur Rahman, *Lakhnau Kanfarans: Khutbat, Tajvizen, Aur Tarikhi Taqriren* (Patna, 1948).

Rahmani, Abdus Samad, *Islami Huquq Aur Muslim League* (Patna, 1937).

Reyaz, Hasan, *Pakistan Naguzeer Tha* (Karachi, 1970).

Rizvi, Anis al Din Ahmad, *Pakistan* (Bareily, 1940).

Said, Ahmad, *Maulana Ashraf Ali Thanvi Aur Tahrik-i-azadi* (Rawalpindi, 1972).

_____, *Azadi-i-Hind Ka Khamosh Rahnuma Darul Uloom Deoband* (Deoband, 1957).

Sajjad, Maulana Mohammad, *Pakistan Ki Cheestan Aur Jamiatul Ulama-i-Hind Ka Wazih Faisla* (Dehli, 1945).

Sandelvi, Muhammad Ishaq, *Islam Ka Siyasi Nizam Jis Mein Islam Ke Siyasi Nizam Ka Asasi Khaka Pesh Kiya Gaya Hai* (Azamgarh, 1957).

Seoharvi, Maulana Hifzur Rahman, *Tehrik-i-Pakistan Par Ek Nazar* (Dehli, 1945).

Shafi, Maulana Mufti Muhammad, *Kangres Aur Muslim League Ke Mutaliq Shari'i Faisley* (Deoband, n.d).

Sherkoti, Mohammad Anvarul Hasan, *Khutbat-i-Usmani, Shaikhul Islam, Maulana Shabbir Ahmad Usmani Ke Milli, Siyasi Aur Nazariya-yi-Pakistan Se Mutallaq Alamanah Khutbat, Maktubat Aur Mukalimat Ka Majmua* (Lahore, 1972).

____, *Anvar-i-Usmani: Shaikhul Islam Allamah Shabbir Ahmad Usmani Ke Ilmi Aur Zati Maktubat Aur Digar Ilmiafadat Ka Majmuah* (Karachi, 1967).

Tayyib, Muhammad, *Islami Azadi Ka Mukammal Program: Khutbah-i-sadarat, Ijlas Jamiatulama Bambai Safar 1364/January 1945* (Deoband, 1945).

____, *Azadi-i-Hind Ka Khamosh Rahnuma Darul Uloom Deoband* (Deoband, 1957).

Thanawi, Ashraf Ali, *Ifadat-i-Ashrafiya Aur Masail-i-Siyasiya* (Deoband, 1945).

Usmani, Shabbir Ahmad, *Hamara Pakistan: Khutba-i-Sadarat Punjab Jamiatul Ulama Conference*, Lahore, 25–27 January, 1946 (Hyderabad, 1946).

____, *Roshni ka Minar* (Multan, 1950).

Zaidi, Raza, *Hindustan Hamara* (Dehli, 1946).

Printed Primary Sources in English

Adhikari, Gangadhar, *Pakistan and National Unity: The Communist Solution* (London, 1943).

Ahmad, Jamiluddin, *Historic Documents of the Muslim Freedom Movement* (Lahore, 1970).

____, *Speeches and Writings of Mr. Jinnah*, 2 volumes (Lahore, 1952).

____, *Some Aspects of Pakistan*, Pakistan Literature Series No. 3 (Lahore, 1946).

____, *Through Pakistan to Freedom* (Lahore, 1944).

____, *The Indian Constitutional Tangle* (Lahore, 1941).

____, *Muslim India and its Goal* (Aligarh, 1940).

____, *Is India One Nation* (Aligarh, 1939).

Ahmad, Kazi Saiduddin, *The Communal Pattern of India*, Pakistan Literature Series No. 2 (Lahore, 1946).

____, *Is India Geographically One?*, Pakistan Literature Series No. 6 (Lahore, 1945)

____, *Politico-Regional Division of India*, Pakistan Literature Series No. 4 (Lahore, 1945)

Ahmad, Rizwan (ed.), *Quaid-i-Azam Papers, 1940* (Karachi-Lahore, 1976)

____ (ed), *Quaid-i-Azam Papers, 1941–42* (Karachi-Lahore, 1976).

Ahmad, Waheed (ed.), *Letters of Mian Fazl-i-Husain* (Lahore, 1976).

AIML, *Report of the Inquiry Committee Appointed by the Council of the All India Muslim League to Inquire into Muslim Grievances in Congress Provinces* (Delhi, 1939).

Ambedkar, B. R., *Thoughts on Pakistan* (Bombay 1941).

____, *Pakistan or Partition of India* (Bombay, 1946).

____, *Thoughts on Linguistic States* (Delhi, 1955).

Azad, M. A. K, *India wins freedom* (Delhi, 1988).

____, *India Wins Freedom: The Complete Version* (Hyderabad, 1988).

Aziz, K. K., *Muslims under Congress Rule: A Documentary Record* (Islamabad, 1979).

A Student of International History, *Are the Indian Muslims a Nation?*, Pakistan Literature Series No. 13 (Lahore, 1947).

Carter, Lionel (ed.), *United Provinces Politics 1936-1937: Formation of the Ministries and Start of Congress Government, Governors Reports and Other Key Documents* (Delhi, 2008).

____, *United Provinces Politics, 1938: Congress in Mid-term: Governors Fortnightly Reports and Other Key Documents* (New Delhi, 2009).

____, *United Provinces Politics, 1939, the End of Congress Ministry: Governors Fortnightly Reports and Other Key Documents* (New Delhi, 2010).

____, *Partition Observed*, 3 volumes (New Delhi, 2011).

Chatterji, Basudev (ed.), *Towards Freedom: Documents on the Movement for Independence in India, 1938*, Parts 1, 2 and 3 (New Delhi, 1999).

Chopra, P. N., *Towards Freedom: Documents on the Movement for Independence in India, 1937* (New Delhi, 1985).

Faziel, Ali Ahmed, *Power Resources of Pakistan*, Pakistan Literature Series No. 10 (Lahore, 1946).

Gopal, S. (ed.), *Selected Works of Jawaharlal Nehru*, 10 volumes (New Delhi, 1973–1982).

Gupta, Amit K. and Arjun Dev, *Towards Freedom: Documents on the Movement for Independence in India, 1941*, Parts 1and 2 (New Delhi, 2010).

Gupta, Parthasarathi, *Towards Freedom: Documents on the Movement for Independence in India, 1943-1944*, Parts 1, 2 and 3 (New Delhi, 1997).

Hasan, Mushirul (ed.), *Towards Freedom: Documents on the Movement for Independence in India, 1939*, Parts 1 and 2 (New Delhi, 2008).

Indian Annual Register, Calcutta, 1932-1947.

Jinnah-Nehru Correspondence, *Including Gandhi-Jinnah and Nehru-Nawab Ismail Correspondence* (Lahore, 1960).

Khan, Nawabzada Liaquat Ali, *Muslim Educational Problems*, Pakistan Literature Series No. 7 (Lahore, 1945).

Kheiri, Muhammad Abdus Sattar, *National States and National Minorities*, Pakistan Literature No. 1 (Lahore, 1945).

Madani, Sayyid Husain Ahmad, *An Open Letter to the Muslim League, Translated by Professor Bright* (Lahore, 1946).

Mahajan, Sucheta, *Towards Freedom: Documents on the Movement for Independence in India, 1947,* Part 1 (New Delhi, 2013).

Manglori, Tufail Ahmad, *Towards a Common Destiny: A Nationalist Manifesto,* Translated by Ali Ashraf (New Delhi, 1994)

Masood, Mukhtar (ed.), *Eyewitnesses of History: A Collection of Letters Addressed to Quaid-i- Azam* (Karachi, 1968).

Maudoodi, Maulana Syed Abu Ala, *The Islamic Conception of State: Being an Address Delivered at Shah Chiragh Mosque, Lahore, October 1939* (Aligarh 1940).

Moon, Penderel (ed.), *Wavell: The Viceroy's Journal* (Oxford, 1973).

MRT, *Nationalism in Conflict in India* (Bombay, 1942).

____, *Pakistan and Muslim India* (Bombay, 1942).

Mujahid, Sharif al (ed.), *In Quest of Jinnah: Diary, Notes, and Correspondence of Hector Bolitho* (Karachi, 2007).

Mukhtar Masood (ed.), *Eyewitnesses of History: A Collection of Letters Addressed to Quaid e Azam* (Karachi, 1968).

Muhammad Yunus, *Industrial Pakistan*, Pakistan Literature Series No. 11 (Lahore, 1947).

Nanda, B. R. (ed.), *Selected Works of Gobind Ballabh Pant*, 17 volumes (New Delhi, 1993–2002).

Panikkar, K. N., *Towards Freedom: Documents on the Movement for Independence in India, 1940,* Parts 1 and 2 (New Delhi, 2009).

Pirzada, Syed Sharifuddin, *Foundations of Pakistan*, 3 volumes (Karachi, 1969–90).

Prasad, Bimal, *Towards Freedom: Documents on the Movement for Independence in India, 1945* (New Delhi, 2008).

Qasimi, Muhammad Reza (ed.), *Jinnah-Liaquat Correspondence* (Karachi, 2003).

Qureshi, Anwar Iqbal, *The Economic Basis of Pakistan*, Pakistan Literature Series, No. 12 (Lahore, 1947).

Qureshi, I. H., *The Development of Islamic Culture in India*, Pakistan Literature Series No. 9 (Lahore, 1946).

____, *The Future Development of Islamic Polity*, Pakistan Literature Series No. 8 (Lahore, 1946).

Saeed, Ahmad (ed.), *Eastern Times on the Qaid-i-Azam* (Islamabad, 1983).

Sarkar, Sumit, *Towards Freedom: Documents on the Movement for Independence in India, 1946*, Parts 1 and 2 (New Delhi, 2007).

Shafi, Ahmed, *The Fiscal Fabric*, Pakistan Literature Series No. 5 (Lahore, 1945).

Sharma, Haridev (ed.), *Selected Works of Acharya Narendra Dev*, 3 volumes (New Delhi, 1998).

Tirmizi, S. A. I (ed.), *Paradoxes of Partition 1937-39* (Delhi, 1998).

Zaidi, Z. H. (ed.), *Jinnah-Ispahani Correspondence, 1936-1948* (Karachi, 1976).

Zaidi, Z. H. (ed.), *Quaid-i-Azam Mohammad Ali Jinnah Papers*, 17 volumes (Islamabad, 1993–2007).

Secondary Sources in English

Abrahamian, Ervand, *A History of Modern Iran* (Cambridge, 2008).

____, *Khomeinism: Essays on the Islamic Republic* (Berkeley, 1993).

Ahmad, Aziz, *Studies of the Islamic Culture in the Indian Environment* (Delhi, 1999).

Ahmad, Jamiluddin, *Quaid-i-Azam as Seen by His Contemporaries* (Lahore, 1976).

____, *Creation of Pakistan* (Lahore, 1976).

____, *Final Phase of Muslim Political Movement* (Karachi, 1967).

____, *Middle Phase of Muslim Political Movement* (Karachi, 1964).

____, *Early Phase of Muslim Political Movement* (Karachi, 1963).

____, *Glimpses of Quaid-i-Azam* (Karachi, 1960).

Ahmad, Z. A., *The Indian Federation: Congress Economic and Political Studies No. 10: Published by K.M Ashraf on Behalf of the Political and Economic Information Department of the All India Congress Committee* (Allahabad, 1938).

Ahmad, Ziauddin (ed.), *Mohammad Ali Jinnah: Founder of Pakistan* (Karachi, 1976).

Ahmed, Rafiuddin, *The Bengal Muslims: A Quest for Identity* (Delhi, 1981).

Alavi, Hamza, 'Ethnicity, Muslim Society and the Pakistan Ideology', in Anita Weiss (ed.) *Islamic Reassertion in Pakistan* (Syracuse, 1986), 21–48.

Al-Rashid, Madawi, Carool Kersten and Marat Shterin, *Demystifying the Caliphate: Historical Memory and Contemporary Contexts* (New York, 2013).

Amin, Shahid, *Event, Metaphor, Memory: Chauri Chaura, 1922-1992* (Berkeley, 1995).

Ashraf, K. M., *Indian Historiography and Other Related Papers* (New Delhi, 2006).

____, Hindu-Muslim Question and Our Freedom Struggle, 2 volumes (New Delhi, 2005).

____, *An Overview of Muslim Politics 1920-1947* (New Delhi, 2001).

____, *Life and Conditions of the People of Hindustan* (Delhi, 1970).

Bayly, C. A., *Origins of Nationality in South Asia: Patriotism and Ethical Government in the Making of Modern India* (New Delhi, 2001).

____, *Rulers, Townsmen and Bazaars: North India in the Age of Imperial Expansion* (Cambridge, 1983).

____, 'Pre-History of Communalism in South Asia', *Modern Asian Studies*, 19(2) (1985): 177–203

____, *The Local Roots of Indian Politics Allahabad 1880-1920* (Oxford, 1975).

____, *Empire and Information: Intelligence Gathering and Social Communication in India, 1770-1870* (Cambridge, 1996).

Bhalla, Alok, *Partition Dialogues: Memories of a Lost Home* (New Delhi, 2006).

Bhargava, Rajeev (ed.), *Secularism and its Critics* (Delhi, 1998).

Binder, Leonard, *Religion and Politics in Pakistan* (Berkeley, 1961).

Bolitho, Hector, *Jinnah, Creator of Pakistan* (London, 1954).

Bourke-White, Margaret, *Halfway to Freedom: A Report on the New India in the Words and Photographs of Margaret Bourke-White* (New York, 1949).

Brass, Paul, *Language, Religion and Politics in North India* (Cambridge, 1974).

Bridge, Carl, *Holding India to the Empire: The British Conservative Party and the 1935 Constitution* (New Delhi, 1986).

Burke, S. M., *Pakistan's Foreign Policy: An Historical Analysis* (London, 1973).

Butalia, Urvashi, *The Other Side of Silence: Voices from the Partition of India* (Durham, 2000).

Chakrabarty, Bidyut, 'The Communal Award of 1932 and its Implications in Bengal', *Modern Asian Studies*, 23(3) (1989): 493–523.

Chandra, Bipan (ed.), *The Indian Left: Critical Appraisals* (New Delhi, 1983).

Chatterji, Joya, *Bengal Divided: Hindu Communalism and Partition 1932–1947* (New Delhi, 1996).

Clymer, Kenton J, *Quest for freedom: the United States and India's Independence* (New York, 1995).

Cohen, Stephen, *The Idea of Pakistan* (New Delhi, 2005).

Coupland, Reginald, *The Indian Problem: Report on the Constitutional Problem in India* (Oxford, 1944).

Custers, Peter, 'Maulana Bhashani and the Transition to Secular Politics in Bengal', *Indian Economic and Social History Review*, (April/June 2010): 231–59.

Devji, Faisal, *Muslim Zion: Pakistan as a Political Idea* (London, 2013).

Dhulipala, Venkat, 'Rallying the Qaum: The Muslim League in the United Provinces, 1937–1939', *Modern Asian Studies*, 44(3) (2010): 603–40.

Douglas, Ian Henderson, *Abul Kalam Azad: An Intellectual and Religious Biography* (New Delhi, 1988).

Euben, Roxanne and Muhammad Qasim Zaman, *Princeton Readings in Islamist Thought: Texts and Contexts from al Banna to Bin Laden* (Princeton, 2009).

Farhat Tabassum, *Deoband Ulema's Movement for the Freedom of India* (Delhi, 2006).

Faruqi, Zia-ul-Hasan, *The Deoband School and the Demand for Pakistan* (Bombay, 1963).

Freitag, Sandria, *Collective Action and Community: Public Arenas and the Emergence of Communalism in North India* (Berkeley, 1989).

Gershoni, Israel and James Jankowski, *Redefining the Egyptian Nation 1930–1945* (Cambridge, 1995).

Ghosh, Papiya, 'Muttahidah Qaumiyat in Aqalliat Bihar: The Imarat-i Shariah, 1921-1947', *Indian Economic and Social History Review*, 34(1) (1997): 1–20.

Gilmartin, David, 'Partition, Pakistan and South Asian History: In Search of a Narrative', *Journal of Asian Studies*, 57(4) (November 1998): 1068–95.

____, *Empire and Islam: Punjab and the making of Pakistan* (Berkeley, 1988).

Gooptu, Nandini, *The Politics of Urban Poor in Early Twentieth Century India* (Cambridge, 2001).

Hardy, Peter, *The Muslims of British India* (Cambridge, 1972).

Hardiman, David, *Gandhi in His Times and Ours* (New York, 2003).

Hasan, Mushirul, *Legacy of a Divided Nation: India's Muslims since Independence* (Delhi, 1997).

____, *India Partitioned: The Other Face of Freedom* (New Delhi, 1995).

____, *A Nationalist Conscience: M.A. Ansari, the Congress and the Raj* (New Delhi, 1987).

____, *India's Partition: Process, Strategy, and Mobilization* (New Delhi, 1993).

____, *Nationalism and Communal Politics in India, 1916-1928* (Delhi, 1979).

Haqqani, Husain, *Pakistan: Between Mosque and Military* (New York, 2005).

Herwitz, Daniel and Ashutosh Varshney, *Midnight's Diaspora: Critical Encounters with Salman Rushdie* (Ann Arbor, 2008).

Husain, Azim, *Sir Fazl-i-Husain: A Political Biography* (Bombay, 1946).

Ispahani, M. A. H, *Qaid-i-Azam As I Knew Him* (Karachi, 1966).

Jaffrelot, Christophe (ed.), *Pakistan Nationalism without a Nation* (New Delhi, 2002).

____, *A History of Pakistan and its Origins* (London, 2002).

Jalal, Ayesha and Anil Seal, 'Alternative to Partition: Muslim Politics between the Wars', *Modern Asian Studies*, 15(3) (1981): 415–54.

Jalal, Ayesha, *The Sole Spokesman: Jinnah, The Muslim League, and the Demand for Pakistan* (Cambridge, 1985).

____, *Self and sovereignty: Individual and Community in South Asian Islam since 1850* (London and New York, 2000).

Jones, Allen Keith, *Politics in Sind, 1907-1940: Muslim Identity and the Demand for Pakistan* (Karachi, 2002).

Jones, Owen-Bennett, *Pakistan: Eye of the Storm* (New Haven, 2002).

Joseph, Pothan, *Looking Back* (Bangalore, 1950).

Kaushik Roy (ed.), *Partition of India: Why 1947?* (New Delhi, 2012).

Kaviraj, Sudipta, *The Imaginary Institution of India* (New York, 2010).

Kaura, Uma, *Muslims and Indian Nationalism: The Emergence of the Demand for India's Partition 1928-40* (Columbia, 1977).

Keer, Dhananjay, *Dr. Ambedkar: Life and Mission* (Bombay, 1971), third edition.

Khadduri, Majid, *The Islamic Law of Nations: Shaybani's Siyar* (Baltimore, 1966).

Khaliquzzaman, Chaudhry, *Pathway to Pakistan* (Lahore, 1961).

Khan, Abdul Rashid, *The All India Muslim Educational Conference: Its Contribution to the Cultural Development of Indian Muslims 1886-1947* (Karachi, 2001).

Khan, Naveeda, *Beyond Crisis: Reevaluating Pakistan* (London, 2010).

Khan, Shafa'at Ahmad, *The Indian Federation: An Exposition and Critical Review* (London, 1937).

Khan, Yasmin, *The Great Partition: The Making of India and Pakistan* (London, 2007).

Khosla, G. D., *Stern Reckoning* (New Delhi, 1949).

Khomeini, Ruhollah, *Islam and Revolution: Writings and Declarations of Imam Khomeini Translated by Hamid Algar* (Berkeley, 1980).

King, Christopher, *One language, Two Scripts: The Hindi Movement in Nineteenth Century India* (Bombay, 1994).

Kruger, Horst (ed.), *Kunwar Mohammad Ashraf: An Indian Scholar and Revolutionary, 1903-1962* (Bombay, 1969).

Landau, Jacob, *The Politics of Pan-Islam: Ideology and Organization* (Oxford, 1994).

Lelyveld, David, *Aligarh's First Generation: Muslim Solidarity in British India* (New Delhi, 1996).

Lia, Brynjar, *The Society of Muslim Brothers in Egypt: The Rise of an Islamic Mass Movement, 1928-1942* (Reading, 1998).

Lieven Anatole, *Pakistan: A Hard Country* (New York, 2011).

Low, D. A. (ed.), *Congress and the Raj* (London, 1977).

Mahmud, Shabana 'Angare and the Founding of the Progressive Writers Association', *Modern Asian Studies*, 30(2) (May 1996): 447–67

Malik, Hafiz, 'The Marxist Literary Movement in India and Pakistan', *Journal of Asian Studies*, 26(4) (1967): 649–64.

Malik, Rizwan, 'Muslim Nationalism in India: Ashraf Ali Thanawi, Shabbir Ahmad Usmani and the Pakistan Movement', in *Pakistan Journal of History and Culture*, Vol. XVIII/2 (1997), 76.

——, *Mawlana Husayn Ahmad Madani and Jamiyat Ulama-i-Hind: Status of Islam and Muslims in India*, unpublished Ph.d dissertation (University of Toronto, 1995).

Metcalf, Barbara D. and Thomas R. Metcalf, *A Concise History of Modern India* (New Delhi, 2006), second edition.

Metcalf, Barbara D, *Husain Ahmad Madani: The Jihad for Islam and India's Freedom* (Oxford, 2009).

——, *Perfecting Women: Maulana Ashraf Ali Thanawi's Bihishti Zewar; A Partial Translation with Commentary* (Berkeley, 1990).

——, *Islamic Revival in British India: Deoband, 1860-1900* (Princeton, 1982).

Minault, Gail, *The Khilafat Movement: Religious Symbolism and Political Mobilization in India* (New York, 1982).

——, 'Urdu Poetry during the Khilafat Movement', *Modern Asian Studies*, 8(4) (1974): 459–71.

Misra, Salil, *A Narrative of Communal Politics – Uttar Pradesh, 1937–39* (New Delhi, 2001).

Mitchell, Richard, *The Society of Muslim Brothers* (New York, 1993).

Mojaddedi, Jawid (tr.), *Rumi, The Masnavi: Book One* (Oxford, 2004).

Moon, Penderel, *Divide and Quit* (Berkeley, 1962).

Moore, R. J., *Endgames of Empire: Studies of Britain's Indian Problem* (Delhi, 1988).

Moraes, Frank, *Witness to an Era* (New York, 1973).

Mujahid, Sharif-al, *Jinnah: Studies in Interpretation* (Karachi, 1969).

Mujeeb, M., *The Indian Muslims* (London, 1967).

Naim, C. M., 'A Sentimental Essay in Three Scenes', *Outlook Magazine*, 11 January 2007.

____, *Ambiguities of Heritage* (Karachi, 1999).

Naipaul, V. S., *India: A Million Mutinies Now* (New York, 1991).

Nair, Neeti, *Changing Homelands: Hindu Politics and the Partition of India* (New Delhi, 2011).

Nandy, Ashis, *The Intimate Enemy: Loss and Recovery of Self Under Colonialism* (Delhi, 1983).

Nasr, S. V. R, *The Vanguard of the Islamic Revolution: the Jamaat-i-Islami of Pakistan* (Berkeley and Los Angeles, 1994).

Nawaz, Shuja, *Crossed Swords: Pakistan, Its Army and the Wars Within* (Oxford, 2008).

Nehru, Jawaharlal, *The Discovery of India* (London, 1956).

Newman, K. J., 'Pakistan's Preventative Autocracy and Its Causes', *Pacific Affairs*, 32(1) (March 1959): 18–33.

Noman, Mohammad, *Muslim India: The Rise and Growth of the All India Muslim League* (Allahabad, 1942).

Page, David, *Prelude to Partition-The Indian Muslims and the Imperial System of Control 1920-1932* (Delhi, 1982).

Pandey, Gyanendra, *The Ascendancy of Congress in Uttar Pradesh: Class, Community and Nation in Northern India, 1920–1940* (London, 2004).

____, *The Construction of Communalism in Colonial North India* (New Delhi, 2004).

____, *Remembering Partition: Violence, Nationalism and History in India* (Cambridge, 2001).

____, *Routine Violence: Nations, Fragments, Histories* (Stanford, 2006).

Philips, C. H. and Wainwright, M. (eds.), *The Partition of India: Policies and Perspectives* (London, 1970).

Powell, Avril A., *Muslims and Missionaries in Pre-Mutiny India* (New Jersey, 1993).

Prasad, Rajendra, *India Divided* (Bombay, 1946).

Qasimi, Muhammad Reza (ed.), *Jinnah-Liaquat Correspondence* (Karachi, 2003).

Qureshi, I. H., *The Muslim Community of the Indo-Pakistan Subcontinent (610-1947): A Brief Historical Analysis* (Gravenhage, 1962).

Qureshi, Naeem, *Pan Islam in British Indian Politics: A Study of the Khilafat Movement, 1918-1924* (Karachi, 2008).

Rao, K. Rama, *The Pen as my Sword: Memoirs of a Journalist* (Bombay, 1965).

Rashid, Haroon-or, *The Foreshadowing of Bangladesh: Bengal Muslim League and Muslim Politics*, 1936-1947 (Dhaka, 1987).

Ravoof, M. A., *Meet Mr. Jinnah* (Lahore, 1944).

Reeves, P. D., B. D. Graham and J. M. Goodman, *Handbook of Elections in UP 1920-51* (Delhi, 1975).

Rizvi, Gowher, *Linlithgow and India: A Study of British Policy and Political Impasse in India* (London, 1978).

Rizvi, Sayyid Mahbub, *History of the Darul Uloom Deoband*, translated into English by Prof. Murtaz Husain and F. Qureshi, 2 volumes (Deoband, 1981).

Robinson, Francis, *Cambridge History of Islam Vol.5: The Islamic World in the Age of Western Dominance* (Cambridge, 2010).

____, *Islam and Muslim History in South Asia* (Delhi, 2003).

____, *Separatism among Indian Muslims: The Politics of the United Provinces Muslims 1860-1923* (Delhi, 1997).

Samad, Yunus, *A Nation in Turmoil: Nationalism and Ethnicity in Pakistan 1937-1958* (New Delhi, 1995).

Sarkar, Sumit, *Modern India, 1885-1947* (Delhi, 1983).

Sayeed, Khalid bin, *Pakistan: The Formative Phase, 1857-1948* (London, 1968).

Shaikh, Farzana, *Making Sense of Pakistan* (New York, 2009).

____, *Community and Consensus in Islam: Muslim representation in Colonial India, 1860-1947* (Cambridge, 1989).

Sho, Kuwajima, *Muslims, Nationalism, Partition: 1946 Provincial Elections in India* (New Delhi, 1998).

Siddiqi, Majid Hayat 'Bluff, Doubt, and Fear: The Kheiri Brothers and the Colonial State, 1904-1945', *Indian Economic and Social History Review*, 24(3) (1987): 230–63.

Siddiqi, Nurul Hasan, *Landlords of Agra and Avadh* (Lucknow, 1950).

Singh, Anita Inder, *The Origins of the Partition of India, 1936-1947* (Delhi, 1987).

Smith, W. C., *Pakistan as an Islamic State* (Lahore, 1951).

____, *Modern Islam in India* (London, 1946).

____, *The Muslim League, 1942-45* (Lahore 1945).

Som, Reba, *Differences within Consensus: The Left and Right in the Congress 1929-39* (New Delhi, 1995).

Talbot I. A., Planning for Pakistan: The Planning Committee of the All India Muslim League, 1943-46, *Modern Asian Studies*, 28(4) (October 1994): 875–89.

____, *Punjab and the Raj 1849-1947* (Delhi, 1988).

____, *Provincial Politics and the Pakistan Movement* (Karachi, 1988).

____, 'The 1946 Punjab Elections, Modern Asian Studies', *Modern Asian Studies*, 14(1) (1980): 65–91.

Taylor, D. and Yapp, M., (eds.), *Political Identity in South Asia* (London, 1979).

Tendulkar, D. G., *Mahatma: Life of Mohandas Karamchand Gandhi* (New Delhi, 1952).

Tomlinson, B. R., *The Indian National Congress and the Raj, 1929–42: The Penultimate Phase* (London, 1976).

Toosy, M. S., *My Reminiscences of Quaid-i-Azam: A Collection of Interviews and Talks with Quaid-i-Azam during November 1942 to May 1943* (Islamabad, 1976).

Troll, Christian, *Sayyid Ahmad Khan: A Reinterpretation of Muslim Theology* (New Delhi, 1978).

Veer, Peter van der, *Religious Nationalism: Hindus and Muslims in India* (Berkeley, 1994).

Weiss, Anita (ed), *Islamic Reassertion in Pakistan: The Application of Islamic Laws in a Modern State* (Syracuse, 1986).

Wilcox, Wayne Ayres, 'The Pakistan Coup d'état of 1958', *Pacific Affairs*, 38(2) (Summer 1965): 142–63.

Winichakul, Thongchai, *Mapping Siam: A History of the Geo-Body of a Nation* (Honolulu, 1994).

Wolpert, Stanley, *Jinnah of Pakistan* (Oxford, 1984).

Zakaria, Rafiq, *Price of Partition: Recollections and Reflections* (Mumbai, 1998).

Zaman, Muhammad Qasim, *Modern Islamic Thought in a Radical Age* (Cambridge, 2012).

____, *Ashraf Ali Thanawi: Islam in modern South Asia* (Oxford, 2008).

____, *The Ulama in contemporary Islam: custodians of change* (Princeton, 2002).

Zaman, Mukhtar, *Students Role in the Pakistan Movement* (Karachi, 1978).

Zamindar, Vazira, *The Long Partition and the Making of Modern South Asia: Refugees, Boundaries, Histories* (New York, 2007).

Ziring, Lawrence, Ralph Braibanti and Howard Wriggins (ed.), *Pakistan: The Long View* (Durham, 1977).

Index

Printed by Printforce, United Kingdom